The Sisters, Servants of the Immaculate Heart of Mary, Scranton, Pennsylvania: 1919-1974

The Sisters, Servants of the Immaculate Heart of Mary, Scranton, Pennsylvania: 1919-1974

by Sister Michel Keenan, IHM

RoseDog Books
PITTSBURGH, PENNSYLVANIA 15222

ISBN # 0-8059-9718-0
Printed in the United States of America

First Printing

For information or to order additional books, please write:
RoseDog Books
701 Smithfield St.
Pittsburgh, PA 15222
U.S.A.
1-800-834-1803
Or visit our web site and
on-line bookstore at www.rosedogbookstore.com

Preface

The history of the Sisters, Servants of the Immaculate Heart of Mary of Scranton, Pennsylvania, from 1845 to 1919 is found in the landmark work of Sister Immaculata Gillespie, IHM, published in 1921 and entitled *The Sisters of the I.H.M.*

This present work continues that history, beginning in 1919 with Mother Casimir Murray's term of office, and ending with that of Mother Beata Wertz in 1974.

Unpublished manuscripts covering the period from 1919-1955 were completed in 1988 and circulated within the congregation. Sisters who have read these manuscripts will recognize that they have been included in this volume. The reader must remember, therefore, that some information regarding the status of particular apostolates in 1988 have changed in the years between then and now. If our sisters have been withdrawn, or a mission closed, that account will appear later in the administration in which it occurs.

Additional research since 2001 has brought together, then, a total of fifty-five years of Scranton IHM history with the addition of the period between 1955 and 1974—the administrations of Mother Kathleen Hart and Mother Beata Wertz

What all of this history will reveal is that the Scranton IHMs were always pioneers, always courageous, hopeful, dedicated, and holy. It will take the reader through the valiant struggles of change, moving from a diocesan to a papal congregation; from monastic to apostolic religious lifestyles; to ever more democratic and inclusive ways of governing; and to the many other monumental changes of Vatican II.

I can only hope that your reading of this volume will do for you what it has done for me: it has filled me with deep gratitude to God for all the IHMs who have gone before us, but also admiration, pride and love for all of today's IHMs who persevered through those tumultuous times and continue the journey.

Vision for the future of this great IHM Congregation can come, I believe, by visiting and revisiting our significant past. I have been blessed to have contributed to that past and that future. As Reverend Shaun McCarty once wrote, "The present and the future grow out of a common history . . . when a group has a dynamic history preserved in living tradition, it is more likely to have a creative imagination in moving ahead." I am grateful to the IHM Congregation leadership in the persons of Sisters Redempta Sweeney, Anne Munley, and Mary Persico for the opportunity to make the IHM story live in print.

. . . .

I wish to acknowledge the assistance given in the completion of the earlier sections by Sisters St. Teresa Healy, Marionette Coll, Harriet Jackson and Espiritu Dempsey. Since 2001, the archivists, Sisters Eleanor Desaulniers and Kathleen McNulty have assisted enormously in locating archival materials, in reformatting, processing and computerizing the earlier typewritten sections. They, together, with Sister Espiritu Dempsey, have patiently persevered in proofreading this document. My prayers of gratitude for their hard work, interest and support will continue.

Sister Michel Keenan, IHM
August 15, 2004

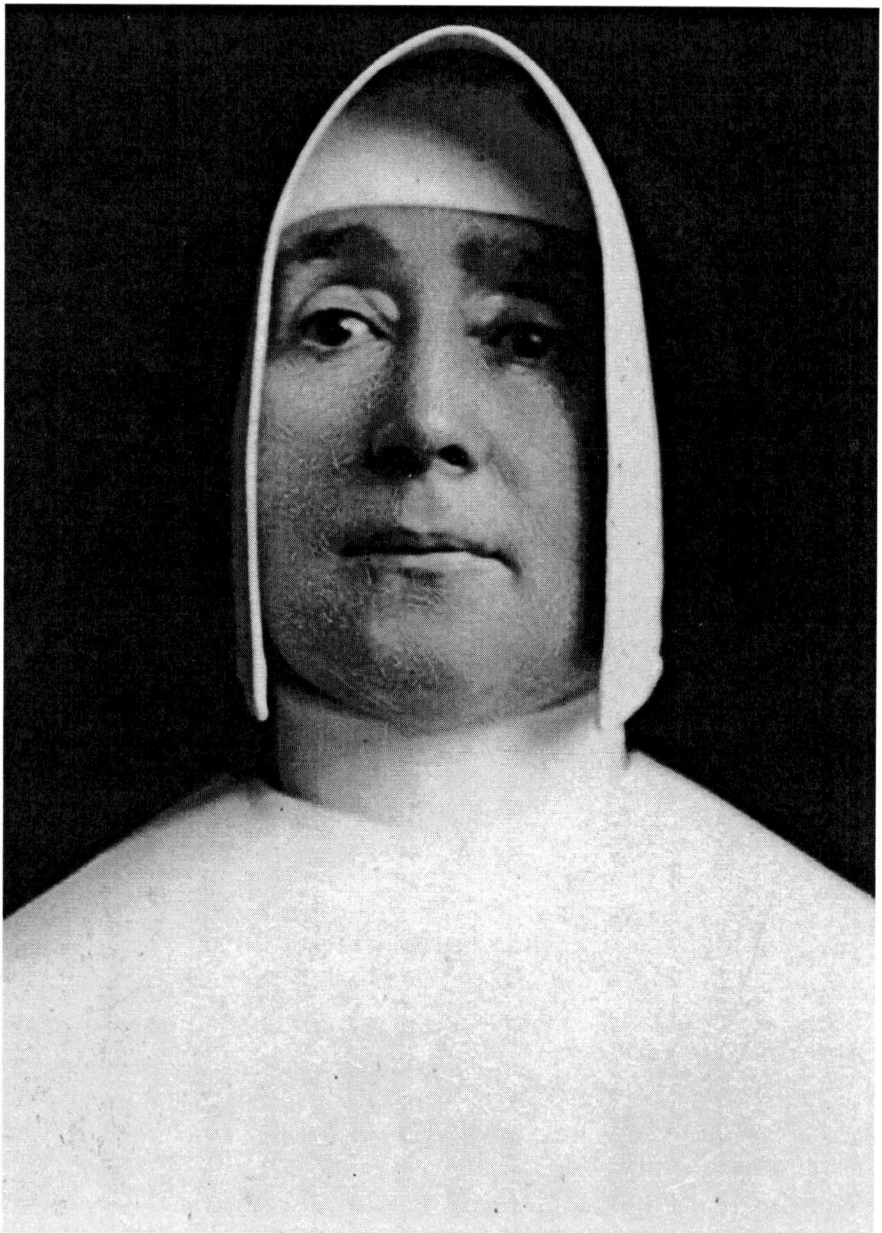

Mother M. Casimir Murray, IHM
1919-1929

BORN:	Ellen Murray, November 10, 1850, Reading, PA
PARENTS:	James Murray and Margaret Dolan Murray
EDUCATION:	A.B., Marywood College, Scranton, PA
RELIGIOUS LIFE:	Entered IHM Congregation, September 29, 1868, at Reading, PA Reception of Habit, December 3, 1868, Reading, PA Profession of Vows, November 22, 1870, Susquehanna, PA
MISSIONS:	St. Joseph's School, Williamsport, PA *Laurel Hill Academy, Susquehanna, PA *Served as Principal of the School and Convent Superior
MEMBER OF THE GENERAL COUNCIL:	Bursar, 1871-1877
SUPERIOR GENERAL:	1919-1929 (died during second term of office)
DIED:	February 16, 1929 – 79 years of age

TABLE OF CONTENTS

Mother M. Casimir Murray
1919 - 1929

TOPIC PAGE

The year was 1919. Mother Casimir Murray accepted her election as seventh superior general of the Congregation of the Sisters, Servants of the Immaculate Heart of Mary of Scranton, Pennsylvania and began ten years of service that were to be truly prophetic years for the future of the Congregation.

The post-World War I atmosphere in which the congregation found itself was electrifying as the nation dealt with such issues as prohibition (passed into law on January 16, 1920); woman suffrage (ratified as the Nineteenth Amendment to the Constitution on August 26, 1920); and a child labor amendment which was submitted to the states, but not ratified. Some of the bishops of the Catholic Church, concerned about the returning World War I veterans, were urging programs related to housing, educational and job training, minimum wage scales, and other reforms. These ideas found their way by February 1919 into a major social publication entitled "The Bishops' Program of Social Reconstruction."

It was a time of Catholic emergence in literature and the arts with such names as Agnes Repplier, Theodore Dreiser, John O'Hara, convert Ernest Hemingway, F. Scott Fitzgerald, James T. Farrell, and Eugene O'Neill coming to prominence. By 1920 there were some eighteen million Catholics in the United States, more than a million of who had served in the armed forces during the war. As Hennessey, SJ, reports: "They (Catholics) emerged from their first extended experience of inter-religious cooperation with heightened self-confidence." (1) So great was Catholic influence becoming that the *Fiery Cross*, a publication of the Ku Klux Klan in one of its 1925 editions queried as to whether "Washington, D.C. might not be renamed 'Piusville' or 'St. Patricksburg'." (2) Across the nation Catholic education grew on all levels. One hundred thirty colleges and universities in 1921 became one hundred sixty-three by 1928, enrolling about one-half of all Catholic college students, as against one-third in 1921. (3) Parishes, high schools, retreat houses, orphanages, hospitals, and other special institutions were multiplying in every diocese.

In this invigorating climate of emerging Catholicism, it was no wonder that Mother Casimir set the congregation also on an expansionist route, as she responded to the requests of bishops and pastors for IHM Sisters. Thirty new missions in ten dioceses were opened—a testimony even then to the Congregation's on-going desire to distribute its ministries and personnel in accord with the principle that "fewer sisters in more places" was to be preferred to "more sisters in fewer places." Thus, the following new locations were established:

1920: Casa Regina, Altoona, Pennsylvania
St. Joseph's Shelter, Scranton, Pennsylvania
St. Ann's, Scranton, Pennsylvania

1921: Nativity, New York, New York (catechetical)
St. Mary's, Avoca, Pennsylvania
St. Patrick's, Oneida, New York
St. Thomas, Ashville, Pennsylvania

1922: St. Paul's, Edgewood, Rhode Island
St. Ephrem's, Brooklyn, New York

1924: St. Dominic's, Oyster Bay, New York
Sacred Hearts, New York, New York
St. Peter of Alcantara, Port Washington, New York
St. Mary's, Upper Marlboro, Maryland
St. Justin's, Pittsburgh, Pennsylvania
St. Thomas, Manton, Rhode Island
Liberal Arts Building, Marywood College, Scranton, PA

1925: St. Agnes Place, Elmhurst, PA

1926: St. Joseph's, New Bern, North Carolina
St. Mary's, Manhasset, New York
St. Raymond's, Lynnbrook, New York
St. Rita's, Dundalk, Maryland.
St. Joseph's Hospital, Carbondale, Pennsylvania

1927: St. Thomas, Archbald, Pennsylvania
Sacred Heart, LaPlata, Maryland
St. Mary's, Goldsboro, North Carolina
Our Lady of Mercy, Washington, North Carolina

1928: St. Bernardine's, Baltimore, Maryland.
Our Lady Queen of Martyrs, Forest Hills, New York
St. Mary-John School, Cresson, Pennsylvania
O'Reilly Residence Hall, Marywood College, Scranton, PA

1929: St. Charles, Sugar Notch, Pennsylvania
St. Paul's, New Bern, North Carolina
Sacred Heart, La Plata, Md. (Secondary School)
Epiphany, Sayre, Pennsylvania

NORTH CAROLINA MISSIONS

North Carolina, with an area of some 52,000 square miles, was considered missionary territory, and is so considered even today. By 1925, the number of Catholics in the state was about 12,000, with only 1,500 of these being blacks. The Diocese of Raleigh was created, and Bishop William J. Hafey, later to become Bishop of Scranton, was consecrated on June 24, 1925. He began at once the task of obtaining priests and religious communities to serve this huge state. At this time there were only twenty diocesan priests and six priests of religious orders. Of this number, only two were working with the black people.

Anti-Catholic feeling was rampant, and only by years of loving service by religious would a better understanding and acceptance of the Catholic Church come about.

Bishop Hafey was especially interested in the evangelization of the black people and in response to his appeal for religious, Dominicans, Passionists, Franciscans, Redemptorists, Josephites and IHMs all generously responded.

Bishop Hafey's original plans for the IHM Sisters had a scope as expansive as his own generous nature, as is reflected in his letter of October 13, 1925, to Bishop William J. Hoban of Scranton in requesting that Mother Casimir be permitted to explore this new apostolate in the Raleigh Diocese. He was looking far beyond grade schools and catechetical instruction as he wrote:

> In the future I believe it will be most prudent to establish a Catholic College for young women in the Eastern part of North Carolina . . . While the establishment of such a College could not be in the immediate future, there is, however, a site now available which can be purchased . . .
>
> Would you at least give Mother M. Casimir permission to view the situation and go into the possibilities of taking it over for future purposes? I understand that the Order is a very efficient one and that the Sisters are all receiving very excellent training. I am sure they will be fitten (sic) to do excellent work in this State of Marvelous Opportunities. (4)

St. Joseph's, New Bern, North Carolina

In 1926 Mother Casimir sent the first IHMs to St. Joseph's, New Bern, where a school had been established for "colored children" and conducted by lay people. They had made praiseworthy efforts, but no doubt because of their own meager knowledge of school management and instruction, the school was forcibly discontinued. It was the foresight and zeal of Reverend Charles Hannigan, SSJ, which resulted in the appointment of Sisters Lucinda Harrington, Sergius O'Donnell, and Marie Gabriel McQuade to teach the black children at St. Joseph's.

Twenty-three black children registered the first day, of whom only one was a Catholic. Gradually the enrollment increased until at the end of the first year there were ninety enrolled, and a convert class of about twenty.

Words reminiscent of Mother Teresa Maxis' early letters were used by one of the sisters to describe the first months of their life at St. Joseph's:

> Early in November we moved into our little unfurnished convent. Its poverty was our joy. Our refectory table was a homemade 6 x 4 which had previously served the carpenters as a work table. We carried our chairs when needed from the classrooms to the Convent. (5)

Commenting on the visit of Reverend Bonaventure McHugh, CP, to their convent, it was said, "Noticing our lack of furniture, he offered to spend the money given him in charity to buy some furniture for our parlor so that we might at least ask our visitors to be seated when they called. The donation was thankfully received." (6)

But the furniture problem was not laid to rest until a friend of Father Sweeney's, Mr. John Stuart of the furniture firm of Stuart and Scanlon in Boston, was apprised of the sisters' needs and provided furnishings for their modest rooms.

The deprivations experienced were not all in the material order, as a further comment made clear. On Christmas morning Father Stephen Sweeney, CP, who was conducting missions at St. Joseph's arrived at the convent and said two Masses in the Chapel "bringing for the first time Our Lord to dwell with us in our Convent home."(7)

By the second year the sisters at St. Joseph's, New Bern, had expanded their work to include a catechetical school at St. Paul's Church, New Bern, and a class for black children in Washington, North Carolina, where Mother of Mercy School was later opened.

It was inevitable that the day would come when integration of black and white students would be a reality. The Supreme Court of the United States in the case of Brown vs. The Board of Education of Topeka declared racial segregation unconstitutional on May 31, 1955, thus "officially" prohibiting segregation. In 1962, this law was put into effect in the

Raleigh Diocese by Bishop Vincent S. Waters, simultaneously merging St. Joseph's and St. Paul's, New Bern, and renaming St. Joseph's secondary school the "William Gaston Regional Catholic High School." This high school was to reach an enrollment of one hundred two students by the year of its closing in 1969. Its smallness had not interfered with its ability to offer high quality education and to merit its continued accreditation by the State of North Carolina. (8)

Mother of Mercy School, Little Washington, North Carolina

On August 30, 1927 four IHM Sisters arrived in Little Washington: Sister M. deChantal McHale, superior, Sister Sergius O'Donnell, Sister Gertrude Marie Jelley and Sister St. Ann Quinn. With their arrival, the school, which housed a chapel and the sisters' residence, became the Catholic Church of Little Washington. On the eleventh of September 1927, Bishop Hafey dedicated these areas and reserved the Blessed Sacrament for the first time in Washington, North Carolina. Although priests had come from Baltimore, Charleston, South Carolina, New Bern and Wilmington, North Carolina, to minister to the needs of a few white Catholics from time to time, provision could not be had for the reservation of the Blessed Sacrament.

Reverend Charles Hannigan of New Bern was given charge of the Little Washington mission which consisted of nine persons—four sisters and five lay persons, all of whom were converts to the Catholic faith. They were Mr. David Keyes and his wife, Stephen Bonner and his wife and Mrs. Louisa Little. Father Hannigan went from New Bern to Little Washington twice a week. Once again, the deprivation of daily Mass and Holy Communion was the greatest hardship experienced by the sisters.

In October 1927, Bishop Hafey purchased the Mallison Home on North Market Street for the convent. The sisters moved into it on January 10, 1928. Reverend Mark Moislein, CP, a golden jubilarian in his seventy-fourth year of life, arrived to act as pastor for both black and white peoples of Washington, North Carolina. Through his zeal and the dedicated work of the sisters the school soon had to be enlarged to provide for all of the students. Not only was their work of education thriving, but they were also attracting converts to the faith. In one year, by May of 1928, four of the non-Catholic students were baptized.

Bishop Hafey visited the school frequently and was deeply appreciative of the work being done. True to IHM heritage in music, the sisters prepared the children in Gregorian Chant, and on December 8, 1927, the first Gregorian Mass ever sung in North Carolina was sung by all-black, all-Protestant students of St. Joseph's School choir in New Bern. Bishop

Hafey commented that he wished it were possible to take that choir to every church and chapel of the Raleigh Diocese and particularly to the Raleigh Cathedral.

The peak enrollment of 113 students was reached in 1968, but fell to 69 by 1972. Due to lack of enrollment the elementary school was closed in June 1973; the high school, which had opened in 1933, had already closed in 1969. The sisters received great praise from the bishop and from the people for the 46-year IHM presence and work in Little Washington. (9)

St. Mary's Elementary School, Goldsboro, North Carolina

Responding to the invitation of Monsignor Arthur R. Freeman, pastor of St. Mary's Church, Goldsboro, North Carolina, Mother Casimir sent sisters to staff the parish school. Sisters Kathleen Hart, superior and principal, Maureen LeFevre and St. Clare Flanagan arrived in Goldsboro on August 27, 1927. They took up residence in a large frame building that had been purchased in June of that year and remodeled to serve as a combination convent and school. The first floor was made into five classrooms; the upper floor adapted to be used as a convent. St. Mary's School, Goldsboro, opened on September 12, 1927, the Feast of the Holy Name of Mary, with a Mass in honor of the Blessed Virgin Mary. The enrollment was forty-five pupils for kindergarten and the first seven grades. In addition to the three sisters, Miss Eunice Freeman was a member of the teaching staff. None of the accounts of this situation enlightens the reader as to how the fact of eight classes and five classrooms was resolved, but one can conjecture that some doubling and even tripling occurred.

Monsignor Arthur Freeman, assigned in 1915, served as pastor of St. Mary's for sixteen years, until April 1931. A long line of pastors succeeded him. Probably the one most entwined with IHM history was Monsignor Edward T. Gilbert who became pastor in 1951. It was he who purchased the property at the corner of Edgerton Street and Jefferson Avenue in planning for the future of a total parish community to include church, school, rectory and convent. As he saw the school enrollment climb to 185 students in 1955, he announced that a new school and convent would be built within a year.

True to his promise, the groundbreaking ceremony took place on April 15, 1956, and by the following December 7 the sisters moved into a new convent. Holy Mass was offered in the convent chapel on December 8, with Monsignor Gilbert presiding, and conducting the blessing of the entire convent following the Mass. "Open house" was held for the parishioners in December.

The several weeks that followed saw a flurry of activity in preparation for the January 6, 1957 “open house” for the new St. Mary’s School. Formal dedication ceremonies, with Bishop Vincent Waters officiating, were held on January 27. Seventy-five priests, including Air Force chaplains from the Seymour Johnson Air Force Base nearby, sisters representing many congregations and members of the laity were in attendance. The local community of St. Mary’s that year included: Sister Jane Kehoe, superior and principal, Sister Rosamund Doyle, Sister Remigia (Elizabeth Mary) Quinlin, Sister Mary Alan (Patricia) Dyer and Sister Catherine Mary Manley.

As the 1958 school year began, the ability of the excellent new facility to attract new students was obvious. Enrollment increased by 100 pupils to a new high of 370. Steady increases are noted: 1960, 450 pupils; 1962, 477 pupils; 1963, the peak was reached with 510 pupils. In 1964 it was necessary to build an addition to the school to provide extra classrooms, audio-visual and storage space, and a faculty room. This addition was completed by November of 1964.

On September 25, 1974, Monsignor Gilbert was stricken with a heart attack. The sisters were able to get him to Wayne Memorial Hospital where he remained for several weeks. He was eventually moved to the Catholic hospital in Pinehurst for further recuperation. It was December 1 before his return to the parish. He spent three more years in active service as pastor and decided to retire on June 13, 1977. Forty-five years of his priesthood had been spent with the IHM Sisters from Scranton; twenty in Washington, North Carolina, and twenty-five in Goldsboro. It was, indeed, the end of an era.

Reverend John J. Harper succeeded Monsignor Gilbert as pastor on July 1, 1977. He turned his attention very early in his pastorate to plans for building a new church, since the school and auditorium had served as St. Mary’s Church since 1978 when the downtown church property was sold. Plans were tabled for several years as fund-raising continued and the support of the parishioners was gained for the project. The groundbreaking finally took place on October 21, 1984.

With the deepest pride Father Harper and his parishioners were able to celebrate the one hundredth anniversary of the original St. Mary’s Church by the dedication of their beautiful new church on January 12, 1986.

As the school gradually grew, adding eighth and ninth grades, there were to be about an equal number of Catholic and non-Catholic pupils. At one point, with the influx of children of Seymour Johnson Air Force Base personnel, the percentage of Catholic students rose to eighty-six. Expanding from five Catholic families in 1889 to some 400 Catholic families in 1986,

St. Mary's Parish growth has impacted the growth of St. Mary's School. The excellent facilities built under the direction of Monsignor John Gilbert in 1956 served 209 students in 1985.

The faculty included four sisters and six full-time and one part-time lay teachers. The religious faculty for 1985—1986 included: Sister Maryla Farfour, superior (a Goldsboro native), Sister Amy Zychal, principal; Sister Mary Ruth Bailey, and Sister Doreen Willis. (10)

St. Paul's Elementary School, New Bern, North Carolina

From the time of the opening in 1926 of St. Joseph's School in New Bern, which provided parochial education for black children, the Sisters, Servants of the Immaculate Heart of Mary had also given catechetical instructions to the white children of St. Paul's Parish, New Bern. Reverend Michael A. Irwin, Pastor, was anxious to establish a parochial school, so in June 1928 he sought additional sisters from Mother Casimir. His seriousness of purpose was evident when in August 1929, he had procured land and erected a three-story red brick building, to be a combination school and convent.

Mother M. Casimir had died on February 16, 1929, having already approved the new venture, but it was natural that some concern and anxiety would be reflected in the March 6 and August 8, 1929 letters from Bishop Hafey to "Sister" Mary William, attempting to determine whether, in light of Mother Casimir's death, sisters would, in fact, be sent to St. Paul's, New Bern. On the feast of St. Augustine, August 28, 1929, the question was answered as Sister Pauline Gallagher, superior, Sister Seraphine Gallagher and Sister St. Helen Sullivan arrived at the new setting. Father Irwin, the pastor, had gone on a pilgrimage to Europe, hence did not know until his return in early October that the sisters were occupying the new convent and that St. Paul's School was in operation, with fifty pupils in six grades.

One account of this situation says, "They agreed to keep the arrival of the sisters and the school news from him until after supper. Just as the meal was about over the good priests told him and one could hear him all over New Bern singing the solemn Deo Gratias." (11)

Sister Pauline was to serve as superior at St. Paul's, New Bern, until 1943 when Sister Marie Imelda Callahan succeeded her.

With the racial integration of black and white students came the merger of St. Joseph's and St. Paul's Schools in 1962-1963. This process went smoothly, however a loss of seventy-one white pupils occurred, leaving an enrollment of 69 black and 72 white children. St. Paul's, New Bern, was to achieve a peak enrollment of 230 pupils in 1980.

Today the elementary school has grown to the point where there are really two "schools". The former St. Joseph's Grade and High School now houses kindergarten through grade four; the original St. Paul's building contains grades five through eight. The total enrollment in 1985 was 209 pupils, with four sisters, six full-time and three part-time lay faculty.

Summary

In summing up this brief account of the founding of the North Carolina missions staffed by IHM Sisters, it seems appropriate to cite the closing paragraph of a letter from Bishop Hafey to Mother Casimir dated May 1, 1928:

> . . . Taking this opportunity to assure you that the coming of your Sisters has been for this diocese perhaps the outstanding blessing from God, and trusting that it will also be a source of great blessing to your Congregation in general, I remain, with best wishes,
>
> Sincerely yours, William J. Hafey, Bishop of Raleigh (12)

Bishop Hafey's grand plans for the Raleigh Diocese were cut short when he was surprisingly chosen as Coadjutor Bishop to the ailing Bishop O'Reilly of Scranton, Pennsylvania, effective October 2, 1937. On March 25, 1938 Bishop Hafey was to become the fourth Bishop of the Diocese of Scranton, upon the death of Bishop O'Reilly. (13)

MARYLAND MISSIONS

Rural education in Maryland was 275 years old when the Sisters, Servants of the Immaculate Heart of Mary accepted the call to serve in Upper Marlboro in 1925. The Jesuits had established a school in 1650 in St. Mary's City that lasted until 1696. By then, the hostility of the colonial government and of the members of the Anglican Church, which was the "established Church" of Maryland by law, made it impossible to maintain a school under Catholic auspices. Catholics were disenfranchised and it was a crime for a Catholic to teach school. There was also a fine of forty shillings a day for every day that a householder would employ a Catholic tutor, and a five hundred dollar fine for sending a youngster to a European college.

Despite these laws, the Jesuits provided Catholic preparatory school education for the boys. Subsequently these boys attended college in Belgium or France; girls were prepared at home for the academies of

Europe. The sacrifices of Catholic families to maintain this system of Catholic education were very great, but it tells a story of the deep desire of Maryland Catholics for this type of education and their dedication to the preservation of the faith in their children. (14)

After the Revolutionary War, when liberty of conscience and education were restored to Catholics, it was no longer necessary for schools to remain hidden, nor to send students to Europe. By the nineteenth century, urged by the Plenary Council of Baltimore to establish a school with every Catholic Church, there was even some activity in this regard in rural parishes. In time to come, the religious orders of women would augment the early work of the Jesuits. The Madames of the Sacred Heart, School Sisters of Notre Dame, Sisters of St. Joseph of Hartford, the Oblates of Providence, the Sisters of Charity from Leonardtown, and the Sisters, Servants of the Immaculate Heart of Mary formed a long chain of dedicated religious teachers reaching from 1870 to the present to bring Catholic education to rural Maryland.

St. Mary's Elementary School, Upper Marlboro, Maryland

The first school in the Archdiocese of Baltimore to be staffed by the Scranton IHM Sisters opened in September 1925. St. Mary's School, Upper Marlboro, Maryland, was also the first Catholic school to be established in Charles County. It was at the invitation of Reverend Francis J. Loughran that Mother Casimir sent Sisters Thomasina Gallagher, superior, Euphrasia Kelley, St. Teresa Healy, Gerard Ford and Jane Marie Ruddy to comprise the first community in the new mission. Father Loughran's long cherished desire to found a parochial school for his widely scattered flock was partially realized in the opening of St. Mary's for the white children. Segregation was still in practice, but it would be only another September before Father Loughran would find a way to offer a Catholic education to the black students as well. (15)

The term "school" must be used with reservations in describing the physical setting in which one hundred twenty newly registered students found themselves as classes began at St. Mary's. At this time the only building was the rectory. Father Loughran housed the sisters here while he himself resided with a parishioner, taking his meals, however, with the sisters. Eventually, the rectory was to become the convent, as the pastor had a small house built for himself. Classes, however, continued to be held in the "convent": the enclosed porch housed the seventh and eighth graders; the dining room, the fourth, fifth, and sixth graders; the parlor, the first three grades; and a small office in the front of the house, barely large enough for a piano and desk, served as the music room. (16) The students learned very early lessons of sacrifice as many of them walked long distances to school and several came by bus or train. Father Loughran was seen daily in his station wagon delivering youngsters to their destination. One account given by a parishioner reminiscing at the sixtieth anniversary of St. Mary's School in 1985, recounts both the hardships and the love that surrounded these youngsters:

> I walked to school every day with my brothers and sisters about five miles each way. At times it was bitter cold and we felt nearly frozen; when we got to school sister would let us sit by the stove to get warm. There were times when Father Loughran would come along and he would stop to pick us up. He would let the tailgate down on his station wagon and the five of us would sit on it and ride to school. The wagon was already full of children he transported back and forth to school each day, but he wouldn't pass us by. (17)

Whatever was wanting by way of physical comforts, there was no doubt that St. Mary's merited the name "school" because of the excellence of its educational offerings. There were outstanding musical programs, spelling contests, plays, and many religious activities to engage the minds and souls of the students. Many of the students evidenced much talent for music and gradually a large music class was formed. Recitals and entertainments left deep impressions on the students and parents, many of who later recalled the events at "Gibbons Hall" with joy.

When St. Mary's opened there were two missions, namely, Rosaryville and Forestville, attended from there by their zealous pastor, Father Loughran. Sister Gerard Ford and Sister St. Teresa Healy took charge of the religion classes in both of these parishes on Sundays after Mass. It was on one such Sunday morning in 1926, after the sisters had returned to St. Mary's, that a raging tornado struck, destroying the Rosaryville mission.

Father Loughran's hope was realized when, in September 1926, two more sisters arrived to open the "colored" school—namely St. Mary's Hall—a large auditorium one block away from St. Mary's. Sisters Servula Healy and Maria Augustine Maher were delighted to find seventy-two children enrolled. Sister St. Teresa augmented the faculty by teaching music one day each week at St. Mary's Hall. She prepared the black children for a Latin High Mass that they sang for the Catholic congregation at Rosaryville.

St. Mary's Hall was not destined for rapid growth and even thirty years later, in 1956, was reported as having only 101 children. (18) The sisters were beginning to inaugurate the diocesan "integration plan" and had enrolled a total of six black children in the white school by the fall of 1957. (19) Full integration of all students in all classes would become a reality in 1963. (20)

By 1985, there were 316 pupils enrolled in St. Mary's School, with four sisters and one part-time and five full-time lay faculty members. (21)

St. Rita's Elementary School, Dundalk, Maryland

The following account of the founding and growth of St. Rita's, Dundalk, Maryland was prepared for the Parish Sixtieth Anniversary booklet, dated September 6, 1986:

> The history of Saint Rita School is deeply entwined in the history of Dundalk as a community. There was no Catholic Church in the vicinity at the time of the official establishment of the area post office, which occurred on November 1, 1928. Area Catholics attended Mass in either Highlandtown or Sparrows Point. As the population grew, the need for a Catholic Church in Dundalk grew as well. With the end of the war residential Catholics sought to establish their own parish church. Within two years, permission was granted by Archbishop Michael Curley to plan a permanent church. Reverend Joseph Weidenhan was assigned to establish the new parish in Dundalk, Maryland.
>
> At this time, Bethlehem Steel Company was offering to donate an acre of land to any church organization, stipulating that a permanent building be erected on the land within a year. Father Weidenhan not only took advantage of this offer, but also had enough foresight to purchase another acre at the same time. Thanksgiving Day has always been a special day at Saint Rita's because it was on that day, November 30, 1922, that the first Mass in Saint Rita's Church was celebrated. Many parishioners can still remember the original wooden structure that faced Dunleer Road.
>
> About eighteen months after the parish was founded, Father Weidenhan was assigned another major task. He received a call from Archbishop Curley requesting that a school be added to the parish. Church benefits were held in order to secure funds for this project, and by November 1925, plans were drawn up for the construction of a modern building with eight classrooms. Saint Rita's parishioners again showed their true Christian spirit. At the request of Father Weidenhan, the men volunteered to clear the

> ground of trees and underbrush to facilitate the digging of the foundation. The ground was staked off on Saturday, February 20,1926. On Monday, February 22, the actual work began.
>
> The cornerstone of the new eight-room school was laid and blessed on May 26, 1926, and on September 6, Saint Rita School opened its doors to one hundred and twenty-six pupils. Formal dedication of the school by Archbishop Curley took place on October 31, 1926. By the end of that school year, the enrollment had jumped to one hundred and eighty-five. Word spread fast that this was a fine school.
>
> The combined efforts of Archbishop Curley and Father Weidenhan had secured as teachers the Sisters, Servants of the Immaculate Heart of Mary of Scranton. (22)

The first community of sisters included Sister Anysia Moran, superior, Sister Paulina Langan, Sister Miriam Therese Rihn, and Sister Francis Marie Butler, with Sister Consilia Godfrey, a novice, being added in October as the enrollment moved up to one hundred and eighty-five students. Sister Caroline Cullin replaced Sister Consilia in December.

St. Rita's reputation for educational excellence continued to grow and four additional classrooms (the annex) were needed, and eventually another building. DeLauder Hall, named for the second pastor of St. Rita's parish, was constructed. This housed a lecture hall, library, two remedial reading rooms, an art room, and a parish meeting room. At its peak, St. Rita's had two classrooms for each grade level, with an enrollment of 969 students in 1959-1960. (23) The little community of five sisters had grown to thirteen (soon to become 15), and lay teachers also augmented these numbers.

Monsignor Weidenhan, the founding pastor, died on October 8, 1958, having lived to see the phenomenal growth of the school to 903 pupils in 1957, and to celebrate his Golden Jubilee of priesthood on October 25, 1956, and his 76th birthday on October 27, 1957.

One of St. Rita's most prestigious awards was to come in 1986 when under the principalship of Sister Beatrice Caulson, IHM, St. Rita's was chosen as one of the best elementary schools in the United States. The National Elementary School Recognition Program Committee selected 270 schools in the nation for this honor, five of which were in Maryland. Awards were based on how schools use resources and meet students' needs, with special emphasis on reading and mathematics achievement. This was, indeed a proud moment for St. Rita's, its 215 students and twelve full-time and three part-time teachers. (24)

Sacred Heart Elementary and High Schools, La Plata, Maryland (Renamed Archbishop Neale Elementary and High Schools)

Natural disasters have a way of unpredictably altering the course of history and of charting a new course of events. Such was probably the case when the "great tornado" struck La Plata, Maryland, on November 9, 1926. Devastation was widespread over much of the southeastern United States. One specific disaster, however, affected the coming of the Sisters of IHM to La Plata in 1927, namely, the total demolition of a public school by the tornado while classes were in session, causing the death of twenty-two children, most of whom were Catholic.

Mother Casimir's affirmative response to the request of the pastor, Reverend Brent Matthews, SJ, of Sacred Heart Parish in Charles County, La Plata, Maryland, resulted in the opening of the second school staffed by IHM Sisters in the then Archdiocese of Baltimore. Bishop Michael J. Curley's purchase of the property of the McDonough Institute for a consolidated parochial school to serve four area Jesuit parishes brought the sisters to a very historic setting.

Maurice J. McDonough, for whom the Institute was named, had been a peddler who died in April 1804, leaving his money for the education of children in the locale in which he had worked. The trustees of the McDonough Charity School Fund, incorporated in 1804, founded the McDonough Institute, an endowed school for both sexes in the fall of 1903, one half mile west of La Plata. The Institute being the only secondary school in the county, equipped with boarding accommodations for girls as early as 1904, and for boys by 1905, was very attractive, especially to students living at a distance. There were three buildings on about thirty-five acres of land. McDonough Institute flourished until 1927 when state aid was withdrawn. (25)

It was in this setting that Sacred Heart School, La Plata, was opened on September 8, 1927, with twenty pupils in seven grades. (By the close of the year there were fifty pupils.) The school had six classrooms and a library completely furnished. The Girls' Hall, erected in 1904, became the sisters' convent. This was a three-story building with an assembly hall, office, reception room, dining room, and rooms to accommodate about forty boarding students. Into this large dwelling came the initial four sisters: Sister Benedicta O'Brien, superior, Sister Seraphia Gallagher, Sister Leo Lehman, and Sister Norberta Streilly. Sisters Maria Immaculate Yahner and Catherine Ruane came later that year. This structure served as the convent until March 2, 1935, when it was destroyed by fire caused by an explosion of the oil furnace. A new convent was built and the sisters were once again settled by August 1935.

Sacred Heart School was to grow rapidly: by September 1943, there were 207 pupils from seven area parishes. Catechetical instruction was conducted by the sisters at Pomfert, Bel Alton, Issue, Rocky Point and Indian Head, Maryland. Since so many of the children in attendance at Sacred Heart School were from other parishes, it was decided in 1948 that these parishes should share the financial support of the school. The school was renamed Sacred Heart Consolidated School. Continued enrollment increases, together with the poor physical condition of the original school, resulted in the decision in 1952 to build a new school, a combination grade and high school, to be named "The Archbishop Neale School" in memory of Archbishop Leonard Neale, second Archbishop of Baltimore and a native son of Port Tobacco, Charles County. Sister M. Edwin Ott became the flrst principal of Archbishop Neale School, a combined grade and high school.

In the educational climate of later years, it is difficult to imagine that a high school would be opened in La Plata on September 8, 1929, with only a freshman class, and that class numbering only seventeen pupils. It is needful to think of the thirty mile distance to Washington, DC, and the lack of public transportation as a major obstacle to attendance elsewhere; it is needful to remember that the stock market crash of 1929 catapulted the world into the most severe economic depression ever known; it is needful to remember, as Hennessey states, that "American Catholics did not easily shake off the alienation and discouragement fostered by the message they seemed to be receiving in 1928." (26) By this comment, he referred, of course, to the bigotry that had beset Catholic candidate, Alfred E. Smith, in his campaign for the Democratic nomination for President of the United States in that year which caused Smith's defeat, and the rude awakening of Catholics to the fact that they were an object of mistrust and suspicion for their faith and their membership in the "Roman" Church. It was still demanded of the nation's Catholic citizens "that they establish the compatibility of their religion with American democratic ideals, laws, and practices." (27)

The action of the Catholic families of La Plata in providing for a secondary level to their parish educational offerings is very much in line with the clarion call issued by Paulist Father James Gillis, editor of the *Catholic World* in the December 1928 issue where he proclaimed "We Catholics shall not wither up and blow away."(28) It was a time both to "dig in" and to "reach out"; it was a time both to claim strengths and strengthen shortcomings; it was a time to gain both moral and intellectual ground. Catholic education was seen as the chief key to these goals.

These were certainly some of the reasons for the opening of Sacred Heart High School in 1929. The Department of Public Instruction of Maryland accredited this school in the following year, 1930.

Each year a class was to be added to the secondary school, but not without obvious difficulties. Mother Casimir had died soon after her letter of January 23, 1929 assuring the pastor, Reverend Charles Hennessey, SJ, that she would provide for the high school: "I think for at least a year one extra Sister ought to make it very easy to begin a high school . . . " (29) Carrying out this promise fell to Mother Mary William who was pressured by Father Hennessey's strong letters to send a sister in time for the opening of school on September 8, 1929, in spite of her statement in a letter of September 1, 1929, that ''I cannot possibly send you this Sister until after the Profession at Christmas . . . "(30)

It is apparent from a subsequent letter that Mother Mary William wished to keep the promise made by Mother Casimir, so Sister Stella Devers was appointed. (31) Although Sister Stella was of frail health she had been carrying a heavy teaching load at Marywood College in Scranton, Pennsylvania, so Mother Mary William felt this change to a small class of fifteen pupils in La Plata would not overtax her. Some time in the spring, possibly in March, however, Sister Stella became ill and could not continue in school at La Plata. There was no sister available to replace her, so it is likely that through the collaborative efforts of the priests and the grade school sisters the first year was completed. Reverend William B. Hannas, SJ, pastor of St. Joseph's Church, Pomfret, Maryland, aided the fledgling high school by teaching dramatics and encouraging athletics among the students, although the school had no gymnasium. There were many strengths considering the small setting: both academic and commercial subjects were offered; there was a fully equipped science laboratory for teaching of chemistry, biology, and general science; a separate building, Brent Hall, was built in 1935 as an auditorium. Above all, there was a strong religious emphasis and many religious and academic activities.

Throughout every subsequent administration of the Congregation there were requests made for additional sisters. The peak of 905 pupils, 159 of whom were high school students, and fifteen sisters in the combined grade and high schools was reached in 1960-1961. The strain on the physical plant by these enrollment increases was obvious: class sizes were unmanageable for good instruction; students on waiting lists had no possibility of admission; there were no private offices for the principals, no gymnasium, no classroom for the music teacher; cartons of unpacked books could not be placed in the library for lack of space. The library, in fact, was used as a classroom most of the time and there was no health room. Continued requests for solutions went unheeded because of financial constraints in the parishes and in the Archdiocese of Washington, DC. There were good intentions expressed by pastors and parishioners, but none of these translated into meeting the basic need for additional space. The suggestion of the IHM Congregation was that Archbishop Neale High School close and that the grade school be expanded to double track for each grade in the existing sixteen classrooms. Amid much protest and sadness this was done in 1975. Archbishop Neale Elementary School continues to thrive, with a 1985-1986 enrollment of 590 pupils in kindergarten through eighth grade. (32)

St. Bernardine's Elementary School, Baltimore, Maryland

A letter to Mother Casimir from Archbishop Michael Curley of Baltimore, dated April 7, 1928, provides the reason for the invitation to the Sisters of IHM to staff the future St. Bernardine's School in Baltimore.

> . . . You were kind enough to give us three communities for small schools in the Archdiocese in Upper Marlboro, Dundalk, and La Plata. I appreciate the generous kindness of the Community, and am now anxious to offer you a real school in the City of Baltimore . . . When you were willing enough to take charge of small schools, which to some Communities are not so attractive, I think that it is only right that I ought to give you consideration when it is a question of something that is really attractive. (33)

It didn't take Mother Casimir long, both to contact Scranton Diocese Bishop Thomas C. O'Reilly to obtain his permission (letter dated April 14, 1928), to respond to Archbishop Curley (letter dated April 15, 1928), and to receive his letter of gratitude for acceptance of the new mission (April 19, 1928). All of this activity was part of the total whirlwind of events that started with the May 12, 1927, request of the people of the Lyndhurst section of St. William's Parish in Baltimore to Archbishop Curley to organize a new parish. Their request was approved that very day and plans for a church, school, convent and rectory began to take shape in rapid order. Within a year, Reverend John A. Smith was appointed first pastor, with the parish plant erection already well under way. The church was the gift of the James Keelty Family, in memory of their daughter, Bernardine, who had died at five years of age. Their only request was that the church be named in honor of her patron Saint Bernardine of Siena. The church was formally dedicated on June 16,

1929. It was a magnificent granite structure, with interior features which included stained glass windows made in Munich, Germany; altars of white Italian marble; tabernacle, sanctuary lamp and candlesticks of French gold. The internal structure of the church was such that no view-obstructing pillars were used, but arched beams instead.

Meanwhile, St. Bernardine's School had opened on September 14, 1928, with one hundred sixty-five pupils in five grades. The first group of sisters assigned were Sister Josepha Hurley, superior, Sister Agathina Murray, Sister Catherine Marie Murphy, Sister Muriel Whalen, Sister Frances Maria Butler and Sister Marie Bernarde Kilcullen.

The spirit of these early years at St. Bernardine's is captured in the words of Sister Muriel Whalen, a member of the first community there. "We were very poor," she said, "when the pastor came to the convent in September to bring us one month's salary in advance, Mother Josepha had only four dollars in her purse to meet all our needs. But the people were generous in providing for us—I recall someone's giving us cartons of shredded wheat; others brought bushels of apples. We had shredded wheat and apple sauce for breakfast for nearly a year!" What could have been looked upon as poverty and sacrifice, Sister Muriel describes in this way: "We had loads of fun . . . it was Mother Josepha's great spirit which supported us." (34)

The convent was not completed at the time of the sisters' arrival, nor would it be completed until Thanksgiving time, 1928. The Flynn family offered their home completely furnished for the temporary use of the sisters. It was no small sacrifice for the Flynn family who continued until late November to reside at their summer home near the ocean. The convent was formally dedicated by Archbishop Curley on January 16, 1929, with fitting congratulations for the people of the parish who had accomplished so much in so short a time. (35)

By July 1929, Father John Smith was petitioning Mother Casimir for two additional sisters so that he could open both sixth and seventh grades in September. Then, the age-old struggle began, for there were never enough sisters to fill the demands being made for their services. To Father Smith's request, Mother Casimir replied: "I have given your note of July 15th careful thought and I find it impossible for me to give you two more Sisters in September. To begin with, it is a waste of time for a teacher to spend her entire day with twelve pupils, another with twenty-one, another with twenty-four." (36)

She then goes on to explain the manner in which the problem could be solved by doubling up certain grades. Needless to say, there was a letter from Father John Smith by return mail expressing his disappointment, saying: "I have been in school work for twenty-four years, and I do not agree with you 'that it is a waste of time for a teacher to spend her entire day with twelve, twenty-one and twenty-four pupils.' The work done in this school last year by your teachers was excellent . . . I do not think they consider their year wasted." (37)

The Silver Anniversary booklet of St. Bernardine's Church reports the conclusion of this above exchange of letters: "In 1929, the sixth and seventh grades were added to the school, and taught in one classroom." (38) It appears that both Sister Josepha and Sister Agathina were reassigned; Sister Wenceslaus became the new superior and teacher of both sixth and seventh grades whose enrollment was quite small; Sister Ellen Marie Loftus replaced Sister Agathina Murray.

The peak days of St. Bernardine's seem to have been reached in 1955 when an enrollment of 845 was recorded. A downward plummet began about 1959, and it was noted in 1963-1964 that the enrollment of 376 students was a decrease of some 400 students in a four-year period.

In order to meet the decline being experienced in both nearby St. Edward's School and in St. Bernardine's and to address the growing social pressures caused by the changing racial balance in these geographical areas, John XXIII Elementary Education Center was established in 1967-1968, merging students from the two parishes, and IHMs and Sisters of the Holy Union of Sacred Hearts, in the St. Bernardine's School building. Special education was also offered.

The enrollment in the new educational center reflected the racial changes, with three Chinese, seventeen white and 268 black children registered. John XXIII had become an inner-city school. (39)

Mounting personal and educational frustrations and tensions led to the withdrawal of the IHM Sisters from this setting in January 1970.

PENNSYLVANIA MISSIONS

From 1920 through 1929 Mother Casimir accepted seven new schools in Pennsylvania, scattered from West Scranton to the western part of the State of Pennsylvania in Pittsburgh. These were: St. Ann's, Scranton, 1920; St. Mary's, Avoca, 1921; St. Thomas, Ashville, 1921; St. Justin's, Pittsburgh, 1926; St. Thomas, Archbald, 1927; St. Charles, Sugar Notch, and Epiphany, Sayre, 1929. The opening of the first of these, St. Ann's, Scranton, has previously been described in Sister Immaculata Gillespie's book, *THE SISTERS OF THE IHM* published in 1921. (40) In addition, Mother Casimir completed two of the new Marywood College buildings, ventured into two social service ministries, opened St. Agnes Place, Elmhurst, for the care of the ill and elderly sisters, and founded St. Joseph's Hospital, Carbondale.

St. Mary's Elementary School, Avoca, Pennsylvania

Forged out of hardships and struggles, the story of St. Mary's, Avoca, is a story of the faith that brought a people from the "Emerald Isle" to Pleasant Valley, Luzerne County, Pennsylvania in the mid-1800s. It was a "time of the troubles" for them in their new land, as it had been in their homeland. Material goods were scant in spite of hard, long hours of labor in the mines and on the railroads.

The "time of the troubles" took various forms like the train car disaster that occurred on October 10, 1888, at Mud Run between Hazleton and Avoca, which killed twenty-seven parishioners of St. Mary's Parish. To memorialize the victims, the town's name was changed from Pleasant Valley to Avoca, a Gaelic name reminiscent of the "sweet vale" of Avoca in their homeland.

The sacrifices which these people made to build their church had to be made over and over again as trouble struck first on October 3, 1893, when a windstorm blew off part of the roof and front of the structure, causing the grand spire of St. Mary's to topple to the ground. Again, on June 12, 1910, a mine subsidence occurred under the church severely damaging the property. People of lesser faith, and a pastor of lesser zeal than Reverend Michael Crane, would have given up, but "assisted by the generous efforts of his people, he (Father Crane) succeeded in repairing the church . . . St. Mary's was again rededicated on September 21, 1913." (41)

Father Crane had cherished the hope of providing a parochial school for the children of his parish, many of whom traveled each day to St. John's in Pittston to attend a Catholic school. In 1919, when he could announce that he had saved $40,000 toward this project, the construction of the school was begun. The following year, on December 27, 1920, Father Crane celebrated the Golden Jubilee of his priesthood. On that occasion the parishioners presented him with a gift of $11,000, which he immediately designated as a starting fund for building a convent for the sisters. To raise such amounts of money in those times and under the circumstances is a great tribute to these devoted people.

On August 1, 1921, Father Crane received the welcome news that the Sisters, Servants of the Immaculate Heart of Mary had agreed to staff the new school. The first group of sisters included: Sister dePazzi Houlihan, principal and superior, Sister Cornelia Tillman, Sister Roseann O'Boyle, Sister Patrice Kearney, Sister Angela McNulty, Sister Jean Marie Swift, Sister Georgina Wertz, Sister Rebecca Doyle, Sister Alphonsus Marie Downey, Sister Hilarion Sullivan, Sister Maura Fleury, and Sister Clementine Gunther. On September 2, 1921, St. Mary's School opened to 500 students in seven grades, undoubtedly a double track system for some grades.

Until the convent was completed on July 23, 1923, the sisters lived in a rented double house under very crowded conditions and, in the poverty of its furnishings, reminiscent of the early days in Monroe, Michigan. Father Crane was not to live to see the completion of the convent. On the bitter cold Christmas Eve of December 24, 1921, his final act of charity was performed as he went to look after the furnace in the basement of the sisters' house. A few hours after his return to the rectory, he died. His forty-seven years of service to St. Mary's Parish were ended.

The first graduation from St. Mary's School took place in that same year, 1923. From that first class there were eventually to be four vocations to the religious life, three priests and one sister, Sister John Francis Marley, IHM. Over the one-hundred-year period from 1874-1974 St. Mary's Parish has had sixty-one religious vocations—thirty-one priests, two brothers, and twenty-eight sisters, nineteen of whom were IHMs.

Enrollment was to fluctuate at St. Mary's School, relating the school to the economic rise and fall of the area's population. By 1955-1956 there were 321 children in eight grades, with a peak of 368 being reached in 1960. The period of the 70s saw steep declines, and attempts to build up the school were made. A kindergarten was introduced as part of the "Save Our School" campaign of the 80s. The sisters were withdrawn in June 1984, leaving behind a legacy of faith and sacrifice that would motivate the parishioners to continue their school with an all-lay faculty and principal. (42)

St. Thomas Aquinas Elementary School, Ashville, Pennsylvania

In the 1900s Ashville, in western Pennsylvania, was a small, quiet mining town with no theater, no public park or water amusements, with few cars, and little interest or outlet to the rest of the world. People rarely met, except at church on Sunday. Since all but four or five families were Catholic, this meant that the whole town had its social meetings at church on Sunday. The Church of St. Thomas Aquinas could have been the focal point of much activity, but the pastor, Reverend F. X. O'Donnell, a priestly and kindly man, was not socially inclined. There were no church societies, no devotions of any kind, or youth programs to bring the people together.

Into this milieu in 1920, Bishop John Joseph McCort of Altoona introduced the idea of building a parochial school. Tension developed between the pastor and the men of the parish, as it was evident that Father O'Donnell had no experience in building and had ideas for a far more costly building than this mining parish could afford. Nonetheless, the men of the parish worked evenings after their own full days in the mines in order to dig the foundation for the school themselves. Meanwhile, Father O'Donnell hired a contractor from Cresson to build the school, and the parish turned against him and would not support it. (43)

The school building was not completed until October 1921, but the sisters arrived and school opened in the parish hall on September 8, 1921. The first sisters included: Sister Annunciata Madden, Sister Mariana Weir, Sister Rosalind Nailen, and Sister Joseph Marie McGraw. Over two hundred pupils registered on the first day, including Protestants, Jews and Catholics, leaving only seven pupils in the Ashville Public School. In a short time this and two other public schools in the outlying areas also closed, since the children living within a radius of four miles attended the parochial school. It was a great event since many had never before seen a sister.

In the spring of 1923 Father O'Donnell was replaced by Reverend James Sass of Loretto, Pennsylvania, who proved to be an excellent manager, but he, too, failed to win the people's support. (44)

The school, however, became the hub for all activities and the sisters received great respect and support. Their efforts were centered on bringing the people together since there were still few church activities. An orchestra was started, plays and recitals given—and even a baseball team was organized. Through friends, the sisters secured some cast off Chicago Cubs uniforms for the boys, and games were arranged with St. Monica's, Chest Springs, and with Sacred Heart and St. Mark's of Altoona. St. Thomas' boys, who called themselves "the sisters' boys" won nearly every game they played, so a great spirit was generated.

The women of the parish scrubbed the school throughout twice a year, making a real day of it that ended with a dinner served by the sisters and some of the women. (45)

Letters from Reverend Stephen P. McGarvey, pastor of St. Thomas' Parish in 1936 to Mother M. Josepha, superior general of the Congregation, described clearly the financial plight in which he found himself. He wrote: "Conditions here are so deplorable that as much as I regret it, I find it necessary to close the school next year. My monthly collection for 1935 amounted to $479.00 and my school collection amounted to $297.00 . . . It is impossible for me to run the school and scarcely possible to run the parish on the contributions received . . . "(46)

A letter from Mother Josepha to Monsignor John Cordori, who was serving as administrator of the Altoona Diocese after Bishop McCort's death, expressed the sadness of the sisters at the proposed closing of the school. Mother Josepha said in part, "I know the conditions in that little town have been very trying since the depression. For that reason I have been glad to give the services of the sisters gratis, and I am willing to continue doing so until times are better . . . " (47)

Monsignor Cordori's response indicated that the Bishop's Council had, in fact, given permission to Father McGarvey in 1935 to close the school if the financial condition did not improve. He felt, therefore, that he, as temporary administrator, could not act in the case. (48)

Thus, St. Thomas School in Ashville was closed in June 1936, after fifteen years in existence. In that time it had nurtured sixteen religious vocations—thirteen to the Sisters of IHM, two became School Sisters of Notre Dame and one a Sister of Charity of Greensburg, Pennsylvania.

St. Justin's Elementary School, Pittsburgh, Pennsylvania

St. Justin's Parish, Pittsburgh, was, in 1925, a newly formed parish taken from part of the very large parish of St. Mary of the Mount, Pittsburgh. The IHM Sisters who staffed St. Mary of the Mount were thus well known to the people whose children either attended St. Mary of the Mount School or received catechetical instruction from these sisters.

Early in 1925 at the request of Reverend John B. Barry, pastor of the newly established parish, Mother Casimir agreed to staff St. Justin's Elementary School, with long-range plans to include also the staffing of a high school. The first sisters sent to St. Justin's were: Sister Hyacinth Tierney, superior and principal; Sister Concilium Lynn, Sister Delphina Healy, Sister Lucinda Harrington, Sister Joachim Lane, Sister Gonzales McGowan, Sister Neumann Murray and Sister Agnes Marie Johnson. Two postulants were also assigned: Margaret Pouloux, later to become Sister Margaret Cecilia and Hannah O'Riordan who became Sister Canice.

The sisters lived in a small house near the school for the first two years at St. Justin's. It was soon clear that even with "doubling up" this house was not adequate. Father Barry moved from the rectory, thus providing the sisters with housing in which each would have her own bedroom, and the two music teachers each had space for their many music pupils.

St. Justin's School was an impressive new building with eight classrooms and a large, very long auditorium, which was built with the intention of gradually being divided and used as high school classrooms. (49)

While the people of this area were mostly middle class, and some even well to do, they were somewhat bitter about having built the parish and school at St. Mary of the Mount and were now being asked to build up a new parish at St. Justin's. This somewhat dampened their enthusiasm about plans and activities at the school in the beginning.

But, as Sister Gonzales said, "We just had to sell ourselves, and in time, through the involvement of the children in academic contests, plays, recitals and their singing at Masses, the people saw the value of the education being provided." (50) According to Sister's account, the youngsters were truly cooperative and interested in their school and the parents very supportive in spite of the huge parish debt.

The private music pupils were so numerous that two teachers had to teach all day and after supper in order to accommodate all. It was well for the sisters that their meager monthly salaries were supplemented by this music income.

In light of subsequent developments at St. Justin's, it is interesting to note the terms of one of the earliest "School Contracts" signed by Mother M. Casimir and Reverend John B. Barry, pastor, on May 10, 1925. It is not so important that the agreed upon salary was thirty-five dollars per month per teacher, since such salaries were usual even into the 1950s for sisters working in parish schools. What is more pertinent in this case is the first point of the contract which states: "The party of the second part (IHM Congregation) agrees to supply such numbers of teachers as the party of the first part (Pastor) may require, which teachers shall be religious sisters belonging to the Congregation of the party of the second part . . ."(51)

Of equal importance was the fourth point of the agreement which reads " . . .This agreement may be cancelled for a just cause by the party of the first part . . . and the party of the second part by giving six months' notice of its intention so to do; said cancellation of agreement not to be made by either party during the course of the school term." (52)

These points became crucial in August of 1930 when it was necessary for Mother Mary William, as successor to Mother Casimir, to write to Father Barry to tell him that "it will be impossible for me to send you more than two high school teachers at this time . . . there are three parochial schools opening in September. It was not until last May that we were called upon to supply Sisters for these schools, and since they are in our own Diocese I must take care of them." (53) An immediate return letter expressed Father Barry's outrage and closes with the sentence, "By the eternal laws of justice I demand that you send us the twelve teachers." (54)

Father Barry had already postponed the opening of the high school in 1929, hence his determination to get it under way in 1930 and his desire to see both the grade and high school fully staffed by religious. The problems of both parties are understandable, and it is obvious that Father Barry considered the contract to have already been null and void when he failed to honor the six months' notice provision. His final telegram to Mother Mary William read: "We have secured another Community. Grateful to your Sisters for their splendid work." (55) It seems that he had, indeed, within three days, procured a full staff of twelve sisters from the Erie, Pennsylvania, Mercy Congregation.

The response from Mother Mary William which closed this five-year association with Father Barry and St. Justin's Parish was simply: "In reply to your telegram just received, we are grateful to you for the favor." Very sincerely yours, Sisters of IHM per Mother Mary William. (56)

As Sister Gonzales explained, "We accomplished a lot in five years and would have loved to continue working with these beautiful children." (57) At the sisters' departure in August 1930 there were 438 pupils in the elementary and seventy-six in the secondary school.

St. Thomas Elementary School, Archbald, Pennsylvania
St. Thomas Post-Graduate Commercial School

The first Catholics had settled in Archbald, Pennsylvania, in 1845. Their strong faith was nurtured by dedicated priests who celebrated Mass in the parishioners' homes once or twice a month. They encouraged those who were able to walk the six miles to Carbondale to St. Rose of Lima Church on the other Sundays and Holy Days. Even after a mission church was erected in 1850, because of the shortage of priests, Archbald Catholics continued to have Mass only twice a month. Such was the dedication and sacrifice of these good people that when their numbers required a new church in 1870, they were able to pay off the entire debt in a period of eight years. This was achieved in spite of the fact that times were bad and the mines, where most of the men and boys were employed, were working only half time.

It was this kind of faith which enabled the Archbald Catholics to sustain a devastating fire which destroyed most of the sanctuary and valuable paintings in their new church on March 15, 1875, just six weeks after its dedication.

It was this kind of faith that supported them again when in 1899 a cyclone struck the town of Archbald and damaged the church steeple, requiring it to be rebuilt. The heart and center of the life of the Archbald Catholic families seemed to be their church. Each succeeding pastor renewed, repaired and increased the beauty of the church property in spite of financial hardships. There was yet another disaster in the spring of 1942 when heavy rains caused White Oak Creek to burst through and flood the area, damaging much of the church property, especially the heating plants.

Against this background and the factors of a six-month strike in 1925, and the onslaught of the great depression, it is amazing that Reverend Michael Manley, pastor from 1924-1935 was able to lead his people to the establishment of St. Thomas Aquinas Elementary School in 1927 and St. Thomas Convent in 1929. (58)

St. Thomas Elementary School building was originally a three story parish hall. Reverend Miles McAndrew's history of the parish comments:

> From 1914 to September 1927, the Parish Hall served the community and the parish in numerous ways. It was in 1927, however, that Reverend Michael F. Manley, Pastor, established St. Thomas Aquinas Parochial School and brought the Sisters, Servants of I.H.M. to Archbald to staff the school when it opened in September 1927. In the parish hall he found a building, relatively new, and easily convertible into a school. (59)

The first sisters came on September 2, 1927. They were Sister Julia Herron, superior and principal, Sisters Edith Ralston, Olive Kelly, Cecilius McHale and Josephine Marie Martin. Four grades were opened that first year, with a total of 368 pupils, 128 of whom were first-graders. The sisters resided on the second floor of a home on Gilmartin Street for one year, then moved to the home of Mrs. Molly Moran opposite the church for a time before the convent was completed in 1929. By then, the fifth and sixth grades had been added to the school, and in 1931-1932 both the seventh and the eighth grades. Thus, 1931-1932 saw the first graduating class from St. Thomas, a class of thirty-nine, with twenty boys and nineteen girls.

In September 1928, Father Manley decided to open a post-graduate commercial program for graduates of the Archbald Public High School in order to provide courses not available to the young people of his parish without traveling to business schools in Scranton. Classrooms and equipment were provided and housed in a section of the convent that became known as St. Thomas Post-Graduate Commercial School. By 1943 a survey showed four hundred graduates of this school well placed in a variety of businesses in scattered geographical locations. This school continued with highly successful business graduates until 1950 when it was closed "due to the fact that all the boys were being called to the service." (60)

St. Thomas Elementary School continued under the staffing of four IHM Sisters and six full-time lay teachers. Its enrollment hovered around the original 368 pupils into the 1970s, but a decline began with the loss of 128 pupils in the ten-year period from 1969-1979. The 1985 enrollment was 156 pupils. Some 200 pupils were enrolled in weekly catechetical instructions. (61)

The combined faith-filled influences of the family, the parish and the school have resulted in many young people's responding to the Lord's call for service through religious life. Forty-seven priests, fifty-three sisters and two religious brothers are natives of St. Thomas Aquinas Parish, Archbald. One of these was to become Mother Marcella Gill who served as superior general of the Sisters of IHM from 1940 to 1955.

Epiphany Elementary School, Sayre, Pennsylvania

In reading the request of Reverend James F. Houlihan, pastor of the Church of the Epiphany, Sayre, Pennsylvania, in August of 1928, Mother Casimir would not have known that the approval she would give for sisters to open a school in Sayre in September 1929 would have to be finalized by her successor. The last year before her death was as dedicated to forwarding Christ's mission and that of the Church as all her years had been. She was in tune with the great desire of Bishop O'Reilly that a Catholic school be established in every parish, as had been mandated by the Third Plenary Council of Baltimore in 1884.

It is not surprising then that Father Houlihan's letter rather presumed that sisters would be provided, as he wrote:

> Dear Mother Casimer (sic): Bishop O'Reilly has approved a six grade school for Sayre and he also gave me permission to have the Immaculate Heart Sisters. The school will open in September, 1929 . . . I will have a fine place ready for the nuns in the way of a school and convent. I also promise that my people will work well with the Sisters and that we will have a fine school." (62)

Not every pastor would be certain he could really rally his parishioners to respond to such promises, but Father Houlihan would prove over his twenty years as pastor of Epiphany Church, Sayre, (1922-1942) that he had such leadership. His continuing optimism and positive support of the sisters was evident in subsequent letters written by him to Mother Mary William in the fall of 1929. (63)

Once sure that the sisters were to open the school in September 1929, he converted the old church on North Elmer Avenue, built about 1890 under the pastorate of Reverend John Costello, into a parochial school. He also converted the old rectory into a convent for the sisters.

Five sisters were assigned, one serving as a free principal, and four teachers, some of whom had double grades. The first faculty included Sister Mary Thomas McAndrew, superior and principal, Sister Devota Walsh, Sister St. Dominic Foley, Sister Clement Shermanson and Sister Benigna Ball, until she became ill with pneumonia in March. (64)

There were 148 students, 28 in first grade, 23 in second, 33 in third,

17 in fourth, 32 in fifth and 15 in sixth grade. In subsequent years the seventh and eighth grades were added, and in 1933 a class of twenty-one students was graduated.

The 1890 church building, which had become in 1929 Epiphany Parochial School, served well until 1963 when the seventy-three year old building was condemned by the Pennsylvania Department of Public Instruction as unsafe. A new site was purchased on Stevenson Street and by August 31, 1964, the new Epiphany School was dedicated. The pastor, Reverend Francis Toolan, deserves much credit for opening this $411,667 structure debt-free. That the new building would be a drawing card for increased enrollment was borne out by the registration of 351 students in eight grades in the first September of the new building's opening. (65)

A new convent was constructed also and the sisters, now seven in number, moved into their new, beautiful home at 627 Stevenson Street, adjacent to the school, in the fall of 1966-1967.

Changing economic patterns in the Sayre area, as well as rising tuition costs at Epiphany School caused gradual enrollment decline. The 1985-1986 enrollment was 197 pupils, with four full-time and one part-time sister faculty, and five full-time and two part-time lay faculty. (66)

St. Mary John Elementary School, Cresson, Pennsylvania

The Sisters of IHM had staffed St. John and St. Mary's orphan homes for boys and girls since January 4, 1909, and September 24, 1917, respectively. Until the year 1928, however, separate grade schools were maintained in each home. St. John's in addition, had a two-year high school that both boys and the girls attended. The burden of providing two complete teaching staffs for the homes, as well as the need of a parochial school for the Catholic children of nearby St. Aloysius Parish, Cresson, resulted in a decision by the Most Reverend John J. McCort, DD, to build a grade school on the grounds near St. Mary's Home. It was a small, one-story brick building and was opened on November 15, 1928. Bishop McCort named it the St. Mary John School. Three hundred children were enrolled on opening day and placed under the teaching staff that included Sister Uriel Hurst, Sister Robert Gerrity, Sister Dunstan Gallagher, Sister Matilda O'Boyle, Sister Irenaeus Turner, Sister Geraldine Tessier, Sister Macaria Mooney and Sister Kevin Maria McMullin. The preschool children of both homes were cared for in the kindergarten by Sister Claudia Whelan.

Reverend Father Strittmatter, pastor of St. Aloysius Church, made provision for the children of his parish to pay a book rental fee of one dollar per year and to furnish their own writing materials. The children of his parish who lived at too great a distance to attend St. Mary John School were provided religious instructions on Wednesday after school and on Saturday morning. Sister Anna Maria Hayes and Sister Myra Haggerty taught these classes.

The high school at St. John's Home was discontinued in 1938, and since there was no Catholic high school in the area, boys and girls of high school age were sent to the Cresson Public High School.

At one point in its history St. Mary John School was able to offer space for students from the nearby Sankertown district. In 1942 the Sankertown Public School was burned to the ground. Acting on the advice of Bishop Guilfoyle, the chaplain of the orphanages, Father Hacala, offered to accommodate the displaced pupils of Sankertown, and the school's Board of Directors accepted his offer. (67)

In light of the fact that the orphanages were built to house 300 children, and in 1961 had about 38, it was decided by then Bishop J. Carroll McCormick to make other arrangements to provide for the orphans and for the Catholic education of Cresson children. St. Mary John School had some 200 pupils in 1961.

The General State Authority of Pennsylvania and the Altoona Johnstown Diocese, represented by the Bishop, entered into a transaction by which the Commonwealth purchased St. John's Home, St. Mary's Home, St. Mary John School and a related recreation park—a total of 147 acres of property—in 1962. The actual date of the takeover of the school was June 15, 1963. The complex was to be used as a youth development center for girls 12 to 18 years of age committed by juvenile courts in central Pennsylvania.

The sisters who had taught at St. Mary John School at its closing were asked to staff the new St. Aloysius Parochial School which opened in 1963. (68)

St. Charles Elementary School, Sugar Notch, Pennsylvania

The area in which Sugar Notch, Pennsylvania, is located was originally settled in 1754 and became incorporated in April 1867. In the early years, most of the population was Catholic of German, Irish, and Polish ancestry. Most of the men were employed at "Number 9 and 10" mines, which were the best producing collieries in the Wyoming Valley. Most of the homes in which they lived were owned by the coal companies. The coming of the railroads made it possible for the area to grow more rapidly as there was increased coal production and shipping by rail.

Up until 1875 Mass was offered by visiting priests in a carpenter shop at "Number 9" colliery on Sundays. Reverend Thomas J. Rea, a native of

County Cork, Ireland, was the first resident pastor, serving about one thousand parishioners.

By 1913 there were two more Catholic parishes, Holy Family and Sts. Peter and Paul, which were established to meet the needs of Polish and Lithuanian Catholic immigrants in the area. (69)

The Very Reverend Walter A. Gorman, pastor of St. Charles Borromeo Parish in 1928 was planning for the construction of a school and convent in the parish. Both structures were large, two-story frame buildings, well built and fully equipped. Besides the classrooms, the school also contained a large auditorium.

When school opened in September 1929, 228 pupils in six grades were in attendance. Simple arithmetic would make it appear that about 38 pupils were in each grade. The fact was, however, that there were three sisters, each with double grades, so one can imagine the "large group" instruction that must have challenged this first faculty. Sister Nepomucene Caffrey, superior and principal, together with Sister Presentation Wilkinson and Sister Laurence Tierney, as many teachers did even into the 50s, taught these large groups of youngsters very well.

Even to 1971, at the time of the withdrawal of the sisters from St. Charles School, the double-grade arrangement continued, with the principal and superior carrying responsibility also for fifth and sixth grades, and the music teacher covering the total school music program, private after-school lessons, and grades three and four. By this time, the enrollment had decreased to about 154 pupils in eight grades. It is obvious from the convent annals that the sisters were willing to continue these arrangements in order to save their school. (70) Attempts at a merger of St. Charles' with St. Leo's School proved unworkable because of space limitations at St. Leo's, hence the closing of St. Charles School in June 1971.

NEW YORK MISSIONS

Nativity Parish Catechetical Instruction, New York, New York

In September of 1921, Mother Casimir responded to a request from Reverend Patrick Quinnan, SJ, pastor of Nativity Parish, New York City, for sisters to undertake catechetical instruction there. Father Quinnan was well known to Mother Casimir because he had been pastor at St. Cecilia's in Wyoming, Pennsylvania, and founded that school prior to his entrance into the Society of Jesus.

In the absence of school and convent facilities at Nativity Parish, it was agreed that the sisters would reside at St. Alphonsus Convent on Thompson Street, with our sisters who lived there, and that they would travel each day to the Nativity parish hall to teach pupils from five large public schools. Since the classes did not begin until dismissal of the schools in the afternoon, the sisters were engaged as sacristans, clerical workers, caring for the church books, the envelope system and statements of monthly contributions of the parish. The sisters appointed for this work were Sister Gerald O'Donnell and Sister Josephine Connerton. Sister Eugene Murray and Sister Oswalda Flaherty, a novice, assisted them later. Subsequent transfers brought Sister Rebecca Doyle to assist Sister Gerald O'Donnell.

Some of the Catholic teachers who brought their pupils from the public schools to catechetical instructions also assisted with the instructions. Miss Cain, Miss Bergen, and Miss Fitzpatrick were among these public school teachers. Especially noteworthy was the assistance given by Miss Kemp, a Jewish woman, who was principal of Public School 63. It is said that on Wednesday and Friday, the days for Catholic instructions, she had a special "Catholic bell" rung five minutes before regular dismissal in order to assemble the Catholic students for instructions.

At the beginning of the third year, several public schools were on half-session because of the overflow numbers of students. This fact made it possible for the sisters to hold some of the catechetical instructions in the morning and early afternoon. Father Quinnan engaged one of the Parish Visitors of Mary Immaculate to assist, thus it was possible to have the classes several times a week.

Father Quinnan had always desired to erect a parish school at Nativity, but was unable to do so because of the transient population and resultant unstable income. It was decided that a day nursery was the only work that could be carried on, so the Missionary Helpers of the Sacred Heart took over this new work. Sister Gerald and Sister Rebecca were appointed to the newly-opened Sacred Hearts High School in 1925, having completed an amazing four years of religious instruction which reached an estimated eight hundred New York City youngsters. (71)

St. Patrick's Elementary School, Oneida, New York

Reverend John McGraw, pastor of St. Patrick's, Oneida, had come there in October 1913. From the beginning of his pastorate he expressed his desire to build a parochial school. It was not until a memorable May 16, 1919, that Father McGraw was able to announce in the *Oneida Dispatch* that property at the rear of the church had been purchased for a parochial school.

From the time of this announcement, through the succeeding two and one-half years, the people of St. Patrick's Parish were busy with this project. In the summer of 1920 Bishop John Grimes laid the cornerstone of the school. Before the winter started, the exterior of the building was completed and work continued on the interior throughout the winter months. The total cost of both school and convent was $163,000, about one third of which was raised through a parish fund drive.

A somewhat unique ceremony marked the opening of St. Patrick's School, Oneida. On Sunday afternoon, September 8, 1921, following the Confirmation service of some 250 children, Most Reverend John Grimes, Bishop of Syracuse, accompanied by about forty visiting clergy, and escorted by the Knights of Columbus, entered the school and blessed each room. The entire congregation and visitors thronged through the school building. The following day the school was less ceremoniously, but more "officially" opened as two hundred children in six elementary grades set to work. Sister Josepha Hurley was the first principal and superior, with the total community including also Sister Pauline Gallagher, Sister Agathina Murray, Sister Clement Schermanson, Sister Cecil Nooney, and Sister Catherine Marie Murphy.

A high school was also opened in 1925 but was discontinued in 1929 because of the failure to obtain New York State approval for the third and fourth year classes, since there was insufficient space in the building. Actually, only one class graduated from this high school. There was another attempt to maintain at least a first year of high school between 1961 and 1968, although the enrollment for that class was only about 25 pupils.

As testimony to the quality of education offered at St. Patrick's and the desire of the parents to have their children in a Catholic school, the enrollment history of St. Patrick's has been a positive one, indeed. The high point was reached in 1960-1961 when 525 pupils from kindergarten through eighth grades were enrolled and eight sisters and one lay teacher staffed this vibrant school. (72)

The gradual decline was to occur almost twenty-five years later when the enrollment dipped to 173 in 1982-1983 and was 179 in the final year of the sisters' presence there. Three sisters, Sister Christina Aldarelli, principal, Sister Antoinette Bosak, primary teacher, and Sister Carolyn Cossack, junior high teacher, were to prepare the seven lay teachers for the continuance of St. Patrick's School under complete lay staffing in 1984-1985. Thus, after sixty-three years of service in St. Patrick's, Oneida, the sisters were withdrawn.

The homily preached by Reverend John H. Comeskey, pastor, at the final appreciation Mass for the sisters on June 9, 1984, is undoubtedly a prophetic message about our role in all of our ministries in the future: to prepare the laity to assume their place in the church's ministries. Father Comeskey compared the sisters to the missionaries of old who brought their own priests and sisters to evangelize new areas, but when the mission area was mature and prepared, the missionaries would move on, leaving the native clergy and catechists to continue their work.

> The IHM Sisters are leaving like the missionaries of old: (a) they have taught your children; (b) they have raised up an active Parents' Club; (c) they have trained our lay teachers; (d) they have laid a solid educational foundation. Now we are mature enough to continue on our own . . . As you leave we say, thank you; we love you; we appreciate all you have done! You have left us a Christian heritage to perpetuate, a solid school to continue, a Christian tradition to appreciate! (73)

St. Ephrem's Elementary School, Brooklyn, New York

Writing history from the vantage point of nearly sixty-five years after the events gives an opportunity to see how the seeds for future happenings were present in that past event. The language and attitude of the 1980s Catholic church emphasize the "Mutual Relationships Between Bishops and Major Superiors of Religious," the language of "collaboration" among bishops, clergy, religious and laity within the Church and ecumenical relationships with those of other faiths. These Post-Vatican II concepts present, in fact, in the early church, were in shadow through centuries of persecution, "holy" wars, struggles between church and state, through intellectual controversies and heresies and the suppression of religious orders. Diocesan thoughts of collaboration and sharing were not that evident in the 19th century United States of America as religious congregations began to flourish and their services were in demand. Individual bishops were quite possessive of these groups of sisters, most of whom were clearly "diocesan" in their establishment and outreach.

It is, therefore, important to note the "whole church" view and the collaborative attitude which led the newly consecrated Bishop William Hoban of the Scranton Diocese to accede to the request of the newly installed Bishop Thomas Molloy of the Brooklyn Diocese for the services of the IHM Sisters in St. Ephrem's School, Brooklyn, New York. The series of letters begins with a request from Reverend Richard Kennedy, pastor of St. Ephrem's, to Mother Casimir early in January 1922. Mother Casimir's response to this "native son" and former pupil of our sisters in Scranton was very positive:

> Your application will, of course, have to receive the approval of our Bishop.I feel confident that he will gladly consent to our

> taking up your work in September. If so, you may look for eight teachers to take charge of your proposed school. (74)

Meanwhile, Reverend Joseph McClancy, Superintendent of Catholic Schools in Brooklyn, was busy contacting Bishop Molloy so that by February 11, 1922 he could write to Mother Casimir:

> I am directed by our Right Reverend Bishop to notify you that he will be pleased to have your community teach in the Diocese of Brooklyn. You are at liberty to convey this request to the attention of Bishop Hoban who in his Catholic outlook on the Church's interest may see fit to allow the favor to Bishop Molloy. (75)

One wonders why Bishop Molloy did not contact Bishop Hoban directly, but whatever the reason, Mother Casimir wasted no time in getting the required permission. By March 1, 1922 she wrote to Bishop Molloy of Brooklyn:

> In conversation with our Right Reverend Bishop last week, the matter of entering your diocese was discussed. Our good Bishop is highly pleased with the recognition you have given to our community and freely consents to permit us to devote our energies to the charges you are about to entrust to us. (76)

It was not common to have a contract in 1922, so it is of historical importance to note some of the provisions of this Brooklyn Diocesan document:

> . . . The Community shall supply, as far as possible, a sufficient number of competent teachers to conduct the work of the school properly . . . Without the explicit consent of the Right Reverend Bishop or the Reverend Rector, lay teachers shall not be employed in any school of the diocese.
> . . . All teachers, except those forty years of age and over, who are in charge of the fifth or a higher grade, shall, after September 1, 1927, hold a high school certificate or its equivalent.
> . . . Schools of eight or more rooms shall have a free principal on or before September 1, 1925. (77)

Other duties of the Sisters were detailed in the contract, such as teaching Sunday school, taking charge of the children's Sunday Mass and children's sodalities, conducting commencement exercises and one other entertainment each year, and keeping the ordinary records of the school.

In return, the rector of the parish was to provide the following:

> . . . a salary of Forty Dollars per month for each teacher and the directress for ten months. If no convent is provided by the parish, each Sister will receive forty-five Dollars per month.
>
> . . . a completely furnished dwelling with "ample and well-ventilated sleeping quarters, a community room and the usual bath, toilet and laundry facilities. . . " Light and heat were also to be supplied.
>
> . . . Holy Communion shall be distributed to them (the Sisters) every morning at a fixed time, not later than seven o'clock.
>
> . . . the Sisters may teach private music lessons in the convent and retain the income derived therefrom. (78)

It is sincerely hoped that the income from the private music lessons was considerable in light of the fact that eight sisters each earning four hundred dollars per year yielded a sparse total indeed. It seems that the Diocese of Brooklyn received far more than it gave in 1922.

With all of these preliminary steps in place, on Labor Day in September 1922, six of the eight appointees for St. Ephrem's left Scranton on the early train to Hoboken, New Jersey, where they were met by the pastor, Father Richard Kennedy. He had the convent in readiness and dinner prepared. A later train brought the remaining two sisters and completed the full community of Sister Nepomucene Caffrey, superior and principal, Sister Fabian Gallagher, Sister Francesca Farrell, Sister Magdala Hogan, Sister Theodora Healey, Sister Damian Howley, Sister Teresita Clarke, and Sister Rosemary Cavanagh.

Their new convent home was roomy and comfortable and contained a beautiful, well-furnished chapel. The school, a large, substantial brick structure, had already been erected, with the lower floor serving for a time as the church. The three upper floors were gradually filled to capacity and utilized as classrooms. The school was opened on September 11, 1922, with a registration of 475 pupils. (79)

Ten years later, in 1932, the enrollment had reached 1065 pupils, and by 1943, there were 1143 pupils and a staff of twenty sisters. It was not until 1950 that Mother Marcella Gill was to write to the pastor, Reverend Edward J. Sweeney, to ask that he consider hiring a lay teacher. (80) The great explosion of students and staff caused a strain on existing building facilities, but it would not be until 1957 that plans for a new convent on the same site as the old one would cause the sisters to move to temporary housing in three locations until the new convent was built and occupied on February 23, 1959. An extension had to be added to the school also. By 1961-1962 there were 1,600 pupils in thirty-two classrooms and a staff of twenty-seven sisters and seven lay teachers.

A gradual decline of these peak enrollments was experienced ten years later and until 1985 when reports show 586 pupils and a faculty of nine full and five part-time sisters and thirteen full and one part-time lay staff. (81)

From the very beginning this school has been known for its educational excellence, with scholarships being awarded annually to its graduates to attract them to area Catholic high schools.

St. Dominic's Elementary and High Schools, Oyster Bay, New York

Reverend Charles Canivan, pastor of St. Dominic's from 1914-1944, was the fourth priest to minister to the Catholics of Oyster Bay in a history that begins in the 1850s. Oyster Bay had no church of its own, so was serviced by Father James McEnroe from Glen Cove. Mass was celebrated at first on Sundays in the home of Matthew Brady. Later a hall on the corner of West Main and South Streets was rented for two dollars a week and provided the place for Catholic worship in Oyster Bay. In 1870 a frame church large enough to seat 250 parishioners was constructed at a cost of $6,000. The first full-time pastor was Reverend Walter J. Power who served zealously from 1900-1914. After his death, Reverend Charles J. Canivan was appointed pastor. Father Charles Canivan was also a native of Scranton, as was Father Richard Kennedy, the pastor of St. Ephrem's in Brooklyn. Father Canivan had actually applied to Mother Casimir for IHM Sisters for his future school several months before Father Kennedy, but he acknowledged that his building plans would not be completed for a year or more. (82)

In making his request, Father Canivan wrote:

> The first thing that came to my mind in considering the organization of the school was, what order of Sisters should be placed in charge of it. Being a native of the Scranton Diocese and knowing so many of its priests, I have heard many excellent reports of the work of the Sisters of the Immaculate Heart in the schools, and decided long ago that when the time came for beginning a school here, that I would have the Sisters of that order take charge of it, if it could possibly be arranged.(83)

By February 28, 1922, Bishop Hoban of Scranton had given approval for this work in the then Brooklyn Diocese. (84) Ground was broken for St. Dominic's elementary school on August 15, 1922, but the school was not in readiness until September 1924. The building, of polished buff brick and Indiana limestone trim, had ten large classrooms, a library, principal's office, health room and gymnasium. It was an ultramodern, well-equipped facility in every respect.

The newly appointed sisters arrived on August 1, 1924, and took up their residence in a large, comfortable dwelling that had been purchased for a convent. The community included Sister Benedicta O'Brien, superior and principal, Sister Eymard Begley, Sister Redempta Doudican, Sister Angelo McNulty, Sister Norberta Streilly, Sister Assunta McCaffrey, and Sister Regina Marie Crane. They were to begin classes on September 8, 1924, with 340 pupils in six grades. The seventh and eighth grades were added in the two succeeding years. The first graduation from St. Dominic's Elementary School saw thirty-nine pupils receive diplomas in June 1928.

The excellence of the grade school and the reluctance of parents to send their children to a public high school encouraged the undertaking of a high school for September 1928. Under the able leadership of Sister Marcella Gill, who had succeeded Sister Benedicta as principal, St. Dominic's High School became a reality. Its small start, with nine boys and fourteen girls, was soon to be turned around as word of the only co-educational Catholic High School on North Shore Long Island spread and applications from far and near were received. The curriculum of St. Dominic's High School included both a classical track to prepare students to meet college entrance requirements and a commercial track for students whose interests were in the business field.

With the introduction of the high school and the rapid increase of the elementary school enrollment, four additional classrooms were constructed on the ground floor. The library was moved to larger quarters on the second floor; a large laboratory was equipped for the teaching of science, and a cafeteria designed to serve daily lunch to some six hundred students was opened.

After four years as principal, and having gained the recognition of the Department of Education of New York State for St. Dominic's High School, Sister Marcella Gill was called to fill the office of assistant to the superior general of the Congregation. (85)

By 1940 it was evident that the high school would need a building of its own. Excavation was begun in April 1941 and the new building was opened in September 1941. The high school was a two-story structure having ten classrooms, a library, a medical office, administrative offices and a science laboratory. In the basement there was a recreation room that doubled as a 500-person seating capacity auditorium. There were bowling alleys and a projection room also.

This was to be the last of Father Canivan's tremendous labors for St. Dominic's. He died on March 14, 1944, greatly mourned by his parishioners and all the people of Oyster Bay who had grown to respect and love him over his thirty years as pastor. Reverend Vincent Short succeeded him.

In 1955 the twenty-four sisters serving the schools at St. Dominic's were living in two inadequate, tumbling-down houses. In the spring of 1955 the foundation for a new convent was begun. The cornerstone for the new four-story convent was placed a year later on April 11, 1956, and the first Mass was celebrated by the pastor, Father Vincent Short, in the new convent on July 19, 1956.

In the meantime, to illustrate the extent of the demand being experienced for entrance into St. Dominic's High School, over 600 eighth-graders from a long list of schools in the area reported on March 30, 1956, to take the high school's entrance examination. The policy was to accept St. Dominic's parishioners first—seventy-five in number—hence, only one hundred applicants could be accommodated. Six additional classrooms were constructed from the space occupied by the ground-floor bowling alleys and two old public school buildings at the corner of Weeks and Anstice Streets were purchased as a building expansion loomed in the near future. In 1957-1958 there were 643 elementary and 660 high school students at St. Dominic's. Correspondingly, a faculty of twenty-five sisters and five lay teachers was required.

Father Short died on July 15, 1964, and was succeeded by Reverend James E. Collins. Another era of building began, as Father Collins constructed a new church and a new elementary school in 1970, and a magnificent high school gymnasium was dedicated on September 10, 1978. (86)

As William F. Shore III, a graduate of the Class of 1973 and chairman of St. Dominic's Golden Anniversary Committee, wrote:

> Apart from St. Dominic's physical plant, accomplished athletic program and distinguished academic achievement, St. Dominic's shall always be remembered by its graduates as a place of love in their hearts. St. Dominic's is imbued with a spirit and dynamism which exists to this day, and we hope for long into the future.(87)

Many Sisters were to come and go at "33rd Street"—one reason being that any sister studying for a Master's degree at Fordham University in New York was required by the University to have at least one year's residence in the city before the degree would be awarded. Many sisters fulfilled this requirement while teaching at Immaculata High School or Sacred Hearts Elementary School.

The beautiful new convent constructed next to the school building was blessed and dedicated by His Eminence John Cardinal Spellman of New York on May 15, 1958. Sister Clare Marie McMenamin who had served as principal and superior from 1928-1942 and again from 1951-1957 was present at the dedication and was praised in an eloquent talk delivered by Reverend Michael F. Dwyer, director of Catholic Charities of the Archdiocese of New York. He said, in part:

> Many people have worked and prayed for this new convent: Monsignor McAvoy and before him Monsignor Congedo; Mother Alma Marie, the present superior, and before her the previous superior, who is here today, Sister Clare Marie. To all we offer congratulations. And to Sister Clare Marie, I wish to offer, in the name of all, a tribute that I know you hold me responsible to render. Every word has a synonym. In the minds and hearts of all who know her, Sister Clare Marie is the "synonym" for Immaculata. The spirit which her community gave to her, Sister Clare Marie gave to this school; first in the seventeen years of her original assignment, and then as superior for six years. We are all instruments in the Hands of God—so is Sister Clare Marie. But we are grateful to God for using her to form the spirit of this wonderful school; and for the sacrifices she made to be a good—very good—instrument in His Hands. We earnestly beg God to bless her.
>
> And may He bless every Sister, Servant of the Immaculate Heart of Mary, in particular those who will dwell in our new Convent of the Sacred Heart. (92)

As convenient and attractive as the convent was on the interior, nothing caused more exclamations than the front door approach with its wrought-iron enclosed garden with grass, trees and flowers growing on East 33rd Street in New York City!

By June of 1966 the now deceased Monsignor Congedo's dream of a school to serve Italian children of Sacred Hearts Parish, Manhattan, had changed. The neighborhood was no longer a family neighborhood, and of the 196 children registered in the elementary school, only forty-seven lived in the immediate area. A letter from Reverend James J. Gilhooley to Bishop John J. Maguire outlines the problems with which the parish was faced:

> The building which serves as a home for both the Sacred Hearts Elementary School and the parish secondary school, Immaculata, is in dire need of extensive renovation and rehabilitation . . . The general thought of this memo is that the elementary school of the Sacred Hearts be closed and that a completely refitted building serve as the home of an enlarged Immaculata High School . . . (93)

This same letter closes with appreciation for the work of our sisters:

> This writer cannot speak too highly of the professional competence, the commitment to Christ and His Church, and the personal graciousness of the women who conduct both our secondary and primary schools. I speak of the Sisters, Servants of the Immaculate Heart of Mary. These Sisters working under the skillful direction of Sister M. Basil (McLane) and Sister M. Gervase (Callahan) have for many years performed a splendid work. It is to be hoped that this work will continue here per omnia saecula. (94)

Thus, Sacred Hearts Elementary School was closed after forty-two years—1925-1967. Many of the children were absorbed in St. Stephen's Elementary School on East 29th Street to which seven of our sisters were assigned in September 1967, continuing to reside at Sacred Hearts Convent and traveling by car, taxi, or walking each day to and from school.

Four years later, in June 1971, our sisters were to be withdrawn from Immaculata High School, bringing to a close forty-three years of service there. A letter from Sister Graecia Mangin, IHM, principal of Immaculata High School at the time, spells out the reasons for the withdrawal:

> Five major factors have brought about a shortage of personnel in the Community. These factors are: numerous deaths and illnesses over the past few years, retirement of many Sisters, as well as the great withdrawals from Religious Life coupled with fewer applicants to enter the Community. These reasons are not individual to the IHMs but are being felt realistically in all levels of Catholic education.(95)

The evaluation report of the nine-member Archdiocesan Team Visitation Committee of March 31, 1971, to Immaculata High School praises the work, loyalty and cooperation of the thirteen full-time teachers (eight sisters and five laymen) and the two part-time priest teachers. Despite the inadequate facilities, the team noted the "lively and happy atmosphere" and ''excellent spirit" and the "personal interest" shown by the teachers and staff for the students. The excellence of the teaching and preparation of the faculty were noted, as was the fact that the curriculum was broad enough to serve the students' needs. (96)

It must have been difficult indeed to leave behind the 131 boys and 201 girls who made up the student body of this inner-city high school, Immaculata. The sisters continue, as of 1987, to serve at St. Stephen's Elementary School, but now reside at St. Joseph's Convent, Waverly Place, New York.

St. Peter of Alcantara Elementary School, Port Washington, New York

St. Peter's, Port Washington, New York, must have seemed a most unlikely spot for a parochial school to eventually flourish when, in January of 1925, thirty-five students in four grades reported for the opening of school. The small community of sisters sent to staff the school consisted of Sister Hilda Brown, principal and superior, Sister St. Clare Flanagan and Sister Philomena Purcell. A large estate-like family dwelling formerly owned by a famous New York attorney, Bert Cochran, had been purchased by the pastor, Reverend Sylvester J. Tobin, to serve as the convent. It was located next to the church. This two story home, crowned with a turret, was set back amid beautiful trees, with a winding roadway leading to a portico-covered front porch that extended almost fully around the house. The house had been neglected and had not been furnished nor cleaned prior to the sisters' arrival. Beds were provided and in the dining area a table and four straight chairs. For some reason, the pastor had thought that the sisters would take their meals in the rectory, but Sister Hilda saw at once the need to get the sisters established in the convent with adequate furnishings, which she succeeded in doing.

The school classes were housed within the convent, with some classes indoors and some on the glassed-in porch.

Difficult as the situation was, with a kitchen coal stove that didn't work, and a gasoline heater with three burners as the only stove, no washing machine, and sheets and tablecloths having to be done by hand, still the greatest hardship was the absence of a chapel and the deprivation of the Eucharistic presence in the convent for some six months. The parishioners came generously to the aid of the sisters in refurbishing the convent. Mrs. McGirr, mother of Sisters Terence and Catherine Patricia, was responsible for the chapel remodeling and furnishings. (97)

These early days at Port Washington were difficult and filled with hard work. The sisters shared the struggles of the people whom they served, who, at that time, were chiefly families of the caretakers who labored on the nearby estates, for example, the estates of the Guggenheim's and the Belmont's. Port Washington was at this time a rather rural area, and the children of the laboring families, mostly of Irish descent, were quite poor.

Cars were unusual then, and Sister Clare Flanagan, one of the earliest members of the Port Washington community, tells of going for a car ride to Manhasset with the brother of one of the sisters. They were "speeding" along through Plandome at approximately twenty miles per hour and were stopped by the police and given a ticket. So much for a little ride in the country! (98)

The number of students increased rapidly, and as grades were added up to the eighth grade, it was soon clear that a larger building would be needed for the school. A campaign for funds was highly successful and ground was broken for a new school on February 22, 1930. The building was of cream-colored stucco and included ten large classrooms, a music room, library, medical room and a large auditorium. A cafeteria and gymnasium were provided in the basement area. (99)

By 1940, the new school had attracted 368 pupils through its excellent programs and high standards of scholarship and religious education.

In another fifteen-year period, there were to be vast changes at St. Peter's. The years 1955-1956 saw the people of St. Peter's realize a grand total of $326,329.83 in a fund drive for construction of a new convent for the sisters. Reverend Jerome Holland, pastor, was responsible for generating great enthusiasm among the parishioners for this project. Ground was broken for a new convent on August 5, 1956. July and August 1955, also saw great preparations being made to receive the 952 pre-registered pupils for September. Six new classrooms, a kindergarten and a music room had been added and equipped with new furniture.

Between the construction of the new convent and the rapid growth of the school which necessitated additional space, the fifties were exciting years at St. Peter's. The number of sisters had grown to sixteen. They were a joyful, grateful community as they moved into the beautiful new convent on Thanksgiving morning, November 27, 1957, to participate at a Thanksgiving Mass said by Father Holland in the convent chapel. The public and official dedication of the convent took place on April 22, 1958, with Bishop Kellenberg of the newly created Rockville Centre Diocese officiating. Eight months later, on December 29, 1959, deep sadness was to enter the life of the parish as Father Holland, after an illness of several months, died. His leadership had enabled so much to be accomplished at St. Peter's. He had lived to see the September 1959, enrollment of a peak 1,045 pupils in attendance at the parish school.

Work began on the construction of a new school in July 1963, under the direction of the new pastor, Monsignor Conerty, but he was to die suddenly on August 13, 1963, without seeing its completion, which came about in September 1964. (100)

The 1960s reflected enrollments in the 900s; the 1970s in the 700s; and the 1980s in the three and four hundred's. St. Peter's continues to attract students to its excellent educational environment. The 1985-1986 enrollment was 364 pupils. (101)

St. Mary's Elementary and High Schools, Manhasset, New York

For fifty-nine years, from 1853 to 1912, St. Mary's Parish, Manhasset, experienced being a mission parish, first of St. Michael's in Flushing, next of St. Mary's in Roslyn, and finally of St. Peter's in Port Washington. As early as July 29, 1853, Reverend John McMahon, resident pastor of St. Michael's, Flushing, had written to Archbishop John Hughes of New York seeking permission to establish a parish in Manhasset and to erect a small church there. His letter presents a rather sorry picture of the people of Manhasset in those early days and the priest's concern for the preservation of the faith:

> I had occasion to write to your Grace a little time ago about the state of the Catholics in this district. For the present it will suffice to say that they are too poor to help themselves; and after so many years of what was perhaps necessary neglect, have too little faith remaining to cause them to exert themselves to the extent of the small powers they possess . . . I do not despair of building such a Church as will meet the present wants of the place and thus preserve many of whom it may be said with the greatest truth that they are almost gone.(102)

It was not until 1857, however, under Reverend James O'Beirne, pastor of Flushing, that St. Mary's was to have its first church. It is said that as soon as the Flushing church was completed in 1856, Father O'Beirne had the old Flushing church moved to Manhasset. It served, hot in summer and cold in winter, despite its pot-bellied stove in the middle aisle, until the present church was opened on August 15, 1917. (103)

It was under the pastorate of Reverend William K. Dwyer (1912-1916) that the sixty-year-old wooden church was replaced by the

Spanish mission-style church and rectory. The latter was completed in the summer of 1916, and the church itself a year later under Reverend Thomas J. Quinn, pastor.

Reverend Ambrose P. Dunnigan became pastor of St. Mary's, Manhasset in 1924. It was he who bought the land marked by the present elementary school frontage, and extending back to Second Street. The property had a large white house that stood on Northern Boulevard. This dwelling was moved to the rear of the new property to face on Second Street and was to serve a variety of needs, first as the original convent of the Sisters of IHM in 1926; next, as the residence of the Marist Brothers from 1950-1957; next, as a residence for the Nursing Sisters of the Sick Poor, and later deeded to Catholic Charities. (104)

Father Dunnigan began the construction of St. Mary's Elementary School in May 1925 and opened it on February 1, 1926. The architecture of the school was Spanish mission-style to match the church. This building contained eight classrooms, a large well-equipped library and a gymnasium. Classes began on February 2, 1926, with 150 pupils in grades one to five. The first community of sisters included: Sister Josepha Hurley, superior and principal, Sister Agathina Murray, Sister Laurentia Flannery, Sister Christina Heyburn, Sister Maria Theophane Allen, and Sister Miriam Catherine Corcoran. In May of that year Sister Christina's death occurred, bringing shock and sadness to the new mission. (105)

It was under Reverend Francis J. Coppinger, pastor from 1928-1932, that additional property was purchased adjoining the school and the sisters moved to a second convent home, this one to be the hub of future additions and renovations as St. Mary's grew and additional sisters were sent to minister there.

The story of expansion all over the United States was also Manhasset's story as initial farm areas became residential suburban centers. Nassau County was then one of the fastest growing counties in the country. Over 5,000 parishioners were located within the bounds of St. Mary's Parish in the 1940s, and eight Sunday Masses were provided to serve their needs in a church they had already outgrown. However true or exaggerated were the words written in 1853 by Reverend John McMahon in describing the dying faith of this area at that time, the vigor of parish life at St. Mary's, Manhasset, over all the later years certainly laid those early doubts to rest. The generosity of the people was evident as in 1941 an addition was opened to the elementary school; in 1947 another extension was made to the convent; and in 1950 St. Mary's High School was completed.

In its first year, 1949, St. Mary's High School operated out of space in the elementary school and the church basement, registering 160 young women and men. By 1954 there were 811 pupils from thirty-four parishes. Six Marist Brothers of Poughkeepsie, New York, were added to the faculty in 1950 to teach the boys, and this number increased to thirteen by 1953. The first faculty of Sisters of IHM to staff St. Mary's High School included Sister Annette Corcoran, principal, Sister St. John Qrtner, Sister Marie Assumpta Clifford, Sister Helen Maria Reddon and Sister Ephrem Carmody. (106)

The parish centennial in 1954 saw the completion of the enlargement and refurbishing of the church, increasing its capacity from 425 to 775. Incorporated into the church enlargement were two more high school and six more elementary classrooms.

By 1957, a new high school was opened for the boys, leaving the original building for the girls. Living quarters for the Marist teaching brothers were provided on the top floor of the new school. Bishop Walter P. Kellenberg, first Bishop of the new Diocese of Rockville Centre, dedicated the new high school on May 27, 1957.

Reports from 1964 show the amazing growth of these high schools. The boys' division had 700 students, with twenty brothers and five laypersons on the staff. The girls' division had 741 pupils, with a staff of twenty-one sisters and six lay faculty. In its three schools, St. Mary's recorded 2,556 students. (107)

These outstanding schools continue to flourish and engage the talents of one part-time and seven full-time Sisters of IHM, together with twenty-one full-time and three part-time lay teachers for 409 pupils in the elementary school. Ten full-time and four part-time IHMs, two full-time Sisters of Charity and thirty-one full-time lay teachers for 675 students serve the girls' division of the high school in 1985-1986. (108)

St. Raymond's Elementary School, Lynbrook, New York

When a parish is old enough to observe its 75th Anniversary, as St. Raymond's did in 1984, it is hard to imagine those early days in 1909 when the first pastor, Reverend Dennis E. Carroll, offered the first Mass for the parish in the Lynbrook Lyceum (now the site of the Lynbrook Medical Center). It is hard to think of St. Raymond's without its magnificent church, but until January 22, 1911, Father Carroll celebrated Mass and held religious classes in the Earle Avenue Firehouse and in a garage on Spencer Avenue while "the little wooden church" which was to be used for the next forty-six years was being constructed. (109)

These were to be years of rapid growth, and by the time of Reverend William J. McKenna's pastorate in 1919 there were thoughts of building a parochial school. Acquisition of the land fronting on Atlantic Avenue, from Carmen to Grant was the first step; raising the funds for the new building, the second step; visiting of many school sites to get ideas for the architectural plan; the letting of contracts; and finally, the groundbreaking in the autumn of 1925. Early in 1926, Father McKenna was asked by the bishop to accept a parish in Brooklyn, so Father Charles Craig succeeded him. It fell to Father Craig to complete the school and to raise the additional funds needed for the project. (110)

The building was not completed until December 1, 1926, but the sisters arrived on September 8 and opened classes on September 14, 1926, in the Sunday School Hall. Four grades were opened that first year with 180 students registered. The first community of sisters included Sister Donald Murray, superior and principal, Sister Marinus Krumenacker, Sister Dolores Marie McNamara and Sister Maria Martin Flanagan. The first convent was the O'Rourke home on Center Avenue opposite Plainfield Avenue.

Father Craig died in 1931 and was succeeded by Father Francis T. Scullin. His first task was to move the sisters' residence from the dilapidated Center Street location to a larger house at 641 Scranton Avenue, about six blocks from the school, where they remained for five years until the building of the new convent in 1937. Father Scullin's term was cut short by death on July 14, 1935, hence his plans had to be taken up by the next pastor, Reverend Francis V. Waters.

A registration of 785 pupils in St. Raymond's School in 1956 was indication of the growing number of families in this suburban parish. A series of building decisions between 1955 and 1961 saw the construction of a new church, the enlargement and renovation of the convent to accommodate seventeen Sisters of IHM, the enlargement of the school to a total of twenty-four classrooms. (111) It was a great tribute to the sisters that the new church contained a special chapel dedicated to them and that the school children donated funds for a commemorative window in this chapel in honor of Mother Teresa Maxis Duchemin.

All of this growth, and a subsequent leveling-off in the 70s and 80s provided the Congregation with the challenge of providing leadership personnel of vision for St. Raymond's School. A succession of outstanding principals provided this leadership: Sister Ricarda Gill, Sister Mary Olive Kelly, Sister Alma Marie Morgan, Sister Maria Thomas Harrington, Sister Mary Dawson, Sister Regina Marie Wilson, Sister Nancy Elder and, in 1985-1986, Sister Ruthanne Gypalo.

Recognition has been given to the great educational efforts of the sisters by the parents, pupils, pastors and bishops. The words of Bishop John McGann on the occasion of the 75th Jubilee of St. Raymond's Parish sum up these sentiments:

> . . . I thank the Lord for His many blessings to the parish over the years . . . the presence of the Sisters, Servants of the Immaculate Heart of Mary, in the parish, and their involvement in St. Raymond's School and in other parish ministries as well. Their presence these many years is both most welcome and very much appreciated. (112)

Our Lady Queen of Martyrs Elementary School, Forest Hills, New York

A census of the Catholic population of Forest Hills, New York, taken in March 1912, reveals only 78 persons, 60 adults and 18 children. However, in 1915, plans for a future parish in Forest Hills, New York, took an initial step when the Catholic Diocese of Brooklyn claimed title to twelve lots on the southwest annex of Ascan Avenue and Hoffman (now Queens) Boulevard. The amazing purchase price was only $14,000. Also, in 1915 a wooden Chapel of Our Lady Queen of Martyrs was built, and in 1917 Reverend Joseph R. McLaughlin was appointed pastor. With the vision and energy of a true spiritual leader, Father McLaughlin had, by 1925, outlined the unified group of parish buildings which now exists, including parish school, church, rectory, convent and additional space for later needs. (113)

On January 5, 1928, ground was broken for the school which was the first of the proposed cluster of buildings. The cornerstone of the school was laid on May 30, 1928, at which time Father McLaughlin announced that he expected the building to be completed for the opening of school in September. No one thought this feat could be accomplished—certainly not Reverend Joseph McClancy, the superintendent of Catholic Schools in the Brooklyn Diocese, for it was not until July 3, 1928, that he wrote to Mother Casimir (as if the date were a year, rather than two months, away) as follows:

> . . . We have arranged for your Community to staff Father McLaughlin's school at Forest Hills next September . . . You will kindly interpret this letter as an official invitation on the part of the Bishop for your Sisters to accept the Forest Hills school . . . (114)

On September 9, 1928, the day before school opened, desks were placed in the classrooms, general cleaning was done, water and light connections were made, and even into the night, barrels, boxes and rubble from construction were being cleaned up and thrown out of the windows into the schoolyard. This beautiful English gothic-style building with its fourteen classrooms, large auditorium, principal's office, library, music room, health room, and science laboratory stood ready to receive its first pupils in the first five grades. Ninety boys and one hundred twenty-one girls, a total of two hundred eleven pupils enrolled, and perhaps no one on that opening day could envision that an over-capacity enrollment of 859 students would, in 1955-1956, fill this school.

The first sisters assigned to Our Lady Queen of Martyrs School were Sister Maria Assumpta Clifford, superior and principal, Sister Marguerite Murray, Sister Malachy McKernan, Sister Simeon Walker, Sister Benedictus Philpott, and Sister Maria Angela Orr. These six sisters seem to have fulfilled to a high degree Father McLaughlin's three-fold requirements for his teaching staff: "They should be spiritual women, cultured ladies, and qualified teachers." (115)

A picture of a typical classroom in Our Lady Queen of Martyrs School in June 1929, shows a class of 39 students and the traditional Old English printing on the blackboard setting forth some profound maxims for daily living: "Humility is Truth" and "Idleness is the Strength of Bad Habits." (116)

In spite of the sobering content of these messages, the atmosphere of this school was one of joy, as related by Sister Benedictus Philpott, one of these first teachers. She was in her first year of teaching and was responsible for grades 1B and 2A, as well as the school music. Sister praised the interest of the pastor in everything being done in the school, the excellence of the faculty of sisters, and the help given to them by a parishioner, Miss Fanning, who was then a public school teacher. She assisted them in the selection of supplementary readers, some of which included fairy tales that could be dramatized by the children. Sister Benedictus' recollections of that year in Forest Hills brought her much joy and, as she expressed it, "I only stayed one year in Forest Hills, being transferred to Marywood, but I loved and enjoyed every day with those children in my first grade." (117)

Sister Benedictus described the people of Forest Hills as generous, appreciative and highly interested in the school. Parents often stopped in on weekends to view the work of the students that was displayed in the school. In reminiscing, Sister expressed pride in all that was accomplished with children who were only in grades one through five. ''Many opportunities were given to the children to assume responsibility and to take leadership, even though they were very young, " she said. (118)

When one thinks of the grand scale on which all of these parish buildings were eventually to emerge, it is difficult to imagine the little country-like chapel which served as the parish church until fire destroyed it in 1929 or to picture a three-story duplex house, one half of which served as the convent in those early days. This three-bedroom home accommodated the six sisters with some doubling up, with only a very small space available for a chapel. It is obvious that the sisters' joy at Our Lady Queen of Martyrs had its source in other than material comforts. Their own goodness and dedication brought forth many blessings, as the small original group of six sisters was to become sixteen by 1943 and twenty-one by 1955 as enrollment in the school escalated.

Our Lady Queen of Martyrs School continues as a vibrant ministry, serving a wide variety of ethnic and culturally diverse students, many of whose parents are employed at the United Nations in New York City.

RHODE ISLAND MISSIONS

St. Paul's Elementary School, Edgewood, Rhode Island

The end of the story of our relationship with St. Paul's, Edgewood, Rhode Island, is stated in a letter dated May 8, 1984 from Reverend Monsignor William J. Carey, Pastor, to Sister Michel Keenan, then superior general of the IHM Congregation. It reads:

> Dear Sister Michel:
> What had seemed so far away when it was first discussed has come. The Sisters of the Immaculate Heart of Mary will be leaving St. Paul's of Cranston on the last day of June 1984 . . . The contribution of the Sisters has been monumental and has filled an exciting chapter in the life of the Christian community of St. Paul's . . . (119)

This was the final historic record of the sixty-two-year commitment by the IHM Sisters to St. Paul's that brought the end of one era and launched another. As the remaining two IHMs, Sister Kathleen Joy Steck and Sister Moira Murray departed, they left behind a vibrant school that is prepared to serve the rich cultural and ethnic diversity of the Providence and Cranston areas encompassed by the parish. Ten lay teachers and two Sisters of Mercy, one of them the principal, continued the staffing of St. Paul's School.

In leaving, the IHMs were aware that the seed that was planted by earlier IHMs had taken root, was flourishing, and will continue. They could reflect upon evidences of change and growth in St. Paul's, and the fact that while the school was founded in 1922 to educate the children of Irish immigrants, third generation Irish were still there in the majority, now walking harmoniously beside minorities made up of 10.4% blacks, 11.8% Haitian, 4.2% Asian, and 12.2% Portuguese. It was consoling to know that over many years the Sisters of IHM had prepared the school for this diversity of population, as well as for the emergence of qualified lay women and men as partners in the ministry of Catholic education.

A flashback to the years 1920-1922 shows that a series of letters was exchanged between Reverend Michael J. McCabe, pastor of St. Paul's since 1907, and Mother M. Casimir about the possibility of securing IHM Sisters for the parish elementary school he planned to build. Father McCabe had no first-hand knowledge of the IHM Sisters, but it is evident from his letters that he was confident in the IHM educational expertise which he had heard about from two Redemptorists, Reverend William Kenna, CSsR, rector of the Mission of Our Lady of Perpetual Help, Roxbury, Massachusetts and Reverend Joseph Turner, CSsR. Father Kenna, as uncle of our Sister Neumann, may have been a bit biased! (120)

The enthusiastic response of Mother Casimir to Father McCabe's request for sisters reveals her pleasure at the prospect of sending pioneer IHMs to this first IHM mission in the New England states. On May 11, 1921, Mother Casimir wrote to Father McCabe as follows:

> Dear Reverend Father:
> Always during the month of May we look for special thought from the Blessed Mother of God. This year she has brought us a great favor—your decision to entrust your precious little ones to our care. I shall dedicate our future work in your school to Mary Immaculate that she may obtain from her Divine Son the help we will need to make your school all that you desire. Father Kenna has spoken so highly of your zeal for souls that we are happy, indeed, to become your co-workers. (121)

Mother Casimir's own zeal for souls is such an over-riding motivation that it almost leaps out from the pages of her letters. She seemed to have a simplicity that was awed by each further request for the services of our sisters and a deep sense of the responsibility assumed in teaching children.

On August 25, 1922, Sister Mary Thomas McAndrew, who had been appointed superior, and Sister Neumann Murray arrived in Edgewood. They were met and warmly welcomed by Father McCabe. As the projected convent was not even begun, arrangements were made with the Sisters of St. Joseph's Hospital for hospitality. In a short time, temporary residence was provided in the home of the Robert McLaughlin family on Massachusetts Avenue. The family remained at their summer home during that time.

In early September, Sister Mary Thomas and Sister Neumann were joined by Sister Oswald Bissell, Sister Immaculate Keefe, Sister

Bonaventure Murphy, Sister Teresina Thompson, Sister Aidan Jordan, Sister Leo Lehman, Sister Georgina Wertz, and later, Sister Mary Francis Legnard.

A temporary altar was erected in the living room of the McLaughlin residence so the sisters could have the privilege of daily Mass. The McLaughlin family was present at the first Holy Mass offered in their home. (122)

The Catholic newspaper of the Diocese of Providence carried the announcement of the dedication of the new St. Paul's School and heralded this event as "the greatest day in the history of St. Paul's Parish, Edgewood" and "the opening of a new era in Catholic education in the southern half of Providence and its suburbs." There seems to be some slight implication of an attitude of surprise at this accomplishment by Father McCabe and the St. Paul parishioners as the article continues:

> . . . It falls to the credit of this young parish, which this summer observed its fifteenth birthday, to open the first Catholic school south of the Cathedral. When the present pastor and founder of the parish, by appointment of the late beloved Bishop Harkins, built the existing Saint Paul's Church, the few and faithful parishioners of those earlier years little thought that St. Paul's would in so few years lead the way on so grand a scale in the march of Catholic education in this section. Some had in mind a new and grander church as years went by, but their pastor declared for a Catholic school to be built before the Church should be supplanted. (123)

These words may be a veiled reference to some of the difficulties encountered by Father McCabe in attaining the fulfillment of his dreams on the occasion of the dedication of St. Paul's School, September 10, 1922. Two of his early letters to Mother Casimir in the spring and summer of 1921 refer to difficulties he was experiencing. Some of these were undoubtedly financial in nature, but there were other unspecified concerns to which his letters made reference:

> I have at length secured the Bishop's consent to have your Sisters take charge of my new school, when I have it built. I won't mention the difficulties which prevented me writing to you long ago. Thank God, I have won out—but the way is beset with other difficulties . . .

> I have set my heart on having a model school here, and have prayed constantly that God would send me the right Order to make it possible. Some of the worst difficulties have been overcome and I feel that the others will quickly pass. Meanwhile let us both pray that it is God's will and that it shall speedily become a reality. (124)

After it became clear to him that the school would not be ready for occupancy until September 1922, Father McCabe again wrote to Mother Casimir expressing his disappointment in the delay but adding, "I am consoled by the fact that I have secured a teaching order, which by all accounts, is able to back up the assertions I have so often made in favor of Catholic education." (125)

To conjecture may be hazardous, but it may have been that the choice of the Sisters of IHM as an unfamiliar religious community to staff this large, new school met with some resistance from some sources in the diocese. It seems also that there was some resistance by parishioners to Catholic education in general, and to the building of a school instead of a church at this time.

In spite of all these real and implied "difficulties" the dedication was presided over by Bishop William A. Hickey and a bronze tablet was set in place, reading, "St. Paul's School—erected through the generosity of the people of Saint Paul's Parish to attest their adherence to the faith of their fathers, and their unalterable conviction that religion and morality are the basis of true education . . . "(126)

Thus, the first Catholic school in Cranston was launched, and on September 11, 1922, school opened with 368 pupils registered in the eight grades. It did not take the IHM Sisters long to be accepted by the new diocese, and at the first Catholic Teachers' Conference, organized by Reverend Cassidy, superintendent of Catholic Schools of the Diocese of Providence four of our sisters were on the program to give lectures and demonstrations in their respective fields: Sisters Leo Lehman, Scholastica Chainey, Rosalie McDermott and Brendan O'Brien.

By 1934 a ninth grade was opened at St. Paul's School and as the total school enrollment increased to over 700 pupils, a third floor was added to the building. There were two of every class from grade one through nine. The number of sisters was increased to seventeen.

Into the 1970s a gradual decline to a one-track school replaced the large two-track enrollment. A concomitant reduction of the number of sisters occurred. (127)

The people of St. Paul's Parish proved to be very supportive of the sisters and of the Congregation's projects over the years. They raised close to $60,000 for the Marywood College Library fund, contributed annually to the Autumn Fair, which eventually cleared all debt on the Novitiate (now the Generalate) Building, and contributed nearly $3,000 after the Motherhouse fire in 1971.

An impressive number of religious vocations have come from this parish, twenty-one of whom entered the Sisters, Servants of the Immaculate Heart of Mary in Scranton.

St. Thomas Elementary School, Manton, Rhode Island

The fifty-six years of service of the Sisters, Servants of the Immaculate Heart of Mary at St. Thomas Parish, Providence (Manton), Rhode Island began in January 1924 when religious education of the children of the parish was initiated at the request of the pastor, Reverend J. J. O'Reilly. The first community of IHM Sisters included Sister Anysia Moran, superior, Sister Alma Marie Morgan and Sister Edith Ralston.

These three sisters began their religious education ministry with two grades in each of three classrooms in the church building. Their work was so well received that it was decided to open a kindergarten the following year, which would serve as the beginning of a parish elementary school. Sister Anysia was succeeded by Sister Maria Loughlin as superior, with Sisters Alma Marie Morgan and Maria Patrick Comer comprising the community in 1925. The initial registration of nine boys and sixteen girls at the opening of school in September 1925 provided little promise of the future growth of St. Thomas School. Even in 1940 when the eighth grade was discontinued, and in 1942 when the seventh grade was also discontinued, the enrollment was only 126 pupils. Some of this early low enrollment can no doubt be attributed to the crowded quarters of the classes in the church building and the need for a more adequate school facility. (128)

Indeed, when the new school was dedicated on September 8, 1955, there was an enrollment of 292 pupils, with five IHMs and one lay teacher as faculty. According to the annals of St. Thomas Convent, "St. Thomas new school with its nine classrooms, all-purpose room, office, clinic room, music room, teachers' room and two lavatories is the dream of twenty-eight years of waiting. It is one of the best equipped schools in the Diocese." (129)

By 1966 the school was to grow to 315 pupils, with seven IHMs and one laywoman serving as faculty. At the time of the sisters' departure in 1979-1980 there was an enrollment of 272 in the school, a solid curriculum was in place, the sisters had received much affirmation for their work from the diocesan supervisor, and they could feel that they were leaving a thriving academic and religious project for those who would follow in staffing St. Thomas School. (130)

Beyond Expansion

While Mother Casimir was busy expanding the schools, she was simultaneously addressing the appropriate preparation of the sisters for the teaching profession. Very early in her first term of office, in an historical letter to the Congregation dated June 13, 1920, using terminology that could have come from the Post-Vatican II era, she addressed for the first time the question of State Teacher Certification for the sisters. She wrote:

> Very dear Sisters:
> In view of some threatening 'signs of the times,' I have deemed it advisable to make provisions to forestall any possible disadvantages that might come to us if the question of certification by the State at some future time should become a reality. I believe that it is necessary for us to begin the work of preparation at once, and the first step will be to establish a system of certification of ourselves. (131)

She then proceeded to outline the existing State certification requirements and set forth a program of study and class work in the convents in the evenings and on Saturdays and a schedule of examinations which would result in her own issuance of a 'certificate' for those sisters who passed successfully. Her deep concern that the sisters not be disturbed by the thought of impending requirements is also reflected in this letter where she promises special help for those who might need it and motivates them, saying, "I do not wish any Sister . . . to feel discouraged or disheartened . . . all that I require is that each Sister will do faithfully what she is able to do." (132)

Thus was inaugurated the simple beginning of a process which was to engage our teaching sisters for decades to come. It was an educational idea whose time was not to come in most congregations for another twenty or thirty years. It was an educational idea that was to launch the Scranton IHMs as outstanding educators then, and in a highly fruitful future.

Marywood College, Scranton, Pennsylvania

Marywood College had opened in 1915 during Mother M. Germaine's term of office and had begun with a small number of students in the motherhouse building. By 1919 growing pains were already being experienced as the growth of Catholic higher education, and particularly the higher education of women, exploded in the United States. Mother Casimir's dream was to construct a triple-building complex to respond to the College's needs—buildings to accommodate administrative offices, classrooms, library, and residence facilities. At the charter meeting of the College Corporation, held on June 2, 1921, the question of providing new college buildings was discussed. First the advisability of seeking another location for the college was placed before the council. Some of the members were of the opinion that it might be well to secure another location for the motherhouse, novitiate and Marywood Seminary, leaving the entire campus at Marywood for the College. In fact, a committee was appointed to look for a site in the suburbs of Scranton for such a relocation, but the search was not successful. Looked at from today's vantage point, it was undoubtedly a blessing that the decision was to erect the projected college buildings on the campus, leaving the motherhouse, novitiate and Marywood Seminary intact.

The site chosen was, in 1921, the location of a flourishing orchard adjoining College Street and Adams Avenue. After a thorough survey with the approval of the Pennsylvania Coal Company, the site was declared safe for the erection of the proposed buildings. The Pennsylvania Coal Company also guaranteed that for the future no mining would take place in that locality.

Plans for the Liberal Arts Building, with two wings for residence halls were drawn up by Mr. John Howley, the architect selected. They were approved and the building contract was given to Boland Brothers. Early in August 1922, the Most Reverend M. J. Hoban, DD officiated at the groundbreaking ceremony. When one observes the size and magnificence of the Liberal Arts Building today, it is amazing to note that it was completed in about two years. The rotunda alone —seventy-two feet in diameter, rising over two stories in height, with its marvelous paintings and inscriptions—is an architectural and artistic feat.

The rapid increase in the enrollment of resident students made the construction of a new residence hall imperative. Fortunately the plans were part of the original plan for the Liberal Arts Building that had provided two wings for residence halls when the need would arise. On September 24, 1926, therefore, construction was begun. The exterior design of the residence building was in conformity with the Liberal Arts Building and constructed to house about two hundred students. The completed residence hall was named O'Reilly Hall in honor of Bishop O'Reilly who, when lack of funds threatened the cessation of the work, lent his assistance so that it might be in readiness for the priests' retreat listed for June 1928. At the close of the retreat, final preparations were made for the coming of resident students in September. Bishop O'Reilly celebrated Mass in the small chapel on the second floor of the residence hall, dedicated it to Our Lady of Perpetual Help, and after Mass blessed the entire building. (133)

In 1964 O'Reilly Hall was renamed Regina Hall, and in 1971 its beautiful 450 student capacity dining room, which had grown too small for the enlarged student body, was converted to the campus chapel.

The Liberal Arts Building and O'Reilly Hall were the initial buildings of what was to become a campus of 23 outstanding architectural accommodations enhancing and supporting the excellent education provided at Marywood College. So voluminous are the records of events over the years, and so important has Marywood College continued to be in the history of the IHM Congregation that its full story is reserved for a history of its own.

Social Service Ministries

In the light of subsequent developments in the ministries that the Congregation would undertake in service to the church, Mother Casimir's decisions to initiate the IHM Sisters into the social service arena were, indeed, prophetic.

One such venture was her acceptance of an invitation to direct "Casa Regina," a home where self-supporting young women might live, attend evening classes, and find an atmosphere of Catholic living. The "Casa Regina" was located in Altoona, Pennsylvania, and under the leadership of Father Garesche, SJ, was formally opened on December 3, 1919. Sisters Anselm Lavey, superior, Sister Herman McLaughlin and Sister Claudia Whalen took charge on January 6, 1920. This work was to continue until 1928 when it seemed no longer needed. (134)

The opportunity for a second social service project came when Bishop Michael J. Hoban, Scranton, asked Mother Casimir for sisters to take over the direction of the Scranton-based St. Joseph's Shelter and Day Nursery. This shelter had been operated since 1915 by a society of laywomen incorporated as the St. Joseph Society, dedicated to works of charity. They had established the St. Joseph's Shelter in a large dwelling near St. Peter's Cathedral for the care of transient women and neglected and orphaned children. The Society's association with the IHM Sisters occurred during the influenza epidemic of 1918 when the sisters assisted in nursing care of the children and mothers who had been stricken. It was natural, then, as the Society's work grew, for them to recommend to Bishop Hoban that the Sisters of IHM be requested to assume management of the shelter. At the Bishop's request, Mother Casimir acquired the shelter building. The sisters, including Sister Mary Clare Howard, Sister Melanie Rowan and Sister Consolata Ball began their work on June 11, 1920.

Eventually, children from St. Joseph's Shelter, together with those from the Scranton diocesan- based orphanages, which in 1935 cared for some 810 children, were cared for at St. Stanislaus Institute, Elmhurst, or at St. Michael's Industrial and Agricultural School at Hoban Heights, Pennsylvania. This reduction in the number of such institutions from six to two by 1968 was a welcome "sign of the times." St. Joseph's Shelter and Day Nursery closed its doors in the summer of 1953. (135)

St. Agnes Place, Elmhurst, Pennsylvania

Mother Casimir's concern for the sisters was also reflected in her love and care of the ill and aging sisters. The need for a home for these sisters became known to Mrs. Agnes Allen Glennon, an alumna of St. John's Pittston, Pennsylvania, and a close friend of the sisters, who donated her estate, a beautiful country residence located in Elmhurst, Pennsylvania, for this purpose. As a home for our aged and ill sisters, it was named St. Agnes Place in honor of the donor.

Sister Monica Quinn and Sister John Baptist Hale were sent to prepare the house for occupancy. The work was completed by July 1925, but the house was not opened until early August of that year. The "summer helpers" included Sisters Isadore Connor, Clara McNulty, Jeromine McCarthy and Everildus Miller, but when September came these sisters left for the schools and the new community became Sister Regis Wynne, superior, Sister Xavier Byrne, Mother Germaine O'Neill, Sister Rosalia Kelly, Sister Loyola Melley, Sister Perpetua Doyle, Sister Lucy Philbin, Sister Ann Scanlon and Sister Demetria Bode.

St. Agnes Place was a quiet, peaceful setting on a very productive piece of farmland. There were bountiful supplies of vegetables, a dairy provided milk and butter, and with the chickens a plentiful supply of fresh eggs. In their new surroundings the sisters felt only one lack in their new home—the absence of the Blessed Sacrament. It was not until January 1926, that their prayers were answered, and it was with deep joy that they participated in the first Mass offered in their chapel by the Auxiliary Bishop of Scranton, Andrew Brennan, assisted by Reverend Gallagher of Dunmore, and Reverend Alphonsus, CP.

A priest from St. Ann's Monastery, Scranton, was appointed confessor for the sisters of St. Agnes Place and St. Mary's Villa, a neighboring home for the aged conducted by the Sisters of Jesus Crucified. The sisters' spiritual needs were well provided for on a daily basis also by the Very Reverend Monsignor Dennis J. Kane, then pastor at Moscow, Pennsylvania. Elmhurst was one of his missions, but he had a singular interest in the aging and convalescent sisters at St. Agnes Place, as did the many pastors who followed him.

Even as today at the Marian Convent the sisters at St. Agnes Place were happy to assume tasks in accord with their physical ability and stamina.

Thus it was that some sisters taught in the novitiate of the Sisters of Jesus Crucified at St. Mary's Villa; some taught catechetical instructions in Moscow; others were involved in household and gardening tasks. (136)

The Marian Convent located on the Marywood campus, was planned during Mother Marcella Gill's term, but was completed and dedicated on April 9, 1956. Since St. Agnes Place was no longer needed, it was sold in 1957 for $22,000 after appraisal by Mr. Maxwell D. Shepherd, a licensed real estate broker of Carbondale, Pennsylvania. By 1987 standards, and in the awareness of the ideal suburban location of this property and the beauty of the main stone and frame house with some eighteen rooms, it would seem that the total appraisal value of $23,400, even in 1957 was very low. The twenty-five acres of land were valued at $100 per acre; the main building of eighteen rooms, judged to be in only ''fair" condition was appraised at $15,000; the barn, in "very bad condition," at $2,000; a three-car garage at $1,500; the caretaker's house, a two and one-half story, seven bedroom frame house, about fifty years old, at $2,400. (137)

With this transaction and the establishment of the Marian Convent, a new era in the care of our elderly and ill sisters had begun.

St. Joseph's Hospital, Carbondale, Pennsylvania

It is difficult to match the courage with which Mother Casimir entered upon new and untried ventures. Her vision can only be appreciated in hindsight as the legacy of this courage is seen in later decades. This is maximally true in the case of the Congregation's entry into hospital work. It was in 1925 that the series of events began which would lead to the building of St. Joseph's Hospital, Carbondale, Pennsylvania.

St. Joseph's Hospital had its beginnings in an old, converted wooden residence on Washington Street which had been known from the date of its founding in 1908 as the Carbondale City Private Hospital, later renamed the Carbondale City Hospital in 1917. The directors of this hospital wished to provide a modern hospital and efficient management to service the health care needs of the Carbondale area population, then some 90,000 in number. With the approval of Bishop Hoban, Mother Casimir accepted this challenge.

By March 1926, the St. Joseph's Hospital and its patients had been transferred temporarily to the available St. Rose Convent building; it was chartered by July 6, 1926; the cornerstone for a new St. Joseph's Hospital was blessed by Cardinal Dougherty of Philadelphia by December 7, 1927; and the new 120 patient-bed facility, St. Joseph's Hospital, was opened to the public on March 19, 1929. These amazing accomplishments were achieved at an approximate cost of $500,000, nearly

$300,000 of which was raised through public pledges. The School of Nursing had also opened in 1926 and was accredited at the time of its first graduating class in 1929.

The first group of sisters assigned to St. Joseph's Hospital was Sister M. Donald Murray, superior and superintendent, Sister Bertha Grady, Sister Melanie Rowan, Sister Magdalen Devine, and Sister Mary Francis Legnard. Sister St. Agnes Moran was added to the group in August 1926. (138)

Given the impact made by St. Joseph's Hospital in the health care field and the developments which have occurred in its services to patients, the size and quality of its religious, medical, and support staff, and the expansion of its physical plant to the present day, it is easy to see the guidance of the Holy Spirit in the insights of Mother Casimir which led to the founding of St. Joseph's Hospital, Carbondale, Pennsylvania.

The fascinating history of this institution merits a complete history of its own. Mother Casimir did not live to see the completion of her plans for St. Joseph's Hospital. She died on February 16, 1929, about one month before its opening, leaving this fine institution, and so many other signs of her leadership and her awareness of the diversity and flexibility in ministry which would be needed by her sisters in an unknown future.

Mother M. Casimir Murray: A Life Fulfilled

Mother Casimir Murray died at Marywood on February 16, 1929, after a full life of seventy-nine years, fifty-nine of which she had spent as a professed religious of the Sisters, Servants of the Immaculate Heart of Mary.

She entered the Congregation in Reading, Pennsylvania in 1868, was professed in 1870, and began her teaching ministry in Susquehanna. In 1871, she was one of the original band of twelve sisters who generously elected to remain in the Scranton Diocese when separation from the Archdiocese of Philadelphia occurred. She was appointed bursar of the new community, and later held a variety of administrative positions.

Mother Casimir was elected mother general of the Congregation in 1919. The ten years of her administration were filled with the development of the Congregation—spiritually, educationally and in the geographic expansion of its ministries. While Mother Casimir's term of office may be recorded historically in terms of this physical expansion, she herself is remembered for her simplicity, humility, kindness, common sense and genuine love for all. Tributes paid to her at her death praised her zeal on behalf of Catholic education, her deep religious convictions, and her courage. One letter said of her, "Her life radiated sympathy, understanding and feeling; it was the life of one who was strong enough to be just, and brave enough to be kind; the life of one prodigal in activity, but at the same time hidden with Christ in God." (139) Reverend Joseph McClancy of Brooklyn wrote: "She was an excellent religious . . . To meet her was to learn the best of the Sisters of the Immaculate Heart of Mary." (140)

The Sisters of the Immaculate Heart of Mary were deeply saddened at Mother Casimir's death for she had been a friend whom they highly esteemed and loved. She was one who knew well the traditions and spirit of the Congregation and embodied them in her daily life.

References

1. James Hennessey, SJ. *American Catholics.* Oxford University. Press, NY. 1981, p. 235.
2. *The Fiery Cross.* Jan. 2, 1925, reprinted in Michael Williams, *The Shadow of the Pope.* 1932, p. 315.
3. Hennessey, op. cit., p. 237.
4. Personal Correspondence between Bishop Hafey and Bishop Hoban, 1925. Archives, IHM Generalate.
5. Unsigned notes on "The Southern Missions," p. 4. Archives, IHM Generalate.
6. Ibid.
7. Ibid.
8. Annals of St. Joseph's, New Bern, NC. Archives, IHM Generalate.
9. Annals of Mother of Mercy, Little Washington, NC. Archives, IHM Generalate.
10. Annals of St. Mary's, Goldsboro, NC. Archives, IHM Generalate.
11. Annals of St. Paul's, New Bern, NC. Archives, IHM Generalate.
12. Mother M. Casimir's Term of Office, Archives, IHM Generalate.
13. Monsignor John P. Gallagher, *A Century of History.* Haddon Craftsmen, Scranton, 1968, pp. 343-344.
14. Horace B. McKenna, SJ. Address on "Rural Education in Maryland" delivered to the Sodality Union of Washington, April 30, 1934.
15. Annals of St. Mary's, Upper Marlboro, MD. Notes of Sr. Immaculata Gillespie, IHM, Archives, IHM Generalate.
16. Personal Interview with Sister St. Teresa Healy, September 8, 1986.
17. Mary Eunice Proctor Butler, ''St. Mary's School Sixtieth Anniversary Memory Booklet," April 1986, p. 5.
18. Annals of St. Mary's Convent, Upper Marlboro, 1956-1957. Archives, IHM Generalate.
19. Ibid., 1957-1958.
20. Ibid., 1964-1965.
21. Statistics from the Office of the Director of Apostolic Planning, 1985-1986. IHM Generalate.
22. Sixtieth Anniversary Booklet, St. Rita's, Dundalk, MD. 1986, p. 1.
23. Annals of St. Rita's, Dundalk, MD. September 1959-June 1960. Archives, IHM Generalate.
24. Statistics in Office of Director of Apostolic Planning, 1985-1986, IHM Generalate.
25. Sister M. Immaculate Gillespie, Collected Notes on Sacred Heart, LaPlata, MD. Archives, IHM Generalate.

26. Hennessey, op. cit., p. 254.
27. Ibid., p. 253.
28. Reverend James T. Gillis, *Catholic World 128* (1928), p. 357.
29. Letter from Mother Casimir to Reverend Charles Hennessey, SM, cited in his letter to Mother Mary William, dated August 31, 1929. Archives, IHM Generalate.
30. Letter from Mother Mary William to Rev. Charles Hennessey, SJ. September 1, 1929. Archives, IHM Generalate.
31. Letter from Mother Mary William to Rev. Charles Hennessey, SJ. Undated, probably Spring 1930. Archives, IHM Generalate.
32. Statistics from the Office of the Director of Apostolic Planning, 1985-1986. IHM Generalate.
33. Correspondence between Archbishop Michael J. Curley and Mother Casimir, April 1928. Archives, IHM Generalate.
34. Sister Muriel Whalen in personal telephone interview, September 18, 1986.
35. Annals of St. Bernardine's Convent, Baltimore, MD. Archives, IHM Generalate.
36. Letter from Mother Casimir to Rev. John A. Smith, July 1929. Archives, IHM Generalate.
37. Letter from Rev. John A. Smith to Mother Casimir, July 1929. Archives, IHM Generalate.
38. St. Bernardine's Church, Silver Anniversary Booklet, 1928-1953.
39. Annals of St. Bernardine's School, 1955-1970. Archives, IHM Generalate.
40. Sister M. Immaculata Gillespie, IHM. *Sisters of the IHM.* Kennedy & Sons, NY, p. 482-483.
41. 100th Anniversary Booklet, St. Mary's Parish, Avoca, PA, pp. 1-4.
42. Annals of St. Mary's Convent, Avoca, PA. 1955-1984. Archives, IHM Generalate.
43. Private Correspondence to Sister Immaculata Gillespie from one of the Sisters, possibly written in the 1940s, unsigned and pages missing because of fire damage. Archives, IHM Generalate.
44. Sister M. Immaculata Gillespie, IHM, Notes and research unpublished. Archives, IHM Generalate.
45. Private correspondence previously cited. Archives, IHM Generalate.
46. Correspondece from Reverend S. P. McGarvey to Mother Josepha, May 6, 1936. Archives, IHM Generalate.
47. Correspondence from Mother Josepha to Monsignor Cordori, May 20, 1936. Archives, IHM Generalate.
48. Monsignor John N. Cordon. Letter to Mother Josepha, June 20, 1936.
49. Annals of St. Justin's Convent. Archives, IHM Generalate.
50. Interview with Sister Gonzales McGowan, September 29, 1986, Marian

Convent, Scranton, PA.

51. St. Justin's School Contract, May 10, 1925. Archives, IHM Generalate.
52. Ibid.
53. Letter dated August 18, 1930 from Mother Mary William to Father Barry. Archives, IHM Generalate.
54. Letter dated August 20, 1930 from Father Barry to Mother Mary William. Archives, IHM Generalate.
55. Telegram from Father Barry to Mother Mary William dated August 23, 1930, 7:46 p.m.
56. Letter from Mother Mary William to Father Barry dated August 24, 1930. Archives, IHM Generalate.
57. Previously cited interview with Sister Gonzales McGowan, IHM.
58. Centennial Booklet 1875-1975, Saint Thomas Aquinas Church, Archbald, pp. 12-18.
59. Reverend Miles McAndrew, SS, quoted in "Fifty Years of Catholic Education", Commemorative Booklet, 1978, p. 3.
60. Reverend Miles McAndrew, SS, "History of St. Thomas Aquinas Parish and Archbald Borough, 1958," p. 62.
61. Statistics from the Office of the Director of Apostolic Planning provided by the Principal of St. Thomas School, 1985.
62. Correspondence from Rev. James Houlihan, Pastor, Epiphany Church, Sayre, to Mother M. Casimir, dated August 25, 1928. Archives, IHM Generalate.
63. Correspondence from Rev. James Houlihan to Mother Mary William, September 1929. Archives, IHM Generalate.
64. Telephone interview with Sister Benigna Ball, November 21, 1986.
65. Commemorative Booklet, 50th Anniversary Celebration, 1929-1979, pp. 11-12.
66. Data from the Office of the Director of Apostolic Planning, 1985-1986.
67. Notes from Sister Anna Maria Hayes derived from the diary of Sister Sebastian, formerly Corinne Hall, a resident of St. Mary's Home, who became an Oblate of Mary in Baltimore, Archives, IHM Generalate.
68. Annals of St. Mary's Home, Cresson, 1961-1963. Archives, IHM Generalate.
69. Kevin Lenahan, "History of Sugar Notch." Composition-paper notes. Annals of St. Charles, Sugar Notch.Archives, IHM Generalate.
70. Annals of St. Charles Convent, 1970-1971 and Correspondence from Sister Willemyn Gambrill to the Congregation Council Members, February 10, 1971.
71. Account written by Sister Rebecca Doy]e and filed with Annals of Sacred Hearts High School, New York, Archives, IHM Generalate.

72. Notes on St. Patrick's, Oneida, NY gathered by Sister Immaculata Gillespie. Archives, IHM Generalate.
73. Annals of St. Patrick's Convent, Oneida, NY, 1983-1984. Archives, IHM Generalate.
74. Letter of Mother Casimir to Father Kennedy dated January 4, 1922. Archives, IHM Generalate.
75. Letter of Reverend Joseph McClancy to Mother Casimir, February 11, 1922. Archives, IHM Generalate.
76. Letter of Mother Casimir to Bishop Thomas Molloy dated March 1, 1922. Archives, IHM Generalate.
77. Copy of Diocese of Brooklyn School Contract signed by the Pastor, by Mother Casimir, and by the Superintendent of Schools for the Bishop of Brooklyn, September 21, 1922. 8. Ibid.
79. Annals of St. Ephrem's, Brooklyn, NY. Archives, IHM Generalate.
80. Letter from Mother Marcella Gill to Father E. J. Sweeney dated May 25, 1950. Archives, IHM Generalate.
81. Statistics from the Office of the Director of Apostolic Planning, IHM Generalate, 1985-1986.
82. Letter from Rev. Charles J. Canivan to Mother Casimir dated November 21, 1921. Archives, IHM Generalate.
83. Ibid.
84. Letter from Mother Casimir to Rev. Charles Canivan, February 28, 1922. Archives, IHM Generalate.
85. Notes of Sister Immaculata Gillespie on St. Dominic's, Oyster Bay, NY. Archives, IHM Generalate.
86. Annals of St. Dominic's Convent, Oyster Bay, NY, 1955-1985. Archives, IHM Generalate.
87. Golden Anniversary Booklet, St. Dominic's High School, May 30, 1980, p. 7.
88. Statistics from the Office of the Director of Apostolic Planning, IHM Generalate, 1986.
89. Notes of Sister Rebecca Doyle. Archives IHM Generalate.
90. Annals of Sacred Hearts Convent, New York, NY. Archives, IHM Generalate.
91. Interviews with Sister Clare Marie McMenamin and Sister Marionette Coll, November 1986.
92. Reverend Michael F. Dwyer. Dedication of the Convent, May 15, 1958.
93. Correspondence from Reverend James J. Gilhooley to Most Reverend John J. Maguire, DD. June 1, 1966.
94. Ibid.
95. Letter of Sister Graecia Mangan to the Parents and Friends of Immaculata High School, January 20, 1971.

96. Evaluation Report of Immaculata High School by Team Visitation Committee for the Archdiocese of New York, March 31 - April 1, 1971.
97. Material prepared by Sr. Immaculata Gillespie, Archives, IHM Generalate.
98. Interview with Sister Clare Flanagan, Marian Convent, November 25, 1986.
99. Ibid.
100. Annals of St. Peter's Convent, Port Washington, NY. Archives, IHM Generalate.
101. Office of the Director of Apostolic Planning, IHM Generalate, 1985-1986.
102. Unsigned papers, St. Mary's Parish, Manhasset, NY and its former pastors, 1853-1943. Archives, IHM Generalate.
103. "A Centennial History of St. Mary's Parish, Manhasset, 1853-1943, p. 5.
104. Ibid., pp.11-12.
105. Annals of St. Mary's Convent, Manhasset, NY. Archives, IHM Generalate.
106. Personal communication with Sister Annette Corcoran, IHM, November 25, 1986.
107. Centennial Booklet, St. Mary's Parish, Manhasset, NY. op. cit., p. 16.
108. Statistics from Office of Director of Apostolic Planning, IHM Generalate, 1985-1986.
109. "The History of St. Raymond's Parish, Reflections," 75th Anniversary Booklet, St. Raymond's Church, 1909-1984, p. 8.
110. Unsigned notes on the "History of St. Raymond's Parochial School," p. 7. Archives, IHM Generalate.
111. Annals of St. Raymond's Convent, 1955-1965. Archives, IHM Generalate.
112. Letter of Bishop John McGann to Reverend William V. Singleton, Pastor, ''The History of St. Raymond's Parish, Reflections," 75th Anniversary booklet, p. 2.
113. "Our Lady Queen of Martyrs School - 50 Years." Jubilee Booklet. p. 9.
114. Letter from Rev. Joseph V. S. McClancy to Mother Casimir, July 3, 1928. Archives, IHM Generalate.
115. Notes collected by Sister Immaculata Gillespie. Archives, IHM Generalate.
116. Golden Jubilee Booklet, Our Lady Queen of Martyrs, op. cit., p. 15.
117. Personal Interview with Sister Benedictus Philpott at the Marian Convent, February 4, 1987.
118. Ibid.
119. Letter from Rev. Monsignor William J. Carey to Sister Michel Keenan, May 8, 1984. Annals of St. Paul's Convent, 1984. Archives, IHM Generalate.
120. Notes collected by Sister Immaculata Gillespie. Archives, IHM Generalate.

121. Letter from Mother Casimir to Rev. Michael J. McCabe, May 11, 1921. Archives, IHM Generalate.
122. Notes collected by Sister Immaculata Gillespie. Archives, IHM Generalate.
123. Clipping from Providence Diocesan Catholic Newspaper, Vol. XLVIII, No. 36, September 3, 1922.
124. Letter from Rev. M. J. McCabe, Pastor, St, Paul's, Edgewood, RI, to Mother Casimir, Ascension Thursday, 1921.
125. Ibid., July 15, 1921.
126. 50th Anniversary Booklet, St. Paul's Church, Cranston, RI, p. 12.
127. Annals of St. Paul's Convent, 1955-1984, Archives, IHM Generalate.
128. Sister Immaculata Gillespie, sources previously cited.
129. Annals of St. Thomas Convent, 1955-1956. Archives, IHM Generalate.
130. Statistics from the Office of the Director of Apostolic Planning, 1979-1980, IHM Generalate.
131. Mother M. Casimir. Letter to the Congregation, June 13, 1920. Archives, IHM Generalate.
132. Ibid.
133. Notes collected by Sister Immaculata Gillespie, IHM. Archives, lHM Generalate.
134. Ibid.
135. Gallagher, op. cit. pp. 392, 394.
136. Annals of St. Agnes Place, Elmhurst, PA. Archives, IHM Generalate.
137. Correspondence from Mr. Maxwell D. Shepherd to Mother M. Kathleen, August 22, 1957.

Mother Mary William Craig, IHM
1929-1931

BORN:	Ellen Craig – August 10, 1871, Pittston, PA
PARENTS:	Patrick and Ann Brown Craig
EDUCATION:	A.B., Marywood College, Scranton, PA
RELIGIOUS LIFE:	Entered IHM Congregation, July 31, 1890 Reception of Habit, August 2, 1891 Profession of Vows, April 3, 1893
MISSIONS OF RECORD:	St. Alphonsus Academy, Tillamook, OR St. Lawrence Elementary School, Portland, OR IHM Academy, Coeur d'Alene, ID *St. Joseph's Elementary School, Danville, PA *Served as Principal of Elementary School and Convent Superior
MEMBER OF THE GENERAL COUNCIL:	First Assistant to Mother Casimir, 1925-1929
SUPERIOR GENERAL:	1929-1931 (completed Mother Casimir's term of office)
DIED:	May 3, 1965

Mother Mary William Craig
1929 - 1931

<u>TOPIC</u> <u>PAGE</u>

> If the Mother Superior die before the expiration of her term of office, the Assistant will be the Mother Superior for the remainder of said term, unless the Right Reverend Bishop should proceed to a new election or nominate the Mother Superior provisionally.
>
> (Rules and Constitutions of the Sister, Servants of the Immaculate Heart of Mary, 1890, Chapter III, Article 10)

Thus it was that Mother Mary William Craig, who had been the assistant to Mother Casimir Murray since 1925, was confirmed by Bishop O'Reilly as the new mother superior in February 1929. Mother Mary William had, at this time, been in the Congregation for thirty-nine years, having entered in 1890. Twenty of those years she had spent in the western missions, having opened St. Alphonsus Academy, Tillamook, Oregon, in 1897; she was sent to St. Lawrence Academy in Portland, Oregon, in 1901 and later to the IHM Academy, Coeur d'Alene, Idaho. As early as 1898 she conducted a six-weeks' summer school for the Sisters of St. Mary of Beaverton, Oregon. She must have seemed a good choice, indeed, since in 1924 and later throughout her term as assistant mother superior she had served as community supervisor of schools. She also served on the corporation of the Sisters of IHM, which then included Marywood College, from the time of her selection as a member on August 18, 1927. All of these experiences, responsibilities, and memberships prepared her well for the decisions and the times which she was to face in the course of her brief term of office 1929-1931.

The "Great Depression" of the 1930s was about to break out in the United States. Signs of economic disaster were apparent on all sides as intermittent unemployment, high interest rates, bank foreclosures for inability to pay debts, depletion of savings, and an atmosphere of panic was building up in the country. The stock market began to crumble on Thursday, October 24, 1929, sending reverberations around the world. People did not want to believe what was happening, and many whose fortunes and future seemed to be wiped out took refuge in irrational acts of crime and even suicide. The optimists tried to say that prosperity was just around the corner, but, as Monsignor Gallagher states, "By the end of 1932, no one was whistling anymore. The breadlines were too long, the suffering was too intense, and the gloom was too pronounced for even the most naive to be fooled any longer."(1)

In describing this period in the Diocese of Scranton under the leadership of Bishop Thomas C. O'Reilly, Msgr. Gallagher comments:

> In the light of the sudden widespread poverty, it was little wonder that Bishop O'Reilly's record of accomplishment did not include a tribute to his prowess as a builder . . . while construction and

> expansion represented one measure of achievement, the avoidance of foreclosure certainly deserved to be considered as another. Within that framework, Bishop O'Reilly's feat was all the more historic. It was his unpleasant task to preside in a time of catastrophe . . . He had to ensure the survival not only of 208 parishes, but also of a complex network of hospitals, orphanages, custodial homes, and schools . . . Not one single mortgage was foreclosed; not one single facility failed . . . Bishop O'Reilly rode out the storm and guided the diocesan structure through intact. (2)

In this description there is a deep parallel to the role of Mother Mary William Craig as she guided the Sisters of IHM during this crucial economic period. Her concern over the impact of the depression is reflected in her Christmas letter to the sisters of the Congregation, the final paragraph of which says:

> Pray, too, dear Sisters, that the little Prince of Peace will during this holy season touch the hearts of those who are responsible for the awful depression, and bring prosperity and happiness to poor suffering humanity. (3)

Under the care of God's Providence, the diligent management of Mother Mary William, the frugality of the sisters in sending the small but steady stipends from the missions, the gifts of donors, and the income from board and tuition of students at the College and at Marywood Seminary, these years saw the Congregation able to restore and refurnish the Motherhouse, to make repairs to Marywood Seminary, to complete, furnish, and pay for O'Reilly Residence Hall (now Regina Hall), to make improvements at St. Agnes Place in Elmhurst, and to make payments of about $100,000 or more per year on indebtedness. The treasurer's report for August 1, 1931, states in part:

> All the furniture and equipment for the new Residence Hall, and for all other buildings, paid in full. All maintenance bills are paid . . . The winter's supply of fuel for St. Agnes Place, Elmhurst, Pa., and for the stores at Marywood, is paid in full . . . The winter's supply of butter for Marywood, and for St. Agnes Place is paid in full. (4)

Another drain on the Congregation's finances was the need for ongoing flushing projects to support portions of the land that had been improperly protected by the coal companies in their mining operations. Mother Casimir had been notified on October 29, 1928, by the mining engineer, Mr. Severin W. Sekol, that a major flushing project was needed under the Marywood buildings. (5) It was a sign of the economic stress already being experienced that Mother Casimir would respond to Mr. Sekol's concerns in November 1928 by writing, "As you already know, we have done some flushing and intend to have our men resume the work in the near future. We are carrying a big debt at present and must do this work of flushing on a smaller scale." (6)

As if the concerns about the underground conditions were not already great enough, word was received by Mother Mary William about five weeks after Mother Casimir's death that the Pennsylvania Coal Company intended to do further mining under the Marywood property. It is apparent from this letter that the Pennsylvania Coal Company had deeded the land to the Congregation on March 1, 1895, but had reserved the underground and mineral rights to itself. The letter from Mr. J. C. Brydon, Vice President of the Pennsylvania Coal Company states in part:

> You are hereby advised that the Pennsylvania Coal Company proposes to mine and remove the coal underlying the premises conveyed by the said Pennsylvania Coal Company to the Congregation of the Immaculate Heart by deed made the first day of March, 1895 . . .
>
> You will note that the coal and other minerals were reserved, with the right and privilege of mining and removing the same as if the Pennsylvania Coal Company remained the owners . . .
>
> This notice is not required to be given to you, and it is given merely for the purpose of informing you and permitting you to take such steps as you may deem necessary to protect your property and persons who may be upon the premises. (7)

It would be some time before the Congregation would actually become involved in huge mine flushing projects on its property, but it was no doubt true, as series of letters on file testify (8) that much time was consumed over the ensuing years in consultation with engineers, attorneys, and coal company representatives. Bishop Thomas C. O'Reilly was also involved, since several church properties and Maloney Home (now Holy Family Residence) adjacent to Marywood, were also affected.

Meanwhile, throughout 1929, 1930 and 1931, requests were continuing to come in to Mother Mary William seeking sisters to staff new schools in a wide variety of locations. Bishop William J. Hafey, then of the Raleigh, North Carolina Diocese, was hoping to open a second school, St.Paul's in New Bern, North Carolina, and was earnestly "checking with

Mother Mary William to see that Mother Casimir's promise of Sisters for September 1929 would be kept." And it was.

In the early fall of 1929 Mother Mary William visited the western missions in Portland, Oregon, and Coeur d'Alene, Idaho. From the correspondence to the Very Reverend H. Schutten, CSsR.in Portland on her return, it is clear that while she was pleased with the work of the sisters on these missions, she was pondering the question, even then, of their continuance. She writes:

> I laid the Western question before the Council and the senior Sisters. All are very much in favor of keeping the Western houses open. In fact, they would consider it a calamity to close these missions. I also took the matter up with our Right Reverend Bishop. He will not disturb these schools, but when I mentioned signing the ten year agreement he laughingly said, 'It will not be necessary. Leave things as they are.'
>
> In regard to opening new schools in the West, it would be impossible just now for there is scarcely a school that has its full quota of Sisters. However, I feel that when the home missions are fully supplied that there will be no objection to increasing the number of schools in the Far West . . . As soon as I can I will send one or two more Sisters to Coeur d'Alene for I see they are much needed. (9)

It must have given Mother Mary William great satisfaction to report this decision to Father Schutten because of her own love of the western missions that she herself had pioneered.

Knowing the needs of the schools from the vantage point of having been Congregation supervisor of schools, however, her responses to new requests over the next two years reflected her concern for replacements for sisters who were ill and for twelve sisters who had died throughout 1928-1929. And so, to Reverend A. R. Cioffi of Brooklyn, New York, to the rector of Immaculate Conception Monastery, Jamaica, Long Island, to Reverend C. J. Bruton, Church of St. Margaret Mary, Rochester, New York, and to Reverend John Wynne of St. Barnabas Parish, Bellmore, Long Island—and possibly many others not recorded—the answer was much the same: ". . .in justice to the schools already opened, and to the zealous pastors who have charge of them, I feel in duty bound to take care of these schools before opening new ones." (10) She also adhered strictly to the sound change made by the Church in not allowing the novices to go out into the classrooms, as had formerly been the case. This change meant that the services of some twenty second-year novices each year were no longer available to augment the number of teaching sisters on the missions. She had so often been faced with the pressure of claims of pastors to real or pretended "promises" made by Mother Casimir that toward the end of her term she began to add a new reason to those mentioned above for not agreeing to send sisters: " . . . this is our election year, and in the present scarcity of help I do not feel justified in making a promise that someone else might not be able to fulfill after August 15th." (11)

The years of Mother Mary William's administration, 1929 through 1931, then, was a period of economic strain and of personnel shortages. It was a time for constraints on expansionism for the Congregation; it was a time for "running a tight ship."

However, during this period three new schools were opened: St. Monica's "colored" School, Raleigh, North Carolina; Sacred Heart of Mary, Jermyn, Pennsylvania; and St. Mary, Help of Christians, North Pittston, Pennsylvania. All of these were opened in 1930.

St. Monica's Elementary School, Raleigh, North Carolina

Bishop William J. Hafey of the Raleigh, North Carolina Diocese, was well aware of the personnel shortage among the Sisters of IHM in Scranton for he had exerted much pressure on Mother Mary William in the months following Mother Casimir's death in 1929 to make sure that sisters would be sent, in accord with arrangements made by Mother Casimir, to the new school in New Bern, North Carolina, in September 1929. Having obtained this request, his next appeal for sisters to staff St. Monica's in Raleigh, North Carolina, was directed to Mother Loyola of the Philadelphia IHMs. Her response must have given him some hope of having sisters to work among the 15,000 black people of Raleigh, but the decision was reversed, and in a letter of April 21, 1930, Bishop Hafey explains the matter to Mother Mary William:

> I had reason to be quite confident that Mother Loyola of Immaculata would be able to send Sisters to begin our work among the fifteen thousand colored people of Raleigh. But His Eminence, the Cardinal of Philadelphia, has decided against the Sisters leaving the Archdiocese. It represents another failure to my many requests. With the property purchased and plans made to begin the building of the school and Priest's house on May l, you can imagine my disappointment . . .
>
> I assured [sic] you it was not my intention to ask you to begin another school. You have done so much that it seems like imposition. Yet now I feel that I must ask you to give the proposed work

> in Raleigh your prayerful consideration . . . Raleigh being the Cathedral city and the Capital of the State, I am convinced that an evidence of the Church's interest in the Colored should be given without delay . . . We could begin with three Sisters hoping for a fourth after the first year . . . (12)

In reply, Mother Mary William assured Bishop Hafey of her desire to assist him in spite of the illness of some twenty sisters who were off duty at the time. She adds, however, that it will depend on Bishop O'Reilly's permission. Needless to say, Bishop Hafey wasted little time in getting that permission and wrote to Mother Mary William in early June that he had seen Bishop O'Reilly at Mount St. Mary's, Emmitsburg, had put the request for three sisters before him, and had assured Bishop O'Reilly of Mother Mary William's interest in the work with the colored in Raleigh. Bishop O'Reilly's reply was that "if you would furnish the Sisters, he would be in every way satisfied." (13) It was left to Mother Mary William to assure Bishop O'Reilly that she could provide the sisters for the Raleigh mission.

Bishop Hafey must have been delighted when the letter of approval arrived from Mother Mary William some two months later which said in part,

> . . .You may expect four Sisters for this new school some day during the week of August 25th. I will wire when they are leaving here. I hope God will bless our first undertaking in your Episcopal City and that the humble work of the Sisters will be instrumental in reaping a harvest of souls for our dear Lord. (14)

Mother Mary William's concern for the welfare of the sisters was evident in her subsequent correspondence with the pastor, Reverend Charles J. Hannigan, SSJ, and with Bishop Hafey about the renovations of the home which was to serve as the convent. She reminds them of the need for good lighting, for the installation of a small laundry, and of the need to procure a good housekeeper for the sisters. In defense of these requests she says, "The work in the schools nowadays is heavy and trying, consequently Sisters need all the help they can get to make their duties outside of the classroom as light as possible." (15)

Father Hannigan needed no prodding to provide everything possible for the little community which included Sister Anysia Moran, superior and principal, Sister Servula Healy, Sister Eleanora Whalen and Sister Benigna Ball. Sister Anysia's first letter to Mother Mary William describes how solicitous Father Hannigan was for them and how beautiful both the convent and the school were. (16)

Actually, the school and the church were combined in one newly constructed brick building. Four large, airy, perfectly equipped classrooms were provided. The dedication of this structure took place on Sunday, September 7, 1930, with a solemn procession of dedication headed by Bishop Hafey, who was accompanied by fifteen priests. Forty-three sisters of different religious orders also participated, including Franciscans, Dominicans, Sisters of Mercy, Charity Sisters, and seventeen Sisters of IHM. More than two hundred non-Catholic black people were in attendance.

On September 8, 1930, Father Hannigan opened St. Monica's School with Holy Mass. One hundred sixty children—all Protestants—were registered in the first four grades. Seventy-five fifth graders had to be turned away. Bishop Hafey visited the school and addressed the children on this opening day.

On the Feast of the Holy Name of Mary, September 12, 1930, the Blessed Sacrament was carried from the school chapel to the convent where Father Hannigan celebrated Holy Mass for the first time. Bishop Hafey, who was to be an interested and frequent visitor, also celebrated Mass for the sisters in the convent chapel on September 14, 1930.

From its very beginnings the challenges at St. Monica's generated much enthusiasm from all concerned—the bishop, the pastor, the sisters, the children, and friends of this missionary project. The sisters must have impressed Father Hannigan with their love of Marywood too, for in an early letter to Mother Mary William he says,

> I have called our blessed estate Marywood. I have in mind that this, Our Lady's Wood, will be, for our community in North Carolina, what the Mother Marywood is to the Order of the Sisters, Servants of the Immaculate Heart of Mary. (17)

It was no small feat for Sister Eleanora Whalen to take on the task of preparing for a Latin High Mass for the feast of the Immaculate Conception, December 8. But, three months of intensive work on the music and the Latin brought about tremendous results. St. Monica's Protestant children were able to sing both common and proper parts of the Mass in Latin in a reverent and beautiful manner. As Father Hannigan described it,

> I do not think it could have gone off any better, even at Marywood. The Mass, the surprising effect of the uniformed choir, and the melody of their voices, and their happy pronunciation of the Church's sonorous language . . . (18)

A simple, beautiful spirit prevailed with so many events, development or improvements being planned as "surprises" either for or by the sisters, the pastor or the bishop. All seemed united in a great desire to serve God and to work zealously that His Name would be made known through St. Monica's School and Church. By the close of the first school year fourteen black people had received the Sacrament of Baptism.

Together with the great praise that came to the sisters for their wonderful work with the school children, there were also some sufferings to be experienced in the bigotry which was rampant at the time. Much effort was put forth to develop leadership for Catholic Action among the black Catholics of the area, who were few in number.

Those first years passed all too quickly, with Mother Josepha Hurley succeeding Mother Mary William in the leadership of the Congregation in August 1931; with Sister Anysia Moran being changed from Raleigh in 1932 to become Mistress of Novices at the death of Mother Mary Clare; with Father Hannigan's leaving St. Monica's to establish another mission for the blacks at Southern Pines, North Carolina, in 1934; and with Bishop Hafey himself being called from his much-loved North Carolina to the Diocese of Scranton, Pennsylvania, in 1937. He was replaced by Bishop Eugene J. McGuinness, another zealous missionary bishop who was much loved by our sisters.

The Dominican Fathers took over St. Monica's Mission in July 1934 and were outstanding in their work with the black people of the parish and with the school children. In the South these years had been exciting, developmental, and growth years, in spite of the depression. In a brief ten-year period the Diocese of Raleigh had increased from 5,900 Catholics to 9,872; from 20 diocesan priests to 53; from 6 religious order priests to 26; from 5 Catholic schools for whites to 16, and from one Catholic school for blacks to 8 schools. These phenomenal advances were certainly due not only to the inspired leadership of Bishop Hafey and his successor Bishop McGuinness, but also to the dedication of the many religious and priests who responded to the call to serve in North Carolina.

St. Monica's was a reflection in miniature of the growth of the faith in the entire diocese. Each year witnessed the conversion and baptism in the Catholic faith of several children from the school and adults from the parish. In January of 1938 there were sixteen children and one adult baptized by Bishop McGuinness. It was obvious from the academic success of the graduates of St. Monica's School that not only were the students receiving knowledge of the Catholic faith and absorbing a religious atmosphere, but they were receiving excellent preparation in all other areas as well. In June 1944, of the six scholarships awarded to graduates of the "Colored High School," four were merited by former graduates of St. Monica's. These scholarships were to Fisk University, Tennessee; Shaw University, Raleigh; North Carolina State, Durham; and St. Augustine College, Raleigh. In the freshman class of this same high school, out of 165 students, the three receiving the highest academic averages were former St. Monica's students. It was significant for black youth of that time that all of the graduates of St. Monica's were continuing their education in various high schools.

St. Monica's reached its peak enrollment of 194 students in 1959-1960. Over the years it had averaged about 170 students per year in eight grades, with a low of 160 students in 1961-1962. The grades were doubled in each classroom, so there were never more than four IHMs on the faculty. The music teacher and the principal who carried two grades in addition to their other duties performed double duty. In the case of Sister Carol Baden, the principal, music teaching and third and fourth grades were all part of her responsibility. (19)

In the interest of forwarding the goals of racial integration in the Raleigh Diocese, Bishop Vincent S. Waters, in 1967, merged St. Monica's School with Sacred Heart Cathedral School that was served by the Newburgh, New York Dominican Sisters. Sister Geraldine, OP, served as principal and Sister Joan Coyne, IHM as vice principal of the racially integrated school. The combined schools opened in September 1967 with an enrollment of 240 pupils in eight grades, and with a faculty of four Dominican Sisters and four IHMs. Prior to the opening of school, meetings were held between the two faculties and a new joint Home School Association with representatives from both schools was formed. The president of the Home School Association and the secretary were from Cathedral, the vice president and the treasurer from St. Monica's.

Great sensitivity and tact were exercised in explaining to the people and students of St. Monica's the reasons for the merger and the changes they could anticipate under the new arrangements. One of these was certainly the adjustment required to meet the tuition level in existence at Cathedral School. Parents were urged not to let the increased tuition be a barrier to their children's attendance at Cathedral School, since a way would be worked out by St. Monica's Parish to assist with the tuition differential. An open house was held on August 27, 1967, to acquaint all with the facilities available at the Cathedral School.

As well prepared as the faculty was for the historic fact of racial integration taking place in their school, it is clear from the IHM community annals that the racial unrest being experienced across the nation had its reverberations in Raleigh, too. Very practical means were utilized to bring the concept of equality into reality. Some of these were based in the ceremonies surrounding faith experiences, for example, the fact that on

December 3, 1967, the Confirmation class of thirty parishioners included for the first time both black and white persons; also, that on May 5 a class of thirteen First Communicants included one white boy, Mark DiMeao, the first white child to receive Holy Communion in a formal First Holy Communion class in St. Monica's Church.

These efforts were augmented by the establishment of a school guidance program in which the sisters conducted individual and group guidance with a view of fostering true acceptance among the students based on the dignity of each one as God's child.

The Diocese for its part, in order to facilitate integration, assigned also new parish boundaries in the city of Raleigh. Since St. Monica's had been established initially to serve the black population, it was now dissolved and integrated into other area parishes, with the St. Monica's area becoming St. Joseph's Parish. Thirty-five years of service by the Dominican Fathers came to an end with the appointment of the new pastor, Reverend Cronan Graves. Even though the IHM Sisters were teaching at Cathedral School, they continued to serve St. Monica's neighborhood and the newly established St. Joseph's Parish. (20) By January 1969 the old St. Monica's School was humming with the sounds of 80 children, as it had been converted to a day care center. The director was Mrs. Mary Sharpe, a former graduate of St. Monica's School.

A letter of January 18, 1972, to Mother Beata from Sister Mary Francis McDonald, superior general of the Newburgh Dominicans who were staffing Cathedral Elementary School in Raleigh with the IHMs, started a flurry of activity, which was to end with the withdrawal of the IHM Sisters from Raleigh. This letter set forth three alternatives for Mother Beata to present to the council for consideration (1) That the Dominicans withdraw two Sisters in June 1972, leaving two for one additional year, and then withdrawing entirely; (2) That the Dominicans withdraw one Sister in June 1972 without guaranteeing any future direction; (3) That the Dominicans or the IHMs should withdraw entirely leaving four Sisters to staff the school of 222 pupils. As a follow-up to the statement of these alternatives, Sister Mary Francis did comment on "the very fine spirit of inter-community cooperation which has come to prevail in the school" (21) which she would regret seeing terminated under the third alternative. She also commented that she favored the first alternative, but should it become a reality, she felt the remaining sisters should all live in one convent. (22) The chief reason set forth for any of the above action was that Cathedral School was overstaffed with its eight teachers and 222 students.

This letter was acknowledged by Mother Beata on January 22, 1972, and the decision of the Central Administrative Assembly to withdraw the

IHMs from Raleigh was communicated to Sister Mary Francis on February 1, 1972. (23) The fact that Sister Mary Francis had asked for a reply before meetings scheduled for February 5 and 6 was probably the reason for the great haste with which this decision was reached. Obviously there was no time for consultation with the sisters in Raleigh and the flood of letters which followed the announcement of withdrawal of the IHM Sisters expressed great sadness, surprise, shock, distress and disappointment on the part of the sisters, the people, and Bishop George Lynch, Auxiliary of Raleigh. All were testimony to the deep love the sisters had for their apostolate, as well as the respect and love that the children and people had for them. One letter summed up the feelings of all quite well: "Your Sisters have been a special blessing to Raleigh's Negro [sic] population. Their loving, generous Christian participation in the total community has generated more of the same among the people they served. Their example and their labors are still greatly needed." (24)

In light of the shortage of sister-personnel across the Congregation it was undoubtedly true that overstaffing of one school was not a wise use of resources. Since the Dominicans had staffed Cathedral School from its beginnings, part of the reasoning behind the Central Administrative Assembly's decision was that if only one Congregation should remain, it should be the Dominicans. That the Central Administrative Assembly did not see this as an opportunity to gain four sisters for other apostolates is reflected in their expressed desire to study the situation and place these sisters in other North Carolina missions if warranted. (25) Sister Angela Mary Parker was assigned to Mother of Mercy School in Washington, North Carolina, and Sister Elizabeth Bullen to Rocky Mount, North Carolina, thus continuing their service to the Raleigh Diocese.

Sacred Heart of Mary Elementary School, Jermyn, Pennsylvania

Sacred Heart of Mary parish school began with the groundbreaking ceremony on March 17, 1930. The John Gibbons Company was general contractor for the building of the school, an eight-classroom brick building. Bishop Thomas C. O'Reilly dedicated the school on August 25, 1930. The following week the first community of sisters arrived and was welcomed to their new convent home by a committee of ladies from the parish who had furnished the convent and who had prepared a delicious meal for the sisters. This first community included Sister Hyacinth Tierney, superior and principal, Sister Inez Farrell, Sister Euphrasia Kelly, Sister Anselmo Murray, Sister Maria Catherine Walsh, and Sister Florita Waters.

The school opened formally on September 15, 1930, with 250 students registered in five grades. In a letter to the Bishop, Reverend Thomas M.

Jordan, pastor, wrote that all but one Catholic family in the parish were sending their children to the parochial school. Father Jordan was an outstanding scholar and educator, hence made the school and the progress of the students his special concern. Each morning he visited the classes for religious instructions. One of his favorite questions, to the delight of the youngsters, was, "What question would you like to ask the professor?" He accomplished much for the parish and the school in his seven-year pastorate, but because of poor health was transferred to St. Dominic's Parish, Parsons, Pennsylvania, where he died February 9, 1942. (26)

Another zealous pastor, Reverend John A. O'Neil, succeeded Father Jordan in January 1938. Under his leadership the large debt was significantly reduced. He continued as pastor until 1971 when he became pastor emeritus, being succeeded by Reverend William J. Egan, who was followed by Reverend William P. Ward in 1974. (27)

During the school year 1961-1962 all eyes were focused on the progress of the beautiful new cinderblock and brick convent which was taking shape from August 1961 through March 1962. Hopes had initially been raised that the completion would come at Thanksgiving time, then for December 8, then for Christmas. But, as with most construction projects, there were delays. These delays only heightened the atmosphere of joyful anticipation that culminated on March 17.

The record states,

> Finally, the long line of trunks being moved across an improvised plank from the back door of the old house to the new one gave sure proof that the long awaited day had arrived. March 17 found the Sisters in corps pushing, carrying, dragging, and balancing anything that had to be moved from the old house. Mr. Pidgeon, our sexton, and his crew managed the heavier articles.
>
> Late that night this congregation of movers could be found nestled snug in their new beds, in roomy new cells, in a beautiful new convent complete excepting the chapel and many little odds and ends left by the workmen.
>
> Within a matter of days, the old house which was now in our front yard, was demolished and removed. (28)

Sunday, March 25, was the open house for the parishioners; so one can imagine the activity in the new convent as the five sisters prepared for this event scheduled for eight days from their moving in. This, and the open house on May 27 for the IHM Sisters in the area, were successful in every way. Some 115 sisters attended a catered buffet supper that was provided in the church auditorium. The new split-level convent, which according to the architect, Mr. George Murray, was to be "monastic, sufficient and convenient," (29) was also beautiful in its simplicity. The enrollment of Sacred Heart of Mary School, Jermyn, hovered around the 200 mark for the twenty-year period 1955-1975, with a low of 185 in 1960 and a high of 219 students in 1956. By 1975-1976 when a decision had to be made about the continuance of the IHM Sisters in the school, the enrollment was eighty students in six grades. Partly because of this, and partly because of the personnel shortage in the Congregation, the announcement of the sisters' withdrawal from Sacred Heart of Mary in June 1976 was made by Father Ward on October 25-26, 1975.

Father Ward, realizing the needs in his parish for religious education for the children after the sisters would leave, wrote to Sister Anne Fulwiler, superior general, requesting the assignment of two sisters to continue to live in the convent in Jermyn and to serve the parish as CCD coordinator and visitor to the elderly and sick, as well as to take the census and provide some of the liturgical music. (30) While it was not possible for the Congregation to respond with two sisters, the request was looked upon favorably as a way to continue the forty-five year presence of IHM Sisters in the parish. Plans were for a sister to be appointed as CCD coordinator and to reside with our sisters in nearby St. Thomas Convent, Archbald, Pennsylvania. (31) This was confirmed by Sister Anne Fulwiler in April 1976, (32) but as it turned out, the Congregation was unable to provide a sister as CCD coordinator for Sacred Heart of Mary Parish. (33)

Father Ward's remarks regarding the closing of the school reflect his gratitude for the work of the IHM Sisters in the parish:

> This parish owes a great debt of gratitude to the Sisters of the Immaculate Heart of Mary who are now in their 45th year of service to this parish and its children . . . The closing of a parish school is a difficult and painful decision. We must prize the graces we have received in its forty-five years of service. We are all challenged to face the future with courage and dedication in the religious education of our children. Our faith tells us that God will provide. (34)

St. Mary, Help of Christians Elementary School, North Pittston, Pennsylvania

Upper Pittston, Church Hill, or North Pittston, as it was called at various times, had the distinction of building the first church erected in Pittston, Pennsylvania. As early as 1849 the ground for the church had been selected, and in 1895 when St. Mary, Help of Christians first became a parish, Reverend John B. Loughran, pastor, built the first church. While it was a small, primitive structure without seats, it was a source of great pride to the parishioners. St. Mary's, Help of Christians, went through many stages in the early days, being at one time a parish in its own right, with a resident pastor, and at another time, being a mission of St. John the Evangelist Church, Pittston.

Soon after the death in 1899 of Reverend John Finnen, pastor of St. John the Evangelist Church, St. Mary's again became a parish church. Reverend John F. Greaves was named pastor. St. Mary's shared in a legacy left by Father Finnen, and with that five thousand dollars built a parish hall that was named Finnen Memorial Hall. This hall was to serve various uses over the years: at one point when the new church was being built, Finnen Hall was used for religious services; at another time, the first floor was converted into a rectory; finally, in 1930, it was converted into a parish school. (35)

It was in June of 1930 that Reverend George J. Dixon, then pastor of St. Mary's, Help of Christians Parish in Upper Pittston, wrote to Mother Mary William:

> St. Mary's Parish has begun the erection of a convent; the school was built years ago and has been practically put into condition to open school. We expect to be ready to open school about the middle of September. We will likely need about four teachers . . . We kindly ask you to put our application on your list for consideration and we trust that you will be able to take care of us at the proper time . . . (36)

The "proper time" was, of course, only three months away, but there seems to be no hint in Mother Mary William's response that this was indeed very short notice on which to plan for the opening of a new school. She writes:

> I am glad to learn from your letter that you will be ready to open your school about the middle of September. It will be a pleasure to send you the number of Sisters you have requested . . . we will feel honored to be permitted to contribute our mite in the building up of Catholic education in your parish . . . (37)

Father Dixon had proposed in his letter to begin by taking children from third to eighth grade, but on this point Mother Mary William suggested rather that "we find it better to begin with the primary and add the upper grades as soon as conditions permit. This gives better results in the end because all the children have had the same training from the beginning." (38)

And so the first six grades were opened on September 8, 1930, with 175 pupils registered. The first group of sisters included Sister Mary Conception Donnelly, superior and principal, Sister Catherine Ruane, housekeeper, Sister Eulalia Walsh, Sister Teresa Maria McGinnis, Sister Demetria Bode, Sister Gerald Maria Holleran, and later in the year, Sister Ina Kenney, a novice, who served as music teacher and assisted in school for three months.

Sister Ina described the convent as ''ideal" in its provision of simple, but adequate space. The deprivation she can recall experiencing was the absence of the Blessed Sacrament since the beautiful convent chapel had not yet been dedicated. The space on the first floor of the former parish hall had been divided into four large classrooms, with the youngsters rather evenly distributed in each room. (39)

By 1931 the seventh and eighth grades were opened, filling the four classrooms with some forty-five pupils each. There were changes in the faculty also, as Sister Leocadia Lynott replaced Sister Mary Conception Donnelly as principal and superior, and Sister Adalbert (Mary) Schelb was assigned for the seventh and eighth grades, as well as for the teaching of music after school. Sister Mary Schelb recalls this, her first mission, quite vividly. The lively, deep faith of the people, the closely-knit families, and the impact of the depression years that left many miners out of work, are part of those recollections. She remembers the interest of the public school teachers, most of whom were Catholic, in St. Mary's School, and also in seeing that the Catholic pupils in the public school attended First Friday Mass and went to confession regularly.

Father Dixon, the pastor, must have impressed everyone with his kindness and love of the sisters. Sister Mary Schelb described him as a short, stocky, white-haired, jovial priest who often visited the sisters at recreation time in the convent, leaving a spiritual thought with them, especially reflections on Our Lady. He was a very deeply spiritual person but not aloof from his people. He kept after the youngsters, motivating them in their studies and in religious living. The youngsters responded well to him, referring to him informally as "Pop" Dixon. (40)

On February 12, 1933, the little community was to experience a great shock in the sudden death of Sister Catherine Ruane. In the most meaningful sense it was a "beautiful death" in that the priest assigned for confessions of the sisters had just left and Sister Catherine went to the community room to do her spiritual reading. It was in that final act that she died. Father Dixon was called and he anointed her there on the community room floor where she had fallen. In minutes, the sisters from St. John's in lower Pittston were present to assist.

By 1956, under the principalship of Sister Harold Mulderig, a preschool was added to the eight-grade system. Sister Rita Mary Mayan, the newly appointed kindergarten teacher, was responsible also for the music class and the choir. At this point the registration numbered only about 145 students, but it was clear that Reverend Andrew P. Maloney, pastor, wished to continue to educate the children of his parish at whatever sacrifice. It was, in fact, in June of 1956 that he requested a ninth grade teacher for 1957, which hinted at his hope to have secondary level education at North Pittston also. (41) It does not appear that this hope ever materialized, however. Father Maloney deserves credit for the continuous physical plant renovation and updating, especially of the school and the church over the eleven years of his pastorate from January 1956 to 1967. Each year the annals of St. Mary's Convent record some action on his part to improve the physical conditions under which the sisters worked: "new lights were put in the halls," "walls and woodwork were painted," "the exterior of the church, rectory and convent were painted," "new desks for grades three through eight," "blackboards refinished," "the ceilings lowered," "new flooring in three rooms," "new library," —and then the cycle of repairs would start again. In spite of the limitations of the physical structure of St. Mary's School, another comment continues to surface over the years in describing the visits of Reverend William Donovan, then the assistant superintendent of schools of the Diocese of Scranton: "Although our school building is far from the best, Father [Donovan] was pleased with the work of the sisters and with the children in general." (42)

In spite of all efforts, the enrollment of the school fell to 122 students in 1960, rose again to 138 students in 1964, but hovered around 135 until 1967 when the diocese, with the approval of the two pastors and the two congregations involved, proposed a merger of St. Rocco's School, operated by the Filippini Sisters, under Reverend Julio Serra, OSJ, pastor, with St. Mary's School. The merged school was named Pittston Catholic Elementary School. Both school buildings were to continue to be used, with a Filippini Sister as principal at the St. Rocco's building, and an IHM as principal at the St. Mary's building. Four members of each Congregation were to serve as faculty, with two of each Congregation being placed in each building. In other words, some IHMs had Sister Giovannina, MPF, as principal and some Filippini's had Sister Agnes McHale, IHM, as principal.

Since many families had children at both locations, it was a great challenge to the two principals to synchronize schedules, events, and school regulations to meet the needs and convenience of the families. The arrangements were further complicated by the need for two sisters from each group of sisters to travel to the other school.

The initial year of the merger 1967-1968 saw 125 of St. Mary's students and 133 of St. Rocco's students, for a total of 258 students in the two buildings. St. Rocco's housed the first four grades and St. Mary's grades five through eight. In 1968-1969 there was a decrease of 20 students, reflected chiefly in declines in the first two grades where St. Mary's children would have had to travel to St. Rocco's, and in the fifth grade where, for St. Rocco's youngsters it would have meant travel to St. Mary's for the first time in their schooling. By 1969-1970 there was a total of 196 students in the two buildings. It was clear to the families, the sisters, and the pastors that even with all the efforts being made to make the merger a success, there were just too many problems to surmount to make it work. The low enrollment, and the many problems related to the arrangements of the merger, topped by religious personnel shortages in the Congregation caused Mother Beata Wertz to withdraw the IHM Sisters from St. Mary's in June 1970. (43) Reverend Edward J. Gerrity who had been pastor since 1967 when the merger was initiated (and who is still pastor at St. Mary's as of this 1987 writing) had a deep appreciation of the work of the sisters. His thoughtful message in the parish bulletin of June 14, 1970 reads in part:

> For forty years now the Sisters have been here at St. Mary's, living a life of consecration . . . No one will ever write a book to tell of their deeds; no one will ever erect a monument or plaque to record their triumphs, but in the many fond hearts of those they taught just the other day, and those they taught in the long years ago, their names will be enshrined forever . . . We owe our Sisters much—how much God alone knows. And I know that all join me in saying that we shall be eternally grateful—which isn't even thanks enough. We hope that it will help to know that they will be remembered where it means most, as we ask God to send more laborers to aid them in doing their part to attend to the great business of the salvation of mankind. (44)

Mother Mary William Craig

After the close of her term of office as superior general, Mother Mary William served the Congregation for thirty-four more years in a variety of capacities, and on various missions. At the time of her death on May 3, 1965, she was 94 years of age, having been born on August 10, 1871, and she had served as a Sister, Servant of the Immaculate Heart of Mary for seventy-five years. In her last years, two serious falls resulting in broken hips limited her physical mobility, but her mind was keen and alert to the end.

Besides the official positions which she held in the Congregation, referred to earlier, and her pioneering of the western missions in the 1890s, she is probably best remembered for her meticulous care in renovating the original motherhouse, and for the refinement of taste with which she furnished Marywood College's first residence hall, O'Reilly (now Regina) Hall. In each mission where she resided there was some reflection of her bent for refurbishing. To this day, there are missions which still set out "Mother Mary William's dishes and fine glassware" for special occasions.

Mother Mary William loved the Congregation, which she fondly referred to as "our dear Order." Her letters reveal a keen understanding of all the work awaiting the availability of more of our sisters, and a deep pride in what they were accomplishing. She was a grateful person, deeply mindful of the many ways in which God was blessing the Congregation, and mindful, too, of those who had preceded her. In one letter she writes, "While we are all united in loving Him and in thanking Him for innumerable blessings bestowed on ourselves and our loved ones, let us not forget the dear departed ones who in great measure made our present joys possible." (45)

She was happy to communicate the change which provided that the sisters could make perpetual vows after three years in temporary vows. It seems that up until December 3, 1930, the privilege of making perpetual vows, although allowed by the Constitutions, had never been claimed. Instead, annual renewals of vows were made. Most Reverend Thomas C. O'Reilly decreed on this date that the provisions for perpetual profession should henceforth be not optional, but mandatory. All of the sisters eligible made perpetual vows on December 8, 1930. Of this event, Mother Mary William wrote:

> Another Christmas is truly another blessing, and surely it is a great blessing for us who on its threshold this year had the great happiness of dedicating ourselves anew and perpetually to the service and love of our heavenly Spouse. Let us try to prove our gratitude for this great grace by greater fidelity in the exact observance of even the smallest rule, and while our hearts during the Christmastide beat in unison with the little Heart of the Infant Christ in Holy Communion, let us renew our offering and say with all possible fervor and love, 'I give myself to Thee forever, O my sweet Infant King.' (46)

Such was the commitment of her own life.

References

1. Msgr. John Gallagher, PhD, op. cit., p. 325.
2. Ibid., p. 328.
3. Letter of Mother Mary William to the Congregation, Feast of St. Eusebius, 1930. Archives, IHM Generalate.
4. Minutes of the Meetings, Board of Directors, Congregation of IHM, p. 56. Archives, IHM Generalate.
5. Letter to Mother Casimir from Mr. Severin W. Sekol, October 29, 1928. Archives, IHM Generalate.
6. Letter of Mother Casimir from Mr. Severin W. Sekol, November 28, 1928. Archives, IHM Generalate.
7. J.C. Brydon, Vice President, Pennsylvania Coal Company. Letter to the Congregation of the Immmaculate Heart, March 21, 1929.
8. Mr. Severin Sekol and J.Rossa McCormick, Construction Engineer. Letters to Bishop Thomas C. O'Reilly, 1932-1937.
9. Mother Mary William. Letter to Very Reverend H. Schutten, C.Ss.R. Portland, OR, 26th Sunday after Pentecost, 1929. Archives, IHM Generalate.
10. Mother Mary William. Letter to Very Reverend Joseph V.S. McClancy, Superintendent of Catholic Schools of Brooklyn Diocese, March 12, 1931.
11. Mother Mary William. Letter to Very Reverend Joseph V.S. McClancy , February 16, 1931.
12. Bishop William J. Hafey, Raleigh, NC. Letter to Mother Mary William, April 21, 1930.
13. Bishop William J. Hafey, Raleigh, NC, to Mother Mary William, June 12, 1930.
14. Mother Mary William. Letter to Bishop Hafey, Eleventh Sunday after Pentecost, 1930.
15. Mother Mary William. Letter to Rev. Charles J. Hannigan, SSJ. Raleigh, NC. August 19, 1930.
16. Sister M. Anysia Moran, IHM. Letter to Mother Mary William, August 28, 1930.
17. Reverend Charles J. Hannigan, Pastor, St. Monica's, Raleigh, NC. Letter to Mother Mary William, September 6, 1930.
18. Reverend Charles J. Hannigan, Pastor, St. Monica's, Raleigh, NC. Lettter to Mother Mary William, December 11, 1930.
19. Annals of St. Monica's Convent, 1967-1968. Archives, IHM Generalate.
20. 50th Anniversary Celebration of IHM Service, booklet, p. 5. Archives, IHM Generalate.
21. Sister Mary Francis McDonald, OP, Superior General, Newburg Dominicans. Letter to Mother Beata Wertz, January 18, 1972.
22. Ibid.

23. Mother Beata Wertz, IHM, Superior General. Letters to Sister Mary Francis McDonald, Newburg. NY.
24. Philip S. Ogilvie, State Librarian. Letter to Mother Beata, February 11, 1972.
25. Mother Beata Wertz, IHM. Letter to Bishop Vincent S. Waters, February 2, 1972.
26. Notes of Sister Immaculata Gillespie. Archives, IHM Generalate.
27 Bulletin of Sacred Heart of Mary Church, October 26, 1975.
28. Annals of Sacred Heart of Mary Convent, Jermyn, Pa., 1961-1962. Archives, IHM Generalate.
29. Ibid.
30. Rev. William P. Ward, Pastor, Sacred Heart of Mary Church, Jermyn, Pa. Letter to Sister Anne Fulwiler, Superior General, July 31, 1975. Archives, IHM Generalate.
31. Sister Mary Martin O'Dea, Sector Superior, Letter to Reverend William P. Ward, February 11, 1976. Archives, IHM Generalate.
32. Sister Anne Fulwiler, IHM. Letter to Reverend William P. Ward, April 14, 1976. Archives, IHM Generalate.
33. Annals of Sacred Heart of Mary Convent, Jermyn, Pa., 1975-1976. Archives, IHM Generalate.
34. Bulletin of Sacred Heart of Mary Church, Jermyn, Pa., October 26, 1975. Archives, IHM Generalate.
35. Notes of Sister Immaculata Gillespie. Archives, IHM Generalate.
36. Reverend George J. Dixon. Letter to Mother Mary William, June 9, 1930. Archives IHM Generalate.
37. Mother Mary William, Superior General, Sisters of IHM. Letter to Reverend George F. Dixon, Trinity Sunday, 1930. Archives, IHM Generalate.
38. Ibid.
39. Conversation with Sister Ina Kenney, IHM, March 16, 1987.
40. Conversation with Sister Mary Schelb, IHM, March 14, 1987.
41. Reverend Andrew P. Maloney, Pastor, St. Mary's, North Pittston. Letter to Mother M. Kathleen, Superior General, June 9, 1956. Archives, IHM Generalate.
42. Annals of St. Mary's Convent, North Pittston, 1959, 1960, 1962, etc. Archives, IHM Generalate.
43. Ibid.
44. Bulletin of St. Mary, Help of Christians Church, North Pittston, June 14, 1970.
45. Mother Mary William. Letter to Sister Madelena and Community, Christmas, 1930.
46. Mother Mary William. Letter to Sister M. Marcella and Community, Feast of St. Eusebius, 1930.

Mother M. Josepha Hurley
1931-1940

BORN:	Delia Hurley – February 8, 1876, Susquehanna, PA
PARENTS:	Thomas Hurley and Helen Maroney Hurley
EDUCATION:	Laurel Hill Academy, Susquehanna, PA A.B., Marywood College, Scranton, PA M.A., Fordham University, Bronx, NY
RELIGIOUS LIFE:	Entered IHM Congregation , October 2, 1901 at St. Rose Novitiate, Carbondale, PA Reception of Habit, April 1, 1902 Profession of Vows, August 2, 1904
MISSIONS:	St. Cecilia's, Wyoming, PA *St. Patrick's, White Haven, PA *St. Patrick's, Oneida, NY *St. Mary's, Manhasset, NY *St. Bernardine's, Baltimore, MD *St. Paul's, Scranton, PA *St. Mary of the Mount, Pittsburgh, PA *Served as Principal of Elementary School and Convent Superior
SUPERIOR GENERAL:	1931-1937 (first term) 1937-1940 (died during second term)
DIED:	December 4, 1940 – 64 years of age

TABLE OF CONTENTS

Mother M. Josepha Hurley
1931-1940

The events of August 4, 1931, were a foreshadowing of participatory and collegial forms of governance in religious congregations everywhere. Prior to this date, Most Reverend Thomas C. O'Reilly, Bishop of Scranton, had sent notice to the IHM Congregation that he would conduct a general visitation of all of the professed sisters, and directed all, with the exception of those missioned in the West, to be present in the chapel at the motherhouse in Scranton for this visitation. It is recorded that on the appointed date, August 4, 1931, some 498 professed IHM Sisters were present, and one of the outcomes was that ''more than a majority of the Sisters asked for approval of election of the General Superior, two assistants (the first assistant to be Local Superior of the Motherhouse at Marywood) and two Councilors, all to be elected by ballot, and a Treasurer, General Secretary and Mistress of Novices to be appointed by the above elected officers with the approval of the Right Reverend Ordinary." (1)

After consulting with the Apostolic Delegation and with instructions from same, the Right Reverend Bishop proposed this motion to the assembled sisters and it was adopted unanimously. (2) These actions were historic for the Scranton IHM Congregation, first, in the matter of electing the mother superior as standard procedure, in place of the occasional appointments by the bishop taking precedence over elections; second, in the enlarging of the council by three members in view of the growth of the Congregation and enlarged duties; third, in the direct appointment by the mother superior and her council of the treasurer, secretary and mistress of novices, without approval of the chapter. These latter actions superceded the existing *Constitutions*, Chapter II, No. 10 which read: "The Mother Superior thus elected shall make choice of such Sisters as she shall in conscience deem most fit for the offices of Sister Assistant, Bursar, and Mistress of Novices, and propose them to the Chapter . . . If all, or any of them, shall not receive a majority of the votes, the Mother Superior shall propose others . . ." (3)

At the Congregation elections held on the following day, August 5, 1931, 498 professed sisters were present and twenty-seven (twelve of these from the West) voted by ballots sent through messengers, as provided in the *Constitutions*. Sister M. Josepha Hurley, IHM, was elected and was confirmed by Bishop O'Reilly as the new mother superior. After her installation, the sisters proceeded to elect Sister M. Marcella Gill, first assistant; Sister Madeleine Loughlin, second assistant; Mother M. Cyril Conway, first councilor; and Sister M. Immaculata Gillespie, second councilor. Later that day, Mother Josepha made the following appointments with the approval of the council: treasurer, Sister M. Irmina

McMahon; mistress of novices, Sister M. Anysia Moran; and assistant mistress, Sister M. Teresa Moran. It must have been decided that one of the council members could serve as general secretary, because this position is not mentioned specifically. (4)

Thus began the nine-year term of office as mother superior of this dynamic, much-loved native of Susquehanna, Pennsylvania. Mother Josepha, who now at fifty-five years of age and in her twenty-eighth year of religious profession, was an experienced administrator and religious superior, and quite capable of assuming the duties of this office.The times were frightening and challenging as the depression of the 30s spread worldwide. The tensions in Europe, which preceded the outbreak of World War II in 1939, were casting their shadow in the form of extremist movements. Hitler's Nazi Party came into power in Germany with its goal of rearmament and the rise of a so-called "Master Race;" German atrocities were committed in the concentration camp holocaust of the Jews and the Polish people in Germany; there was Civil War in Spain by 1936; the Italians, under Mussolini, had turned Fascist and had teamed up with Hitler's Nazi regime against France; Germany annexed Austria, took Czechoslovakia, teamed up with Soviet Russia, and invaded and divided Poland between them. The Russians took Lithuania, Latvia, and Estonia in 1939 and defeated Finland in 1940. Throughout the dark days of the war, Sir Winston Churchill was prime minister of England and provided inspiring leadership. The United States was assisting the war effort behind the scenes on the side of France and England until December 11, 1941, when Germany and Italy declared war on the United States.

World War II would eventually end, with the landing in 1944 of the allied troops under General Dwight D. Eisenhower on the Normandy Beach in France. Mussolini's regime had already collapsed in 1943 and the Germans surrendered in 1945.

What all of this meant throughout the years of Mother Josepha's terms of office was sacrifice, with shortages of food and construction materials, as well as man-power for the many tasks which faced the Congregation. Her deep gratitude and her strong faith that God would provide, and her concern for the distress caused by war and economic depression are evident in her Christmas letter of 1931 to all the sisters:

> . . .while the whole world is suffering and many are in need of the necessaries of life, we, the favored spouses of our dear Lord, realize perhaps better than ever before, the hundredfold we are enjoying in return for the paltry things of earth which we renounced by our holy vows. Let us, therefore, try to prove our gratitude to God

> by greater fidelity in His holy service, and let us pray that peace and prosperity may soon return to gladden the hearts of our poor distressed people. (5)

She set to work at once with courage, reorganizing the motherhouse and Marywood Seminary, which with the completion of the liberal arts building at Marywood College had newfound space previously occupied by college classes. Her first project was to provide, in accordance with Canon Law, appropriate space for the postulants and novices of the Congregation. Most of the two upper floors of the southwest wing of the motherhouse was given over to the postulancy and novitiate. All of the rooms were repainted and refurnished, new crucifixes and pictures hung, and new statues of Our Lady and a Christmas Crib scene were added. The library was enlarged, reclassified, and new books added. Classrooms were furnished with new desks and equipment. The course of study was revised to meet the new requirements for teacher certification, which through the efforts of Bishop O'Reilly had been secured for all the novitiate normal schools of the Scranton Diocese. The foresight and planning of Mother Casimir had also prepared the Congregation for this eventuality.

The next project undertaken under Mother Josepha's guiding hand was the beautifying of the grounds of the motherhouse, seminary and college. The driveways were asphalted, four outdoor tennis courts were laid out, and a large athletic field plotted. At the upper end of the field, an elevated terrace was constructed to serve as a stage for outdoor plays and other events. Shrubbery and trees, gifts of the Long Island and Oregon missions, were planted to beautify the grounds. To the shrines already erected on the grounds, Mother Josepha added one more, that of her patron, St. Joseph. At the time it was located on a knoll overlooking the grounds; this land has settled considerably, but the shrine of St. Joseph still stands and figures prominently in relation to the college's fine arts center built in 1985.

Mother Josepha's enthusiasm was caught up by the Roger Bacon Chemical Society members at the college as they launched a landscaping project of their own related to their scientific studies. This included the pool, flower gardens, sundial, and a rustic park in the ravine adjacent to the science building. A generous donor, Mr. Pasquale Adonezzio of Pittston, Pennsylvania, provided the funds for a statue of Our Lady, sculpted by Mr. Rossi in Italy. This beautifully simple depiction of Our Lady as a young girl with braided hair was given ecclesiastical approbation to bear the official title of "Our Lady of Marywood." An outdoor replica was purchased for the rustic outdoor shrine and the marble sculpture transferred to the second floor of the rotunda of the liberal arts building where it is clearly visible to all even today. (6)

As Mother Josepha's spirit and the resultant "refurbishing" of the buildings and grounds was a source of pride to all, so her dismay and disappointment spread to all concerned when the extensiveness of damage to Marywood property from underground mining operations became known to her. For the seven years from 1932 through 1939 a series of letters from mining engineers to Bishop O'Reilly, copies of which were sent to Mother Josepha, reported on a regular basis the conditions underneath the Maloney Home (now Holy Family Residence), Nativity Church, Marywood College, and the motherhouse. These letters, especially during 1932, reflect an obvious desire on the part of the bishop and of his mining engineer, Mr. J. Rossa McCormick, to protect these properties from further encroachment by the coal companies. Safety supports were not being maintained and extensive "robbing of the coal pillars," which had been left as supports, was going on, either by so-called "bootleg" miners, or by the coal companies themselves. Efforts were aimed at obtaining legal agreements to require the coal companies to make restitution for damage done to surface buildings and grounds, as well as to require more careful mining practices in the future. (7)

It was during this period also that the newly paved asphalt roads buckled and began to show deep "pot holes" as a result of weakening of underground support. The tennis courts, too, were not usable because of similar problems. To further complicate matters, a cave hole about forty feet deep broke open beyond the cemetery on the college campus, revealing a mine fire that had been smoldering for some time. Fumes from the fire were invading the entire region, so there were complaints from the neighborhood and fear of the fire's spreading. As Mr. J. Rossa McCormick reported, "This fire had grown to such proportions that the citizens felt their lives were menaced by the fumes of the gases given off." (8)

It seems that not only was the Pittston Coal Company partly responsible for the undermined conditions which caused the cave-in, but that many other parties also had been using this area for dumping rubbish, ashes, and all kinds of debris—the Dunmore Borough, area residents, and the Marywood maintenance crew themselves could all be faulted for the conditions which resulted in combustion and fire. All parties concerned were involved in the expense of extinguishing this fire by bulldozing and flushing.

In March 1933, Mother Josepha exacted a very strict, detailed agreement from Mr. Severin Sekol as he began borehole work for another client in the area behind the science building. Her concern for the projects he had already completed is apparent in her restriction of access over congregation land to "such places as shall be agreeable—and no other places (and particularly, the party of the first part shall not use the concrete drive on the said premises)." (9) She was also concerned about disruption of the college, as she specifies that the hauling of materials would not be done on Sunday, "and at no time shall materials be hauled thereto that would interfere with the peace and quiet of the proper conduct of the said college." (10)

Continually during the years from 1928-1932 both Mr. Severin W. Sekol and Mr. J. Rossa McCormick, mining engineers, had recommended extensive flushing projects be done beneath the Marywood property. Mother Casimir and Mother Mary William had both postponed these warnings because of the great cost. Since they were continuously engaged in small flushing projects on the property, they probably did not realize the extent of the problem. By 1937, agreements were being reached which involved the Borough of Dunmore, the City of Scranton, and representatives of the Hudson Coal, the Pennsylvania Coal, the Glen Alden, Green Ridge Coal, and the Pittston Coal Companies. These agreements required more careful mining in the future and reasonable repairs to be made by the coal companies to all lands and buildings damaged by mining operations. (11) These agreements were finally completed by 1939. Mother Josepha's expression of gratitude has a bit of tongue-in-cheek humor as she writes to the president of the Pennsylvania Coal Company: ". . . Our gratitude to you, dear Mr. Connolly, for this protection is in proportion to the anxiety we experienced for many years from fear of mine caves . . . " (12)

Meanwhile, throughout most of 1935 and 1936 Mother Josepha and her council showed great faith in the future of the college and motherhouse on their original locations as they set to work in earnest to complete the liberal arts rotunda. In September 1935, permission was sought from the bishop to contact an architect and arrange for ideas to be submitted for the murals, painting and decoration of the domed ceiling. Permission was given in October of 1935 and a contract was negotiated with Professor Gonippo Raggi of East Orange, New Jersey, by November 22 of that same year.

The original agreement, which included twenty-four columns in scagliole on the first and mezzanine floors, twelve colored Italian marble column bases, a four-foot, six-inch colored marble wainscoting around the entire rotunda, decoration of the dome and entablatures under the dome, all electrical work and fixtures, and repairing of existing terrazzo floors, — all of this was contracted for a total of $47,908! (13) Mother Josepha could, therefore, write to Bishop O'Reilly:

> . . . I feel we can carry this indebtedness without interfering with our other outstanding obligations, for we will be permitted to make payments when we can, and there will be no interest charges. We hope to make monthly payments until the whole is paid . . . (14)

One can imagine the humility of this great woman as she asked the contractors for such payment arrangements as these, and as she then reported them to the bishop. It is easy to imagine the perseverance with which she pursued these endeavors. The rotunda project grew to include a decorative vestibule entrance with stained glass windows and oak doors, and changes in materials to strengthen and support both the ceiling and the floor of the rotunda. As the total price climbed to $63,387, she was not overwhelmed. Although Professor Raggi had to wait nearly a year for the last installment of $7,873, it was made on May 9, 1938, bringing this stage of the work on the rotunda to completion.

The magnificence of this work remains today as testimony to the outstanding architect, Mr. Anthony J. DePace of New York, to the Roman artist-painter, Professor Gonippo Raggi, and to the creative genius of the many minds contributing to the concept that took shape. It is unbelievable to observers of later generations that a plan of such scope could have been executed for so little cost. The decoration of the dome was done at a cost of $10,000; the twenty-four panels with quotations from St. Thomas Aquinas' *Summa Theologica* for seventy-five dollars each, or $1,800; and the sixteen figure paintings at one thousand dollars each, or $16,000. The total of this part of the project was $27,800! (16)

While a complete description of each panel and medallion portrait is available, this account will address only the central ideas portrayed.

> The general conception of the decoration was inspired and based on the two fundamental principles for which the Congregation of the Sisters of the Immaculate Heart of Mary was founded: namely, the sanctification of its members and the religious education of youth. (17)

It portrays the work of Marywood College, then, as a religious education institution supporting the arts and sciences. In the center of the dome of the rotunda, the Holy Spirit is represented, symbolizing that faith inspires, enlightens and governs the work of the IHM Congregation and Marywood College. Four figures central to the Congregation's history are painted around the central symbol: the Immaculate Heart of Mary, patroness of the Congregation; St. Alphonsus whose spirituality is lived by the Congregation; Father Louis Florent Gillet, CSsR., founder of the Institute; and a kneeling figure of a Sister, Servant of the Immaculate Heart of Mary.

The principle virtues of Christian life are portrayed in figures representing each: Faith, Hope, Charity, Prudence, Justice, Temperance, Fortitude, and Chastity. Murals on the first floor depict various gospel scenes: the Good Shepherd, the laborers in the vineyard, the martyrdom of St. Stephen, and the ten virgins. The chief arts and sciences are depicted by figures and emblems, showing their integration with religion and their contribution to a total Christian education.

One can imagine the awe and amazement with which visitors to the college as well as the students responded to this magnificent work. The silver jubilee of the college occurred in 1940, and the rotunda must have been the focus of interest for that celebration.

It is obvious, also, how much energy and time must have been expended by Mother Josepha, as president of the college, to the needs and interests of this growing, dynamic institution. It must be remembered that simultaneously she was actively expanding the visibility of the congregation by opening eighteen new missions in some eleven different dioceses.

1933	St. Agnes Elementary School, Woodlawn. MD
	Nativity Elementary and High Schools, Scranton, PA
1934	Mount Carmel Elementary School, Asbury Park, NJ
	St. Matthew Elementary School, E. Stroudsburg, PA
1935	St. Mary Elementary School, Dunmore, PA
1936	St. John the Evangelist Elementary School, Binghamton, NY
	1937 Our Lady of Good Counsel Catechetical Center, Inwood, NY
	1938 Holy Angels Elementary School, Hays, Pittsburgh, PA
1939	St. Agnes Elementary School, Lock Haven, PA
	St. Ann Catechetical Center and Elementary School, Devon, CT
	St. Edward Elementary School, Twin Falls, ID
	Our Lady of Perpetual Help Elementary School, Rocky Mount, NC
	St. Agnes Elementary School, Washington, NC
	St. Francis Elementary School, Munhall, PA
	St. Edward Catechetical Center, Barnesboro, PA
	Our Lady of Mount Carmel Catechetical Center, Barnesboro,PA

1940 St. Ignatius Catechetical School, Kingston, PA
1941 Our Lady of Good Counsel Elementary School, Inwood, NY

St. Agnes Elementary School, Woodlawn, Maryland

Woodlawn, Maryland is a suburb of Baltimore about five miles from the central city. The parish of St. Agnes, Woodlawn, was made up of poor and middle class people whose principal occupations were as dockworkers at the Baltimore harbor where large ships came in and out. Some also worked at the Baltimore and Ohio Railroad shops.

St. Agnes School had been for several years under the charge of the Sisters of the Incarnate Word of Texas. At the time of their withdrawal from St. Agnes at the close of the school year in 1933, Reverend Ignatius Fealy, Pastor, began a search for replacements for his school. It was, indeed, the "eleventh hour," August 13, 1933, when he wrote of his need to Mother Josepha, " . . . Father Joseph Wiedenham of St. Rita's Church, Baltimore, has told me that you might be able to supply our school with four teachers for the coming year . . ." (18)

St. Agnes School was to be the sixth school in the Archdiocese of Baltimore staffed by the Sisters, Servants of the Immaculate Heart of Mary, Scranton. By September 1, 1933, Mother Josepha had signed and returned the school contract that provided for a salary of "thirty-five dollars per month for twelve months" for each of the four sisters. (19) Father Fealy wasted no time in returning the contract and expressing his hope that "the worthy Sisters may reach here for Masses on Sunday, so the parents may see we are ready to start on Thursday the 7th." (20) This letter, written on Thursday, could possibly have reached Scranton on Saturday, or perhaps was not delivered until Monday. In any case, the sisters arrived at their new mission on September 6, 1933, and were well received. The new community included Sister Clarissa Dunleavy, principal and superior, Sister Oswald Marie Hopkins, Sister Ambrose Walker and Sister Julitta Mahon. By September 12 Father Fealy wrote to Mother Josepha:

> . . . Your Sisters are truly grand and they are repeating that they are truly happy. On the other hand we are very fond of them too. At Mother Clarissa's request I bought five new mattresses and pillows for $70, so you see I am trying to make them comfortable. God knows they need refreshing repose after their day's toil. (21)

His anxiety about finances was already apparent as, in addition to the above, he mentioned the amount of painting and renovation he was having done in the school, and that more would be done when funds were available. He also mentioned that he had paid the sisters half of the September salary, seventy dollars, out of income from the Harvest Festival. Then came the pointed question, which related to the twelve-month contract he had signed only twelve days previously, "If the Sisters do not stay here during the summer, will I have to pay them for July and August just the same?" (22)

School opened on September 11 with 190 pupils registered in eight grades. The opening High Mass was sung by the school children who gave evidence of good musical training. Since each sister had two grades in a classroom, which meant forty-five or more pupils, it would have been a much greater challenge had not the children been well trained and so responsive. The pastor was very much interested in the school and gave considerable time to it. Every Monday morning during the school year a special High Mass was offered in which the school children participated and were responsible, with the sisters, for the singing. After the Mass, Father Fealy gave a special religious instruction to the children. (23)

The question of the summer salaries for the sisters remained unanswered until a second request was made by Father Fealy:

> . . . I beg to ask if in the contract that I signed you will require that I pay for the months of July and August? Inasmuch as I have to conduct the school and parish on a budget and the income is becoming more and more restricted, I should like to save here. The $280 that I would save by the elimination of those two months would just about see me through, otherwise I must endeavor to save the money or raise that amount in some other way . . . (24)

Mother Josepha acquiesced to Father Fealy's request with her great generosity of spirit:

> . . . In regard to the payment of the salary, it is customary, under ordinary circumstances, for it to run on during the twelve months of the year, because the Sisters have no other means of support and their expenses do not decrease during the summer months. However, during this depression we must make allowances, and you will not be required to pay salary during the two summer months until normal conditions return. (25)

This generous gesture, so typical of Mother Josepha, brought forth the deep gratitude of Father Fealy, and by August 1934 he showed his good will by sending a gift of twenty-five dollars to Mother Josepha for the needs of the congregation with the promise of donating more when better conditions returned. (26)

But, "better conditions" were not to return for some time at St. Agnes Parish. This good pastor was to be plagued by financial worries over the years. The very size of the parish property, with its new stone school containing a large auditorium-gymnasium, the church, rectory, and the stately twelve-room convent—all must have required great outlays of funds for utilities and on-going maintenance. The depression was taking its toll, leaving hundreds of families with little or no income. Franklin D. Roosevelt was elected in 1933, but it would take time for the New Deal programs of economic and social reform to be enacted and begin to reverse the great depression.

The economic troubles of St. Agnes Parish, Woodlawn, Maryland, exemplified the broader scene across the nation and the world. Most Catholic school children did not have the required tuition money and the burden fell to the pastors to decide whether they could in some way continue to operate their schools. This is evident in Father Fealy's 1936 communication to Mother Josepha:

> Dear Good Mother: We are so strapped for funds this year that I beg you to let us have only three Sisters for the next school year. The bus I cannot very well dispense with and I cannot ask you to reduce the salary of the good Sisters. Certain children can pay both tuition and transportation and will not do so, and these I shall not be able to take back. It is unfortunate, I know, but I see no other course. About thirty-three pupils per class should not be too much for each teacher. (27)

Mother Josepha's reply is worth citing in fu1l, since it reveals her common sense approach to things as well as her generous nature, and her concern for the Catholic education of the children involved:

> Dear Father Fealy,
> I am surprised to learn from your letter that you intend to drop a number of your children from the school, in fact, the announcement came like a thunderbolt, for I had admired your zeal so much during the entire depression that I could never imagine such a thing now when everything is becoming more hopeful.

> Surely, dear Father, you will not punish the children for the fault of their parents, if fault it may be called, for I doubt that these poor people are yet able to pay off the many obligations that accumulated during the past trying years.
>
> I am very willing to send back four Sisters and require salary for three, rather than deprive these precious souls of the benefit of a Catholic education. Instead of dropping your children you should try to increase the registration, and thus guard your little ones from the dangers that surround them in schools where God is unknown.
>
> Assuring you of my desire to cooperate with you in saving these children, and hoping to hear from you soon and favorably, I remain in the Immaculate Heart of Mary, Very sincerely yours, (28)

We can only assume that Father Fealy was delighted with Mother Josepha's offer since no further correspondence on the matter was retained. One thing is certain—there has been insufficient praise given for the courageous people who saw Catholic education through its depression years in this country. That St. Agnes School, or schools like it, might have floundered in the 30s would indeed have prevented thousands of children of future years from attaining the excellent Catholic education which they received. By 1955, St. Agnes School had an enrollment of 769 pupils, with twelve sisters and two lay teachers. There were by then two sections of every grade except the sixth grade.

Father Fealy had died April 15, 1942, and was succeeded by Reverend Maurice Roche. Sister M. Clarissa Dunleavy, having completed the customary six years in 1939, was succeeded by Sister Leonard Connell. Later principals included Sister Lucian Reddington, Sister Joseph Gabriel Welsh, Sister Evangeline Conmy, Sister Ignatius Brown, Sister Sarita Gesler, Sister Marie Elise Regan, Sister Maria Thomas Harrington, Sister Nora Clarke, Sister Rosemaron Rynn and Sister Nancy Marie Elder.

In anticipation of further growth in the already crowded school and convent at St. Agnes', the pastor in 1956 provided a full addition to the convent which nearly doubled its capacity, adding nine bedrooms, dining room, kitchen, four bathrooms, a sewing room and sun parlor. Two more classrooms were added to the school by the fall of 1958, which by this time was burgeoning with 1,025 pupils. From this time, until the peak year, 1964, when there were three sections of each grade, for a total of 1,300, there was continuing growth in St. Agnes School. The faculty grew accordingly, numbering nine lay teachers and fifteen sisters, in addition to the music teacher and the principal. (29) The once rural setting of this parish and school has been transformed into a very busy and well-developed suburb of Baltimore. Much of the out-mobility from the residential areas of Baltimore is probably due to the changing racial make-up of these areas.

Rising costs of parochial school education and decrease in family size over the 70s and 80s gradually impacted the earlier growth patterns of St. Agnes School. Gradual declines in enrollment were experienced and by 1980-1981, for example, there were 526 students served by fourteen lay teachers and eight teaching sisters. This school continues its excellence in education and as of 1986-1987 has 459 students. (30)

One could only wish that Mother Josepha and Father Fealy could have lived to witness the fruit of their early struggle.

Nativity of Our Lord, Elementary and High Schools, Scranton, Pennsylvania

The parish of the Nativity of Our Lord is geographically identified with the earliest history of the Catholic Church in Scranton. On the site it presently occupies, the first church in Scranton was erected in 1847 to serve the Irish and German immigrants of the "Slocum Hollow" area, once called also the village of Harrison. Prior to this, Father Henry Fitzsimmons of Carbondale and Father Andrew Sullivan, working out of Carbon County, provided occasional Masses in the houses of the people. Starting with a gift of land from the firm of Scrantons and Platt, the iron manufacturing company for which most of the area people worked, Father Patrick Prendergast, the pastor of Carbondale and Wilkes-Barre, saw the opportunity to establish a chapel for this growing section of his territory. The Irish and German people of the area contributed their labor and built a frame church, thirty-five feet long, twenty-five feet wide and fourteen feet high, having a seating capacity of 200. Father Prendergast named the chapel St. Bonaventure's. There was no resident pastor for this mission chapel for several years. (31)

The present magnificent Church of the Nativity was built in 1903. Reverend James A. O'Reilly who had been pastor of the Cathedral Parish for some fourteen years was named pastor of "the new Catholic Church in South Scranton" on February 2, 1902. By October 1903, the new congregation had a designated place, St. John's Hall, in which to assemble for Sunday Masses. By this time the pastor informed his parishioners that their parish was to be "The Nativity of Our Lord" parish and their goal was to construct a church. Ground was broken on May 23, 1904, with large crowds in attendance, and a few months later, on August 1, 1904, Bishop Hoban, assisted by over thirty priests and in the presence of over 5,000 laity, laid the cornerstone. By July 16, 1905, the basement was completed and dedicated for services. But the beloved pastor, Father James O'Reilly, was not to see the completion of his magnificent plans. He died following surgery on the pancreas on May 26, 1907. He is buried beneath the sanctuary in Nativity Church. The new pastor was Reverend Dr. John J. Loughran. The rectory was completed in 1909 and the upper church was dedicated on November 29, 1914. (32)

A complete parish group of buildings had been planned by the people and their pastor to include a rectory, convent and school, all of a similar granite and of Gothic architecture to harmonize with the church.

On March 17, 1932, Bishop Thomas C. O'Reilly blessed the site for the new school and convent and turned the first shovel-full of earth. By November 6, 1932, he officiated at the laying of the cornerstones for the two new structures. Nearly a year later, on September 6, 1933, the school and convent were solemnly consecrated by His Eminence Dennis Cardinal Dougherty, Archbishop of Philadelphia, with Bishop O'Reilly celebrating the High Mass and with the sermon on Catholic education preached by Bishop Thomas Molloy of the Brooklyn Diocese. Bishop Molloy gave much praise to the pastor and parishioners of Nativity Parish for the evidence of their faith and their sacrifices in the outstanding structures they had provided. (33)

The school and convent were outstanding structures then and now. Designed in Gothic style to harmonize with the church and rectory, the walls were constructed of granite brought from quarries near Allentown, with carved and molded limestone from Indiana, a trim around the windows and doorways.

The design of the school was unusual in its inclusion of an 800-seat auditorium, kitchen, meeting rooms, and the principal's office on the first floor and all of the classrooms on the second and third floors. Sixteen classrooms were planned, a large library, a medical room, and teachers' room. The school building was connected with the convent by means of an enclosed passage.

The convent was designed to house twenty sisters and was well laid out to be both beautiful and functional. The chapel is known as a "gem of architecture," with its altar of Italian rosato marble with beautiful glass mosaic inlays, above which is a rose window picturing the Nativity of Our Lord. The railing is of hammered Swedish wrought iron. Six side windows have medallions containing scenes from the life of the Blessed Virgin Mary. The chapel seats about forty persons and has a small balcony that opens off the second floor corridor. (34)

It must have been an awesome experience for our sisters to have been part of such demonstrations of the presence of "church" as was witnessed in Nativity Parish with the completion of these buildings. Because of Bishop O'Reilly's interest in them, because the pastor, Rev. Dr. Loughran, had previously been chancellor of the diocese for eight years, and because of the historic nature of the very site of the Nativity buildings, it seemed that several bishops, hundreds of priests and thousands of the faithful turned out for each event. But the pomp and circumstance would finally end and the sisters would get about the business of opening school.

Registration of children in the first four grades was held on September 11, 1933. About 270 pupils were enrolled, distributed over six classrooms since there was a sufficient number for two first grades, two second grades, and one each of grades three and four. Classes were officially begun on September 12, 1933. The school was tuition free in its early years, but lacked nothing by way of equipment or supplies. Its outstanding faculty included Sister Brigida Strome, superior and principal, Sister St. Helen Sullivan, Sister Maria Raymond Grogan, Sister Maria Angela Orr, Sister Gaudentia Pelland, and Sister Joseph Maher. Sister Aimee Pencovich was also a member of this community, rendering that most vital service of preparing the meals for the sisters. Sister Brigida was to refer to this group as "the originals," for they had the distinction of remaining at Nativity for the nine years in which she was there as principal. (35)

Rev. Dr. Loughran was very solicitous for the sisters and from his first conversation with Sister Brigida tried to exact a promise regarding three matters which he deemed most important: first, that no sister would ever leave Nativity Convent without sufficient money; second, that there would never be a cracked dish on the table; and third, that no sister would scrub floors in the convent or the school. Perhaps there was never a cracked dish on the table, but as Sister St. Helen Sullivan relates, the sisters were without money most of the time, and Dr. Loughran would never, much to his consternation, persuade Sister Brigida that the sisters should not scrub their own convent floors!

It seems that this pastor exercised a great control over the stability of his faculty because of his insistence that a new school would succeed best if there were no changes. His annual May visit to "Marywood" for the first seven years of the school's existence resulted in the same announcement each year, "No sister is changed."

Even Sister Maria Angela Orr, who had just completed her degree in Home Economics and was promised to that department of the college "after one year," remained at Nativity School for nine years. Sister St. Helen Sullivan was there for seventeen years. (35) Other faculty of those early years included Sister Pius LaRocque (1934-1945); Sister Ambrose Walker (1935-1948); Sister Clare Kelly (1936-1941); Sister Franzchen Yahner (1938-1940); and Sister Marita Gill (1939-1943). (36)

The school children of Nativity were known for the excellence of their liturgical singing and many a visitor was brought by the pastor, Dr. John Loughran, to hear the children sing Gregorian Chant at the High Masses. The sisters also emphasized speech, with choral speech becoming a specialty throughout the school. There was even a private class of sixty pupils for speech work in the school. An excellent orchestra was also built up gradually because of the number of pupils involved in private music lessons.

A new grade was added each year until 1938, and after the eight grades were completed Dr. Loughran made preparations to equip the projected high school. A triple science laboratory was installed for instruction in biology, chemistry and physics, and a library with a shelving capacity of 5,000 books was furnished and equipped by the Gaylord Company of Syracuse, New York. The first 1,000 books had been carefully selected and the plan was to add some 1,500 books each year. By 1940 the school included the sophomore year of high school and the total enrollment was approximately 560 pupils, 160 of whom were high school students. Three of the six "original" sister-teachers, Sister Maria Angela, Sister Joseph and Sister Gaudentia, were gradually moved to the high school. Plans were also laid for the junior and senior years to be added, and the inclusion of the business department in the fall of 1940. Dr. Loughran had already begun negotiations for the business equipment when his untimely sickness and death occurred in 1940. With his death there seemed to have come an abrupt end to the existing high school classes and to all plans for expansion to the junior and senior years. The students transferred to St. Mary's, St. John's or to the public high schools of the area. (37)

Rt. Rev. Monsignor William Farrell, LTD, succeeded Dr. Loughran as pastor of Nativity. Sister Brigida Strome remained as principal of Nativity School until 1942. Subsequent principals included Mother Beata Wertz, Sister Teresa Moran, Sister Maria Theophane Allen, Sister Consolata Maria Hedderson, Sister Pius LaRocque, Sister Claranne Nolan, Sister Victoire Moran, Sister Gertrude Hopkins, Sister Agnes McHale and Sister Mary Alice Kane. (38)

Nativity School was to house high school students once again in 1963 when St. Mary's Assumption High School was closed. Since there was no space for these students at South Catholic, the solution was to utilize Nativity School for all South Catholic freshman students; St. Mary's High School for all sophomores; and South Catholic for juniors and seniors. The consolidation of 128 St. Mary's students took place, bringing the total South Catholic High School enrollment to 568. This arrangement continued until 1966 when the construction of a new, enlarged facility enabled all of South Catholic High School to be under one roof. (39)

Some fluctuations in Nativity's school enrollment were offset in 1970 by the closing of St. John's School in Southside and the merger of these pupils with Nativity Parish pupils, bringing the enrollment to 425 students. Fluctuating numbers of sisters constituted the Nativity local community, as the faculty of South Catholic High School was partially housed at Nativity and at St. John's Convents from the beginning of the school in 1947 until 1972, when St. Mary's Convent (now IHM Convent on River Street) was purchased by the Board of Pastors as a faculty house for the Sisters of IHM. (40)

At the time of the Golden Jubilee of Nativity Parish it was noted that a total of sixty-three religious vocations had emerged from Nativity Parish: 32 priests, one religious brother and 30 sisters, 25 of whom were IHMs. God has certainly blessed the vibrant faith of these families. (41)

This outstanding school continues to thrive, having added a kindergarten in 1982-1983 and repeating its 1933 history by having two first grade sections again in 1984. The enrollment in 1986-1987 was 396 pupils. (42)

Our Lady of Mount Carmel Elementary School, Asbury Park, New Jersey

Our Lady of Mount Carmel School in Asbury Park was the first venture of the Sisters of the Immaculate Heart of Mary in the Trenton, New Jersey Diocese. This parish was only thirty years old when our sisters came in 1934 and had been served by five different pastors during that period. The Trinitarian Fathers were invited by Bishop James McFaul of Trenton to serve the parish in 1912, and Reverend Anthony Giovannini, OSST, was appointed by his religious congregation. This zealous priest was fired with the missionary spirit that had taken him previously to assignments in Italian Somaliland in Africa, service as master of novices for the Trinitarians, and provincial for the congregation in Rome. His dreams for the development of the Italian parish of Our Lady of Mount Carmel were on a grand scale, but it was not until 1923 that he was able to construct the parochial school on Bangs Avenue. It was the basement of this structure that served as the parish church until the new church was built in 1951—fourteen years after his return to Rome, and ten years after his death in Rome in 1941. (43)

The Bangs Avenue school was originally placed under the charge of the Maestrine Philippini Sisters and later under the direction of the

Missionary Sisters of the Sacred Heart. At the withdrawal of this latter group, it was Monsignor J. J. O'Hara of Bradley Beach, New Jersey, who suggested to Father Giovannini that he investigate obtaining the Sisters of the Immaculate Heart of Mary for his school. In considering this request, Mother Josepha must have discovered that the convent was actually too small for the number of sisters required and that extensive cleaning and painting were needed. Because of Father Anthony Giovannini's lack of facility in speaking and writing English, it was Monsignor O'Hara who conducted correspondence with Mother Josepha in regard to the sisters' coming. Evidently the enlargement of the convent had to be deferred because, as Monsignor O'Hara wrote, "Our Bishop is very happy to have you take care of Mount Carmel School. But he made . . . a rule not to permit one dollar of new debt anywhere. He explained to Father Giovannini that if the matter were placed before you that the Sisters would gladly make the best of the situation this year with the hope that conditions will clear up." (44) The "conditions" referred to, of course, were the economic depression condition that had caused so much suffering everywhere. True to her generous nature, Mother Josepha's reply indicated her willingness to send the sisters and to wait for the additional rooms until conditions might improve. (45)

Subsequent correspondence reveals, however, that even though general economic conditions improved, it would be a later pastor, and then only under direct orders from Bishop William A. Griffin of Trenton in August of 1946, who would join the convent to a house in the rear in order to provide adequate space for a chapel, community room, dining room and individual rooms for the sisters. (46)

The little community of four sisters who arrived by car in Asbury Park, New Jersey, on August 28, 1934, however, were not overly concerned about space. Sister Neumann Murray, superior and principal, Sister Liguori Farnon, Sister Mary John Bates and Sister Carmelita Charette entered upon their new mission with openness and a good sense of humor. Sister Neumann's account of their arrival and first evening at the convent reveals their pioneering spirit and their acceptance of the positive and negative aspects of the situation. Monsignor O'Hara of Bradley Beach, New Jersey, their benefactor from the first day, had provided a new Kelvinator frigidaire as a gift and had stocked it with butter, eggs, bacon and soft drink. The pastor arrived with bushel baskets of peppers, potatoes and tomatoes—as Sister Neumann commented, "The poor priests can't do enough for us
. . . " It was evidently a setting in which it would be easy to practice poverty, as described by Sister Neumann:

> The five cells are very nice—the bed, chair and stand comprising the furniture. A small new rug at each bed, and a crucifix on the wall. Each bed was made up with two sheets, and a colored crinkly spread—blue, green, pink, lavender and yellow. No blankets, so we used our cloaks to keep us warm, and over them the new rugs. Even then we were freezing almost. (47)

With directness and foresight, Sister Neumann presented her needs to Mother Josepha: "I sincerely hope you'll be good enough to send us some cash to get started. The food, etc. is high here due to the aristocratic summer resort—and then too the three C.O.D. trunks from N. Carolina and one from Renovo will cost plenty . . ." (48)

But her hopeful attitude was an over-riding characteristic as she summed up the situation, "It will take time and money, but the place will be comfortable I'm sure. School will probably take the same." (49)

The pastor, Father Anthony Giovannini, proved to be most solicitous for the sisters' welfare, providing them with a weekly order of meat and other necessities to augment their thirty dollars per month per sister income. The Redemptorist Fathers, too, who came from St. Alphonsus Retreat House, West End, New Jersey, as confessors for the sisters, were very generous. They provided a new altar for the chapel, a dining room table, a community room table and chairs of light oak, and a set of Devonshire dinnerware. (50)

The school opened to 160 pupils in eight grades with ceremonial blessings of the classrooms and of new playground equipment. The meaningfulness of these blessings became better known to the sisters when they began to work with these youngsters. As Sister Neumann said, ''The youngsters evidently never knew discipline so we have our hands full . . . We have laughed for two weeks—but it is a reality just the same . . . I hope the examiners won't come here . . . I really think everything will come around in time, but it will take patience and hard work." (51)

As an interior support for their arduous educational efforts the sisters brought their concerns to their common prayer together in their little chapel. The absence of the Blessed Sacrament was a keen spiritual suffering for them, so by October a letter was sent by Mother Josepha to Father Giovannini expressing her gratitude to him for all he was doing for the sisters, but urging him to approach the bishop for permission for the sisters to have the Blessed Sacrament in their chapel. She made a persuasive argument, saying,

> We have convents in three Archdioceses and nine Dioceses, and there has never been any question of denying the Sisters the great

> comfort of having the Blessed Sacrament in their chapels. If the sleeping room above the chapel interferes with this privilege, we will gladly close this room. (52)

This pastor's delay in this matter related to his reluctance to approach a very strict Bishop unless an emergency required it. However, later correspondence reveals his desire also to have the sisters very much present to the people of the parish. He wrote to Mother Josepha at one point asking that the sisters be permitted to receive Holy Communion on Sundays and holy days, as well as at daily Mass, in the church instead of in the convent "in order to encourage others and to give good example." (53)

Difficult as these beginning days at Mount Carmel may have been for our sisters, Father Anthony was most supportive of their work, and he and his priest assistants were generous with their time in giving instructions in religion throughout the school. One priest also taught Italian in the seventh and eighth grades and two of his pupils, the Capanelli twin boys, won a trip to Italy in 1934 for their fluency in Italian.

The children at Mount Carmel were naturally gifted in music and in art and were encouraged by Father Anthony who loved Italian operatic music and by Sister Carmelita, the music teacher, who prepared them for public entertainments. Prizes were also won by students for their work in art. The school rapidly became the focal point of parish activity. (54)

Whatever his idiosyncrasies, it must have been a sadness to everyone to see Father Anthony Giovannini leave Mount Carmel for Rome a few days after the parish celebration of the silver anniversary of his pastorate on February 17, 1937. He would spend the remaining four short years of his life in Rome. He died on December 8, 1941.

The new pastor, Father Marcellino Romagno, came to the parish in February 1938. At this time there were about 500 families in the parish so he realized that the old basement church was inadequate and that his first task was to build a new church. This goal was not achieved, however, until 1951, and five years later, in 1956, the adjacent rectory was completed. (55)

The school was gradually growing in size, with 354 pupils registered in the 1940s; by 1962-1963, 550 pupils; and by 1966-1967, over 600. (56) Increasing numbers of pupils caused a concomitant increase in sister-teachers, causing in turn a need for enlarged school and convent facilities by 1962. The school that had been built in 1923 was not only too small, but was also showing its forty years of age. Repairs that were crucial were made to both the convent and the school, and gifts from benefactors, especially the Nicholas Aldarelli and Sam Scanio families, kept the sisters supplied with needed electrical appliances, vestments for the chapel and other necessities.

Groundbreaking for the new school and convent was held on July 1, 1962, with Reverend Marcellino Romagno, pastor, officiating. Construction of the twelve-room school actually started on August 27, 1962. The eighteen-room convent, with chapel, eleven bedrooms, community room, refectory, parlors, kitchen and laundry was begun on October 29, 1962.

As obedience would have it, Sister Georgina Wertz, who had served for six years as principal and superior, was transferred in June of 1961, and Sister Celesta Sinisi, who had served at Mount Carmel for fifteen years, was changed in June 1963, and appointed superior at East Stroudsburg, Pennsylvania. Sister Catherine Patricia McGirr was the new superior and principal in September 1963, when the new school and convent were opened. The dedication of these two new facilites took place on September 21, 1963, with Bishop George W. Ahr officiating, assisted by Father Romagno, pastor. The occasion was marked by Solemn Benediction and a dinner at which sisters who had previously served at Mount Carmel were present, together with the sisters from Holy Spirit and St. Peter Claver Parishes, and the priests from the area. (57)

Gradual changes in the nature of the parish affected the school enrollment which declined to 334 by 1973-1974; to 318 by 1982-1983 and to 288 in 1986-1987. Although smaller, the school continues its vibrant contribution to the Catholic education of the youth of Our Lady of Mount Carmel Parish.

St. Matthew's Elementary School, East Stroudsburg, Pennsylvania

The first Catholic Church in East Stroudsburg was built in 1868 and was serviced at that time as a mission by the priests of St. Catherine's, Moscow, which did not become a full-fledged parish itself until 1884. St. Matthew's Parish, East Stroudsburg, was founded on July 4, 1902, having as its first resident pastor Reverend Francis Craft, who, at age 53, had already lived what others less robust in nature would have considered a very full life. At age thirteen he participated in the battle of Gettysburg as an officer's mascot; at twenty-one, he went to France to fight in the Franco-Prussian War; later, he fought in the Cuban Ten Years' War of Independence—a revolution which ended in failure. Returning home, he settled down long enough to study medicine and earn his MD degree. Renouncing his Presbyterian background, he became a convert to the Catholic faith, responded to the call of the priesthood and was ordained in 1883 by Bishop Martin Marty of Sioux Falls, Dakota Territory. He served as a missionary to the Sioux Indians for fifteen years.

As "medicine-man," "spiritual father" and occasional warrior engaged with his beloved Sioux in their skirmishes, Father Craft was honored among the Indians. As Monsignor Gallagher says, "Father Craft won their hearts forever in the summer of 1890 when he ventured perilously close to the front line at the battle of Wounded Knee Creek and almost lost his life through a knifing which penetrated his right lung." (58)

At the age of forty-nine Father Craft returned to the east and for four years went into a semi-retirement, worn out by the rigors of his vigorous careers. In 1902 he accepted the pastorate of St. Matthew's Parish as a new and welcome challenge, one that would occupy his attention for eighteen years—until his death on September 11, 1920. Reverend John J. Butler succeeded Father Craft as pastor.

As Stroudsburg expanded rapidly, especially with the increasing number of Catholic students attending the state-supported Stroudsburg Normal School, Father Butler saw the need for a new church to replace the 1868 structure. His plans included construction of a church, school and convent. Ground was broken for these present structures on June 12, 1932; the cornerstones were laid on October 29, 1932, and the dedication of this complete plant took place, with Bishop Thomas C. O'Reilly officiating, on July 8, 1934. (59)

Meanwhile, in March 1933, Father Butler had written to Mother Josepha for sisters to staff the new school which he thought would open in September 1933. It was his thought that the first four or five grades would be opened at first, with a plan to add a grade each year. His estimate was that some 120 pupils would register when the school opened. As for the teaching faculty, he expressed high hopes, saying, "The Bishop said that we should have a faculty equal, at least, to that of the State Teachers College which is a short distance from our church, school and convent . . . and . . . of course we shall need a music teacher. (60)

It appears that he achieved his wish in the arrival of Sister Alphonsus McGoldrick to serve as principal and superior, Sister Alma Marie Morgan, Sister Rose Irma Spillane, Sister Ursula Burns and Sister Lucy McGrath on August 28, 1934. The interior of the convent was not yet complete, and Sister Lucy recalls that Father Butler's greeting was, "I told them not to send the Sisters yet!" (61) On September 8, 1934, the school was formally opened with four grades and approximately 160 pupils.

There was great interest in both music and art among the students, and in a year's time an excellent orchestra had been organized. By 1936 a children's choir had also been inaugurated. At the practical level, a home economics department was added in 1936 and students showed great interest especially in sewing classes.

Because there were only six rooms in the school, it was not long before classes had to be doubled. Sister Lucy McGrath mentions that in 1937 she had seventy-two children in grades one and two. She refers also to the fact that many of these youngsters were too poor to afford their school clothing, and it was the pastor, Father Butler, who saw to it that money was provided to Sister Lucy to purchase clothing for them. (62)

Good relationships existed with Stroudsburg Normal School, both in the sisters' serving as moderators for the Sodality which was composed largely of students from the Normal School, and in St. Matthew's serving as a practice-teaching opportunity for these future teachers. Since physical education has always been a prime major for college students at Stroudsburg, these college students frequently taught physical education classes at St. Matthew's.

St. Matthew's School reached eight grades and had its first graduating class by 1939. There were twelve girls and sixteen boys in this class for a total of twenty-eight graduates.

Sister Felicitas Ryan became principal and superior in 1940. Her administrative abilities and foresight were strong assets as the school experienced steady growth in small space. Sister Elsie Miller who was assigned to St. Matthew's from 1940-1944 recalls that space was at such a premium that the second floor main hall had to be used as a classroom for some forty fifth-grade students. The students were well behaved, and under the excellent instruction of Sister Eleanora Whalen achieved very successful dramatic and musical productions.

Sister Elsie recalls also that a good number of the students were from families who were poor enough to be found in the food lines each month when the school served as a distribution center for government surplus food, such as flour, cheese, prunes and other staples. (63)

Father John Butler passed away on June 2, 1943, after several months of illness. He was succeeded by Reverend Harold Durkin on June 28, 1943.

Father Durkin saw to the renovation of the school and also fully equipped and furnished a kindergarten in 1947. His support could always be counted on, and under his pastorate the school experienced a steady growth, reaching 337 by 1955-1956 and 397 by 1960-1961. Father Durkin died on September 8, 1961, and was succeeded by Monsignor Thomas J. Cawley who had been chaplain for thirteen years at St. Joseph's Children's and Maternity Hospital staffed by our own sisters in Scranton.

Other principals who served St. Matthew's Elementary School include Sister Teresa Clare McAuliffe, Sister Joanella Ryan, Sister Celesta Sinisi,

Sister Marie Lourdes Vanston, Sister de Sales Williams, Sister Gabrielis Marley, Sister Johanna Antenner, Sister Ann Belz, Sister Agnes Mary Devitt and Sister Laurentia Mayan (to 1987).

In anticipation of the opening of Notre Dame High School, the pastor, Monsignor Cawley, built an addition to St. Matthew's Convent, renovated existing rooms and dedicated a new convent chapel over a period of two years—1963-1965. The temporary inconvenience soon gave way to a beautifully refurbished and enlarged convent, waiting the arrival of the high-school faculty. By the fall of 1968, Notre Dame High School was completed. Its first faculty, all of whom resided at St. Matthew's Convent, included Sister Immaculee Cavanaugh, first principal, Sister Helaine O'Dea, Sister Joanne Pickard, Sister Mary Frances Krystofik, and as librarian, Sister Antonina Williamson. Sister Antonina was replaced by Sister Angelisse Boyce in 1969-1970; other additions that year were Sister Elizabeth Collins, Sister Patricia Tippen and Sister Jean Leonard. At this time there were four Sisters in the elementary and eight in the high school. (64)

In 1968 St. Matthew's Parish was divided and a new parish, St. Luke's, was formed. Psychologically, this may have had some impact on the school's enrollment, as a slight decline was experienced. (64)

Given the strategic location of Stroudsburg in its proximity to New Jersey, to New York City and to the Pocono Mountain resort area, these schools were bound to have a mobile population, but given also the growth of Stroudsburg as a college town—the original Normal School now has become Stroudsburg University—young families of students and older families of college staff and faculty members assure a bright future for both schools. St. Matthew's current (1987) problem is whether to build an addition to the school or to construct an entirely new, larger building. Two hundred fifty-eight students in six grades, happy to be recipients of its excellent programs and religious environment, now bulge its small space. (65)

St. Mary of Mt. Carmel Elementary School, Dunmore, Pennsylvania

A proud and generous tradition characterizes the parishioners of St. Mary of Mount Carmel, Dunmore, Pennsylvania. Descendants, for the most part, of the early Irish Catholic families, they had absorbed and been schooled in a strong, living faith. Having been originally established in 1856 as St. Simon's Parish, the name was changed to St. Mary of Mount Carmel when a new church was built in 1874 by the pastor, Reverend Gerald McMurray. It seems that church name-changes to honor the titles of Our Lady were the thing to do, since in 1873 Father Moses Whittig, vicar general of the diocese, and obvious "trend-setter," in relocating his North Scranton parish, St. Thaddeus Chapel, to William Street, changed the name to St. Mary's Church of the Most Holy Rosary (later to be called Holy Rosary Church). Not to be outdone, in 1874 Reverend John Schelle of St. Bonaventure's Parish in South Scranton, changed the name to St. Mary's Church of the Assumption. Holy Rosary did set the pattern for the building of a Church of St. Mary of Mount Carmel in Dunmore. Both were of permanent brick construction with a capacity of about 850 people. Father Schelle's church was already nine years old when it was renamed. (66) In any case, Our Lady is honored in the dedication of these architectural masterpieces in her name.

This was not to be the only connection St. Mary's would have to the persons and offices of the Scranton Diocese. Reverend Andrew J. Brennan who had been chancellor of the diocese from 1908-1923 while serving as auxiliary bishop to Bishop Michael J. Hoban and serving also from 1916-1924 as pastor of St. Peter's Cathedral, was appointed in October 1924 as pastor of St. Mary's, Dunmore. This zealous priest and indefatigable worker managed to continue as auxiliary bishop and to serve St. Mary's superbly until his own appointment as Bishop of Richmond, Virginia, came on May 28, 1926. Even then, he continued as pastor at St. Mary's until December 16, 1926, because of the ailing condition of the seventy-three-year-old Bishop Hoban to whom he had been a "right-hand man" and friend for over twenty years. Bishop Hoban died on November 13, 1926, and Bishop Andrew J. Brennan was consecrated Bishop of Richmond, Virginia, on December 16, 1926, two days after his forty-ninth birthday.

As the years went by, both the pastors and parishioners recognized the need for a parochial school. In 1934, during the pastorate of Reverend Michael E. Loftus, land was purchased across from the church, and ground was broken in August 1934 for St. Mary of Mount Carmel Elementary School. In spite of the fact that the economic depression had taken its toll on the financial stability of most parishes of the diocese, it seemed that

> "Ironically, the depression was in itself a factor which accounted for the emergence of the five new structures at that period of time (Nativity, Scranton; St. Matthew's, East Stroudsburg; Holy Rosary, Duryea; St. Anthony's, Throop; and St. Mary's, Dunmore). In each instance, the pastor had been most fortunate in the placement of his financial reserves during the roaring twenties. As a direct result of their luck and/or prudence, they

> managed to keep their accounts in tact despite the rash of bank failures . . . When the worst of the panic subsided they found themselves in the midst of a happy coincidence wherein the value of their dollars was high while the cost of what they wanted was low. For them the opportunity to build had come at last. (67)

Both the school and the convent were near completion within the year and on September 2, 1935, were dedicated by Bishop Thomas C. O'Reilly. The sisters assigned were Sister Evangeline Conmy, superior and principal, Sister Maria Aquina O'Toole, Sister Raymond Rafferty, Sister Bernardine Rinkavage, and Sister Francis Marie Butler as cook. Four grades were opened on September 4, 1935, with an enrollment of one hundred eighty pupils. (68)

A nearly completed school and convent caused some confusion on the first day of school as large planks served as walkways over which active youngsters bounded with little concern for the obvious dangers. Discovering that the school lavatories were not yet ready for use, the principal dismissed the students for the remainder of the day. Since the convent was not ready for occupancy, Mother Josepha arranged for the sisters to reside at the motherhouse at Marywood and insisted that they not miss their dinner, which was served at noon. It was necessary, therefore, for the school janitor to take the sisters to Marywood each noon and to pick them up again at about 12:40 p.m. to return to St. Mary's. Meanwhile, Father Loftus, the pastor, assumed the playground supervision! This schedule continued from late August until December 31, 1935, when at long last St. Mary's Convent was completed. (69) The convent was, and remains even today, a beautiful, serviceable structure.

Sister Raymond Rafferty was at St. Mary's from its opening in 1935 until 1945. In that period she witnessed its significant growth, reaching 391 students in eight grades by 1939. Classes were very large, and she recalls getting to know the youngsters very well because, while she started as the third grade teacher, she moved up with her class to fourth, fifth and eventually to eighth grade with them. She recalls that the children were well trained, with many of them interested in music. She had a fifty-boy liturgical choir and forty music pupils whom she taught on an "after school" schedule.

Father Michael Loftus did not live to see St. Mary's first graduation class. He died in 1937, having served as pastor for ten years at St. Mary's. His successor was Reverend James F. Gilloegly who was appointed in 1938. The first graduating class on June 16, 1940, numbered thirty-five students. Several of these went on to Marywood Seminary or to St. Paul's

High School as scholarship recipients. Father Gilloegly, as Father Loftus before him, was very much interested and involved in the school. He encouraged the students and was exceptionally kind and generous to the sisters.

Sister Evangeline Conmy served as superior and principal of St. Mary's until 1941, being succeeded by Sister Neumann Murray for a one year term, 1941-1942; Sister de Pazzi Houlihan followed Sister Neumann in 1942. Subsequent principals of St. Mary's School include: Sister Alma Marie Morgan (1948-1951); Sister Maria Loughlin (1951-1957); Sister Christine Clarkin (1957-1963); Sister Stella Devers (1963-1969); Sister Sarita Gesler (1969-1971); Sister Noralene Calpin (for two months in 1971); Sister Norma (Rosemary) Casey (1972-1983); Sister Therese Petz (1983-1985); and Sister Eileen Clinton who assumed principalship in 1985. Sister Maria died on January 12, 1957, at 6:30 a.m. after having felt ill only one half hour before. She would have been a diamond jubilarian had she lived until February 2. On February 4, Sister Madelena Gilroy was appointed the administrator at St. Mary's School and Convent.

By 1957 there were eight full-time sisters in addition to the principal and one lay teacher at St. Mary's. With the opening in 1965 of Dunmore Central Catholic High School (now Bishop O'Hara High School) located only a few blocks from St. Mary's, it was inevitable that St. Mary's community would be augmented by sisters appointed to teach at the high school. Thus it was that Sister Samuel McKeown and Sister Albertus (Anne) Fulwiler were sent to Dunmore Central Catholic to teach mathematics and science, respectively. Meanwhile, Reverend Raymond Larkin, pastor, had begun refurbishing the convent, furnishing the third floor bedrooms, carpeting the first and second floor halls and remodeling the kitchen.

Eventually, the IHM Sisters were to be requested to supply an assistant principal for the high school. From 1973-1975 Sister Mary Elizabeth Ehling held this post; from 1975-1981, Sister Maria del Rey Shevlin; and in 1981-1982, Sister Claudette Naylor, who became Principal in 1985.

Absorbed in the building of the high school, Father Larkin's attention may not have been focused on what was gradually occurring in the declining enrollment in St. Mary's Elementary School. By 1969-1970 it was down by about seventy-five students, and in 1971-1972 the total enrollment was down to 235. Classes were small for those years, and from the primary grades' registration all indications were that the school would shortly be in trouble. Grade one had only thirteen pupils; grade two, 21, and grade three, 22. In light of these problems, the Congregation's administration suggested to the then pastor, Monsignor

Joseph G. Quinn, that the pupils of St. Mary's could be accommodated at St. Clare's, St. Paul's and St. Anthony's Schools and that St. Mary's Elementary School building be used as an annex for Dunmore Central Catholic High School. (70)

A letter from Monsignor Quinn to then Bishop J. Carroll McCormick tells of his concerns about the school's continuance and his inability to explain the decline in enrollment, having been pastor only two years. (71) Evidently he felt that he should be given an opportunity to improve the situation before the sisters would be withdrawn, because a subsequent letter of February 5, 1972, from Bishop McCormick to Mother Beata Wertz, superior general, makes a plea for its continuance, especially since it was a "feeder" school for the high school. (72) The school remained open, struggling for survival. Monsignor Quinn was in fragile health and became inactive when stricken with a brain tumor in November 1973. He died in January 1974 and was succeeded by Monsignor Charles W. Heid, then pastor of Our Lady of the Snows Parish, Clarks Summit.

Under Monsignor Heid's vigorous leadership the school began to grow again. At the time of his retirement in 1986 there were 293 students enrolled at St. Mary's. (73)

St. John the Evangelist Elementary School, Binghamton, New York

The excellent reputation of the IHM Sisters in the Diocese of Syracuse prior to 1936 had truly gone before them. Bishop John A. Duffy directed that an invitation be sent to Mother Josepha to increase the presence of our sisters in the diocese. He was asking her to accept in the fall of 1936 a proposed catechetical center, and a future parish elementary school at St. John the Evangelist Parish in Binghamton, New York.

The following letter from Reverend David C. Gildea, Superintendent of Schools for the Diocese of Syracuse, tells the story of "our call" to Binghamton:

> Dear Mother Josepha:
> Before the opening of St. Ambrose School in Endicott, you expressed a willingness in a letter of February 4, 1934, to send Sisters to staff the new school. At that time commitment had already been made for the teaching faculty.
>
> A week ago property was purchased in St. John the Evangelist Parish, Binghamton, for a new elementary school to be erected in that community in about four years. In the meantime, a social-catechetical center is contemplated for the parish, to be operated until the school is built. At least three Sisters are

required for this parochial activity which is scheduled to begin next September. A fitting convent will be ready to house those who engage in this work. Cognizant of the splendid work which your sisterhood is doing in this diocese, the Most Reverend Bishop directs me to invite another group of your Community into this section of New York State to engage for a time in the social-catechetical work and eventually in the regular school program in the parish of St. John's. I am certain that your acceptance of the invitation will please Bishop Duffy.

Perhaps you are familiar with the section of Binghamton included in St. John's. Situated in the southern part of the city where the last generation has witnessed a rapid building growth in a pleasing atmosphere, St. John's already boasts a beautiful new church and ample property for its other buildings. Parochial success is already fixed and the outlook is equally bright.

All concerned would be pleased to receive your affirmative answer.

Sincerely yours in Christ, (74)

Mother Josepha's prompt response, dated July 10, 1936, indicated her great desire to accept another mission in the Syracuse Diocese, especially with the potential it promised of a future elementary school location. (75)

Thus it was that on October 31, 1936, four sisters arrived to take up residence in an apartment at 11 Livingston Street until the convent at 7 Livingston Street would be ready (not until the Spring of 1937, as it turned out.)

Sister Olive Kelly, Sister dePaul Dougherty, Sister Mary John Bates and Sister Francis Marie Butler, the latter to serve as housekeeper, constituted the first community. Change impacted the little group almost at once, with Sister Olive being replaced by Sister Gerald O'Donnell by November 2.

The enrollment for the first year reached 340 pupils, the majority of whom came from nearby Lincoln School, some from Longfellow and Franklin Schools. About sixty of this number came from the Binghamton Senior High School on the released time program. By the third year, 1939, the curate of the parish obtained permission from the public school authorities to give instructions at the senior high school. Junior high school students were bussed directly to the catechetical center from their school. Released time scheduling of students from the public elementary schools resulted in an increased enrollment for a total of 450 pupils in 1940.

Reverend Joseph Wilmes, pastor, was most supportive of the catechetical work of the sisters and was familiar with the students. In observance of Father Wilmes' golden jubilee of priesthood in July 1941 the catechism classes presented a special program in his honor. It was only four months later, on November 18, 1941, that Father Wilmes died suddenly. Reverend Clement D. Shaughnessey succeeded him. Having had much experience in catechetical work among children, Father Shaughnessey at once gave his attention to the program and attendance continued to increase. He himself instructed the Confirmation class, and the sisters, with the aid of young women of the Sodality, instructed the remaining grades.

In January 1942, the sisters extended their ministry to conduct catechetical classes also at the Vestal Center School Building. Pupils from first grade to and including senior high school received instructions every Thursday afternoon at this center. Approximately 115 pupils were reached in this manner.

Sister Gerald O'Donnell remained in charge of this work in Binghamton and Vestal until 1942 when Sister Constance Roche replaced her. Sister dePaul Dougherty had been transferred in 1938, having been succeeded by Sister Ann Dolora Cullen; Sister Mary John Bates was replaced by Sister Teresita Clarke in 1939. Sister St. Andrew Connor was sent as an assistant with the classes in 1941. Other sisters who served in catechetical work here were Sister Maria Rose O'Malley, Sister Carmelina Fabbri, Sister Nativite Layden and Sister Malachy McKernan. (76)

The hope Mother Josepha had expressed to Bishop John Duffy in 1936 that one day there would be a parochial school in St. John's Parish was thirteen years in coming to reality, but by August of 1948 Monsignor David Gildea was once again in communication with the Congregation, this time to discuss plans for the new school to be opened in September 1949. Both Mother Josepha and Bishop Duffy had gone to their eternal reward, but they were remembered as many hundreds of parishioners, clergy and religious assembled to witness the dedication of the new $300,000 school building by Bishop Walter A. Foery on September 18, 1949.

Classes had begun on September 7 with an enrollment of 246 pupils in the kindergarten and the first four grades. Work continued on the school even as it opened in order to complete the full eight grades of the total building by the end of the year. The first sisters included Sister Evangeline Conmy, principal and superior, Sister Maronita Egan, Sister Marcelia Brennan, Sister Imelda Sharpe, Sister Charity Moran, Sister Cecile Gallagher, Sister Marella Moran and Sister Doreen Carmello. (77)

Unbelievable growth in enrollment was experienced at St. John's School. In six short years, by 1955-1956 the records show 696 pupils in kindergarten through eighth grade and a faculty of ten sisters and two lay teachers. Undoubtedly the pressures from financial and spiritual responsibilities took their toll on Monsignor Shaughnessey and on February 14, 1958, his illness forced him into "Pastor Emeritus" status. He was succeeded as pastor by Reverend Robert P. Driscoll from Johnson City. His work seemed to be cut out for him as he began in earnest to prepare for additions to the school and convent to meet the anticipated continued growth. By the school year 1959-1960 there were thirteen classrooms in operation, and in 1961-1962 with the addition of a ninth grade in the previous year, the total enrollment rose to 700 pupils. The faculty included eleven sisters and four lay teachers.

The short-term provision of a ninth grade came to an end with the graduation of 57 students in 1963 and the availability of a new Catholic Central High School, Seton Catholic, in Binghamton. (78)

The outstanding support which had been experienced by the sisters from the time of their arrival in 1936 continued. Monsignor Driscoll announced his retirement as pastor as of July 1, 1976, and was succeeded by Reverend Thomas J. Kiernan. His vision of St. John's Parish included support for the school and also outreach to children and adults for religious education and renewal. He had witnessed the effectiveness of the director of religious education, Sister Anne Pickard, who served in Our Lady of Sorrows Parish, Vestal, and Sister Marion Irving at St. Catherine's Parish, Hillcrest, both of whom resided at St. John's Parish Convent.

So it was that in the fall of 1982 Father Kiernan appointed the first director of religious education at St. John's, Sister St. Germaine O'Neil. With the addition of Sister Johanne Barry, newly selected principal of Seton Catholic Central High School, in residence also at St. John's, this local community was launched upon a wave of the future which would eventually see many such diversified-ministry groups of sisters forming community for religious life.

Many deaths occur in the Congregation each year and all are significant losses to the local community and to the Congregation as a whole. One such significant loss came to St. John's on October 25, 1983, in the shocking accidental death of Sister Marion Irving whose death followed a fall in her niece's home. Sister never regained consciousness, but lingered in a coma for one week in Lourdes Hospital, Binghamton. In reflecting back on the events, one of the sisters wrote in the annals, ''As Sister Marion had been so healthy and vitally alive, her sudden death was a great shock. The absence of her warm, exuberant presence left a void which we experienced often throughout the year." (79)

The excellent and dedicated ministries of our sisters at St. John's continue. The school in 1986-1987 had an enrollment of 546 students and a faculty of twelve sisters and twenty-one lay teachers. (80)

Our Lady of Good Counsel Elementary School, Inwood, New York

The story of thirty-three years of service by the Sisters of the Immaculate Heart of Mary at Our Lady of Good Counsel, Inwood, New York, began with a letter in 1937 from Reverend John F. McGowan, parish assistant, to Sister M. Marcella Gill, then assistant to Mother Josepha Hurley. This letter had as its purpose to communicate to the Congregation that the pastor, Father Francis Agius, "is considering the Sisters of the Immaculate Heart for the religious and catechetical work in our parish" and that "Father Agius is anxious to get at least four nuns or if possible five to help us with our work of training the children." (81) The further specifications were that "one of the Sisters would have to know Italian and Father would also like to have one Sister who knew music." (82)

By November 17, 1937, a contract had been drawn up with the pastor agreeing to the usual diocesan requirements, and Mother Josepha agreeing to provide five sisters for a total of 160 dollars per month. In addition a five-point paper was signed detailing the "conditions under which we would like the Sisters here to do their work in this parish." These included the sisters' caring for the sanctuary of the church, developing a boys' and a girls' choir, two hours of missionary work in the morning four days a week, visiting families and renewing parish life and church attendance. The catechetical instruction was to be held from three p.m. until six p.m. four days per week and Saturdays from 9:30 a.m. until noon. In the summer, the classes were to be held from nine a.m. until eleven a.m. Sunday duties included presence at the children's Mass at 9:30 a.m., followed by instructions until 11:15 a.m. (83)

In actuality, only three sisters were provided initially: Sister Zita McGlynn, superior, Sister Malachy McKernan and Sister Rosa Recktenwald. Sister Eustace Hanley joined these in December, was replaced by Sister Gerardus Turi in March, and Sister Vera Nallin was added to the group in May, thus bringing the total in that first year to five sisters.

While Good Counsel Parish had no parochial school in 1937, it did have a convent large enough to house seven sisters. The convent was located on Redwood Avenue, a short distance from the church. The sisters received a warm welcome into their convent home on Saturday, December 4, 1937. Mass was celebrated in the convent chapel and the Stations of the Cross were blessed and erected in the chapel. The arrival of the sisters was announced at all the Sunday Masses and an invitation extended by the pastor for all to attend the ceremony of blessing of the convent. Sister Zita describes the event in a letter to Mother Josepha:

> What a crowd came. They were packed in the house and lined up on the street awaiting their turn to get indoors. The last of them left at 5:30 p.m. . . Benediction was given from an altar erected at the front entrance to hundreds of people . . . The ladies of the Altar Society served cake and tea to more than four hundred. (84)

Father Agius had certainly judged the needs of his people rightly in setting up a catechetical center. More than 450 children were in attendance at Sunday school the very first week. The end of the year report dated June 13, 1938, showed a total of 478 pupils under instruction and two choirs, one of 35 boys and another of 40 girls formed and trained to sing the Mass and Vespers under the direction of Sister Rosa. Father Agius himself took the high school boys for instructions in the evenings. As things developed, classes in sewing, art and recreational activities were offered in addition to religious instruction on Saturdays.

In 1938, Sister Vera was replaced by Sister Aquinas McMenamin, and by 1940 only two of the original five remained. Sister Anna Murphy had replaced Sister Rosa in the music work, Sister Philippa Carroll was appointed superior and Sister Marie Rose O'Malley had replaced Sister Aquinas. Only Sister Malachy and Sister Gerardus had a three year longevity at the time of Father Agius' letter of October 1940 to Mother Josepha expressing his pleasure with the work of the sisters, but his disappointment with regard to so many changes. These concerns quite probably never reached Mother Josepha since she was at this time, and for several months, experiencing the excruciating pain from cancer that would lead to her death on December 4, 1940.

It was Mother Marcella Gill, who had been her assistant, who completed Mother Josepha's term, and it was she who, after learning of Father Agius' desire to begin a parochial school, motivated him to make Good Counsel School an outstanding school from the beginning. She made many prudent suggestions to him about seeking the advice of Monsignor McClancy, the diocesan superintendent of schools, early on. Quite forthrightly she also asked Father Agius to undertake the building of a new convent since the existing residence was already too small and too far distant from the school. Her concern for the sisters and for the good of their pupils is revealed when she writes:

> The present convent is too far distant from the school to insure good work. After making a trip to and from daily Mass and at least four more trips to and from school daily, you can realize how much valuable strength and energy are consumed, thus

> making the Sisters less able to do good work.This is particularly true in bad weather. Some good teachers who were sent there had to be changed for this reason.
>
> A convent close to the school has many advantages, particularly that of giving the teachers an opportunity to spend their spare minutes in decorating blackboards and preparing little devices that will make the work more interesting for the pupils. (86)

Her suggestions regarding the convent were not immediately realized, but the pastor's ambition to have a parochial school took form in the erection of a small, five-room school that opened on September 8, 1941, to 136 students (74 boys and 62 girls) in five grades.

The sisters sent to staff the school were: Sister Beata Wertz, principal and superior, Sister Sergius O'Donnell, Sister Elvira Manze, Sister Maronita Egan and Sister Terence McGirr. According to one account,

> There were many things lacking in those opening days, but the inspiration received from association with the children who in many cases have little of the comforts of this life, made one realize at every turn that Lady Poverty was sending her blessing. We noticed this particularly in the constant growth in friendliness among the people we came to serve. Many visitors coming into the school at dismissal time have said, 'These children never want to go home.' (87)

Indeed, school was an exciting and interesting place to be, with many diversified activities—art, music, drama—in addition to the regular curriculum. Regular weekly assemblies to which every class contributed something of spiritual or educational value challenged these youngsters to their creative best. Great stress was also placed on the accuracy of the children's religious knowledge so that they in turn could impart this knowledge to their parents and assist their return to the practice of their faith.

Father Agius continued as a vibrant spiritual leader of Good Counsel Parish until his death on January 24, 1958. He had been pastor for twenty-three years and had seen his parochial school grow to 367 pupils and a continuing catechetical group of 250 students. Needless to say, an annex to the original school was a need that he provided for in 1956.

Reverend William Galloway succeeded Father Agius and proved himself to be a strong supporter of the school and a much-loved pastor. Over the years he carried out many renovations to the convent and the school, adding twelve rooms to the school in 1961-1962. The school reached its peak enrollment of 560 students in 1968-1969 at which time there were two sections of each grade, one through eight. Eleven lay teachers and nine IHM Sisters staffed this school at its closing in 1970 in the pastorate of Reverend Raymond David.

The thirty-three year presence of the Sisters, Servants of the Immaculate Heart of Mary at Our Lady of Good Counsel, Inwood, New York, came to an abrupt end at their withdrawal on November 13, 1970. It is apparent from the records that much anguish and pain accompanied this decision, which seemed appropriate in light of the many injustices being experienced and the inability to find a resolution to them.

Holy Angels Elementary School, Hayes, Pennsylvania

Holy Angels was the fourth mission of the Sisters, Servants of the Immaculate Heart of Mary in the Pittsburgh Diocese. The Vincentian Sisters of Charity had staffed the school previously, but at their withdrawal an invitation was sent to Mother Josepha from the pastor, Reverend Michael J. Vitale, with the approval of Bishop John F. Dearden. (88) The typical contract provided in those years shows a salary of thirty dollars per month per sister. (89) It can be assumed that among the first community there was at least one sister who taught private music lessons to augment this small remuneration. The original community included Sister Alma Shelly, superior and principal, Sister Bernita McDonough, Sister Edwarda Wilson and Sister Alois Ortner.

The sisters arrived on August 27, 1938, and school was opened with a High Mass on September 6, 1938. The enrollment for the eight grades was 169 pupils. The school was a two-story building which would see much renovation and even an addition as it was expanded to receive 314 pupils by 1955-1956.

Memories of those early years at Holy Angels focus on the generosity of the parishioners in assisting the sisters renovate, furnish and equip the convent in order to make it livable. The pastor's interest in the upkeep of both the school and the convent was not consistent and sustained. After thirteen years of patient endurance of these conditions, an exchange of letters between Mother Marcella and Bishop Dearden in 1951 pointed to the fact that the Congregation felt that the only resolution was to withdraw the sisters from Holy Angels. (90) Reverend Thomas Quigley, superintendent of the Pittsburgh Diocesan Schools, and Bishop Dearden both appealed to Mother Marcella to have the sisters remain. Father Vitale was changed and a new pastor, Father Savage, replaced him.

In the spring of 1952 the matter was favorably resolved and a decision was made to have the sisters continue at Holy Angels' School. Father

Savage was very positive about his assignment in spite of the great challenges and set out to provide for the needs that were evident. The convent was refurbished, an addition made to the school, a church hall was renovated for classroom space, and a new rectory was built adjoining the school. The five years of Father Savage's pastorate were fruitful, but he was transferred in 1957 to St. Scholastica's Church and replaced by Reverend Michael Carmody in December 1957.

From 1957 through 1964 when Father Carmody was transferred to Blessed Sacrament Parish, there was only growth and expansion, so a prime concern centered on finding additional space for school. In 1959 there were two first grade classes so a large area was opened up in the basement to provide for a primary level area. 1959-1960 saw a complete renovation of the school, providing tile floors throughout, installing fire escapes, and painting inside and out. By this time there was an enrollment of 427 pupils with six sisters and two lay teachers in the school. In 1960-1961 Father Carmody, desirous of keeping his promise to do something about the sisters' housing proposed a switch of residences between the priests and sisters. Thus the former parish house (rectory) was completely refurnished for the sisters, and after some renovations of the old convent, the priests exchanged residences with the sisters. In March of 1964 Father Carmody was transferred leaving incomplete his great plans to relocate this parish, to one day have completely new parish buildings and a school for 1,000 students.

His successor was Reverend Dennis Doran. A brief year and a half later, on September 20, 1965, Father Doran met his death in a terrible fire which erupted in the rectory (former convent) in the early morning hours. Father Aranowski, the assistant pastor, awakened to the sound of fire sirens and saved his life by jumping out the window to safety. This incident was made doubly sad in the fact that Father Doran's eighty-five-year-old mother was still living. The sisters brought her to the convent and cared for her through her days of sorrow. The wake for Father Doran was held in the convent and large numbers of parishioners came to pay final tribute to Father Doran over the day and one half of the wake at the convent, after which he was transferred to the church. One account recalls some of these events:

> The Knights of Columbus were the guard of honor. Sisters from city communities with whom he had been connected in a variety of ways came to pray at his side. It was a great consolation to his dear mother to see them all. She knew many of them personally, as did his sisters. His family remained here (at the convent) while the body was here. (91)

Monsignor Paul Lackner was named Father Doran's successor. He arrived to take up his duties as pastor on October 27, 1965. With the rectory demolished, the priests moved into a house in the area close to the church. Monsignor Lackner responded to the need among the parishioners for thoughtfulness and healing as a consequence of the sudden loss of the former pastor, Father Doran. He anticipated many of the needs of the sisters and shared in their personal sorrows as several sisters lost family members in death. Also, at the death of Sister Finbarr Daley on April 7, 1968, he traveled to Marywood to offer the final Mass of Requiem with the sisters. Sister Finbarr had been on active duty at Holy Angels until stricken with a heart attack on April 3. It was a year in which she had lost both a brother and a sister in death before her own came.

The final chapter of IHM presence at Holy Angels in Hayes is a puzzling one. Throughout 1966-1967 correspondence with the Congregation indicates that the pastor, Monsignor Lackner, was pleased with the work of the sisters in the school. Several of his requests concerned further work in which he desired the sisters' services—in taking the parish census; in beginning a summer program in remedial reading and the teaching of other subjects; in offering summer religious education. (92) Some of these activities materialized, some did not, due to the need of the sisters to make retreat, attend summer school, take care of their health, and take a few days' relaxation.

The possible transgression of the fine line between interest and interference by the pastor in the administration of the school could have been a cause of tension were it not for the virtue of the principal, Sister Mary Arthur Meinzer. The account of one such incident in the 1967-1968 annals is an example:

> . . . In December our pastor, Monsignor Lackner, informed us that at his invitation three faculty members of California Teachers' College in California, Pennsylvania, would come on December 17 to evaluate Holy Angels School. Of course, this caused the normal anxiety as we were all aware of the physical limitations of our school building. However, we received favorable evaluation and this was a welcome prelude to the Christmas holidays. (93)

The commendations of the evaluating team covered all salient educational points— personal enthusiasm, cooperation, textbooks, testing programs, library materials, attendance of staff at workshops. Recommendations included provision for smaller class sizes, for a fulltime principal (Sister Mary Arthur was also teaching), and a K-6 organization if finances became problematic in the future. The need for improving the existing school facilities was noted more than once. (94)

Reverend David Crowley succeeded Monsignor Lackner as pastor. In assessing the extensive renovation needed in the school and the predictable financial outlay for lay teachers in the future, he decided to close the school. This decision was reached in 1969, but the superintendent of schools of the Pittsburgh Diocese insisted that at least one year's notice be given to the parishioners. This was done, and in June 1970, thirty-two years of IHM presence at Holy Angels' School came to a close.

Father Crowley promised the parents that he would provide bus transportation at the expense of the parish so that the children could continue their Catholic education at St. Michael's School. This promise was carried out. This seemed providential in that it was the Vincentian Sisters of Charity who had originally staffed Holy Angels who at this time staffed St. Michael's. Things had, in a sense, come full circle for them. (95)

St. Agnes Elementary School, Lock Haven, Pennsylania

> With the opening of St. Agnes School, Tuesday, September 6 (1938), a new sisterhood, the Sisters, Servants of the Immaculate Heart of Mary, will be in charge of the teaching. The new Sisters have already arrived at St. Agnes Convent. (96)

Indeed, the "new sisters" had arrived on August 25, 1938. They included Sister Maura Fleury, superior and principal, Sister Dolores Ryan, Sister Virgine Maurer, Sister Hosina (Genevieve) McCloskey and Sister Nora Clarke. The "new" Sisters were not coming to a new mission, however. St. Agnes School had opened in 1881 and had been staffed by the Glen Riddle Franciscans for fifty-seven years. The withdrawal of these sisters opened the door for the pastor, Reverend Donald Wagner, a former pupil of the IHM Sisters in Renovo, Pennsylvania, to pursue the possibility of our sisters' staffing St. Agnes School, Lock Haven. It seemed natural that this request would come, since our sisters were already located at nearby Immaculate Conception Parish in Lock Haven where they staffed both an elementary and a secondary school. The coming of the sisters to St. Agnes' would provide for greater community contact in the area.

Father Wagner's first exploratory letter (97) must have received favorable consideration, for on May 31, 1938, he wrote to Mother Josepha stating Bishop Guilfoyle's approval of the IHM Sisters' coming to St. Agnes. His letter was quite forthright, describing in some detail the needs of the Italian families of his parish, most of whom were economically poor, but desirous of having their children receive the education that they themselves had not received. "Thus we need," he said, "above all, teachers who can be sympathetic with their mode of living and condition of life." (98) He had previously written, " . . . for the first four grades we need Sisters who are strict disciplinarians." (99)

The statement from an older version of our *Constitutions* seems to be just the right balance for what he had in mind, "Those who teach . . . shall seek to make themselves beloved by their pupils by governing them with firmness tempered with mildness." (100)

Since there was no church organist, and the choir was composed of girls from the school, he also indicated the need for the sisters to take charge of the music.

The school had five large classrooms and opened with a registration of 176 students, in grades one through eight. The sisters were very well accepted from the beginning both by the pastor and by the parents and children. Their relative youthfulness and vigor were needed for the challenges that were present. The disastrous flood of 1936 had damaged extensively the church, school and convent, and everyone's energy was directed at survival until the physical plant could be restored. The school auditorium was being used for Mass. By December 22, 1938, Father Wagner had completed the renovation of St. Agnes Church that was rededicated by Bishop Richard T. Guilfoyle, Bishop of Altoona.

St. Agnes School was to become one of the best equipped schools in the State of Pennsylvania as the pastor and the sisters, with the assistance of the Parent Teacher Association worked on the replacement of textbooks and school equipment. Parish suppers, raffles, and donations somehow yielded the funds necessary for school projects.

Father Wagner was transferred to the pastorate of St. Mary's Church, Altoona, and was succeeded in February 1941 by Reverend Charles H. Hipp, former teacher of foreign languages at Altoona Catholic High School. Father Hipp must have been a combination of scholar and social actionist. He was a graduate of St. Francis College, Loretto, and had studied further at Freiburg, Switzerland; he was also a strong advocate on behalf of the underprivileged. His work was cut out for him at St. Agnes where so many deserving poor were located. (101)

With the elimination of the Works Progress Administration in the post-depression years, most school lunch programs were dropped because of lack of funds to pay for personnel. Later, this would become a volunteer effort in most Catholic schools, but this concept had not yet replaced the "government-supported" worker concept. Father Hipp was highly enterprising in procuring additional government aid, supplemented by a small fee from the children, to keep the lunch program going. Since many mothers were working in order to support large families, it was of great assistance to them. Some 150 luncheons were served daily at St. Agnes School.

Father Hipp was also most generous in giving encyclopedia sets and many books to the school library.

Soon after his arrival in the parish Father Hipp began the renovation of the convent that had also been left in a dismal condition by the 1936 flood. Sister Cornelia describes the improvements in these words:

> Remodeling different rooms, and treating the entire house to the cheerful tonic of ivory paint and beautiful paper, made a pretty and comfortable home for the Sisters. A devotional chapel replete with a liturgical altar, new prie-dieu's and beautiful carpet replaced its defaced predecessor. New rugs and furniture, and well chosen pictures have transformed the old begrimed building into a new and cheerful abode. (102)

Up until 1946, nearly all of the children of the parish attended St. Agnes School, hence the need for classes in religion outside of school time was minimal. However, when a change of policy occurred in the State of Pennsylvania in 1946 denying transportation on public school buses to children attending private schools, the children from a distance had to attend public school. Father Hipp then provided religion classes for these children after school and had men from the parish pick them up at their school and take them to St. Agnes' School for instructions. On Sunday mornings he provided breakfast for them. Father Hipp was succeeded by Reverend John J. Burkardt as pastor.

As the years went on, the school flourished and by 1955 the enrollment was 264 pupils. All grades, except first and second, were double until that year when a lay teacher was hired for third grade, giving some relief to Sister Juliette Flannery who had originally been scheduled for third and fourth grades, and music, together with serving as superior and principal.

Evidence that the sisters were also very active in catechesis was seen in the fact that in 1958 in addition to the Confirmation class of 150 children, there were sixty adults confirmed, among whom were twenty adult converts.

By the school year 1959-1960, a peak enrollment of 300 students was reached. Father Burkardt had pleaded, and received, a seventh sister, and together with one lay teacher, finally all classes first through eight had their own classroom. Such progress would have been welcomed by prior faculty members of St. Agnes School, but was cause for rejoicing among the faculty present that year which included Sister Marie Imelda Callahan, superior and principal, Sister Berenice Cauley, Sister Serenus (Katherine) Rolley, Sister Vera Nallin, Sister Berchmans (Eileen) Miller, Sister Gracilda (Rita Lorraine) Burke, Sister Maria Goretti Timperio and Mrs. Mary Shive.

In spite of annual threats of floods, and another major flood in March 10, 1964, which damaged the newly dedicated St. Agnes Church, the school continued to grow. The next milestone in the school's history was the announcement in 1967 that St. Agnes School was to be consolidated with Immaculate Conception School in Lock Haven to form the new Consolidated Catholic Schools of Lock Haven. This was part of a larger plan of consolidation in the Altoona Diocese that saw twenty-eight Catholic elementary schools merged into seven. Based as it was on the fiscal and religious personnel realities of the time, and as projected into the foreseeable future, the plan had much merit. Since enrollment in the seventh and eighth grades of both schools had declined, these grades were dropped and the new school became a 1-6 grade school.

The closing of the 50-year-old small Catholic high school at Immaculate Conception occurred at the same time, making space available for a total, comprehensive elementary school. The location of the school at Immaculate Conception related to the better condition and size of the buildings since the school had been built in 1961 and occupied in January 1962. It also had a better and safer location during the flood season. Two hundred twenty-five pupils registered in the new six-grade consolidated school in the fall of 1967. Only one of the sisters formerly at St. Agnes School had been transferred to Immaculate Conception to the consolidated school, namely, Sister Laurana Burns. Her presence proved to be a helpful link in the transition. Sister prepared the children from St. Agnes for their First Communion that took place at St. Agnes Church so their parish identity was not lost in the school consolidation. (103)

There were several transfers at Immaculate Conception also in August of 1967. Sister Teresine (Eleanor) Desaulniers, who had been principal and superior, and high school teacher, since 1962 was replaced as principal and superior by Sister Virgine Maurer. Sister Virgine had responsibilities also for the sixth grade and for the music. The total faculty consisted of five sisters and one lay teacher. Evidently, the transition caused no major difficulties, except for the fact that most classes were far too large, some in excess of forty pupils. Predictably, this would level off in years of declining births in the years ahead. By 1972 there were 170 pupils in six grades.

Seventy-six years of service at Immaculate Conception School were to terminate in July 1978 as our sisters were withdrawn and prepared both the convent and the school for the arrival of the Sinsinawa Dominicans from the Milwaukee, Wisconsin, province of their congregation.

The final IHM community included: Sister Eileen Miller, superior, Sister Pulcheria Longe, principal, Sister Paul Marie Viedeffer, Sister Yolanda Bravin and Sister Roberta Mary Harding. (104)

St. Ann Catechetical Center and Elementary School, Devon, Connecticut

In the spring of 1938, Reverend John F. Ryan, pastor of St. Ann's, Devon and of St. Gabriel's at Wildemere Beach, Connecticut, applied to Mother Josepha for sisters to open a religious education center for the children of these parishes. The frustration he was experiencing is evident in his appeal, "For the past two years I have been searching high and low for four nuns for catechetical instruction and parish visitation. And I have been unsuccessful . . . would it be possible for you to do anything for me in this regard?" (105)

Mother Josepha and Mother Anysia Moran, then directress of novices at Marywood, traveled to Devon to assess the situation. At this time Father Ryan offered the rectory on Naugatuck Avenue for the housing of the sisters. He himself and the assistant pastor, Reverend Cornelius Looney, were willing to take up temporary residence on the shore front, renting a cottage at No. 7 Seaview Avenue, Laurel Beach, for some months, and later moving to 32 Broadway, Wildemere Beach. The chief works that Father Ryan wished the sisters to do were parish visitation, catechetical instruction of children on a daily basis, and instruction of women converts.

The new mission was approved by Mother Josepha and three sisters arrived on Saturday, October 1, 1938: Sister Mary Martin Cawley, Sister Maria Rose O'Malley, and Sister Reparata Callan. Leaving Scranton by train from the Lackawanna Station at 10:30 a.m., and arriving at Hoboken, New Jersey, at 2:30 p.m., the sisters were met by Father Looney and taken by car to Devon. Since the housing arrangement was considered "temporary," the priests had removed only essential personal belongings from the rectory. This meant that the house was completely furnished and that all utensils, table and bed linens, and even the complete library was left for the use of the sisters. The house was small, but manageable. (106)

During 1938-1939 the sisters held catechetical classes in which 423 children of grade-school level, 90 of high school and 30 pre-school youngsters were instructed. They engaged in parish visitation, visitation of the sick, instruction of adult converts, and instruction of both children and all parishioners in Gregorian Chant for singing at the Masses. In June of that year, Sister de Neri McLane was sent to assist with the summer religious instruction classes. (107)

It was Father Ryan's great concern to remedy the living conditions of the sisters as soon as possible. So it was that he informed the parishioners by letter almost a year in advance that his intent was to break ground for a convent in the spring of 1940. His deep appreciation of the work of the sisters was expressed in his inimitable style, detailing the history and ministries of the Congregation's three branches, and extolling the educational preparation and expertise of the sisters and his gratitude that some community was able to respond to the needs of his parishes.

> The Order of the Immaculate Heart of Mary was under no obligation whatsoever to send four highly trained and holy women to the Diocese of Hartford, which itself could not supply the need, to minister unto the needs of the parishioners of St. Ann's and St. Gabriel's . . . yet we feel we are under obligation to furnish them a decent home wherein they may find the only enjoyment which is permitted to them. The old rectory can scarcely be deemed a suitable home for them. (108)

True to his promise, Father Ryan obtained the approval of Bishop Maurice F. McAuliffe of Hartford for the convent project, and ground was broken on Low Sunday, 1940. Three weeks later, on April 21, 1940, Father Ryan met his death following an accident. This was a tragedy and shock for all. It had been planned that the new convent would be ready in time to coincide with the termination of the lease on the rented cottage being used by the priests. With Father Ryan's death, work on the convent ceased for several months, so this plan could not materialize. The sisters therefore returned to Marywood on May 29, 1940, making way for the return of the priests to the old rectory. The Bishop was assured that they would return in the fall. In June 1940, Reverend Joseph L. Kinney became pastor of St. Ann's and work was resumed on the convent.

The sisters returned in September 1940. The community included Sister Mary Martin Cawley, Sister Reparata Callan, Sister Aquin O'Brien and Sister Franzchen Yahner. A house was rented for them since the convent was not yet completed. This house was located on the dividing line of the two parishes, a half-mile from either church and a quarter of a mile from the bus line. Because the situation was again "temporary," the Blessed Sacrament was not placed in the house. All hopes were focused on the months ahead when at length their convent home would be completed. Writing to Mother Josepha, Sister Mary Martin's hope and humor were evident:

> I know you are desirous to hear how this portion of your flock is getting along. Not too bad in many ways though there are a few inconveniences which also give us a taste of holy poverty and the 'stern reality' of the common life. Out of it all we have plenty of good fun and laughter particularly when we have to keep on schedule for our baths, as hot water is one of our deprivations. (109)

This beautiful spirit, so characteristic of our sisters, is reflected also in their commitment to the tasks at hand and to the ministry that had brought them to Devon. Their hope was to be in the new convent by Thanksgiving, but it was December 31, 1940, before the cornerstone was laid in a quiet, brief ceremony that included only the pastor, Father Kinney, his assistant, Father Cornelius Looney, and the four sisters. The furnishings were placed during the week of January 15, 1941—chairs, tables and kneelers were made at St. Michael's Industrial School, Hoban Heights, Pennsylvania. The liturgical altar and bronze tabernacle were gifts of the Ryan family and were inscribed in memory of the former and beloved pastor, Father Ryan.

Many special gifts from parishioners provided candelabra, crucifixes, Stations of the Cross, electrical fixtures, and kneelers. Open house for the laity was held on January 19. The first Mass to be offered in the new convent chapel was celebrated by Father Kinney on January 25, 1941, and the joy of the sisters was complete in the presence of the Blessed Sacrament in their convent after five months of experiencing this deprivation. It was a solemn occasion also since everyone felt Father Ryan's dream had been realized and that the convent would always be regarded as a memorial to him.

The work of the sisters and priests was greatly blessed as, by 1943, 521 elementary level pupils were in attendance. Sister Mary Nicholas Scanlon was added to the local community. Instructions were given once a week for the primary level and twice a week for Grades 3 to 8 inclusive. All grades were double, except 2, 5 and 6. The course of study included the Catholic faith catechism, bible and church history, teaching of prayers, use of the missal, training in Gregorian Chant, choir and hymn practice. The pastor provided a children's lending library in addition to other books and periodicals in religion. Father Kinney looked after the religious instruction of the high school students of St. Ann's Parish; Father Looney, those of St. Gabriel's. It was assumed early on that these educational endeavors were the forerunners of a parochial school. (110)

Eleven years later, a new pastor, Reverend Francis P. Breen, initiated the first step toward the goal of a parochial school in writing to Mother

Kathleen Hart to relate his plans for a school with kindergarten through eighth grades. "Before I make my plans, I would like to have your assurance that I will have your sisters to staff the school when it is complete," he wrote. (111) Evidently his request was well received, for a year later, on June 6, 1955, ground was broken for the proposed school. It was decided to start the first and second grades in the convent classroom as of September 1955; they were on half sessions until the school was ready in January 1956. Meanwhile, a decision had to be made about the public school religious instructions, for the practice had been that these children were released from school at ten, twelve and three o'clock to attend religion classes. Once the parochial school would open, this would no longer be possible, so it was decided to take as many classes as possible after school on Monday, Tuesday, and Wednesday, and on Sunday mornings after the nine o'clock Mass.

St. Ann's School opened officially on January 30, 1956, with 192 pupils in five grades. Sister Helaine O'Dea was superior, principal and fifth grade teacher; Sister St. Walter (Ann) Hughes, fourth grade; Sister Virgine Maurer, third grade; Sister Rosalind Doyle, second grade; and Sister Carolus Maloney, first grade. The school was modern in every respect, having an "intercom" system throughout, a 500-seat assembly hall with stage and complete kitchen facilities, health room, teachers' lounge and library, in addition to eight large classrooms. The assembly hall on the ground level had a separate entrance so as to be used when needed independently of the school for parish activities.

On April 22, 1956, Bishop Henry J. O'Brien of Hartford conducted the formal dedication. Some two thousand people attended.

The school enrollment grew steadily with a capacity enrollment of 310 pupils being reached in 1970. Six sisters and three lay teachers staffed the school at this point, including Sister Rose Angela Ruddy, superior and principal, Sister Casimira Kent, Sister Hermine Krug, Sister Mary Arthur Meinzer, Sister Joanne Campanini and Sister Margretta (Jane) Snyder. In addition to the capacity numbers in the regular day school there were over four hundred students in religious instruction classes after school. (112)

Various factors were at work by 1975 which caused the Congregation administration to introduce discussions with Reverend Edward Rooney, pastor, and with Reverend James G. Fanelli, superintendent of schools for the Hartford Diocese, about the future of St. Ann's School, Devon. The Congregation was experiencing a decline in vocations, coupled with illnesses and deaths among our sisters, so much thought had to be given to the distribution of the sisters among the many ministry commitments existing. The enrollment had declined to 247 pupils by this time. Suggestions were made to withdraw from St. Ann's since St. Gabriel's School was only one mile distant; or to reduce the number of sisters required in either school by arranging for four grades to be served in each school; or to gradually reduce IHM presence by two sisters per year through 1976-1978 leaving one sister as principal, who could live with IHM Sisters in Bridgeport for 1978-1979. Four years' notice would thus be provided to the parish in the hope that other religious might be found to staff the school jointly with our sisters, or to bring about some arrangement for its survival. (113)

In actuality, the convent was closed on August 5, 1977, with the last community being Sister Agnes McHale, Sister Celestina Langan, Sister Daniela McCarthy and Sister Anine Hopkins. Sister Agnes continued as principal with an all-lay faculty for 1977-1978, residing with our sisters at St. Ambrose Convent, Bridgeport. It had been hoped that a new principal would be found during that year to work with Sister Agnes before her departure, but as of June 23, 1978, when the school closed, no principal had yet been named.

Mt. Carmel and St. Edward Catechetical Center, Barnesboro, Pennsylvania

The influence of Pennsylvania's strong ethnic presence within the Catholic Church is evident in the very interesting history which found two Barnesboro pastors, located just five blocks from one another, both seeking sisters the same year for identical ministries in their parishes. Reverend Charles Smyth, TOR, presided over a mainly Italian parish, Mount Carmel; Reverend Michael Brett described St. Edward's as "a Congregation of some two hundred families, and in this community of five Catholic Churches, is better known as the Irish Congregation." (114) The latter had, in fact, a goodly number of people of Slovak, Polish, and Hungarian heritage, (115) but was probably somewhat conditioned by the pastor's own Irish background and that of his two priest-brothers, also resident at Mount Carmel, to view the scene through "Irish" eyes.

It appears that Mount Carmel Parish had taken the lead in responding to Bishop Guilfoyle's plan for providing religious education for Catholic children who could not, because of great distances involved, attend a Catholic school. The people of Mount Carmel Parish were supportive of the efforts of their zealous pastor. Because the parish could not provide a convent, Father Smyth arranged for two sisters of the Immaculate Heart of Mary to reside at Spangler and commute to provide religious instructions daily to the youngsters of his parish from 2:30 p.m. to 5:00 p.m. Sisters Willemyn Gambrill and Dolores Ryan were appointed for this work. This arrangement continued from September until June 1937. The pastor and people of Mount Carmel were anxious to have "their own" sisters in residence, so a dwelling was finally secured and they set to work to furnish and equip it before the arrival of the sisters. Meanwhile, the pastor of St. Edward's, Reverend Michael Brett, had requested two sisters, thus bringing to four the total needed for the two parishes.

The original four who set out from Scranton by train for Altoona, and thence to Barnesboro on August 28, 1938, included: Sister Thomasina Gallagher, superior, Sister Willemyn Gambril, Sister Servula Healy and Sister Margaretta Mullin. The latter two were appointed to serve at St. Edward's; the pastors had agreed that all four would reside at the Mount Carmel Convent. Much excitement and concern clouded their arrival, as Sister Servula was stricken with a heart attack that evening. Barnesboro must have seemed like the end of the earth as the little group gathered their strength and assessed their situation. Mother Josepha was contacted and she responded by sending Sister Vera Nallin to assist at Mount Carmel. Meanwhile, Sister Willemyn was sent with Sister Margaretta to St. Edward's where the work had gotten off to a much-delayed beginning. After her hospitalization, Sister Servula remained at Mount Carmel until her recuperation was complete, but was then transferred. (116)

A contract of sorts for both parishes carried a detailed description of the expected activities of the sisters on seven days of the week and several evenings: daily religious instructions and extensive secretarial work, care for the altar linens and decoration of the church, keeping records of parish weekly collections, looking after bingo or card party tickets and receipts, addressing and mailing out Christmas, Easter and other feast day greetings to parishioners and friends, in addition to instructing the children in singing, training altar boys, visitation of parish families, and training the children for at least two entertainments per year. (117) "There was nothing left in the St. Gregory hymnal to teach them," commented Sister Willemyn, of the intensity of their endeavors. Subsequently, because of Father Smyth's request that a parish census be taken, Sister Marie Louise Langan, who had facility in the Italian language, was added to the Mount Carmel community. And all of this for thirty dollars per month per sister was quite a bargain, even in 1938!

For twelve years these arrangements continued with much strain on both pastors and sisters in trying to meet the growing needs of the two parishes. At one point it was proposed by the Congregation that three sisters be shared, as a unit, to conduct the programs at the two parishes, but the pastor of Mount Carmel would not consent to not having "his own" Sisters. (118)

With the shortage of sisters it became necessary in 1950 to withdraw from Barnesboro. (119)

St. Edward's Elementary School, Twin Falls, Idaho

Something very important about the nature of the Congregation becomes obvious as it is noted that the new missions opened by Mother Josepha from 1933-1938 were located in nine different dioceses. It is not surprising, then, that she would respond positively to a request to send sisters to a somewhat remote spot in southern Idaho, Twin Falls. She was following predecessors who had already established our sisters in Coeur d'Alene, Idaho, in the Boise, Idaho Diocese (encompassing the entire State of Idaho) and in the Archdiocese of Portland, Oregon.

In a letter dated June 17, 1939, Bishop Edward J. Kelly of Boise wrote to Mother Josepha explaining that the Sisters of Holy Cross were having difficulty staffing their schools and would welcome another congregation's replacing them at St. Edward's, Twin Falls. They were anxious to make final arrangements before July 1, so this left Mother Josepha with less than ten days for a reply. (120) She sent a telegram with her affirmative response, promising to supply four sisters for the school. (121)

Bishop Kelly's letter hints at the fact that the school and convent are not in prime condition as he describes them as "temporary," and "cannot be replaced for about five years when the debt will be off the church." (122)

Pictures reveal that the convent which the sisters lived in from 1939 to 1945 was a very small house of one floor with an attic dormitory. The white frame building which housed grades 3-8 was the old church building; grades one and two were in a small frame ''annex" to the main building. The school and convent were located seven blocks from the church.

To this setting came Sister Ursulina Shaughnessy, superior and principal, Sister Canice Reardon, Sister Noel Michalek and Sister Henry Kennedy. They left Scranton by train on August 22, 1939, and arrived in Spokane, Washington, on August 25. Here they were met by some of the sisters from the IHM Academy in Coeur d'Alene, Idaho, some thirty-five miles distant. The welcome greetings for the newly arrived "sisters from the East" were warm, indeed, and after three days of riding on the train, the rest and hospitality of the next two days were appreciated. On August 27 they set out for Twin Falls where they were welcomed on arrival by the pastor, Reverend H. E. Heitman. (123)

Twin Falls, Idaho, at that time was a town of some 12,000 people, having about 1,000 Catholics. This was, and still is, a very religious area, having many religious denominations represented, the highest percentage of which are Mormon. Churches and church-related private schools are common in this area.

Our sisters seem to have been well received from the beginning, although they themselves had some concerns about their acceptance, in view of the departure of the Holy Cross Sisters. With hard work and much energy expended they gradually turned their poor dwelling into a comfortable convent home. (124)

The simplicity of the surroundings is evident in this account, written a year later:

> . . . There was not even an altar linen or anything else left here when we arrived; we had to get a small supply from the church before we could have the Blessed Sacrament in the house, but when after three or four days, He came to make His home with us, it gave us such happiness that nothing else made any difference to us . . .
>
> The house was anything but orderly; the dormitory upstairs was like a barracks and would give one chills to look at it much less to sleep in it . . . We moved the furniture around until it finally looked neat and roomy; the new arrangement also did away with the necessity of getting traffic lights to warn us of danger to our corns . . . Next we moved the chiffonier from the refectory which is also our community room when the dishes have been removed . . . The result is a neat, comfortable home, but certainly nothing fashionable or beautiful about it. (125)

A spirit of humor and uncomplaining good will prevailed, with hard work both in the convent and the school as routine. Sister Ursulina's realistic appraisal was that "There does not seem to be much hope of either a new school or convent for a good many years yet. The debt is $23,000 and must be paid first. They paid $2,000 of it this year, and at that rate it will take at least eleven years to pay it off." (126)

Monsignor Joseph P. O'Toole followed Father Heitman as pastor in 1941. Desirous of having the sisters settled in a new convent before Sister Ursulina's six years were completed, when she would be leaving Twin Falls, he accomplished the purchase of a beautiful, large dwelling located near the church, in May of 1945. Sister Ursulina lived in this convent for one month before her departure.

As the first superior and principal of St. Edward's her influence must be noted: it is clear that she guided the little community prayerfully and happily through some hard times and together they established the beginning of an outstanding reputation as religious teachers which would continue through the years. Both Monsignor O'Toole and Bishop Kelly were filled with praise for what had been accomplished in those first six years. Knowing that he could not alter the fact that Sister Ursulina's term was up and she would be leaving, the Bishop's words were meaningful, " . . . If you leave your spirit here, it will be enough."

Sister Rosamund Wyvill followed Sister Ursulina as superior and principal, dedicated to the continued excellence of the school and to the development of the young sisters under her care. In October 1945 she relayed news of plans for the new school to Mother Marcella, writing, " . . .he (Monsignor O'Toole) has bought a house near the church for his rectory . . . The next move is toward the school. He expects to start soliciting by going from house to house. He said that we would not see much of him in school from now until Christmas." (127)

Monsignor O'Toole succeeded in centralizing the locations of the church, convent and school in the same block when the new school was built next to the church in 1947.

By 1955, the golden jubilee year of St. Edward's Parish, there were 388 pupils in the school and a faculty of eight sisters, including Sister Marie Bernarde Kilcullen, superior and principal, Sister Bernita McDonough, Sister Maron (Mary) Rassley, Sister Joan of Arc (Jacquelin) Servick, Sister Infanta Bronzie, Sister Mary Mark Carnes, Sister Mary Martin O'Dea and Sister Mariel Dougher.

Nineteen hundred fifty-five was the year also of Bishop Edward J. Kelly's death. It was on April 21 at 6:45 a.m. that he was stricken by a heart attack and died. On April 23 Monsignor O'Toole, pastor of St. Edward's was named administrator of the Diocese of Boise, retaining his duties as pastor. On August 29, 1956, Bishop James J. Byrne was installed as the new Bishop of Idaho.

The little school that started out with 135 pupils was attracting students from miles around and its continued growth seemed assured: 1958-1959 saw 385 pupils; 1960-1961, 396; and 1961-1962, 405. Meanwhile Monsignor Edmund R. Cody replaced the ailing Monsignor O'Toole as pastor; and once again a change of bishops occurred, as Bishop James J. Byrne became Bishop of Dubuque, Iowa, on March 7, 1962. He was replaced by Bishop Sylvester Treinen, who was installed on August 9, 1962. (128)

Over the years the sisters had taught instructions and summer school classes of religious education in Buhl, Idaho, about eighteen miles from Twin Falls. In 1960, the pastor of six months, Reverend Jerome T. O'Connor, having inherited nearly completed convent, school and rectory buildings from his predecessors, wrote to seek the help of the Congregation in obtaining sisters:

> I have written over one hundred and twenty letters to different orders of sisters; last summer I drove from one state to another

> trying to get sisters . . . Mother, will you please say you will accept the school and send me two sisters to open it in September 1961? . . . If I don't open it, I may as well move out. This is no exaggeration. (129)

Had there not been a general shortage of sisters in the Congregation to meet existing commitments, this sincere appeal would have evoked a positive response, chiefly because of the long association of our sisters with the parishioners of Immaculate Conception Parish in Buhl, Idaho. The story has a happy ending in that Father O'Connor did get another congregation, the Sisters of Mercy, to staff the school.

Unusual aspects of the annals of St. Edward's include accounts of 3,000-mile car trips "commuting" back and forth to and from Scranton; two-day retreat journeys to Coeur d'Alene, Idaho, to join with other IHM Sisters in the West; visits to such exotic places as Sun Valley, Magic Valley, Galena Summit and Big Wood River; seeing a real, live rodeo complete with cowboys, bucking broncos, and steers; baked boar roasting; picnics in the Canyon; and "drop-in" visits from the Bishop of Idaho. (130)

All of these "unusuals" were integrated with the more typical and "usual" IHM life so that we can all recognize ourselves in this description:

> This was a year of surprises and joy. A retreat centered around devotion to the Holy Spirit set the tone and spirit for the rest of the year. After that week, permeated with the Spirit of love, the Sisters set out loving, learning, teaching, giving, and living Christ in a daily round of activity, prayer and joy, through a year that breathlessly kept pace with a rapidly changing world, and terminated in a new beginning (131)

The new year, 1971, brought the news that IHM Sisters would be withdrawn from all of the IHM missions in the West—Coeur d'Alene, Portland, Gresham and Twin Falls, because of a shortage of personnel. The finality of it all brought deep sadness, for not only were the IHMs departing, but also no congregation could be found to send replacements. Some of what both the people and the sisters in Twin Falls were experiencing is captured by Sister Mary Zita (Carolyn Mary) Cossack:

> Over the years the non-Catholics as well as the Catholics have come to love the Sisters and to consider the school a real asset to the community. We can't go into a store, bank, library, hospital or

> meeting without people stopping to express their concern about the Sisters' leaving. It is very humbling to see grown men with tears in their eyes . . .
>
> I know that 'for those who love God, all things work together unto good,' and the pain and sacrifice have been so great, only a great good can result . . . God is doing something new. It will be wonderful like everything else He does . . .(132)

This faith-filled, yet disappointed, attitude characterized the pastor, Monsignor Edmund Cody, Bishop Sylvester Treinen, the sisters, and the people of St. Edward's. Their shock at the possible loss of their school caused them to put forth many alternatives, such as dropping the seventh and eighth grades, thus requiring only four sisters. The bottom line was to seek a reconsideration of the Congregation's decision and to express their deep concern that their children would be without a Catholic education. (133) But, the Congregation did not see a reversal of its decision as possible.

The final group of sisters at St. Edward's included Sister Kathleen Kelley, superior, Sister Mary Zita Cossack, principal, Sister Monique Dissen, Sister Myles Boyd and Sister Maria Goretti Timperio.

In 1977 Sister Bernita and Sister Mary Zita returned for a six-week summer session. Their ministry included religious instructions, visiting the sick of the parish and taking the census. Sister Bernita had been stationed at St. Edward's for nineteen years, in six of those she served as principal; Sister Mary Zita was there for ten years, serving as principal in the last two years of the school's existence. Reverend Perry W. Dodds, a former student and graduate of St. Edward's, was pastor in 1977. His joy at having the sisters back, even for the summer, was unbounded. His appreciation was expressed as follows:

> I can only capsulate my feelings by saying that I have never seen in my eighteen years in the priesthood such an outpouring of affection on the part of a people toward sisters . . . We were absolutely overjoyed at the prospect that the Sisters would be able to return next summer—that a summer program in Twin Falls could be viewed as an on-going apostolate. (134)

This summer ministry at Twin Falls continued until the summer of 1985 with various sisters in different summers accompanying Sister Bernita, among them Sister Immaculata Norton, Sister Maria Goretti Timperio, Sister Mary Rassley, Sister Johanna Antenner, and Sister Greta Collins.

Our Lady of Perpetual Help Elementary School, Rocky Mount, North Carolina

It is always a challenge to capture the flavor and spirit of a particular geographical locale in which the Congregation has chosen to minister. This is particularly true of the South, unless one has personally spent some time there, or can make the history come alive by providing a background or context.

Rocky Mount, the city, is in the eastern part of the State of North Carolina, being known, in fact, as the "Gateway to Eastern North Carolina." It is built on the famous "Tobacco Trail," the shortest route between Maine and Florida. The Rocky Mount tobacco market is famous, but other southern products such as corn and cotton are also successfully cultivated.

In 1939, Rocky Mount had an estimated population of 28,000, with only 145 of these Catholics. Yet, as early as 1892 the Sacrifice of the Mass was celebrated in Rocky Mount in the private home of a Catholic family. By 1910 the first church and rectory for Our Lady of Perpetual Help Parish were constructed on Franklin Street at the site of the present school hall and sixth and seventh grade classrooms. With so few Catholics in the town it is at first surprising to note that there was a second Catholic Church in the town, Immaculate Conception Church for the blacks. This church was dedicated December 23, 1942, and its first pastor was Reverend Joseph A. Ellison, CSsR. At its opening there were only about seven Catholic families in attendance. When one recalls the deep historical antagonism that existed between southern blacks and whites, the fact of separate churches is not surprising. (135)

In spite of the small number of Catholics, Monsignor Peter McNerney, pastor of Our Lady of Perpetual Help Parish, resolved to establish a Catholic school. Early in 1939, therefore, he applied to Mother Josepha for sisters and when he was assured that he would receive them, he set about obtaining property to house the new project. A large, stately, typical southern mansion, the Brewer estate, at 328 Hammond Street became available for purchase at this time at a cost of six thousand dollars. By today's standards this price was practically a gift, but even this small amount represented a large debt for the tiny parish. Without assistance from a group calling themselves the "Northern Friends of the Southern Missions" and an immediate gift of one thousand dollars from the Catholic Daughters of America for furnishing of the building which was to serve as both school and convent, the little parish could never have supported this ambitious project. (136)

The presence of the Blessed Sacrament completed the joy the sisters were experiencing in their beautifully remodeled convent home. "Our apartment is fitted out in a style quite foreign to monastic simplicity, but in excellent taste. So it won't bother us too much," wrote Sister Sergius to Mother Josepha. " . . . I know I have not done justice to its description, but I have not seen anything like it before in the South." (137)

September 5, 1939, was the official opening date of the school. Thirty-three children from kindergarten through fifth grade were registered. There was at first some reluctance of families to send their children to the "unknown" school; it would have to prove itself first through its students gaining recognition in competitive academic events, and in gaining acceptance of its graduates into the next higher educational level in the public schools. But, for the saintly pastor, Monsignor McNerney, and for the sisters, it was reward enough to witness the Palm Sunday Confirmation of seventeen youngsters and the First Holy Communion ceremony of eight.

When school opened on Labor Day 1940, the enrollment had grown to 52 pupils. With few exceptions, the families of these children paid a small tuition of about five dollars per month. Music lessons were in great demand, as students wished to be part of the Thanksgiving, Christmas and spring performances which drew large audiences of parents, friends and neighbors, most of whom were protestant. "The work is progressing, slow but sure, [sic] each public performance makes a wider circle of admirers and the June recital finds all available space occupied." (138) In addition to these programs, Sister Redempta Doudican conducted the kindergarten and developed a junior choir which, building on the work started by Sister Adalbert (Mary) Schelb in the summer of 1939, was well trained and able to sing the major parts of the Mass in Latin, for the Sunday liturgies.

The highlight of the month of October 1940 was the visit of Mother Josepha to the South. It was her first and last visit to Rocky Mount, and it must have been a journey taken out of deep love for her sisters laboring so far from "home," for already the illness which would claim her in less than two months had made its painful inroads in her body. Knowing how ill she had been for several months, the sisters must have indeed appreciated her visit to them. What she witnessed in the labors of the sisters was the fruit of her great "yes" to the call to minister in these southern missions. She saw the high standard of performance being attained by the students; and the melting antagonistic attitudes through the sisters' patience and kindness. It was a fact, as Sister Sergius had described it to Mother Josepha, that "We continue to be a 'laughing stock' for the people who see us for the first time; once we were 'cussed at,' but generally, people are more and more courteous and friendly." (139)

By 1947 the enrollment had grown to 74; 34 boys and 40 girls. There were 36 music students. Evidence of the impact of the sisters was seen in the converts numbering fifteen.

The parish had outgrown the little white church on Franklin Street by 1950. So, after two years of anticipation in watching the plans turn into reality, the present red brick structure was erected. The solemn blessing took place on November 12, 1952. The new church provided also some temporary expansion space for the school as the kindergarten was moved from the old Brewer house to the auditorium of the church. (140) All signs pointed to the need for a new school also, so 1956 became the year in which a fund drive was launched for this purpose. Pledges of $73,000 over a three-year period were made by the parishioners, and even the school children raised $322. Encouraged by this cooperation, Reverend Charles B. McLaughlin, pastor, entered upon this second building project. The groundbreaking for the new school took place on October 23, 1956.

This kind of faith-filled forging ahead in providing Catholic education in the South was quite courageous in light of the fact that the impact of the May 31, 1955, Supreme Court decision regarding racial integration of the schools was not yet clear. Mother of Perpetual Help School had already, in September 1955, experienced the withdrawal of the children of twenty white families when two black students were accepted. Only two of the twenty families were Catholic, but it provided a hint of things to come and pointed to the need for extensive education of the people in preparation for a future which would include broader integration. (141) In actual fact, the application of black children to the school was so gradual, only three applied by 1958-1959, that no further unpleasant incidents are recorded.

Development went forward on all fronts with the complete renovation of the convent, landscaping of its yard with lawn and shrubs, and the completion of the new school. September 15, 1957, was a banner day on which the school was blessed and dedicated by Bishop Vincent S. Waters. High Mass was sung by the school children; Monsignor Edward T. Gilbert, then superintendent of schools for the Raleigh Diocese, preached the sermon. Among the visiting communities of religious who were present were: The Oblate Sisters and the Sisters of Divine Providence from Wilson, North Carolina; Precious Blood Sisters from Kinston; Mercy Sisters from Jacksonville; Dominicans from Raleigh; and IHMs from Goldsboro, New Bern, and Raleigh. It was a spirited occasion for the little community of sisters at Our Lady of Perpetual Help that year: Sister Donelda Fox, superior and principal; Sister Honor Lenihan, Sister Melissa Hester, and Sister Marie Elise Regan. (142)

In the spring of 1963 news came of the transfer of Reverend Charles B. McLaughlin, pastor, to St. Leo's Church, Winston-Salem, North Carolina. What was not known then became clear a year later when on April 15, 1964, Father McLaughlin was consecrated Auxiliary Bishop of Raleigh to assist Bishop Waters. Bishop McLaughlin was later to become Bishop of St. Petersburg, Florida.

Reverend James Jones served as administrator of Our Lady of Perpetual Help Parish for several months until the appointment of Reverend Thomas F. Kerin in September 1963. So much development had occurred in the parish under the fifteen-year pastorate of Father McLaughlin that Father Kerin, in his four-year pastorate, was not faced with any major physical plant problems. However, by 1972, under the pastorate of Reverend John Weidinger, permission was obtained from Bishop Waters to demolish the Brewer estate convent and build a new one. This meant that the sisters would move into a rented house until the completion of the new convent. A two-bedroom house for this purpose was located at 1305 West Thomas Street, about two miles from the church and school. The brief description of the August 1972 activity states simply: "The week of August 28, 1972, found the sisters packing, involved in faculty meetings, beginning school (August 30), moving into their rented home (August 31), and greeting their first visitors, the sisters from Washington, North Carolina." (143)

The new convent was ready for occupancy on May 18, 1973, and open house was held for the parishioners on May 27. It was not until Easter, the following April, that all of the furnishings for the chapel were complete. A parishioner, Mr. Terinelli, had made the main altar and Sister Babette Opferman's woodcarvings were mounted on the altars and lector stand. The statue of the Blessed Virgin Mary was a gift from our sisters in Washington, North Carolina, when they closed their convent. After Easter the official "open house" of the new convent was held. As it happened, only Sister Honor Lenihan, Sister Leonette Bower and Sister Dorothy Lyons, of the sisters who had previously been stationed at Our Lady of Perpetual Help, were able to be present for the celebration. The local community included Sister Patricia Mary Gallagher, superior, Sister Carol Loughney, Sister Ann Parker, and Sister Elizabeth Bullen.

The new convent was designated as the location of one of the Congregation's formal summerhouses of prayer that year. Sister Kathleen Newett was in charge of the summer program that opened on June 17, 1974.

With the new convent completed, it was as if Father Weidinger's work was complete. He had served as the only resident priest in Rocky Mount, and in spite of his seventy-six years had accomplished much for the parish. However, it was evident that more and more frequently other priests from outside the area were being called upon to render needed liturgical services. He retired on November 1, 1975. Reverend Robert Lawson was appointed pastor. (144)

There were 200 pupils registered for the 1977-1978 school year. Twenty-two years with much growth had passed since the "new" school was built. For a time, the seventh and eighth grades were dropped because of low enrollment, but the desire was to have a seventh grade once again. So, in 1979-1980, parish needs and school needs were met in a combined facility, which would house the sixth and seventh grades and the parish hall. This modern building is air-conditioned and is the envy of the other classes during the hot weather.

June of 1980 was especially memorable for one person, namely, Sister Dorothy Welsh, who had completed two years at Rocky Mount as fourth grade teacher and advisor to the Elder Adult Group of the parish. She was being transferred to Lourdes Community at the IHM Generalate in Scranton. These two years at Rocky Mount brought her service in the Raleigh Diocese to a total of twenty-six years. (145)

There is great pride in the parishioners and the children of OLPH in their school. *The Sunday Telegram* of February 3, 1985, ran a full-page article on the school, citing the fact that each teacher is fully certified and that the school itself is accredited both by the NCEA and by the State of North Carolina. Besides the emphasis on basics in education, it was noted that the school has a computer system, music, band and art programs, as well as a supervised after school program which provides for children whose parents cannot pick them up until 5:30 p.m. each school day. The article also quotes a mother of two students whose comment was, "There is a lot more to our school than academics. The child here develops self-confidence because he is in a comfortable environment where everyone is working together. You can see it on the playground where the older children look after the younger ones. It is the spirit here. It's lots of love." (146)

An enrollment of 239 students was recorded for 1986-1987 as this vibrant school continues under the able leadership of Sister Mary Mark Lowery, principal, Sister Myra Gilbart, superior, Sister Joyce Marks and Sister Maria Goretti Timperio. (147)

St. Agnes Elementary School, Washington, North Carolina

"Little Washington," North Carolina, was not unknown territory to the Sisters, Servants of the Immaculate Heart of Mary, since we were already well established there, having accepted Mother of Mercy School in 1927 in order to provide for the religious education of black children. It is an interesting historic fact that the blacks had their own church and school at that time and the white population, of which there were few practicing Catholics, worshipped in a small room which was the chapel in Mother of Mercy Convent, but had no Catholic school.

During the summer of 1929, Bishop William J. Hafey bought a home on North Market Street and Tenth which was to be the future convent for our sisters in Mother of Mercy Parish. The sisters moved into this home on June 25, 1930. Their former convent became St. Agnes School for white children.

Meanwhile, also, white Catholics moved into a church of their own which was dedicated October 13, 1929, by Bishop Hafey. The church was named St. Agnes Church and was built as a memorial to Mrs. John Cogan of Brooklyn, New York, mother of Reverend John Cogan, a former classmate of Bishop Hafey's at Mount St. Mary's, Emmitsburg, Maryland. The Cogan family took an on-going interest in the little church over the years. St. Agnes Church was one of several missions of Mother of Mercy Parish, having no pastor of its own until September 1931 when Reverend Edward T. Gilbert was appointed resident pastor.

As superintendent of Catholic schools in Eastern North Carolina, Father Gilbert had seen much evidence of the relationship of growth in Catholicism to the establishment of Catholic schools. So, after several years, in the spring of 1939, he sent a request to Mother Josepha for one sister to come to St. Agnes to open a kindergarten, and thus begin a school that would add a grade each year, if conditions warranted its continuance. This realistic approach was based on the fact of the small size of the white Catholic congregation at St. Agnes at the time. Mother Josepha responded by sending Sister Gioia de Zerman to begin the kindergarten at St. Agnes Academy in September 1939, and to reside with the IHM Sisters at Mother of Mercy Convent.

The classroom was located in the rectory building. Four pupils were enrolled that first year. Sister Gioia's enthusiasm and expertise worked wonders in the town of "Little Washington," causing the school's reputation to spread and attracting new students. It is said that since the school had no hall or stage, entertainments were given by the children on the porch where they were visible to all passers-by. Especially noted was the entertainment given in June when the little kindergarteners had their commencement exercises in caps and gowns. This had the town talking for a week following the event! (148)

When the sisters returned for school in September 1940 and Sister Gioia was not among them, great sorrow and consternation resulted. Sister Rosalind Doyle had been sent in her place. Father Gilbert, pastor, wasted no time in expressing his thoughts on the matter in writing to Mother Josepha:

> . . . Sister Gioia did good work here. It is regrettable that you found it necessary to make a change for we, who know the great difficulties confronting the Church in the South and are familiar with southern mentality, are convinced that real, steady progress will be made only when the same talented workers are allowed to remain in the field to combat daily those devastating forces which the weapons forged and sharpened alone by experience can subdue. (149)

It was not that Father Gilbert did not appreciate Sister Rosalind, but it is evident that he would have been more comfortable with someone he had come to know over the previous year, and was aware of the impact such change would have on the school. However, in September 1940 there was an increase in both kindergarten and first grade enrollment. By the following year, the enrollment continued to grow. Mother Josepha showed her support of this very small seedling mission by adding Sister Laurana Burns to the faculty for first and second grades, thus allowing Sister Rosalind to devote full time to the kindergarten. Sister Rosalind was transferred in 1941, being replaced by Sister Rosalie Martin.

Nineteen forty-three to 1944 was called a "banner year" because an enrollment of fifty-five pupils in four grades was recorded. Sister Laurana was transferred, but Sister Gioia returned and Sister Teresa Clare McAuliffe arrived for third and fourth grades.

Sister Teresa Clare recalls that although the number of pupils was small, they were very active in regional and state-wide musical and oratorical contests, very often bringing back awards. Father Gilbert set high standards, as did the sisters. The parents entered actively into what was going on in the school; many came to observe every Friday afternoon when "open house" was held at the school. (150)

By the following year, 1944-1945, Father Gilbert, witnessing an enrollment of sixty-three pupils, and supported by Bishop McGuiness' desire to see a free-standing Catholic school building for white children in Washington, North Carolina, began solicitation of funds for this purpose. (151) He must have known that the school would have a much larger enrollment by the time he would be financially able to put up the new building, for, indeed it was 1956 before the new K-8 grade school was built. (152) By then Monsignor Gilbert had been pastor in Goldsboro for four years.

In August 1945, Father Gilbert moved into a lean-to room off the garage while building a two-room cinder block dwelling to serve as a rectory. Thus, the second floor of the former rectory, now St. Agnes Academy, was made available as the convent for the sisters teaching at St. Agnes. (153) The racial problem being what it was in those days, it was meaningful to St. Agnes Academy to have its own sisters, "the white Sisters," as separate from the so-called "black Sisters," the IHMs serving at Mother of Mercy.

In 1956-1957 there were four sisters at St. Agnes Convent for the first time. These were Sister Maria Dominic McDonald, who taught kindergarten; Sister Moya (Joan) Ciraula, first and second grades; Sister Justine (Audrey) McHale, third, fourth and fifth; Sister Geralda, sixth, seventh and eighth. Sister Geralda, as superior and principal, must have welcomed the coming of Sister Maria Dominic to relieve her of the kindergarten duties that she had also previously carried. (154)

September 1958 saw the entrance of Jane Hardison into religious life in the IHM Congregation. Jane had graduated from St. Agnes in 1954 and had completed her last three years of high school at Washington High School. Much joy prevailed over her entrance especially since she was the first religious vocation from St. Agnes.

The biggest change in the thirty-three years of existence of St. Agnes School occurred with the opening of the1963-1964 school year. This can best be described by the sisters of Mother of Mercy Convent who experienced it:

> . . . For the first time, our neighbors next door, the Sisters of St. Agnes Convent, would not be with us. For the first time there would be one pastor of all Catholics in Washington, and for the first time the Catholic school would be integrated. (155)

The new pastor was Reverend James R. Jones and the Mother of Mercy local community that was to manage the integration and merger of St. Agnes and Mother of Mercy included Sister Nadine Moran, superior and principal, Sister Vincent de Paul Bonanza, Sister St. Laurence (Loretta) Mulry, Sister Paschal Fitzgibbon, Sister Karen Marie O'Neill and Sister Redempta Sweeney. Their commentary demonstrates their awareness of the historical importance of this step toward integration and of the potential for difficulty involved in the process. The annals report as follows:

> In most places integration is a process of sprinkling a few Negroes [sic] among the established white society. But not so

> here! When registration was completed the grade school tallied forty-nine Negroes and seven whites, and the high school, seventeen Negroes and six whites . . . When you consider our integration of whites into an established Negro institution, then we feel that as small as it was, it was highly successful. (156)

It was decided to move all of the grade school classes to St. Agnes Grade School and while Mother of Mercy High School was being renovated, to utilize the former St. Agnes Convent for the high school classes. Transporting desks and equipment from one building to another was no easy task.

By Holy Week in the spring 1964, integration was becoming more visible in the church also. All the services were held at Mother of Mercy Church, with some of the white teenagers joining in with the black choir of Mother of Mercy. Evidence of the good will of the people of St. Agnes is seen in their invitation to the sisters of Mother of Mercy to attend a Communion breakfast with the St. Agnes Guild on May 3. "Left without what they considered 'their Sisters,' they adopted us 'colored Sisters' and proved themselves very hospitable company." (157)

Registration improved over the next few years, totaling 113 pupils in 1968. However, as the public schools gradually became integrated also, many of the non-Catholic students left because of tuition costs, athletic opportunities, or a variety of other reasons. When, in 1972-1973 the enrollment dropped to 69 pupils, the Congregation decided to withdraw the Sisters from Washington, North Carolina. The high school had already closed in 1969. The merged St. Agnes/Mother of Mercy School closed on May 30, 1973. The four sisters serving there at the time were Sister Edith Marie (Patricia) Smith, Sister St. Francis Lyons, Sister Eileen Egan and Sister Angela Mary Parker. Writing to these sisters, Bishop Vincent S. Waters noted the nineteen years of service of our sisters at St. Agnes prior to its integration with Mother of Mercy and summed up the "Little Washington" experience, saying,

> We see you leave us now with much sadness, yet we know that in addition to the fine curricular studies you imparted to our children, they also received from you cultural opportunities which extended themselves to drama and music. Most important of all was the religious instruction they received in the Faith, which we hope will always live on with them. (158)

St. Francis Elementary School, Munhall, Pennsylvania

St. Francis was the fifth school to be accepted in the Diocese of Pittsburgh, Pennsylvania, by the Sisters, Servants of the Immaculate Heart of Mary. The pastor, Reverend Charles Moosman, made his request through Sister Alma Shelley, then superior and principal at Hays, Pennsylvania.

The Sisters of Divine Providence who had staffed the fifty-year-old St. Francis School for over thirty years were withdrawn in June 1939. Although the enrollment was quite small, it was the pastor's hope that this would change and that some of the attitudes, which had prevailed on the part of various ethnic groups toward this historically German parish, could gradually be altered. The many nationalities in this section could have been an enriching factor, but served, rather, to divide the people and caused competitiveness rather than cooperation.

Into this setting came three of our sisters—Sister Edwin Ott, to serve as superior and principal, Sister Jamesine Hopkins and Sister Honorine Walsh. School opened on September 5, 1939, with some forty-nine pupils registered in all grades except seventh, for which there were no pupils. One of the factors in the low enrollment was certainly that of distance, since most of the children came from surrounding towns and from other parishes, such as Whittaker, Homeville, and Homestead Park, and had to come by bus or other transportation. Many parents were unwilling or unable to pay the daily cost of transportation to and from St. Francis School.

The training which the children had received from the prior community of sisters was evident in their general responsiveness to the sisters, and especially notable in their ability to sing the High Mass every morning, as well as Benediction on Friday and Sunday evenings. There seemed to be an atmosphere of unrelieved burdensomeness, however, in the brief observations recorded: "There was no formal opening . . . We do not have a program of any kind for pupils graduating from the eighth grade. Certificates of graduation, medals, etc. are awarded in the classrooms." (159) The implication is that this is the way it had been, and perhaps was the way the pastor wanted it. It seems, however, that Father Moosman was very gracious to the sisters and provided well for both school and convent: "Both are quite comfortable and very well cared for," wrote Sister Edwin to Mother Josepha. (160) Our presence at St. Francis, Munhall, was to be short-lived in any case. As early as December 1943, Mother Marcella sounded the first notice of the Congregation's intent as she wrote to Father Moosman:

> . . . Your registration runs about fifty pupils. In some of our large schools a Sister has sixty or seventy in one grade. For this reason I am anxious to withdraw the Sisters from St. Francis School at the close of this school year, but I will take no further action until I hear from you again. I would hesitate to do this if I felt the children would be deprived of a Catholic school education, but since there are other parochial schools in the neighborhood who could easily accommodate this number, I feel you might be glad to be relieved of the worry and expense of a school at this time. (161)

Several exchanges of letters between Father Moosmann and Mother Marcella followed in January, February and March 1944. Father Moosmann continued hopeful that after the war (World War II, 1939-1944) conditions for families would improve and that his parish would experience new growth. Yet, he acknowledged that "we are sure of only three for September, and perhaps a few others who are not of the parish." (162) By return mail, Mother Marcella reiterated her belief that the sisters should be withdrawn. (163)

Father Moosmann must have received great pressure from the people, especially from those parents having children in the school, for in March he again made an earnest plea for reconsideration of the decision. This heart-breaking appeal revealed that he had come to understand that the people felt it was his fault that the sisters were being withdrawn because of his harsh attitude toward the school children. "Perhaps that is true," he wrote, "since there is so little cooperation in the homes . . . My intentions were good. Since the war, children get less attention at home from parents as to religion, and even before, it was not overly much . . . Thus it did overwork my nerves trying to overcome this indifference and lukewarmness on the part of parents and children, but I intended no harm." (164)

His last point was to make known the fact that he expected to be changed from St. Francis Parish soon, and that the school and parishioners should be given another chance under the direction of a younger priest. This touching letter called forth a warm, concerned response from Mother Marcella who wrote:

> Dear Father, my only reason for withdrawing the Sisters was the small number of children in the school who, I thought, could be cared for in neighboring schools. I have never heard critical remarks from Sisters or people regarding you. Far from blaming

> you, I have often pitied you for the struggle you have in trying to keep your school.
>
> After reading your letter I could not refuse your request. I shall be glad to leave the Sisters with you for another year . . . (165)

Over the ensuing years efforts were made by the Congregation and by Reverend Thomas J. Quigley, PhD, superintendent of schools for the Diocese of Pittsburgh, to bring about a merger of area ethnic schools, but this was never brought about because it was not the wish of the people.

The problem of low enrollment continued, and Father Moosmann continued as pastor of St. Francis Parish. The IHM Sisters completed not only 1944-1945, but also 1945-1946 under these conditions. A final letter expressing our regret at leaving, and encouraging Father Moosmann to have the parents place their children in nearby Catholic schools, was sent by Mother Marcella in May 1946. (166)

Thus ended the brief seven year history of our Sisters at St. Francis, Munhall, Pennsylvania.

St. Ignatius Catechetical School, Kingston, Pennsylvania

Little did Mother Josepha realize when she decided to open a catechetical school at St. Ignatius, Kingston, Pennsylvania, in 1940 that except for the seven years between 1977-1984, this ministry would continue to thrive into the present (1987)—over four decades later.

Reverend J. J. McGuckin was pastor of St. Ignatius Parish and the Mission Chapel of St. Ann's in Kingston at the time. He had become pastor in 1938, but in the short five years before his death on December 6, 1943, he would make a lasting imprint on St. Ignatius' Parish, especially in its growth in physical facilities to serve the youth of the parish. He purchased the former Black Diamond American Legion Post Home on Market Street as a recreation center. St. Ignatius Community Hall, as it was called, was a vibrant center, not only because of its athletic programs, especially the bowling teams, but especially because it provided space for the development of an excellent scouting program.

It was Father McGuckin who directed the renovation of St. Ignatius Church and advised the Scranton Diocese in the purchase of the huge John Vaughan estate at Vaughan's Corners, Kingston, which he had planned to develop as an orphanage or foundling home. Later, instead, it was converted into a public park and opened to the use of the general public. In 1940 he purchased the former Newell Homestead at 840 Market Street, Kingston, as the residence for the Sisters, Servants of the

Immaculate Heart of Mary.

It had been his dream, as it had been also a dream of pastors who preceded him, to one day have a Catholic school in St. Ignatius Parish. Land had been purchased for this purpose as far back as 1905 in the pastorate of Reverend M. E. Lynott. This property was held for twenty-one years, and then was sold in March 1926. Later, Father Lynott purchased a parcel of land on Maple Street, opposite the church, with the intent that one day a school would be erected there. It would be 1954 before this land would, indeed, be used as the site of a school, West Side Central Catholic High School.

But, on September 6, 1940, with the coming of the Sisters of IHM, to open "The St. Ignatius Catechetical School of Kingston, Pennsylvania" and a kindergarten, it was clear that a parish grade school was not in the plan for the immediate future, if ever. The first group of sisters were: Sister Alphonsus McGoldrick, superior, Sister Theresa Gabriel Dolan, Sister Rose Francis Brown, music instructor, Sister Carina McCaffrey and Sister Helaine O'Dea.

It did not take this excellent group of teachers long to organize an outstanding program of religious education. One account states, "As catechists the Sisters of the Immaculate Heart of Mary established an enviable reputation that had a most effective influence on the parish." (167)

In addition to religious instruction for grade and high school level youngsters in the afternoons and evenings, there was regular instruction in liturgical singing. Over seven hundred young people were involved in these classes. Gradually, a lending library of religious books was built up; a glee club and a dramatic club were formed; retreats were offered at the convent by a priest to area women; adult converts were instructed; a parish census was taken and a kindergarten established! Most of these activities took place in St. Ignatius Convent in the first year, but in September 1941, the school board of the Pringle and Larksville School Districts granted permission to the sisters to hold catechetical classes in the public school building at 3:30 p.m. This gave many school children living at a distance from the convent the opportunity to attend religion classes.

A Eucharistic Congress of the Diocese of Scranton was held in May 1941 at Wyoming Seminary Stadium. All decorations were taken care of by the sisters, in addition to preparing the children to participate in the ceremonies. Sister Rose Francis prepared the children for the Mass and procession, singing and directing the assembled group for the occasion. One hundred eighty-three sisters and all the clergy who attended were served dinner in the convent. (168)

Sister Maria Thomas Harrington succeeded Sister Alphonsus McGoldrick in 1943. In that year, too, the pastor, Father McGuckin, died on December 6. Reverend Martin F. Boylan served as interim administrator until Reverend Joseph S. Gaigon was appointed pastor. The involvement of the sisters in the life of the parish and in the activities of the youth was really remarkable, considering that their contacts were on a part-time basis. In 1943-1944, for example, the high school students put on three one-act plays for the public, and even took their performance to St. Michael's Industrial School in Hoban Heights.

This same year a Day of Recollection was begun for members of the senior class. It was given annually on one of the Sundays during May and was held at the convent. Father Gaigon conducted the retreat day, or had a Passionist, Maryknoll, or Holy Cross priest in for the day. Appproximately forty students attended this retreat each year. The youngsters took an active role in raising funds for their lending library, which shortly had over 700 books. They also were devoted to the support of the missions. During Catholic book week each year they distributed pamphlets and posters in places of business, in the public library and in the main waiting room of Nesbitt Hospital. Trips were arranged by the sisters for the high school students who wished to visit Catholic colleges such as Catholic University of America, Villanova and Marywood College. Formal dances were scheduled by the catechetical school in order to provide opportunities for Catholic young people to meet, and also to have the sisters become better known in this very non-Catholic area. (169) The enthusiasm that prevailed is evident in Sister Maria Thomas' account. It is obvious, too, that the work most precious to the hearts of the sisters was that of preparing the children for the reception of the sacraments:

> We have brought into the Church ten families within the past three years. This was accomplished through the instruction of the children. Besides these families, five adult converts have come into the Church and about nine children between the ages of ten and fourteen have made their First Holy Communion in our convent chapel during the course of the year. This, of course, is apart from our regular Communion class which usually numbers 80-90 annually. (170)

Spurred on by the pronouncements of the popes regarding the value of Catholic education, Bishop William J. Hafey was determined to establish a Catholic high school in the Kingston area. Father Gaigon, as pastor of St. Ignatius Parish, was most supportive of the idea because of the distance his parishioners had to travel to a Catholic high school. Having obtained approval of the Kingston Borough Board of Adjustors at a public hearing on January 16, 1952, construction work soon began at the corner of North Maple Avenue and Hoyt Street on the land purchased in 1926 by Monsignor M. E. Lynott. Upon the school's completion it was named West Side Central Catholic High School and its newly appointed principal, Reverend Edward L. Collins, STL, took charge on June 24, 1954.

The history of this high school has been ably written by Sister Zita Maria Kane, IHM, in a work entitled "Bishop O'Reilly High School, Kingston, Pennsylvania, 1954-1980." No further account of it will be given here except to note that the opening of the high school added new life to St. Ignatius Convent with the coming of five additional IHM Sisters. These included: Sister Joseph Marie McGraw, who was to serve as prefect of studies at the high school; Sister Miriam Therese Rihn, director of music; Sister Marita Gill, Sister Venarda (Mary) Wren and Sister Angelisse Boyce. They were part of a faculty which included three Mercy Sisters, two each of the Bernardine, Christian Charity and Cyril and Methodius communities, three lay teachers and four part-time priests in addition to Father Collins, principal. (171)

Work at the catchetical school continued for all Catholic children attending public school. Sister Benedictus Philpott came as superior in 1955, remaining until 1960, at which time Sister St. Teresa Healy was appointed. In addition to Sister St. Teresa, two sisters continued to staff the catechetical school, Sister Damian Howley and Sister St. Andrew Connor until 1965-1966, when Sister Paschal FitzGibbon replaced Sister Damian. Other sisters who served the Kingston Catechetical School were Sister Paulette Morrison, Sister Cecilia Kielty, Sister Gonzales McGowan, Sister Celestina Langan, Sister Dolores Mary McErlean, Sister Edwardine Travers, Sister Muriel Whalen and Sister Miriam Catherine Corcoran. In 1972 Sister Maris Law was appointed director of religious education and coordinated lay teachers in the religious education classes. This continued through 1976-1977, but sister was not replaced in 1977-1978 because of the shortage of sister personnel. At the request of Monsignor James T. Clarke, pastor of St. Ignatius Church, our sisters again took up this work. Sister Norita Corrigan assumed the position of director of religious education for the parish in 1984-1985. (172)

In addition to the fruitfulness of the ministries of our sisters at St. Ignatius Convent, there has been an added gift to the Church in the fact of forty-four religious vocations, fourteen priests and thirty sisters to seven congregations, including five to the Sisters of the Immaculate Heart of Mary. (173)

Mother M. Josepha Hurley

Early in January 1938, the symptoms of the illness that was to make the last years of Mother Josepha's life a veritable martyrdom began to make themselves felt. Mother bore her sufferings silently and with heroic fortitude and during the intervals between the attacks tried to carry on her work as usual, especially the visitation of the schools. (174)

Her last visitation, as was noted earlier, was made to the schools in the South. Soon after her return on November 24, she grew rapidly worse, and on Friday, November 29, 1940, she received the last sacraments. A few days before her death, Bishop William J. Hafey visited her and, in consoling her, spoke of the heavy burden she had borne as mother superior of the Congregation. Her response was characteristically honest and humorous, ''Yes, the work has been hard, but I've had lots of fun, too." (175)

Her Christmas letters to the Congregation revealed her beautiful simplicity and her desire to encourage humility, simplicity, sacrifice and fidelity among the sisters. (176) These virtues closely paralleled those which she herself possessed to a very high degree.

One writer said of Mother Josepha:

> Throughout her long life as a religious Mother M. Josepha has been an indefatigable worker, distinguished in particular for gentleness and generosity. She was an exemplary religious, a great-hearted, whole-souled, womanly woman, respected by her associates, revered by her Sisters, and universally loved by the children in the many schools of her community. (177)

The funeral Mass for Mother Josepha was celebrated in the chapel at the Marywood Motherhouse on the eve of the Feast of the Immaculate Conception of Our Lady. Most Reverend William J. Hafey, Bishop of Scranton, pontificated. The sermon was preached by Monsignor Martin J. O'Connor, then pastor of St. Peter's Cathedral in Scranton and vicar general of the Diocese. Mother Josepha, in her humility, would have been embarrassed at the words of praise of her which were spoken by so many, and written in cards and letters to the Congregation administrators by hundreds more, letters from civic and church officials, religious congregations, from businessmen, friends, students—all of whom felt that they had lost a friend. But two things she would have appreciated, and perhaps even deemed appropriate, in all her simplicity: first was the fact that the theme selected for the sermon of her funeral Mass was taken from the Act of Consecration to God which she had spoken on her profession day: "Behold, My God, I am entirely Thine." (178) In August of 1904 she had pronounced these words that had come to full reality for her on December 4, 1940, as she placed her life before her God. She would have approved of the focus on these words instead of on herself.

Loving the sisters as she did, Mother Josepha would have appreciated also the fact that she was laid to rest among them. She was buried at the feet of the beautiful statue of Our Lady that she had arranged to have erected a short time before in the sisters' plot at St. Catherine's Cemetery, Moscow, Pennsylvania. (179)

References

1. Record of visitation and elections written by Rev. Martin J. O'Connor as witness. August 5, 1931. Archives, IHM Generalate.
2. Ibid.
3. *Constitutions and Rule of the Sisters, Servants of the Immaculate Heart of Mary, Scranton.* (1890 Edition) Archives, IHM Generalate.
4. Notes of Sister Immaculata Gillespie. Archives, IHM Generalate.
5. Letter from Mother M. Josepha Hurley to the Sisters of IHM, Christmas, 1931. Archives, IHM Generalate.
6. Notes of Sister Immaculata Gillespie. Archives, IHM Generalate.
7. Letters from Mining Engineers to Bishop O'Reilly, 1932-1937. Archives, IHM Generalate.
8. Letter from Mr. J. Rossa McCormick to Bishop O'Reilly, September 13, 1932. Archives, IHM Generalate.
9. Contract between Mr. Severin Sekol and Mother M. Josepha as President of Marywood College, March 13, 1933. Archives, IHM Generalate.
10. Ibid.
11. Letter from Cadwalloder Evans, Jr. of the Hudson Coal Company to Stanley J. Davis, Mayor, City of Scranton, August 13, 1937. Archives, IHM Generalate.
12. Letter from Mother M. Josepha to Mr. H. A. Connolly, Pennsylvania Coal Company, October 10, 1939. Archives, IHM Generalate.
13. Contract between Professor Gonippo Raggi and the Sisters, Servants of IHM, Marywood College, November 22, 1933. Archives, IHM Generalate.
14. Letter from Mother M. Josepha to Bishop O'Reilly, September 1935. Archives, IHM Generalate.
15. Letters from Professor Gonippo Raggi to Mother Josepha, July 30, 1937 and May 9, 1938. Archives, IHM Generalate.
16. Letter from Professor Gonippo Raggi to Mother Josepha, March 9, 1937. Archives, IHM Generalate.
17. Notes of Sister Immaculata Gillespie. Archives, IHM Generalate.
18. Letter from Rev. Ignatius Fealy, Pastor, St. Agnes Church, Baltimore, to Mother Josepha Hurley, Superior General, August 13, 1933. Archives, IHM Generalate.
19. School Contract, September 1, 1933 signed by Rev. Ignatius Fealy and Mother M. Josepha. Archives, IHM Generalate.
20. Letter from Father Fealy to Mother Josepha, September 1, 1933. Archives, IHM Generalate.
21. Letter from Father Fealy to Mother Josepha, September 12, 1933. Archives, IHM Generalate.

22. Ibid.
23. Notes of Sister Immaculata Gillespie. Archives, IHM Generalate.
24. Letter from Father Fealy to Mother Josepha, January 24, 1934. Archives, IHM Generalate.
25. Letter from Mother Josepha to Father Fealy, February 3, 1934. Archives, IHM Generalate.
26. Letter from Father Fealy to Mother Josepha, August 1, 1934. Archives, IHM Generalate.
27. Letter from Father Fealy to Mother Josepha, July 6, 1936. Archives, IHM Generalate.
28. Letter of Mother Josepha to Father Fealy, July 19, 1936. Archives, IHM Generalate.
29. Annals of St. Agnes Convent, Woodlawn, Maryland, 1955-1965. Archlves, IHM Generalate.
30. Statistics from the Office of the Director of Apostolic Planning, 1986-1987. IHM Generalate.
31. Gallagher, Rev. John P., PhD. *A Century of History*, 1968. pp. 74-76.
32. Golden Jubilee Booklet, Church of the Nativity of Our Lord, 1903-1953, pp 13-55.
33. Notes of Sister Immaculata Gillespie. Archives, IHM Generalate.
34. Golden Jubilee: Booklet, op. cit., pp. 62-66.
35. Notes of Sister M. Brigida Strome, IHM on Nativity of Our Lord School, 1933-1942. Archives, IHM Generalate.
36. Conversation with Sister St. Helen Sullivan, IHM, March 26, 1987.
37. Ibid.
38. Annals of Nativity Convent, Scranton, PA, 1955-1986. Archives, IHM Generalate.
39. Kane, Sister Zita Maria, IHM, *South Catholic/Bishop Klonowski High School*, pp. 16-17. Archives, IHM Generalate.
40. Annals of Nativity Convent, op. cit.
41. Golden Jubilee Booklet, op. cit., pp. 96-97.
42. Statistics from the Office of the Director of Apostolic Planning, 1986-1986. Archives, IHM Generalate.
43. 75th Anniversary Booklet, Our Lady of Mount Carmel Church, Asbury Park, NJ, p.1.
44. Letter from Monsignor John J. O'Hara to Mother Josepha, August 8, 1934.
45. Letter from Mother Josepha to Monsignor John J. O'Hara, Bradley Beach, NJ, August 11, 1934.
46. Letters from Bishop William A. Griffin, Bishop of Trenton, NJ, to Rev. Marcellino Romagno, OSST, pastor, Mount Carmel Parish, June 8 and August 17, 1946. Archives, IHM Generalate.

47. Letter from Sister Neumann, IHM, superior, Asbury Park, NJ, to Mother Josepha, Superior General, undated, but possibly written August 29, 1934. Annals. Archives, IHM Generalate.
48. Ibid.
49. Ibid.
50. Notes of Sister Immaculata Gillespie. Archives, IHM Generalate.
51. Letter from Sister Neumann, IHM, to Mother Josepha, undated, possibly at close of first week of school in September 1934.
52. Letter from Mother Josepha to Rev. Anthony Giovannini, October 20, 1934.
53. Letter from Rev. Anthony Giovannini to Mother Josepha, March 14, 1936.
54. Notes of Sister Immaculata Gillespie. Archives, IHM Generalate.
55. 75th Anniversary Booklet of Our Lady of Mount Carmel Church, Asbury Park, NJ, p. 1.
56. Data from the Office of the Director of Apostolic Planning, IHM Generalate.
57. Annals of Our Lady of Mount Carmel Convent, 1958-1965. Archives, IHM Generalate.
58. Gallagher, Rev. John P., *A Century of History*, Haddon Craftsmen, Scranton, PA, 1968, pp. 305-306.
59. Notes of Sister Immaculata Gillespie. Archives, IHM Generalate.
60. Letter from Rev. John T. Butler, Pastor, St. Matthew's, East Stroudsburg, PA to Mother Josepha, March 22, 1933.
61. Sister Lucy McGrath, IHM, notes on reverse side of photograph of first Sisters at East Stroudsburg, PA.1934.
62. Notes on reverse side of class photograph of first and second grades, St. Matthew's, East Stroudsburg, PA. Archives, IHM Generalate.
63. Recollections of Sister Elsie Miller as communicated in telephone conversation on April 7, 1987.
64. Annals of St. Matthew's Convent, East Stroudsburg, PA, 1955-1970. Archives, IHM Generalate.
65. Data from the Office of Director of Apostolic Planning. IHM Generalate.
66. Gallagher, op. cit., pp. 145 and 481.
67. Gallagher, op. cit., pp. 274-275.
68. Notes of Sister Immaculata Gillespie, Archives, IHM Generalate.
69. Recollections of Sister Raymond Rafferty provided in telephone conversation, April 8, 1987.
70. Annals of St. Mary's Convent, 1955-1986, Archives, IHM Generalate.
71. Letter from Monsignor Joseph G. Quinn to Bishop J. Carroll McCormick, February 4, 1972, Archives, IHM Generalate.
72. Letter from Bishop J. Carroll McCormick to Mother Beata Wertz,

February 5, 1972, Archives, IHM Generalate.
73. Data from the Office of Director of Apostolic Planning. IHM Generalate.
74. Letter from Rev. David C. Gildea, Superintendent of Schools, Diocese of Syracuse to Mother Josepha, July 2, 1936, Archives, IHM Generalate.
75. Letter from Mother Josepha Hurley to Bishop John A. Duffy of Syracuse, July 10, 1936, Archives, IHM Generalate.
76. Notes of Sister Immaculata Gillespie, Archives, IHM Generalate.
77. Telephone conversation with Sister Maronita Egan, June 19, 1987.
78. Annals of St. John the Evangelist Convent, Binghamton, New York, NY. 1955-1986, Archives, IHM Generalate.
79. Annals of St. John's Convent, Binghamton, New York, 1983-1984, Archives, IHM Generalate.
80. Data from the Office of Director of Apostolic Planning, IHM Generalate.
81. Letter from Rev. John F. McGowan to Sister Marcella Gill, March 3, 1937. Archives, IHM Generalate.
82. Ibid.
83. Agreement signed by Rev. Francis J. Aguis and Mother Josepha, November 17, 1937. Archives, IHM Generalate.
84. Letter from Sister Zita McGlynn to Mother Josepha, Feast of St. Nicholas, 1937. Archives, IHM Generalate.
85. Letter from Rev. Francis J. Aguis, April 28, 1941. Archives, IHM Generalate.
86. Letter from Mother Marcella Gill to Rev. Francis J. Aguis, April 28, 1941. Archives, IHM Generalate.
87. Notes of Sister Immaculata Gillespie. Archives, IHM Generalate.
88. Letter from Rev. Michael J. Vitale, Pastor, Holy Angels, Hays, PA, to Mother Joseph, August 12, 1938. Archives, IHM Generalate.
89. Contract between the Congregation of Sisters, Servants of the Immaculate Heart of Mary and Holy Angels Parish, September 1, 1938. Archives, IHM Generalate.
90. Letter from Mother Marcella to Bishop John Dearden, September 26, 1951 and response of September 29, 1951. Archives, IHM Generalate.
91. Annals of Holy Angels Convent, 1965-1966. Archives, IHM Generalate.
92. Annals of Holy Angels Convent, 1966-1967. Archives, IHM Generalate.
93. Annals of Holy Angels Convent, 1967-1968. Archives, IHM Generalate.
94. Letter from Ruth Barry, Joseph Kulikowski, and Rose Dalaidi, Evaluations from the Division of Teacher Education, California Stare College of PA, January 22, 1968.
95. Information from Sister Mary Arthur Meinzer, former principal of Holy Angels School, received May 5, 1987.
96. Cited from *The Lock Haven Express*, September 5, 1938. Archives, IHM

Generalate.
97. Letter from Rev. Donald Wagner, Pastor, St. Agnes Parish, Lock Haven, PA, to Mother Marcella, assistant to Mother Josepha, March 20, 1938. Archives, IHM Generalate.
98. Letter from Rev. Donald Wagner to Mother Josepha, May 31, 1938. Archives, IHM Generalate.
99. Op. cit., Wagner, March 20, 1938.
100. *Constitutions of the Congregation of the Sisters, Servants of the Immaculate Heart of Mary, Scranton, PA*, 1960, Chapter XVIII, Article 169, p. 50. Archives, IHM Generalate.
101. Notes of Sister Cornelia Tallman, provided to Sister Immaculata Gillespie, July 1947. Archives, IHM Generalate.
102. Ibid.
103. Annals of St. Agnes Convent, 1955-1967. Archives, IHM Generalate.
104. Ibid.
105. Letter from Reverend John E. Ryan, Pastor, St. Ann's, Devon, CT, to Mother Josepha, June 24, 1938, Archives, IHM Generalate.
106. Notes of Sister Immaculata Gillespie, Archives, IHM Generalate.
107. Letter of Reverend John E. Ryan, Pastor, St. Ann's, Devon, CT, to parishioners, June 22, 1939, Archives, IHM Generalate.
108. Ibid.
109. Letter from Sister Mary Martin Cawley to Mother Josepha, October 1, 1940,

Archives, IHM Generalate.

110. Notes of Sister Immaculata Gillespie, Archives, IHM Generalate.
111. Letter from Rev. Francis P. Breen, Pastor, St. Ann's, Devon, CT, to Mother M. Kathleen, Superior General, June 26, 1954.
112. Annals of St. Ann's Convent, Devon, CT, 1955-1975, Archives IHM Generalate. 113. Correspondence from Sister Kateri Nicolaus, IHM, Coordinator of Apostolic Works for the IHM Congregation, to Reverend James Panelli, Superintendent of Schools, Hartford, CT, Dec.1975—June 1978 and replies. Annals of St. Ann's Convent.
114. Letter of Reverend Michael Brett to Mother Josepha, May 3, 1938, Archives, IHM Generalate.
115. Notes of Sister Immaculata Gillespie, 1947, Archives, IHM Generalate
116. Conversation with Sr. Willemyn Gambrill, IHM, May 11,1987.
117. Notes of Sr. Immaculata Gillespie, Archives, IHM Generalate.
118. Letter from Reverend John P. McEntire to Mother Marcella, February 10, 1950, Archives, IHM Generalate.
119. Letters from Mother Marcella Gill, Superior General, to Reverend Charles Smyth, TOR, Pastor of Mount Carmel Parish, March 24, 1950 to Rev. John

P. McEntire, Pastor, St. Edward's and Bishop Richard T. Guilfoyle of the Altoona Diocese. Archives, IHM Generalate.

120. Letter from Bishop Edward J. Kelly, Boise, Idaho, to Mother Josepha, June 17, 1939. Archives, IHM Generalate.
121. Letter from Mother Josepha to Bishop Kelly, July 1, 1939, referring to telegram sent. Archives, IHM Generalate.
122. Letter from Bishop Kelly, op. cit.
123. Notes of Sister Immaculata Gillespie, 1974. Archives, IHM Generalate.
124. Letter from Sister Ursulina Shaughnessy to Mother Josepha, November 17, 1939. Archives, IHM Generalate.
125. Letter from Sister Ursulina Shaughnessy to Mother Josepha, January 11, 1940. Archives, IHM Generalate.
126. Ibid.
127. Letter from Sister Rosamund Wyvill to Mother Marcella, October 18, 1945. Archives, IHM Generalate.
128. Annals of St. Edward's Convent, Twin Falls, ID, 1955-1962. Archives, IHM Generalate.
129. Letter from Rev. Jerome T. O'Connor, Pastor, Church of the Immaculate Conception, Buhl, ID, to Mother Beata Wertz, December 12, 1960. Archives, IHM Generalate.
130. Annals of St. Edward's Convent, Twin Falls, ID, 1960-1967. Archives, IHM Generalate.
131. Ibid. 1966-1967.
132. Letter from Sister Mary Zita Cossack to Mother Beata Wertz, Superior General, April 24, 1971. Archives, IHM Generalate.
133. Letter from Mr. Otto Florence, Jr., President of St. Edward's Parish Board to Mother Beata, January 29, 1971. Archives, IHM Generalate.
134. Letter from Rev. Perry Dodds, Pastor, St. Edward's Parish, to Sister Anne Fulwiler, Superior General, September 9, 1977. Archives, IHM Generalate.
135. Notes of Sister Immaculata Gillespie, 1947. Archives, IHM Generalate.
136. Notes of Sister Sergius O'Donnell, Superior and Principal, OLPH, Rocky Mount, NC, Archives, IHM Generalate.
137. Letter from Sister Sergius O'Donnell to Mother Josepha, Superior General, about September 1, 1939. Archives, IHM Generalate.
138. Notes of Sister Sergius O'Donnell, op. cit. probably about 1947. Archives, IHM Generalate.
139. Letter from Sister Sergius O'Donnell to Mother Josepha, January 1940. Archives, IHM Generalate.
140. 75th Anniversary Booklet (1910-1985) of Our Lady of Perpetual Help Church, Rocky Mount, NC, p. 1
141. Annals of OLPH Convent, Rocky Mount, NC, 1955-1956. Archives, IHM

Generalate.
142. Annals, op. cit., 1957-1958. Archives, IHM Generalate.
143. Annals, op. cit., 1972-1973. Archives, IHM Generalate.
144. Annals, op. cit., 1973-1976. Archives, IHM Generalate.
145. Annals, op. cit., 1977-1980. Archives, IHM Generalate.
146. *The Sunday Telegram*, Rocky Mount, NC, Feb. 3, 1985. Archives, IHM Generalate.
147. Statistics from the Office of the Director of Apostolic Planning, 1986-1987.
148. Notes of Sister Immaculata Gillespie, 1947, Archives, IHM Generalate.
149. Letter from Reverend Edward Gilbert, Pastor, St. Agnes Parish, Little Washington, NC, to Mother Josepha, August 30, 1940, Archives, IHM Generalate.
150. Conversation with Sister Teresa Clare McAuliffe, May 26, 1987. IHM Generalate.
151. Letter from Reverend Edward T. Gilbert to Mother Marcella, October 4, 1944, Archives, IHM Generalate.
152. 50th Anniversary Booklet of IHM Service in North Carolina, p. 4, Archives, IHM Generalate.
153. Ibid.
154. Annals of St. Agnes Convent, Washington, NC, 1955-1957, Archives, IHM Generalate.
155. Annals of Mother of Mercy Convent, Washington, NC, 1963-1964, p. 1, Archives, IHM Generalate.
156. Ibid., p. 1-2.
157. Ibid., p. 5.
158. Letter from Bishop Vincent S. Waters of Raleigh to Sister Edith Marie, Principal and Superior, Mother of Mercy Convent, Washington, NC, June 6, 1973, Annals.
159. Notes of Sister Immaculata Gillespie, 1947, Archives, IHM Generalate.
160. Letter from Sister Edwin Ott to Mother Josepha, September 12, 1939, Archives, IHM Generalate.
161. Letter from Mother Marcella to Reverend Charles F. Moosmann, Pastor, Munhall, PA, December 30, 1943, Archives, IHM Generalate.
162. Letter from Reverend Charles Moosmann to Mother Marcella, February 2, 1944, Archives, IHM Generalate.
163. Letter from Mother Marcella to Reverend Charles Moosmann, February 5, 1944, Archives, IHM Generalate.
164. Letter from Reverend Charles Moosmann to Mother Marcella, March 10, 1944, Archives, IHM Generalate.
165. Letter from Mother Marcella to Reverend Charles Moosmann, March 20,

1944. Archives, IHM Generalate.
166. Letter from Mother Marcella to Reverend Charles Moosmann, May 27, 1946, Archives, IHM Generalate.
167. St. Ignatius Church Centenary Booklet 1885-1985, Kingston, PA, p. 15.
168. Notes of Sister Immaculata Gillespie, 1947, Archives, IHM Generalate.
169. Notes of Sister Maria Thomas Harrington, 1943-1946, Archives, IHM Generalate.
170. Ibid., p. 3.
171. Kane, Sister Zita Maria, IHM, *Bishop O'Reilly High School Kingston, Pennsylvania, 1954-1980*, p. 4.
172. Annals of St. Ignatius Convent, Kingston, PA, 1955-1985, Archives, IHM Generalate.
173. Centenary Booklet, St. Ignatius Church, Kingston, Pa., 1885-1985, p. 42.
174. Notes in Archives, IHM Generalate.
175. Notes of Sister Immaculata Gillespie, 1947, Archives, IHM Generalate.
176. Christmas letters of Mother M. Josepha Hurley, 1931-1939, Archives, IHM Generalate.
177. *The Catholic Light*, December 6, 1940.
178. Ibid.
179. Notes on the death of Mother Josepha, Archives, IHM Generalate.

Mother M. Marcella Gill, IHM
1940-1955

BORN:	Katherine Gill, December 22, 1877, Parsons, PA
PARENTS:	John Gill and Marie Nolan Gill
EDUCATION:	A.B., Marywood College, Scranton, PA M.A., Marywood College, Scranton, PA
RELIGIOUS LIFE:	Entered IHM Congregation, July 2, 1896 at St. Rose Novitiate, Carbondale, PA Reception of Habit, February 2, 1897 Profession of Vows, July 15, 1899
MISSIONS:	Holy Rosary High School, Scranton, PA *St. Joseph's High School, Renovo, PA *Most Holy Rosary High School, Syracuse, NY *St. Dominic's High School, Oyster Bay, NY *Served as Principal of High Schools and Convent Superior
MEMBER OF THE GENERAL COUNCIL:	1931-1940 – First Assistant to Mother Josepha
SUPERIOR GENERAL:	1941-1943 (completion of Mother Joseph's term) 1943-1949 (first term) 1949-1955 (second term)
DIED:	September 14, 1955 – 77 years of age

TABLE OF CONTENTS

Mother M. Marcella Gill, IHM
1940-1956

Continuity, with the strength and vitality that had become familiar to the Congregation through the nine years of Mother Josepha's terms of office, seemed to be the atmosphere and theme that prevailed after her death.

The *Constitutions* of the Congregation supported this mood in their provision that:

> If the Mother Superior die before the expiration of her term of office, the Assistant will be the Mother Superior for the remainder of said term, unless the Rt. Rev. Bishop should to a new election or nominate the Mother Superior provisionally. (1)

Bishop Hafey made clear that he did not intend to exercise the options provided by sending a letter to Mother Marcella Gill who had served as the First Assistant under Mother Josepha from 1931-1940, the full period of Mother Josepha's time in office. The letter stated, in part:

> This letter will confirm your succession to the late Mother Josepha in the office of General of the Sisters, Servants of the Immaculate Heart of Mary, with Motherhouse of St. Mary's, Scranton. (2)

Confirmed also, in the same letter, were the following: Sister Madeline Loughlin, first assistant; Mother Cyril Conway, second assistant; Sister Immaculata Gillespie, first councilor. These successions were undoubtedly acceptable to the Congregation at large also, since these were sisters who had been elected by the Congregation in 1937.

The second councilor, appointed at a later date, was Sister de Pazzi Houlihan. (3)

Other appointments which retained continuity with Mother Josepha's administration were: Sister Irmina McMahon as bursar; Mother Anysia Moran as mistress of novices and Sister Teresa Moran as assistant mistress of novices and director of postulants.

Thus was set into motion the administration of Mother Marcella Gill. Had she known in December 1940 that she would serve as mother general until 1955, the longest period in the history of the Congregation, she would certainly have been reluctant to begin the long journey. Seasoned by forty-one years in the Congregation in which she had proven herself to be an able teacher, principal, superior and administrator, she had keen insight into the tasks that lay ahead for her as leader of a growing Congregation.

It was a time for the judgments of experienced leaders and for the optimism that springs from firm faith in God. Mother Marcella Gill was able to project these qualities in an atmosphere of uncertainty that was part of living during World War II: Adolf Hitler's German troops were marching across Europe; Churchill as prime minister; Stalin's Russian troops had invaded Poland and the Scandinavian countries; and the government of France had fallen to the Germans. Franklin D. Roosevelt, president of the United States, found himself being maligned by some Catholics and supported by others as he tried to forge an alliance with the Soviets to bring the war against the Germans to a halt. Catholic leadership was divided about the wisdom of the U. S. participation in the war: some, like Dorothy Day of the Catholic Worker Movement, Rev. John LaFarge, Editor of *America*, Reverend James Gillis and Monsignor Fulton Sheen and several mid-western and western bishops were definitely pacifist and isolationist in their views. The prominent Church leaders like Cardinal Mundelein of Chicago, Cardinal Francis J. Spellman of New York and many others strongly supported the president. Quoting President Roosevelt, Cardinal Spellman reiterated " We really cannot longer afford to be moles who cannot see, or ostriches who will not see." (5)

Yet, what many could see was that the struggle was really between Nazism and Communism and that the only weapons against these ideologies were education and persevering prayer. To education and to persevering prayer Mother Marcella called her sisters. Her first Christmas letter to the Congregation, written perhaps only a week after coming into office, shows her awareness of the times. She wrote:

> There is a loud echo of Good Friday in Christmas this year, Calvary instead of the Crib. Let us be mindful of the fact that the roaring planes are making a desperate effort to silence the voice of the Christ Child, and that the god of war lists his victims while the God of Peace knocks at the door begging for admittance . . .
>
> Let us, contrary to the spirit of the world, see not the defeat of Good Friday in a today, but let us rather see it as . . . a magnificent prelude to a rebirth of faith and love for God. (6)

Indirectly, she reveals her own sadness at the loss of her close associate, Mother Josepha, when she adds:

> In our Christmas this year, there will be a loneliness, which we all experience, Christmas without our beloved Mother Josepha. Yet, I feel that it is wrong for us to mourn for her who, I am

> confident, is celebrating Christmas with the Holy Family in Heaven.

She then challenges each Sister to personal holiness and to perseverance in the commitment made at profession as she writes,

> As she (Mother Josepha) looks down on each one of us, may she turn to Christ and say the words quoted by Monsignor O'Connor in her funeral sermon, 'My God, she is entirely Thine.' (7)

Mother Marcella's first year as superior general ended with another major war as the Japanese bombed Pearl Harbor on December 7, 1941 and the United States declared war on Japan.

Six months later, on June 6, 1942, a deep personal sorrow was again to enter Mother Marcella's life. It was on that date that her long-time friend and her second assistant on the council, Mother Cyril, was taken in death. After sixty-six years of religious life, Mother Cyril, at eighty-two years of age, was not only a symbol of the vigorous past of the IHM Congregation, but also a reminder of the serenity and beauty of a life lived fully for the Lord.

Having entered the IHM Novitiate at St. Cecilia's in Scranton from Pittston, Pennsylvania in June 1876, she was professed on August 27, 1878. Subsequently she served at St. Patrick's Orphanage, Scranton; Laurel Hill Academy, Susquehanna; St. Cecilia's, Scranton; and as superior and principal at St. Paul's, Scranton from 1895-1901. Meanwhile, she had also been elected bursar of the Congregation in 1889, a position she managed while at St. Cecilia's.

In 1901, at the age of forty-one years, she was elected superior general. She completed the second of two full six-year terms in 1913, and then became superior and principal of St. Mary of the Mount School in Pittsburgh where she served for sixteen years. In 1929 she became principal and superior of St. John's School in Pittston, Pennsylvania. In 1931 she was elected as first councilor of the Congregation in Mother Josepha's administration and served also as directress of Marywood Seminary. She became second assistant to Mother Marcella in 1940, continuing in this position and as directress of Marywood Seminary until her death in June 1942.

As Superior General from 1901-1913 she had opened many new missions, stretching the Congregation to western Pennsylvania and western United States. She had completed the building plans of Mother Crescentia for the motherhouse and Marywood Seminary and within six years could

report that the Congregation was debt-free. She had responded to the needs of Slovak and Lithuanian immigrants by founding the Sisters of Sts. Cyril and Methodius and the Sisters of St. Casimir who revere her to this day. She saw to the higher education preparation of her Sisters for their professional work and to their proper certification.
One tribute to Mother Cyril summed it up saying:

> Mother Cyril was the epitome of initiative and of enterprise. She gave supreme treatment to rich and poor alike. She had a fertile mind with a desire to solve problems, and a patience and a persistence that carried her along. Mother Cyril was like a finely cut diamond, sparkling, light, serene, warm, sweet and friendly. She had given over sixty years of faithful, humble, distinguished, noble service to the work of her Community. Like the valiant woman of Holy Scripture her own works praise her. (8)

Mother Marcella's concern for peace in the world would be the subject of her Christmas letters over the following four years as many of the families of the sisters experienced war casualties. In writing to the sisters she asked, "Does it not seem fitting, then, that as a community we unite in prayer and plead with God to have pity on the world?" (9) In addition to prayer, Mother Marcella urged the sisters to personal sacrifice and to the sound instruction of the young so as to prepare them to deal with rampant erroneous theologies and philosophies. She wrote:

> Christianity today faces a most serious crisis. False doctrines, immorality, disbelief and paganism confront our youth on all sides. It is our sacred duty to prepare these precious souls to correspond to the designs of God in their regard. We must train them to be faithful in the discharge of their obligations to God, to themselves and to their neighbor. The accomplishment of this God-given task requires, first of all, our own personal sanctification which is to be acquired by the many spiritual helps so generously placed at our disposal and particularly by prayer and sacrifice. (10)

At that point, "Apostolic Spirituality" had not yet received its name or a refined explication by the Church, but Mother Marcella's letter shows that she understood its essential message and could have given the first course in it.

In spite of the wars, and often because of them, the Church in the United States was expanding as servicemen and their families engaged in the unsettling business of moving about the country. Easterners found new beauties in the West; westerners found the East to be more than an "asphalt jungle;" northerners grew to like the southern hospitality, and southerners just wanted to get back home. In this new atmosphere of mobility it was not unusual over the coming years that Mother Marcella would receive requests for the services of our sisters from far-flung locations, such as a request from the Bishop of the Archdiocese of Portland in Oregon to accept another school, Blessed Sacrament in Portland. (11) Another request came to her from Bishop Charles D. White of Spokane, Washington, encouraging her to take one or more schools there. (12) Even San Antonio, Texas was heard from in a request from Rev. Eustace Struckhoff, OFM to teach in a Mexican parish there that had over 1,000 children. (13) Bishop Edward J. Kelly of Boise, Idaho, got a word in, too, as he asked that the General Chapter note his vote for a western province. (14)

Mother Marcella would respond to a call for sisters in the far west later on, but her first venture was taken in order to meet the needs of young children of women working in the defense plants in and around Williamsport, Pennsylvania.

Costello Nursery School, Williamsport, Pennsylvania

In 1942 a small kindergarten was in operation on Saturdays only in St. Joseph's School, Williamsport. Monsignor Frank P. McHugh was pastor of Annunciation Church, Williamsport, at the time and was receiving many requests to enroll pupils for the entire week, since many mothers of small children were working in defense plants in and around Williamsport. Father McHugh saw the need of a nursery school rather than an extended kindergarten to meet this need. He also saw the possibility that a non-sectarian nursery school might overcome some of the strong prejudice then existing toward Catholics in Williamsport.

Bishop Hafey approved Father McHugh's plans and personally assisted him in the selection and purchase of the home in which the nursery school would be located. A large three-story dwelling on Campbell Street in Williamsport, known as the "Banker Graham" property was chosen. Renovation began on August 1, 1942, in order to comply with state standards for nursery schools; the second and third floors were converted into quarters for the three sisters whom Mother Marcella had promised.

The school was opened on September 14, 1942, and named "Costello Nursery School" in memory of a former pastor of Annunication Parish. Sister Georgina Wertz was in charge with Sister Jane Frances Keating and Sister Michael Donnelly assisting. (15) A note from Sister Georgina to Mother Marcella indicates that the sisters did not move into the Campbell

Street house until December 6, and even then the chapel was not yet completed. (16) They had, no doubt, been residing with our sisters at St. Joseph's Convent, Williamsport. At the opening of the nursery school there were only seven children, but very soon there was an average of fifty children per day as word spread about the loving care and the excellent program being offered. Children between the ages of two and six years, about 75% of them non-Catholics, were accepted. The daily hours of operation of the nursery school were 6:00 a.m. to 6:00 p.m. The nurse put the early arrivals to sleep on cots until time for morning inspection. There is no doubt that the later concept of "day care center" was already operative at the Costello Nursery School of 1942.

As the first nursery school in Pennsylvania to begin operation under the Defense Program for Child Care under the federal Works Progress Administration (WPA) auspices, the Costello Nursery School was a unique operation. All personnel were paid through the WPA, so teachers, a nurse, the cook, janitor and other helpers were all on the federal payroll.

As early as October 15, 1942, a federal government supervisor, a Mrs. Pinkham, visited the school, evaluated it as an A-1 nursery school and urged the hiring of a kindergarten teacher to be paid under the program funds. WPA support continued until April 30, 1943, at which point application was made through the Pennsylvania Council of Defense in Harrisburg for funding under the Lanham Act. Only two of eighty applications received grants—the Costello Nursery School was one of the two awardees.

On January 16, 1943, Sister Michael Donnelly, who had been assigned to work one-half day in the office and one-half day with the children, fell and broke her ankle. Soon after, Sister Monice Sullivan was sent to replace her.

Celebrating the first birthday of the Costello Nursery School in September 1943, the local newspaper ran an article and pictures of the children with Sister Georgina. That the work had earned the respect of the area people is evident from what was written:

> One year ago the Costello Nursery School opened its doors to the children of war-pressed working mothers . . . Today there are more than fifty youngsters depending on the non-sectarian nursery school for daily-supervised care. Their mothers spend long hours at war work, but are content that the children are safe. (17)

The article continues quoting Sister Georgina:

> Not all soldiers wear uniforms. These tots are soldiers too—they get up as early as six o'clock in the morning and part with their

mothers every working day in the week, just so that the war can be won. (18)

Having served a wartime need, once the war was over the need for Costello Nursery School no longer existed. Quite inconspicuously and without fanfare it was closed in 1946.

St. Bernard's Elementary School, Hastings, Pennsylvania

St. Bernard's, located in a country setting between Altoona and Pittsburgh in Pennsylvania, is a mission to which the Sisters of IHM have returned four times since its opening in 1915. Bishop Garvey of Altoona had originally invited Mother Germaine to send sisters to teach in the parish school, which was under the jurisdiction of the Benedictine Fathers. Father Marcellus Rettgen, OSB, was pastor at the time. This school was highly successful, registering about five hundred pupils in its initial stages. By 1921 high school classes were added, but this proved to be financially prohibitive, hence was discontinued in 1925. Commercial classes beyond eighth grade had been offered, but they too were discontinued because of crowded conditions in the school (19)

There seemed to have been no problem with retention of a good enrollment. Sister Inviolata Durkin, former principal, reported that in the years in which she was there (1932-1935) there was an average of 320-350 pupils, with as many as 410 in 1934—a confirmation year.

The closing of the school on June 5, 1935, was because of the inability of the parish to maintain a school and pay on a church debt of $45,000. These were hard times in this region since most of the people worked in the mines, and of the three collieries, two were inoperative for months and the third was working only two days a week.

The solution seemed to be to close the school for a time, rent the building to the public school, rent the convent as a two-family home, and use the income for the payment of the debt. This was done. The convent furnishings were stored in other IHM convents in Spangler and Ashville for the day the school and convent would reopen. (20)

And, re-open it did! Father Matthias, OSB, had worked for several years to clear the debt and managed to reduce it considerably. By February 1942, a request was made by the new pastor, Father Vincent Schlemnee, OSB, to Mother Marcella to send sisters to teach in the summer vacation school and to prepare for the re-opening of St. Bernard's as a catechetical center in September 1942.

Father Vincent must have included a request for other services from the sisters also because in one exchange of letters with him, Mother

Marcella clarified the extent to which the sisters would be involved in caring for the church. She wrote:

> I will be glad to have the Sisters take care of the sanctuary, the vestments and altar linens, but we are not permitted to do scrubbing or heavy manual work in churches. No doubt the vestments need mending and touching up and the sisters will be able to do this. (21)

St. Bernard's reopened as a catechetical center on September 8, 1942. Sister Aluigi Devers was appointed superior, with three other sisters constituting the community: Sister Ann Elizabeth O'Donnell, Sister Edna Lambert, and Sister Germana Radley. Six hundred fifty pupils attended classes at three locations—St. Bernard's (which continued as a public school at this time), the public high school building about eight blocks from the convent, and a two-room country school. Classes were scheduled before school in the morning, after school, in the evenings and on Saturday and Sunday mornings in order to accommodate all grade levels in all locations.

Sister Aluigi described the children in this way, " All the children, whether from the borough or township schools, are most respectful and well mannered and very eager to learn their religion." (22)

In the second year Sister Germana was changed and Sister St. Catherine Keefe came in her place. In addition to the catechetical instruction, both Sister Aluigi and Sister St. Catherine taught piano lessons to augment the twenty-five dollar per month per sister stipend which they received. Sister Ann Elizabeth's every free moment was spent in making and mending vestments and linens for the church.

It is obvious from the exchange of letters that Father Vincent was difficult to get along with and seemed, in spite of the growing financial stability of the parish, to be in no hurry to reopen the school. There was evidence as early as December 1944 that the bishop had considered its reopening in September 1944. (23) This did not occur however, and later, with a new pastor, Father Raymond, the matter was again considered but not brought to completion, although Mother Marcella had promised additional sisters to staff a six or eight-grade school when it reopened. (24)

In April 1949, another new pastor, Reverend Adalbert Klosch, OSB, wrote to Mother Marcella setting forth his hopes to obtain sisters in sufficient number to reopen the school—grades one through six. He had done some genuine planning, having conducted a parish survey that revealed that 220 pupils would be registered for the six grades. He was aware that much would have to be done in getting the school plant ready and for the teachers to order books in time for a September opening, but his eagerness was apparent. (25)

St. Bernard's parochial school reopened in September 1949. The sisters continued to serve the religious education needs of the children not attending the parochial school in addition to their regular teaching, but the catechetical center as such was discontinued. The group of sisters who comprised the community included: Sister Ambrose Walker, superior and principal, Sister Ann Helene Coyne, Sister Edna Lambert, Sister Avila (Mildred) McCloskey, Sister Gerardine Francis, Sister Mary Bede Douglas, and Sister St. Catherine Keefe who remained for full-time private music lessons. Both Sister Ambrose and Sister Ann Helene had fond recollections of this mission and praised Father Adalbert for his great zeal and interest in the youngsters. Sister Ambrose recalled that Father Adalbert was a keen mathematician and would keep the children alert with his rapid-fire questions on the subject. (26) Sister Ann Helene remembers his appreciation of all that the sisters were doing. Although Sister Ambrose had a five-pronged role of superior, principal, sixth-grade teacher, church sacristan and after-school music teacher, Sister Ann Helene remarked, "We were a very happy community."(27)

Father Adalbert was to continue as pastor until June 1957, completing eight years at St. Bernard's. His transfer to St. Joseph's Church, Covington, Kentucky, left a greatly saddened parish and school at St. Bernard's. Reverend Stephen Wendell, a native of Pittsburgh, filled his pastorate. With the death of the assistant pastor, Father Alvin Andrea, OSB, on June 23, additional shock came to the parish. Father Andrea had celebrated the children's Mass on Sunday and was found dead in his room early on Monday morning.

These sorrows, together with the earlier death of Bishop Guilfoyle on June 10, overshadowed the activities of school and parish that year. (28) Most Reverend Howard J. Carroll of Pittsburgh was consecrated Bishop of the Altoona-Johnstown Diocese on January 22, 1958, but his tenure was to be very brief as the Lord called him in death in the spring of 1960. Bishop J. Carroll McCormick was named to succeed him on June 25, 1960. The ceremony of installation was held on September 21, 1960. His tenure was relatively short also as he was named in 1965 to be Bishop of the Scranton Diocese.

St. Bernard's remained a vibrant mission and its parish over the years was blessed with many vocations to the religious life, six of whom became Sisters, Servants of the Immaculate Heart of Mary. These were Sister Armella Nelson, Sister Mary Denise Thomas, Sister Clementine

Gunther, Sister Cyprian Weakland, Sister Marie Immaculate Yahner, and Sister Serenus Yahner.

As a part of the Congregation's master plan approved by the General Chapter of 1978, at the close of the 1979—1980 school year the sisters were withdrawn from St. Bernard's. The sisters serving at St. Bernard's that year were Sister Dorothy Lyons, principal, Sister Hermine Krug, Sister Elise Frank, superior, Sister Moira McMonagle, and Sister Mary of the Angels Whalen. The school remained open, staffed by two Mercy Sisters and the lay faculty. (29)

But this is not the end of the association of the IHMs with St. Bernard's School. Continued requests from the pastor, Rev. Daniel Woefel, OSB, and the need of three of our sisters who had elderly ill mothers residing in this area, brought about our return to St. Bernard's in June of 1984. Sister Mary Elaine Peters, RSM, continued as principal and resided in the convent with the IHM community which included Sister Florine Madigan, superior and first grade teacher, Sister Elsa Eckenrode, third grade teacher, and Sister Lenore Thomas who served as director of religious education for four rural parishes.

Sister Elaine's mother died during the year, hence she accepted a new assignment for 1985-1986, leaving the principalship open. Sister Florine was appointed principal and Sister Elsa was elected superior. There was one addition to the community, namely, Sister Franzchen Yahner who served in the area of support services for the local community. (30)

The work of our sisters at St. Bernard's is obviously not yet completed. The school's enrollment for 1986-1987 was 181 pupils and the school continues with two sisters and a lay faculty. (31)

Holy Name of Mary Convent, Montrose, Pennsylvania

The opening of the Holy Name of Mary Convent in Montrose, Pennsylvania in September of 1942 had a special significance for the Sisters, Servants of the Immaculate Heart of Mary in the Scranton Diocese. The surrounding region was hallowed by the memories of the initial coming of Mother Teresa Maxis Duchemin and the first group of sisters from Monroe, Michigan in 1857 to nearby St. Joseph; by the imprint of Bishop John Neumann, now a canonized saint of the Church; and by the dedicated missionary activity of Reverend John Vincent O'Reilly who served not only old St. Joseph's, but the entire northeast Pennsylvania region.

The extensive plans of Bishop William J. Hafey in the 1940s included the establishment of a home in Susquehanna County for the ill and aged priests of the Scranton Diocese. His own great love of the country atmosphere motivated him to purchase the Russell estate at Silver Lake where the Trinitarian Fathers had agreed to establish a hospice-style facility for the care of the priests. They were also to serve as spiritual directors and assist in the spiritual care of these residents. In addition to the Russell estate, the Bishop also purchased a nearby dairy farm, which would provide for the dairy product needs, as well as for fresh fruit, vegetable and poultry supplies for the hospice.

This background is provided here because of its relationship to the arrangements made for the sisters when they came to serve at Montrose. Bishop Hafey had also purchased the former home of George Lathrop of Philadelphia in Montrose. This home was built over ninety-four years previously by a Dr. Henry Drinker, one-time president of Lafayette College, and tradition says that the first Mass ever celebrated in Montrose was said on the grounds where this home is located. The bishop had in mind that this home would serve as the convent, a center for catechetical literature, a kindergarten and music school. Since it was envisioned that for some time there would be no other income for the sisters, the arrangement was that fees charged for the kindergarten tuition and for music lessons, augmented by the milk, butter, eggs, poultry, fresh vegetables and fruit from the farm would provide for the needs of the sisters. The faith is planted and nourished in a variety of settings and under various circumstances, and the bishop undoubtedly had some insight into the need for the sisters to be independent of the support of the people, at least in the beginning. It was a well-known fact that Catholics in the Montrose area were in the minority, and their numbers were lost among strong Baptist Bible Christians and Episcopalians. The people were not happy to hear that the bishop had purchased the Lathrop home, and that soon there would be sisters living there and kindergarten children running about.

But the sisters did come, and the Lathrop home became Holy Name of Mary Convent and was opened on September 8, 1942, to receive fifteen kindergarten children, only five of whom were Catholic. The beautiful twenty-one room home was soon transformed: a chapel was furnished in one of the rooms on the second floor; the beautiful bright sun-parlor was fitted out as a lending library for catechetical materials; music rooms and kindergarten spaces were appropriately equipped. Many of the rooms were already more than adequately furnished by the Lathrop family and the parish supplied the rest of the furnishings. The first community of sisters at Montrose included Sister Alma Marie Morgan, superior, Sister Rose Irma Spillane, music teacher, and Sister Francella Shaughnessy, kindergarten teacher. It is interesting to note that initially Sister Bernadette Burns was assigned to Montrose as music teacher but stopped at St. Joseph's Hospital in Carbondale for what she thought was a minor health problem. Her sudden and unexpected death occurred on September 22, 1942. Hers was the first death notice the new community received. Sister Rose Irma was sent to Montrose in her place.

In addition to the kindergarten and music lesson activities at the convent, the sisters taught catechetical instructions at such country places as St. Joseph, Friendsville, Little Meadows, Springville and eventually Brooklyn, Pennsylvania. In the summer, additional sisters who assisted in preparing the Confirmation and First Holy Communion classes for the following year's ceremonies augmented their numbers. The summer work, in fact, proved to be central to their financial support, since these pastors usually offered a stipend for the sisters' services over the summer. The five dollars per month per pupil tuition in the kindergarten and the one-dollar per lesson for the music, even with supplies from the farm, would not have sustained them especially since cookies and milk had to be provided for the children daily from the tuition money. But, as Sister Francella recalls,

> We were not ever really without . . . after a few months the people of Montrose accepted the Sisters, especially as they witnessed the work they were doing, and they were generous in bringing vegetables and fruit, both summer and winter. The Sisters did a lot of canning and made jams and jellies for use over the winter also. The goodness of our sisters from other locales was also in evidence and groups like the Marywood College Mission Guild would send donations especially at Christmas time. (32)

Besides all this, Bishop Hafey was not one to fail to follow up on something he had begun. He was a frequent visitor to the convent, and would often come unannounced, would walk in and open the refrigerator and cupboards to see what supplies the sisters had, and would himself provide for their needs if warranted. In addition to the activities already named, the sisters organized the Sodality of the Blessed Virgin Mary Study Club, a choir, and visited the sick and elderly of the parish. It was no wonder that they became a familiar sight in Montrose and endeared themselves to the people.

Changes came to the Montrose community in 1943, as Father Martin Maher, the pastor, was transferred to St. John's, Susquehanna, amidst the many tears of the parishioners and children who loved him dearly. Reverend Thomas P. Monahan was appointed pastor. His generous and jovial nature soon won him the respect and love of all. (33) Sister Rose

Irma was also changed that year and she was replaced by Sister Wilhelmina Hill as music teacher.

Father Monahan was very concerned about the sisters' support, and while he had no resources from which to establish a regular salary for them, he offered to share his Mass stipends with the sisters if Sister Wilhelmina would play the organ and Sister Francella would sing for the Masses, which they did!

Reverend Joseph Corcoran followed Father Monahan as pastor. His missionary bent was responsible for the spread of the catechetical programs to additional towns of the area. He personally went before the school boards to obtain released time for Catholic students to attend religious instructions. He purchased a house in Springville in order to have teaching rooms and a chapel available for year-round instructions by the sisters. One of the families of the parish lived on the second floor of this house in order to care for it.

It is difficult to believe the anti-Catholic feeling that existed only nine miles distant from Montrose in Brooklyn, Pennsylvania. Initially, the Odd Fellows organization permitted the use of their meeting rooms for instructions, but under the protests of the public, instructions were moved to a store, then to a garage, and later to an abandoned cider mill, and finally to a private home. Father Corcoran accompanied the sisters to the various sites where religious instructions were being given and supported their efforts in every way. Some evidence of the effectiveness of their ministry lies in the fact that in the first twelve years of the sisters' presence in the Montrose area there were three IHM vocations: Sister Eva Marie Zlotucha, Sister Thomas Aquinas Kielceski and the former Sister Marilyn DeWitt. (34)

The kindergarten enrollment hovered around eighteen pupils until 1955-1956 when twenty-seven were registered. By 1963, there were thirty-eight, and a high point was reached in both the 1964-1965 and 1965-1966 terms when fifty-three children were enrolled. However, this tapered off again to sixteen by 1969-1970. (35) Certainly, this and the fact that both public school and private kindergarten classes were available provided strong arguments for not continuing the kindergarten.

The catechetical programs, which served both public high school and grade school students, had by this time been confined to one day per week in accord with the released time arrangements made by the public school system. However, with the shortage of sister-personnel it was no longer feasible to assign four sisters to Montrose for this work. (36)

Keeping the faith alive and vibrant in these small country parishes which had no Catholic school was a work which was very dear to Bishop

Hafey, as well as to the Congregation. It was not easy, therefore, for the little community to close the door in 1970 on this ministry that had provided twenty-eight years of instruction to the young people of the area. The final group of sisters included Sister Miriam Catherine Corcoran, superior, Sister Marie Bernard Kilcullen, Sister Maronita Egan and Sister Dorothy Donovan. (37)

Sisters who had served this mission as superiors from 1942 to its closing were Sister Alma Marie Morgan, Sister Rachel Farrelly, Sister Wilhelmina Hill, Sister Lucinda Harrington, Sister Maurine LeFevre, Sister Benedictus Philpott, and finally, Sister Miriam Catherine Corcoran. (38)

St. Matthew's, (Woodcrest), Wilmington, Delaware

Today's observer of the beautiful physical plant—church, rectory, school and convent—which have been developed in St. Matthew's Parish, Wilmington, Delaware, could not easily imagine the difficulties experienced by our sisters at the time of their first coming to Delaware in 1942. One has to think about St. Matthew's as a newly founded parish and the dedicated pastor, Reverend John J. Foley, with no assistant to rely on, overworked yet striving to accomplish the commission given to him by the bishop to build a complete parish complex. This vast building project was underway, with the school nearing completion when the sisters arrived on August 24, 1942. The classrooms were in readiness, but the plan called for the convent to be located on the top floor above the school. This area was just open space at that point, and was being utilized for the parish Sunday Masses since the church was still under construction.

Father Foley must have had some apprehension about the situation into which he was inviting the sisters as their first introduction to the State of Delaware, the Wilmington Diocese and St. Matthew's Parish. He went personally to the Wilmington train station to meet and welcome the sisters, who from that moment on were his sisters. The group included Sister Brigida Strome, superior and principal (as well as fifth grade teacher); Sister Adrienne Wells, kindergarten and music teacher; Sister Maria Rita Ruddy, teacher of first and second grades; Sister Clarice Gallagher, third and fourth grades; and Sister Maria Angela Orr, sixth and seventh grades. On that first day Father Foley took the sisters to the small home on Curtis Avenue, which he had purchased to serve as their residence until the convent above the school was completed. This dwelling was located across from the rectory and about three blocks from the school.

Sister Brigida noted at once the absence of a chapel in this house. Father Foley, who had become accustomed to the inconvenience of offering Mass, first in the local fire station, then above the school, or in a small chapel adjoining the rectory, proposed that the sisters, too, could use the rectory chapel. Sister Brigida's first request of Father Foley on that August afternoon was that the ground floor bedroom of the house, intended for her use, be converted into a chapel and that the space above the garage be used for her bedroom. (39)

Whatever the inconveniences of the days that followed with the sounds of construction everywhere, Sister Maria Angela Orr remembers these times with fondness: "We had happy days and we laughed a lot over things that happened each day. I wouldn't give up one of those early days, they were difficult, but we had good community life and we loved and served the Lord well." (40) She recalls the great love and appreciation the people had for the sisters and their generosity at a time when the sisters' stipend was only thirty dollars per month per sister.

It was well that Sister Brigida had insisted on the temporary arrangements for a chapel in the original little house because it was not until January of 1946 that the new convent above the school was completed and the sisters were able to leave the little house on Curtis Avenue behind. Sister Albrette Rouleau who was stationed there at the time recalls the wintry day of their moving—a day on which regular classes were held concurrently with the moving project! (41) By this time Sister Brigida, whose twelve years' canonical time as superior had been completed (she had been superior for nine years at Nativity in Scranton), was no longer at Wilmington. Sister Maria Angela, too, had been transferred to St. Agnes, Baltimore, where she served as principal and superior from 1945-1951 before returning to St. Matthew's in these capacities in 1951.

Meanwhile, Sister Edwin Ott was appointed in 1945 and served until 1947; Sister Kieran Helring followed her as superior and principal from 1947-1951.

The original 140-pupil kindergarten through seventh grade school, called the Woodcrest Catholic School, was later christened "St. Matthew's School" and was to grow rapidly. April 18, 1956, saw 550 pupils and nine sister faculty members rejoicing that a new wing of seven classrooms had reached completion, expanding the capacity of the school. Several small classrooms had also been enlarged. This renovation also removed all classrooms from the convent and provided space for four additional bedrooms and an added bathroom in the convent.

Sister Juliette Flannery became principal and superior in 1957-1958. Five hundred eighty-three pupils were registered in K-8, so for the first time since the opening of the school a lay teacher was added to the faculty. The following year, with 683 pupils registered, a second lay teacher joined the nine on the faculty.

The well-sown academic and spiritual seeds were beginning to bear special fruit as two former graduates of St. Matthew's, Geraldine Vannicola (now Sister Angelique) and Theresa Angela Greggo entered the IHM Congregation in 1959, and Mary Ann Adams (now Sister Mary Ann) followed in 1960.

By 1962, a peak enrollment of 795 pupils was reached and two classrooms were added in the church basement. The faculty now numbered ten Sisters of IHM and five lay teachers. (42)
Sister Juliette's term was completed in June 1963 and Sister Agnella Murtaugh was appointed superior and principal. Ten teaching sisters and five lay teachers constituted the faculty, thus allowing Sister Agnella to devote full time to administrative duties.

The following year, on September 26, 1964, Father John Foley who had been pastor since the opening of St. Matthew's Parish, died. This dedicated priest burned himself out in building up, both physically and spiritually, St. Matthew's Parish. He was deeply mourned and left a lasting imprint on the children and people of this parish.

Monsignor Eugene J. Biggins was appointed to succeed Father Foley as pastor. One of his early decisions, seeing the crowded conditions of the eleven sisters in the convent atop the school, and the bulging classrooms, augmented by two separate mobile units, was to build a new convent for the sisters. By April 1966 he presented to the sisters the plans for the new two-story brick structure, to be located on the corner of Maryland and Victoria Avenues. Due to the subsequent ill health of Monsignor Biggins and the death of Bishop Michael Hyle, there were unavoidable delays in forwarding the plans. However, on January 22, 1968, the sisters were told to begin to take some personal and other lightweight materials to the new convent. On January 23 a large moving van arrived to complete the move. The official dedication took place on February 11, with open house for the sisters of the Wilmington Diocese on February 17, and for the parishioners on February 18. Open house for the IHM Sisters from nearby states was held on March 16 and 17, with approximately 150 Sisters attending. Monsignor Biggins, due to a March 11 surgery, was unable to join in the celebration.

It had been a very full year for all, especially for Sister Helen Hemmer who was in only her second year as principal and superior at St. Matthew's. Twelve sisters now resided in the convent, including Sister Eamon O'Neill, diocesan reading consultant. Six lay teachers, in addition to Sister Helen and ten teaching IHMs, served as faculty. By 1969-1970 Sister Helen would have an assistant principal, Sister Domitilla (Mary) Sweet. Four additional sisters would reside at St. Matthew's as the new

St. Mark's Diocesan High School opened and the faculty residence was not yet constructed. These included Sister Mary John (Jean) Conaty, Sister Ignatius (Ann) Seguljic, Sister Isabel Schratwieser, and Sister Dolores Filicko.

By 1970-1971 the office of superior was separated from that of principal and Sister John Francis Marley was appointed superior of the house and fourth grade teacher. Sister Roberta Peters was named principal, with seven lay teachers and ten IHMs as faculty members. St. Mark's Faculty House was dedicated on September 20, 1970, by Bishop Mardaga, so the four IHMs who formed part of that faculty group left St. Matthew's to take up residence at St. Mark's. (43)

Over subsequent years the Lord was to call many of our sisters to suffering as physical illness was a frequent visitor to this house. Most notable of these was the patient suffering of Sister Elizabeth Buschman. She was hospitalized in January 1978, returned in February to teach small groups of primary students in the convent parlor until the close of the school year. On November 7, 1979, she had surgery for a cancerous condition, recovered, and returned to half-day teaching from January to June 1980. The following school year found her actively engaged in teaching, preparing the children for First Holy Communion, being a member of the adult choir and parish Liturgy Committee, and of the Diocesan Religious Education Committee. In her twenty-fourth year of religious profession, and after five years at St. Matthew's, she died on August 19, 1981. Her funeral Mass was held at St. Matthew's Church. She had enriched the sisters of this local community, the pupils she taught, and the parish and diocese she served so well. (44)

While there was some expected decline in the enrollment of St. Matthew's School, registration was maintained at about 525 pupils in the early 1980s. New signs of life were found in the fifty-pupil kindergarten newly established in 1980 under Sister Sharon Kelly, IHM, and the prekindergarten founded in 1982 and located in the basement of the convent. With the opening of this latter facility, Sister Elizabeth McEneaney took over the kindergarten in the school.

Additional sisters who served as principal at St. Matthew's were Sister Mary Martin O'Dea, Sister Karen Braun, Sister Timothy Smyth, and Sister Amy Zychal.

This vibrant school continues with an enrollment of 472 in 1987-1988, a faculty of seven full-time and two part-time IHM Sisters and thirteen full-time and two part-time lay teachers.(46)

The founding of new missions was only one of the many activities which made demands on the time and abilities of Mother Marcella. Of central concern to her was obtaining approval for the *Constitutions* of the Congregation.

Revision of the *Constitutions*

The period from December 1933 to August 1943 crossing through the administrations of Mother Josepha and Mother Marcella represents a significant period in the history of the Sisters of the Immaculate Heart of Mary of Scranton as regards the updating and approval of the *Constitutions*. Mother Marcella, serving as assistant to Mother Josepha through most of that period, would have been familiar with the steps that had been taken to obtain approval of the Rule. But this work had never been completed.

While the Congregation had been founded in 1845 in the Diocese of Detroit, Michigan, the coming of the sisters to Pennsylvania in 1857 placed them in the Philadelphia Archdiocese, which then included Scranton. In 1868 Bishop James F. Wood of Philadelphia obtained permission of Pope Pius IX to divide his large diocese; thus the Scranton Diocese was formed and Very Reverend William O'Hara, Vicar General of the Philadelphia Archdiocese was appointed first Bishop of Scranton, July 12, 1868.

On August 15, 1871, the houses of the Congregation, which were located within the Scranton Diocese, were declared by Bishop O'Hara to be independent and were erected into a Scranton Diocesan Congregation. By the time Mother Josepha came into office in 1931 the influence of Bishop Thomas O'Reilly in the affairs of the Congregation was quite strong, as was evident in the election process of that very year of her election when the Bishop's proposal, although insightful for the future, did supersede the existing *Constitutions.* This alternative was not equally acceptable to all the sisters. (47) It was also true that the Congregation was already a multi-diocesan-based institute. Mother Josepha, in arranging for the revised Rule to be taken to Rome by Bishop O'Reilly in 1933, must have known that the Redemptorist canonists (48) were preparing a format, which would be interpreted in Rome as an application for the Decree of Praise and temporary approbation as an Institute of Pontifical Right, not as a Diocesan Institute. (49)

With this background in mind it is interesting that in 1940, Monsignor O'Connor pointed out to Mother Marcella that the Italian original which had been worked on in 1934 in Rome viewed the Congregation in this way, that is, as applying to be of Pontifical Right. However, Roman Canonist, Reverend Robert Sposetti who did the 1934 revisions, provided a translation of the Italian original, which considered the community as diocesan. Commenting on this, Monsignor O'Connor says, "You will note that the translation considers the community as a Diocesan one and as I explained to you, this is the wish of the Most Reverend Bishop." (50) It is apparent that in the interest of completing the approval process, Mother Marcella accepted Bishop Hafey's wish in the matter.

Anyone who has worked on documents such as the constitutions understands what transpired over the next three years, as every word and its meaning was given a thorough scrutiny by those working on the updating of the *Constitutions* and *Book of Customs* of the Congregation. Reverend William V. Greene, a Redemptorist and Doctor of Canon Law from Mount Saint Alphonsus in Esopus, New York, and Reverend Edward C. Daly, OP, of the Dominican House of Studies in Washington, DC, and member of the Apostolic Legation, were selected for the work. Monsignor (eventually, Archbishop) O'Connor worked very closely in the matter also, acting as liaison among all parties concerned. Many exchanges of letters over this period indicate the great desire of Mother Marcella to complete the revisions, honoring the suggestions of the canonists, and meeting her own deadline; namely, to have the revised *Constitutions* to the sisters at the time of the General Elections in August of 1943. By March 1943 the revisions were completed, and Father Daly spelled out what it meant to be officially a congregation of diocesan right as he indicated the next steps in the process:

> The text will become the law of your Congregation when the Bishop promulgates it for you, after he hears from the other interested Bishops, [those in all dioceses where our Sisters were residing]. For effectiveness is enough that he determine the date when the text becomes obligatory; for the Bishop is the legislator for the congregation of diocesan right. It suffices that you transmit copies to the local superiors for their subjects with notice of the date of obligation which the Bishop predetermined. It is not necessary to deliver the text through a General Chapter whose acceptance is not required to make the text your law. (51)

Twelve bishops and three archbishops thus had to send in to Bishop Hafey their approval of the proposed Constitutions. In order of their response from April through July 1943, they were Bishop Leech of Harrisburg; Bishop McGuiness of Raleigh; Archbishop Spellman, New York; Bishop Fitzmaurice, Wilmington; Bishop Boyle of Pittsburgh; Bishop Kelly of Boise, Idaho; Bishop Foery of Syracuse; Bishop McAuliffe of Hartford; Archbishop Michael Curley of Baltimore and

Washington, DC; Bishop Griffin of Trenton; Bishop Guilfoyle of Altoona; Bishop Keough of Providence, Rhode Island; Archbishop Howard of Portland, Oregon; Bishop Molloy of Brooklyn, and Bishop Hafey of Scranton. (52)

Four of these had submitted the material to their own diocesan canonists who, of course, came up with additional observations and suggested changes. These were all submitted to the coordinators of the project and many of the suggestions incorporated into the revised document. At long last, the fully revised copy was sent to the printer on July 26, 1943. While it was a disappointment to Mother Marcella who had hoped to distribute the new *Constitutions* at the first General Chapter meeting of the Congregation on August 4, 1943, it was nonetheless a tremendous tribute to her persevering, yet genteel, prodding that all parts of this huge project would come together, and indeed that the printer's promise to have the copies ready for all the sisters by August 15 was kept. (53) The Feast of the Holy Angels, October 2, 1943, was set by Bishop Hafey as the official date of promulgation of the new *Constitutions*. (54) In announcing this to the Congregation, Mother Marcella wrote:

> My dear Sisters, if we faithfully observe our Constitutions and the Customs of the Congregation, so full of wisdom and the religious spirit, we will surely attain the perfection required by our holy calling, and more effectually become fit instruments of God for the accomplishment of the secondary object of our Congregation, the salvation of souls, through the various works in which we are engaged . . . (55)

The First General Chapter—August 4, 1943

It was an historic moment in the Congregation when, prior to the General Chapter of Elections of August 5, 1943, the capitulars to the Chapter were called to meet as the First General Chapter. The newly revised *Constitutions,* approved by the Bishops, but not yet promulgated to the sisters at large, nor indeed to the Capitulars themselves, prescribed that:

> Before the election of the new Superior General takes place, the Superior General whose term of office is expiring, or the First Assistant, as the case may be, shall render to the General Chapter an exact account of the administration of the common property of the Congregation as well as of its financial condition during the time that has elapsed since the last General Chapter. She shall

> also make a report of the personal, temporal, and disciplinary status of the Congregation. (56)

Mother Marcella was very generous in offering praise to the sisters for their faithfulness to their religious obligations and to their duties in the apostolate; she was also quite candid in addressing areas that were in need of improvement, especially as regards charity, reconciliation, and poverty. Her report also addressed the progress made in the revision of the *Constitutions* and the process utilized to obtain their approval.

The status of the institutions of the Congregation, the education of the sisters and their appropriate certification, the novitiate, a statistical summary of the membership and missions of the Congregation and a financial statement were all included in Mother Marcella's report. As required by the *Constitutions* a committee was appointed to examine the financial report and submit corrections or approval. This committee included Sisters Borgia, Ildephonsus and Macarius.

At the close of her report, Mother Marcella also announced the gift of Miss Ella McCarty in the amount of $49,000 for the erection of a "practice house" on campus for the Home Economics Department of Marywood College. This house later was named McCarty Hall. (57)

The General Elections of August 5, 1943

Ninety-nine capitulars, including the six ex-officio members of the Congregation's administration, and Mother Mary William Craig as a former superior general, assembled in the Motherhouse Chapel at Marywood for the election of the superior general, her two assistants and two councilors. The ninety-nine ranged from the three oldest elected members of the Congregation: Sister Borgia Boylan, Sister Ildephonsus McCarthy and Sister Macarius McDonnell, to the youngest elected members: Sister Laurana Burns, Sister Jovita Loomis and Sister Cor Mariae Schroth who also served as secretary to the Chapter.

Mother Marcella Gill was elected to the office of superior general. Having completed Mother Josepha's second term, she now began her own six-year term. Sister Irmina McMahon was elected first assistant; Sister Eugenia Kealy, second assistant; Sister Madeline Loughlin, first councilor; and Sister Sylvia Morgan, second councilor. (58)

That same day, August 5, 1943, a council meeting was held at 1:15 p.m. at which Sister Madeline was selected as general secretary of the Congregation; Sister Aquina Whalen, as general bursar. Mother Anysia Moran and Sister Teresa Moran were reappointed as mistress of novices and assistant mistress of novices, respectively.

Later, at 1:40 p.m., the second meeting of the General Chapter of 1943 was held, at which the newly elected superior general, Mother Marcella, presided. The committee appointed to review the financial statement reported their "unqualified approval."

In an unprecedented show of participatory government, Mother Marcella then asked for recommendations from the sisters. One capitular brought up the matter of charity and its relation to "uniformity in regard to observance" of the *Constitutions.* Another spoke of the need for an assistant to the superior in houses where there are a large number of sisters. Mother Marcella noted that the new *Constitutions* had provision for these matters.

Further suggestions were sought by Mother Marcella regarding material for the *Book of Customs* that was then under revision. It is due to the suggestion of Sister Macarius that the custom of observing Saturday as a free day in our Congregation was initiated. This was the only issue put to a vote, and it carried and was incorporated into the revised *Book of Customs* in 1943! (59)

Immaculate Conception Chapel School, Scranton, Pennsylvania

In 1943 Immaculate Conception was still a mission chapel of St. Peter's Cathedral Parish, having one pastor, Reverend Francis A. Costello, and one parochial school, Cathedral School, founded in 1872 as the first Catholic School in Scranton and originally named St. Cecilia's Academy. The children from the Petersburg and Hill sections of the parish who attended Catholic school were enrolled in the downtown facility. Religious instructions were also provided at the Cathedral School for those attending public schools. In 1923, the Mission Chapel of the Immaculate Conception was built. While it was not yet a parish in its own right and had no resident pastor, the chapel became the center of worship for Catholics from the Hill Section, and its auditorium also provided a convenient location in which to hold religious instructions for the children. The Sisters, Servants of the Immaculate Heart of Mary who had served as teachers at the Cathedral School from its opening in 1872 serviced the Mission Chapel as sacristans and religious education teachers from the time of its opening in 1923. (60)

In 1941, Monsignor Martin J. O'Connor (later, Archbishop) as pastor of Cathedral Parish acquired the old Bayard Taylor, No. 35 public grade school, located at the corner of Taylor and Olive Street, from the Scranton School District. This building was a three-story, red brick structure with ten classrooms and two spacious halls. It was in complete disrepair at the time of its purchase, but under the direction of Monsignor O'Connor, extensive improvements were made—the tower which surmounted the school was taken down; the iron fence that surrounded the property was removed and the grounds landscaped; classrooms and halls were painted; desks sanded and refinished; and new blackboards set in place. At the time of the purchase of the school, two vacant lots across from the property on Olive Street were also purchased. This land was graded and sodded and playground equipment installed. New cement walks were laid. These playground facilities were made accessible to all the children of the neighborhood. (61)

A year before the school was officially opened to students for a regular full-time session, religious instructions were offered twice weekly in the school building. In the summer of 1942 both kindergarten and catechetical instructions were held there. The sisters engaged in this work included Sister Francella Shaughnessy as kindergarten instructor; Sister Margrete Kelly, Sister Maris Law and Sister Rosalita Smith taught religion to the various grade levels of children. These sisters lived at Cathedral Convent and commuted by the day to the Chapel School building. (62)

Monsignor O'Connor had been made Auxiliary Bishop of Scranton, so his pastorate was given into other hands. He had prepared well for a successor and the many matters for which he had been responsible were transferred with relative ease. By September 7, 1943, all was in readiness for the opening of Chapel School. Monsignor Francis Costello, newly designated pastor of Cathedral Parish, celebrated a votive High Mass in honor of the Holy Spirit in Immaculate Conception Mission Chapel. Following the Mass, two hundred children from kindergarten through fourth grade marched the two blocks from the Chapel to the school under the watchful eyes of Sister Ricarda Gill, who served as principal of both Cathedral and Chapel Schools, and the five sister-faculty members. These included Sister Ignatius Brown, Sister Grata (Barbara) Brow, Sister Timothea (Jane) Driscoll, Sister Vera Nallin and Sister Carmelita (Jane) Berube.

Sister Ignatius was to spend only two months there since she was transferred to Coeur d'Alene, Idaho, in November 1943. Sister Maria Theophane Allen took her place at Chapel School. (63) Since 1938 Sister Ricarda had served as principal at Cathedral School, where the enrollment was about 600 pupils, so perhaps she took it in stride that she was now being asked to add 200 to her expert care!

The foresight shown in planning for and opening Chapel School is evident in the fact of its growth to almost six hundred students by 1958. The numbers of students exceeded the space limitations, so the then pastor,

Monsignor Robert A. McNulty, announced that the eighth grade would henceforth be located at Cathedral School on Wyoming Avenue and that children who were not members of Cathedral Parish (or the Mission Chapel) would also transfer to the Cathedral School. But even with these arrangements the Chapel School still enrolled nearly five hundred children. Nine sisters and one lay teacher comprised the faculty at that time.

On August 28, 1958, Monsignor McNulty also announced that Miss M. Pauline Casey had given her home at 612 Clay Avenue to the Cathedral Parish for the use of the Sisters, Servants of the Immaculate Heart of Mary, as a convent. Miss Casey had given this property to the Bernardine Sisters in 1943, but in withdrawing their sisters from the faculty of South Catholic High School in 1958, the Bernardine Sisters returned the property to Pauline Casey. These events were providential for our sisters, since the growing faculty at Cathedral High School would have soon brought about the need for an additional residence to accommodate the faculty of Immaculate Conception Chapel School.

The Casey residence was located two blocks below the school in the beautiful hill section of Scranton. Its twenty rooms readily accommodated the needs of the nine sisters who took up residence there on Saturday, August 30, 1958. The local community included Sister Rose Francis Brown, superior and principal, Sister Miriam Eugene Carroll, Sister Constantine Proulx, Sister Marquita Sealey, Sister Greta Collins, Sister Charlene Templeton, Sister Rosaria Joyce, Sister Eugenius (Teresa) O'Malley and Sister LaSalette Connell.

Monsignor McNulty on Sunday, August 31, 1958, celebrated the first Mass in the new convent. A Jesuit priest, Reverend Joseph P. Logan, was appointed chaplain, thus providing daily Mass in the convent for the sisters.

Pauline Casey continued to show her extreme generosity by having the exterior of the convent painted and by purchasing a new electric stove for the kitchen. Generous gifts and donations were made also by parishioners and by the families of the sisters to provide chapel, kitchen, library and other materials for the convent. (64)

Chapel School continued to grow as a K-7 grade school, reaching a peak of 514 pupils in 1962-1963. By 1966, declining enrollment at the downtown Cathedral Elementary School, however, resulted in the decision to close the Cathedral Elementary School, transfer grade seven from the Chapel School to the Cathedral High School building, thus creating a junior and senior high school complex; and to provide for Cathedral and Chapel elementary students a K-6 setting at the Chapel School.

While these actions were logical due to the shifting population of the downtown parish with an enrollment of 184 students, 121 of whom were in grades 7 and 8, it was obvious that the end of an era had come. St. Peter's Cathedral Grade School building had been, over a 94-year span a most significant spot in the history of the Sisters, Servants of the Immaculate Heart of Mary. The original building on this spot was opened and blessed on July 2, 1872, by Bishop William O'Hara, first Bishop of Scranton, and on September 8, 1872, it was named Saint Cecilia's and became the motherhouse and novitiate of the Congregation, transferring from Susquehanna, Pennsylvania. On September 26, 1872, St. Cecilia's Academy was opened as a resident and day school and became the first school founded in the diocese by Bishop O'Hara. The sisters resided on the fourth floor of this structure above the school, with no elevator to ease their ascent. Portress duty was reserved for the young and agile!

At the time of the decision to close Cathedral Grade School in 1966, it was decided to retain this 92-year-old structure as a convent for the Cathedral High School faculty until further plans could be made. (65)

On June 17, 1967, Immaculate Conception officially became a full-fledged parish, separate from Cathedral Parish. The word "Chapel" was dropped from the name of the parish. The first pastor of the newly created parish was Reverend (later, Monsignor) Leo W. Gildea. (66)

The deteriorating physical condition of the Chapel School building was a serious financial drain on the parish and became also a safety concern of the parents of school-aged children. Throughout 1970 and the spring of 1971 there was much discussion about the future of the school as the enrollment dropped to 160 pupils, K-6 grades. There were additional costs also as three lay teachers were hired to augment the four sister-teachers. An exchange of letters between Bishop J. Carroll McCormick and Mother Beata Wertz in December 1970 and January 1971 indicate the Bishop's desire and the Congregation's willingness to continue this school. (67) And, as the annals report, "Easter recess brought happy news. The Church Bulletin announced that our Reverend Bishop did not want the school closed and repairs would be planned." (68)

Monsignor Gildea was replaced as pastor by Reverend (later, Monsignor) William Purcell on September 8, 1971. Aware of the enormity of his tasks, Father Purcell, nevertheless, began with great enthusiasm and with the support of the parishioners to renovate the school. During the week of January 7, 1972, teams of parishioners painted classrooms throughout the building. New desks were placed in the first five grades and new tile flooring was laid. Bishop McCormick visited the school on May 2 and expressed his approval of all that had been accomplished. Open house was held on May 7 for all parishioners, both to affirm the labor that many had contributed and to conduct information and public relations efforts on behalf of increased enrollment for the school.

The beautiful twenty-room former Casey home that served as the Immaculate Conception Convent was also in constant need of repairs and refurbishing. In the summer of 1972, Father Purcell and his volunteers tackled the job of painting the convent inside and outside. At this point there were only four full-time sisters and one part-time sister assigned to Immaculate Conception. It was not surprising, then, that there was talk of selling this large home and moving to a smaller house. On May 3, 1973, talk became reality and the pastor purchased a new convent home at 817 North Irving Avenue. The Casey home (Clay Avenue Convent) was sold to Mr. Richard Walsh. The summer of 1973 was spent moving from 612 Clay Avenue to the new convent on North Irving Avenue with cleaning, packing, unpacking, and rearranging the order of the day. The move was completed on August 10. Father Purcell, pastor, offered the first Mass in the new convent on September 1 and on September 10 Bishop McCormick blessed the entire house.

The reality of a low enrollment in the fall of 1973 of only 135 pupils and continuing rumors that Immaculate Conception was going to close, together with the Bishop's exhortation to the sisters to strive to keep Immaculate Conception School open, caused concern for the little community, which now included Sister Rose Angela Ruddy, principal and superior, Sister Cecile Gallagher and Sister Jean Coughlin. Their number was increased by one when a postulant, Suzanne Campbell, was assigned for third grade. (69) Their concerns were not unfounded, for on September 18 Sister Rose Angela, as principal, attended a Congregation meeting at which she learned that our sisters were to be withdrawn from several schools, including Immaculate Conception, at the close of the school year. The annals describe shock and disbelief, even numbness, as the emotions characterizing the pastor, sisters and parishioners as they received this news. (70) The plan was that students from Immaculate Conception School would be bused to St. Clare's and St. Paul's Schools in Green Ridge, utilizing the busing system of the Scranton Public School District. Insofar as feasible, books, equipment and materials from IC would be transported to St. Clare's and St. Paul's over the summer. It is not difficult to imagine how the sisters spent June of 1974 as they readied the school building for occupation by personnel of the Northeast Educational Instruction Unit #19 on July 1. The building was to be prepared to be a school for the handicapped in September 1974.

The Irving Avenue Convent, too, had to be dismantled, after only one year of occupancy by our sisters. The statues and the monstrance from the chapel had been the gift of Sister Greta Collins' family. These were given to our convent on River Street in Scranton. Furnishings belonging to the parish were, of course, left behind, but disposing of books and materials belonging to the community was a large task. Many spiritual reading books were given to the Passionist Sisters at St. Gabriel's Monastery.

Father Purcell, no doubt inundated by the events of the year, was not present at the final closing of the convent. He had left on July 5 to serve as chaplain with the Armed Forces of the 109th Division for two weeks.

> On Sunday, July 14, Father Callahan removed the Blessed Sacrament from our Chapel. Sisters Rose Angela, Maria Rita, Leo Marie and Henry were in attendance . . . On Monday, July 15, Fathers Meckwood and Callahan visited us to say goodbye, to thank us for the work of the IHMs through the years, and to wish us well. The rest of the day was spent completing those inevitable last minute items. Finally, at 4:30 p.m. we closed the doors and returned the keys to the rectory. (71)

The thirty-year presence of our sisters at "the Chapel" had seen a long line of religious women, rendering quality educational service under the leadership of outstanding principals including: Sister Ricarda Gill, Sister Paulette Morrison, Sister Alma Shelley, Sister Alma Marie Morgan, Sister St. Helen Sullivan, Sister Rose Francis Brown, Sister Bernita McDonough, Sister Carol Baden, Sister Honor Lenihan and Sister Rose Angela Ruddy.

In tribute to all of the sisters who had served at "Chapel" School an unidentified woman wrote a story for the *Scrantonian* in 1981 as the old building, upon the decision of Father F. Allan Conlon, pastor, and his parishioners, faced the wrecking ball of the M & S Demolition Company of Old Forge. The writer renews many happy memories of the old school, and asks:

> Was it the magic of the building or the people who staffed it that created the aura? I think it was both. I think the school starved for the special touch of the IHM Sisters, with their optimism and spirit. For although the original heating registers in each room were engraved August 1, 1870—the official birth of the building—I feel now that it must not have taken its first breath until 1941 when the Diocese of Scranton bought it and the Sisters came. But that is only my feeling, and there is no one else here to debate it with this quiet morning . . .(72)

Sacred Heart Catechetical Center/Elementary School, Mount Holly, New Jersey

In February of 1943, Mother Marcella responded affirmatively to the request of Bishop William A. Griffin, first Bishop of Trenton, for sisters to open a catechetical school in Sacred Heart Parish, Mount Holly, New Jersey. The Bishop described the work as "missionary because of the present large number of mixed marriages with corresponding lapses in the practice of our holy faith." (73) It was missionary also in that this one parish served the Catholic population in an area of approximately 1,200 square miles and included Hainesport, Medford Lakes, Rancocas, Masonville, Jobstown, Pine Grove, Red Lion, Brown's Mills and Four Mile Colony, in addition to Mount Holly. Reverend George E. Duff was the pastor at Mount Holly, the only permanent parish in the 1,200-mile area with a resident pastor.

The first difficulty encountered by the Bishop and Father Duff was to find a residence for the sisters. The War Production Board would not permit any building because of the shortages of building materials, so a search was begun for the purchase or rental of a house, which would not be too remote from the church. As the end of August 1943 approached with no housing for the sisters having yet been identified, the offer of Miss Clementine Mehl, 129 Madison Avenue, Mount Holly, to share her home with the sisters on a temporary basis was regarded as the only immediate solution. The second floor apartment had two large bedrooms and one small bedroom. The Bishop had also promised that a small chapel would be provided in a first floor parlor room. Miss Mehl's original good will in the matter was evident in the fact that she would accept no rent from the pastor for this apartment, and had expressed the possibility that she might, in time, donate the entire property to the church for the use of the sisters. (74)

Thus it was that in September 1943 five sisters took up residence in the convent on Madison Avenue, some six blocks from the church. The initial community included Sister Alphonsus McGoldrick, superior, Sister Carlotta Kaschalk, Sister Stella Devers, Sister Christina Murphy and Sister St. Margaret Montague. It is obvious that the small quarters afforded the sisters no privacy, little opportunity to assemble as a community, no space for the evening religious instructions for the high school students, and, possibly most difficult of all the absence of the Blessed Sacrament in their residence. Whatever the problems, Mother Marcella noted in her March visit that the tabernacle arrived the day she was there. (75)

In spite of these difficulties the sisters kept before them the purpose for which they had come and they set about their missionary endeavors.

For the first few months census-taking was their main work, and each morning the sisters set out carrying their census cards, their lunches and their catechisms, so as to be able to show the families what the children would be studying. Once the Catholic families had been identified, classes were organized wherever groups of children could be gathered together—in the homes, the general store, or on the farms. The work bore fruit almost at once in the numbers of children attending classes, but also in the return of fathers, mothers and grandparents to the practice of their faith. (76) Before the close of that first year Bishop Griffin had come to Mount Holly for Confirmation; First Holy Communion had taken place; the children had been prepared for Forty Hours and Holy Thursday processions, as well as to sing a Gregorian Chant High Mass.

Meanwhile, Sister St. Margaret had been changed to another mission and because of the crowded conditions at Miss Mehl's residence, no sister was sent to replace her. After Mother Marcella's March 30 letter to the Bishop about the unsatisfactory housing arrangement and Miss Mehl's own growing discomfort with it, there was an immediate response on the part of the Bishop. Sister Alphonsus had informed the Bishop of the untenanted Judge Davis property on 310 High Street, and he had already looked into it by mid-March. It seemed that the government had the property and had already begun to convert it into apartments for military personnel from nearby military bases. Amazingly, the Bishop and Father Duff were able to persuade the United States War Housing Administration to stop the work on the property and to permit Mrs. Davis to sell the property to the Church instead. It included a twenty-two-room mansion with surrounding land of four acres beautifully landscaped with beautiful shrubs and trees.

This property is a story in itself. The mansion was an historical landmark in Mount Holly, having been built originally in 1832 by Nathan Dunn, a world traveler and collector, who had made his fortune in Canton, China, as a merchant and trader. He lived in China for about twelve years and on his return settled in Mount Holly, having a local architect, John Notman, design a home for him that came to be known as the "Chinese Cottage." The house was modeled on homes of Chinese aristocrats, with added touches of the English cottage architecture of the early 1800s. The property included twenty acres of land and gained renown, not only for its architecture, but also for the beauty of its landscaped grounds. Nathan Dunn imported exotic shrubs and trees from China, Japan and other countries to enhance the property. Subsequent owners, Franklin S. Levis and John D. Johnson, had made many modifications. Levis expanded the second story and added a third. Johnson added a south wing for a ballroom, a brick carriage house, and covered the entire first floor with Pompeian brick. At the time of its purchase as the future sight of the Mount Holly Regional Catholic School in June 1944, it was a twenty-two room mansion with magnificent leaded stained glass windows, huge carved doors, exquisitely carved stairways, Grecian chandeliers, brass gas lamps, inset mirrors above the many fireplaces and in the doors, and intricate wood carvings in woodwork throughout the house. It was, and still is, an elegant house. (77)

The Bishop's vision was that this mansion would serve as both the regional Catholic grade school and the convent, and certainly there was ample room for his plan in 1944. A complete remodeling was undertaken and the lower floor was transformed into four large classrooms, a kindergarten, music room, an auditorium and a chapel. The second and third floors were converted into living quarters for the sisters. What was once a large basement and bowling alley became a modern cafeteria for the children.

When school opened to kindergarteners and the first four grades on September 11, 1944, needless to say, the work begun in the summer was not completed. For another month the noise of hammers and saws continued while numerous workmen scurried about. But Mount Holly Regional Catholic School became a reality by solemn dedication by Bishop Griffin on October 15, 1944. Clergy from most of New Jersey were present, as were dignitaries from surrounding towns. The Commanding General and his aides from Fort Dix also attended. Parishioners and students rejoiced at the realization of what had been for so long only a dream for them. (78) The expected eighty pupils for the opening of the school turned out to be 144! With characteristic ingenuity the sisters quickly made the necessary adjustments to accommodate all. The larger problem was that just two days after school opened a state law passed excluding private and parochial school children from public school transportation. With so many children in attendance from far-flung areas, it was necessary for Bishop Griffin to come to the rescue by lending money for the purchase of parish buses from funds of the Diocesan Society for the Conservation of the Faith. As Sister Alphonsus wrote,

> One of the three zealous pastors, while waiting to procure buses, drove cars himself, and, aided by obliging parishioners, the children were brought back and forth to school. Before long, we saw, with feelings of just pride, our own yellow buses, bearing the title 'Catholic School Coach' started on the long routes of picking up our scattered children. (79)

The faculty for the school and for the catechetical work of the three parishes and their missions had been amply provided for since Mother Marcella sent seven sisters to Mount Holly in September 1944. Additions to the four sisters already there included Sister Patricia Cavanagh, Sister Carina McCaffrey and Sister Lucy McGrath. (80) The end of the regular school day was the commencement of another work for the sisters, for each day children in nine centers were provided catechetical instructions. On Saturday mornings several sisters gave instructions to the mentally retarded children at the Four Mile Colony in Brown's Mills. Sunday, too, was a busy day as the sisters attended the different churches to be with the children at Mass. In the afternoon, sodality choirs were trained so that liturgical music could be sung at Holy Mass. This missionary ministry entailed many personal sacrifices by the sisters, but the ever-increasing numbers of adults who attended Holy Mass and received the sacraments motivated them to continue their efforts with the children. (81)

Grade five was added to the school in September 1945 and grade six in 1946. This continued expansion necessitated the leasing of the Royle Mansion at 234 High Street as a convent for the sisters. Thus for the second time in three years the sisters were faced with moving. Most of the summer of 1946 was spent in readying their new convent home, but Sister Alphonsus was not destined to reside there for she was succeeded in August 1946 by Sister Brigida Strome as superior and principal. The facility at 310 High Street was bulging as over 500 children in six grades filled every available space. As it became apparent that the needs for future space could not possibly be satisfied in the old "Dunn Cottage," the pastor, Reverend James S. Foley, approached Bishop Griffin with the idea of building a new school. The Bishop thought the idea extremely extravagant and agreed only to look for another property that could be renovated to take care of the overflow of students. Sister Brigida, an experienced school administrator, did not see the advisability of the Bishop's plan, but bided her time and launched a prayer crusade, especially directed to Mother Francis Xavier Cabrini, to assist them in obtaining a new building for their school. The school children even placed medals in the ground on the site of the future school, as had Mother Cabrini in her lifetime for her hoped-for projects. It seems that both heaven and earth conspired to change Bishop Griffin's mind and soon the southwest corner of the grounds were humming with construction. The sisters moved back into the original convent at 310 High Street as they saw that the new school would be ready by September.

On October 17, 1948, just four years after the original convent-school had opened, Bishop Griffin dedicated the new school building in proud recognition of the growth of his original concept of a regional Catholic grade school. It was a special joy for Bishop Griffin, for the pastor, Father Duff, and for the sisters, most of whom were among the original group that started the Mount Holly mission. Additions were Sister Laetitia Caulson, Sister Ignatia Murphy and Sister Albertus (Anne) Fulwiler. The new school had six classrooms, all on one floor, and was constructed so as to permit the addition of a second floor, if needed.

June 17, 1949, was the date of the first graduation from Mount Holly Regional Catholic School. Bishop Griffin was on hand to present thirty-six eighth grade graduates with their diplomas.

An ever-increasing enrollment made it necessary in 1950 to drop the kindergarten, to restrict new registration to first grade, and to direct the 125 pupils from the Medford area to other schools. The new pastor, Reverend Joseph V. Kozak, appointed in June 1950, had two additional classrooms constructed in the basement of the school. By the time this latest addition was made to the school, Sisters Gioia deZerman, Francella Shaughnessy, Espiritu Dempsey, Nivard (Patricia) O'Brien, Helen Hemmer, and Isabel Schratwieser had each taught for a period at the Regional School. Sister John Berchmans (Josephine) Joy was sent in May 1952 to assist the sisters at this busy time of year.

In August 1952, Sister Raymond Rafferty was appointed superior and principal to succeed Sister Brigida Strome whose term was completed. Having come to Mount Holly in 1945, Sister Raymond was well prepared to assume her new position. New to the faculty that year were Sister Maria Gerald Shanley, Sister Benedicta Berendes, Sister Francis deSales (Michlyn) Grella and Sister Marya Foley. (82)

In July 1953, construction was begun on a second floor addition of six classrooms to the existing school building. In September school opened once again to the accompaniment of cement mixers, drills, hammers and saws. When the school addition was blessed and dedicated in May 1954, there were some new faces. Bishop Griffin, a friend indeed, and initiator of the Mount Holly concept, and of our sisters' presence there, had died. His successor, Bishop George W. Ahr entered enthusiastically and quickly into his new role and became a staunch supporter of the school also. Among the sisters, Sister Julie Pfister and Sister Bernardinus (Gloria) Frank were recent assignees.

By 1958 there were 650 students in the school, with eleven sisters and two lay teachers as faculty. Having completed a total of thirteen years at Mount Molly, six of which she served as superior and principal, Sister Raymond was changed. Sister Cecily Wittig succeeded her. During her principalship the enrollment continued to climb, reaching 800 students in

1960-1961 when two additional classrooms were opened, bringing to sixteen the number of classrooms in use. The peak of eleven sisters in 1959-1960 fell to ten with six lay teachers augmenting their number in 1960-1961. A fifty-pupil per grade maximum was set—a heavy load, indeed, for all teachers. Both the 800-student enrollment and the ten sisters and six lay teachers continued up to 1964-1965.

Sister St. Mark (Mary Mark) Lowery succeeded Sister Cecily as superior and principal in 1964. The enrollment, which was to decline slowly to 600 students by 1969-1970, was 735 students as school opened in 1964. With faculty numbers holding stable, it was possible to decrease class sizes and address more significantly the individual needs of students. As always, the extra task of teaching religious instructions to children not attending the Catholic School was embraced. It is noteworthy that five sisters and seven lay teachers taught instructions after school at Sacred Heart, two sisters continued to work at Hainesport, four sisters taught the children at Fort Dix on Saturdays and three sisters assisted evenings with the Neumann Club and high school student instructions. Each year there were the three locations for First Holy Communions, and periodically there were two or three Confirmation ceremonies.

The school continued to flourish with students excelling and capturing prizes for speaking, debating, writing and community service. It is a great side effect of the work of the faculty at Mount Holly that many young men and women entered the priesthood and religious life. Four of these are IHM Sisters, namely, Sister Marguerite Green, Sister Rosemary Goulet, Sister John Michele Southwick and Sister Eileen Egan.

Sisters who served as principals from 1970 to 1987 include Sister Robert Mary Murphy, Sister Daniel Mary Heisey, Sister Virgine Maurer and Sister Fidelis Flannery. In that same period the superiors were Sister Gracette Baker, Sister John Francis Marley, Sister St. Germaine O'Neil, Sister Eileen Egan, Sister Joanella Ryan, Sister Kathleen Hassett and Sister Thelma Gutt.

In 1987 Mount Holly Regional School had 543 students with nine sisters, three of whom instruct small groups, and fifteen lay teachers. (84)

St. Ambrose Catechetical Center/Elementary School, Bridgeport, Connecticut

The Sisters, Servants of the Immaculate Heart of Mary were not strangers to the pastor and people of St. Ambrose Parish, Bridgeport, when they went to establish a Catechetical School there in 1944. Our sisters from Devon had taught religious instructions in summer sessions prior to 1944, commuting from Devon. St. Ambrose Parish, located in the eastern section of Bridgeport, had been established only about fifteen years at the time of the sisters' coming in 1944. It was located in an area surrounded by large industrial plants, chief of which were General Electric and the Remington-Dupont Companies. Jobs were plentiful since these plants were operating on a twenty-four hour daily working schedule to meet the demand for war supplies manufactured here. It was an area that had been all too suddenly industrialized, hence lacked the housing, stores, and other services to support an influx of laborers and their families. A housing project called "Success Park" was built by the federal government and located in this section of Bridgeport. The people were of diverse nationalities with a slight predominance of the Slavic races. They were hard working, frugal themselves, yet generous with the Church.

There was no Catholic school in St. Ambrose Parish at this time, but Rev. Thomas P. Mooney, pastor, was determined to meet the religious education needs of the growing numbers of young people in his parish through the joint efforts of religious and lay instructors. Thus it was that he sought and obtained permission from Bishop Maurice F. McAuliffe to establish a Catechetical School and to seek the Sisters of IHM for this work. In February of 1944 he wrote to Mother Marcella to convey the Bishop's approval of the proposed project. (85)

Father Mooney's plan was to purchase a house at 460 Mill Hill Avenue adjacent to the church, make the necessary alterations, and have all in readiness as a convent for the sisters in August. Since the house he had in mind was already rented, it may not have been a simple matter to procure it. In any case, four sisters were appointed for the new mission: Sister Mary Martin Cawley, superior, Sister Mary Grace McCarthy, Sister Franzchen Yahner, and Sister Rita Marie Byrne. Since the convent was not ready, initially they resided with our sisters in Devon and commuted daily to Bridgeport to arrange for the scheduling of classes, ordering of books, and the numerous chores entailed in getting ready for school. Seeing the slow pace of the workmen engaged in the convent renovations, the story is told that Sister Mary Martin gave them fair warning that the sisters would be moving in "ready or not." And on October 14, 1944, that is exactly what happened! There was no furniture in the house upon their arrival but she saw to it that beds were ordered that day and delivered for use by the sisters that very night. Items found in the kitchen included a small hot plate, a set of dishes, and a bushel of apples. (86)

The convent was at length completed and the chapel was beautifully furnished from the generous gifts of the people of the parish. The altar was dedicated as a memorial to the members of St. Ambrose Parish serving in the nation's armed forces, five of whom had lost their lives at that time. Bishop McAuliffe and several priests were present for the solemn blessing of the convent on November 29, 1944. The Bishop's presence was especially significant, since it was his last official and public action. He entered the hospital on December 3 and died within three weeks, a victim of overwork and exhaustion from his rigorous wartime schedule and impaired health. The sisters from St. Ambrose were present for the final prayers at his bedside.

In spite of these unsettled beginnings, the work of the sisters met with immediate success in the great numbers of children who registered for the Catechetical School. There was a released time program for the public school youngsters from Hall, Edison, Stonybrook and Summerfield Schools. A total of 750 children were taught over the five afternoons each week. In addition, there were two sessions of religious instructions on Sundays. One sister estimated that about 1,200 different students were contacted each week. (87) The services of the four sisters were augmented by thirty-five volunteer lay instructors.

The people of St. Ambrose Parish were very happy with the work of the sisters. Their gratitude was often expressed in their generosity and help to the sisters. At that time the contract under which the sisters worked was for $450 for ten months per sister. It would have been impossible for them to live on $1,800 a year had it not been that, as Sister Thaddeus who was there from 1950-1952 recalled, all of their fresh vegetables and meat were given to them without charge by generous store owners from the parish. (88)

From the time of the sisters' coming for the Catechetical School, it was part of the plan that one day St. Ambrose Parish would have a parochial school. Father Mooney, pastor, was taking no chances, however, on whether sisters would be available when his school building was ready. In June 1950 therefore, he wrote to Mother Marcella about his plans to complete his school by September 1952 and his hope to open eight rooms in the new building. (89) He was assured by a return letter of July 10, 1950, that " I shall do my best to have the quota in readiness for St. Ambrose's School." (90)

Meanwhile at the Catechetical School, Sister Mary Martin had been followed as superior by Sister DeNeri McLane (1949-1950) and Sister Thaddeus Kelly (1950-1952). This work continued until the opening of the school in 1952, and even then some released time pupils continued to come for instructions until the program was discontinued. The sisters watched the gradual emergence of the new St. Ambrose Parish School, a two-story brick building of sixteen classrooms, with auditorium and lunchroom space on the ground floor. In the summer of 1952, just prior to the school's opening the sisters who were at St. Ambrose for catechetical work also took an interest in the new school and helped to prepare for its opening by covering books and decorating both the blackboards and the expansive tack board space in the halls. (91)

In order to provide residence space for the additional sisters who would arrive for the opening of school in September 1952, the pastor purchased a second house next door to the original convent. In 1954 there would be an enlarged dining room and kitchen added and the garages would be replaced to provide a passageway connecting the two houses.

Eight sisters staffed the first four grades at the opening of the school in September of 1952. These included Sister Elizabeth O'Sullivan, principal, Sister Franzchen Yahner, Sister Carmelita (Jane) Berube, Sister Ann Marie Foley, Sister Margaret Russell, Sister Therese Culhane, Sister Cornelius Scanlon, and Sister Paschal FitzGibbon. A Mrs. Rourke served as librarian that first year, but was added to the teaching staff in 1953. The classes were large, with about forty students in each class, for a total of about 300 students.

In each subsequent year of his pastorate, Father Mooney predictably sent in his spring request for two additional sisters as each grade was added and two sections were needed. He was not satisfied to have a lay teacher in his school because of the expense, and sought also a "lay sister" to relieve the financial burden of paying a "domestic" in the convent. (92) He was actually asking for four sisters that year, and it was understandable that Mother Marcella's reply would attempt to apprise him of the lack of realism in his request, in light of the shortage of sisters. She wrote in reply:

> . . . as I foresee a continued shortage of teachers, I can only promise to do my very best to send you two sixth grade teachers . . . Father, if the present fourth grade teacher is satisfactory, I would suggest that you keep her next year. You will not be the only one who will have to employ a lay teacher. Even in the Scranton Diocese, where it was an unheard of thing, pastors are now forced to hire lay teachers . . . If I give you two Sisters, Father, it will be more than I will be able to give anyone else . . . (93)

September 1955 saw the enrollment in seven grades grow to 700 pupils with two sections of each grade. The principal, Sister Elizabeth, twelve other sisters and one lay person all taught classes of about fifty pupils each in sixteen classrooms, three of which were newly arranged in the basement area.

At the beginning and end of the 1955-1956 school year two key figures in the founding and development of St. Ambrose School were to be taken in death. Mother Marcella Gill, after some months of illness, died on September 14, 1955, and on June 30, 1956, Monsignor Thomas P. Mooney, pastor since the beginning of the parish, died. (94) The rapid growth of his parish and school had probably taxed his strength over the years. While he did not live to see the first eighth grade graduating class, he had lived to see the success of his labors in the dynamic parish life, the renewed congregational singing, the success of the school, and the excellent continuing program of religious instruction for the public school children. Reverend Thomas F. Henahan was named pastor in late September 1956 and arrived on October 5. He had been a school principal for ten years at St. Augustine's School, hence had a keen interest in the school at St. Ambrose's.

Monsignor Mooney's last letter requesting additional sisters had been sent to Mother Kathleen, successor to Mother Marcella. In it, he praised the work of the sisters, both in the regular classrooms and in the catechetical instructions provided three times a week to various groups of youngsters. His hope was to obtain two eighth grade teachers and a seventh grade replacement teacher for Sister Elizabeth so that she could devote full time to her duties as principal. Mother Kathleen, too, had to remind the good pastor that his was only one of one hundred schools she had to staff. She wrote,

> It would give me much joy were I able to send you all the Sisters you state are needed in Saint Ambrose School; but I am glad to promise you one more Sister for your school staff. This addition may appear small from the point of view of your school needs; but it is large when viewed from the point of view of our limited supply and the pressing needs of the one hundred schools we serve. (95)

Thus it was that the 1956-1957 school year witnessed 800 pupils in the full eight grades and fourteen sisters and two lay teachers as staff. These included Sister Elizabeth O'Sullivan, principal, and Sisters Dominica Gurrell, Paulita (Katherine) Broderick, Anna Maria Foley, Franzchen Yahner, Margaret Russell, Nativite Layden, Therese Culhane, Madeleine Merritt, Mary Lena (Theresa) Fitzgerald, Josaire Brady, Anton (Jeanne) Albrittain, Rosemaron Rynn and Bernard Mary (Ann Marie) Lynott. The lay teachers were Mrs. Catherine Rourke and Mrs. Biers. The first graduation was held on June 9, 1957, with 83 students receiving diplomas.

In 1958, Sister Joel O'Rourke replaced Sister Elizabeth as principal and eighth grade teacher. A full-time music teacher was added, namely, Sister St. Clare Flanagan. Sister Marietta Smith replaced the latter the following year because of illness. The school continued to attract about 800 pupils and had fourteen sisters and eventually three lay teachers until 1963-1964 when there were thirteen sisters. Sister Joel was transferred in June 1964 to Coeur d'Alene, Idaho, to serve as principal of the elementary school. Sister Andre Davoren who served as principal from 1964 until 1970 replaced her in Bridgeport.

There were many developments at St. Ambrose in this period, not the least of which was the move from the three houses into a new convent. 1966-1967 was called the "Year of Moving" as the sisters were scattered with five residing at Holy Name Convent, Bridgeport, with the Sisters of St. Cyril and Methodius; four were living with our sisters in Devon and four with the Collins family at Fairfield. A temporary convent was obtained on Barnum Avenue by the end of October. This must have been an interesting neighborhood with "Honest John's Swap Shop" and a scrap metal plant as neighbors! (96) On February 18, 1967, much joy accompanied the move to the new convent at 460 Mill Hill Avenue, across the street from the school. The dedication ceremonies took place on March 5. "Open House" was held for the parishioners on May 12, for the area religious on May 7, and for the IHM Sisters on May 20.

The school's enrollment decreased to about five hundred students in the late 60's, but maintained itself well into the 70s. Sister St. Pius Kirsch (Mary) was principal for one year in 1970-1971. She was followed by Sister Eva Marie Zlotucha who was principal from 1971-1980 in a time of decreasing religious teachers and increasing lay teachers. By 1979 there were eight sisters and nine lay teachers on the faculty. Sister Jane Ellis followed Sister Eva Marie as principal in 1980-1981 and served in that capacity until 1986. Under her leadership and with the cooperation of six IHM teachers and nine lay teachers, St. Ambrose School became the first Catholic School in the Bridgeport Diocese to be accredited by the State of Connecticut. (97)

The 1986-1987 registration was 459 pupils. Sister Beatrice Caulson became principal in 1986. (98)

St. Ann Elementary School, Nyack, NY

It is evident from the correspondence in early 1944 between Monsignor William R. Kelly, diocesan superintendent of schools for New York, and Sister M. Brendan O'Brien, the Congregation's supervisor of schools, that the Sisters of the Immaculate Heart of Mary from Scranton were held in high regard and sought after as teachers. This was true in initiating an IHM presence at St. Ann's, Nyack, New York. It is interesting to note that an exchange of some six letters took place between March and May of 1944 which included Bishop William J. Hafey's permission for Mother Marcella to accept St. Ann's, Monsignor Kelly's concerns for the renovation of the convent and school, and Sister Brendan's reports on the progress being made. No correspondence is recorded from the pastor of St. Ann's, Reverend John Farrelly, who seems to have been the recipient of a parade of distinguished diocesan and congregation visitors, all prodding him into action regarding the physical conditions of the school and convent. (99)

The Sisters of Charity of Mount St. Vincent, New York, were leaving St. Ann's School for the second time, having initially opened St. Ann's School in 1892, and having been withdrawn in 1897. After the withdrawal of the Dominican Sisters, the Charity Sisters returned in 1920 and remained until 1944. Their leaving was a source of deep regret to many parishioners who had themselves been educated by these sisters. One can surmise that the atmosphere surrounding our acceptance at St. Ann's was somewhat strained. However, in the appointment of Sister Octavia Walsh as superior and principal, and a faculty which included Sister Terentia McNulty, Sister Stanislaus O'Donnell, Sister Johnita Hines, Sister Moira McMonagle, Sister Martina Williams, Sister Cornelius Scanlon and Sister Hilary Meehan, a good mixture of experience and youth was provided for St. Ann's Parish School in Nyack. (100)

Sister Hilary Meehan recalls that very hot August 24 when the eight sisters, fully clad in the required outdoor attire of the times which included cloak, veil and gloves, took the bus to New York City, then the ferry, the subway to 168 Street, and another bus on to Nyack. They arrived in the early evening, but apparently were not expected on that date, for no one was there to meet them and they walked up the hill to the convent, carrying their suitcases. Having no access to the convent, they went to the rectory where a very surprised Father Farrelly, the pastor, met them. He provided them with the keys for the convent and later returned with some groceries for their evening meal.

It was well that the sisters had some sustenance for the shock they received in touring the convent that they soon realized was not ready for their arrival. There was no furniture in the house except a tiny iron cot covered with a thin mattress in each bedroom. Father Farrelly sent over a box filled with sets of sheets, but there were no pillows or blankets that first night.

The following days were spent in procuring the many utensils and furnishings needed, cleaning and bringing order into the situation. It is difficult to imagine this old convent, located on the site of the present beautiful school. It was a two-story structure with an attic that housed three small single bedrooms; two double bedrooms, two single rooms and a bath were located on the second floor. The dining room and kitchen were in the basement, and a small chapel, music rooms and parlors were on the first floor.

If the convent was a shock, the school's condition was a disaster! The old school was across the street from the convent next to the rectory. Originally a four-classroom school with double grades, it had been enlarged by building a gallery over the auditorium in which two grades were located. A small separate building housed the kindergarten and first grade, but these classrooms were separated by a partition that did not reach completely to the ceiling. Over seventy students were registered in 1944 for the kindergarten.

With heroic effort things were put into order by the opening of school on September 11, 1944, with 355 pupils in attendance. A private music class of 36 pupils was also organized. The sisters found the children most responsive and attributed much of the ease of the transition to the preparation received by the students from the Sisters of Charity. The parents, too, were found to be most supportive. It being the Diamond Anniversary of the foundation of the parish, the sisters were quickly thrust into many preparations for this celebration. It was also a year for Confirmation to be administered so the large class had to be prepared by the sisters and the strange sounds of "Ecce Sacerdos" and "Confirma hoc" soon became familiar to the youngsters.

As Sister Hilary summarized that first year,

> It was difficult physically, but rewarding in the fact of beginning something. There was nothing to start with but we could see something being accomplished with these wonderful children. We didn't think of the discomfort, but of the challenge that was there. (10l)

The elderly Father Farrelly died in 1945 of a heart attack. Reverend Michael J. Murphy succeeded him.

By the 1955-1956 school year the enrollment had grown to 485 pupils with eight sisters and one lay faculty member. Sister Bernadette Carmody had been serving as superior and principal since 1950, so it was encouraging news to her to learn from Monsignor Giblin, then pastor, that plans were underway for a new school and convent. Difficulties in procuring the desired property, however, prevented the project from being started that year.

In the summer of 1956 the four sisters who were home for the summer were moved to a summer cottage on the Hudson with the thought that the cottage could be used as a temporary convent while the new convent was being built. This plan was abandoned, however, because of the inconvenience of traveling back and forth to church and school. So the sisters returned to the old Jefferson Street Convent on September 20. In early March 1957, Monsignor Giblin sold the summer cottage for $42,500 and was thus able to purchase property adjacent to St. Ann's Church as the site for the new convent. A fundraising drive with a $150,000 goal opened on May 24 and by June 14 a total of $200,000 had been received. The speedy erection of the convent was guaranteed.

Sister Bernadette had been transferred to St. John's Convent, Silver Spring, Maryland, leaving the office of superior and principal in the hands of Sister Catherine Patricia McGirr. It seems that 1956-1957 had been a banner year in every way as St. Ann's School now boasted an enrollment of 497 pupils. (102) The year 1957-1958 was one of expectation with the groundbreaking for the new convent occurring on July 26, the Feast of St. Ann. The ceremony included an outdoor procession of the Blessed Sacrament in which the members of the congregation took part, carrying lighted candles and singing the Lourdes hymn. On December 19 the excavation for the new convent was begun. Little progress was made during the cold and snowy months that followed, but in March progress began again. By the end of June, the first and second floor exterior brickwork was completed. The expectation was that the new convent would be ready for occupancy in the late fall. Indeed, an elaborate ceremony was held on July 27 when His Excellency, Bishop Michael Fearns, officiated at the solemn blessing of the cornerstone of the new structure. Once again there was a Eucharistic procession, this time including the Knights of Columbus, the Holy Name Society, Boy and Girl Scouts, Monsignori, clergy, religious and parishioners. Sisters of Christian Doctrine, Sisters of Charity, Dominican Sisters from Blauvelt and Sparkhill and IHMs were present. A buffet lunch was served to all the guests by the parish. Work continued throughout the year and on March 24, 1959, Monsignor Giblin blessed the entire convent from attic to cellar. The annals for that year record the joy of the sisters on first seeing the completed convent:

> We were spellbound when we saw the interior of our convent completely furnished and with magnificent taste. The chapel, community room and refectory were air-conditioned. (103)

On April 27, 1959, the Blessed Sacrament was taken to the convent chapel. The sisters moved into their new home that very afternoon!

"Open House" for IHM Sisters was held on June 6 and over one hundred sisters responded. Among the many donors of memorials for the convent chapel were Helen Hayes, whose contribution was $10,000; Chester Fabrini, $3,600 for the tabernacle; and Mrs. Haire, $3,000 for the organ.

Celebration continued with colorful dedication ceremonies on September 19. The entire archdiocese was being made aware of the new St. Ann's School it seems, for His Eminence, Francis Cardinal Spellman, over one hundred Monsignori, religious organizations from a variety of locations together with parishioners, clergy and religious were again assembled for ceremonies at the convent and in the church. Sister Brendan O'Brien, congregation secretary, and Sister Aquina Whalen, bursar, represented Mother M. Kathleen on this occasion. (104)

Monsignor Giblin did not let his parishioners become accustomed to many months without a major project occupying their attention. In November 1960, he announced a fund-raising project of $250,000 toward the construction of a new school to replace the existing structure that was built in 1894. The new school was to be built on the site of the old convent on Jefferson Street, so on Holy Thursday morning 1961, a bulldozer demolished the 100-year-old convent. A certain nostalgia was felt as a fire was set to the remains and by 5:00 p.m. that day there were only smoldering embers of our beginnings in Nyack.

Monsignor Giblin was not to see his plans for the new school brought to completion, however, for on April 3 he received word of his transfer to St. Raymond's in the Bronx. As his last official act as pastor, he officiated at the groundbreaking ceremony for the new school. He left for St. Raymond's on April 15 knowing how respected and beloved he was at St. Ann's.

Monsignor John J. Kane succeeded him as pastor, arriving on April 16, 1961. He took up the task of completing the school and in the presence of the entire student body and faculty conducted the ceremony of laying the cornerstone on November 21. The small building formerly used for the kindergarten and first grade was demolished on June 25, providing a playground area adjoining the school. (105)

The new school year, 1962-1963, saw the coming of Sister Daniela McCarthy as successor to Sister Catherine Patricia as superior and principal. Eight sisters and one lay faculty member, Mrs. Julia O'Brien, staffed the school. The magnificent new seventeen-room school opened to 464 pupils on September 9, 1962. Nine classrooms, the library, faculty room, cafeteria, offices and the meeting room were in daily use; several classrooms were able to be reserved for catechetical instructions for released time classes.

This was a significant year also in the fact that the former beloved pastor, Monsignor Charles Giblin, died on March 20. To the sisters he was not only a pastor, but also a friend and benefactor.

The new school was solemnly blessed and dedicated by His excellency the Most Reverend John J. Maguire, Vicar General of the Archdiocese of New York, on October 27, 1963.

The interest of the parishioners in their new school was demonstrated by their continued support through fund raising activities. By February 14, 1964, they were able to procure an 1800-volume addition to the library.

St. Ann's School was to continue over the years under the principalships of Sister Donelda Fox (1968-1970), Sister Sabine Higgins (1970-1974), Sister Rose Angela Ruddy (1974-1975), Sister Audrey McHale (1975-1977), Sister Jane Ellis (1977-1980), Sister Mary Bride O'Malley (1980-1985), and Sister Theresa Petz (1985-1988). This proved to be an exceedingly challenging school in which to administer and to teach as the make-up of the parish was changing and the school gradually became 95% Haitian in its population. Adjusting to the culture and language was difficult for both pupils and teachers; communicating with non-English speaking parents was still another problem. Throughout this period, there were deep financial problems in the parish, and with the declining number of sisters available, the increased cost for lay teachers in the school was an added burden.

The Sisters of IHM and the Archdiocesan school officials were committed to the survival of this very special school, however, and in spite of many hardships, including the doubling of several classes to save on teachers, this school continues. Its enrollment was 103 in 1986-1987. (107)

The locale nearby St. Ann's, Nyack, has furnished many outstanding opportunities for the spiritual development of our sisters. Among the centers which provided retreats and/or days of recollection and recreation were: The Monastery of Togoste in Suffern, Blessed Sacrament Monastery, the Sacramentine Sisters in Yonkers, the Sparkhill and Blauvelt Dominican Sisters' Houses of Prayer, and the Marydell Camp in Nyack.

St. Peter's Catechetical Center, Wellsboro, Pennsylvania

St. Peter's Parish in Tioga County, Pennsylvania, was founded in 1879, with mission locations at St. John the Baptist in Antrim and Sacred Heart in Morris, Pennsylvania. Before St. Peter's Parish was organized in 1879,

Reverend P. J. Murphy, pastor of Blossburg, celebrated Mass occasionally in Wellsboro in the home of Michael Conway. The Catholic community at Blossburg had the distinction of receiving a visit from Bishop (now Saint) John Neumann five times; his travelogue showed a Confirmation visit to Wellsboro on June 17, 1858. The building that was renovated for St. Peter's Church was formerly the Wellsboro Academy, renowned for its many famous graduates.

In 1879 Father John McDermott was appointed first resident pastor. His successor in 1889 was Father Michael J. Manley who during his time as pastor earned these words of praise written in an 1897 history of Tioga County: "Father Manley is a popular priest, a very eloquent speaker, and one of the hardest working priests in the Diocese of Scranton." (108)

Consistent with his efforts to provide catechetical instructions for the youth of other parts of the Scranton Diocese, Bishop William J. Hafey was desirous of establishing in Wellsboro a Catechetical Center. As this idea germinated, he purchased the former residence of Attorney and Mrs. Thomas Murphy. This very attractive residence, surrounded by spacious lawns, and set with shrubbery and beautiful trees, was redecorated and furnished as a convent and catechetical center by Reverend Thomas Kelly who became pastor in 1942. The plan was to provide religious instruction of grade and high school pupils, to conduct a nursery school, kindergarten and classes in music.

St. Peter's Catechetical Center was opened in September 1945. Mother Marcella appointed four sisters to this work: Sister Lucian Reddington, superior, Sister Reparata Callan, Sister Sabina McHale and Sister St. William Lynch. The sisters arrived on August 19, having been escorted by the pastor, Reverend Thomas Kelley, who went to Marywood to pick up the sisters and drive them to Wellsboro. The sisters' arrival must have occasioned much interest on the part of Catholics and non-Catholics alike, since they were the first religious in all of Tioga County. The convent and catechetical center was sparkling in its new paint and furnishings. The chapel furnishings had been provided by the Kelley family in memory of Reverend John Kelley, brother of the pastor and of two of our sisters, Sister Clare and Sister Margrete (now deceased). The following account quite accurately describes the stages of development in the attitudes of the Wellsboro townspeople toward the sisters:

> The Sisters were probably the first nuns who had ever put in an appearance in Wellsboro and their reception by the community at large was somewhat mixed at first. However, they worked so much with both Catholic and non-Catholic people, particularly

> through the operation of the kindergarten as well as instruction classes, that contacts were made which resulted in establishing a good rapport between Sisters and people . . . (109)

Writing to Sister Immaculata Gillespie shortly after the opening of this mission, Sister Lucian Reddington noted that there was an enrollment of seventy pupils in the catechetical school and twenty pupils in the kindergarten, mostly non-Catholics. There were, in fact, only six Catholic pupils among the twenty. The private music pupils were also mostly non-Catholics.

In addition to the work in St. Peter's Parish, the sisters serviced the mission churches at Blossburg, Antrim and at Morris, being taken there by car by the assistant pastor, Reverend Henry Korpusik, every Sunday.

Sister Sabina McHale was in charge of the singing for the children's Mass each Sunday and also trained a special choir for special feasts such as Christmas and Easter. (110)

The parish Sodality of Our Lady was also under the direction of the sisters. This gave them greater contact with the young women of the parish and the opportunity to assist in their religious development through religious discussions. The meetings of the Sodality were held in the catechetical center. Through openness and hospitality toward the various parish groups utilizing these facilities, bonds of friendship grew.

A letter to Mother Kathleen written by one parishioner, Margaret L. O'Leary, sums up quite well the esteem in which the Sisters were held in Wellsboro:

> Our parish is in a predominantly Protestant town and in all of our county there had never been any religious order until the 'Sisters in Blue' arrived eleven years ago to open a catechetical school and kindergarten in Wellsboro. They still are the only religious order in large and sprawling Tioga County but what a difference in the attitude of the townsfolk of Wellsboro! When the Sisters came in 1945 they were regarded for the most part with suspicion and hostility. . . The Sisters now are almost universally loved and respected by the non-Catholics of our town and as for the parish — well, they are firmly instilled in our hearts and nothing can dislodge them . . . The Sisters, with their serene and dedicated life, their just-right touch of firmness and gentleness, have brought many narrow-minded citizens to a truer realization of the truth of our holy faith, their visits to the sick, the bereaved—whether of our faith or not—have brought commendation to them. Their wonderful work with the little ones of our town and parish has been crowned with high success. (111)

At a later date, Reverend Leo J. O'Malley, pastor, wrote in a similar vein to Mother Beata Wertz:

> It is impossible to tangibly calculate the tremendous work done in our community—in our parish—by the Sisters, Servants of the Immaculate Heart of Mary in the nineteen years they have been assigned to our parish. Not only do they profoundly influence our parishioners and their children, but this same influence is felt by those outside the Faith, and the good done for souls is immeasurable. (112)

Over the years the sisters continued to be engaged chiefly in serving some forty children in the kindergarten nursery school, teaching about forty private music pupils, and reaching out to over two hundred youngsters in catechetical instructions at Wellsboro, Blossburg, Tioga, Antrim and Morris. Three sisters constituted the small community until 1974 when the Congregation appointed Sister Margot Worfolk as campus minister at nearby Mansfield State College. As time went on the sisters also served as part of the ecumenical ministerium of Wellsboro and Mansfield, regional coordinators for youth ministry and for the CERT program, participants in the Meals on Wheels Program of the area, and visitors to the hospitals and nursing homes. The wide range of their activities brought them into contact with many people and earned them deep love and respect.

It is no surprise, then, that when it became necessary in 1976-1977 to inform the parishioners that the Congregation could no longer staff the kindergarten nursery school, there was great opposition. The pastor, Father Hannigan, felt he could not afford to hire a lay teacher for this work, nor to keep the convent open to house the sisters for the other works in which they were engaged. (113) By May, Father Hannigan must have reconsidered, for the church bulletin of May 16, 1977, carried this announcement:

> As of June, St. Peter's nursery and kindergarten will close. The Sisters, Servants of the Immaculate Heart of Mary have informed us that they are now unable to give us a kindergarten teacher . . . Fortunately, we will retain three Sisters in the parish who will expand their teaching on primary, secondary and adult levels and aid in other parish works. (114)

At its closing in June 1976, there were thirteen nursery and thirteen kindergarten students.

The 100th Anniversary of St. Peter's Parish was to be observed in 1979. In preparation for this event, both the convent and the rectory were moved into newly renovated residences on Central Avenue close to the church, which had been built in 1969 in the pastorate of Reverend John J. O'Brien. Open house was scheduled for the parishioners on September 24 and for the sisters on October 14. In September of this centennial year of St. Peter's, Father Hannigan was transferred. Reverend John T. Albosta was appointed pastor.

In 1984, the Congregation's overall shortage of sisters once again took its toll on St. Peter's, Wellsboro, in the announcement of the withdrawal of the sisters at the close of the year. On Sunday, May 6, the decision was conveyed to the people of the parishes served in the area. Sister Theresa Thayer described the general feeling:

> Shocked and heartbroken is the only way to describe the people's reaction. Endless expressions of gratitude, love for the Sisters and a deep sense of loss poured out from everyone as the days passed between May and August. On May 22 the parish held a dinner to express thanks and say goodbye. A Mass of Thanksgiving for all the Immaculate Heart Sisters have given to the community will be offered at a later date. Father John Albosta, pastor, is having a plaque made based on our community seal which will be hung in the church in memory of our Sisters. (115)

Thus closed the 39-year-old chapter of IHM presence in Wellsboro where some forty-five of our sisters had served under the leadership of twelve different superiors:

Sister Lucian Reddington, 1945-1951
Sister Bernita McDonough, 1971-1973
Sister Maria Gabriel McQuade, 1951-1957
Sister Carol Baden, 1973-1975
Sister Marie Adele Lynam, 1957-1963
Sister Margaret Russell, 1975-1977
Sister Pius LaRocque, 1963-1965
Sister Maris Law, 1977-1981
Sister Maria Angela Orr, 1965-1969
Sister Jane Driscoll, 1981-1983
Sister Romuald Doyle, 1969-1971
Sister Sarah Landis, 1983-1984

St. Patrick's Catechetical Center, Milford, Pennsylvania

Pike County lies east of Lackawanna County, with Wayne to its north and Monroe to its south; the Delaware River and the State of New Jersey lie on its eastern boundary. Within Pike County are such tiny towns as Milford, Matamoras, Shohola, Lackawaxen, Greeley, Bushkill and Dingman's Ferry.

As early as 1840 this area had been served by traveling priests, one of whom was Reverend James Maloney of Honesdale, who ministered to scattered Catholic families, offering Mass in private homes. In Milford, Mass was offered in the Revogre home on Broad Street, the later site of Paul's Bakery. The parish of St. Joseph's, Matamoras, the only Catholic parish in Pike County at the time, was founded in 1892. St. Patrick's, Milford, was a mission of St. Joseph's, as were Lackawaxen, Shohola, Greeley, Mill Rift, Parker's Glen and Dingman's Ferry. Reverend William J. Trevis was sent by Bishop O'Hara to organize the Pike County missions. His regular Saturday afternoon mission trip included taking the Milford stage to connect with the Mountain express at Port Jervis, on to offer a first Mass in a little school house by the river at Parker's Glen, then catching the milk train to Lackawaxen for a second Mass, and journeying back to Milford.

It is hard to believe that St. Patrick's, Milford, did not become a parish until 1946 (116) when Bishop William J. Hafey officially designated it as such and assigned Reverend Vincent J. Mahon as its first pastor in residence in Milford. It was Bishop Hafey's intent that the establishment of a catechetical center at Milford would provide religious education opportunities for the children and adults of this very protestant area. To this end, Bishop Hafey purchased a house owned by Chester and Edith Dissinger on the corner of High and Fourth Streets in Milford for St. Patrick's Parish on April 4, 1946. The deed records that the purchase price was $8,500—by today's standards a giveaway for such a beautiful house and four prime lots. The record also states that the property would not be available until June 15, 1946. (117) On September 12, 1946, the new mission was opened. Mother Marcella and Sister Irmina were present when Sister Rose Irma Spillane, superior, and Sister Regina Barrett arrived from Scranton by car. Sister Alphonsus McGoldrick came by car from New York later that day. The convent was far from ready for their arrival. As Sister Regina describes it:

> Not one room was actually settled. The small dining room table had unopened cartons of housewares and furnishings piled high atop it; the living room had one or two chairs and a rug which

> was far too large for the size of the room; beds were set up, but not made; there was nothing in the refrigerator, so the sandwiches brought by my sister served as our supper. (118)

The house had not been remodeled nor adapted to its new triple function as catechetical center, kindergarten and convent. It would take time before each room could be properly furnished. Sister Alphonsus took upon herself the furnishing and care of the chapel, a small room to the right of the first floor foyer. Sister Rose Irma and Sister Regina had brought altar linens from Marywood, so these were in readiness. The convent was blessed on September 14 and the first Mass was offered by Father Mahon in the convent chapel, ready or not, on September 24, 1946. (119) The Blessed Sacrament was not reserved there, however, until about Thanksgiving time.

On September 30 the kindergarten opened in one of the second floor bedrooms with Sister Regina in charge. Five children, only one of whom was Catholic, enrolled on opening day, with a gradual increase to eight by January. The proceeds from the kindergarten amounted to about fifty dollars per month that went to the pastor. Sister Rose Irma purchased a piano from community funds and by January there were six private music pupils, three of whom were kindergarten pupils. It was difficult to attract music pupils because the Milford Public School offered free lessons on band and orchestra instruments and some of these music teachers also taught piano lessons.

A total of sixty-seven pupils were enrolled that first year in the catechetical instructions. The children from Milford and Dingman's Township came to the convent for their instructions; children from the other missions gathered on Saturday mornings at St. Joseph's Church, Matamoras, where the sisters were taken by Reverend John Carroll, pastor of St. Joseph's. (120)

It was a good beginning and the hardships that accompany any new venture were present. The predominantly non-Catholic environment was a new experience for the sisters, but they only heard about, and did not experience, the hostility that was supposed to be present toward them. As Sister Regina recalls, the sisters did much to dispel these negative attitudes by their own kindness and friendliness to all. She credits Sister Rose Irma's efforts for the changes that occurred within the Catholics themselves as they grew from being ''ashamed of being Catholic" to a new pride in their faith, their parish and their school. The convent was open to all and the children especially enjoyed the spirit of joy and celebration they experienced there. The beautiful front foyer with its stately fireplace was the center for many a hot dog roast for the youngsters. The third floor attic became a social room that was often decorated for children's parties.

Bolstered by the generosity and enthusiasm of the numbers of Catholic families who came to the Milford area for the summers, a special session of the kindergarten was run in the summer. Additional sisters were sent also for the large turnout in the summer catechetical programs at each mission. The hospitableness of the sisters was known also to the summer theater troupes that frequently practiced for their performances on the shady lawn of the convent, since the theatre was located across the street. On Thursdays they were usually offered a substantial picnic supper on the lawn.

In a short time the upstairs bedroom kindergarten was no longer adequate, so the pastor remodeled the convent basement with knotty pine paneling, making one large area separated from the convent activities for the kindergarten. (121)

In spite of the affirmation of Catholics and non-Catholics alike for the wonderful work of the sisters at Milford and in the surrounding areas, their impact on great numbers was not to be the measure of their success. Even by 1954-1955 the kindergarten had only five Catholic children among its nineteen enrollees; six Catholics were enrolled in 1955-1956 out of a total of 29.

A turning point in the interest and enthusiasm of the people seemed to occur with the dedication of the new St. Patrick's Church in Milford on June 30, 1957. That August the three sisters were all newly appointed: Sister Maria Gabriel McQuade as superior, Sister Anita Mary Shaughnessy and Sister Inviolata (Lois) Buckley, and they were delighted to see the beautiful new church and its spacious, modern kindergarten annex. Registration for classes was announced in the local newspaper and thirty-seven pupils, seventeen of whom were Catholic, were enrolled. Catechetical classes increased to 105 students at Milford and 103 at Matamoras. These numbers would have been even greater, but on July 1, 1957, Reverend A. R. Mulligan of Shohola had opened a new convent (St. Ann's). Unable to secure additional IHM Sisters for Shohola, after the summer session was completed, he contracted with the Graymoor Sisters from Garrison, New York, to teach religious instructions to the children of his parish. This was a disappointment to the sisters from Milford who had taught at Shohola both winter and summer for ten years. (122)

The zeal of the sisters was very great as they reached out to potential converts for individual instructions; to another setting at Dingman's Ferry where they were refused the use of the public school, but held classes in the home of Mrs. Esther Reilly for a time. They also organized a children's choir, trained altar boys, and gave instructions at the Margaret Duer Judge School for Exceptional Children and prepared these children for reception of the sacraments.

The highpoint in kindergarten enrollment was reached in 1961-1962 when forty-six pupils were enrolled. While the people in general were more positive in their attitude toward the sisters, there was simultaneously a very competitive spirit among the churches which revealed itself in competing appeals to high-school-level youngsters for attendance at social affairs. Attempts to form a youth group failed, but the sisters continued to arrange events, such as a day of recollection at Cresco, a bus trip to West Point with a CYO group from Hawley, Pennsylvania, and other spiritual and social gatherings of the youth of the area.

By 1966, efforts at ecumenism were more common. One outstanding example was the Union Prayer Service that was held on October 2, 1966, at St. Patrick's Church, Milford. It was an historic occasion, which saw Catholic, Methodist, Presbyterian, and Episcopal clergy, together with about 350 men and women gathered to pray together. It was recalled that not since 1813 had people of different faiths gathered together in prayer. At that time some Trappist monks who had walked to Pike County from Baltimore to assess land they had inherited there, had said Mass on a huge rock, with Catholic and non-Catholic settlers gathered around.

Having served as pastor for twenty-five years, since the opening of the parish and the arrival of the Sisters of IHM, Father Vincent Mahon retired on October 29, 1972. The new pastor was Monsignor Michael J. Kennedy. At the close of that year there were changes among the sisters, too, as the superior and music teacher, Sister Mario Killeen, and the kindergarten teacher, Sister Kathleen Paulus, were changed. For 1973, the community included Sister Carolyn Cossack, superior and kindergarten teacher, Sister Agnes Cecilia Mangan, music, Sister Nancy Abbott, and Sister Elsabet Carden, catechetical instructors.

The kindergarten was closed in June 1978, Sister Annamae Haran being the last of a long series of excellent kindergarten teachers at Milford. Subsequent superiors at St. Patrick's, Milford, included Sister Mary Howard Krotzer, Sister Mary Sheehan, and Sister St. Germaine O'Neil. In the early 80s, under the pastorate of Reverend Joseph Weber, the ministry of the sisters was considerably extended. Their catechetical service to Milford, Matamoras, Shohola, and Dingman's Ferry was augmented by the Follow Christ program for youth, ministry to the senior citizens which included visits to the sick in the nursing home, hospital, and in private homes, census-taking, Eucharistic ministry and ecumenical activities. The convent chapel was a welcome spot for any interested persons to join in the prayer of the sisters, and the convent grounds were a focal point for picnics and other social get-togethers for the young people. (123)

With the center of activity being St. Patrick's Parish and Convent, it is understandable that the pastors of the other parishes in which the sisters provided catechetical instruction once a week would feel somewhat neglected. The shared financial support of the sisters and the convent among the four parishes became a point of contention to the extent that at least two of the parishes expressed a desire in November 1981 to withdraw from continuing the service and support of the sisters. The Bishop of the Diocese who observed that 300 children and their families, as well as the sick of the parishes, were beneficiaries of the sisters' ministries did not approve this unusual suggestion. Father Joseph Weber, pastor of St. Patrick's, Milford, expressed the results of a March, 1981 meeting of the four pastors:

> . . . The pastors want to continue cooperatively to have three Sisters at St. Patrick Convent to carry out the work they are now doing in the four parishes . . . We are pleased to have found a way to continue having the good witness and works of the Sisters in Pike County. (124)

How the financial matters were resolved is not known, but part of the resolution of communications problems was to designate one sister as "coordinator" for each mission parish. This called for some adjustments among the sisters, but they were willing to strive to make the situation viable. Perhaps one strong indication that the cooperation among the four parishes was to be short-lived was the transfer of Reverend Joseph Weber from Milford.

The new pastor was Reverend Joseph Bonner. By early October 1981, it was clear that he saw the closing of the convent as inevitable in light of the desires of the other three pastors to make their programs more individually centered with their own directors. It was understandable that the sisters' time could not be shared equally among the four parishes because of distances to be traveled, bad weather conditions throughout the winter months, scheduling of students. St. Patrick's, Milford, was unable to assume the total support of the sisters at that time.

On June 27, 1982, Sister St. Germaine O'Neil, Sister Maris Law and Sister Dorinda Dougherty closed this chapter of IHM presence in Milford. Father Bonner was transferred to Muncy, Pennsylvania, turning St. Patrick's Parish over to Reverend William Hines. (125)

Mother Marcella and the Congregation's Domestic Concerns

While the number of new missions being established was increasing, Mother Marcella was also occupied with deep concerns on the home front at Marywood. Monthly and even weekly throughout 1940 and 1941, letters were exchanged with representatives of the Pennsylvania Coal Company about safeguarding the grounds under the motherhouse and college buildings from further subsidence from mining of supportive remaining coal pillars. Mother Josepha, too, had directed much attention to this matter.

The good news relayed through Bishop Hafey on December 18, 1940, was that the Pennsylvania Coal Company had deeded to Marywood College all of the coal underlying the thirteen acres on which college buildings were then located. The bad news was the accompanying admonition that flushing projects should be begun at once to fill in the existing voids. (126) At least the deeds assured the Congregation that no further mining would be done in those particular sections.

Plans which Mother Marcella and her council had for the expansion of Marywood College's buildings had to be delayed until funds could be found for the mine flushing project which would assure the safety not only of existing structures, but also of additional buildings. One estimate placed the cost of the project at roughly $90,000.

With vision and determination Mother Marcella pursued the possibility of obtaining additional property, specifically the lots facing Washington Avenue, presently a campus area behind the Fine Arts Center. Her plan, which indeed eventually was realized, was to build an auditorium, music and art building facing Adams Avenue with ample property beyond it to Washington Avenue. The Congregation already owned the lots on Adams Avenue, but they were not part of the thirteen-acre subsurface deeded earlier to the Congregation. In 1941 the Pennsylvania Coal Company still owned the underground rights beneath both the Adams and Washington Avenue lots and made no apologies for its plans to continue mining there. (127) The lots on Washington Avenue were subsequently purchased from the Pennsylvania Coal Company for $15,000. (128)

During the 1940s, the fiscal expertise of the Congregation's administrators, supported by the generosity of the mission houses and the sacrifices of individual sisters, enabled the Congregation to reduce its debt substantially and to add considerably to the building fund for the future construction of new college buildings. It is important to remember the conditions prevailing in the world at the time in order to appreciate what was accomplished. From 1941-1945, the United States was involved in World War II in Europe and with Japan as a result of the bombing of Pearl

Harbor by the Japanese on December 7, 1941. Shortages of all materials needed in the war effort were experienced by those at home. President Franklin D. Roosevelt, who had been effective in bringing the country out of economic depression in the 30s was in his fourth term as president. Many conferences and negotiations were held with Britain's Prime Minister Winston Churchill and Russia's Josef Stalin. These conferences laid down plans for post-World War II Europe. President Roosevelt died in 1945 and Harry S. Truman, then Vice President of the United States, completed his term. The war with Japan was ended when the United States dropped atomic bombs on Hiroshima and Nagasaki, destroying these cities almost in their entirety and causing incalculable long-range nuclear effects among the Japanese people and their land. All of this war activity took its toll on the home front in the absence and death of servicemen and women, the consequent need of women workers, and shortages of products in demand that caused inflated prices and a high cost of living everywhere.

The struggles of one religious Congregation may seem insignificant in the context of these world events, but it was a time for hope, for courage and determination in faith that the leadership of the Congregation had.

In light of the shortages of steel and other building materials, a decision was made by Mother Marcella and her council in May 1946 to postpone the building plans for Marywood College and to utilize some of the money for the badly needed flushing projects to secure the underground of the campus buildings. (129) Having received bids from five firms, the contract was drawn up with the Severin Sekol and Sons Company of Scranton on July 31, 1946. The actual amount paid for this flushing project was $69,498.30. (130)

Before Marywood College opened in September 1946, it was necessary to locate additional residence space for the increased number of students. The one existing residence hall, O'Reilly Hall (now, Regina Hall), was filled to over-capacity. Sister Sylvia Morgan, then president of the College and second councilor, described the situation to Mother Marcella:

> The number of students enrolled in the College and Seminary (Marywood) this year is unprecedented. On account of inadequate accommodations in classrooms and dormitories many students had to be refused. The purchase of a house on College Street, opposite the Chaplain's House, has relieved the congestion to some extent. Accommodations for a number of students were secured in homes in the vicinity of the College. A second residence hall is absolutely

> necessary. The contemplated new Novitiate Building would relieve the congestion in the Seminary. (131)

The records reveal that the Shautz home at 1420 College Avenue, later named St. Mary's Hall, was purchased for $13,500. It was resold in 1952 for $15,000. (132)

Sister Sylvia's statements above reveal also the extent of the planning that was underway about the college and the novitiate long before hope of new buildings became a reality.

Extensive redecoration of the motherhouse chapel was contracted for on May 26, 1947, with Professor Gonippo Raggi and Sons of Orange, New Jersey, who had previously worked on the College Rotunda. Professor Raggi was also asked to renew the rotunda paintings at this time. The two projects were completed at a cost of $26,092.67! (133)

Flushing, redecorating and building projects were not the only order of the day. With the growth of Marywood College, it became apparent that the superior general of the IHM Congregation should no longer serve also as president of the College. Sister Sylvia Morgan, IHM, was, therefore, appointed president of the College in 1943. Sister Immaculata Gillespie, who had served in an outstanding manner as dean of Marywood College for twenty-eight years, retired from this position. Bishop Hafey was to describe her later as "she of the light heart and great vision." Her great contributions as dean were followed by her writing and publication of the *History of the Sisters of IHM* from its 1845 beginning to 1920. Sister Cuthbert Donovan, IHM, in 1943 succeeded Sister Immaculata as dean.

Other significant milestones in the Congregation's history were also occurring. Outstanding among these were, of course, the official approval of the *Constitutions* and *Customs* of the Congregation and their publication in 1943; and the Centenary of the Congregation whose official dates of observance for the Scranton IHMs were September 26, 27, and 28, 1945.

Correspondence on record indicates the extensive planning throughout all of 1944 for all the details of this event. Bishop Hafey obtained the Most Reverend Amleto Giovanni Cigonani, Apostolic Delegate to the United States at the time, as celebrant of the Mass for the occasion. Bishops, vicars of religious, chancellors and major superiors of congregations in all of the dioceses where our sisters were located were invited. Heads of colleges and representatives of local, state and national government were also extended invitations. Congratulations and letters of commendation for the work of our sisters flowed in from all parts of the country.

One can imagine the hours of preparation for all aspects of the centenary observance. Musicians, artists, librarians and historians were all focusing their great talents on this magnificent occasion. Sister Paulinus Sullivan, IHM, poet of recognized distinction, wrote "For Mary Immaculate," an inspiring canticle that subtly combined recognition of the wartime era with the peaceful hopes of our religious Congregation. The second verse of that work follows:

> "A troop formed but a century ago
> To serve you whom the centuries serve.
> We know not ancient wars. Our glory is to gain
> For you, strategic, rich and fair terrain
> This latter day of difficult, strange war,
> Lady, whose banner fluttering from afar
> Is that of one whose heel bears down the foe.
> Woman, star-helmeted, warrior aglow
> With slaying purity, we consecrate anew
> Our fealty, our arms and lives to you."

Sister Davida Sullivan, IHM, another Congregation poet, also wrote a composition in ten parts, which was recited by the novices in verse choir at a program presented on September 26 for the community. This work was entitled "Heaven in Mary's Immaculate Heart."

The novices and postulants of the Congregation entered fully into preparations for the celebration, especially for their program honoring the Apostolic Delegate. Sister Camillus (Mary) Kelly, then of Marywood College's speech and drama department, was polishing up the novices' choral speech recitations; Sister Scholastica Chainey, then supervisor of music for the Congregation, was writing the music to accompany the words of "Heart Immaculate," written by a novice, Sister Aquin Theobald. Dr. Wanda Persichetti of the foreign language department of the College was trying diligently to prepare inexperienced linguists to deliver in flawless Italian a short greeting to the Apostolic Delegate and to sing two songs in Italian. Chosen for the special Italian greeting were three novices: Sister Celesta Sinisi, Sister Florent (Margaret) Loftus, and Sister Dolorosa (Regina) Barrett. Sister Michaeline Macedonio, then a postulant, and Sister Immaculata Norton gave other special greetings. Words like "Reverendissimo" and "Ecelenza" were ever afterwards associated with them by their peers! (134)

It is evident from the musical program for the Pontifical Mass celebrated by the Apostolic Delegate, the Most Reverend Amleto Giovanni

Cicognani, that the music department of the College under the leadership of Sister Lucretia Gilroy had used their considerable gifts in presenting outstanding music. Sister Maria Cecilia MacMillan, a talented organist, played for the occasion, introducing the program with an organ processional, "Prelude and Fugue in C Minor" by Bach. The recessional she chose was "Finale from Sixth Symphony" by Vierne.

The Latin proper and Ordinary of the Mass, as well as the four-part "Ave Maria" at the offertory and the four-part Palestrina "Magnificat" finale were sung by the A Capella Choir of the College, trained and directed by Sister Davidica Kildea. (135)

The sermon, preached by the Right Reverend Edward B. Jordan, DD, Vice Rector of the Catholic University of America, paid high tribute to the Congregation's members, living and deceased, and looked perceptively to the future in saying:

> The years that lie ahead will open to this Congregation wider and wider fields of endeavor, and new demands will be made upon its members. To meet these they will need to know the story of the past, but above all they will need to be imbued with the spirit, the enthusiasm, the faith, the hope, the love of God and neighbor that have characterized the lives of their predecessors. Thus equipped and thus inspired, they must hope to equal and perhaps surpass the achievements of a century that is now drawing to a close . . . (136)

The centenary year was a time for remembering our roots, as stories of the early days in the little old log cabin in Monroe were repeated. It was a time to thank God for the many blessings of the first hundred years and to seek His continued guidance for the years ahead. Great joy greeted the announcement that Bishop Hafey had granted daily exposition of the Blessed Sacrament in the motherhouse chapel for the entire year. From after Mass in the morning until the four o'clock afternoon benediction, this privilege was observed for the Centenary Year, renewing that charismatic love for the Blessed Sacrament planted in our sisters by Father Gillet and Mother Theresa.

The General Chapter of 1949

Nineteen forty-nine was a banner year for Mother M. Marcella! She marked her seventy-second birthday that year, and it was the year of the golden jubilee of her religious profession that had taken place on July 15, 1899. Several letters on file, and comments made by her at council meetings, indicated that she felt that this general election year for the Congregation would bring a successor into her position. But that was not to be the case. On August 6, 1949, the General Chapter assembled to elect a superior general, first and second assistant, and first and second councilors. Bishop William J. Hafey presided at the election of the superior general. The tellers were Sister Germaine McCormick and Sister Joyce McQuaide. Sister Eugenia Kealy was secretary. There were 103 members of the Chapter, in accord with the process for election at that time.

Mother Marcella Gill was re-elected as superior general and Bishop Hafey confirmed the election.

Mother Marcella presided over the remaining elections which resulted in the following: Sister Kathleen Hart, first assistant; Sister Mary Martin Cawley, second assistant; Sister Cuthbert Donovan, first councilor; and Sister Alphonsus McGoldrick, second councilor. (137)

The messages of congratulation which poured in from Church officials, other religious congregations, and the sisters themselves indicated the depth of support which was given to Mother Marcella's re-election. Her own response to one such message reveals the manner in which she regarded it:

> I had hoped that I might be relieved of the burdens of office, but since God has decreed otherwise, I can but say, 'Fiat' and depend on Him for help and guidance. (138)

Marywood College Building Program

Mother Marcella's humble dependence on God was evident as she set to work at once on the unfinished agenda of the college building plans. As early as October 25, 1949, she wrote to Henry D. Dagit and Sons, Philadelphia architects, confirming her desire to begin as soon as possible. Volumes of correspondence were necessary before the plans were completed, the bids sent out on the project and the Philadelphia firm of McCloskey and Company selected for the construction by September 15, 1950. Their bid indicated that the estimated cost of the four-building project would be close to two million dollars. (139) In 1949, this was a courageous venture, indeed!

Once again Mother Marcella was faced with concerns about the underground support for the planned structures, having received warnings from the mining engineer, Mr. Severin Sekol, about the still unsafe conditions in areas beyond the thirteen acres already flushed in 1946. (140) It was, therefore, decided to confine the new structures to these sites.

Nor were the historic groundbreaking ceremonies for the four buildings delayed. Bishop Hafey was on hand to officiate at these ceremonies held on October 7, 1950. The spot now occupied by Immaculata Residence Hall was the site where the crowd gathered to hear Bishop Hafey, Judge John Murphy, as chairman of the Board of Advisors of the College, and Reverend Thomas Horan, chaplain, commend the sisters for their foresight in establishing and extending the services of Marywood College by the construction of the Fine Arts Building, Physical Education Building, Immaculata Residence Hall and the Science Building.

Throughout all of 1950 and 1951 until the completion of these buildings in 1952, extensive correspondence was had between Mother Marcella and the two Philadelphia-based companies, Dagit and McCloskey. Exactly two years from the date of the October 7, 1950, groundbreaking, the formal dedication of the completed buildings occurred—October 7, 1952. Bishop Hafey again officiated, Archbishop Patrick O'Boyle of Washington, DC gave the principal address, and Judge T. Linus Hoban, as chairman of the Advisory Board, extended the good wishes of that body. (141)

One would have imagined that not much else was getting done, but that was certainly not the case as Mother Marcella traveled to make visitation of the widely scattered missions of the Congregation and saw to the Congregation's extended apostolic contributions through the opening of additional locations as well.

St. Hugh's Catechetical Center, Hughesville and Resurrection, Muncy, Pennsylvania

To the uninitiated to the geography of Pennsylvania in the Williamsport area it is important to visualize this area as approximately two hours south and west of Scranton, depending on the route one takes. Exactly, where are the towns of Muncy and Hughesville? Traveling from Scranton south on Interstate 81, then west on 80, the town of Muncy will be reached fifteen miles south and east of Williamsport; Hughesville is about the same distance directly east of Williamsport. The two towns are roughly five miles from each other. At the time that Mother Marcella was considering sending sisters to the Hughesville/Muncy location in 1948, our sisters had already been in nearby Williamsport since 1878 and in the Immaculate Conception and St. Agnes, Lock Haven, locations since 1902 and 1938 respectively. This was not unfamiliar territory, therefore, and it was obvious that both Bishop Hafey and the pastor of the Church of the Resurrection in Muncy, Reverend Gerald J. Bischof, were excited over the prospect of adding sisters to this "outpost" area of the Scranton Diocese. (142)

A formal contract for the services of the sisters at thirty-five dollars per month each had been drawn up and signed in July 1948, but it is evident from the records that the sisters did not actually come to the area until August of 1949. The *Muncy Luminary*, the daily newspaper, had this report on August 18, 1949:

> The first Catholic sisters ever to reside in the lower part of Lycoming County moved into the Catholic mission of St. Hugh's at Hughesville on Wednesday, preparatory to taking up their duties of operating a kindergarten and catechetical center there . . . The superior nun is Sister Marie (sic) Thomas, who has just completed two three-year terms at St. Ignatius School, Kingston, and there are two others, who will assist Sister Marie with the work here. (143)

Sister Maria Thomas, in a letter to Mother Marcella, revealed her own amusement at what had appeared in the paper. She doesn't comment on being termed "the superior nun," but says:

> The enclosed article we have laughed at every time we read it. Imagine saying I 'completed two three-year terms.' It sounds as though I was in the reform school with the 'bad girls' in Muncy. I do not know who wrote the article but I know you will enjoy it. (144)

The "two others" to which the article referred were Sister St. Margaret Montague and Sister Agatha (Mary) Roche. Sister Thomasita Nash had come also as a visitor in the first days of the sisters' arrival at St. Hugh's Convent in Hughesville and it was well that she was there for she was quickly pressed into service. As Sister Maria Thomas relates,

> There is a coal stove which we will have to manage ourselves—that means build the fire, get our wood and coal and empty the ashes, etc. There is no janitor of any description. Sister Thomasita . . . has been a gem—she is showing us how to keep a fire in it which is an art. (145)

The accounts of those first weeks in Hughesville reveal the ingenuity of the sisters as they made habitable a veritable "empty" house. The fifty dollars borrowed from Sister Aquina Whalen, congregation bursar, upon their departure from Marywood was depleted in short order as cleaning materials were purchased, together with mops, brooms, brushes and pails. A washer and electric sweeper, rugs and badly needed furniture, table linen, altar linens, blankets and sheets were ordered and the house began to look like a convent home. Once Sister Thomasita's services as "keeper of the coal stove" were no longer available, Sister Maria Thomas purchased a two-burner hotplate on which they did their cooking for several months. Monsignor Frank McHugh of Williamsport presented an electric stove to the sisters in time for their congregation feast, December 8!

Sister Maria Thomas had a way of winning people over and of seeing through the projects she had in mind. St. Hugh's Convent was definitely a challenge at which she intended to succeed. One room of the convent on the right side of the entrance was set aside for the chapel and within a month's time the sisters had beautified this room. The tabernacle was a gift of Judge John E. McGeehan of New York, as were the Persian throw rugs. Once Father Bischof's Church in Muncy was completed, the predieus, altar and other furnishings formerly used for Mass in the rectory were given to the sisters for the convent chapel. Father Bischof said Mass daily in the convent chapel so that the sisters would no longer need to find a daily ride to Muncy.

Another large room on the first floor of the convent was designated for the kindergarten, which was taught by Sister Agatha (Mary) Roche. This room had its own entrance from an outdoor porch, hence was convenient for the entrance and exiting of the kindergarteners. The kindergarten had been well furnished with tables and chairs made by a local furniture factory. Sister Agatha had just come from the novitiate where, as a second-year novice, she had been responsible for the Marywood Seminary kindergarten. Since the Marywood kindergarten had been closed that year, she brought numerous supplies, books and decorations from that source. Seeing the poverty of the beginnings of the Hughesville mission, it was fortunate, indeed, that she had been given these treasures to start the kindergarten at Hughesville. The seven pupils who registered that first year were well provided for in every way.

Once Father Bischof saw the whirlwind of activity created by the three sisters, he himself got involved in painting the house, recruiting students for the kindergarten and even transporting children from Montgomery to and from Hughesville for school. Soon there were twelve, eighteen and twenty students, as well as an influx of music pupils. By 1954 the space for the kindergarten was too small so the large woodshed adjoining the kitchen was renovated for the kindergarten and the former space made into a classroom for catechetical instruction. A second music teacher was also needed since Sister Agatha could not handle the increase of both kindergarten and music pupils. Sister Katherina (Kathryn) Birdsall was sent as the second music teacher. (146)

Sister Maria Thomas' six years as superior at Hughesville came to a close in 1955 when she was transferred to St. Ephrem's, Brooklyn. Whatever her subsequent achievements, and there were many, none could be more appreciated than her efforts in Hughesville. The editor of *The Muncy Luminary,* Mr. Robert N. Wilt, wrote an unpublished article, which captures the esteem in which Sister Maria Thomas and the sisters were held:

> Hughesville had seen most of its nuns only in the world of cinema and literature, and was strangely ignorant of the ways of the Catholic world. It had only a few Catholic families, no church, and no close affiliation with the Catholic faith. But that was six years ago. Last week Sister Maria Thomas left Hughesville for a new assignment. But she left not as a stranger. No six years of anyone's life could have been better spent in the education of a community to the Catholic faith . . .
>
> In Hughesville, the sight of Sisters walking down the streets is no longer awesome. It has meant to most people that those good women are out again on an errand that will do someone some good . . . (147)

Sister Marie Adele Lynam succeeded Sister Maria Thomas as superior at Hughesville. The catechetical center continued its growth, numbering a total of ninety pupils in 1955-1956. The lending library of religious materials was expanded to some 400 volumes and included audio-visual materials as well. The kindergarten numbered thirty-three pupils by 1957-1958.

The year 1958-1959 was significant in that the sisters moved from Hughesville to Muncy. This was a reasonable move in that most of the Catholic population was in Muncy, and many of the children attending the kindergarten were coming from Montgomery, beyond Muncy. It was appropriate also that the sisters would now be located in a residence adjacent to the Church of the Resurrection. Sister Sabina McHale was superior and Sister Leonnette Bower, kindergarten teacher, at this time.

On April 26, 1961, Father Bischof was transferred to St. Mary's Assumption Church, Pittston, Pennsylvania. This was a big change since Sister Maria Aquina O'Toole was only in her first year as superior at Muncy and had already experienced other setbacks in the illness in October of Sister Marietta Smith who was replaced by Sister Henrita McArdle, who, in turn, was hospitalized in February for a time. In fact, the newly appointed pastor, Reverend Jacob Wideman, had just had emergency surgery at Mercy Hospital in Wilkes-Barre, so his arrival was delayed. Sister Catherine of Sienna (Kathleen) Paulus, a junior professed sister at the time, seemed to be the hardiest of the group. She was to continue as kindergarten teacher until the close of the 1962-1963 school year, at which point the kindergarten was well established with 35 pupils, the catechetical classes totaled 144 students, and there were 22 music pupils. Father Wideman had renovated the chapel, kitchen, and bathrooms and had had the exterior of the convent painted.

Sister Thelma Gutt had replaced Sister Maria Aquina as superior in 1961-1962. The first inklings that our sisters might not be remaining long at Muncy came in a letter from Mother Beata to the pastor on Monday of Holy Week. The appeal of the pastor and sisters for this mission to remain open withheld the inevitable for a few more years, until June 1966. Sister Miriam Catherine Corcoran was superior for that final year 1965-1966, and after two changes of sisters that year, saw to the closing of the mission at Muncy with the aid of Sister Melissa Hester and Sister Inviolata (Lois) Buckley. (148)

In summing up the experiences of the sisters in the Hughesville/ Muncy area, one must recognize the break-through that occurred in bringing a better understanding and openness to Catholicity in this very non-Catholic area. Through kindergarten-aged children a new appreciation was built for the sisters' expertise as educators; in the catechetical education of youngsters from first grade through senior high school, new involvements of the people in the practice of the Catholic religion were brought about, and "the Church" was, in a real sense, re-established.

For the sisters themselves there were the challenges of poverty, of feeling ''foreign" in one own's land, of making many golden opportunities for community celebrations with the sisters from nearby locales. A deepening sense of the meaning of sharing and Congregation caring came as they were recipients of so many gifts from our sisters who generously supplied the things they lacked. There was a sense of accomplishment as adult converts were made, as students were prepared for First Holy Communion and for Confirmation, and as prejudice toward them gradually turned to appreciation.

St. John the Evangelist Elementary School, Silver Spring, Maryland

St. John's Parish, both in Forest Glen and in Silver Spring, Maryland, is so central to the story of the Catholic Church in the United States that the name "Bethlehem of the Church in the United States" has been applied to it. It is difficult to fathom that the Maryland Colony founded in 1634 on principles of freedom of religion by Cecil Calvert, the second Lord Baltimore, could have departed so quickly and to such a great extent from being the "Land of Sanctuary" dreamed of by its founder. The famous Act of Toleration of 1649 lasted only until 1654 when the Puritans overthrew the Calvert's regime. By 1688 the Catholic Calverts were deposed and in 1691 Maryland became a British royal colony. The Church of England was established by law in 1692 as the state religion. The denial of complete rights of citizenship for Catholics began in 1718 and lasted until after the Revolutionary War. This included the right to erect their own churches; hence religious services were held in private chapels in the homes of Catholic people. Catholics were compelled to pay taxes for support of the Church of England; they had no voting rights, could not participate in public life, and were forbidden to conduct schools for the religious instruction of their children. (149)

It was a time of turmoil for the Catholic Church in the United States, and in England as well. The Jesuit order had been suppressed in England in 1773. Thus it was that Reverend John Carroll, SJ, who had been away from home for twenty-five years, set sail from England in the spring of 1774 to return to serve the spiritual needs of his own people. He took up residence in his mother's house in Rock Creek, Maryland. One account reads as follows:

> Certainly he did not shirk work in his new field, and he began at once to visit all the Catholic homes in that part of the Old Maryland mission. A room in his mother's house was set aside as a chapel for the Catholics of the surrounding country and the people gathered to hear Mass and revive their faith. (150)

But, as the historian John Gilmary Shea observes:

> The little congregation at Rock Creek grew so rapidly that it was soon necessary to prepare special building; and the erection of St. John's Church was begun about a half a mile from the residence.(151)

While no date for this building is given, it became official church property after his brother Daniel's death on May 7, 1762, when two acres of the estate were willed to John Carroll for use of the Roman Catholic congregation worshipping in the church that had been built there. It has been claimed by some that this first St. John's, quite possibly built with his mother's money, was built as early as 1774; others claim 1787 and 1783. (152)

In any case, in 1784 Reverend John Carroll was named superior of the missions in the United States of North America. In this capacity, he performed the duties of a bishop by special dispensation of the pope. He visited all of the Maryland, Virginia, Pennsylvania and New York missions. There is no record of his visitation of the territory beyond the Alleghenies to the Mississippi River. He was called to England and consecrated bishop on August 15, 1790, so that he might assume the See of Baltimore that had been established the year before in 1789. He had moved from his mother's home to St. Peter's Parish, Baltimore, in 1786 and remained there until he died in 1815.

St. John's Parish was served by Jesuit missionaries from Whitemarsh and Georgetown. It was a mission of St. Mary's, Rockville, for over one hundred years and had been served by seventeen different pastors from Rockville over that period. The appointment, therefore, of Reverend Charles Oscar Rosensteel, as the second resident pastor of St. John's, Rock Creek (Forest Glen), on November 2, 1898,—the first having been Reverend John Carroll—was greeted with great affirmation. He had already, as pastor of St. Mary's, Rockville, taken a great interest in the Carroll Chapel (St. John's) and had witnessed the growth of Catholicity in the Forest Glen area which led him to construct a new St. John's Church in 1893 about one hundred yards north of the old frame church, which had been built by Monsignor Beward J. McManus in 1850, to replace the deteriorating original Carroll Chapel. Father Rosensteel's idea was to build a more permanent structure of brown sandstone and thus to memorialize Archbishop Carroll who had spent twelve years of his priestly life there. James Cardinal Gibbons of Baltimore laid the cornerstone of the new St. John's on May 11, 1893, and dedicated it on May 5, 1894, amid great celebration that included the Confirmation of eighty-five candidates. (153)

Thus the roots of today's St. John's Parish were planted firmly by saintly founders.

> Father Rosensteel, it is to be noted, during the years of his service at St. John's, fifty-two fruitful years, labored singly and alone, without the aid of a curate. Refusing parishes in both Baltimore and Washington, he asked to be allowed to remain a country pastor. This was a life of great hardship and many privations, in a time when travel was slow and tedious—roads often impassable from the depth of the mud or the height of the snow—and parishioners were few, widely scattered and often poor. (154)

Father Rosensteel would never recognize his "country" parish, teeming with mainline Gecrgia Avenue traffic today. But his great spirit would have adjusted to whatever was needed in the service of his parishioners, for in his own day he was the first pastor to ride a motorcycle and one of the earliest to drive a car in order to reach his parishioners! In his eightieth year, 1936, he retired and Reverend Joseph T. Kennedy succeeded him as the third pastor of St. John's. Father Rosensteel left Forest Glen in April 1939 because of failing health and died at the home of his sister in Johnstown, Pennsylvania, on June 13, 1940, at the age of eighty-six. He is buried in the cemetery at St. John's, Forest Glen.

It was in the pastorate of Reverend Joseph T. Kennedy that Father Rosensteel's dream of having a parish school was to be realized. As far back as 1931, Father Rosensteel had saved $44,585.58 toward the school. Father Kennedy, mindful of the rapid expansion of the population in the area after World War II, and citing the fact that some 4,000 homes were under construction within St. John's Parish area, in July 1948, appealed to Archbishop Patrick O'Boyle that he be allowed to build a parish school. Permission being granted, Father Kennedy next looked for an appropriate site. Since not enough land was available near the church in Forest Glen, the pastor sought other property. The J. A. McGeever property at 10501 Georgia Avenue, consisting of 8.8 acres, at a total cost of $65,000 was procured on May 16, 1949.

It is significant that only five weeks later a letter was sent from Archbishop O'Boyle inviting the Sisters, Servants of the Immaculate Heart of Mary of Scranton to staff the planned school. He wrote, in part,

> The School itself will be a one-story building, since there is plenty of ground available. I really believe, Mother, that this will be one of our finest school establishments in Washington, and I would be highly honored and pleased if the Sisters of the Immaculate Heart would be good enough to take over this school in September 1950. (155)

In the months that followed, the first ten classrooms and the auditorium were under construction. By March 1950, Archbishop O'Boyle, having heard from Father Kennedy of St. John's that Mother Marcella intended to send six sisters in September, wrote to express his hope that sisters would staff all grades from kindergarten through sixth grade. That would mean seven, not six, sisters. In reply some very likeable human traits in Mother Marcella were evident as she wrote:

> Despite the fact that your letter contained a request for one more Sister, a request which I dread receiving these days because of the prevailing scarcity, yet the gentle, considerate tone of the petition

> conquers me, and I am of a mind to acquiesce in the matter; I will place a community of seven in Saint John's Parish. (156)

The McGeever residence served as a chapel for a time until the auditorium was completed. With the arrival of the sisters, however, the McGeever residence became the convent. It was a colonial style wooden house of about eleven rooms, which had been kept in very good condition by the McGeevers. It provided ample space for the seven IHM Sisters assigned: Sister Amata Jordan, principal, superior and fifth grade teacher; Sister Adrienne Wells, music and kindergarten teacher; Sister Bernard Cunningham and Sister Paracleta Gallagher, first grade; Sister Dorinda Dougherty, second grade; Sister St. Leonard (Mary) Newett, third grade; and Sister Raymonda Farry, fourth grade.

The distribution was as follows: two kindergarten sessions; three first grades with about ninety pupils in all; two second grades, and single grades from third through fifth grades. The seven sisters had to be augmented by two lay teachers to reach out to the great influx of pupils. But Sister Amata and her teachers were equal to the challenge. The school building was not yet complete, hence the opening of school was delayed, thus giving them time to prepare and organize for the large groups to come. Surrounded as it was by construction, the convent seemed like the only secure and finished structure—and even it had no outdoor steps, just planks laid precariously as a means to reach the porch. (157)

By 1953 and again in 1956 the school had to be enlarged, bringing the structure to eighteen classrooms, a library, school offices and the auditorium which was used as the church. This latter arrangement also suffered from inadequate space, making it necessary to have First Communion ceremonies on two separate days, with some eighty First Communicants in each group.

As a response to the continued growth in numbers of Catholics in the Wheaton-Silver Spring area, the pastor of St. John's, Reverend Joseph Kennedy, advocated continued division of the parish and the creation of new parishes. St. Catherine's was thus established in 1951 and St. Andrew's in 1959. For his twenty years of insightful planning for St. John's Parish and the surrounding areas, Father Kennedy was made a Domestic Prelate on January 29, 1956. (158)

St. John's School earned a reputation for excellence early on. Its annual book fairs were well supported by families and friends and by the 1955-1956 school year the library had some 2,300 circulating volumes. Monsignor Spence (later, Bishop), as superintendent of Catholic Schools for the Archdiocese of Washington, selected St.

John's as the recipient of a special program to be operated under the auspices of the music department of the Catholic University of America. All students in the fourth grade were to receive free piano lessons under the direction of a Dr. Weber from the University. Four pianos were delivered cost-free to the school and set up in empty spaces for use of the pupils. Sister Adrienne assumed the responsibility for student practice. (159)

Sister Amata's six-year term of new beginnings ended in 1956. Sister Bernadette Carmody succeeded her. In preparation for the new year the pastor had refurbished the 100-year-old convent, painting it both inside and out, reupholstering some of the furniture and replacing many of the draperies. By this time there were twelve sisters on the staff at St. John's including Sister Bernadette Carmody, Sister Cecilius McHale, Sister Maria Imelda Callahan, Sister Pulcheria Longe, Sister Rosalie Martin, Sister Paracleta Gallagher, Sister Angelica LeStrange, Sister Ita (Catherine Anne) Mullaly, Sister Angelus Mills, Sister Francis Regis Vagt, Sister Cordis Houston, and Sister Michael Mary Donovan.

Knowing the extensiveness of the summer's refurbishing of the convent, it is distressing to read that on February 20, 1957, at about 10:30 p.m. the sisters were aroused by a heavy smell of smoke. It was eventually determined by the firemen that an over-heated furnace caused the charring of the wooden beams above it. The Blessed Sacrament was removed by one of the priests, and the sisters were evacuated, as were the sacred vessels and vestments and some personal belongings, to the school building. The sisters returned to the convent at 2:30 a.m. to find the fire out, part of the community room floor torn up, and everything permeated with smoke. Since the boiler had to be replaced, the convent was to be without heat for several days, so after school that day some of the sisters went to stay with our sisters at Little Flower Convent, and some were housed at the Washington Retreat House.

This event was a natural prelude to the announcement of a fund drive for a new convent, as part of larger plans for a new church and rectory as well. So successful was the drive for the funds for the convent that within six weeks the goal of raising $250,000 was surpassed by $101,278 for a total of $351,278. Groundbreaking for the new convent was held on June 13, 1960. Less than a year later, on Easter Sunday, 1961, Monsignor Kennedy, pastor, blessed the beautiful new convent. Easter Monday was moving day for the sisters. The annals contain this description of the day:

> Easter Monday Holy Mass was offered for the last time in our old convent. Moving day was filled with excitement. Together with the generosity and good will of all, it will be remembered as a

> day of great joy. The presence of the Most Blessed Sacrament permeated spiritual life throughout our new convent when Monsignor Kennedy placed It in reserve in our beautiful chapel Easter Monday afternoon. The first Holy Mass was offered the following morning. (160)

The usual "open house" tours filled much of the rest of the month of April, with adult parishioners, students, clergy and religious of the area being graciously received by our grateful sisters. The old convent served one last important role as it was burned to the ground by the Montgomery County Fire Department on April 9, 1961, as part of a fire-fighting training exercise.

Meanwhile, a peak of 1,070 students had been reached in the school enrollment, with a faculty of thirteen sisters and three lay teachers. June 10, 1961, saw the graduation of 116 eighth-graders. These numbers in the school were indicative of the continuing growth of St. John's Parish and the need for an adequate parish church. Having liturgical services in two locations—at Forest Glen and in the school auditorium—was proving most inconvenient, and once the new rectory would be completed, the center of parish life would move to the Georgia Avenue location. Throughout the winter months of 1961, work progressed on the new church, a striking edifice built at the highest point of the property. The exterior is of salmon-rose-colored brick with limestone trim with a 40-foot high white enameled metal and gold pinnacle topped with a gold cross. The front of the church is totally covered with a magnificent marble mosaic of the crucifixion scene with St. John and Mary, the Mother of Jesus, as prominent figures. Both interior and exterior features of this church are inspirational to worshippers and passersby on busy Georgia Avenue. They are also a tribute to Monsignor Kennedy, pastor at this time. (161)

At the conclusion of the Easter Vigil Services in the school auditorium, the Blessed Sacrament was removed to the new church where public services were to be held for the first time at 8:00 a.m. Easter Sunday, 1962. The boys' choir of St. John's School sang the High Mass of Thanksgiving on Easter morn. It was not until May 27, however, that Archbishop Patrick O'Boyle was available to come to St. John's for the formal dedication of both the convent and the church. Forty-two IHM Sisters from the area were present for the ceremonies and for a catered luncheon later. (162)

One cannot but be impressed in reading the annals of St. John's Convent with the involvement of the sisters in catechetical work beyond their regular classroom teaching; in their participation in the on-going religious vocation activities of the Archdiocese, and in their regularly scheduled trips to Marywood with bus loads of young women to attend the religious reception ceremonies of future IHMs. The fruit of these activities was the entrance into the Congregation of Sally Smith (Sister Anne Mary) and of Ann Knight (the former Sister Carmella), as well as many vocations to the priesthood.

It is notable also that this convent has served over the years as a place of hospitality for many sister-visitors to Washington, DC, whether recuperating from surgeries at renowned medical centers nearby or visiting Washington for business or personal reasons. Several sister-students were in residence at St. John's also as they pursued educational programs at the Catholic University of America or other area institutions. Among these were Sister Kathleen Toner, Sister Dorothy Haney, Sister Ann Lucille Bohn, Sister Anne Fulwiler and Sister Eleace King.

The sisters of St. John's enjoyed many spiritual and professional benefits in being situated in such an active Archdiocese in the nation's capital. Under the leadership of principals like Sister Amata Jordan, Sister Bernadette Carmody, Sister Donelda Fox, Sister Norma (Rosemary) Casey, Sister Marella Moran, Sister Eunice Corcoran, and Sister Kathleen Lannak, there were innovative programs in the school and attention to developments in educational theory and practice.

Monsignor Kennedy retired as pastor in July 1968 and lived at St. John's as pastor emeritus until his death on January 5, 1975, at eighty years of age. Monsignor Harry E. Echle succeeded him as pastor in 1968, but another pastor was again appointed in November 1970, namely, Monsignor Louis W. Albert. Monsignor Albert was an experienced administrator and was the right choice for the financial and reorganization needs of St. John's at the time. In three years' time he had managed to motivate the parishioners so that the debt was completely paid off.

The changing picture, which was a foreshadowing of the future profile of many local communities, is exemplified by the membership of St. John's local community in 1978-1979:

Sister St. Mel Wright, Superior	Primary teacher
Sister Maria Magdala O'Boyle	Tutorial
Sister Maria Andrew Allen	Private Music Pupils
Sister Francis Gabriel Lenihan	Primary teacher
Sister Eunice Corcoran	Principal
Sister Annchen Caulson	Intermediate
Sister Anne Fulwiler	Student
Sister Alexius Fitzgerald	Primary/Library

Sister Mary Newett	Spanish Ministry
Sister Anne Mary Smith	Pastoral Ministry
Sister Joan Katoski	Music teacher
Sister Mary Ann Adams	Junior High
Sister Agnes Panik	Intermediate (163)

And even this picture with a total of thirteen sisters, eight of whom served in the school, would rapidly change as the decisions of the General Chapter of 1978 became operative and discussions began in 1980 about the plan to decrease the number of sisters in the schools because of the shortage of teaching personnel. By 1981-1982 St. John's would have six sisters in the school and five sisters in other ministries of service in the parish or archdiocese, and by 1986-1987 there would be seven sisters in a variety of ministries outside the parish, four sisters in St. John's School and one sister in ministry to the elderly of the parish.

Changes such as these call for flexibility and versatility among all involved in the situation. Certainly Monsignor Albert absorbed most aspects of these changes very well. He retired from his pastoral duties in July 1983 and was succeeded by Reverend Oliver Mehady, pastor as of this writing. Superiors at St. John's who assisted in facilitating these many post-Vatican II changes include Sister Felician Hurley, Sister Helene Hicks, Sister St. Mel Wright, Sister Joan Katoski, Sister Anne Fulwiler and Sister Catherine Mary Manley. (164)

Holy Trinity Elementary School, Poughkeepsie, New York

Pioneering in the 1950s may not have presented the same kind of hardships as those experienced by pioneers at earlier periods; there were, nonetheless, hardships and sacrifices to be experienced even in so lovely a place as Poughkeepsie in Dutchess County in the beautiful Hudson Valley of New York State. The mission at Poughkeepsie probably should have opened in 1953 instead of 1952, but with the new Holy Trinity School completed, except for outdoor landscaping, Reverend Leo J. Gregg, pastor, was confident that a place of residence for the sisters would be available on time. Such was not the case, however, when Sister Brigida Strome, the newly appointed principal and superior of Holy Trinity, together with Sister Stella Devers arrived on August 16, 1952.

"Home" for them for the next two weeks would be Saint Mary's Convent where the Newburgh Dominicans offered gracious hospitality. What was to become (and is today) Holy Trinity Convent was at that point an occupied house with a tenant not quite ready to leave. Over subsequent weeks and months, it would be vacated, renovated, and enlarged to serve as convent home for the first community of six IHM Sisters in Poughkeepsie. These were Sister Brigida Strome, Sister Pius LaRocque, Sister Stella Devers, Sister Phyllis McCarty, Sister Albrette Rouleau and Sister John Berchmans (Josephine) Joy.

During the interim, the sisters made the best of the situation of living in the parish hall. The little kitchen, which ordinarily was used for parish activities, became their kitchen and dining room. Curtained separations marked off each sister's space in the hall, with a bed, chair and wash pail as their only furnishings. They assembled in the church each day for their prayers and made their spiritual reading together in the school.

As the opening of school approached, it was necessary for the sisters to vacate the parish hall, since it was to be used for a school cafeteria. So, the next move was to accept the hospitality of the Franciscan Sisters at Saint Francis Hospital, Poughkeepsie. They were able to offer our sisters three double bedrooms in the nurses' residence near the hospital and the opportunity to use the chapel in the Franciscans' residence, as well as to take breakfast and dinner with them. Approximately six weeks were spent under this housing arrangement, with a driver from Holy Trinity Parish taking the sisters to school each morning in the parish station wagon. Usually, the return trip was made by taxi.

On October 12, 1952, the sisters moved into the convent. Although unfinished—without radiators or sinks installed in the eleven bedrooms, with no laundry facilities connected, and without completion of the chapel, it was, nonetheless, "home." December 8, the actual and official date of the completion of the convent, didn't seem that far away. (165) The Holy Sacrifice of the Mass was offered by Father Gregg for the first time in the convent chapel on December 8, 1952, and the permanent location of the Blessed Sacrament here became a reality. It seems that "life" in any new location begins for our sisters from the date of the coming of the Blessed Sacrament.

However, much of life at Holy Trinity was well underway, for September 8 had seen the enrollment of approximately four hundred children in kindergarten through sixth grade. Two lay teachers augmented the staff of six IHM Sisters. On September 14, 1952, they witnessed the dedication of the beautiful, sprawling one-floor school building of Vermont stone. His Eminence, Francis Cardinal Spellman, Archbishop of New York presided. With all of these events crowding their days, this first year passed. An insightful summary appears in the annals:

> The work of the first year progressed, and, through the grace of God, much good was accomplished both with the children of the new Holy Trinity School as well as with the five hundred or more

> children in catechetical classes. Preparations for Christmas, First Holy Communion, Holy Week, May Crowning, and Forty Hours brought with them their rich spiritual reward. (166)

So great an increase in enrollment in the school occurred in the second year (1953) that one classroom had to be set up in the parish hall, which became labeled the "school annex." A decision was also made to eliminate the kindergarten so as to gain additional space. The growth of the school and the spiritual influence of the sisters in the parish were obvious to all when some three-hundred middle-grade youngsters were part of the Confirmation ceremony in May 1954. Bishop Joseph M. Pernicone administered the Sacrament and offered commendations to all on their excellent preparation, noting in particular the children's singing of the Gregorian chant.

In September 1954, the increased enrollment again necessitated adding a classroom in the "school annex." These makeshift solutions led to the construction of eight new classrooms and a large, modern gymnasium. This project was underway when school opened in September 1955, but no one seemed to mind the blasting, bulldozing and drilling noises in the awareness of the possibilities for additional space when the project was completed. And it was well that the new wing was ready for the 1956 impact of seven hundred youngsters. The "school annex" was now reconverted to the school cafeteria, a much-needed facility since all of the children carried their lunch. Most children were transported to school by bus; in fact, twenty-one busses were in use daily—eighteen provided by the public school system, and three for the rural areas provided by Holy Trinity Parish.

As the growth of the school continued, so the faculty had nearly doubled by 1956, totaling eleven sisters and four lay teachers. Concerned about the costs of a growing lay faculty, Monsignor Gregg arranged for four Marist Brothers to teach the boys in grades five through eight in Holy Trinity School as of September 1957.

Great and good things had been accomplished in the first six years and Sister Brigida could end her term as principal and superior with confidence that Holy Trinity School had received an excellent foundation, both in facilities and faculty. Sister Gertrude Hopkins succeeded Sister Brigida in the fall of 1958, having a faculty of eleven IHM Sisters, four Marist Brothers and two lay teachers.

In 1959-1960 the school reached its enrollment peak of nine hundred pupils. That these numbers of students were being well taught and the diversity of their talents was being developed is evident in the prizes and awards they were capturing in a wide variety of contests—essay, poetry, music festivals, and ten awards in the 1959-1960 Catholic Youth Organization Art contest. It is evident also from the descriptions of the activities of the faculty that these were teachers who were involved in a variety of in-service programs, updating their teaching skills and being introduced to new concepts through such means as the Regents Educational Television Programs for classroom and in-service use. (167) It was no wonder that there was a waiting list of applicants for this fine school.

In 1962-1963 Holy Trinity Parish was divided, with the new parish of Saint Martin dePorres being created. Plans were made also to have an elementary school in that parish by the fall of 1964. The Marist Brothers were withdrawn at the close of the 1962-1963 school year because of needs in their congregation's high schools. This meant an increase in the lay faculty at Holy Trinity School, but the parishioners assumed this burden in the interest of having a Catholic school education for their children. Eight lay teachers and ten IHM Sisters composed the faculty for 1964-1965 under the leadership of the new principal, Sister Margaret Russell. This was again a very full year with the peak number of 92 eighth-graders graduating.

In November of 1965, the pastor, Father Gregg, was hospitalized at the Albany Medical Center until Christmas Eve, when his return brought joy to the sisters and the entire parish. His poor health, however, continued and his presence at school and parish functions became limited. His death in the summer of 1966, therefore, did not come as a shock to our sisters, but as a loss of the good and interested friend of fourteen years.

The coming of Bishop Joseph Pernicone, Vicar o£ Dutchess County, as pastor of Holy Trinity marked the beginning of a tradition of sorts in having a bishop as pastor in this location. He would become pastor emeritus on June 14, 1978, having observed the Golden Jubilee of his ordination on December 17, 1976. Bishop Pernicone's retirement year would coincide with the 25th Anniversary of Holy Trinity School which saw the return of some twenty IHM Sisters who had formerly served there. While Bishop Pernicone had been appointed as pastor by Francis Cardinal Spellman of New York, the next pastor of Holy Trinity was appointed by Terence Cardinal Cooke, for Cardinal Spellman had died on December 7, 1967. It was Bishop Anthony Mestice who assumed the pastorate on October 14, 1978. (168)

It is apparent that through the efforts of these fine pastors and the dedication of the sisters a spirit of openness and hospitality prevailed. At various times members of the Sparkhill Dominican Sisters served the school and parish and lived with our sisters in Holy Trinity Convent. Excellent rapport also existed between the faculty at Holy Trinity and the Dominicans teaching at the newer St. Martin de Porres Parish School. Much credit is due to the attitudes created by principals and superiors over the years. Beyond those already named, there were also these principals: Sister Geralda McNamee, 1970-1972; Sister Rosarii Hemmer, 1972-1976; Sister Clotilde Cullen, 1976-1982; Sister Mary Ellen Downing, 1982-1986; and Sister Jean Louise Bachetti, 1986-present writing.

Sisters who served as superiors at Holy Trinity from 1972 to the present include: Sister Leo Marie McDermott, 1972-1975; Sister Angelique Vannicola, 1975-1977; Sister Felician Hurley, 1977-1980; Sister Dorothy Lyons, 1980-1981; Sister Hubertine Gallagher, 1981-1984; and Sister Lorraine Studley, 1984-1988. (169)

The number of IHM Sisters serving at Holy Trinity was the same in 1987 as in 1952—six sisters. There have been peak times when as many as eleven IHM Sisters were there, but there were never fewer than five. Some sisters should be especially named for the longevity of their service to Holy Trinity, such as Sister Dorinda Dougherty and Sister Grace Madeline Dusch who served for eleven years.

This mission continues to be a vibrant location for the ministries of our sisters. In 1987-1988 the enrollment of Holy Trinity School was 282, being served by six IHMs, one Dominican and eleven lay teachers. (170)

Holy Name of Jesus Catechetical Center/Elementary School, Forty Fort, Pennsylvania

An 84-year-old parish has seen a great amount of history, and its development and flavor are intertwined with that of its locale. Thus Holy Name of Jesus Parish reflects the development of the boroughs of Swoyersville and Forty Fort, Pennsylvania, with a beginning of less than one hundred families and a growth to over one thousand. In the late nineteenth century, Luzerne County was known to be one of the finest naturally endowed regions in Pennsylvania. The northern anthracite coalfields stretched for over sixty miles and a tide of immigrant people—English, Welsh, Irish and German—settled near the mines as a way to make a living. Forty-five percent of these were born in Ireland and about sixteen percent in Germany. These two groups included some 61,000 Catholics in Luzerne County. (171) To serve the religious needs of these people there was a great expansion of church buildings over the last twenty-five years of the nineteenth century.

Among these new churches was Saint Ignatius Church in Kingston, Pennsylvania, built in 1885. Since this was to become the parent church to the mission of Holy Name of Jesus Parish in Swoyersville, it is noteworthy.

Since so many of St. Ignatius parishioners resided in the Borough of Swoyersville (incorporated in 1898) and in Forty Fort (incorporated in 1886), Reverend John P. O'Malley, pastor of Saint Ignatius Parish, held services in the Shoemaker Street schoolhouse in the borough for these people. It was during Father O'Malley's administration that a plot of land at the corner of Shoemaker Street and Watkins Avenue was purchased by Bishop Michael J. Hoban for the Holy Name of Jesus Parish, Forty Fort. The deed is dated December 21, 1899. (172)

Holy Name of Jesus Church was built as a mission of Saint Ignatius Parish, Kingston, under the pastorate of Reverend Michael E. Lynott. Construction was begun in 1903 with Bishop Hoban laying the cornerstone on Thanksgiving Day of that year and the former pastor, Reverend John P. O'Malley, preaching the sermon. The church was completed in April of 1905 and Father Lynott celebrated the first Mass in the new church. Within a month the status of Holy Name of Jesus as a mission church was to change, as Bishop Hoban announced the creation of a new parish, separate from Saint Ignatius, Kingston, and having its own pastor. Reverend Patrick C. Hurst thus became the first official pastor of Holy Name of Jesus Parish, Swoyersville.

Father Hurst resided at St. Ignatius Rectory in Kingston from May 1905 until February 1906. During this time the new church was destroyed by fire. He first set about the building of a rectory on the corner of Shoemaker and Watkins Avenue adjacent to the site of the church. Father Hurst was not to see the completion of his efforts at rebuilding Holy Name Church. He was transferred to St. Peter's Cathedral Parish in Scranton leaving the task to Reverend Joseph P. McHale, the new pastor.

Holy Name of Jesus Church was rebuilt and was rededicated by Bishop Hoban on September 26, 1909. Holy Mass was celebrated in the new edifice on that date. (173) It seems significant that no mention is made of the presence of Father Hurst for any of these dedication services.

Father McHale was to serve as pastor until 1917. He was succeeded in January 1917 by Reverend Martin J. Fleming who served until the appointment of Reverend Aloysius Boylan as pastor on June 20, 1950.

Father Aloysius Boylan was a planner and a builder. His first plan was to extend the parish plant into the Forty Fort section of the parish, since sixty-five percent of the parishioners were residents of the Borough of Forty Fort. At a cost of $36,500 he was able to purchase three properties along Wyoming Avenue. The plan was eventually to replace the forty-one-year-old wooden frame church, and possibly to erect a school.

In June of 1952 a house at 1212 Wyoming Avenue was purchased for $25,000 with the hope of obtaining the Sisters of IHM to begin a preschool program and assist with the already well-established catechetical program of the parish. Father Boylan was a Carbondalian and received his elementary education at St. Rose Academy in Carbondale, and as a priest had served with IHM Sisters at St. Mary's, Avoca, St. Leo's, Ashley, and St. Ann's, Tobyhanna. He was also well aware of the work of the sisters at the catechetical center at St. Ignatius, Kingston, and of the assistance given by Sister Maria Thomas Harrington to the lay people of Holy Name Parish in initiating their catechetical program. It was no surprise, then, that in July of 1952 Father Boylan contacted Mother Marcella Gill, inviting her to visit the parish and to assess the possibilities of utilizing the new house at 1212 Wyoming Avenue, Forty Fort, as a combination school and convent.

Mother Marcella responded affirmatively after her visit to the site, and by July 20, 1952, Father Boylan was able to assure his parishioners that a commitment had been made by Mother Marcella to send sisters to Holy Name Parish in August 1952. (174) The first contract signed by Father Boylan and Mother Marcella was dated August 15, 1952, and specified $40.00 per month per sister for twelve months.

The three sisters assigned to Holy Name were Sister Rose Irma Spillane, Sister Mary Nicholas Scanlon and Sister Annamae Haran. Two rooms on the first floor of the convent were equipped for the kindergarten class, which in that first year numbered fifteen. The first child registered was Beatrix Simon, daughter of Mr. and Mrs. William Simon of Forty Fort.

The impact of the sisters was so immediately successful that petitions were made for the addition of a first grade class in 1953. Sister Ellen Marie Loftus was beginning a six-year term as principal and superior at Holy Name and met the many challenges presented. Another room in the convent at 1212 Wyoming Avenue was converted into a classroom to add the first grade, but only eighteen pupils could be accommodated in the space available. Within one week of the announcement that a first grade would be opened, the full quota of eighteen was reached. September 1954 saw a repetition of these events, as a third classroom was made available for grade two. A total of sixty pupils was thus accommodated in the "convent school."

It was obvious that this process could not continue indefinitely. Bishop Hafey's permission was obtained for the building of a Catholic school in Forty Fort. On May 1, 1955, announcement was made by Father Boylan that two properties at 45 and 47 Center Street in Forty Fort had been purchased for $26,000. Plans for the new school began at once. From the beginning, the architectural firm of Lacey, Atherton and Davis of Wilkes Barre expressed its concern about constructing a school in Forty Fort where the possibility of subsidence because of past mining beneath the site and the potential of flooding from the nearby Susquehanna River were to be reckoned with. After the death of Bishop Hafey, it was with patient perseverance that Father Boylan and the architects worked to persuade Bishop Jerome Hannan and the Diocesan Building Consultors of the special construction needs in Forty Fort. (175)

Meanwhile, September 1955 found eighty-five pupils from kindergarten through grade three crowded into the convent. When one visits this residence today and observes the limited space in the first floor rooms, it is almost unbelievable that this many children were educated there. The delay in the building plans into the1956-1957 school year, and an enrollment of 102 pupils precipitated the decision to move the kindergarten to the small bungalow on the Regan estate at 1133 Wyoming Avenue a block from the convent. This location was quickly named "Sister Annamae's Workshop." (176)

There was great rejoicing when the groundbreaking for the $300,000 two-story school finally occurred on April 4,1957. Bishop Jerome D. Hannan officiated and Father Aloysius T. Boylan turned over the first spade of dirt. Less than a year later, on February 2, 1958, Holy Name of Jesus School was formally blessed and dedicated. The 16,000 square foot building of special lightweight construction and with special built-in protection against subsidence, floods and fire, included eight classrooms, a library, clinic and office.

Classes were begun in the new school on Tuesday, February 4, 1958. During the months that followed the original school (the convent) was fully restored and furnished to accommodate the enlarged faculty of four sisters: Sister Ellen Marie Loftus, Sister Annamae Haran, Sister Ann Patricia Elmore and Sister Marian (Mary Louise) Conlon.

The rapid growth of the school and the increased duties associated with that growth did not deter the sisters from reaching out to over 400 students in catechetical instructions and preparation for First Holy Communion and Confirmation.

A children's choir was developed and private music pupils were also instructed. "Open School Days" were held each year at which time a book fair was held. Books were purchased, and then donated to the school. Through these contacts with children and parents, the sisters were gradually breaking down many of the antagonisms that existed against Catholics in the area.

In 1958-1959 there were seven grades, kindergarten through grade six with a total of 200 pupils in the new school. Sister Ann Patricia had forty-three pupils in first grade. Sister Carolyn Dukehart had replaced Sister Marian, and Sister Gerlinda Griffin brought the number of sisters to five.

Sister Elsie Miller succeeded Sister Ellen Marie Loftus as principal and superior in the fall of 1959. Sister Elsie had just become familiar with her new surroundings when, on October 15, the disruption of a mine subsidence occurred. The scene was described as follows:

> . . . after the movement of the earth was over, the school looked like a tilted steel box, high at one end, low at the other . . . two panes of glass snapped and the blacktop paving in the school yard opened in several places. In the interior of the building, four interior gypsum board panels buckled at the exterior wall joint and six square feet of ceramic tile in the lavatories had sheared vertically . . . (177)

Summing up a detailed description of the damage, the record states, "built in a conventional manner the school would have been reduced to a pile of bricks by the subsidence, leading to a total financial loss." (178) Father Boylan's words reflected the thoughts of all concerned as he spoke at the following Sunday's Mass: "A building can be rebuilt. We must look at the bright side and be grateful that no persons were in the building at the time of the disaster." (179)

The speed and efficiency with which the Sardoni Construction Company worked was a significant factor in preventing further damage to the building. It was the last week of April 1960 before repairs were completed and the building declared safe for the return of the students who, in the intervening seven months, had been attending St. Cecilia's School in Exeter. Classes resumed in Holy Name of Jesus School on Monday, May 9, 1961. The first eighth grade graduation was held in June of that year.

Sister Paulina Langan became the new principal and superior in the fall of 1961. Sister Annamae Haran who had become a much-loved kindergarten teacher over her nine years at Holy Name of Jesus School was transferred to Chapel School in Scranton. Her replacement was Sister Sharon Brady. Together with Sisters Ricarda Gill, Harold Mulderig, Josellen (now, Helene) Hicks, Ann Patricia Elmore and Lambert Rossi, the number of sisters was now seven. Two lay teachers augmented the sisters in serving the 280-pupil school.

Sorrow visited the little community of sisters in the summer of 1963 as word reached them that Sister Ricarda had taken a stroke while on retreat at Marywood. After hospitalization she recovered sufficiently to go to the Marian Convent for further care. She was able to visit the sisters at Forty Fort on January 23, but it was less than three weeks later, on February 11, 1964, that Sister Ricarda died.

The school stabilized in enrollment under the principalships of Sister Evangeline Conmy (1967-1970) and Sister Raymond Rafferty (1970-1974). The school continued to graduate 25 to 28 pupils each year. That effective instruction was being provided was evidenced in the awards being captured by students in art exhibits and science fairs, as well as in the national honors for achievement being awarded to ten students of the seventh and eighth grades by the National Educational Development Testing Program in 1971-1972. Father Aloysius Boylan was an interested and amiable pastor who generated much good spirit everywhere. He seemed to love to be with the school youngsters and enjoyed their programs, socials and competitions.

The usual closing of the convent for the summer months occurred on June 18, 1972, as the sisters departed for their annual retreats, for home visits, or for summer study. But this was to be no ordinary year, as five days later, on June 23, 1972, the raging Susquehanna River, whipped by Hurricane Agnes, smashed through dikes and barriers causing devastation throughout Wyoming Valley.

Eighty percent of Swoyersville Borough was flooded because of the broken dike near Forty Fort cemetery. The muddy water flowed up Slocum Street from Forty Fort and by the time the river receded some 1,957 homes were inundated. The damage at Holy Name of Jesus Convent was about $20,000; the school, covered with 27 feet of water, sustained $300,000 in damage. The rectory and church basements received another $30,000 in damages. Ninety-five percent of the parishioners were left homeless.

It was no time for despair. Ways had to be found to bring hope, encouragement, and help to the area. The return of the sisters and their many IHM helpers each day brought comfort to the people. Sister Ann Marie Lynott, Sister Margaret Burke and Sister Marion Tarone made heroic efforts to clean the mud from the cellar and first floor of the convent. Many other sisters, among them Sister Eileen Egan, Sister Marianne Knight and Sister Mary Ann Adams, came to assist in the school. Father Boylan and his assistant, Father Edward Lyman, also worked daily in the school. Monsignor Thomas Horan with many of his parishioners from St. Rose Parish, Carbondale, came to help clean the school. So also did Sister Hilary Meehan and her sisters from St. Thomas Convent, Archbald. Sister Raymond Rafferty, principal of Holy Name of Jesus School, commuted daily from St. John's Convent, Pittston, to work at restoring the school. Early in August she was joined by Sister Maria James McNamara, Sister Rosella Salvato and Sister Rose Regina Mainguth.

Resurrection Parish in Northeast Philadelphia, under its pastor, Father William Sailer, involved themselves in the cleanup of Holy Name under the "adopt-a-parish plan" of recovery. They collected $13,130.79 that Monsignor Boylan graciously accepted. It must be remembered that Holy Name Parish had an $86,000 debt prior to the flood. (180)

The generous charity of the Congregation was everywhere in evidence as clothing, food, housing, and physical labor were given without stint throughout the flood area. The Congregation waived the payment of the sisters' salaries for the year. Of this, Monsignor Boylan wrote:

> We have been getting along to date, managing to pay our bills, principally because the Sisters of the Immaculate Heart of Mary, through their Generalate, have notified us that the salaries of the Sisters and the upkeep of their residence will be borne by the Sisters of Marywood in Scranton from August 1972 to August 1973. This is a magnanimous gesture on the part of the Sisters. Six Sisters at $205 each per month—$1,230 a month. For the 12 months this means $14,760. This figure does not include the art teacher and music teacher also subsidized by Marywood. $25 a month each is $50 a month—$600 a year. Grand total is $15,360. (181)

Soon emergency legislation was passed and federal grants and loans became available for purposes of restoration.

The sisters of Holy Name School, who had been living temporarily at St. John's, Pittston, and St. Cecilia's, Exeter, were able to return to the convent on September 10, 1972. The annals record their situation:

> The only room on the first floor, which we were able to use, was the kitchen. We were happy to be able to enjoy that, especially when we realized that our loss was nothing compared with the losses suffered by the parishioners and the other people in the valley. (182)

Needless to say, restoration work continued throughout the year. Once heat was restored to the school, the school year could begin which it did on September 26th. It was amazing that so much was accomplished so that this was possible.

Such disasters take a human toll that cannot be measured in terms of life and death. Illnesses caused by the stress, physical exhaustion, and anxiety over the future were to reveal themselves over the months and years to come. Such was no doubt the case for Monsignor Aloysius Boylan as he entered Mercy Hospital, Wilkes-Barre, for surgery on September 21, 1972. While he was able to resume his duties in October, he decided to retire to St. Joseph's Villa for priests in Scranton, in May 1973, having served superbly as pastor of Holy Name of Jesus Parish for twenty-three years. He was given a testimonial dinner by the parishioners on July 15, 1973. It was recalled at that time that a parishioner had once said of him, "A man who can walk down the aisles of his church and call every child of his six hundred families by his first name is doing an important job." (183)

Monsignor Edward T. Sullivan succeeded Monsignor Boylan as pastor on September 4, 1973. His tenure was to be brief as he was transferred two years later in 1975 to become pastor at St. John the Evangelist Parish in Wilkes-Barre. Reverend William J. Wheeler replaced him.

Sister Clotilde Cullen who had been appointed principal in September 1974 was transferred to become principal of St. Ann's School, Nyack, New York, in 1976. Sister Jacqueline Cunningham who also had a two-year tenure followed her as principal at Holy Name of Jesus. Sister Margaret Mary Kane became principal in 1978 and Sister Ritamary Mayan replaced Sister St. Henry Haiss as superior of the local community.

In 1978-1979 an upsurge occurred in the enrollment of the school, with close to two hundred students. By 1979-1980 there were 215 pupils enrolled as a new kindergarten was opened. Once again, however, there was turnover as the pastor, Reverend William J. Wheeler, was transferred to Immaculate Conception Church, Taylor. Reverend Martin J. Dacey was appointed the new pastor. He set about in earnest to complete renovations to the chapel and parlor in the convent. At the close of this year, Sister Margaret Mary Kane was named to the principalship of the Montessori School at Our Lady of Grace in Manhasset, New York. Sister Carlita Bird was appointed principal of Holy Name of Jesus School. There were to be only four sisters assigned for 1980-1981. These included Sister Ritamary Mayan, Sister Mary Barbara Campbell, Sister Rosemary Tasselli, and the principal and eighth grade teacher, Sister Carlita.

It was in September 1980 that Father Dacey was informed of the decision of the Congregation to withdraw from Holy Name of Jesus School by 1984. One can imagine that Father Dacey may have experienced some relief in hearing this news, so overwhelming were his financial obligations as an outcome of the long-range problems associated with the 1972 flood. The four-year notice did provide ample time for plans to be made about the future of the school. The number of sisters was reduced to two for 1982-1983 and they were housed with the IHM Sisters at St. Ignatius Convent, Kingston.

In the final year of IHM presence there, only the principal, Sister Carlita, was appointed. She continued to reside at St. Ignatius Convent until the close of school in June 1984. (184) The Sisters of Mercy of Dallas, Pennsylvania, had moved into Holy Name of Jesus Convent in 1982 when the remaining IHMs had moved to Kingston. At the IHM departure in 1984, Sister Mary Felice, RSM, was added to their community and accepted the principalship of Holy Name of Jesus School. She served for two years and was followed by Mr. Joseph Casciano as principal in 1986-1987. (185)

Our Lady of Grace Elementary School, Greensboro, North Carolina

> Please be aware of the gratitude of this parish for the years of service given by so many Immaculate Heart Sisters to our school and parish. Through all the joys and sorrows of these 26 years much has been accomplished to build the Kingdom of God in the minds and hearts of our parishioners. The Spirit of your Congregation will always be a part of our parish as our history continues to develop. (186)

In these words, the new pastor of Our Lady of Grace, Greensboro, North Carolina, Reverend William N. Pharr, acknowledged the decision of the Congregation to withdraw from this mission in June 1980. This word had been conveyed by letter to Bishop Michael Begley of Charlotte, and in personal visits to the prior pastor, Monsignor Francis M. Smith, and to the sisters in April 1979. This withdrawal action was directly related to the master plan drawn up by the General Chapter of 1978 after having considered the declining personnel of the Congregation. The positive aspect in selecting Our Lady of Grace in Greensboro was the recognized potential of this school to continue as an all-lay teacher Catholic school. Not only was the parish able to afford this financial outlay, but also with 24 lay teachers of the twenty-eight-teacher total in the school already, it had been demonstrated that lay leadership was strong and that Our Lady of Grace School could continue without an IHM presence. These facts did not lessen the painfulness of the experience, as parents of school children, members of the Board of Education, Bishop Begley, the pastor, and the sisters—all made their appeals for a reversal of the decision.

But on July 5, 1980, the four remaining IHM Sisters, Sister Maryla Farfour, principal of Our Lady of Grace School, Sister Lisbeth Hartnett, Sister Anne Manion, and Sister Mary Howard Krotzer said their last goodbyes in Greensboro.

Thus closed the nearly 27-year history of IHM ministry at Our Lady of Grace—a history which had begun in 1953, but had been preceded by several very gracious letters from Reverend Arthur R. Freeman, the first pastor, describing the location and attributes of Greensboro, North Carolina, and inviting Mother Marcella to staff the school which was, in 1952, only in the mind of Bishop Waters and Father Freeman. (187) Mother Marcella must have expressed interest in the proposal, but also the unavailability of any sisters for 1953. Father Freeman, undaunted, sought a commitment of sisters for 1954, writing these words of praise:

> On my part, I hold such esteem for the spirit and the high standards always maintained by the Immaculate Heart of Mary Sisters, that I would do anything within my power to have our children here enjoy the privilege of being under their tutelage.(188)

This sincere expression must have moved Mother Marcella, for the next communication from Father Freeman, nearly a year later, speaks to the matter of the priests' moving from the rectory at 201 S. Chapman Street so that the sisters could occupy this lovely dwelling as their convent. The priests moved to a rented residence two blocks from the church. (189) It is easy to see why Father Freeman would not wish to write to Mother Marcella to say that the school was not yet completed and there was as yet no convent as of August 6, 1953.

A school contract was signed by Mother M. Marcella and Father Freeman, pastor, providing forty dollars per month per sister for ten months. Sister Clotilde Cullen was appointed principal and superior of the new school, as well as teacher of the seventh and eighth grades. Sister Thomas Aquinas Kielceski taught fifth and sixth; Sister Marysia Reilly, third and fourth; Sister Anna Maria Foley, first and second; and Mrs. Robert Killam, kindergarten. Reverend Francis M. Smith, then pastoral assistant, taught religion classes. Sister Clotilde and Sister Marysia also taught music after school.

Marysia Reilly (Sister Marysia) recalls that many of the parishioners of Our Lady of Grace were relocated "northerners" who moved from the Philadelphia area when Western Electric Company moved to Greensboro. The locale in which Our Lady of Grace Parish and School were located was an affluent, beautiful suburb, surrounded by large, expensive homes. But, as Marysia observed, the sisters had very little in the beginning, and the income from private music pupils was really needed for their living. Both Sister Clotilde and Marysia taught music after school every day and on Saturday. Gifts were sent to them also from other IHM missions and from the sisters' families. Many parishioners were very generous, in particular, Mrs. Aurelia Guffy, a neighbor, who often brought them food, took them shopping, or to Congregation or educational meetings.

Mr.McFalls, a pharmacist, was remembered for collecting funds for a washer and dryer for the convent. It seems that the sisters had been doing the washing, including table and altar linens, by hand until Mr. McFalls came to the rescue. (190)

It must be remembered that Our Lady of Grace Parish was established only one year before the arrival of the sisters, Monsignor Freeman having been appointed its first pastor in April 1952. Our Lady of Grace Church is historic in itself as the gift of a non-Catholic, insurance company executive, Julian Price, in memory of his Catholic wife, Ethel Clay Price. With a Brooklyn, New York, architect, Henry V. Murphy, Mr. Price had developed plans for the church before his death on October 25, 1946, just three years to the day after his wife's death. Over $400,000 was designated in Mr. Price's will for the construction of the church. This amount was augmented by an additional $300,000 from the Price family—Mrs. Joseph M. Bryan, a daughter, and Ralph Clay Price, a son.

The Church of Our Lady of Grace was commonly known as the Ethel Clay Price Memorial Church, and at its dedication on September 14, 1952, was described as "a masterpiece of construction perfection" and "as one of the outstanding shrine-edifices in the United States, dedicated to the Blessed Virgin Mary." (191) The dedication attracted many bishops, clergy, religious, civic officials and persons of different faiths. Over 4,500 visitors responded to the "open house" invitation of the pastor a week before the dedication and were given guided tours by members of the Legion of Mary, who explained the architecture and the artistic symbols in the church.

Thus, Our Lady of Grace Parish, having the largest church in the Diocese of Raleigh, became a focal point and a model for Catholic activity in the Diocese. Bishop Vincent S. Waters of Raleigh, as co-planner of this church with Mr. Price, was to be a frequent visitor to the site. The sisters, arriving the following year, had no foreknowledge of the challenges that lay before them, but their efforts were to measure up, and exceed even the highest expectations that the pastor, bishop and parishioners had for them.

Meanwhile, during the late months of 1952 and until September 1953, Our Lady of Grace School was under construction. The sisters were expected in August 1953, and somehow most of the deadlines were met.

Our Lady of Grace School was officially dedicated on November 15, 1953, by Bishop Vincent S. Waters of Raleigh. The ceremonies began in the beautiful Price Memorial Church of Our Lady of Grace with the major address given by Reverend Boniface Bauer, OSB, of Belmont Abbey, North Carolina. Much effort had gone into preparations for this occasion as the sisters readied students from sixth, seventh and eighth grades of the school as a choir to sing several selections during the ceremonies.

The $185,000 two-story structure had four classrooms on each floor, with a principal's office on first floor and the library and health room on second floor. The auditorium and the kitchen were on the ground floor of the building. The concrete blocks on the interior were painted in varying light colors. The floors, of concrete, were covered with asphalt tile; stairways were of terrazzo. The exterior of the school was designed to blend with the architecture of the magnificent parish church. Like the church, the school was built of Salisbury granite with Indiana limestone trim. Exterior doorway arches match the Gothic style of the church. (192)

By 1956, there were 254 pupils at Our Lady of Grace School and a waiting list of both Catholic and non-Catholic children. Anxious parents wanted their children to be part of the growing reputation for excellence of Our Lady of Grace School. Annual music festivals, piano recitals and oratorical contests, which brought out the latent gifts of the children were resulting in awards and bringing accolades on the teachers.

The opening of the 1957-1958 school year saw the addition of a fifth sister to the little community which now included, Sister Clotilde Cullen, principal and superior, Sister Rose Regina Mainguth, Sister Marysia Reilly, Sister Thomas Aquinas Kielceski, and Sister Helena Heaney. This addition allowed for the separation of seventh and eighth grades, as Sister Rose Regina was assigned the seventh grade. With a total of 278 pupils crowding the school, it is easy to see the importance of the decision in 1958-1959 to initiate all single grades. With the addition of Sister Maria Pacis (Joan) Coyne, Mrs. Joseph Quinn for third grade, and Mrs. Richard Prokop for fifth grade, the faculty now numbered eight.

The tremendous spirit of community which existed among the sisters ministering in the southern missions was evident in the many descriptions of travels to teachers' institutes, feast days, sharing on significant religious or national holidays, cooperating for the success of diocesan programs, and enjoying a few vacation days together at the ocean.

As the 1959-1960 school year opened, the community still numbered six, but three new sisters were among them. Sister Raymond Rafferty replaced Sister Clotilde as principal and superior; Sister Eugenio (Clare) Belz was the new music and sixth grade teacher; and Sister St. Ephrem (Teresa) Raftery, music and first grade teacher.

Steady progress was made in the growth of the school to 290 pupils by 1961-1962. The convent had been beautifully refurbished for the sisters' return in August. But the year closed on a sad note as the surprising news of Monsignor Freeman's change to Saint Mary's in Goldsboro, North Carolina, was received on June 8, 1962. By June 12, Monsignor

Peter McNerney of Our Lady of Mercy Parish, Winston-Salem, took up residence as the new pastor of Our Lady of Grace. (193)

September 1962, saw a new principal and superior also—Sister Emeline Hastings. Three hundred-four pupils awaited the returning faculty. The new pastor, Monsignor McNerney, had wasted no time over the summer transforming the first floor classrooms and hall in the school from dull gray to bright two-tone colors. The convent's exterior and second floor had received a fresh coat of paint also. September 26, 1962, brought news of Monsignor Arthur Freeman's death. All who knew him, not least of whom were the Sisters of IHM, mourned this saintly priest, who had been the first pastor of Our Lady of Grace Church where he had served until three months before his death. The year with its many activities rolled on and ended with plans for a needed addition to the convent being set into motion. At an estimated cost of $33,000 a new chapel and sacristy, four bedrooms, bathroom, utility room, cedar closet and extended kitchen were to be added. Needless to say, this construction was not completed upon the return of the sisters on August 23, 1963. Monsignor McNerney and his assistant had moved to the older part of the convent and offered the rectory to the sisters for five days. While the sisters returned to the convent on August 28, it would be two months before the work was actually completed.

The October 26, 1963 entry in the annals reads:

> . . . As the Sanctus bells joyfully sounded in our convent home once again, each Sister longingly awaited the precious moment when Our Lord would be present on the altar. This first Mass was offered by our pastor, Monsignor Peter McNerney. (194)

"Open House" on October 27 brought hundreds of visitors and benefactors to whom the sisters proudly and gratefully showed the ample residence they now had. On November 16, fifteen sisters from the other southern missions accepted invitations to come to Our Lady of Grace for Sister Emeline's feast and to see the new convent.

The tenure of Monsignor McNerney as pastor was to be short. As the school grew to 322 in 1964-1965 and to 362 in 1965-1966, the challenges of the growing parish were beginning to tax his failing health. On May 18, 1966, he announced his transfer to Trym, North Carolina. His replacement as pastor was to be the newly consecrated Auxiliary Bishop, Charles B. McLaughlin, who took up residence at Our Lady of Grace on June 12, 1966.

Over the summer while the sisters were "up north," Bishop McLaughlin turned his attention to beautifying the chapel of the convent. A new altar, rose-colored carpeting, and wood paneling of the cinder-block walls, were the major renovations. It was September 30 before this work was completed, so the sisters made their spiritual exercises in the church for about five weeks. Their joy at the privilege of once again having the Blessed Sacrament in their convent home is reflected in the annals for September 30, 1967: "We had Holy Mass in our convent chapel for the first time since returning. Our dear Lord is with us again. Thanks be to God!" (195)

The separations that come to those in mission in the Church never become routine; each one is a reminder of our pilgrim state. This was true at Our Lady of Grace as the sisters received word of Bishop McLaughlin's call to be the first Bishop of the newly established Diocese of St. Petersburg, Florida. There was rejoicing for the honor bestowed on him, but there was sadness in losing their pastor after only eleven months with him. The sisters made the long trip to St. Petersburg on June 14, 1968, and attended the ceremonies for the establishment of the Diocese of St. Petersburg and the Episcopal Installation of Bishop McLaughlin on June 17.

Sister Emeline completed her six years as principal so there were more "goodbyes" as she and Sister Rose Regina, who had served at Our Lady of Grace for eleven years, began their journey "north" to take up new assignments. Sister Mary Edward Loftus was appointed principal; Sister John Francis Marley, superior, and the community now included Sister Rose Francis Brown, Sister Maria Raymond Grogan, Sister Paschal FitzGibbon and Sister John Marie Christiansen. (196) The new pastor was Monsignor Michael Carey.

The declining enrollments that were typical in the 1970s were seen at Our Lady of Grace also as 1969-1970 saw 230 pupils registered. Recognizing that much of the decrease was occurring in seventh and eighth grades, the Central Administrative Assembly, in light of the acute shortage of sister-personnel, decided to no longer assign sisters to the seventh and eighth grades of Our Lady of Grace School. Sister Mary Edward Loftus, principal, was notified of this in November 1970, to become effective for the 1971-1972 school year. (197) This decision meant either the transfer of seventh and eighth graders to other schools or the hiring of additional lay teachers. Our Lady of Grace opted to make its school K-6 for the time being.

The illness of the pastor, Monsignor Michael Carey, and his death on October 7, 1971, brought sorrow again to the sisters and the parishioners. Monsignor Michael J. Begley had been named administrator of the parish in August and was now named pastor, but this, too, was to come to an abrupt end when he was appointed Bishop-elect of the newly created Diocese of Charlotte, North Carolina, on November 29, 1971. Receptions and programs were held by the parish in his honor. Then, on January 12, 1972, hundreds of people, including the sisters journeyed to Charlotte for the double ceremonies of the establishment of the Diocese of Charlotte and the Episcopal Ordination of Bishop Begley. (198) Reverend Francis Smith, who had been the assistant pastor under Monsignor Arthur Freeman in 1953 when the IHM Sisters first went to Greensboro, was named pastor on January 23, 1972.

Sister Janet Rossiter replaced Sister Mary Edward as principal in September 1973. Her sister-faculty included Sisters Mercille Schneider, Babette Opferman, Nadine Foley and Doreen Willis. The enrollment was once again climbing, and reached 376 by the opening date of school, August 26, 1974. This was an increase of 146 pupils over the 1969-1970 figures. One must remember, however, that by this time also, Our Lady of Grace was a nine-grade school. Father Smith's plans for the school resulted in the construction of an imposing building that enlarged the capacity of the school and created a parish activity center under the same roof. This building was dedicated on November 14, 1976.

Sister Dolores Banick was to follow Sister Janet Rossiter as principal in September 1978, but this assignment was short-lived as the incoming congregation administration chose Sister Dolores as director of novices. This meant that on August 30, Sister Dolores left to assume her new position, and Sister Maryla Farfour was named from the faculty of Our Lady of Grace as acting principal. Further confusion was engendered when Sister Jeanne Tubach, who had been assigned to teach grade five, was re-elected sector superior for the Western Sector. Her departure was on October 20. A replacement for her was not possible until January when Sister Mary Leva was sent to teach religion and music in the junior high grades.

The 25th Anniversary of Our Lady of Grace School was observed during the week of December 11 to 18 with many returning former teachers and students joining in the celebration. The joyful tone of these days was to be muted when in the spring of the year the Congregation Administrators visited Our Lady of Grace bringing the news of the withdrawal of our Sisters at the close of the next school year, in June 1980. (199)

Sister Maryla Farfour was confirmed as principal for 1979-1980 and a series of family illnesses and personal reasons resulted in the transfers of Sister Patricia Smith, superior (now deceased) and Sister Mary Leva. Sister Lisbeth Hartnett replaced Sister Patricia and Sister Mary Howard Krotzer was assigned in Sister Mary Leva's place. Sister Anne Manion brought the final group to four.

The difficulty of withdrawal was compounded when a new pastor, Monsignor William N. Pharr, was appointed for Our Lady of Grace in

March of 1980. His understanding of the need for the decision, his patience in seeking out alternative solutions to retain Our Lady of Grace School, and his gratitude for all the sisters were doing, were deeply appreciated by the Congregation administration which, in turn, tried very hard, without success, to locate another congregation to replace the IHMs. Monsignor Pharr's brief experience with our sisters led him to state,

> The cooperation of the sisters has been super in helping us prepare for the transition to an all-lay school next year. Because of the foundation they have laid, we are able to approach the future of our school with much optimism. (200)

Shirley Hovey of the faculty was named by Monsignor Pharr and the Board of Education to be principal of the all-lay faculty for 1980-1981.

Mr. Richard Farwell was named coordinator of religious education for the school, signaling the importance of the school's continuing focus on religion. Mr. Farwell would reside in the former convent; the convent chapel was to be the center for class liturgies. The final sentiments of the sisters are well expressed in these words:

> We alternate greetings and goodbyes. In between the beginning of this year and the end we experienced many opposites: happiness—sadness; laughter—tears; work—play . . . As our final days at Our Lady of Grace drew near, we were confident and satisfied that our school would continue with a lay principal and an all lay faculty (the first in the Diocese of Charlotte). We were sad because we had to leave people we loved and work that was both challenging and rewarding. (201)

St. Agnes Catechetical Center, Forest City, Pennsylvania

Forest City, Pennsylvania is located north of Carbondale, but in the southernmost part of Susquehanna County. It was built in such a way that most of the residential area was situated on the hillside, with an excellent view of the countryside and adjacent mountains.

This small town is the home of five Catholic churches. One of these, St. Agnes, is a territorial parish, while St. Anthony of Padua, Sacred Heart of Jesus, St. Joseph's and St. Michael's are ethnic parishes. Monsignor John P. Gallagher explains the term "territorial" in this way:

> Territorial parishes were those in which the pastor assumed responsibility for the people living within a specifically limited area. (202)

It was the Bishop of the Diocese who created such a parish and spelled out the geographical boundaries.

Ethnic parishes, on the other hand, developed within these geographical boundaries because of the inability of the various immigrant groups to speak English and to adjust to the practice of their religion in any but their native tongue.

Thus, ethnic groups which had their own clergy when they immigrated, established separate parishes and built their own churches, maintaining their own language and customs in liturgical services and in the administration of the Sacraments.

The territorial parish of St. Agnes, Forest City, was established in 1892. By 1894, the Lithuanian people had founded St. Anthony of Padua Parish. In 1904, two additional groups established ethnic parishes—the Polish, at Sacred Heart of Jesus, and the Slovenians at St. Joseph's. Ten years later, Sacred Heart Parish was also to have an elementary school, as the pastor, Reverend James Gryczka, brought the Bernardine Sisters of St. Francis to Forest City in 1914. The fifth Catholic church was established by the Slovak people as St. Michael's in 1921. (203)

It was into this culturally diversified environment that the Sisters of the Immaculate Heart of Mary were called to serve in 1953. Reverend Leo J. Craig was pastor of St. Agnes Parish when sisters were requested to assist with the catechetical work of the parish. Mother Marcella responded by sending Sisters Ann Dolora Cullen, Pierina Kennedy and Paschal FitzGibbon on November 16, 1953. Sister Agnessa McLaughlin had originally been assigned, but sudden illness sent her to the hospital, hence Sister Pierina was sent. Father Craig and the members of the Altar and Rosary Society were present to welcome the sisters. Two days later, on November 18, 1953, the sisters began their classes at St. Agnes.

The story of the Sisters of IHM in the Forest City area is one of continuously expanding services from 1953 to 1970 when the five Forest City parishes and Pleasant Mount were being provided with catechetical instructions for both grade and high school youngsters. It was as early as April 26, 1954, that Father Joseph Kelley, pastor of St. James Parish, Pleasant Mount, sought the sisters' assistance. That summer, Sisters Ann Dolora Cullen, Austin Murdock and John Eudes Briscoe conducted a three-week summer school at Pleasant Mount.

Beginning in September 1954, Reverend John Kameen, pastor of St. Mary's, Waymart, also sought the sisters' help in preparing his parishioners for the sacrament of Confirmation. Sisters Ann Dolora and Paschal were the teachers, assisted on Sundays by Sister Graecia Mangan who came from Carbondale.

Father Kameen was not going to relinquish such help easily, and seeing the good work of the sisters, requested them to teach a two-week summer session in July of 1955. Sisters Ann Dolora, Austin and Benedict Hore were the teachers. Father Kameen's relationship with the IHM Sisters was to be put on a more permanent basis when, in August 1955, he was transferred to St. Joseph's Parish, Forest City, and became a near neighbor to St. Agnes Parish. One of his first acts as pastor was to procure the teaching services of the sisters for his parish (204)

That fall also, grade school children from St. Cecilia's Parish, Hilltop, (a mission of Father Kelley's) were added to the weekly schedule of instructions.

In addition to preparing the children for the reception of First Holy Communion and Confirmation, amazing results were achieved in their education in Church music. On August 1, 1956, a combined group of one hundred-thirty children from St. Agnes and St. Joseph Parishes sang a Gregorian chant high mass in St. Joseph's Church.

With the opening of the 1956-1957 school year, Reverend John Madaj, pastor of Sacred Heart Parish, Forest City, requested the services of the IHM Sisters also. The Bernardine Sisters had been serving this parish from 1914 to 1955, at which time they were withdrawn for other needs of their Congregation. During 1955-1956 Father Madaj was without teaching sisters, but was happy to receive a positive response to his request for teachers from Mother Marcella. What it actually meant was once again extending the outreach of the sisters at Forest City—and these three, Sisters Ann Dolora, Paschal and Angelo McNulty, with some lay assistants, rendered outstanding service with seven hundred children.

On January 23, 1957, the little community was saddened by the death of Father John Kameen, pastor of St. Joseph's Church. Father Kameen was followed by Father Albin Satkowski, who, as an alumnus of St. John's High, Pittston, Pennsylvania, became an instant and most appreciative friend of the sisters. (205)

It is interesting to note that, in spite of the fact that the sisters were instructing children from the various Forest City parishes together, when the time came for Confirmation or First Holy Communion, each parish held its own ceremonies. In fact the record reveals that on September 28, 1958, Bishop Jerome Hannan conducted Confirmation in four different churches in Forest City, starting at 9:30 a.m. and finishing at 9:00 p.m. Fourteen days later he conducted Confirmation ceremonies in St. James Parish, Pleasant Mount. Needless to say, the sisters were present for each group. A total of 166 youngsters had been prepared.

Father Joseph Kelley died on March 22, 1959, and Father Harold Mulrooney succeeded him as pastor of St. James, Pleasant Mount, on June 2, 1959.

It is evident that the sisters instilled a great love of the Blessed Virgin Mary into the hearts of their students. A very active Legion of Mary group was in existence from the beginning of our sisters' presence in Forest City. Annual May crownings were well attended in all the parishes, as were annual retreat days for the high school students. These retreats were usually given by Passionist priests from St. Ann's Monastery in Scranton or Sacred Heart Priests from Kilroe Seminary, Honesdale.

Father Leo Craig, Pastor of St. Agnes Parish, Forest City, with whom our sisters had been associated since their arrival in 1953 seemed like the one certain pillar in the changing Church scene in the Forest City area. But the sisters were to lose this dear friend also when, after being afflicted with a stroke on August 2, 1964, he died on October 8. His death was experienced as a great loss to the parish, but also to the entire region.

Reverend Andrew J. McGowan was appointed administrator of St. Agnes Parish, but because of his other duties did not reside there, nor was he able to offer Holy Mass there except on Sundays. He arranged for Father Vildac S.Giroux, SCJ, of Kilroe Seminary to say Mass at St. Agnes Church two days a week. Father Giroux became interested in the sisters and usually spent some time with them after Mass and eventually offered one Mass each week in the convent chapel. This was a rare privilege since the sisters were accustomed to having Mass in their chapel only twice a year, on Christmas and Easter.

It was January 27, 1965, before a new pastor was appointed to St. Agnes, Forest City. The former pastor of St. Andrew's, Blossburg, Pennsylvnia, Reverend William J. Burke, became the new pastor. He was to have only a short time to be associated with Sister Marie Andrew Allen who had been the superior at St. Agnes Convent since 1959 and had served so well for nine years as catechetical instructor. She was transferred to St. Mary's Convent, Manhasset, New York. Sister Maris Law replaced her as superior.

Father Burke was to be pastor only two years, but in that brief time he accomplished the renovation of the convent, and achieved remarkable results in meeting the spiritual needs of rural families who were away from the Church. He exerted great energy in appealing to the young people of St. Agnes Parish to attend catechetical instructions and retreats. There were some one hundred-fifty high school students who attended the retreat days during his pastorate.

Reverend Thomas Carlin succeeded Father Burke who was transferred to Hawley, Pennsylvania, on June 17, 1967.

The sisters exerted every effort to unite the various parishes through the work and social activities conducted for the young people. In September 1969, they initiated a meeting with the five pastors of the Forest City parishes and the pastor of Pleasant Mount to attempt consolidation of catechetical instructions for all students. Amazingly, all pastors were present except one who, because of illness, could not attend but sent a lay representative to the meeting. A program was worked out which involved the sisters five days per week, including Sunday. This unified program certainly motivated the parents to send their children to instructions, and the resultant enrollment was 375 in the elementary grades and 230 in the high school classes. Sisters from area schools and seminarians from Kilroe, as well as laywomen of the parishes, were enlisted as instructors. The sisters kept in close touch with the significant events in the lives of their students, providing for religious and social celebrations in the parishes for high school graduates, eighth-grade graduates, and for special awards or honors students had received. The sisters were guests at Sacred Heart Polish Church for the annual Epiphany Wafer Supper. Christmas festivities saw them stretching their presence to participate at several different parishes where they had prepared the children for programs.

Meanwhile, the sisters also kept up significant community relationships by enjoying days of retreat, feast days and holidays with the sisters in Jermyn, Carbondale, Archbald, and Olyphant and with several Scranton houses. Their own little convent often housed visitors, but usually "one at a time" for overnight stays.

Sister Maris Law, having served at St. Agnes for six years, was transferred to St. Ignatius, Kingston, in August 1971. Sister Lucian Reddington replaced her as superior, with Sister St. Andrew Connor and Sister Ivan Pollack as the local community. (206) Illness was to cut short Sister Lucian's tenure at St. Agnes, however, and on October 29, 1973, Sister Mario Killeen replaced her.

Most of the time between November and the end of January of 1973 the convent was torn up as Father Carlin began a thorough renovation of the entire structure. On February 2, 1974, "open house" was held for the parishioners, with Father Carlin and the sisters proudly conducting the tours.

In addition to training all of the youngsters for liturgical singing, Sister Mario had two special choirs, the junior and adult choirs, which sang for special feasts, such as Christmas Midnight Mass. There were always three or four First Holy Communion and Confirmation ceremonies, as well as May crownings at each parish, and other special events, renewed certification courses, religious education conferences and ecumenical meetings, which kept the sisters in a somewhat perpetual motion state.

Father William J. Egan who had been pastor at Jermyn replaced Father Thomas Carlin, pastor, on September 3, 1974.

Sister Marie Louise Langan became superior in 1977 and served in this capacity until the fall of 1982 at which time Sister Mario was elected superior of the little community that included Sister Marie Louise and Sister Germaine McCormick. (207)

Due to illness, Sister Marie Louise was hospitalized in Scranton for six weeks in the winter of 1983-1984. From there she was transferred to the Marian Convent. In the fall of 1984, Sister Robertine Fox was added to the community. Sister Germaine was elected superior and continues in that capacity as of this writing (1987-1988).

The pastor, Father Egan, suffered a slight stroke in January 1985, and was hospitalized for a week, but returned to the hospital on June 3 and decided to retire to St. Joseph's Villa in Dunmore on September 4, 1985. A few months later, on December 27, 1985, Father Egan died. Some seventy priests attended his funeral, as did hundreds of Forest City parishioners and friends. Reverend Austin E. Flanagan, who succeeded Father Egan as pastor of St. Agnes in September 1985, was to have a single year's tenure. The shortage of priests in the Scranton Diocese was the reason for Bishop James C. Timlin's decision to begin the merger of ethnic parishes in the small towns of the Scranton Diocese. The first step toward merger was to appoint one priest as joint pastor of several churches. On August 10, 1986, therefore, Bishop Timlin offered Mass at St. Agnes and informed the parishioners that Father Joseph S. Sitko, who already served as pastor of Sacred Heart, St. Michael, and St. Anthony Parishes of Forest City, would also serve St. Agnes. Daily Masses were then scheduled in alternate months at St. Agnes and Sacred Heart Churches. The small inconveniences experienced by the sisters in these new arrangements are part of the bigger picture of the "signs of the times" for the Church. Sister Mario and Sister Germaine continue to serve at St. Agnes. Sister Mario coordinates the religious education program and continues to be involved in church music, as well as in the instruction of private piano pupils. Sister Germaine is assigned to prayer ministry. She served as local community secretary, representative to the district, vocation contact person and local coordinator. (208)

St. Henry's Elementary School, Gresham, Oregon

Gresham, Oregon is located twelve miles east of Portland, just five miles from the famous Columbia River, in a valley with scenic Mount Hood towering as a backdrop forty miles away.

The Sisters, Servants of the Immaculate Heart of Mary had served in a more westerly part of the Archdiocese of Portland, namely, Tillamook, Oregon from 1897 to 1903. They were well known as educators in Portland, Oregon, where they had taught in St. Andrew's from 1909 to 1921, and were teaching in St. Lawrence Parish School and in Central Catholic Boys' High School in the 1950s when Reverend Augustine A. Meyer, pastor of St. Henry's, Gresham, began his search for sisters.

What would attract the Congregation to extend its services into this little town of then 3,100 people, and into a parish of 380 families? Certainly it was unique to be called into the heart of a multi-million dollar berry-producing region—the strawberry capital of the world, to be at the hub of the holly, nursery stock and commercial flower-raising business. Gresham was a thriving shopping center for some 40,000 people living outside of Portland, Oregon, working on the farms, in the logging or sawmill industry, or in food processing plants. All of this life and potential for growth was reflected in St. Henry's Parish. An average of nine baptisms a year between 1913 and 1952 precipitated into 203 Baptisms in 1952-1954. The 1950 census showed a 30% population increase in Gresham in four years. As Father Meyer wrote to Mother Marcella, " I really feel that this parish has a fine future . . . " (209)

In the fall of 1951, the groundwork for additional IHM Sisters serving in the Archdiocese of Portland, Oregon, had been laid by the personal visit to Marywood of Reverend Martin Thielen, superintendent of Catholic Schools of the Archdiocese. It was during that visit that Mother Marcella indicated a willingness to provide additional sisters at some future time. The closeness of that "future time" was clear a few months later in a December 1951 letter from Archbishop Edward Howard of Portland:

> . . . It seems advisable that the Sisters should be assigned to St. Henry's Parish in Gresham. This parish is in good financial condition and should be able to provide a suitable school and convent by September 1953. (210)

The written appeals of Father Meyer, a hard working, determined, and holy priest, were also difficult to ignore. Once he received the slightest hope that sisters might be forthcoming, he set his plans for building a school into high gear, launched a fund drive raising 50% of the total needed, and bought a house to be the future convent for the sisters. That the coming of sisters to St. Henry's was central to his plans for the future is obvious, as he writes:

> I look forward eagerly to the change in the whole parish when the good effects of our school will become evident, and from many sources I have heard nothing but compliments about the Immaculate Heart Sisters, and the observation that they are parochial minded. I will certainly welcome their assistance in the parish. I think they will find my people quite unspoiled—very wholesome, and deeply reverent, with a strong affection for those who have dedicated their lives in the service of God. (211)

Sending sisters into a welcoming and promising environment was not the principal motivation of Mother Marcella, however, since sisters were in great demand everywhere and in short supply. Her motives are clearly related to apostolic ministry and community life concerns as she writes:

> While sending sisters for your school will mean a sacrifice, since we never seem to have enough teachers to supply even the ordinary demands, I feel that God will bless us for taking another mission in the far West. Then, too, as our numbers in the western missions increase, the Sisters laboring there will not feel so isolated. (212)

This foresight and generosity of spirit were characteristic of Mother Marcella.

As the months of 1952 rolled on there were many exchanges of letters between diocesan officials in Portland and Mother Marcella. Several of these letters related to providing residence for the two sisters teaching at Central Catholic High School at St. Henry's upon completion of the convent. Archbishop Howard had first suggested this to Mother Marcella in his 1951 communication with her. The pastor, Father Meyer, was happy to include extra rooms in his plans. The sisters concerned were Sister Justitia Downes and Sister Barbara Dumont, who were residing at St. Lawrence Convent in Portland with the five IHMs who staffed St. Lawrence Elementary School. It seemed an appropriate distribution to add the two Central Catholic High School teachers to the two sisters to be sent to St. Henry's for the new four-grade school. Further, with the cramped conditions at St. Lawrence Convent, with seven sisters using one bathroom, with no shower facilities available, and with five sisters sleeping in a beaverboard dormitory arrangement, the plan seemed logical.

However, letters from Reverend William L. Whalen, principal of Central Catholic High School, and from Reverend Martin Thielen, superintendent of schools, set forth some of the difficulties in locating the sisters at such a distance from the high school, and made clear that Sister Justitia, a Portland native, had "expressed a definite preference for remaining at St. Lawrence." (213)

Mother Marcella settled the matter in a letter of September 27 acceding to these appeals and resolving the imbalance of sisters at St. Henry's by favoring Father Meyer with a third sister. (214) Thus, Sister Liguori Farnon, superior and principal, Sister Agnes McHale and Sister Genoveva Chainey were sent to open St. Henry's School, Gresham, Oregon, in September 1953. Four double grades were opened, and Sister Genoveva served as full-time music teacher.

Sister Agnes McHale recalls the people of St. Henry's as hardworking, mostly middle-class families who came from the outlying areas around Gresham. Father Meyer had organized the furnishing of the convent by providing the stores in town with lists of items that would be needed. The generosity of the people was such that everything was provided—the kitchen was completely equipped; table linens, bedding, and many thoughtful touches throughout the house were provided.

The convent was remarkable for its provision of adequate closets, storage, laundry, and freezer space adjacent to the kitchen, six ample bedrooms, a beautiful chapel, parlors, kitchen and dining room. The windows in the community room looked out on a beautiful view of snowcapped Mount Hood. While the convent was not complete at the time of the sisters' arrival, the workmen were busy evenings finishing the floors and the three unused bedrooms. (215)

Actual construction of the school had begun on January 14, 1953, so it was an amazing accomplishment that both the school and the convent were nearly completed in August. With 900 square feet of floor space, the school provided at that time four classrooms, faculty and health rooms, office and reception rooms. The exterior of both convent and school presented a striking appearance, being finished in vertical redwood siding and red brick. The auditorium was completed by November 1953 and contained both athletic facilities and provisions for stage productions and parish social functions.

Although there were only 82 pupils in four grades at the opening of school and 110 in catechetical classes, the sisters found themselves very busy as they moved into both school and convent. They planned, organized, attended professional and spiritual meetings, and called forth all their domestic talents as they prepared, canned and froze all the marvelous food products—tomatoes, corn, peaches, apricots, cherries, and much more—as the seasonal fruits ripened and the people generously provided the sisters with ample supplies. This tedious work was truly appreciated in the heart of winter when these fruits and vegetables would not otherwise be available.

Father Meyer was more than attentive to the sisters' needs. As a master woodworker himself, he prepared many surprises to enhance the beauty of the convent. He handcrafted the community room table, the pews for the chapel, and the brackets that held the sanctuary lamp. He enjoyed the cheerful and energetic spirit of the sisters and found endless ways to show his appreciation for their work in the parish.

It was April 4, 1954, before Archbishop Howard's schedule permitted him to conduct an official dedication of St. Henry's School and Convent. But this had given the sisters time to prepare the pupils for their part in the program. The IHMs, too, contributed to the program by singing "Heart Immaculate," a hymn composed by Sister Scholastica Chainey, IHM, with words written by Sister Aquin Theobald, IHM. The occasion of the dedication was marked by the presence of many visiting clergy, religious and laity. The IHM Sisters from St. Lawrence in Portland assisted in serving a buffet luncheon in the convent for the many guests. (216)

The school year 1954-1955 saw an enrollment of 138 pupils. Sister Sarita Gesler replaced Sister Genoveva whose health was not good. It was obvious that the trend of increasing enrollment was to continue, so the fall of 1955 saw the assignment of an additional sister, Sister Camilla Kirsch, to St. Henry's. Mother Kathleen Hart had been elected at the close of Mother Marcella's term in June 1955. Mother Kathleen had visited Gresham in 1953 when the school and convent were just being completed and had talked at length with Father Meyer about his hopes and plans for the future. Being aware of the anticipated growth, she did not hesitate to supply an additional sister, and, indeed, when school opened on September 6, 1955, there were 163 pupils in six grades. Four sisters were already not enough. Nor was the four-room school any longer adequate. Ground was broken in March 1956 for an addition to the school.

In light of the planned expansion, Father Meyer promptly wrote to Mother Kathleen requesting a fifth sister and backing up his request with the fact that he had built a convent large enough to accommodate a full complement of sister-faculty for St. Henry's. The happiness of the sisters who were already there, and his desire to do all he could for them and for the school provided a strong case for his request. But Mother Kathleen was unable to spare a sister for Gresham that year. Father Meyer's disappointment was reflected in his words:

> I still refuse to believe it! I still feel so confident that we are going to get another sister that I refuse to accept your letter as final. Here in Gresham we feel that God won't let us down. (217)

School opened in September 1956 with four sisters and one lay teacher, Mrs. Doris Buckley. Two hundred pupils were registered in grades one through seven.

In the fall, 1957, Sister Noel Michalek was transferred from St. Thomas School in Coeur d'Alene to St. Henry's, Gresham. This brought the sister-faculty to five, with one lay teacher, Mrs. Margaret Okrasinski. The enrollment was 234 pupils in eight grades. The school, now four years old, was beginning to sense its impact in the local area. Students were entering contests and winning prizes; they were participating in radio broadcasts, and offering annual entertainments to the public. The teachers were participating in workshops, and were receiving high marks from visiting supervisors from the Diocese and from the State of Oregon. So, the first eighth-grade graduating class was sent forth on June 5, 1958, with much to be proud of at St. Henry's and with a firm foundation for the next level of education.

Sister Camilla was transferred to Lock Haven, Pennsylvania, at the close of the 1957-1958 school year, having served at St. Henry's for three years. Sister Paracleta Gallagher replaced her. Father Meyer was bracing himself for the change yet to come at the close of the 1958-1959 school year when Sister Liguori's term of six years would end. He had come to rely heavily on her, and it was certainly evident that her leadership had brought excellent development to the school.

School opened in September 1959 with an enrollment of 250 pupils. Sister Therese Culhane had been appointed superior and principal; Sister Noel returned to Coeur d'Alene; and Sister Clement Schermanson was transferred from St. Lawrence, Portland, to Gresham. A second lay teacher, Mrs. Gloria Starret, had to be hired. The activity of the sisters increased with the growth of the school and of the after school CCD classes. There were preparations for First Holy Communion and Confirmation ceremonies; the instruction of adult converts brought forty adults into the Confirmation class in this particular year; in addition there were book fairs, conventions, and involvement in Diocesan and Congregation life. (218)

Again, in February of 1960, Father Meyer pleaded with Mother Kathleen for another sister. Since his request could not be honored and the enrollment reached 276, there had to be additional doubling of grades, with a fifth-sixth and sixth-seventh combination. The distance of

Gresham from Portland posed a transportation problem for many potential lay faculty, so the problem of procuring good lay teachers was growing acute. It was probably disconcerting to Father Meyer to see each day for a week the six extra sisters who were staying at St. Henry's. This temporary residence arrangement was made to accommodate the Portland sisters who were moving from St. Lawrence Parish until their new convent at St. Anthony's in Portland opened on December 8, 1960. These sisters from St. Henry's were present for the first Mass celebrated in St. Anthony's Convent and, as they expressed it, had the thrill of seeing the sanctuary lamp lighted in another convent home. (219)

In August 1961 Sister Sarita and Sister Paracleta were transferred to eastern missions. Sister Sarita had completed seven years, having been at St. Henry's since 1954; Sister Paracleta had served there since 1958. Sister Gracilda Burke and Sister Aline Farrell were sent as replacements. A third lay teacher, Miss Carol Monlux, was added to the faculty.

There was no dearth of activity as the sisters extended themselves to diocesan education projects, serving on curriculum and textbook committees. There were many opportunities for enrichment as they attended liturgical conferences, subject-matter workshops and Congregation meetings.

October 12, 1962, was an eventful day as a hurricane devastated the Portland area. The front porch of St. Henry's Church was blown off and two large windows in the school were broken. It was fortunate that power and water in the church, convent and school were not affected, as was the case in most of the area. The sisters from St. Anthony's were guests once again until their electricity and water were restored. (220)

June 18, 1963, saw Sister Agnes McHale depart from St. Henry's for the East. The people of the parish seemed to take her change with deep nostalgia because, as they said, "She was the last of the first Sisters." (221) It must have been a difficult move for her, too, since she had served at St. Henry's for ten years. Of her years in Gresham, Sister Agnes said, "I loved it, and while we worked hard, it did a lot for me, too. (222)

September 1963 saw, not only a replacement for Sister Agnes, but an additional sister, bringing the little community to six. They included: Sister Therese Culhane, principal and superior; Sister Clement Schermanson, Sister Aline Farrell, Sister Christina Murphy, Sister Gracilda Burke and Sister Casimir Bougher. The two lay teachers in the school were Mrs. Okrasinski and Mrs. Fagan.

This was to be an exciting year as the groundbreaking and construction were begun for the new St. Henry's Church and the realization of another of Father Meyer's cherished dreams. It was also a year for travel as the sisters at St. Henry's planned a car trip to California, and the St. Anthony's sisters planned a trip in their six-passenger station wagon to Scranton. These were highlights in their lives, especially the trip East, with all the Congregation ties being renewed over the summer.

The opening day of school in 1964 found a faculty of six sisters and two lay teachers, with Sister Eva Marie Zlotucha replacing Sister Gracilda who had been transferred to Bellefonte, Pennsylvania.

October 18, 1964, was the date of the dedication of the new St. Henry's Church. Many visitors came from surrounding areas, since the architecture and liturgical art of the new structure had received wide publicity in both Catholic and secular papers. Archbishop Edward D. Howard was principal celebrant of the Mass, with deacons and sub deacons representing the Holy Cross Fathers from Portland University, the Franciscan Fathers, and the diocesan clergy. Benedictine priests and brothers served in a variety of ceremonial capacities. St. Henry's men's choir sang for the Mass, and the school choir, directed by Sister Eva Marie, sang the offertory hymn. (223) The church, elegant in its simplicity and open space, was considered to be exemplary of the Church's new decrees on liturgical art after the Second Vatican Council. Reverend John Domin, a diocesan priest and head of the Sacred Art Commission in Portland, had this to say:

> A result of collaborative effort by all, together with pastor and Sacred Art Commission, they (the art work of the church) are valid expressions of a living architecture and a living art for a living faith, in the interest of making that faith more meaningful and satisfying. (224)

Father Domin was referring to the fact that the new St. Henry's, its landscape, architecture, windows, altar, candlesticks, tabernacle, sanctuary lamp, baptismal and holy water fonts, and crucifix were all works of local artists and reflected their living faith.

It was an historic and proud day for St. Henry's Parish. Thirty-six visiting religious sisters were also on hand for the occasion and were served a buffet luncheon in the convent, prepared by the school's Mother's Club and served by the eighth-grade girls.

Sister Therese Culhane's six years at St. Henry's having been completed in June 1965, she was transferred to Little Flower School in Bethesda, Maryland. Sister St. Bernard (Kathleen) Lannak replaced her as superior and principal in September 1965. Sister Aline and Sister Christina were also transferred; Sister Mercille Schneider and Sister Mary of Nazareth (Mary) Dawson came from the East to replace them.

On February 5, 1966, Archbishop Howard retired after completing forty years as Ordinary of the Archdiocese of Portland. Archbishop Robert J. Dwyer succeeded him. Sisters Monica Byrne and St. Bernard represented the Sisters of IHM at the installation ceremonies of the new archbishop. All of the sisters at St. Henry's would have the opportunity of meeting Archbishop Dwyer on April 16, 1966, when he administered Confirmation to 120 children and 35 adults. (225)

Weary, yet invigorated by their summer car trip to Scranton, the sisters took up their work for the 1967-1968 school year. Sister Rosalian Armbruster had replaced Sister Casimir Bougher, and an additional lay person, Mr. Darel McMahon, had been hired for sixth, seventh and eighth grade science classes. This arrangement gave the principal the ability to function as a free principal in the afternoon for the first time at St. Henry's. With 320 children enrolled in eight grades, this was an important change.

Visitors came and went in a steady stream: in October, the regional superior, Sister Georgina Wertz, and her companion, Sister Joyce McQuaide, were welcomed; in November, the sisters from St. Anthony's were Thanksgiving Day guests. Sister Felicitas Ryan, Congregation school supervisor, arrived in Holy Week, enroute to the NCEA Convention in California. All of these were joyful and stimulating experiences of the 1967-1968 year. But several gatherings were full of sadness as farewell dinners were held for the IHMs of St. Anthony's and Central High School, Portland, who were being withdrawn from the West in June 1968. On May 12, five of the Coeur d'Alene Sisters, Sisters Noel Michalek, Mariel Dougher, Gertrudis Porter, Christina Murphy and Bernard Cunningham drove to Portland to say their farewells. The following weekend Sisters Bernita McDonough, Miles Boyd and Joan of Arc (Jacquelin) Servick made the trip from Twin Falls, Idaho, to Portland for their farewells. In spite of the distances separating the sisters in the West, there was an evident bond among them, and their sadness at the departure of these sisters was understandable. Perhaps they were also reading the "handwriting on the wall" for their own missions in the not-too-distant future.

The year 1968-1969 saw Sister Christina Aldarelli replace Sister Rosalian at St. Henry's. It was a year that was to close with the transfers of Sisters Eva Marie and Mary Dawson. But in the intervening months the school was alive with activity as the pupils were capturing prizes in mathematics, science, poetry and physical education contests. Sister Cor Immaculatum, art supervisor for the Congregation, visited the school and gave generously of her talents to assist the teachers. Sister Nora Clarke, sector superior, and Sister Jane Kehoe visited in the spring, as did Sister Christina Aldarelli's mother.

Newcomers in 1969-1970 were Sister Josann Gallagher and Sister Lauren Conk. There were 323 children registered in the school. This was to be a year of much travel as the sisters from the West participated in the Congregation's Institute for all superiors and in the education survey committee. Sister St. Bernard (Kathleen Lannak) flew East at the end of January for these activities. Then in late February, Sisters Aloysius Schermanson, Bernardus Dwyer, Robert Mary Murphy and Christine Marie from Coeur d'Alene, and Sister Kathleen Kelley from Twin Falls came to Gresham to meet with Sister St. Bernard about conducting the education survey in each school. These links with the activity of the wider Congregation were important to the sisters in the West and kept them in tune with developments and changes in the Congregation. (226)

Meanwhile, because of the onset of serious illness, Father Meyer had lessened his involvement in both the parish work and in the school. While he had turned over many duties to his able assistant, Father Gregory Gage, Father Meyer was faithful in his expressions of gratitude to the Congregation for the sisters. In April 1970, he wrote to Mother Beata:

> I am very pleased and delighted with our fine group of good Sisters. Not only in the classroom is there a good spirit and obvious dedication, but away from the classroom they all seem so spirited, lighthearted, congenial and joyful. They truly seem like a family! (227)

What better compliment could he have given them?

In an attempt to comprehend the events of 1970-1971 which led up to the withdrawal of our sisters from St. Henry's, and indeed, from all of our schools in the West—St. Edward's, Twin Falls, St. Pius X, Post Falls, St. Thomas School and the IHM Academy in Coeur d'Alene, Idaho— in June 1971, one must try to enter into the pain and struggle of both the Congregation administrators and that of the sisters serving in these missions. In the face of serious declines in numbers of sisters because of illness, deaths and departures, the administration was faced with hard decisions regarding its commitments. It must be recognized that because of the distance involved, all of the western missions were in some way tied together in the minds of those in the East; the West was a generic category that scarcely differentiated the various scattered locations. Given this concept, it was probably not surprising that the motion made in the Central Administrative Assembly meeting of November 27, 1970, was to withdraw from all our schools in the West. (228) Specific needs and positive elements in the individual situations seemed to have little bearing on the decision in the over-riding need of the Congregation for additional personnel. And while these needs were understandable and withdrawals involved a total of eight missions across the Congregation in 1971, the years have not erased the shock experienced by the sisters in the western missions.

Mother Beata Wertz had visited each mission in 1967 and again in the fall of 1970, affirming the sisters in their ministries and supporting the pastors in their planning for the future. At a district development assembly held in Coeur d'Alene, Idaho, in November 1970, it was decided that a questionnaire regarding sisters' availability for service in the West should be developed and sent to the administration for distribution to the sisters across the Congregation. As one sister explained, "If the response was negative, then we were realistic enough to see the handwriting on the wall. But, if it were positive, then we should go on with our commitment to the West." (229) In addition to this proposal, the minutes show that the sisters set forth nine reasons to support the continuance of the western missions. (230) The timing of these two actions, one by the sisters in the West, and the other, about a week later, a decision by the administration to withdraw from the western missions, cannot be overlooked.

The questionnaire was not sent out, but in January 1971 (two months later), Sister Nora Clarke, sector superior, and Sister Anne Fulwiler, director of apostolic works, arrived in Portland to impart the withdrawal decision in person to the sisters and to the pastors. The situation at St. Henry's, Gresham, was complicated by the fact that Father Meyer had been diagnosed as having cancer of the bone and was absent from the parish for a short vacation. Father Gage, the assistant pastor, agreed to tell Father Meyer when he met him at the airport on his return. A formal follow-up letter was sent to all parties concerned on January 29, 1971, and set a June withdrawal date. It appears that the shortness of notice and lack of input by pastors and sisters in the decision led to the strong negative feelings engendered.

Two requests were made by Father Meyer. The first was that Sister Kathleen Lannak and Sister Mercille Schneider remain for one year to ready the school for continuance with an all-lay staff. Receiving no response to this by early March, he instructed Father Gage to ask for two sisters to remain to organize a CCD Program for the parish. (231) There is no record of the response given to this request. Undoubtedly, the horrendous fire at the Motherhouse in February 1971 was understandably the focal point of all attention and action at the time. The ramifications of this shattering, historical event at Marywood were probably not fully understood or appreciated by those so far removed from it. And this was also true for St. Henry's, steeped in shock and sorrow at the sisters' departure.

> When we left, the people went out of their way to express their gratitude, but their disappointment, too. It was like a wake! Each one of the Sisters went over to say good-bye to Father Meyer as he was now completely bedridden due to the cancer . . . He was dead within the year! 232)

The good work of our Sisters in the Portland Archdiocese was affirmed by Reverend Emmet Harrington, Secretary of Education when he wrote:

> I do wish to tell you that the Immaculate Heart Sisters are close to my thoughts and prayers. I have enjoyed working with them, not only at St. Henry School where they seem to be very happy and did excellent work, but also at Central Catholic High School. . . If at some other time you are able to furnish some Sisters to work in the Archdiocese of Portland where we feel the climate and atmosphere of education is strong and healthy, be assured of a real welcome. (233)

Little Flower Elementary School, Bethesda, Maryland

Reverend Edward J. O'Brien, a native of Covington, Kentucky, ordained in 1932, recipient of a PhD. in Sociology from the Catholic University of America, director of catholic charities for the Baltimore/Washington Archdiocese until 1942, and pastor of several diocesan parishes, was sent in 1948 to found Little Flower Parish in Glen Echo, now Bethesda, Maryland.

At first, services were held in a chapel on MacArthur Boulevard. One parishioner recalls that Father O'Brien rented a house on Namakagan Road for the rectory and was often seen running across busy Massachusetts Avenue to church services in what is now the auditorium. (234) Seeing the large, beautiful physical plant that constitutes Little Flower Parish facilities today, it is difficult to imagine this area without its magnificent cathedral-like church, the fine rectory, convent and sprawling colonial-style school. What is today a parish of nearly 1,400 households had its simple beginnings in the pastorate of Father Edward J. O'Brien in 1948. A spirit that is today described as "generous and friendly" was evidently cultivated by this first pastor who was described as "so generous he'd not only give you the shirt off his back, but his undershirt too!"

Because of its convenient location as a suburb of the nation's capital in Washington, DC, Little Flower Parish grew rapidly and attracted to its residential boundaries the families of diplomats, senators, congressmen/women, cabinet officers and many other dignitaries and business men and women, as well as professionals in the many colleges and universities of the area. As one writer says:

> At Little Flower Church in Bethesda, diplomats are just part of the parish family and at the Sign of Peace people are not surprised to find themselves shaking hands with Secretary of State George Shultz . . . or (former) Speaker of the House Thomas (Tip) O'Neill, who has been worshipping there for years.
>
> Edmund and Jane Muskie are long-time parishioners and the former Senator, Secretary of State and Vice Presidential candidate said, "We came in 1959, when I was a newly elected Senator, and our first obligation was to find a place to send the children to school." (236)

The school the Muskies selected was, of course, Little Flower School, which had opened on October 1, 1953, and was staffed by the Sisters of the Immaculate Heart of Mary of Scranton, Pennsylvania. It was on August 16, 1953, that Sister Maria James McNamara, superior and principal, Sister Marcelia Brennan, Sister Josanna (Joan) Paskert, and Sister St. Patrick McAndrew arrived to open Little Flower Convent and School. Murphy's law appears to have taken over Father O'Brien's activities, for it seems that whatever could happen, did happen in his futile efforts to complete the convent and the school buildings on time. Neither the convent nor the school was ready for occupancy when the sisters arrived. Fortunately, the sisters were able to turn to the IHM Sisters at St. John's, Silver Spring, and to their pastor, Monsignor Kennedy, for hospitality for nearly two and one-half months. Sister Amata Jordan, superior and principal at St. John's, was very welcoming and understanding of the situation these sisters were experiencing, for she and the sisters opening St. John's just three years before this had endured similar conditions until their school was completed.

Sister Maria James McNamara recalls the situation with clarity, describing the sisters' daily commute at the height of the morning traffic as they crossed town to get to the "school." Classes opened on October 1, 1953, in Little Flower Chapel and in the Glen Echo Fire Department Hall. Two hundred thirty pupils from grades one through six crowded into these two locations. Her recollection, and that of Sister Joan Paskert, was of the positive receptivity of the people and the willingness of the parents of the school children to cooperate with the sisters. Great praise was given to the children, the lay teachers—Mrs. W. Berg and Mrs. E. Wagner—to the parishioners, and to the hard working sisters, as everyone tried to make the best of a difficult situation. The pastor's forte did not seem to lie in the construction of buildings, and it seemed that the architect was in no hurry to bring things to completion. The year 1953 was not yet a time when it was usual for sisters to be asked for input, especially not about what was needed for a convent. Pastors and architects were the "experts" in these matters. Evidence that the sisters' advice was needed became apparent, however, as the convent progressed. One casual question posed by Sister Maria James as to why there was no sacristy adjoining or near the chapel revealed that the architect thought that the priest would come fully vested for Mass from the church to the convent chapel. (237)

By early November the convent was sufficiently completed for the sisters to take up residence, as well as to accommodate the classes from the Fire Hall until the school would be completed. While this consolidation brought convenience of one sort, it brought additional work to the sisters who had to clean the convent thoroughly each day after the school children left.

All of this did not deter the sisters from their goal of having an excellent school. The sisters prepared 175 children for Confirmation and 75 for First Holy Communion that spring. Sister Joan Paskert had organized a Boys' Choir that would make its first public appearance on Easter. By early December the new school was far enough along to begin classes in the proper setting. The pastor, Father O'Brien, and his assistant, Father Hughes, led the children from the convent to their new classrooms. There was much exploration and joy at the new facility.

On May 16, 1954, Archbishop Patrick O'Boyle dedicated the church, school and convent.

In 1954-1955 there were 360 pupils, an increase of 130 pupils over the opening year. The seventh grade had been added and an additional sister, Sister Olive Kelly, was assigned to Little Flower. Some changes occurred among the lay teachers who now were three in number and included Mrs. O'Dea, Miss Mary McIntyre, and Mrs. Berg as art teacher.

Grade eight was added in 1955-1956, and the enrollment climbed to 465 pupils. Sister Olive Kelly moved up from seventh grade with her 35 pupils who would become the first graduation class from Little Flower School on June 2, 1956. Sister Maria Raymond Grogan was added to the faculty. Construction was underway before the end of the year to add four classrooms and a gymnasium to the school.

With the influx of an additional 100 pupils in 1956-1957, for a total of 565, the new space was utilized immediately, although its dedication did not occur until Bishop John McNamara's arrival on October 24 to administer the Sacrament of Confirmation to 200 children of the parish. In May of that year, Father O'Brien had to resign because of poor health. Monsignor Henry F. Graebenstein was appointed pastor on June 8, 1957.

Sister Joan Paskert was transferred to Olyphant in 1957 and replaced by Sister Martin Marie Stanwich. The high enrollment necessitated a double track of classes for the first time. Seven sisters and five lay teachers composed the faculty. By the end of Sister Maria James' term in 1959 ground had been cleared for four additional classrooms. Evidence of the growth being experienced by Little Flower Parish was seen in the 103 First Communicants, 205 Confirmandi, and 56 eighth grade graduates—all parish children.

Sister Brigida Strome as new superior and principal at Little Flower in 1959-1960 found a thriving school of 750 pupils and a faculty of eleven sisters and seven lay teachers. The local community included Sisters Olive Kelly, Maria Raymond Grogan, Mary Ruth Samon, St. Mark Lowery, St. Patrick McAndrew, Angela Mary Parker, Martin Marie Stanwich, Mary Howard Krotzer, Helenita Hicks and Maria Regina Loures. The school continued its tradition of excellence in music for liturgical functions in the parish, as well as for entertainment. It was beginning to establish also the ability of its students to win prizes in county and state contests, and to receive high school scholarships. In an area where competition for acceptance into Catholic high schools was very keen, all 56 Little Flower graduates received acceptance. (238)

A grateful pastor and parish responded by supporting the sisters as religious and professional women. The original convent was enlarged by the addition of eight bedrooms with four bathrooms adjoining, and a recreation room paneled in mahogany. A generous parishioner provided a television set for the recreation room. Father Graebenstein blessed the new addition to the convent on November 6. In mid-November another convenience was given to the sisters by the parish, namely, a Chevrolet sedan. Permission had been given for sisters to drive, so the gift of a car was deeply appreciated.

The school term 1961-1962 was also a banner year in the development of the school, as the expansion of classroom libraries became the focus of all efforts. Sister Brigida had procured
1,000 books as the start-up for what would eventually be a central school library. The youngsters, highly motivated as avid readers, were very enthusiastic about the project.

An atmosphere of growth and progress seemed always to be a part of Little Flower Parish. The building of a suitable rectory for the priests was long overdue, but April of 1963 was to witness the completion of this imposing brick structure. Two years later, on March 21, 1965, ground was broken for the erection of the new church. The annals give this description of the event:

> . . . The pastor, Monsignor Graebenstein, insisted that Sister Brigida turn a spadeful of soil. He graciously aided her and at this precise moment the photographer snapped a picture. Of course, this was the picture that appeared in the diocesan newspaper, The Catholic Standard, much to the chagrin of Sister Brigida, but to the glee of the Sisters. (239)

Sister Brigida's six years had seen much internal development in Little Flower School, with a stabilizing of its enrollment growth in 1965. The faculty included twelve sisters and seven lay teachers, remarkable for their teaching ability, creativity and enthusiasm.

As Sister St. William Lynch assumed her new duties as principal and superior at Little Flower, she was joined by five other new faces on the faculty. These were Sister Therese Culhane, Sister Isidore (Elizabeth) Grace, Sister Benedicta Berendes, Sister Miriam Frances (Agnes Mary) Devitt, and Sister Ruthanne Gypalo. The new Sisters joined Sisters Gabrielle Driscoll, Mary Hugh Placilla, Angela Mary Parker, Helene Hicks, Agnetta Casey, and Thomasina McQuaide to complete the even dozen. Six hundred fifty pupils were enrolled at Little Flower.

The influence of the completion of Vatican Council II was felt by the sisters as Congregation-wide study and discussion of the *Documents of Vatican II* were initiated. Many additional opportunities for spiritual and intellectual development existed in the Washington, DC area of which the sisters took advantage. Six sisters from Little Flower enrolled in a Moral Theology course, which was being offered for religious by Dunbarton College of the Holy Cross. Additional professional development engaged various sisters in Saturday morning courses: Sister St. William attended the Catholic University of America; Sister Agnetta attended American University for Sociology; and Sister Gabrielle went to the District of Columbia Teachers' College for Mathematics.

With Washington, DC the location of so many outstanding educational institutions and the center of so much convention activity, it was not surprising that Little Flower Convent received many visitors. One regular guest for feast days and holidays was Sister Espiritu Dempsey from Marywood who was a full-time student at Georgetown University pursuing her doctoral degree in linguistics. Supervisors for the Congregation: Sister Eleanora Whalen, music supervisor; Sister Felicitas Ryan, Sister Sheila Reilly and Sister Nora Clarke, school supervisors; and Sister Cor

Immaculatum Heffernan, art supervisor, were annual visitors, as was the then regional superior, Sister Georgina Wertz.

Meanwhile, construction on the new church progressed. Disappointment reigned when it was far from ready for Christmas Midnight Mass. But on Sunday, March 12, 1967, the church was open for visitation by the public. The exquisite beauty and vastness of this Cathedral-like structure was overwhelming. The carpeting was not laid until after the "open house," so the following week saw what seemed like miles of carpet laid. Finally came the day—Palm Sunday—March 19, 1967, when Mass was celebrated for the first time in the new Little Flower Church.

On Good Friday the Stations of the Cross were hung. From twelve noon until ten minutes to three the workmen labored at placing the Stations. At three o'clock, Monsignor Graebenstein blessed the Stations and then the assistant, Father Travers, led the Way of the Cross for the congregation. (240)

The building of Little Flower Church seemed to bring to a peak the marvelous pastorate of Monsignor Graebenstein. He had accomplished so much in his thirteen years as pastor that it was with great sadness that the parishioners received the word of his retirement on June 3, 1970. They welcomed Monsignor Joseph Coyne as their new pastor, but rejoiced to know that Monsignor Graebenstein would remain at the rectory in "Emeritus" status. When the Golden Anniversary of his ordination came in May of 1972, there were five days of celebrations as the school children honored him in their spring festival program and participated in a special liturgy for him; the sisters held a dinner in the convent for all the priests to honor Monsignor Graebenstein; and the parish celebrated this milestone anniversary for their former pastor with a special Mass on May 25.

In 1971-1972, it was also a year for getting to know all the new faces at Little Flower. Besides the new pastor, Monsignor Coyne, there was a new principal, Sister Helene Coyle; a new superior, Sister Kathleen Kelley; and Sister Jan Marie Kalyan, a new music teacher. In addition, Sister Gaudens Opinsky was in residence as a student attending American University.

More celebrations were to occur in 1973-1974 as the parish commemorated its silver jubilee on September 30, 1973. An eloquent sermon was preached by Monsignor John Tracy Ellis, Church historian from the University of San Francisco. Two golden jubilees were observed among the sisters, namely, Sister Corona McDonald's on October 20 and that of Sister Mary Patrick Burke on April 27. These sisters deserved well the many plaudits they received for their dedication and religious spirit. Tributes were also given at the closing of this 1973-1974 school year as

Sister Gabrielle Driscoll was transferred after eleven years at Little Flower, and Sister Agnes Mary Devitt after nine years. (241)

September 1974 brought several new sisters to Little Flower. Sister Felician Hurley was welcomed as the new superior; Sister Callista Ryan as director of religious education in the parish; and Sisters Kathleen Newett, Ann Dolora Grayeski, and Jean Coughlin for the teaching staff.

History was being made in the Washington Archdiocese as Archbishop William Baum consecrated two new Auxiliary Bishops, Thomas Lyons, former diocesan superintendent of schools, and Eugene Marino, a member of the Society of St. Joseph, the first black bishop of the Washington Archdiocese. Other new activities in the sisters' lives included participation in the parish census-taking and family-group meetings. Some sisters were involved on the parish council, in the choir, and in-home Masses scheduled by lay groups. Many sisters observed World Hunger Week activities at the Lincoln Memorial in Washington, DC, visited the Home for Incurables and Westward Home, joined the Right to Life march at the nation's Capitol, and assisted at S.O.M.E. (So Others Might Eat) soup kitchen. Touching the lives of families more closely brought a sharing of their joys also at Baptisms, Confirmations, First Communions and weddings. Two private weddings were held in Little Flower Convent Chapel. Also, a newly ordained priest, Reverend George A. Stallings, a former pupil of the IHMs at St. Joseph's School, New Bern, North Carolina, said his first Mass in the convent chapel. His later expression of gratitude captures the spirit, not only of the Little Flower local community, but also of all our sisters for whom he had such deep respect. He wrote:

> . . . As you know, I feel a special affection for the IHM Sisters of Scranton. It is not I who should be acknowledged or congratulated on having been ordained to the priesthood, but rather those who took a risk and gave themselves to me in order that I, too, might experience the joy of living. But, most importantly, I think the IHMs conveyed to me that what I received from the Lord is not meant to be concealed but to be given to others so that they, too, can experience that same joy and consolation which comes from a knowledge and love of the Lord Jesus. For this, I am thankful to the Lord and your Order. . . . (242)

The year 1975-1976 saw five new assignees as Sisters Mary Hubert O'Boyle, Fidelmia Lynch, Mary Alice Wheatley, and Noelie Kilmer became part of the faculty of Little Flower, and Sister Paulette Furness, a student at the Catholic University, was affiliated with this local community. Sister Elizabeth Grace had been transferred after ten dedicated years of first-grade teaching at Little Flower. Sister Jan Marie Kalyan had served for four years, and Sister Jean Coughlin, entering into the nursing profession at this time, had served for one year.

The Congregation elections for sector superior in 1978-1979 took place immediately after the General Chapter but were not completed until October. The results of these elections had an impact on Little Flower Convent and School as the principal, Sister Helene Coyle, was elected sector superior of the Southern Sector. There was a mixture of sadness and rejoicing among the sisters, but only sadness and frustration as far as the pastor was concerned. His first concern was to obtain a principal, and since the school year was already underway, his choice was to select someone already at Little Flower who was familiar with the school, the children and parents. Sister Mary Alice Wheatley was appointed as principal for one year, expressing her desire to return to first grade teaching the following September. Sister Kieran Williams was temporarily moved from her position as music teacher to replace Sister Mary Alice in first grade. Since Sister Helene, as sector superior, was to continue to reside at Little Flower when she was not traveling in the Southern Sector or at Marywood for meetings, all depended upon her interest and consultation in school matters at Little Flower. Needless to say, the process of election of sector superiors was never held at so late a date thereafter. (243)

Sister Mary Alice Wheatley stepped down readily in 1979-1980, welcoming the new principal, Sister Nancy Elder. The 1980-1981 school year was ushered in with another change of leadership, as Sister Eva Marie Zlotucha replaced Sister Nancy Elder as principal. It was to be another very active year as students appeared on television, prepared winning posters, presented recitals and received awards in a variety of contests: the American Legion Essay, the Lions Club Essay, Diocesan Vocation Essay, CYO oratorical and the Optimist Club oratorical contests. The Montgomery County Science Fair saw seven Little Flower School students awarded prizes.

This was also the year of Sister Ina Kenney's golden jubilee celebration, a beautiful occasion, which served as the prelude to jubilees to come. Sister Mary Hubert O'Boyle would celebrate her 60th jubilee and Sister Eva Marie, her 25th in 1981-1982; Sister Mary Patrick Burke held her diamond jubilee on April 7, 1984; and Sister Virgine Maurer, her golden jubilee on March 28, 1987.

These celebrations, as well as the many opportunities for retreat days, conferences, renewal lectures, involvement in work with the poor, and faithful participation in the district assembly activities provided support and unity for the busy apostolic life of the sisters.

Additional superiors, not previously mentioned, who served at Little Flower Convent include Sisters Kathleen Newett, Jeanne Albrittain, Ritamary Mayan, and Josephine Joy.

No account of this mission would be complete without special mention of two Little Flower "traditions" which existed in the persons of Sister Mary Patrick Burke and Sister Mary Hubert O'Boyle. They were twin blessings, and their hospitality was experienced by hundreds of visiting Sisters over the years as breakfast, lunch or a snack was set out with apparent ease by these two "experts." Having come to Little Flower in 1970, Sister Mary Patrick taught full-time in the school until January 1, 1978, when, having achieved 54 years of full-time teaching, she "retired" to continue as a private music teacher until 1987. She retired to the Marian Convent in the fall of 1987.

Sister Mary Hubert had come to Little Flower School in 1975 where she served as librarian until 1980. At that time she was assigned to the prayer apostolate, remaining in residence at Little Flower Convent until 1986. Sister Mary Hubert died on December 17, 1986, at the Marian Convent.

In today's parlance, it can be said that they were "the right stuff," and for all times, they exemplified that joyful, loving, self-sacrificing spirit which is an IHM Sister.

St. Clare's Elementary School, Scranton, Pennsylvania

Planted deeply in the history of St. Paul's Parish, Scranton, Pennsylvania, are the roots that supported its expanding branches, St. Clare's School, Convent and Church, dedicated on March 20, 1955. The same faith and generosity built these St. Clare structures which originally built a hemlock-log chapel as the first place of worship for some three hundred St. Paul's parishioners in 1887; replaced it in 1890 with a combined church, school and parish hall; built a convent for the sisters in 1898; built a new, three-story, fifteen-classroom grade/high school building which also housed the church in 1928; and completed a new, $375,000 church in 1952, debt-free. Under the leadership of zealous and dedicated pastors, the faith of the people of St. Paul's Parish was nurtured and spread. One of these, Monsignor John J. Vaughan, pastor from 1940 to 1971, was to preside over this parish in the years of phenomenal growth in both parish and school. The Green Ridge area of Scranton in which St. Paul's is located is an attractive and popular residential area, hence the influx of residents and the growth of the parish. In addition, it was Bishop William J. Hafey's desire that there be smaller, almost neighborhood-like Catholic churches and schools established in the various areas of the city of Scranton.

Thus it came to be that within a block of the Marywood College campus and the Motherhouse of the Sisters of IHM, that St. Clare's Convent, School and Church were erected. The first building in this triad was St. Clare's School, which opened on September 8, 1954, with 93 pupils in the first three grades. The faculty included Sister Eunice Corcoran, principal and first grade teacher; Mary Ann Zlotucha, an IHM postulant (Sister Eva Marie), grade two; and Sister Rosemary Cavanaugh, grade three. Sister Eunice had spent many years as an outstanding first grade teacher at St. Paul's, hence was well known and well received as principal and first grade teacher at St. Clare's.

St. Clare's School was officially dedicated on March 20, 1955, upon the completion of St. Clare Church. Bishop Hafey had died on May 12, 1954, and was succeeded by Bishop Jerome D. Hannan on September 30, 1954. It was Bishop Hannan, then, who officiated at the ceremonies of dedication of St. Clare's. Monsignor John J. Vaughan, pastor of St. Paul-St. Clare Parish, offered the solemn High Mass, with two natives of the parish, Reverend James Clarke and Reverend F. L. Dacey, serving as deacon and sub-deacon, respectively. Scores of people visited both the church and the school on that date.

It would be three and a half years later, February 10, 1958, before St. Clare Convent would be built. In the interim the sisters resided at St. Paul Convent and at the motherhouse at Marywood, just a few blocks away. And it would not be until June 16, 1967, that St. Clare's would become a parish in its own right, independent of St. Paul's, and having its own pastor and rectory.

But these matters in no way deterred the growth and development of St. Clare School. In its second year, 1955-1956, grade four was added and a total of 149 pupils was enrolled. The faculty in that year included Sister Eunice Corcoran, principal and grade four; Sister Rosemary Cavanaugh, grade three; Sister Leo Lehman, grade two; Sister St. Genevieve (Joanne) Pickard, grade one; and Sister Maryla Farfour, music teacher at Marywood Seminary, who served generously as part-time music teacher at St. Clare's. Sister Dorette Coleman was added to the faculty in 1956-1957. With five grades the school now enrolled 217 pupils. This competent faculty was to experience a deep loss, however, with the sudden death of Sister Rosemary on January 30, 1957. She had been on duty until a few days before she died, having administered the Diocesan mid-year examinations to her pupils on Friday, January 25, and leaving school in apparently good health. She became ill on Monday morning and died on Wednesday, January 30, at St. Joseph Hospital, Carbondale, Pennsylvania. Her funeral was held from St. Clare Church with Monsignor Vaughan as celebrant. Students, relatives, and friends felt the shock of her death and the loss of such a dedicated religious and talented teacher.

Mrs. James T. McGrail (Madeline Casey), a graduate of Marywood College, taught the third grade in Sister Rosemary's place for the remainder of the year.

In 1957-1958 sixth grade was added, with a total school enrollment of 294 pupils. The first grade was inundated with 64 students, second grade with 57, and a general state of overcrowding caused many applicants to be turned away.

St. Clare Convent was completed and blessed on February 10, 1958. This well planned and highly functional structure was finished on the exterior in a cream-colored brick to match the school and the church, completing a physical plant of which the people could be justifiably proud. The convent chapel was small, yet complete, and was conveniently located on the first floor. A large kitchen, with separate dishwashing pantry adjoining, dining room, parlors, two music rooms and a good-sized, screened-in outdoor porch completed the first floor. There were ten private bedrooms, several bathrooms, and the community room on second floor. Fortunately, the basement was also completed, providing future space for use by the school.

"Open house" was held for the sisters of the area on February 15. About 125 attended the luncheon that was served by the members of the St. Paul-St. Clare Guild. A steady stream of visitors to St. Clare Convent began almost at once, with council members, supervisors, and countless sisters being offered IHM hospitality. Monsignor Vaughan added to the flood of visitors, proudly bringing many clergy and lay friends to view his latest accomplishments.

It was soon apparent to the faculty of St. Clare's that they were strategically situated to benefit from the numerous cultural, spiritual and intellectual advantages of the nearby Marywood College campus. It would be recognized early on by the College, too, that St. Clare School was a rich resource as a practicum for aspiring college students in elementary education, art, music, communications, religious studies, and other programs of the College. Students from St. Clare have participated in demonstration classes and institutes in reading, music and other subjects at the College.

By 1958-1959 there were 338 pupils in St. Clare School, and in 1959-1960 when the full eight grades were complete, there were 410 pupils. The regular curriculum was supplemented with many enriching activities, and music ranked high among these. An orchestra, band, and glee club were formed, in addition to private music lessons in instrumental and piano for many youngsters. Thirty-six eighth graders, the first graduates of St. Clare School, completed their elementary school education on June 15, 1960. Ten went on to the Scranton Preparatory School, four girls to Marywood Seminary, and the remainder to St. Paul's High School. (245)

Sister Eunice Corcoran served as principal until 1962 at which time she was transferred to St. Ephrem's School, Brooklyn, New York. Sister Harold Mulderig became the new principal and superior of St. Clare's in August 1962. The faculty included six sisters and two lay teachers. In addition to Sister Harold, the sisters were: Sister Raymonda Farry, Sister Mariam Pfeifer, Sister Oswald Maria Hopkins, Sister Germana Radley, and Sister St. Aloysius Wilson.

As had been their practice since the opening of St. Clare's, the sisters, in addition to their regular classroom duties, taught catechetical instructions in the parish on Wednesdays and Sundays. Catholic children from the nearby Pennsylvania State School for the Deaf were also instructed.

On March 9, 1964, it was the first time that St. Clare's had its own Confirmation service separately from St. Paul's. There were 187 youngsters confirmed by Bishop Jerome D. Hannan. First Holy Communion, however, was still held at St. Paul's, with 82 St. Clare children included.

The year 1964-1965 was, undoubtedly, the peak enrollment year for St. Clare's School. The physical facilities were strained to the limit as 433 children (212 boys and 221 girls) began the school year. There were six IHM Sisters, namely, Sister Harold Mulderig, principal and eighth grade; Sister Oswald Maria Hopkins, third grade; Sister Moira McMonagle, second grade; Sister Madeleine Millets, sixth grade; Sister Mariam Pfeifer, fifth grade; and Sister St. Aloysius, first grade. Lay teachers included Mrs. Michael Sedonic, seventh grade; Mrs. James O'Donnell, fourth grade; and Mrs. Buckley, assisting in sixth grade.

This was a banner year also as Monsignor John Vaughan celebrated his twenty-fifth anniversary as pastor. The school pupils joined in a musical tribute to him at a special function in March 1965. On August 17, 1965, Sister Oswald Maria underwent surgery for cancer. Upon recovery, she obtained the doctor's permission to return to her teaching, although she was aware of the terminal nature of her condition. The annals give an insight into this period in sister's life:

> Sister returned to the work she loved—teaching God's little ones. Each day found her in the classroom giving her best, even though she was suffering intensely. Sister remained in school until after the mid-term examinations. With her papers corrected and reports finished, sister knew that, because of her failing health, she could not face another semester of work. (246)

On January 22, 1966, Sister Oswald Maria entered the hospital, and after three more weeks of intense suffering, died on February 12, 1966.

The year 1966-1967 brought some important changes to the Scranton Diocese and to St. Clare's. Bishop J. Carroll McCormick was appointed on March 3, 1966, as successor to Bishop Hannan who had died of pneumonia on December 15, 1965, while in Rome to attend sessions of the Second Vatican Council. (247)

Bishop McCormick visited St. Clare's early in his term, on September 9, 1966, and was accompanied by Monsignor Vaughan through the convent, school and church buildings. It may have been no surprise, then, to learn that St. Clare's was to become a separate parish, and no longer a mission of St. Paul's. Monsignor Robert A. McNulty was appointed first pastor of St. Clare's Parish on June 1, 1967. Since there was no parish rectory, a property was acquired across the street from the church on N. Washington Avenue. This had been a family home, so extensive renovations were required to make it into a suitable rectory for the pastor and his assistant, Reverend William Feldcamp. On April 4, 1968, "open house" was held for the parishioners so that Monsignor McNulty could express his gratitude for the beautifully renovated residence.

In 1969-1970 a practical change occurred which relieved the overcrowded conditions at St. Clare School. St. Clare's became a one-six grade school with 222 pupils; seventh and eighth grade students began attending classes at St. Paul's Junior High School. Thus space became available to set up a library and a listening room in two former classrooms. A departmental curricular program was set up for grades four, five and six with Mrs. Sedonic teaching social studies, Mrs. Ratchford, mathematics and science, and Sister Marie Eileen (Catherine) Luxner, music. Sister Rosarii Hemmer became superior and principal. In addition to the four faculty members, St. Clare's Convent housed Sister Sheila Reilly, the Congregation education consultant, two sister-students in attendance at the Marywood College School of Social Work, and Sister Teresina Thompson, in prayer ministry.

At the close of the year, Sister Rosarii was assigned as principal of Holy Trinity School in Poughkeepsie, New York. Sister Joan Marie Thompson as principal, superior and teacher of grade two followed her at St. Clare's. Two full-time and one part-time lay teachers assisted the four sisters; besides the principal, these included Sister Miriam Eugene Carroll, Sister Bernadette Horan, and Sister Catherine Luxner. The local community had the ministry diversity in 1971-1972 that would characterize it from then on, and which would begin to be increasingly descriptive of most of the Congregation's local houses. Sister Sheila, congregation education consultant, Sister Willemyn Gambrill, diocesan education consultant, and Sister Immaculate Severino, Marywood College music instructor, were part of the St. Clare local community. As Sister Joan Marie commented, "We had a very fine spirit; the diversity of ministries in which the sisters were engaged only added to the spirit." (248)

Late September of 1973 brought the news that St. Clare School was to become a kindergarten through grade three school in 1974, absorbing the children in these grades from Immaculate Conception and St. Paul's Parishes. St. Paul's was to become a grades four through eighth school. To accommodate this new arrangement, some changes in teachers were necessary. Sister Joan Marie continued as principal, but initiated the new kindergarten; two first grade teachers were needed, so, in addition to Sister Maria Rita Ruddy, Sister Dolorosa Loughney was added. Four lay teachers completed the faculty. Two sessions of the kindergarten were conducted each day for separate groups of students; grades one, two and three were each large enough to warrant double sections.

Several changes of principals and superiors occurred over the ensuing years: Sister Mary Alice Kane replaced Sister Joan Marie in 1975, with Sister Paula Baier as superior; Sister Marian Flannery, a Marywood College science faculty member in residence at St. Clare's became superior in 1976-1977; Sister Jeanne Gallagher became principal in 1977 and served in that capacity until 1981 when she was succeeded by Sister Mary Elizabeth Costello. Sisters serving as superior at St. Clare's in that period were Sister Claranne Nolan, Sister Maria Thomas Harrington, Sister Kathleen Kelly, and Sister Cecilian White. (249)

September 23, 1983 was a tragic and frightening day for St. Clare Parish as the church sustained heavy fire damage—the work of an arsonist. Daily and Sunday Masses were scheduled in the basement of the church as major renovations got underway. It was December 17 before these were completed and the Pontifical Mass of Rededication of the church could be held. The new Ordinary of the Diocese, Bishop John O'Connor, officiated. There were many congratulations for Monsignor Robert McNulty on his good taste in the redecorations. Beautiful stained-glass doors completed the overall enhancement of the church. The following December 9 witnessed the celebration of Monsignor McNulty's fiftieth anniversary of ordination to the priesthood, so this refurbished church provided a fitting setting for the event.

It had long been a hope of the Congregation to have St. Clare's School become more closely tied to the teacher-preparation activities of Marywood College and to the "demonstration school" concept. Having already established this concept in the Early Childhood Center located at the IHM Generalate building at Marywood, under the direction of Sister Regina Barrett, it seemed that a logical extension to the next three grades might be possible at St. Clare's. Monsignor McNulty agreed to try out the unique arrangement of utilizing Sisters Regina Barrett and Marilyn Muro of the Marywood Early Childhood Center as principal and vice principal, respectively, of St. Clare School while they continued their commitments also at Marywood. This ambitious undertaking throughout 1985-1986 found teachers absorbed in many meetings and in-service activities, with Sisters Regina and Marilyn working untiringly to bring out the potential of this special all-primary level school. Dedicated and hardworking as they were, it was agreed that they were being stretched a bit too far. In the fall of 1986, therefore, Sister Ann Marie Lynott was appointed principal of St. Clare School. It was a year of many changes as Monsignor Robert McNulty retired to St. Joseph's Villa and Monsignor Joseph Fadden assumed the duties of pastor on September 10. It was the year of preparation for accreditation by the Middle States Association, so Sister Ann Marie had her work cut out for her as she worked with her faculty to attain the coveted approval. Spring days brought the good word that St. Clare's had earned Middle States Accreditation for ten years.

Since 1974 when St. Clare's first became a K-3 school, it has continued to enroll an average of 235 pupils. Sister St. Henry Haiss served as superior from 1984 through August 1987. In 1986-1987 the local community consisted of the following nine sisters: Sister Ann Marie Lynott, principal; Sister St. Henry Haiss, superior and grade one; Sister Nancy Christiano, grade three; Sister Ellen Carney, business manager, IHM Congregation; Sister Electa Schmidt, communications office manager, IHM Congregation; Sister Maria Gerald Shanley, receptionist, Marian Convent; Sister Kathleen Kelley, nurse's aide, Marian Convent; Sister Rosemary Goulet, assistant administrator, Marian Convent; and Sister Florence Langan, graphics art department, Marywood College. (250)

Our Lady of Peace Elementary School, Clarks Green, Pennsylvania

As with so many other parishes, Our Lady of Snows, Clarks Summit, Pennsylvania began as a mission church. It is hard to imagine with the current size and rapid development of Our Lady of Snows that at its founding on October 4, 1899, it was a mission church of St. Patrick's Parish, Nicholson. In fact, it was not until March 1, 1911, that Our Lady of Snows was established as a parish in its own right. (251) Reverend Edward J. Flood was appointed its first pastor by Bishop Michael J. Hoban. (252)

The present church building was dedicated on May 31, 1931, by Bishop Thomas P. O'Reilly. It was built of solid rock out of the blue fieldstone that was excavated from the site. The stained glass doors at the main entrance of the church retell a unique story that occurred in the year 325 in Rome, from which originated the title of Our Lady of Snows. There was an elderly couple living in Rome who had a dream, which kept repeating itself, of a beautiful woman whom they believed was the Blessed Mother. They told their dream to Pope Liberius who recommended that they wait, and if it were a genuine appearance of Our Lady, an unmistakable sign would be given. On August 4, 325, snow began to fall on the Esquiline Hill of Rome. This event was interpreted as God's affirmation of the Council of Ephesus' declaration that Mary was the Mother of God. The Basilica of Saint Mary Major was built by Pope Liberius and was dedicated on August 5, 451 to commemorate the miraculous snowfall and to honor Mary as the Mother of God. (253) The title of Our Lady of Snows originated in this ancient story and was chosen by the early parishioners as the name of their parish.

The pastor of Our Lady of Snows Parish at the time of the coming of the IHM Sisters to this parish was Reverend Charles Heid, who had been appointed only a year before, on September 17, 1953, to succeed Monsignor Robert McNulty. At the time of Father Heid's appointment he was forty-two years old and had been ordained for seventeen years. Having resided at the Cathedral for fourteen of those years, Father Heid obviously came to the attention of Bishop Hafey who had given him several challenging responsibilities along the way. For ten years the newly opened Scranton Diocesan Guild Studio was under his prudent management. Working with the well-known Pauline Casey, he earned her praise as "a priestly gentleman and gentlemanly priest." Father Heid was also placed in charge of the construction of the Diocesan Catholic Youth Center in 1949, continuing its direction for two years even after he became pastor at Our Lady of Snows in 1953.

With these experiences as part of his background, it should have been no surprise that Bishop Hafey's plan was to put Father Heid in charge of having a Catholic school built in Clarks Green. Monsignor McNulty, the prior pastor, had already purchased the land on North Abington Road. "Announce that you're going to build a school," said Bishop Hafey to Father Heid. Hoping to have some time to win over his new parishioners to the idea, Father Heid agreed that the project was timely and he would make it part of his future planning. Little did he know that the Bishop's timing of the announcement was set for the first Sunday of Father Heid's pastorate of Our Lady of Snows! And, as we now know, one year later,

Our Lady of Peace School was a reality. (254) But the initiator of these plans, Bishop William Hafey, was not to see them come to fruition. His death occurred on May 12, 1954, less than four months before the school's dedication.

By the time of the arrival of the IHMs in August 1954, Our Lady of Peace School was already nearing completion. Unaccustomed, however, to having their own parish school initially, there were mixed emotions among the people. Most people were proud of the magnificent new Our Lady of Peace School and welcomed the expected quality and Catholicity it would bring; a few took a ''wait and see" attitude, foreseeing the competitiveness that would develop between the private and public schools of the area.

Father Heid had purchased the home of Mr. and Mrs. John J. O'Leary to be used as a convent for the sisters. It was conveniently located at 404 North Abington Road in Clarks Green next to Our Lady of Peace School. This home was of adequate size for the first group of sisters in 1954, which included Sister Joseph Gabriel (Dorothy) Welsh, superior and principal; Sister Maria Andrew Allen, Sister Jeanette (Ann Helene) Coyne, Sister Pulcheria Longe, and Sister Anselm McShea. The O'Leary's had left behind many of the furnishings for the first floor of their lovely home, so there were some rumors circulating about the "palatial living" of the sisters at Our Lady of Peace Convent. The "palatial living" turned out to extend chiefly to the first floor oriental rugs and some living and dining room furniture. A former tiny den that was planned as the chapel had barely turn-around room. In order to remedy this crowded situation, one of the bedrooms was taken for a chapel and the sisters doubled up in the sleeping rooms.

Mass was celebrated for the first time in the convent chapel on August 20, 1954, at which time Father Heid placed the Blessed Sacrament in the tabernacle. The annals report: "The Sisters said the Te Deum after Mass in thanksgiving for the sacramental presence of Our Lord." (255)

Our Lady of Peace School was dedicated on August 29, 1954, at 3:00 p.m. Since Bishop Jerome D. Hannan was not installed at St. Peter's Cathedral in Scranton until September 30, 1954, Monsignor (later, Bishop) Henry J. Klonowski, in his capacity as administrator of the Diocese, laid the cornerstone and formally dedicated the school to Our Lady of Peace. Monsignor Thomas J. Cawley, then editor of *The Catholic Light*, the diocesan newspaper, preached the dedication sermon.

The initial school building had eight classrooms, a kindergarten, music room, faculty room, library, two offices, and a combination auditorium and gymnasium on the ground floor. The cafeteria and kitchen were located on the lower floor.

School opened on September 8, 1954, with an enrollment of 196 students in kindergarten and the first four grades. Sister Pulcheria taught kindergarten youngsters in the mornings and third grade in the afternoons so that Sister Maria Andrew, the third grade teacher, could teach music in the afternoons. Sister Dorothy taught fourth grade in addition to her duties as principal. Sister Anselm taught first grade. (256)

From the beginning, the sisters were befriended by generous parishioners who, in those days before sisters were permitted to drive, offered their services to transport the sisters to meetings, retreats, and social outings. Parents with children in the school were especially helpful as volunteers for the library, cafeteria and fund-raising projects. Many of the families in Clarks Green had previously lived in Scranton where they were familiar with the work of the IHM Sisters in various parishes.

Since Our Lady of Snows was such a large parish, there was a wide diversity of professional, business, farming, and factory workers represented among the families of the parish. Sister Anselm describes many of the children of those first years at Our Lady of Peace School as "country youngsters." Our Lady of Peace School had its own buses that made the rounds to pick up these pupils each school-day morning. Sister recalls that her life was very busy because by October of that first year the sisters were already reaching out through catechetical instructions to the many children still attending public schools. Sister Jeanette (Ann Helene), Sister Pulcheria and Sister Anselm taught instructions at both Dalton (at what is now "The Dalton House") and at Our Lady of Snows Church on two afternoons each week after school. This meant riding the school buses with the youngsters after school to get to their destination, teaching until 5:00 p.m., and getting a taxi or a ride with a pastor or parishioner to arrive home in time for dinner. Sister Maria Andrew taught music after school, so Sister Dorothy's work as chief cook was cut out for her on these days. (257) The cooking chores were minimized, however, when, according to Sister Dorothy, a non-Catholic woman, Mrs. Dempsey, formerly from North Carolina, came to the convent seeking work as a cook. She was an excellent cook, having been in a catering business before her husband's death. Her only concern in working at the convent was that the sisters would try to convert her to Catholicism. Having received assurance from Sister Dorothy that she need not be concerned, Mrs. Dempsey accepted the sisters' invitation to visit the convent chapel whenever she wished. She had deep worries about her own future since she was not materially well off, and gradually she would be found each afternoon praying in the chapel, as close to the tabernacle as she could get. Sister Dorothy's words to her, "God will take care of you," came true as Mrs. Dempsey returned to her family in North Carolina before her death. (258)

The sisters' lives, while restricted in the many ways required of religious at the time, certainly exemplified the apostolic spirit. As both Sister Anselm and Sister Dorothy explained, Our Lady of Peace Convent was a very happy place, with simple pleasures such as a Sunday afternoon walk to Lourdesmont, attendance at professional meetings and celebrating feast days. Their ministry was very demanding, but their success was obvious in the growth of the school each year. The affirmation of Father Heid, the pastor, was seen in his delight at bringing a steady stream of visitors to see the new school, its pupils, and the sisters. For his part, Father (now, Monsignor) Heid was always available for school functions and was anxious to provide whatever was needed for the school and the convent. (259)

In September 1955, the fifth grade was added, bringing the enrollment to 260 pupils. Since the Congregation could not provide an additional sister, a lay teacher, Mrs. Robert Vogelbacker, was hired to teach the kindergarten.

By January 1956, it was necessary to begin renovations to the convent, which would provide three bedrooms on the third floor, thus relieving the crowded conditions and providing for the coming of additional sisters to Our Lady of Peace.

The distance between the convent and Our Lady of Snows Church made it necessary in the beginning for the sisters to go by taxi to daily Mass. When it became known that the Cure d'Ars Hospice for ill and elderly priests was located nearby, arrangements were made with the director, Father Frederick Lawrence, a Trinitarian, to have the priests who were able come to Our Lady of Peace Convent to say Mass. A Trinitarian religious brother would drive one of the priests each day. This became another ministry of healing and helping for the sisters as they tried to bring joy and encouragement to these priests. When the Hospice was moved to Moscow, Pennsylvania, in the spring, 1957, the sisters began a special devotion to Our Saviour's Holy Face for the intention that priests would be found for their daily convent Mass. As the annals report: "Our prayers were answered with a call from Father Heid saying that he had made arrangements for the Maryknoll Fathers to say Mass each weekday morning, including Saturdays, during the school year." (260) The Maryknoll Fathers were located only a few miles away at what was then called "Venard," the Maryknoll Minor Seminary. These buildings were later sold by the Maryknoll Fathers and became what is today a greatly expanded campus of the Baptist Bible College.

Sister Dorothy was to complete her work at Our Lady of Peace at the close of this third year, having nurtured this new endeavor to a

330-student enrollment in kindergarten through sixth grades. The faculty, with the addition of Sister St. Michael (Michael) McArdle, now numbered six sisters and one lay teacher.

Sister Stella Devers became superior and principal in 1957-1958. The community of sisters numbered seven: Sister Stella Devers, Sister Maria Andrew Allen, Sister Katrina Kondzer, Sister Jeanette Coyne, Sister St. Michael McArdle, Sister Anselm McShea and Sister Josepha Marie Darminio. By early October the plastering, painting and general renovating of the first and second floors of the convent were completed. The sisters welcomed a new dining room and chapel on the first floor, and two new bedrooms and baths on second floor. On November 23, the generous donors of the chapel, Mr. and Mrs. F. David Clarke, attended Mass in the chapel with the sisters. The memorial plaque at the entrance to the chapel was inscribed:

> This Chapel, dedicated to Our Blessed Lady, is the gift of Mr. and Mrs. F. David Clarke in memory of William C. Sherman and James Herbert Hook. (261)

An open house was held in the convent on November 24 so that the parishioners could witness the renovations that their generosity had brought about.

Our Lady of Peace reached its full eight grades in 1958-1959 and recorded an enrollment of 455 pupils in kindergarten through eighth grades. Two lay teachers, one in kindergarten and one in fifth grade, joined the six sisters. Regular evaluations by the Congregation and the diocesan assistant superintendent, Reverend William L. Donovan, provided testimony of the quality education being offered. As 37 eighth-grade graduates were sent forth and readily accepted at high schools of their choice, the good work of the teachers at Our Lady of Peace School was further confirmed.

With renovations year after year it was as if the convent were gradually being completely made over: 1959-1960 saw a beautiful new kitchen installed as a gift of Mr. Vincent Piazza; and in 1961-1962 when the number of sisters reached eight, the work of adding six bedrooms, with tiled sinks, built-in wardrobe closets and rock maple furniture was completed. A solarium connecting this section to the original house provided the finishing touch. This room had Danish furniture and overlooked an outdoor patio and pleasant view of the property.

In this same year, 1961-1962, sixteen classrooms were added to the school. In the fall of 1962 eleven of the sixteen classrooms were put to use, as the first three grades were double grades. Grades six, seven and eight had the privilege of occupying the new classrooms, which were described in the annals as "equipped with every convenience, and a credit to the foresight and wonderful building ability of our beloved pastor." (262)

Growth seemed to be occurring on all sides and the services of the sisters were constantly sought for additional endeavors. At the request of Reverend Carl Cummings, pastor, St. Patrick's Church, Nicholson, another site for catechetical instructions had been added in the fall of 1959. To provide for the special religious events in the lives of the children from Our Lady of Snows, Dalton, and Nicholson required two separate Masses for some 150 First Communicants and two separate Confirmation ceremonies for 300 confirmandi. The increase in the number of sisters required is seen in the fact that three sisters, Sister Thomas More Kane, Sister Sean Lavelle, and Sister Regina Pacis (Joan) Coyne taught at Dalton on Tuesday afternoons; Sister Casimir Bougher and Sister Thomas More, on Monday afternoons at Our Lady of Snows Church; and four Sisters, Sister St. Lawrence (Loretta) Mulry, Sister Casimir, Sister Sean and Sister Regina Pacis taught at Nicholson on Sunday mornings.

Sister Alma Marie Morgan was appointed principal, superior and eighth grade teacher in September 1963. One of Sister's first projects was to explore the possibility of a parish-owned car being made available to the sisters. A fund drive was soon underway under the leadership of the Christian Mothers Society, and a Ford country sedan became the first convent car at Our Lady of Peace on October 30. Driver training had been initiated for the five youngest sisters on September 10. (263)

A new milestone of growth was attained in 1966-1970 when the school enrollment reached 638, with ten sisters and seven lay teachers as faculty. In addition to the regular demands of the classroom and catechetical instructions, there were school science fairs, oratorical contests, and art exhibits; there were piano recitals, glee club performances, music festivals, and religious observances. Summer brought new faces among the sisters and new outreach activities. Sisters Myra Gilbart, Johnellen (Eileen) Clinton, and Mary Liam Horan taught the children of migrant workers reading and arithmetic, as well as preparing them for their First Holy Communion and Confirmation. These activities took place at the migrant camps near Tunkhannock.

By 1968-1970 when Sister Alma Marie completed her time at Our Lady of Peace, the Congregation had adopted a policy of separating the offices of superior and principal. Thus, Sister Eunice Corcoran became the new principal; Sister Ethel Marie Gavin, the superior and eighth grade teacher.

On January 15, 1974, word was received from Bishop Hafey that Monsignor Heid was to be transferred from Our Lady of Snows to become pastor of St. Mary of Mount Carmel Parish in Dunmore. Just at the point when Monsignor Heid's work may have become lighter as Our Lady of Snows Parish was being divided into two separate parishes, he was being called to new challenges as the pastor of St. Mary's, Dunmore. Ever responsive to the many and varied calls he received from Bishop Hafey, Monsignor Heid left his post of twenty-one years, after saying a farewell Mass at the convent on January 24, 1974.

A building and lot were purchased adjacent to Our Lady of Peace Convent to serve as the site for the new St. Gregory's Church. The territory of St. Gregory's Parish was to include Clarks Green and Waverly; Our Lady of Snows Parish was to encompass the Clarks Summit and Chinchilla areas. Monsignor Charles J. Zazzera was named pastor of St. Gregory's and Reverend Joseph Fadden, pastor of Our Lady of Snows. Since Our Lady of Peace School had pupils from these parishes, as well as from Our Lady of the Abingtons where Reverend Joseph Hickey was pastor, the three pastors formed the Board of Pastors administering the overall policy and finances of the school.

As the construction of St. Gregory's Church and rectory progressed, the parishioners were working at becoming a parish. The new pastor, Monsignor Zazzera, took up temporary residence in a home that was available next door to the convent. Sunday and daily Masses for St. Gregory's Parish were offered in the auditorium of Our Lady of Peace School to help establish this new parish identity. Almost a year and six months from the establishment of St. Gregory's as a parish —on July 27, 1975—groundbreaking for the new church was held.

Meanwhile, at the close of the 1975-1976 school year Sister Eunice Corcoran, principal, was transferred to St. John the Evangelist School in Silver Spring, Maryland. Sister Marella Moran succeeded her as principal of Our Lady of Peace School. Sister Celeste Parry became superior of the local community for 1976-1977.

These new school and local community leaders had not yet arrived at Our Lady of Peace Convent when the significant ceremonies of the dedication of the new St. Gregory's Church were held. The blessing of the main altar and Stations of the Cross took place on August 14, 1976. Cornerstone ceremonies, the solemn blessing of the church, and the Pontifical Dedication Mass were held on Sunday, August 15, 1976. (264)

A series of changes occurred which included the transfer of Monsignor Zazzera and the appointment of Monsignor John Louis as pastor in September 1977. Also in that year Sister Marcelia Brennan was appointed superior of the local community, with the transfer of Sister Celeste Parry to Port Washington. In the following year, 1978-1979, Sister Mary Dawson from St. Raymond's School, East Rockaway, New York, replaced Sister Marella as principal. Nine sisters and eleven lay teachers constituted the faculty. Observance of the 25th Anniversary of Our Lady of Peace School began on April 23, 1979, with a full week of activities, which included Parents' Day, Children's Day, Teachers' Day, an evening for graduates, and a dinner for past and present faculty and administrators. The three pastors concelebrated a Mass with Monsignor Heid in Abington Stadium on May 17 to close the celebrations. Reverend Joseph Fadden observed the 25th Anniversary of his ordination and was raised to the rank of Monsignor during this same eventful year. Monsignor Louis gave a memorable gift, a ceramic chalice brought from the shrine of St. Francis in Assisi, to the sisters for the convent chapel.

Sister St. Francis Lyons was elected superior of the local community of ten sisters in September 1979. She would serve in this capacity for four years, until 1983. The members of the local community in 1979-1980 were: Sister Eleanora Whalen, Sister Maria Rita Ruddy, Sister Henriette Kramer, Sister Honor Lenihan, Sister Dolorosa Loughney, Sister Mary Dawson, Sister Janet Milan, Sister Lenore Thomas, and Sister Mary William Philbin.

It was on August 30, 1979, that Sister Janet Milan was diagnosed by the doctors at Geisinger Hospital in Danville as having multiple sclerosis. Physical therapy three times a week at the Marian Convent enabled Sister Janet to keep active until December 6 when she went to the Marian Convent. Her long struggle with debilitating weakness, inability to walk, then support with braces, would eventually culminate in what is, at this writing, a miraculous remission. But this was not known in 1979 as her presence and ministry at 0ur Lady of Peace School and convent were brought to a close. (265)

On November 16, 1980, the fiftieth anniversary of Our Lady of Snows Church was celebrated with a special Mass. Bishop J. Carroll McCormick of Scranton was the chief celebrant. St. Mary's Center in Scranton was the location of the parish dinner and festivities.

The close of the school year brought the inevitable changes among the religious faculty. Sister Mary Dawson was appointed as curriculum director in the Diocesan Catholic Schools office of Rockville Centre, New York. Sister Henriette was transferred to Cresco; Sister Ann Eulaine McHale, to St. Patrick's, Scranton; and Sister Maria Rita Ruddy, to IHM Convent, River Street, Scranton. Replacements included Sister Mary Feldcamp, principal, Sister Eugene Coyne, Sister Madeleine Merritt, and Sister Aloisa McHugh.

The opening of the school year 1981-1982 saw an enrollment of 520 pupils at Our Lady of Peace School. Involved in special peace and justice outreach activities themselves, the sisters communicated a spirit of generosity that was emulated by their pupils who raised $3,000 for the missions, in addition to their many service projects.

The accounts in the convent annals of prayer, ministry, special projects and building renovations are interspersed generously with accounts of celebrations of pastors' birthdays, of sisters' feast days, of occasions like the "triple jubilees" of Sister St. Francis Lyons, Sister Ann Belz and Sister Patricia Rooney on April 23, 1983; the golden jubilee of Sister Pius LaRocque on February 11, 1984; the silver jubilee of Sister Margaret Benfield in October 1985; the silver jubilees of Monsignor John Louis, pastor, St. Gregory's, Sister Mary Alice Wheatley and Sister Angelique Vannicola in February, April and May, respectively, 1987. There was a continuing concern for the inclusion of the sisters at the Marian Convent, either by taking the youngsters' shows to them, or by bringing the sisters to the youngsters at Our Lady of Peace School. One such occasion occurred on May 16, 1985, when twenty-six sisters from the Marian Convent attended a liturgy prepared by the first graders at Our Lady of Peace. Luncheon was served in the school cafeteria after the Mass for these guests.

Sister Mary Feldcamp served as principal for five years through 1985-1986; this latter being the year of the Middle States Association accreditation visits, after nearly two years of preparation. The good news of the accreditation was received the following October and was announced by the new principal, Sister Marianne Knight, to a new pastor, Reverend John Bendik, now pastor of Our Lady of Snows Parish and administrator of the school and convent. Father Bendik had replaced Monsignor Joseph Fadden who was appointed pastor of St. Clare's Parish, Scranton.

In addition to the principal ministry of the sisters in Our Lady of Peace School and the catechetical instructions at each of the three parishes, two members of the local community extended the IHM influence in special outreach ministries. Sister Margaret Benfield served as director of the Drug and Alcohol Program for teenagers at Lourdesmont; Sister Anna Tantsits served as director of religious education at Our Lady of Snows Parish. (266)

It is no wonder that Monsignor Heid could reiterate in 1988 his sentiments of the opening days of Our Lady of Peace in 1954:

> The advent of the Sisters of I.H.M. changed the complexion of the whole parish—homes, church and school in countless positive ways. (267)

Recent additions to the local community included Sister Mary Denise Thomas who served as superior and third grade teacher in 1983-1984; Sister Marylin Grosselfinger who came to Our Lady of Peace for music education in 1983 and served as superior from 1984 to 1988; Sister Rita Lorraine Burke, a junior high teacher; Sister Mary Enda O'Donnell, first grade; Sister Evangelista Lipple, third grade; Sister Ann Marie Lynott, fourth grade; Sister Mary Alice Wheatley, first grade; Sister Angelique Vannicola, fifth grade; and Sister Juan LaBarr, small group instruction.

It is evident that it takes both youthful vigor and seasoned experience to sustain the IHM presence to meet the challenges of three thriving parishes as is done at Our Lady of Peace.

Mother M. Marcella Gill, IHM

The Feast of the Exaltation of the Holy Cross, September 14, 1955, was impressed on the hearts of a saddened Congregation of the Sisters, Servants of the Immaculate Heart of Mary of Scranton as Mother M. Marcella Gill died. Her death occurred just three months after she had completed a vigorous fifteen years as superior general of the Congregation. For the fifty-nine years of her membership in the Congregation she had given her all. Her work was done.

Mother Marcella Gill was born in Parsons, Pennsylvania, on December 22, 1877, and was baptized Katherine Gill in St. Mary's Church, Wilkes-Barre. Her father, John Gill, was born in Ireland; her mother, Marie Nolan Gill, was a native of Hawley, Pennsylvania. The Gills were married in St. John the Evangelist Church, Pittston, Pennsylvania.

After graduation from high school, Katherine Gill entered the novitiate of the Sisters, Servants of the Immaculate Heart of Mary on July 2, 1896, at its early location in Carbondale, Pennsylvania. She was professed on July 15, 1899, receiving the name in religion of Sister Marcella. Her first teaching assignment was at Holy Rosary High School, Scranton, where she met with great success over the nineteen years she spent there. In 1918, she was appointed principal and superior of St. Joseph's High School, Renovo, Pennsylvania. In 1920, Mother Marcella was appointed principal of Most Holy Rosary High School, Syracuse, New York, where she remained until 1926, when she was assigned in these same leadership capacities to St. Dominic's High School, Oyster Bay, New York.

At the time of her election as assistant to the superior general, Mother Josepha, on August 6, 1931, Mother Marcella was already a proven and capable administrator, greatly loved and respected by the sisters and by all who knew her in the various locales where she had served. Her knowledge of the educational systems in the various dioceses where she had previously served was a great asset to Mother Josepha.

Nine years of service by the side of so astute a leader as Mother Josepha served only to enhance Mother Marcella's own gifts. She was well prepared upon Mother Josepha's death in 1940 to assume the remaining three years of Mother Josepha's term of office. That she would also serve two full six-year terms of office of her own probably never occurred to this humble woman whose motto was to live one day at a time fully for the Lord. One account, written after Mother Marcella's death in 1955, summed up her fruitful life as follows:

> As teacher and principal, Mother Marcella is well remembered for her fine scholarship and her gentle character. In her office as superior general, her keen insight into the needs of her sisters and her deep understanding of the problems of teaching and school administration enabled her to guide and direct the efforts of her community in the best interests of over thirty thousand pupils taught in the schools staffed by the Sisters, Servants of the Immaculate Heart of Mary in five Archdioceses, and twelve Dioceses.
>
> Mother Marcella was president of Marywood College from 1940 to 1952. Under her leadership and fine vision, a great college expansion program was inaugurated and six new college buildings were planned and constructed. These fine functional buildings testify to her wise planning and able administration. (268)

These comments may seem to place her out of the reach of the ordinary, but it would not be true to picture Mother Marcella that way. While somewhat formal in her bearing, she had a warm, friendly disposition and found time in her busy schedule to enjoy the sisters. She was present every Sunday morning after breakfast for a conference with the novices. Her explanations of the *Rule* and the *Customs* of the Congregation revealed to the novices her own love of and dedication to religious life.

Mother Marcella's insight into the future needs of the Congregation is obvious in her concern to establish a fitting home for our sick and aging sisters. In her report to the Third General Chapter in June 1955, she states:

> Since our home for the sick and aged Sisters at Elmhurst does not offer adequate accommodations for our increasing needs, His Excellency, Most Reverend Jerome D. Hannan, endorsed permission given by our former Bishop, Most Reverend William J. Hafey, to erect a new convent for our infirm and aged Sisters on the Marywood property.. . . Accordingly, ground was broken

> October 7, 1954. The building, which will offer accommodations for eighty Sisters, will cost approximately $1,142,000. (269)

At once she details how the Congregation will manage this new cost. She has the good news to share that a fund had been set up for this project as early as 1944 and that gifts and donations amounting to $250,000 have now accumulated! The remaining $872,000 needed will be borrowed from the Emigrant Industrial Savings Bank of New York at a fixed interest rate of 3 1/2% per annum. (270) This was Mother Marcella, the business woman, at work. The memories that Sister Marita Gill has of her aunt, Mother Marcella, are personal treasures which catch more fully the scope of Mother Marcella's personality. Sister Marita writes:

> To know Mother Marcella was to love her. She dearly loved every member of her family and was vitally interested in all their activities. By her caring and example she always tried to keep all the members closely knit, loving and helping one another.
>
> In my early years, sisters didn't visit their families unless there was sickness or death. This meant that my parents, my four brothers and I would frequently go to visit at different convents. Since Mother Marcella had a great love for all the family, in her gentle way she would make us aware that we should not only visit her but also our other three aunts, Sister Ricarda, Sister Madelena, and Sister Ethelbert.
>
> When Mother Marcella celebrated her Silver Jubilee, she wanted the family present. As a young family, we traveled to Most Holy Rosary Convent in Syracuse. Twenty-five years later, the Golden Jubilee celebration at Marywood included her grandnieces and grandnephews, present with the family.
>
> My profession and the ordination of my brother, Father Nicholas, CP, were important days in her life and she encouraged all the family to be present at both. On such occasions she would always remind us to thank God for the blessings He had given to the family.
>
> Mother Marcella was a very special person in my life. She was always in the background loving and caring, but not interfering in any way in my undertakings. She was First Assistant at Marywood while I was a student at Marywood College, and later when I was a novice in the Congregation. She made me understand that she was there if I needed her, but I had my own life to live.
>
> Throughout the years, Mother Marcella taught me many lessons by her loving care, gracious, friendly manner, and by her example.

> She made me realize that God has to be first in my life; that each day will bring sorrows as well as joys, but that God will always be there to sustain me in my difficulties, and that He will be with me until we, as a family, are united in our heavenly home. (271)

The respect and graciousness which Mother Marcella had shown to others during her lifetime were rendered bountifully to her at her death as hundreds of people crowded the Marywood Motherhouse Chapel and the college grounds for her funeral on September 16, 1955. Bishop Jerome D. Hannan of Scranton offered the solemn requiem Mass. Sixty-nine priests from the various dioceses where the Sisters of IHM were located were present, as well as hundreds of sisters. Mother Marcella would have been happy that six of her nephews were pallbearers and that her beloved sisters constituted the choir for the solemn Mass of burial.

She closed her life as she closed her final report as superior general, in a spirit of gratitude and faithfulness. She wrote:

> . . . I am grateful to Almighty God for all the graces He has showered upon us, and to all the sisters who have cooperated with us so faithfully. God grant that we will all make every effort to maintain the spirit of our saintly founder, Father Gillet. Once that spirit is lost, we will cease to be true Sisters of the Immaculate Heart of Mary. God bless you, one and all. (272)

References

1. *Rules and Constitutions of the Sisters, Servants of the I.H.M., 1894.* Chapter III, Article 10, p. 33.
2. Letter from Bishop William J. Hafey, Diocese of Scranton, to Mother Marcella Gill, Superior General, December 9, 1940. Archives, IHM Center.
3. Ibid.
4. Record of Appointments, 1940. Archives, IHM Center.
5. George Q. Flynn, *Roosevelt and Romanism: Catholics and American Diplomacy, 1937-1945.* (Westport/London, 1976), p. 78.
6. Mother Marcella Gill: Letter to the Congregation, Christmas 1940. Archives, IHM Center.
7. Ibid.
8. Ibid.
9. Mother Marcella Gill: Letter to the Congregation, Christmas 1942. Archives, IHM Center.
10. Mother Marcella Gill: Letter to the Congregation, Christmas 1944. Archives, IHM Center.
11. Letter from Archbishop Edward D. Howard of Portland, Oregon to Mother Marcella, December 31, 1941. Archives, IHM Center.
12. Letter from Bishop Charles D. White, Spokane, Washington to Mother Marcella, September 22, 1950. Archives, IHM Center.
13. Letter from Rev. Eustace Struckhoff, OFM, South San Antonio, Texas to Mother Marcella, March 14, 1949. Archives, IHM Center.
14. Letter from Bishop Edward J. Kelly, Boise, Idaho to Mother Marcella, June 1, 1949. Archives, IHM Center.
15. Notes of Sister Immaculata Gillespie. Archives, IHM Center.
16. Letter from Sister Georgina Wertz to Mother Marcella, December 6, 1942. Archives, IHM Center.
17. *The Williamsport Sun*, undated, 1943. Archives, IHM Center.
18. Ibid.
19. Letter of Sister Aluigi Devers, Principal of St. Bernard's, Hastings, PA, to Sister Immaculata Gillespie, 1945. Archives, IHM Center.
20. Letter of Sister Inviolata to Sister Immaculata Gillespie, February 7, 1944. Archives, IHM Center.
21. Letter of Mother Marcella to Rev. Vincent Schlemner, OSB, Pastor, St. Bernard's, Hastings, PA, March 12, 1942. Archives, IHM Center.
22. Letter of Sister Aluigi Devers, Superior, St. Bernard's, Hastings, to Sister Immaculata Gillespie, 1945. Archives, IHM Center.
23. Letter of Rev. Vincent Schlemner, OSB, Pastor, St. Bernard's, Hastings, to Mother Marcella, Dec. 29, 1944. Archives, IHM Center.

24. Letter of Mother Marcella to Sister Aluigi, Superior, St. Bernard's, Hastings, Jan. 30, 1947. Archives, IHM Center.
25. Letter of Rev. Adalbert Kolsch, OSB, Pastor, St. Bernard's to Mother Marcella, April 30, 1949. Archives, IHM Center.
26. Telephone conversation with Sister Ambrose Walker, St. Patrick's Convent, Scranton, June 11, 1987.
27. Telephone Conversation with Sister Ann Helene Coyne, Marian Convent Superior, June 11, 1987.
28. Annals of St. Bernard's Convent, Hastings, 1957-1958. Archives.
29. Ibid., 1958-1980. Archives, IHM Center.
30. Ibid., 1984-1986. Archives, IHM Center.
31. Statistics from the Office of the Director of Apostolic Planning, 1986-1987. Archives, IHM Center.
32. Interview with Sister Francella Shaughnessy, IHM, Marywood College, June 17, 1987.
33. Letters from Sister Alma Marie Morgan, Superior, to Sister Immaculata Gillespie, undated, probably 1945. Archives, IHM Center.
34. Interview with Sister Francella Shaughnessy, IHM, previously cited.
35. Annals of Holy Name of Mary Convent, Montrose, PA, 1955-1970. Archives, IHM Center.
36. Letter of Mother Beata Wertz to Rev. Norman J. Irwin, Pastor, Holy Name of Mary Parish, Montrose, PA, May 21,1970. Archives, IHM Center.
37. Annals of Holy Name of Mary Convent, Montrose, PA. 1969-1970, Archives, IHM Center.
38. Personal Interview with Sister Francella Shaughnessy, June 16, 1987.
39. Personal Interview with Sister Maria Angela Orr, June 30, 1987, IHM Center.
40. Ibid.
41. Telephone conversation with Sister Albrette Rouleau, July 1, 1987.
42. Annals of St. Matthew's Convent, Wilmington, DE, 1958-1963.
43. Annals, op. cit., 1963-1971.
44. Annals, op. cit., 1971-1982.
45. Annals, op. cit., 1982-1987.
46. Statistics from the Office of Director of Apostolic Planning, IHM Center.
47. Letter of Bishop Martin J. O'Connor, Auxiliary, Scranton Diocese to Rev. Edward C. Doyle, OP, Canonist, Dominican House of Studies, Washington, DC, March 2, 1943. Archives, IHM Center.
48. Letter of Mother Josepha to Reverend Charles Reilly, CSsR, Esopus, NY, December 11, 1933. Archives, IHM Center.
49. Letter of Monsignor Martin J. O'Connor, DD., Episcopal Representative for Religious, Scranton Diocese, to Mother Marcella, December 21, 1940. Archives, IHM Center.

50. Ibid.
51. Letter of Rev. Edward C. Daley, OP, to Mother Marcella, March 28, 1943, Material on General Chapters. Archives, IHM Center.
52. Letters from the various Bishops to Bishop William J. Hafey, Bishop of Scranton, April – July, 1943. Archives, IHM Center.
53. Report of the Superior General, Mother Marcella Gill, to the First General Chapter, August 4, 1943, p. 2. Archives, IHM Center.
54. Letter of Bishop Hafey to Mother Marcella, September 7, 1943. Archives, IHM Center.
55. Letter of Mother Marcella, Superior General, to the Congregation, September 24, 1943, Material on General Chapters, Archives, IHM Center.
56. *Constitutions of the Congregation of the Sisters, Servants of the Immaculate Heart of Mary, Scranton, PA.,* 1943, Chapter IV, Art.199, p.58.
57. Report of the Superior General, Mother Marcella Gill, to the First General Chapter, August 4, 1943, Material from General Chapter 1943, Archives, IHM Center.
58. Record of Elections, 1937—1986. Archives, IHM Center.
59. Minutes of the Meeting of the General Chapter, August 5, 1943. Archives IHM Center.
60. Article taken from *The Catholic Light*, Scranton Diocesan Newspaper, September 3, 1943, p. 10.
61. Ibid.
62. Personal conversation with Sister Francella Shaughnessy, June 17, 1987.
63. Notes of Sister Immaculata Gillespie. Archives, IHM Center.
64. Annals of Immaculate Conception Convent, 1958-59. Archives, IHM Center.
65. Article by Bill Halpin in the *Scranton Times*, May 16, 1966. Archives, IHM Center.
66. Survey Report from Immaculate Conception School, Scranton, PA, 1969. Archives, IHM Center.
67. Letter from Bishop J. Carroll McCormick to Mother Beata Wertz, December 23, 1970 and reply of January 9, 1971. Archives, IHM Center.
68. Annals of Immaculate Conception Convent, Scranton, PA. 1970-1971. Archives, IHM Center.
69. Annals of Immaculate Conception Convent, Scranton, PA. 1971-1974. Archives, IHM Center.
70. Ibid., 1973-1974.
71. Ibid.
72. Unidentified writer, *The Scrantonian*, Summer, 1981.
73. Letter from Bishop William A. Griffin of Trenton Diocese to Mother Marcella, February 8, 1943. Archives, IHM Center.

74. Letter from Bishop William A. Griffin to Mother Marcella, September 8, 1943. Archives, IHM Center.
75. Letter from Mother Marcella to Bishop Grinnin, March 30, 1944. Archives, IHM Center.
76. Annals of the Sisters, Servants of IHM in Mount Holly, NJ, 1943-1952, p. 2. Archives, IHM Center.
77. Description of Nathan Dunn's "Chinese Cottage" in *Burlington County Herald*, Mount Holly, NJ, March 25, 1976. Archives, IHM Center.
78. Annals of the Sisters, Servants of IHM in Mount Holly, NJ, 1943-1952, p. 4. Archives, IHM Center.
79. Sister Alphonsus McGoldrick, "After 95 Years . . . A Hope Realized," *Journal of Religious Instruction,* June 1945.
80. Convent Annals, op. cit., p. 4. Archives, IHM Center.
81. Ibid., p. 5.
82. Ibid., p. 8-10.
83. Ibid.,p. 11.
84. Statistics from the Office of Director of Apostolic Planning, October 1987. IHM Center.
85. Letter from Rev. Thomas P. Mooney to Mother Marcella, February 22, 1944. Archives, IHM Center.
86. Recollections of Sister Franachen Yahner, IHM, in telephone conversation, July 13, 1987.
87. Ibid.
88. Telephone conversation with Sister Thaddeus Kelly, IHM, July 13, 1987.
89. Letter from Rev. Thomas P. Mooney, Pastor, St. Ambrose Parish, Bridgeport, CT, to Mother Marcella, June 27, 1950. Archives, IHM Center.
90. Letter from Mother Marcella to Rev. Thomas P. Mooney, July 10, 1950. Archives, IHM Center.
91. Telephone conversation with Sister Thaddeus Kelly, IHM, July 13, 1987.
92. Letter of Rev. Thomas P. Mooney, Pastor, St. Ambrose Parish, Bridgeport, CT, to Mother Marcella, January 13, 1954. Archives, IHM Center.
93. Letter from Mother M. Marcella to Rev. Thomas P. Mooney, January 20, 1954. Archives, IHM Center.
94. Annals of St. Ambrose Convent, Bridgeport, CT. 1955-1956. Archives, IHM Center.
95. Letter from Mother Kathleen Hart, Superior General, to Monsignor Thomas P. Mooney, February 29, 1956.
96. Annals of St. Ambrose Convent, Bridgeport, CT. 1966-1967. Archives, IHM Center.
97. Annals of St. Ambrose Convent, Bridgeport, CT. 1985-1986. Archives, IHM Center.

98. Statistics from the Office of Director of Apostolic Planning, IHM Center.
99. Letters from Sister Brendan O'Brien to Mother Marcella, March 9, April 23, May 9 and May 22, 1944; to Monsignor William R. Kelly, May 20, 1944; and from Bishop William J. Hafey to Mother Marcella, May 17, 1944. Archives, IHM Center.
100. Notes of Sister Immaculata Gillespie. Archives, IHM Center.
101. Personal interview with Sister Hilary Meehan at Marywood College, September 2, 1987.
102. Annals of St. Ann Convent, Nyack, NY, 1956-1957. Archives, IHM Center.
103. Annals of St. Ann Convent, Nyack, NY, 1957-1959. Archives, IHM Center.
104. Annals of St. Ann Convent, Nyack, NY, 1959-1960. Archives, IHM Center.
105. Annals of St. Ann Convent, Nyack, NY, 1961-1962. Archives, IHM Center.
106. Annals of St. Ann Convent, Nyack, NY, 1962-1986. Archives, IHM Center.
107. Statistics from the Office of Director of Apostolic Planning, 1987.
108. Nancy and Stephen Bickham and Betty Frazier, The Story of St. Peter's 1879-1979,Chapter I, p. 14.
109. Sister Maris Law, IHM and Sister Jane Driscoll, IHM. 1939-1959, The Story of St. Peter's Parish, Wellsboro, PA, 1879-1979.
110. Letter from Sister Lucian Reddington to Sister Immaculata Gillespie, undated, probably written in 1945. Archives, IHM Center.
111. Letter from Margaret L. O'Leary to Reverend Mother M. Kathleen, August 24, 1956. Archives, IHM Center.
112. Letter from Rev. Leo J. O'Malley, Pastor, St. Peter's, Wellsboro, to Mother Beata Wertz, June 24, 1964. Archives, IHM Center.
113. Letter from Rev. Thomas J. Hannigan, Pastor, St. Peter's, Wellsboro, to Bishop J. Carroll McCormick, April 16, 1976. Archives, IHM Center.
114. Parish Bulletin, St. Peter's, Wellsboro, PA, May 16, 1976. Archives, IHM Center.
115. Annals of St. Peter's Convent, Wellsboro, PA, 1983-1984. Archives, IHM Center.
116. Pike County Dispatch, June 24, 1982. Archives, IHM Center.
117. Copy of official Deed registered in Pike County Court House, April 4, 1946. Archives, IHM Center.
118. Personal interview with Sister Regina Barrett, IHM Center, Marywood, September 23, 1987. Archives, IHM Center.
119. Letter from Sister Rose Irma Spillane to Sister Immaculata Gillespie, July 3, 1947. Archives, IHM Center.
120. Letter from Sister Rose Irma Spillane to Mother Marcella Gill, January 1947. Archives, IHM Center.
121. Personal interview with Sister Regina Barrett, September 23, 1987. Archives, IHM Center.
122. Annals of St. Patrick Convent, Milford, PA, and St. Ann's, Shohola, PA, 1955-1958. Archives, IHM Center.

123. Ibid., 1958-1982.
124. Reverend Joseph O. Weber, Pastor, St. Patrick, Milford, PA. Letter to Sister Michel Keenan, IHM, Superior General, March 2, 1981.
125. Annals of St. Patrick Convent, Milford, PA, 1981-1982.
126. H. J. Connolly, President, Pennsylvania Coal Company, Scranton, PA. Letter to Bishop Hafey December 18, 1940.
127. H. J. Connolly, President, Pennsylvania Coal Company, Scranton, PA. Letter to MotherMarcella, IHM. March 26, 1941 and July 28, 1947.
128. Quinquennial Report of the IHM Congregation to the Sacred Congregation for Religious, Rome, Italy, 1946-1950 (ref. Question 87A).
129. Minutes of General Council Meeting, May 1946.
130. Report to the Board of Directors of Marywood College, 1947 and 1948.
131. Minutes of General Council Meeting, September 1946.
132. Minutes of General Council Meeting, September 25, 1952.
133. Professor Gonippo Raggi. Letter to Mother Marcella, IHM, January 29, 1947.
134. Conversations with Sister Michaeline Macedonio, IHM, Sister Celesta Sinisi, IHM, and Sister Regina Barrett, IHM, October 7 and 9, 1987.
135. Conversation with Sister Reginald Patterson, IHM, October 9, 1987.
136. Rt. Reverend Edward B. Jordan, DD, Vice Rector of the Catholic University of America,Washington, DC, Sermon delivered at Centenary Pontifical High Mass, September 26, 1945.
137. Minutes of the Chapter of Elections, August 6, 1949.
138. Mother Marcella Gill, IHM. Letter to Monsignor Joseph McClancy, Superintendent ofSchools, Brooklyn Diocese, NY, October 17, 1949.
139. M. H. McCloskey, Philadelphia, PA. Letter to Henry D. Dagit and Sons, Philadelphia, PA. September 12, 1950.
140. Mr. Severin Sekol. Letter to Mother Marcella Gill, IHM, November 1, 1950.
141. Program of Dedication of Marywood College Buildings, October 7, 1952. Marywood College Archives.
142. Reverend Gerald J. Bischof, Pastor, Resurrection Church, Muncy, PA. Letter to Mother Marcella Gill, IHM, July 28, 1948.
143. *The Muncy Luminary*, Muncy, PA. August 18, 1949.
144. Sister Maria Thomas Harrington, IHM. St. Hugh's Convent, Hughesville, PA. Letter to Mother Marcella Gill, IHM, Feast of St. Jane, 1949.
145. Ibid.
146. Conversation with Sister Mary Roche, Marywood College, Scranton, PA, October 26, 1987.
147. Article sent to *The Catholic Light*, Scranton Diocesan Newspaper by Robert N. Wilt, Editor, *The Muncy Luminary*, Muncy, PA. August 1955.
148. Annals of St. Hugh's and Resurrection Convents, Hughesville and Muncy,

PA, 1955-1956.
149. Monsignor Francis J. Lauriola, Editor. *The History of St. John's Parish 1774-1984*. Silver Spring, MD, p.2-3.
150. Ibid., p. 7.
151. Ibid., p.11.
152. Ibid., p.5.
153. Ibid., p.21.
154. Ibid., p.25.
155. Archbishop Patrick A. O'Boyle, Washington, DC, Letter to Mother Marcella Gill, IHM. June 27, 1949.
156. Mother Marcella Gill, IHM. Letter to Archbishop Patrick A. O'Boyle, Feast of St. Agapitus, 1950.
157. Annals of St. John the Evangelist Convent, Silver Spring, MD, September 1950.
158. Solemn Dedication Booklet of the Church of St. John the Evangelist, Silver Spring, MD, May 27, 1962, p.l0.
159. Annals of St. John the Evangelist Convent, 1957-1958.
160. Ibid., Easter Sunday, 1961.
161. Solemn Dedication Booklet, op. cit., May 27, 1962, p.11.
162 .Annals of St. John the Evangelist Convent, 1962.
163. Ibid.,1978-1979.
164. Ibid., 1950-1990.
165. Annals of Holy Trinity Convent, Poughkeepsie, NY, October 12, 1952.
166. Ibid.
167. Ibid., 1959-1960.
168. Ibid., 1978-1979.
169. Ibid., 1972-1988.
170. Ibid.., 1987-1988.
171. Monsignor John P.Gallagher, PhD. *A Century of History of the Scranton Diocese, 1868-1968,* p. 137.
172. Sisters Annamae Haran, IHM and Rosella Salvato, IHM. "An Historical Study of Holy Name of Jesus Parish, Forty Fort-Swoyersville, PA. Thesis: Marywood University Library, Scranton, PA. p.18.
173. *The Catholic Light*, Scranton Diocesan Newspaper. September 26, 1909.
174. School Contract Agreement signed bv Reverend Aloysius Boylan, Pastor, and Mother Marcella Gill, IHM, August 15, 1952.
175. Sister Annamae Haran, IHM. Letter to Sister Michel Keenan, IHM. 1988.
176. Annals of Holy Name of Jesus Convent, Forty Fort, PA, 1956-1957.
177. Ibid., 1959-1960.
178. Ibid.
179. Reverend Aloysius Boylan, Pastor, Holy Name of Jesus Parish. Sermon to

parishioners. October 17, 1959.
180. Annals of Holy Name of Jesus Convent, 1972-1973.
181. Holy Name of Jesus Church Bulletin, January 7, 1973.
182. Annals of Holy Name of Jesus Convent, 1972-1973.
183. Testimonial to Monsignor Aloysius Boylan, July 15, 1973.
184. Sister Michel Keenan, IHM, Superior General. Letter to Reverend Martin J. Dacey, Pastor, Holy Name of Jesus Parish, April 12, 1983.
185. Annals of Holy Name of Jesus Convent, 1984-1985.
186. Reverend William N. Pharr, Pastor, Our Lady of Grace Parish, Greensboro, NC. Letter to Sister Michel Keenan, Superior General, October 12, 1979.
187. Reverend Arthur R. Freeman, Pastor, Our Lady of Grace Parish. Letter to Mother Marcella Gill, IHM. September 23, 1952.
188. Ibid., October 28,1952.
189. Ibid., August 6, 1953.
190. Conversation with Marysia Reilly, September, 1988.
191. Archbishop Amleto G. Cicognani, Apostolic Delegate to the United States. Address given at the dedication of Our Lady of Grace Church, September 14, 1952.
192. *North Carolina Catholic*. Nazareth, NC, November 27, 1953.
193. Annals of Our Lady of Grace Convent, 1961-1962.
194. Ibid., 1963-1964.
195. Ibid., 1967.
196. Ibid., 1967-1968.
197. Central Administrative Assembly. Letter to Sister Mary Edward Loftus, IHM, Superior and Principal, Our Lady of Grace, Greensboro, NC, November 14, 1970.
198. Annals of Our Lady of Grace Convent, 1971-1972.
199. Sister Michel Keenan, IHM, Superior General. Letter to Reverend Francis M. Smith, Pastor, Our Lady of Grace Parish, April 13, 1979.
200. Monsignor William N. Pharr, Pastor, Our Lady of Grace Parish. Letter to Sister Michel Keenan, IHM, June 8, 1980.
201. Annals of Our Lady of Grace Convent, 1979-1980.
202. Monsignor John P. Gallagher. *A Century of History: 1868-1968*. p. 150.
203. Ibid., p.206-207.
204. Annals of St.Agnes Convent, Forest City, PA. 1955-1956.
205. Ibid., 1956-1957.
206. Ibid., 1970-1971.
207. Ibid., 1982-1983.
208. Ibid., 1987-1988.
209. Reverend A. A. Meyer, Pastor, St. Henry's Parish, Gresham, OR. Letter to

Mother Marcella Gill, IHM, December 27, 1 951.
210. Archbishop Edward Howard, Archdiocese of Portland, OR. Letter to Mother Marcella Gill, IHM, December 10, 1951.
211. Reverend A. A. Meyer. Letter to Mother Marcella Gill, IHM, September 24, 1952.
212. Mother Marcella Gill, IHM. Letter to Reverend A. A. Meyer. January 5, 1952.
213. Reverend Martin Thielen, Superintendent of Schools, Archdiocese of Portland, OR. Letter to Mother Marcella Gill, IHM, August 20, 1952.
214. Mother Marcella Gill, IHM. Letter to Reverend A. A. Meyer. September 27, 1953.
215. Recollections of Sister Michel Keenan, IHM.
216. Sister Agnes McHale, IHM. Telephone conversation. October 6, 1987.
217. Reverend A. A. Meyer, Pastor, St. Henry's Parish. Letter to Mother Kathleen Hart, IHM, March 16, 1956.
218. Annals of St. Henry's Convent, 1959-1960.
219. Ibid., 1960-1961.
220. Ibid., 1962-1963.
221. Ibid.
222. Sister Agnes McHale, IHM. Personal conversation. October 10, 1987.
223. Annals of St. Henry's Convent, 1964-1965.
224. Reverend John Domin quoted by Beth Fagan in "Sacred Art Attuned to Revised Worship " *The Sunday Oregonian*. Portland, OR. Section Two, p 1, October 18, 1964.
225. Annals of St. Henry's Convent, 1965-1966.
226. Ibid., 1969-1970.
227. Reverend A. A. Meyer, Pastor. Letter to Mother Beata Wertz, IHM, Superior General, April 24, 1970.
228. Central Administrative Assembly Minutes. November 27, 1970.
229. Idaho District Development Assembly Minutes, Fall, 1970.
230. Ibid.
231. Reverend Gregory A. Gage, Assistant Pastor, St. Henry's Parish. Letter to Mother Beata Wertz, IHM, March 9, 1971.
232. Sister Kathleen Lannak, IHM. Letter to Sister Michel Keenan, IHM. January 29, 1988.
233. Reverend Emmet Harrington, Secretary of Education, Archdiocese of Portland, OR. Letter to Mother Beata Wertz, IHM, February 16, 1971.
234. Mary Conway. Article on Little Flower Parish, Bethesda, MD. *The Catholic Standard.* 1983.
235. Ibid.
236. Ibid.
237. Annals of Little Flower Convent, 1953-1954.

238. Ibid., 1954-1960.
239. Ibid., 1964-1965.
240. Ibid., 1966-1967.
241. Ibid., 1973-1974.
242. Reverend George A. Stallings, Jr. Our Lady Queen of Peace Church, Washington, DC. Letters to IHM Sisters, Little Flower Convent, Bethesda, MD, September 26, 1974.
243. Annals of Little Flower Convent, 1978-1979.
244. Annals of St. Clare Convent, Scranton, PA. 1954-1955.
245. Ibid., 1959-1960.
246. Ibid., 1965-1966.
247. Ibid.
248. Ibid., 1971-1972.
249. Annals of St. Clare Convent, 1976-1984.
250. Ibid., 1986-1987.
251. 0urLady of Snows Parish Directory, April 1988, p.1.
252. Golden Jubilee Booklet of Our Lady of Snows Church, 1961, p.1.
253. Parish Directory, op.cit. p.1.
254. Conversation with Monsignor Charles Heid, Pastor, Our Lady of Snows Parish, April 19, 1988.
255. Annals of Our Lady of Peace Convent, 1954-1955.
256. Ibid.
257. Interview with Sister Anselm McShea, IHM, April 12, 1988.
258. Interview with Sister Dorothy Welsh, IHM, April 12, 1988.
259. Ibid.
260. Annals of Our Lady of Peace Convent, 1956-1957.
261. Ibid., 1957-1958.
262. Ibid., 1961-1962.
263. Ibid., 1963-1964.
264. Dedication Booklet, "The Church of St. Gregory," Clarks Green, PA. 1976.
265. Annals of Our Lady of Peace Convent, 1966-1979.
266. Ibid., 1980-1988.
267. Conversation with Monsignor Charles Heid, Pastor, April 19, 1988.
268. *The Catholic Light*, Scranton Diocesan Newspaper, September 22, 1955.
269. Mother Marcella Gill, IHM. Report to the Third General Chapter of the IHM Congregation. June 1955, p.7.
270. Ibid., p.8.
271. Sister Marita Gill, IHM. Letter to Sister Michel Keenan, IHM, April 18, 1988.
272. Ibid., p.9.

Mother M. Kathleen Hart, IHM
1955–1962

BORN:	Helen Hart, June 20, 1891, Ashley, PA
PARENTS:	James B. Hart and Mary Sullivan Hart of Boston, MA
EDUCATION:	B.A. Degree, June 1925, Marywood College, Scranton, PA Teacher Certification in English and Science
RELIGIOUS LIFE:	Entered IHM Novitiate, September 8, 1908 Reception of Habit, October 15, 1910 Profession of Vows, August 2, 1912
MISSIONS:	St. Mary of the Mount High School, Pittsburgh, PA St. Joseph Elementary School, Spokane, WA St. Paul High School, Scranton, PA St. Leo High School, Ashley, PA South Scranton High School, Scranton, PA St. Patrick Elementary School, Oneida, NY Served as Principal and Superior at: St. Mary, Goldsboro, NC St. Bernardine, Baltimore, MD Our Lady of Queen of Martyrs, Forest Hills, NY St. Ann, Scranton, PA Marywood Seminary, Scranton, PA Served as Supervisor of Schools, Scranton Diocese 1944–1946
MEMBER OF THE GENERAL COUNCIL:	1947–1955
SUPERIOR GENERAL:	1955–1961 (first term) 1961–1962 (second term)
DIED:	January 31, 1962

TABLE OF CONTENTS

Mother M. Kathleen Hart, IHM 1955-1962

TOPIC **PAGE**

Mother Kathleen Hart was elected superior general by the delegates to the General Chapter of 1955 and confirmed in office by the Most Reverend Jerome D. Hannan, Bishop of Scranton.

Her predecessor, Mother M. Marcella Gill, had laid the groundwork for the 1955 Chapter in a letter to the Congregation dated April 2, 1955. In this letter she described the duties and responsibilities of delegates, the procedure for sessions, and the date for the elections on June 27, 1955. The serious state of Mother Marcella's health prevented her presence at the opening of the session on June 26, at which the first assistant, Sister Kathleen Hart, presided. (1)

At the Chapter of elections on June 27, 1955, Mother Marcella, having completed fifteen years as superior general, resigned her office in accord with the procedure specified in the Constitutions of 1943:

> At the Chapter for the elections of the Superior General, the former Superior General resigns her office into the hands of the Most Reverend Bishop, or his delegate . . . He shall then transfer the authority (pro tempore) to the First Assistant by giving her the keys to the convent. (2)

Mother Marcella's final report to the Chapter pointed a direction for the agenda, and set the stage for the Extraordinary Chapter of 1957, which she would not live to see. Her death occurred September 14, 1955. It was her successor, Mother Kathleen Hart and the council members, who would give leadership to the realization of her vision. The new administration included Sister St. Mary Orr, first assistant; Sister Beata Wertz, second assistant; Sister Alphonsus McGoldrick, first councilor; and Sister Mary Kevin Nagle, second councilor. (3)

General Chapter of Affairs

A priority question for consideration by the delegates of Chapter 1955 was whether the Congregation should apply for papal approval of its Rules and Customs, thus becoming a Papal Institute. The words of Mother Marcella's final report gave support to this change:

> Up to the present time, our Institute has never petitioned the Holy See to obtain the status of a Papal Congregation. In the past several years the increased attention given to this matter in directives emanating from the Sacred Congregation of Religious would seem to indicate that the Church is encouraging steps in this direction. Our Constitutions were revised in 1943. *The petition*

> *for papal approval was never presented to the Holy See because Bishop Hafey did not favor our seeking it.* In all probability Bishop Hannan, who is a noted canonist, will sanction our seeking it. Naturally, the Constitutions will need more revision before steps can be taken to have them approved. (4)

Since the Congregation was serving in eighteen dioceses/archdioceses, it was ready for this step, the effect of which would be primarily to replace the jurisdiction of bishops with that of the Sacred Congregation of Religious in Rome.

That the Congregation was ready was evident when on June 27, 1955, at the Third Session of Chapter 1955, ninety-six of the one hundred delegates voted in favor of seeking papal approval. Committees were formed to study specific chapters of the Rule and Customs before the next Chapter would convene. (5)

Extraordinary Chapter of 1957

Mother Kathleen, in a letter dated March 19, 1957, announced that an Extraordinary General Chapter would be held from June 29–July 2, 1957, to discuss and approve the proposed revisions to the Rule, Customs and Manual of Prayers. In her opening remarks, Mother Kathleen referring to Pope Pius XIIs words to the First National Congress of Religious in the United States in 1952 said, "It would seem that this General Chapter should have only one primary purpose, to return to or regain the original spirit of our Congregation. If secondary purposes, such as methods and means arise, we are justified in accepting them only to the extent that they help to deepen and strengthen the religious life." (6)

In explaining the process to be used so that the delegates would have wide participation in the discussions, she noted that nine sectional committees had been set up, each with an appointed chair, and each with assigned specific chapters of the Constitutions and Customs for discussion. A recorder was appointed for each group who was to report to the entire assembled Chapter. These reports would become the basis of continued discussion by the entire Chapter. The general secretary would record those revisions which received affirmative approval by the delegates and prepare them for presentation and voting at the Plenary Session on the final day of the Chapter.

It was obvious that Mother Kathleen wished the elected delegates to play an active role in Chapter 1957 as the work of revision moved forward.

Speaking to the delegates at the same opening session on June 29, 1957, Bishop Jerome Hannan encouraged the Congregation's seeking of papal approval for the Constitutions and Customs. He said, "It is the intention of the Church that all Congregations be under the guidance and control of the Sacred Congregation of Religious." Addressing the concern of some that this move would diminish the sisters' dedication to the local ordinaries, Bishop Hannan said further, "You should have nothing but joy in applying for approval . . . I believe that the Holy See will be edified by the Constitutions, Customs, and Manual of Prayers you send to Rome for approval. The Constitutions are your law; they are based on the Canons of the Church."

And, again paralleling Pope Pius XII, "in your deliberations you must strive to preserve the spirit of your Rule; try to retain or regain the spirit of the Congregation . . . Generations of religious of the past are looking at us today and saying: These laws have served us well." (7)

The delegates were also convinced that "these laws served us well," for they completed the work of revision during the four days of the Chapter. Nine changes in the Constitutions were proposed; seven were approved. There were fifteen proposals for changes in the Customs; fourteen passed. The one rejected was that our sisters be permitted to drive cars. Twenty-five proposed changes in the Manual of Prayers were approved. Some minor changes proposed by Bishop Hannan were incorporated.

Provision for moving the papal approval forward was made by several motions at the closing session. Sister Mary Kevin Nagle moved that "the delegates accept the proposed Constitutions, Customs and Manual of Prayers as amended, with the recommendation that the necessary editing be done before the final copy is submitted to the Sacred Congregation of Religious." The motion passed by a unanimous vote. Other motions gave Mother Kathleen and the council the authority to accept the new Constitutions when finally approved and to promulgate them as superseding the previous Constitutions. (8)

The tedious work that followed the Chapter can hardly be imagined as Mother Kathleen, the council members and Sister Brendan O'Brien, the Congregation general secretary, painstakingly prepared the voluminous materials required by the Sacred Congregation of Religious. Responses had to be provided to some two hundred questions about the Congregation, in addition to the work of revision noted above.

An enormous breakthrough in this work came when at the suggestion of Mother Maria Alma, superior general of the Philadelphia IHMs, the assistance of Reverend Bernard Ransing, CSC was obtained. (9) Father Ransing was an American Holy Cross priest, who resided in Rome, serving as secretary general of the Holy Cross Congregation, and assisting at the Sacred Congregation for Religious. As it turned out, Father Ransing was also a University of Notre Dame classmate and close friend of Reverend Thomas Culhane, CSC, brother of Sisters Marthine and Therese of the Scranton IHMs. When contacted by Mother Kathleen, Father Ransing was more than happy to be of help. (10) His letters, often weekly, from December 1958 through 1961, and over the ensuing years, gave precise direction to the process of preparing the documents required by the Sacred Congregation for Religious in Rome. He became, in fact, a lifelong advocate and friend of the IHM Congregation.

Because of Mother Kathleen's determination and Father Ransing's assistance, the Rule, Customs and Manual of Prayers were ready for submission to Rome on May 2, 1958, less than a year after the close of the Extraordinary Chapter of 1957. Subsequent letters reveal the optimism and joy of Mother Kathleen at the progress Father Ransing was reporting as the revised Constitutions made their way through the detailed approval process in Rome. However, frustrating changes in consultors, problems in capturing in Italian certain English texts, the extended summer vacation months in Rome, a move of the offices of the Sacred Congregation, and many more factors all caused delays. (11)

Mother Kathleen's patience in awaiting the approval of the Rule is noted in a December 16, 1959 letter to Father Ransing:

> You were indeed kind to let me know that we must check our own optimism in the matter of the good news we expect to hear from you. Always we have every confidence in your generous interest. The good report for which we pray will be all the more appreciated because of our great longing. We are not disappointed; only more eager to hear the good tidings. (12)

When finally, on June 26, 1960, a cablegram from Father Ransing brought news of the approval of the Constitutions, Mother Kathleen wrote:

> I hope that some of the joy and gratitude your cablegram evoked in us found echo in your heart. Humbly we thank God for His goodness throughout the process of the approval of our Constitutions . . . May God's reward to you be exceedingly great. (13)

News of the final long-awaited step, the signing by His Eminence, Valerio Cardinal Valeri, of the Decree of Praise came on December 2, 1960, in a cablegram to Mother Kathleen from Father Ransing. Mother Kathleen's cable reply was brief, but meaningful: "A fervent Magnificat echoes through our entire community today. Our prayers express our gratitude for your untiring and selfless labor in our cause." (14)

On December 16, 1960, Mother Kathleen informed each of the fourteen bishops in whose dioceses our sisters served that the Scranton IHM Congregation had received the status of a papal congregation as of November 21, 1960. Congratulatory letters poured in from all across the country–from bishops, from each of the local convents, and from major superiors of other congregations. (15)

Mother Kathleen's gratitude to Father Ransing was often expressed over the years, and her letter of December 20, 1960 revealed once again the depth of that gratitude, her sense of relief, and her joy in accomplishment of the goal that at times seemed so elusive. She wrote:

> You have undoubtedly some idea of the joy that was ours when the official copy of our Constitutions and the precious Decree of Praise came to us a few days ago. You know too that our gratitude to you is sincere and lasting. Your unceasing effort in our cause and your competent help elicit our deepest gratitude. What a splendid benefactor you are to our Congregation. Without you, we might be still groping to reach the status of a Papal Congregation. Our fervent prayers of thanks rise to heaven for you. (16)

Buildings and Land

While it may seem that the five years spent by Mother Kathleen's administration in securing the approval for the revised Constitutions and attaining the Decree of Praise as a papal congregation were about all that could be accomplished, such was not the case. Several other major projects were claiming attention at the same time. Historical timing has a way of dictating priorities to which attention must be directed. So it was with several property matters facing Mother Kathleen and the council. Congregation-owned and newly acquired properties were to claim much time and attention. These included the following eleven sites.

Marian Convent, Scranton, Pennsylvania

Ground was broken for a new home for the sick and aged sisters on October 7, 1954, during Mother M. Marcella's last term in office. In her final report to the Chapter of June 1955, Mother Marcella had stated:

> Since our home for the sick and aged at Elmhurst does not offer adequate accommodation for our increasing needs, His

> Excellency Most Reverend Jerome Hannan endorsed permission given by our former Bishop, Most Reverend William J. Hafey, to erect a new convent for our infirm and aged Sisters on the Marywood property. (17)

The plan was for a $1,142,000 structure to care for eighty sisters. Mother Marcella's foresight in this matter was clear as she revealed that as early as 1944, she had set up a fund for this purpose that by 1955 had accumulated $250,000. The remaining $872,000 was to be borrowed at three and one-half percent per annum interest from the Emigrant Industrial Savings Bank of New York.

Mother Kathleen carried forward assiduously this project, which was so badly needed. Just one year later, on April 9, 1956, the completed Marian Convent was dedicated. Bishop Hannan presided and praised it "as a work of charity which the Congregation has given on behalf of its members." He expressed the value of the prayer ministry that would exist there, saying, "The prayer of those who will live here is needed, as well as the efforts of those members of the order who are on the firing line, in the hospitals and the classrooms." (18)

Monsignor Thomas Cawley, editor of the Scranton Diocesan newspaper, *The Light,* in his column, "The Spotlight" expressed the same thought regarding the Marian Convent. He wrote:

> By so doing, the Immaculate Hearts have acted justly, charitably and wisely . . . they have demonstrated their awareness and appreciation of the contribution these Sisters have made to the Order. But they have indicated something else . . . they have indicated how they esteem the prayers, sufferings and intercessory powers of these good women . . ." (19)

Mother Marcella's role in the planning of this building was memorialized in the gift of the Marywood College Alumnae who provided a rope bell in the foyer outside the Chapel of the Immaculate Heart of Mary in the Marian Convent.

One week after the dedication on April 16, 1956, the new reality of life and professional care at the Marian Convent began as twenty-eight sisters were moved from St. Agnes Place, Elmhurst, to the Marian Convent. On April 23, an additional thirteen sisters were moved from St. Joseph's Hospital in Carbondale to the Marian Convent. The total of forty-one sisters quickly brought the new facility to fifty percent of its capacity. Mother Kathleen appointed Sister Alphonsus McGoldrick as first superior and administrator. In this capacity, she served from 1956 to 1961, the year of her death. (20)

Speaking of the Marian Convent in her report to the General Chapter of 1961, Mother Kathleen enunciated a truth which has come to be well-known to all IHM Sisters over the years: "Only in eternity will we be able to gauge accurately the fruit of this most happy venture on the part of the Congregation. It has been a joy to witness the peace, contentment, and security of our dear aged and ill sisters. The Marian Convent is a power-house of prayer, a source of grace and blessings for the entire Congregation." (21)

St. Agnes Place, Elmhurst, Pennsylvania

After moving the older sisters from St. Agnes Place, Elmhurst, Mother Kathleen's attention turned to possible uses for this property. When the Marian Convent opened in April 1956, she obtained permission from Bishop Hannan to house thirty sisters at St. Agnes Place for summer study. This plan lasted only one summer, however, since the structure which had served as a home for our ill and aged sisters for thirty-one years, having been purchased from the W.L. Connell family of Scranton in 1925, was in need of extensive renovation. There were also inconveniences related to procuring priests for Mass and general difficulties of transportation. St. Agnes Place was actually too small to accommodate sizeable numbers of sisters. (22)

The council, therefore, agreed unanimously on July 17, 1957 to place the property on sale. Obtaining the approval of Bishop Hannan and the Apostolic Delegate for the sale, as well as getting two appraisals of the property, took more than a year. Finally, on August 25, 1957, St. Agnes Place, which was appraised at $23,400, was sold for $22,000. It is interesting to note that it was not until September 5, 1957 that the permission to sell arrived from the Apostolic Delegate. (23)

Marian Hall, St. Joseph's Hospital, Carbondale, Pennsylvania

Anticipating the demolition of old St. Rose Convent, Carbondale, which had been the residence for the student nurses at St. Joseph's Hospital, Mother Kathleen and the council approved the request of Sister Cor Mariae, administrator, for the building of Marian Hall adjacent to the hospital. It was completed in 1956 at a cost of $700,000, which was borrowed from the Emigrant Bank of New York City. At the time the building was being completed, Mother Kathleen was a patient in the hospital for a short period. She toured the facility with Sister Cor Mariae who writes this anecdote in her *Autobiography:*

> On the way back to the hospital, I remember saying to her "Now, Mother, I want you to know that three-fourths of me are in that building. There is only one-fourth of me left." Her answer was "Never mind singing your Nunc Dimittus; you have a lot of work to do yet." (24)

And, of course, she did. Sister Cor Mariae was only sixty-six years old and would serve twelve more years as administrator of St. Joseph's Hospital. Marian Hall served as the nurses' residence until 1971 when the nursing program became a non-resident (day) program. The building was a welcome location for physicians' offices and as space for the Northeast Tri-County Mental Health Unit Clinic. The library was retained and some rooms continued as instructional space.

Council minutes indicate that approval was also given on January 30, 1956 for extensive improvements in St. Joseph's Hospital's obstetrics, pediatrics, operating and recovery rooms, and for kitchen equipment and a new cafeteria. A Ford Foundation Grant of $44,000 made many of these renovations possible. (25)

Old St. Rose Convent, Carbondale, Pennsylvania

A significant chapter of Congregation history and a Carbondale landmark, old St. Rose Convent, had become a beloved dinosaur by 1957. The large estate was purchased from Captain and Mrs. William Brennan and served as the Congregation's motherhouse and novitiate from 1876 to 1902 when Mount St. Mary's in Scranton was built. Besides its role as motherhouse and novitiate, St. Rose Convent had been at one time a boys' boarding school; was utilized as a hospital from 1926–1929; was the convent home for the sisters teaching at the nearby St. Rose School; and served as a residence for student nurses from St. Joseph's Hospital, as was noted above.

The parish had built the new St. Rose Convent in 1957 to house the sisters teaching at St. Rose Elementary and High Schools. It was left to Mother Kathleen and her council to decide the disposition of the nearly one hundred year-old St. Rose Convent. Bids were sought on the cost of demolition of the structure and the price that might be paid by an interested firm for the salvageable materials. The three and one-half story building had a total of 334,000 cubic feet of space, much of it containing oak floors. The Shepherd Real Estate Agency of Carbondale submitted a bid on May 7, 1957 to pay .015 cents per cubic foot or $5,000 for the salvage, with the Congregation paying for the razing. In light of another bid from E. A. Bloxham of Forest City, Pennsylvania, agreeing to pay $1,000 for the structure and assuming all costs for the razing, the council authorized the demolition to them on July 19, 1957. The Congregation assumed $400 in costs for grading and finishing work after the razing.

The annals of the St. Rose Convent community for 1957 indicate that on July 29, 1957, the sisters made one "last visit to old St. Rose." (26)

Our Lady of Lourdes Convent, Tobyhanna, Pennsylvania

A letter from the chancellor of the Scranton Diocese, Monsignor Joseph Madden, to Mother Kathleen dated August 26, 1957, brought news of a very generous offer. The offer was from Mary Elizabeth Lynch whose family home was near St. Ann Church in Tobyhanna, Pennsylvania. Miss Lynch, then a captain in the Air Force, stationed in Japan, wished to donate her family home as a convent for the IHM Sisters. The home was situated on ten acres of land. It had four bedrooms and a bath upstairs, five rooms and bath downstairs, and was completely furnished. (27)

Alert to the potential for service in an area having no Catholic schools at the time, and aware of the ideal location as a country respite for the Sisters, Mother Kathleen wasted no time in holding a council meeting, obtaining approval, and by the very next day, August 27, 1957, sending a return letter to Monsignor Madden accepting Miss Lynch's offer. (28)

Eight months later, on April 23, 1958, Our Lady of Lourdes Convent in Tobyhanna opened. The first group of sisters included Sister Leo Lehman, superior, Sister Mary Dawson, and Sister Roselda (Roberta) Peters. Sister Leo's time there was fruitful but short as an aggravated asthma condition weakened her heart, causing her death on November 24, 1961.

The work of the sisters included several nearby mission parishes–South Sterling, Pocono Pines and Gouldsboro to provide catechetical instruction for the children. Thus, Our Lady of Lourdes became the catechetical school for the Pocono area, serving some 141 children each year, for ten years, until 1968. With the opening of Pocono Catholic Elementary and High School in Cresco, Mother Beata withdrew the sisters from Tobyhanna noting the shortage of sisters and the new opportunities for students in Cresco.

Legal arrangements were made through Attorney Harold C. Edwards of Stroudsburg in July 1968 to transfer the title to the property back to Miss Lynch. (29)

IHM Academy, Coeur d'Alene, Idaho

The IHM Academy in Coeur d'Alene, Idaho was one of only three high schools in the state. St. Theresa's, Boise, and St. Gertrude's, Cottonwood, were the other two.

The old Fort Sherman buildings in Coeur d'Alene, dating back to the 1890s were to serve well as convent, boarding school and as the IHM Academy elementary and high school for more than fifty years. Mother Cyril Conway and Sister Clement Kearns, first Academy superior, could not have imagined that the Fort Hospital and Administration Building, purchased in 1905 at a government auction for $1,500, and the Post Opera House, a gift of Jack and R.B. Stack, would be the base from which over half a century's legacy of faith, education, and loving dedication would emerge.

From the simple beginnings in 1903 in a building known as St. Cyril's School, it was evident that the Sisters of IHM were outstanding educators. These first sisters were Sisters Clement Kearns, Dositheus Cawley, Justine Duffy, and Maria Loughlin. (30)

By the 1940s, the overcrowded classrooms became a great concern. In 1944 and 1945, letters between Mother Marcella and Sister Vincent Burke, local superior, indicate their belief that a new grade school should be built by the local Redemptorist Parish, St. Thomas. There was at least one suggestion by Mother Marcella that the parish should build both grade and high schools in which the IHM Sisters would serve on a salaried basis.

These ideas were pursued to the extent of Sister Vincent's presenting a case for a new parish elementary school in a letter to Bishop Edward J. Kelly of the Boise Diocese. He, in turn, expressed his support in a letter to the Redemptorist pastor, Reverend A.C. Dittrich. With a parish free of debt in 1945, Father Dittrich began to set aside funds for the new school. With the change of pastors in the interim, St. Thomas Grade School became a reality in 1950.

As early as 1953 Bishop Kelly had written to Sister Mary Kevin Nagle, then local superior in Coeur d'Alene, to assure his support for a building plan for a new Academy High School and a new convent. In a letter of April 29, 1953, he gave permission for a fund-raising campaign for this purpose. He wrote:

> Everyone realizes the temper and nature of your present school building, which originally was old Fort Sherman, dating back to the primitive days of Idaho history. We ask that God may bless every donor towards this most worthy cause that you plan to carry into effect immediately. (31)

"Immediately" came several years later after the larger picture made its impact on local Coeur d'Alene projects. Mother Marcella died in 1955 and the General Chapter of 1955, which elected Mother Kathleen, also elected Sister Mary Kevin to the council. The fact was that major figures in the picture had changed.

To provide the dynamic, energetic and persevering leadership for the development of the IHM Academy in Coeur d'Alene, Mother Kathleen sent Sister Rebecca Doyle as principal and superior in 1955. Without the aid of later technologies, such as fax machines and e-mail, Sister Rebecca managed to put communication between Coeur d'Alene and Scranton on a very fast track!

By December 5, 1955, Mother Kathleen was responding to Sister Rebecca's building project plans, which included the girls' boarding school, a new academy, a gym and auditorium, and a two-story convent for the sisters! It was obvious that in addition to the funds that the sisters had saved over the years, a fund-raising campaign would be needed. A letter from Mother Kathleen dated December 8, 1955 gave the council's permission for the fund drive, subsequent to having received the approval of both Bishop Jerome Hannan of Scranton and Bishop Edward J. Kelly of Boise.

Bishop Kelly would not live to see the Academy completed. His death on April 21, 1956 was a shock to the entire diocese. Bishop Kelly was succeeded by Bishop James Byrne, who would also prove to be a supportive advocate in all endeavors that lay ahead for the IHM Sisters, especially in Coeur d'Alene. (32)

Plans for the building program moved on. Later in 1955, the Building Committee selected the architect, Mr. Carroll Martell. In August 1966, a loan of $200,000 was finalized from the Coughlin Company of Denver, Colorado.

One piece of the total building project, namely, the gymnasium and auditorium, was set in place as Mr. Larry Brown of Northwest Lumber Company, Coeur d'Alene, generously donated funds for this building which was named for him. In July 1956, the convent porch along the Coeur d'Alene Avenue side of the property was taken down to make way for the new gymnasium/auditorium. This building had special interest because it was the first gym the Academy had in its long history and because of the unusual wood selected for its interior: fine-grained cedar wood lining the lower walls and course-grained cedar on the upper walls. Between the lofty beams, finished in soft driftwood, celetex white tile added to both the beauty and the acoustics. (33)

The year 1957 was an historic one as significant endings and beginnings occurred for the IHM Academy, its students, and faculty. Graduation exercises were held as usual, but nostalgia prevailed as graduates realized that May 27, 1957 was the last day of school in the old Fort Sherman Building, which had housed the Academy for fifty-four years.

So much promise lay ahead, however, as the new Academy moved toward completion and the fall term of 1957 saw one celebration after another. Open house was held on August 25; the new Academy opened for classes on September 5; and on November 4, Bishop James Byrne of Boise dedicated and blessed the school. Sisters on the high school faculty were Sisters Kevina (Joan) Mooney, Spiritus (Kathleen) McNulty, Teresine (Eleanor) Desaulniers, and Barbara DuMont. Sisters Aloysia Shermanson and Timothy Smyth were the music faculty. Sister Rebecca Doyle was principal. (34)

Meanwhile, not skipping a beat, Sister Rebecca had obtained Mother Kathleen's permission to proceed with plans to build a convent for the sisters. There was general awareness of the declining conditions under which both the sisters and the boarder girls were living in the old Fort Sherman buildings. Permission for the new convent and girls' boarding school was given in March 1957. Two months later, Sister Rebecca, faced with the debt on the Academy project, yet eager to proceed with the convent building, asked Mother Kathleen to consider granting a Congregation loan of about $300,000 for the convent project. This request was denied at a council meeting on July 28, 1957.

Again, in answer to Sister Rebecca's appeal for Congregation assistance, the council's action on January 22, 1958 deferred for at least a year any possibility of a loan. It was clear that existing Congregation debt, and the pressing need for a new novitiate building prevented the Congregation from involvement in the Coeur d'Alene building projects. (35)

Anticipating Sister Rebecca's disappointment at these replies, Mother Kathleen wrote:

> No doubt you will be disappointed with our decision, but you must realize that we have to consider the over-all picture of the finances of the community . . . I appreciate the fact that you are anxious to complete the work you have begun. In God's providence He will make this possible if we are patient and place our trust in Him. We are not unmindful of your tireless efforts and the fine things you have already accomplished. (36)

Sister Rebecca must, indeed, have known many discouraging days in this situation, but she ran a "tight ship," setting aside for the time being her great desire to see a new convent and boarding school built. The salary of the eight sisters teaching in St. Thomas Grade School, together with the income from the boarders and the music lessons given all day every week day by Sisters Aloysia Shermanson and Timothy

Smyth provided funds to live on and even savings to pay down the debt on the new Academy building. By March 15, 1959 the debt had been reduced to $167,000 on this $500,000 project. In March, and again in November, Sister Rebecca proposed that the Congregation assume the remaining debt, which at that point was down to $145,000. The council did not approve her request.

Sister Rebecca's spirit was never idle as she thought of ways to take at least small steps toward continuance of the building plans. Her letter to Mother Kathleen dated September 28, 1960 requested permission to tear down the old high school building separating it from the former grade school section and boys' boarding quarters. This was the old Fort Sherman Opera House that had been moved to the spot in 1905. Sister Rebecca rightly observed that this section was obstructing the view of the new Academy, was an expense to continue heating, and would have to come down eventually for further building. She wrote:

> May we, then, Reverend Mother, have permission to go ahead with this project? It would provide that little extra ray of hope and expectation on the part of the sisters and the people, which would be psychologically good at this point. (37)

Mother Kathleen's prompt response dated September 30, 1960, granted Congregation permission, noting the need to also secure the permission of Bishop Byrne. It was not until February 14, 1961 that the old high school was finally dismantled, thanks to the laborious work of the members of the St. Vincent de Paul Society of the parish. (38)

On August 4, 1961, Sister Rebecca, having completed her tireless and fruitful term of six years as principal and superior at Coeur d'Alene, returned to the East. Sister Avellina Ryan, herself an early graduate of the IHM Academy, and former faculty member, was appointed in Sister Rebecca's place and arrived on August 23, 1961.

Within the space of seven months several stark realities faced Sister Avellina. On January 31, 1962, Mother Kathleen died of a heart condition after weeks of illness; on February 8, 1962, the buildings housing the sisters and girl boarders were condemned as unsafe by the Fire Department and an order issued that they be evacuated at the close of the semester; and on March 7, 1962, Bishop Byrne was named Archbishop of Dubuque, Iowa. (39) Events beyond human control would thus expedite the building of the new convent, and a new cast of major players would bring the drama to completion. The dreams of Mother Kathleen, Sister Rebecca, and Bishop Kelly would be realized.

IHM Novitiate Building, Scranton, Pennsylvania

The building for which Mother Kathleen is best remembered is the IHM Novitiate. (40) By October 1955, the council minutes reflect Mother Kathleen's plan to provide candidates and novices with enlarged space in a new building. The influx of some forty-five postulants yearly, and approximately eighty novices in the novitiate at a given time in the two-year cycle, resulted in extremely crowded conditions at the motherhouse.

In 1955, the purchase of part of the Apawana Golf Course as a future site for the new novitiate was discussed. This property was adjacent on the East to existing Congregation property and was situated on an elevated knoll above the other campus buildings. Two years later, on December 17, 1957, after the sale of St. Agnes Place, Elmhurst, the council minutes refer to the fact that the money from the sale of St. Agnes Place had been "invested in the Corn Exchange Bank of New York to purchase land from the Pennsylvania and Hudson Coal Companies for a new novitiate." (41)

Successful negotiating over the next six months ended with the acquisition of forty-eight acres of land by June 13, 1958. The total cost of the land was $48,286, which was paid for from savings. As with any large building project in the Scranton/Dunmore area, concern arose about underground conditions due to years of mining activity by the coal companies. Acting on information that a mine fire was burning underground somewhere in the vicinity, Mother Kathleen arranged for extensive studies to be done by professional engineers. Having determined that the area was protected by thick firewalls underground, the engineers pronounced the land safe for building. (42)

The plans and cost estimates of several architects were considered. In March 1959, Mother Kathleen and the council chose the architectural firm of Valverde and Franco. (43) It was estimated that the novitiate building would cost approximately $1,500,000. Initial expenses were met from the Building Fund, but from June 1961 through January 1962, $562,000 was borrowed from Northeastern Pennsylvania National Bank and Trust of Scranton. An additional $225,000 was borrowed in February and May 1962. (44)

To help meet the challenge of this financial burden, Mother Kathleen organized a group of men in 1958 that became known as the "Fathers and Friends of the Marywood Novitiate." At its height, there were three hundred members, most of whom were fathers of novices or postulants. These men were represented in twelve states and hundreds of cities, especially in New York and Pennsylvania. The presidents of the "Fathers and Friends" up to the time of the dedication of the building included Edward P. Rock, 1958–1959; Joseph A. Rooney, 1960; William G. Connolly, 1961; and

Aloysius J. Wilson, 1962. The largest annual project of the association was the Marywood Autumn Fair, held over three days in October. The IHM Sisters and many friends donated handmade gifts and baked goods for the booths at the fair. The novitiate building dedication booklet comments:

> Under the well-organized leadership of the Fathers and Friends, the Autumn Fair constitutes an inspiring and encouraging manifestation of the generous support of business and professional donors, as well as thousands of friends who patronize its activities. (45)

This organization continued until 1974, having sponsored the Marywood Autumn Fair for ten years, and subsequently conducting fund drives which featured Guy Lombardo Concerts, IHM Sisters Musicales, and dinners for the public, for a total contribution of $891,102. After each of the successful Autumn Fair events from 1958–1961, Mother Kathleen made known her deep appreciation of the work of the Fathers and Friends by letter and in her address at the yearly gratitude banquet. In 1958, for example, she wrote:

> Your fine help in planning, and in executing these plans resulted in what was a really phenomenal affair. Full well we know that we of ourselves could never have achieved the success that your valuable help insured. We are most grateful to you and will ever hold in loving memory the record of your generous help . . . Again, permit me to thank you, as I pray that you who have done so much for our beloved Order will be abundantly blessed by God. May you and your dear ones reap God's abundant reward. (46)

Groundbreaking for the new building took place on May 30, 1960. The dedication booklet describes this event as "a triumphal day for the Fathers and Friends of the Marywood Novitiate." Undoubtedly, that could be said also for Mother Kathleen who, in spite of the pouring rain, "with undampered spirit . . . put her hand to the shovel turning the soil with comparative ease to the unsuppressed amusement of attending clergy and members of the community council, witnesses to the groundwork done by His Excellency." (47)

The architects, Valverde and Franco, must have spent many hours with Mother Kathleen as every detail of the 103,000 square foot contemporary, functional novitiate was developed. The spiritual focus of the novitiate was addressed, as a magnificent chapel became the dominating element of the "H" form plan. Features of the chapel included a custom-designed pipe organ and stained-glass windows portraying biblical events in the life of the Blessed Virgin Mary, as well as one window depicting Congregation history. With a seating capacity of four hundred, the chapel was designed to provide space for large groups attending receptions and professions of postulants, novices, and junior professed sisters.

Other dimensions of the life of a postulant and novice were given attention in well-lighted classrooms and a library; a well-equipped kitchen where the fine art of cooking for large groups would be learned; and spacious dining, dormitory, laundry, and recreational areas.

Mother Kathleen had been closely involved in the planning of the novitiate, including the communication of her desire that the dormitories be constructed in such a way that each novice and postulant would have a window in her sleeping area. And this was done. What did not occur according to her wish was the subject of several letters to and from Bishop Hannan regarding the use of oil instead of coal in heating the new building. Bishop Hannan, anticipating a negative reaction from area people if coal were not the fuel of choice, was quite emphatic in his refusal of support for the use of oil. Mother Kathleen set forth cogent reasons for the change, chief among which was the initial and future expense of using coal. She did, however, accede to the bishop's wishes after receiving the following statement from him:

> Should you and your council decide on the use of oil instead of coal and should there be any censure of this action, I will not hesitate to disavow responsibility for the decision, even publicly, if the extent of the censure threatens to alienate a significant number of Catholics. (48)

After Mother Kathleen's letter of January 16, 1960, assuring Bishop Hannan of compliance with his wishes, the Bishop wrote: "This assures that neither I nor your Congregation will be confronted with the resentment of our Catholic working people." (49)

Mother Kathleen, as superior general of a congregation of some eleven-hundred sisters, having spiritual and temporal responsibilities of such great magnitude as her life story reveals, demonstrated the humility of greatness in a situation where her judgment could well have been upheld and supported. Interestingly enough, the heating system would have to be converted to natural gas and oil in subsequent years!

Mother Kathleen made many visits to the site of the new novitiate as it progressed. But she was not to see the completed fruit of her efforts. She was hospitalized in October 1961, and while she continued working from her hospital room until her death on January 31, 1962, she did not live to participate in the festive dedication on May 30, 1962 of her favorite project, the IHM Novitiate. On that occasion Mother Beata Wertz paid tribute to Mother Kathleen, saying:

> . . . we rejoice in the dedication of this splendid building. It is a monument to our revered Mother M. Kathleen, who devoted herself wholeheartedly to its planning and construction. Every detail was of vital interest to her. Always in our memories, it will express to us the zeal with which she toiled in the care of our novices and postulants. (50)

Our Lady of Grace Convent, Manhasset, New York

In spite of Mother Kathleen's deep involvement in several other property projects, as was seen in the foregoing, she did not hesitate to respond to yet another large endeavor. On January 6, 1959, J. Peter Grace, Jr. of Manhasset, New York offered the Congregation a gift of land and buildings adjacent to his estate. Mr. Grace was head of W. R. Grace and Company, which owned a fleet of thirty-five ships; chemical plants in Canada, Europe and Australia; the Grace National Bank of New York; oil drilling in Libya; and other business ventures.

He intended to purchase the fifty-one acre Cornelius F. Kelly estate adjoining his own, and offered to the Congregation the large, French provincial home and six acres of land surrounding it. Additionally, this included a caretaker's building, stables, and an outdoor pool. The first floor of the chateau had eight large rooms, including a magnificent library, sun parlor patio, and a ballroom that was subsequently converted to the chapel. The second floor had eight large bedrooms and five bathrooms. The basement boasted an English taproom, game room, and powder room. Six bedrooms, two baths, a dining and a sitting room were once the quarters of servants. A few hundred feet from the main house was a ten-car garage and two five-room apartments, in addition to the guesthouse and pool mentioned above. (51)

Seeing many potential uses for this property as a place for spiritual renovation for professed sisters, as a temporary solution to the space needs of the postulants and junior professed sisters, and a possible future provincial house, if required by Rome, Mother Kathleen, nine days after Mr. Grace's offer, sent a letter to Bishop Hannan seeking his permission to accept. Five days later, on January 20, 1959, Bishop Hannan's affirmative reply arrived. (52) On February 1, 1959, approval of the council was recorded. (53) Thus Our Lady of Grace Convent became a reality.

Since the Congregation was not yet a papal institute, in addition to the foregoing actions, there were approvals required from the apostolic delegate and from Bishop P. Kellenberg of the Rockville Centre Diocese in which the property was located. There was also a need to inform Reverend John K. Sharp, St. Mary Parish, Manhasset, and pastor of the nearest local parish.

The council minutes of March 15, 1959 note the approval of Bishop Kellenberg, subsequent to Mother Kathleen's personal visit to him at St. Agnes Cathedral Rectory in Rockville Centre, New York on February 18, 1959. (54) It was a difficult decision for Bishop Kellenberg, since his policy restricted acquisition of tax-exempt property to religious communities in his diocese. He made it clear that the exception in this case was because of "the long and splendid record of I.H.M.'s in the Rockville Centre Diocese." He was referring to the fact that the IHM Sisters had served at St. Dominic, Oyster Bay, since 1924; at St. Peter, Port Washington since 1925; and St. Mary, Manhasset since 1926.

Even with Bishop Kellenberg's approval, there were still several hurdles to overcome. Both the town of North Hempstead and the Village of North Hills had tax exemption policies and zoning laws that applied to use of the property. Since North Hills' zoning law restricted use to "single family dwelling purposes," the legal issue became whether the sisters would constitute a "family." Since no definition was given in the law, Attorney J. Oakey McKnight of Mineola, New York, rendered this opinion that solved the zoning question:

> . . . if the Ordinance did not restrict by definition the use and occupancy to members of a single family related with degrees of consanguinity or affinity," then the Sisters could be considered a family. (55)

The right to tax exemption on the property was obtained from the town of North Hempstead, the Village of North Hills and the School District of Nassau County during April 1959. This was a considerable concession since the property's replacement value had been appraised at $800,000.

In all these matters Mother Kathleen was astute–working with lawyers, businessmen, and bishops. She also had a homey, simple way of endearing herself to those whose help she needed. She became friends with Mrs. Grace (Margaret), the wife of Peter Grace and mother of eight children who attended St. Mary School in Manhasset where the IHM Sisters taught. Mr. Grace was a strong supporter of parochial school education, although he himself attended public schools. His sentiments were expressed in these words:

> I came to feel that I had missed something . . . a religious education seems to me more important than ever today, in the face of the empty materialism that prevails in so much of the world. So I decided to send my own children to parochial schools. (56)

Sister Paul Joseph McArdle, IHM, principal of St. Mary High School in Manhasset, played a key role in cultivating Mother Kathleen's interest in the Grace property. She could see opportunities for the Congregation's presence there, as well as the value of the gift itself.

Mrs. Grace became a strong intermediary contact between Mother Kathleen and Peter Grace who was frequently out of the country on business. It was Mrs. Grace who guided the first tour of the Kelly estate for Mother Kathleen and three council members on January 15, 1959, and who opened her home for subsequent meetings with legal representatives regarding the Kelly estate.

By April 20, 1959, the chief attorney for Peter Grace, Mr. John J. Meehan of Forest Hills, New York, submitted a proposal for the conveyance of the property to the IHM Congregation. The council approved these arrangements on May 8, 1959, and Bishop Hannan also approved in a letter dated May 15, 1959. (57)

So it was that within a five-month period a host of legal requirements had been met, approvals by Church and civil authorities obtained, and the deed and title delivered by Mr. Grace to Mother Kathleen. Plans began at once for occupying the main house in late June 1959. Sisters from nearby IHM convents gave many hours to the task of readying the house. The summer of 1959 was already scheduled for a Spiritual Renovation Program for two groups of "fourteen to eighteen years professed Sisters," about thirty-five sisters in each group for July and August.

Sister Maria Angela Orr was appointed first superior of Our Lady of Grace Convent and Sister Clotilde Cullen, mistress of renovation. Sisters Ignatius Brown, Norbert (Marlyn) DeWitt, and Mariam Pfeifer were assigned to assist during the July renovation program. In August, the four replacement helpers were Sisters Roselda (Roberta) Peters, St. Leo (Joanne) Madden, Sharon Brady, and Mary Faber (Mary Helen) Slavinskas. (58)

Mother Kathleen, together with Sister St. Mary and Sister Beata, was present to welcome the renovants. The interest of Mother Kathleen in the renovation of the sisters continued as a priority, and she found great joy in knowing that the Congregation now had an appropriate, spacious center for the physical and spiritual renewal of the sisters.

In order to ease the space problems at the motherhouse, Mother Kathleen obtained Bishop Hannan's permission for the forty-five postulants who had entered in September 1959 to complete their postulancy at Our Lady of Grace Convent. On December 10, the forty-five, along with their directress, Sister Gertrude Marie Jelley, left from Marywood by Greyhound bus, arriving at their new home in the early afternoon. Sisters Maria Angela Orr, Kotska Sick and Charles Marie Meehan welcomed them. Mother Kathleen had selected four excellent guides for the postulants' introduction to religious life in the IHM tradition and spirit. (59)

By May 20, 1960, the first group of postulants returned to Marywood. Their departure signaled the restart of the cycle of June and August renovation arrivals, followed by the December 29 arrival of the second group of postulants. This scheduling would continue until the opening of the new novitiate building in May 1962.

The Congregation is indebted not only to Mr. and Mrs. Peter Grace for their initial gift of this property and their on-going interest and support of it, but also to the hundreds of women who were members of the IHM League over the years. These women made possible many equipment replacements and beautified the interior by their gifts of furniture, lamps, pictures, drapes, and other household items. The families of many IHM Sisters were also generous donors to Our Lady of Grace Convent.

St. Joseph's Children's and Maternity Hospital, Scranton, Pennsylvania

The long history of St. Joseph's Center, dating from its founding as St. Joseph's Society in 1888, saw many location changes, name changes, and clientele changes. For many, May 1900 was the major step as the main part of the present building at 2010 Adams Avenue, Scranton, the site donated by Mr. John B. Smith, was completed. By October 1909 the two wings were constructed and by 1920 the name changed to St. Joseph's Children's and Maternity Hospital. (60)

From the time of Mother Mary Francis in 1889 to the present, St. Joseph's has provided loving care for infants, unwed mothers, orphans, and neurologically impaired children and young adults. In Mother Kathleen's time, fifty-five years after the initial construction of St. Joseph's, major renovation was the order of the day. Beginning in 1956, aided by a grant of $106,800 from the Ford Foundation, $231,000 in bequests and gifts from donors, and a loan of $140,000 from the Scranton Diocese, a three-year project of repairs and renovations was carried out.

The kitchen, the laundry, and areas occupied by the children were completed in 1959. (61)

Administrators of this facility since the 1950s have included Sisters Christine Clark, Naomi McCloskey, Maria Dolora Legnard, Marian Denise Walsh, Vincentia Dorsey, and Therese O'Rourke. Numerous IHMs have served on the staff over the years as full-time or summer-time assistants. In 2004, the IHM staff members include Sisters Mary Kay Faliskie, St. Francis Lyons, Ann Walsh, Kathleen M. Kelly, and Jean Toolan.

Additional property and buildings would be added over the years to the original St. Joseph's Children's and Maternity Hospital, but the dedication of the sisters to the care of the children and young adults remains its hallmark.

Old Motherhouse and Marywood Seminary, Scranton, Pennsylvania

The year 1957 was one of repairs and renovations in the old motherhouse and Marywood Seminary building. The fifty-five year-old building was showing its age. The council approved roof repairs in the amount of $4,796 on May 17, 1957, having been previously approved by Bishop Hannan on April 26, 1957. (62)

Sisters who as postulants had the task of carrying huge containers of water for dishwashing in three refectories three times a day would be happy for the postulants of 1958 that as of December 1957 cabinets and sinks were finally installed, at least in the "professed" refectory! Sisters who resided in the "old motherhouse" were well aware of the electrical and plumbing projects, which were an on-going necessity in this aging building. Sister Josephine Brennan used to say jokingly that at the third floor bathroom sinks one could wash one's face and feet at the same time!

Marywood College Expansion 1960–1963, Scranton, Pennsylvania

In Mother Kathleen's report to the General Chapter of 1961, a detailed account of the growth
of Marywood College was given. From a student enrollment of thirty-four local women in 1915, the college had grown to 1,276 students from twenty-one states and seven foreign countries in 1961. The faculty numbered ninety-nine, of whom forty-nine were IHM Sisters. (63)

With this growth in mind it was easy to understand why the council on July 7, 1960 approved the expenditure of $25,000 for the construction of a mezzanine floor in the library. This addition nearly doubled the book and seating capacity of the college library. (64)

On December 26, 1961, the council received a report from Sister St. Mary Orr, president of Marywood College, on the expansion needs of the college. (65) With enrollment increasing by one hundred students each year, existing residence halls were overcrowded, and nearly two hundred students were residing in off-campus housing. The need for a new student residence, additional dining space, and a student activity center was obvious. Mother Kathleen and the council gave approval for plans to proceed. A federal government loan of $2,000,000 would be procured, and the Congregation would be obliged to provide $240,000 toward the construction costs. (66) Mother Kathleen's keen interest in the construction of these buildings was apparent, but when they were completed in 1963, it would be a new superior general, Mother Beata, and the council who gave the names of Madonna Hall, Nazareth Hall, and Emmanuel Hall to the new residence hall, student center, and chaplain's residence, respectively. (67)

New Missions: 1958–1960

Just as today, in Mother Kathleen's time there were so many requests for the services of our sisters that even with some 1100 sisters to draw from, affirmative responses to requests were few. Mother Kathleen thus hoped to support existing missions, replacing sisters who were ill or no longer able to teach. Therefore, only the following missions were opened during Mother Kathleen's seven years as superior general:

1958 Our Lady of Lourdes, Tobyhanna, Pennsylvania (discussed previously)
1959 Christ the King Elementary School, Dunmore, Pennsylvania
1959 St. John the Baptist Elementary School, Pittsburgh, Pennsylvania
1960 St. Anthony Elementary School, Portland, Oregon
1961 St. John the Evangelist Elementary School, Clinton, Maryland
1961 Pocono Central Catholic Missions, Cresco, Pennsylvania

Christ the King Elementary School, Dunmore, Pennsylvania

Reverend Michael J. Quinn, pastor of Christ the King Parish in Dunmore, Pennsylvania wrote to Mother Kathleen on December 17, 1957, requesting sisters for the school he hoped to open the following year. (68) On May 9, 1958, Mother Kathleen responded promising two sisters for September 1959. (69) This promise was kept and Sisters Muriel Whalen and Michael Marie Hartman opened the new school in the auditorium of Christ the King Church on September 9, 1959. There were sixty-six pupils in three grades. Sister Muriel served as principal and taught grades two and three; Sister Michael Marie taught grade one. The sisters resided at Marywood and commuted daily.

The pastor had purchased a four-room public schoolhouse on Monroe Avenue in Scranton, a short distance from Christ the King Church, but renovations were not completed until December 6, 1959. On this date the new school was blessed by Monsignor John J. Vaughan, pastor, St. Paul Parish in Scranton, joined by Father Quinn, pastor of Christ the King and the assistant pastor, Reverend Thomas Carlin. On December 7, 1959, the students reported to the new Christ the King School. (70)

In addition to their regular teaching, the work of the sisters in preparing pupils for reception of the sacraments was evident. Only two months after the sisters' arrival, on November 8, 1959, Bishop Jerome Hannan confirmed 108 children from the parish, many attending public schools, as well as Christ the King students. By May 1960 there were fifty-three children in the First Communion class.

Each year saw additional students enrolling at Christ the King School. In 1960-1961 there were ninety-eight pupils and a third sister, Sister Joan Marie MacDonald was added as first grade teacher. Sisters Michael Marie and Muriel each moved up a grade.

The fifth grade was added in 1961—1962 with Sister Muriel moving up with a double class once again. There continued to be only three sisters as the total faculty with Sister Michael Marie being replaced by Sister Marcelline (Ann) Seeley in grades two and three. The first lay teacher, Mrs. Elizabeth Regan, was hired temporarily in mid-October when Sister Joan Marie became seriously ill. By February 12, Sister Bernard Marie Fee joined the faculty and replaced Mrs. Regan. (71)

In 1962–1963 enrollment reached 149 pupils in six grades. Four sisters were assigned: Sister Marcelline Seeley, grade one; Sister Doreen Willis, grades two and three; Sister Ethelreda McNamara, grade four; and Sister Muriel Whalen, principal and grades five and six. The four classrooms in the school were fully utilized. (72) Faculty changes again occurred in 1963–1964 with Sister Teresa Mary Gilhool assigned to grades one and two; Sister Ethelreda, grade three; Sister Angelica LeStrange, grades four and five; and Sister Muriel, grades six and seven. The enrollment had reached 172 students. (73)

From 1964–1965 through 1967–1968, Sister Norma (Rosemary) Casey served as principal and eighth grade teacher. Sisters Joseph Mary Minogue, Flora Long, Angelica LeStrange, and Karen Marie O'Neill comprised the faculty. (74)

In the final year of Christ the King School, 1968–1969, Sister Marie Helene Parks was appointed principal. Mother Beata's decision to withdraw the sisters was based on declining enrollments, proximity of other Catholic schools, and staff difficulties under double-grade teaching conditions. The ten years of IHM presence at Christ the King had been fruitful in developing the spiritual and educational life of the students and the entire parish.

St. John the Baptist Elementary School, Pittsburgh, Pennsylvania

In the seven-year period from 1955-1962 when only three schools and one catechetical center were opened by Mother Kathleen, it was a tribute to the pastor, Reverend Joseph A. Raynak, and to the people of St. John the Baptist Parish that their request for sisters received a positive response. Receiving the news on January 12, 1959, Father Raynak wrote to Mother Kathleen that very day:

> Today I received the very good news that you have consented to staff our new school. I am immensely pleased because now we are assured that the school will open in September and because I have heard so many fine things about the Sisters of the Immaculate Heart of Mary. (75)

Father Raynak knew just how to get things done for the coming of the sisters. There was a large home on the parish grounds, which would be remodeled by the men of the parish to serve as a beautiful convent capable of housing five sisters. Father Raynak contacted Sister Edwin Ott, superior at St. Rosalia's Convent, Pittsburgh to advise him on the convent furnishings.

On August 19, 1959 the sisters assigned to this new mission arrived at the Pittsburgh Airport where Father Raynak welcomed them and drove them to their new home. Sisters Gabrielle Driscoll, superior and principal; Martina Williams, Sharon Brady, and Mary Daniel Griffin were to initiate a history of service in which the IHM Sisters would be involved, in changing roles, to the day of this writing in 2001.

Upon arrival, the sisters were amazed at the work that the parishioners had done. "The rooms were beautifully arranged and furnished. Everything was in perfect order," according to the annals. (76) Everything outside was as perfect as inside, with spacious well-kept grounds dotted with flowering trees and bushes. Just across the lawn the school was conveniently located.

St. John the Baptist Parish had built its school with an eye to the future. While only four grades would open in September 1959, the school had two floors and eleven large classrooms. In addition, there was a large multi-purpose room to be used as a cafeteria and auditorium.

The sisters had their work cut out for them since they had less than two weeks to prepare for the dedication of the school and convent. Open house was to be held on September 2, 1959, and the opening of the new school on September 3.

Bishop John J. Wright of the Pittsburgh Diocese officiated at the blessing and dedication ceremonies. The women of the parish prepared and served dinner for more than two hundred guests. After the ceremonies and dinner, open house continued until 6:00 p.m.

It must have been a weary group of sisters who welcomed 400 students in grades one through four on September 3, 1959. The school opened with a double track of each of the four grades. Sisters Sharon Brady and Mary Daniel (Carole) Griffin taught the two first grades: Sister Martina Williams and Mrs. Theresa Lobert, second grades; Mrs. Gloria Griffin and Miss Faye Steele, third grades; Sister Gabrielle Driscoll served as principal and taught one of the fourth grades. (77)

In the space of five short months the excellence of the education being offered at St. John the Baptist School was recognized after Monsignor John McDowell, superintendent of Catholic Schools for the Pittsburgh Diocese, visited the school and wrote this evaluation:

> Your teaching staff is good and they are following the diocesan program with good care and success. I have nothing but the highest words of praise for your staff and school program. (78)

The pastor, Father Raynak, also expressed his appreciation and support of the sisters' first year in getting the new school off to a good start. On August 6, 1960, he wrote to Mother Kathleen:

> It might please you to know that all of us were glad to have the new school and to have it staffed by the Sisters of the IHM. Personally, I was very pleased with the work of Mother Gabrielle, Sister Martina, Sister Sharon, and Sister Mary Daniel. The world puts so much stock in the price tag, yet there are some things that you can't evaluate, such as the work of your Sisters here at St. John's. Only the recording angel in heaven can mark the true value. (79)

But the sisters were to have only this one year with their dedicated and generous pastor, Father Raynak. He suffered a severe heart attack and died on August 31, 1960. The first anniversary of the dedication of the school on September 3 became the occasion for Bishop Wright's return to officiate at Father Raynak's funeral. It was a very sad chapter in the history of St. John the Baptist Parish. By November 7, 1960, the new pastor, Monsignor Joseph Findlan, had assumed his new duties. (80).

The story of St. John the Baptist School is one of continued growth in faculty, in student enrollment, and in children prepared for the sacraments of Holy Eucharist and Confirmation. In 1962 six classrooms and a faculty room were added to the school. By 1963 there were eight sisters and six lay teachers on the faculty. A sizable extension was constructed to the convent, enlarging its housing capacity to ten sisters and a guest room. (81)

Over the years from 1959–1997 eleven sisters led the school as principal. These included Sisters Gabrielle Driscoll, Timothy Smyth, Raymond Rafferty, Mary Mark Lowery, Maria Regina Loures, Mary Bride O'Malley, Mary Feldcamp, Alice Marie McCormick, Eleanor Kalafut, Joanne Madden and Kieran Williams. Sister Alice Marie and Sister Joanne each carried this role for seven years, the latter presiding over the decline from six IHMs on the faculty in 1990 to two by 1995-1996. (82) St. John the Baptist School had felt the serious impact of the shortage of religious vocations and the aging of the IHM Congregation and sisters were no longer available for the school. However , until 2003, two sisters still serve this vibrant parish–Sister Dorothy Lancor as minister to the sick and bereaved; and Sister Jane Meehan as minister to the homebound. Their ministries would end in 2004.

Saint Anthony Elementary School, Portland, Oregon

The sequence of events, which led to the opening of a new mission in St. Anthony Parish in Portland, Oregon, begins at St. Lawrence Parish in Portland. Opened in 1903 by Mother Cyril Conway, old St. Lawrence was served by the IHM Sisters for fifty-seven years before the 1960 Urban Renewal Project of the City of Portland took over miles of land and buildings extending from the waterfront of the Williamette River to Third Avenue, where the convent, school, church, and rectory stood.

The annals of St. Lawrence Convent for 1957-1958 mention the fact that city planners projected that the entire plant would be demolished in about two years. (83) So it was no surprise to the sisters when, on April 28, 1960, Reverend Martin Thielen, superintendent of Catholic Schools for the Portland Archdiocese, came to the convent to discuss a new location for the community. Residing at St. Lawrence at the time were four sisters teaching in St. Lawrence School: Sisters Ignatius Browne, Gertrudis Porter, Bernita McDonough, and Mary Mark Carnes. In addition, there were two sisters teaching at Central Catholic High School, namely Sisters Immaculata Norton and Charisse Hayes.

Father Thielen's proposal was that the IHM Sisters would eventually be located in Harmony, Oregon at Christ the King Parish that was part of a larger nearby Milwaukie, Oregon parish. There was, however, to be an intermediate step when the sisters would serve at St. Anthony's School in Portland, which was on the brink of closing because of financial problems. With this plan in mind, Father Thielen made the trip to Scranton and obtained Mother Kathleen's approval for the relocation of the sisters. (84)

Reverend James Carroll, administrator of St. Anthony Parish, was delighted at the prospect of having four IHM Sisters for the school and two additional for Central Catholic High School residing in his parish. But his almost impossible task was to find suitable lodging for six sisters. His first thought was to turn the rectory into a convent but the projected cost was exorbitant. It was Sister Ignatius who asked, "Why don't you start from scratch and build a convent? If you have to spend thousands of dollars, you will at least have something permanent in the end." Two days later, Father Carroll announced that he had received permission from Archbishop Edward Howard to build a convent! Ground was broken on August 22, 1960. (85)

Of course, the convent would not be completed for the opening of school in September, ten days later. Because of this the sisters continued to reside for the next three months at St. Lawrence Convent, commuting daily the short distance of six miles to St. Anthony's. Pupils from St. Lawrence School, now closed, traveled by bus augmenting the classes at St. Anthony's.

Back at St. Lawrence Parish, a series of events had begun. On October 11, 1960, the interior furnishings of St. Lawrence Church and School were auctioned off. Demolition crews from the city of Portland razed both the church and school on October 31. During the following month the sisters prepared for departure. On November 28 and 29 professional packers moved their possessions to St. Anthony Convent. The sisters stayed at St. Henry Convent in Gresham until December 5, 1960 when the new convent in St. Anthony Parish was in complete readiness. In Gresham they were right at home with five other IHM Sisters: Sisters Therese Culhane, Clement Shermanson, Paracleta Gallagher, Agnes McHale, and Sarita Gesler.

It is always difficult to leave long-established missions, and while the old convent was about to fall down on its own, many sisters could recall hours of scrubbing, painting, and wallpapering to keep it up over the years. This might explain why their joy in moving was tempered by their memories as was recorded in the 1959-1960 annals:

> We do indeed feel sad to leave the old Parish of St. Lawrence where our sisters have labored so zealously for the past fifty-seven years. Saintly women have labored hard and long here at St. Lawrence. They have left a beautiful religious spirit and an enviable scholastic record. Many of the city's leading Catholic men and women in the professions and in all walks of life has been graduated from St. Lawrence School. The traditions and

> scholastic records set by our predecessors have been faithfully carried on even to the present day–one third of this year's graduating class (the last to leave St. Lawrence's) received over ninety percentile ratings enabling them to be in the honors group of Portland's high schools. (86)

But life goes on and the sisters soon adjusted to their new convent and school in St. Anthony Parish. The new convent, including furnishings, had been built at a cost of $80,000–a major investment for working families of St. Anthony's. The original building had six bedrooms, community room, refectory, a beautiful chapel boasting an altar designed and built by Reverend Glen Schlatter, chaplain at Marian Home, Sublimity, Oregon; a kitchen of birch and stainless steel with built-in appliances, laundry, work room and storage area, and a spacious patio. (87)

The six migrant sisters from tumbledown St. Lawrence were overwhelmed by the beauty and simplicity of their new convent home. As Sister Immaculata Norton commented recently, "It was as if someone very poor had married a rich man and suddenly had everything heaped upon her." (88) The sisters had nothing but praise for their pastor, Father Carroll, who somehow found a way to provide whatever was needed, even delivering a new station wagon to their door a few days after their arrival. The parishioners' generosity also knew no bounds as they filled the pantry shelves with staples and the freezer with meat, poultry and fish. The IHM Sisters from Gresham, too, shared their donated fruits and vegetables with the new St. Anthony's mission. There was a strong community bond between the two groups of sisters.

The joy of the sisters was complete when on December 8, 1960, three days after their arrival, Father Carroll placed the Blessed Sacrament in the tabernacle in their convent chapel. The Feast of the Immaculate Conception was celebrated with Exposition and Benediction.

Archbishop Howard blessed the convent on February 16, 1961. IHM hospitality at its best was observed as the sisters prepared and served dinner for the archbishop and ten priests who had accompanied him. Open house for the sisters of all communities serving in the area was held on May 20, 1961. (89)

Father Carroll wasted no time in obtaining assurances that the Sisters of IHM would be staying at St. Anthony's beyond the two-year "stopover" plan, which would have taken them to Harmony, Oregon. Prior to the blessing of the convent, he had visited the archbishop on February 6, 1961, and brought back news that there was a "possibility" of the sisters remaining. Covering all bases, however, he made a trip East in April 1961 to confirm the "possibility" with Mother Kathleen and the council. According to the annals, he "was very much impressed with Reverend Mother Kathleen and her Council and was happy to tell us that he was almost sure we were staying at St. Anthony's Parish." (90)

In 1961-1962 the little St. Anthony community had two personnel changes. Sister Darius (Barbara) D'Auria replaced Sister Bernita McDonough, and Sister Eamon O'Neill replaced Sister Immaculata Norton at Central Catholic High School. Sister Bernita's new mission was Immaculate Conception School in Scranton, Pennsylvania where she served as principal and superior. Sister Immaculata was to begin a long, outstanding career at Marywood College, Scranton. (91)

Archbishop Howard, now over eighty years of age, continued his interest in St. Anthony's coming with five priests to bless the newly landscaped grounds in August 1961 and enjoying a home-cooked dinner at the convent. Both he and Father Carroll were generous in their praise of the work of the sisters. Reports from the supervisor of schools for the Archdiocese of Portland and from Sister Felicitas Ryan, IHM, school supervisor, reflected the positive influence and professionalism of the school and its faculty.

In 1961-1962 annals speak to the extreme of emotions experienced by the sisters throughout the Congregation, but especially at St. Anthony's, more than three thousand miles from the motherhouse in Scranton. In late June 1961, there was elation and gratitude expressed over the reelection of Mother Kathleen as superior general for a second term of six years. Seven months later, in January 1962, the death of Mother Kathleen brought shock and deep sorrow to the sisters. (92)

There would be many changes over the years ahead including the resignation of Archbishop Howard in 1966. In the same year came the deaths of Father Carroll, the pastor, and Sister Ignatius Browne, former superior, who had been changed in August 1965 to Baltimore, Maryland. (93)

St. John the Evangelist Elementary School, Clinton, Maryland

In coming to St. John the Evangelist Parish, Clinton, Maryland, the IHM Sisters were aware of the historic aura pervading the area. Originally part of the Baltimore Archdiocese, established in 1789 by Pope Pius VI as the first See in the United States, its jurisdiction included all the territory east of the Mississippi River. Its first bishop, elected by the priests was John Carroll, SJ, cousin of the historic signer of the Declaration of Independence, Charles Carroll of Carrollton, Maryland. (94)

The strong Catholic faith planted by Cecil Calvert, second baron of Baltimore, in 1634, would flourish and the new Baltimore colony would become the first settlement in the New World guaranteeing religious freedom for all faiths. (95)

From this large Baltimore Archdiocese many new Sees would be carved, including the Archdiocese of Washington, DC. Pope Pius XII established this Archdiocese in 1939 and appointed Archbishop Michael J. Curley, DD, as first resident archbishop. He was succeeded by Archbishop Patrick O'Boyle in 1948. The new Archdiocese of Washington, DC, included the city of Washington, DC, and five adjacent counties—Calvert, Charles, Montgomery, St. Mary's and Prince George's. It is in Prince George's County that St. John the Evangelist Parish, Clinton, Maryland, is located. (96)

Founded in 1875 by Reverend John J. Conway of Piscataway, St. John the Evangelist Parish was a vibrant part of a farming community whose dream was one day to provide a Catholic school for their children. This dream became a reality in 1961 after 85 years of waiting. Reverend Francis X. Walsh, as parish administrator during the illness of the pastor of twenty years, Monsignor Casimir Losinski, was responsible for bringing the long-awaited dream into being. Letters from Archbishop Patrick O'Boyle and from Father Walsh, dated in September and December 1960, expressed their appreciation to Mother M. Kathleen Hart, superior general, for agreeing to send IHM Sisters to staff the planned school. This decision of Mother Kathleen and the council was announced to the IHM General Chapter delegates on June 25, 1961. (97)

At this time, St. John the Evangelist parish included some 600 families, with about 500 school-aged children, many of whom commuted into Washington, DC, to attend Catholic schools; and many others attended public schools in the area. Some 400 children were in attendance at weekly catechetical instructions held in the church. Plans for the new school developed as a five-acre plot of land adjacent to the church grounds was donated by Mr. and Mrs. B. K. Miller, parishioners. The school was to be a one-story rambler type, having eight classrooms, library, faculty room, health room, and principal's office, but would await full utilization, starting with grades one through four.

So it was that Sister Laurentia Mayan, Sister Maron (Mary) Rassley and Sister Paracleta (Irene) Gallagher arrived on August 21, 1961, at St. Mary's Convent, Upper Marlboro, Maryland, to reside with other IHMs while construction of the new convent and school at Clinton was nearing completion. Two weeks would pass before the sisters would spend their first night on September 6 in the new convent. It was many months later before the signs of workmen and construction would be gone both from the convent and the school. But the final outstanding result was worth the wait. Nothing deterred the opening of school on September 7 with 220 students enrolled in four grades. The first faculty included: Sister Paracleta (Irene) Gallagher, grade one; Sister Maron (Mary) Rassley, grade two; Mrs. John Walton, grade three; Sister Laurentia Mayan, grade four, principal and superior. (98)

From the beginning of St. John's School, the gratitude of the pastor and parishioners was extraordinary. On October 1, the parish conducted a shower for the sisters, overwhelming them with gifts for the convent—dishes, television set, electric polisher, vacuum cleaner, and many other useful items. Meanwhile the pastor, Father Walsh, had installed a new refrigerator in the kitchen, redwood sliding doors between the refectory and community room, a 2000-pound marble altar in the chapel and drapes for the entire first floor of the convent. Throughout the year parishioners would donate generously with gifts ranging from a new station wagon to catered dinners, and a deep freezer filled with food.

By November 11, a "semi-readiness" state was achieved for the dedication of the convent and school. Patrick Cardinal O'Boyle, 55 priests and 56 sisters were present at the luncheon that followed. Sister Beata Wertz, assistant to Mother Kathleen Hart, and Sister Brendan O'Brien were present from Marywood. (99)

Many usual and unusual first-time events are recorded in the 1961 annals: the first Mass in the convent on November 11; the first Exposition and Benediction of the Blessed Sacrament on December 8; the delivery of a seven-foot Christmas tree on December 23; blessing of the Stations of the Cross and altar stone in the chapel on December 29; First Holy Communion for 113 children on April 15; May Crowning procession of some 500 children on May 6; and Confirmation of 212 pupils and 13 adults on May 12 were celebrated. (100) These latter three events would be annual recurrences, but held special meaning for the IHMs and the parishioners in this first year.

The six years of Sister Laurentia's term as principal and superior of St. John the Evangelist School were expansionist years. The original three IHMs were augmented each year, bringing the number of sisters to seven by 1966-1967. Two lay teachers were also on the faculty.

Many changes occurred in 1966-1967 affecting both the school and the parish. The much loved pastor, Reverend Francis X. Walsh, was transferred to Nativity Church, Washington, DC. His contributions to the parish in establishing a new school and convent, and the construction of a new rectory would not be forgotten. Reverend John Lubey replaced him. In this year also Sister Laurentia's departure as principal and superior brought Sister Rosemaron Rynn to these assignments in Clinton. (101)

Again in 1972-1973, both the pastor, Reverend John Lubey, and the principal, Sister Rosemaron Rynn, were transferred. Reverend Alphonsus Smith, pastor of Newtown, Maryland, exchanged places with Father Lubey. Sister Lisbeth Hartnett replaced Sister Rosemaron. (102)

It was not until 1974-1975 that the offices of principal and superior of St. John the Evangelist were separated. In that year, Sister Marthine Culhane was appointed superior and seventh grade teacher, and Sister Lisbeth Hartnett was assigned as a non-teaching principal. Having a so-called "free" principal was a necessity in a school of over 400 pupils, with individual class sizes averaging fifty pupils. At this point there were actually eight IHMs at St. John the Evangelist Convent, six of whom were full-time faculty members. Sister Thomas Maria Anglin, a golden jubilarian, served part-time as a tutorial instructor, and Sister Wendan McCaffery taught private music pupils. Classes were very large, yet a long waiting list left many parish children still seeking admission. In addition to their regular classroom teaching, the sisters conducted catechetical classes after school and on the weekends. Sisters Marthine, Barbara Nogiewich and Gregory Marie Schwalenberg also visited the Americana Nursing Home weekly.

Archbishop William Baum, later Cardinal, had succeeded Patrick Cardinal O'Boyle in 1973. On September 12, 1974, he consecrated as bishops, Monsignor Thomas W. Lyons, former superintendent of schools in the Washington, DC, Archdiocese, and Reverend Eugene A. Marino, the first black bishop for the Archdiocese. The IHMs participated in this event.

After a short term as pastor, Reverend Alphonsus Smith was transferred. The sisters prepared a home-cooked dinner on October 29, 1974, to express their gratitude to him for his many kindnesses. Reverend Thomas Schaefer was assigned as pastor and arrived on November 6, 1974.

The Feast of Pentecost brought Archbishop Baum and all the former pastors of St. John the Evangelist Parish to celebrate the centenary of the parish in first-class style. These and other ecumenical celebrations enriched the lives of the sisters, as did their many involvements in IHM Congregation activities. With many spiritual and cultural resources available to them in the Washington, DC, area, the sisters also enjoyed visits to retreat centers, the National Shrine of the Immaculate Conception, national landmarks, the Smithsonian Institute, the Air and Space Center, and the Kennedy Center for the Performing Arts. (103) Close relationships existed between the Clinton IHMs and all other convents in the Maryland and Washington, DC, areas that brought the IHMs together often.

St. John's School continued to flourish under the capable and dedicated IHM principals—Sister Ann Marie Lynott followed Sister Lisbeth from 1979-1984 and Sister Florence Ann Marino from 1984-1995.

In 1986, the twenty-fifth anniversary of the founding of St. John's School, a massive addition to the initial building was dedicated. The new Educational Center project was approved by Archbishop James Hickey at a cost of $960,544, including architect's fees. Having been in the planning for several years, by February 19, 1984, the parishioners had already pledged over $500,000 toward the construction. Groundbreaking was held on June 2, 1985, and the building opened in September 1986. The building was highly functional, including a new library, computer center, science room, catechetical offices, study and meeting rooms and lavatories. To all of this, a brand new pastor, Reverend Thomas P. Kelley, was assigned. (104)

St. John the Evangelist School continued to register about 300 pupils in eight grades and a kindergarten, but by the 1991-1992 school year there were only three IHMs serving in the school in addition to the principal, Sister Florence Ann Marino. Sister Ann Parker, principal at Star of the Sea School in Indian Head, Maryland, and only IHM in that school, resided with the sisters at St. John's until her resignation from Star of the Sea in 1992.

In 1994-1995 only three IHMs served in the school: the principal, Sister Florence Ann Marino, Sister Kathleen Newett, office assistant, and Sister Alexius Fitzgerald, librarian. Three other ministries were represented among the sisters at St. John Convent: Sister Eileen Clinton, director of sacramental programs, St. Matthias Parish, Lanham, Maryland; Sister Nancy Elder, director of curriculum, Archdiocese of Washington, DC; and Sister Ann Parker, director of religious education, St. Anthony Parish, North Beach, Maryland. The description of the activities of these sisters as a community reveals their grasp of and commitment to diversity in their prayer life, ministry, and every day interactions with one another. (105)

This was to be the last year at St. John's for Sister Florence Ann Marino, who had served as principal for eleven years, from 1984-1995. An article by Cinnamon Burnim in *The Catholic Standard* in the spring of 1995 quotes Sister Florence Ann about her love for St. John's and how difficult it will be to leave. The article also speaks of her accomplishments.

> Under the leadership of Sister Florence Ann, St. John's School has grown and flourished. Some of the accomplishments are the addition of a new school wing and kindergarten classes, the earning of

Middle States Accreditation, making major advancements in the technology program and the continued development of a strong curriculum. (106)

For her part, Sister Florence Ann would undoubtedly shrug off the praise and give credit to the pastor, Father Pollard, and to the dedicated faculty members.

August 1995 found four of the IHM community off to Monroe, Michigan, to celebrate the Sesquicentennial of the IHM Congregation's founding. Their travelogue account of the trip is a piece of history in itself, revealing their pride in the IHM Congregation and the impression made by the people and places they experienced. Since Sister Florence Ann Marino was to take up a new ministry in St. Petersburg, Florida, the travelers made their way home through eleven states and totaled 3,039 miles before returning to Clinton, Maryland, ten days later. (107)

Celebration of the IHM Sesquicentennial continued with festivities in Baltimore on September 9, 1995. The new principal at St. John the Evangelist, Sister Jean Louise Bachetti, added to the local celebration by presenting the IHM story to the students and teachers at St. John's with students assuming the roles of Mother Theresa and Father Gillet.

The little community was saddened, yet rejoiced with Sister Nancy Elder who was to move to Palm Coast, Florida, in August 1995. Her mission was to establish a new convent in St. Elizabeth Ann Seton Parish in preparation for the opening of a new school in the fall of 1997. In the interim she would serve as spiritual director of education. (108)

The fall of 1996-1997 brought additional changes to St. John's community. Sister Eileen Clinton began a new position in the Diocesan Catholic Schools Office as curriculum director and coordinator of the Southern Maryland schools. She continued to reside at St. John's, but was sorely missed in the school. Sister Mary Rita Smith was added to the local community on December 7, 1996, after securing a position as pastoral associate for nearby Andrews Air Force Base. This meant that six IHMs were in residence at St. John's, with three in the school—Sister Jean Louise Bachetti as principal, Sister Alexius Fitzgerald, librarian, and Sister Kathleen Newett, office assistant. There were 263 students enrolled in the school, thirty of whom would graduate on June 6, 1997. Seventeen of these received the Presidential Award for Academic Excellence. (109)

As described in the 1998-1999 annals, this local community had an extraordinary understanding of community life. Their community life statement includes such statements as: "Bringing home the experience of our ministries, we show interest and concern for each sister's ministry . .

. " "In opening our home to our co-workers we share our charism of joy." "As we make a home for ourselves, we respect each other's needs and enjoy each other's company."

In line with these statements, various groups shared the use of the convent chapel, both laity and religious of other congregations. The convent was often used for meetings of faculty groups, chaplains of various religious denominations, air force personnel, and other friends. (110)

In 1999-2000 there were only five IHMs at St. John's Convent. As Sister Ann Parker was needed for family ministry, she continued her work at St. Anthony's Parish, North Beach, Maryland, but resided at home with her father. At this time also, Sister Eileen Clinton's father, living in Mountain Top, Pennsylvania, was very ill. Frequent trips were made by Sister Eileen until her father's death on December 24, 1999. By March 2000, possibly overtaxed by these emotional and physical strains, Sister Eileen decided to move from Clinton to Silver Spring so as to reduce her daily commutes to her work via the beltway. This decision left only four IHMs at St. John's Convent. (111)

The year 2000 would also be the year of Sister Alexius Fitzgerald's retirement after 52 years of teaching, including fifteen years as librarian and media center specialist at St. John's School. Her work was acknowledged by Robert J. Kealey, EdD., Executive Director of the National Catholic Education Association's department of elementary education. He wrote, in part, "You have been a jewel in Catholic education and one who has certainly made a difference in the lives of so many children." Recognition was also given by the Maryland House of Delegates, the Governor and the Senate of the State of Maryland. The pastor of St. John's, Reverend Thomas Pollard, gave a significant tribute to Sister Alexius also, saying, in part, "On behalf of all those lives she touched, I wish to thank Sister Alexius for the gift of her service to our parish and to our school, and assure her that we will hold her in our prayers and in our hearts." (112)

Honors were also given in this year 2000 to Sister Jean Louise Bachetti, first on May 4 from the Archdiocese of Washington, DC, for her efforts in procuring textbook funding for non-public schools of the State of Maryland; second on May 9, Sister was honored as Parish School Administrator of the Year by the Prince George's County Catholic Business Network. (113)

The biggest event of the year 2000, however, was the celebration on June 4 of the 125th Anniversary of the founding of St. John the Evangelist Parish. James Cardinal Hickey, spiritual leader of the Washington, DC, Archdiocese from 1980-2000, was present for the occasion, with Bishop David Foley, former pastor and Bishop of Birmingham, Alabama, assisting at the outdoor Mass at 1:00 p.m. An informal potluck picnic for families followed. Many of the thirty-eight IHM Sisters who had previously served at St. John's were also present. (114)

The school year 2000-2001 opened with only three IHMs in residence at St. John's, with Sister Jean Louise Bachetti continuing as principal and Sister Kathleen Newett as part-time receptionist at the school. Sister Mary Rita Smith's role as pastoral associate at Andrews Air Force Base also continued. The registration of 265 students from kindergarten through eighth grade maintained the more desirable class size in the school. While keeping St. John's School open was a high priority for the parish, it was no small financial fete to support nine lay faculty members, to keep the school's equipment and materials current, and the building itself in good repair. Father Thomas Pollard, pastor, had a huge financial challenge, and there were times, but for the generosity of volunteer individual parishioners, that the convent itself was in serious disrepair. (115)

The little community of IHMs at St. John's was augmented to four by Sister Mary Newett's arrival on August 13, 2001. Her new ministry was in pastoral care at the Greenspring Retirement Village in Springfield, Virginia. Her presence was also a great support to her natural sister, Sister Kathleen Newett.

The year 2001-2002 was to be one of shocking natural and man-made disasters. The entire nation was put into a state of fear by the terrorist attacks of September 11, 2001 which leveled the Twin Towers in New York City, destroyed parts of the nearby Pentagon and killed passengers aboard all four destructive planes, the fourth of which went down in Somerset, Pennsylvania. The sisters, like most Americans, offered their prayers and assistance to the many friends and relatives who were affected both remotely and proximately from these attacks.

In October, having not yet recovered from the September fright, the Washington Metro Area experienced an anthrax attack through the US mail system. Members of Congress and postal workers seemed to be the prime targets, however, many others suffered serious symptoms from the anthrax and five people died, including one parishioner from St. John's. (116)

On April 28, 2002, a severe tornado struck LaPlata, Maryland, where Sisters Helene Fee and Jane Duke were stationed at Archbishop Neale School. The convent was damaged, but the school was a complete loss and had to be torn down. Fortunately, the sisters were not injured and at the invitation of the IHMs in Clinton, made their way through storm and debris from LaPlata to Clinton. IHM hospitality reached out for a four-month period, not only to the sisters, but also to their cat, Tangles, who had been saved from the tornado. Accounts of the rebuilding of Archbishop Neale School and the spirit of the parishioners and sisters are recounted in the LaPlata annals. (117)

This would be the final year of Sister Jean Louise Bachetti's service as principal at St. John's School. On January 12, 2002, she informed the pastor, Father Pollard, that she would be spending the following year on sabbatical, studying spiritual direction and theology at Loyola College campus in Columbia, Maryland. A parish farewell was held on June 8, 2002, with a potluck dinner in the church hall. Much praise and appreciation was expressed to Sister Jean Louise for seven years of leadership as principal of St. John's and for her many activities in the archdiocese and parish. (118) Thus ended forty-one years of IHM principalships at St. John's.

But the school would go on, and on June 28, 2002, Sister Jean Louise turned over the keys of the school to its first lay principal, Mrs. Susan Scott. On August 2, Sister Jean Louise moved from St. John's Convent to an apartment on New Hampshire Avenue, Silver Spring, shared with Sister Angela Kim and Sister Annmarie Sanders. Once again, St. John's Convent had only three IHMs, with only Sister Kathleen Newett serving in the school. (119)

The parishioners of St. John's honored Sister Kathleen Newett on May 1, 2003, as she celebrated the fiftieth jubilee of her profession as an IHM. In the church bulletin, the pastor
Father Pollard wrote:

> This spring Sister Kathleen is celebrating the 50th anniversary of her religious profession. Sister Kathleen has spent 19 of those years at St. John's giving motherly love to others. Once a teacher, now Sister Kathleen works in the school office. Our whole parish community extends its gratitude and affection to Sister on this milestone in her life. (120)

The community and her family celebrated again on June 15 with dinner at a Japanese restaurant in Waldorf, Maryland. As of this writing in 2004, Sister Kathleen remains as the only IHM Sister serving at St. John's School, with Sisters Mary Newett and Mary Rita Smith in residence.

St. John the Evangelist School continues to thrive, with 240 students in kindergarten through eighth grades. It is staffed with fifteen full-time and three part-time faculty, and serves the students well with teacher aides, a school nurse, and custodian. (121) The dedicated parishioners have caught the spirit of the more than 540,000 Catholics in the

Archdiocese of Washington, now only 65 years old, yet enveloping 106 Catholic schools, educating more than 34,500 children. Leadership of this large and diverse segment of the Catholic Church is now in the hands of Theodore Cardinal McCarrick, consecrated on January 3, 2001 and made cardinal on February 21, 2001. (122)

Pocono Catholic Missions, Cresco, Pennsylvania

A study of the map of the Pocono Mountain region of Pennsylvania reveals that this part of the Scranton Diocese, southwest and southeast of the city of Scranton, is dotted with resort towns and rural villages. Names such as Mount Pocono, Canadensis, Pocono Pines, Pocono Summit, South Sterling, Blakeslee Corners, Tannersville, Promised Land, Brodheadsville, and Cresco are familiar to travelers today. Yet in 1909, St. Mary of the Mount in Mount Pocono was the only Catholic Church in the area, with missions to many of the above towns. St. Ann's Parish in Canadensis was formed in 1913; Our Lady of the Lake, Pocono Pines in 1920; St. Joan of Arc, Pocono Summit in 1921 and St. Mary Magdalen, South Sterling in 1922. Reverend Patrick J. Boland, first pastor at Mount Pocono said the first Mass at each of these newly founded parishes. Christ the King Parish, Blakeslee Corner was founded in 1938; Our Lady of Victory, Tannersville, 1948; Our Lady of Fatima, Promised Land, 1951; and Our Lady Queen of Peace, Brodheadsville, 1954. (123)

With all these Catholic communities established, it was a natural sequence that planning for a Catholic school would follow. Right Reverend Monsignor Connell A. McHugh, pastor of St. Mary of the Mount Church since 1926, initiated the dialogue with Mother M. Kathleen Hart, IHM, in 1958, inviting her and members of the IHM Council to visit the proposed site of a new elementary/secondary school in Cresco, three miles southeast of Mt. Pocono. After her visit, Mother Kathleen wrote to Monsignor McHugh on September 30, 1958, praising his foresight and expressing appreciation for the tour they had received. (124) It is obvious from her enthusiasm that she would find a way to send IHM Sisters to staff this new school.

A year later on September 27, 1959, construction began on the 40-acre site selected by Monsignor McHugh. The convent plans called for twenty private rooms, chapel, two music instruction rooms, two parlors, community room, dining room, kitchen, recreational lounge and library. The school building was designed to accommodate both elementary and secondary grades by placing the facilities to be shared in the center. These included the chapel, library, administrative area, principal's office, guidance department, priests' office, and medical-dental suite.

The elementary school consisted of ten classrooms, book storage, and lavatories. The primary classes were especially designed with their own entrances, exits, and lavatories.

The high school consisted of four homerooms, an elevated lecture room, science, business, home economics, and art departments. There were separate and fully equipped laboratories for each of the sciences, as well as a photography laboratory with processing equipment. There was a complete television system with projection studio and outlets in every room to utilize closed and regular circuit television instruction. The auditorium/gymnasium, cafeteria, kitchen, faculty dining room, music instruction area, athletic department, snack bar, and shower-locker rooms were separated from the classroom section by a concourse approach. (125)

One can image the stir and curiosity aroused by the construction of this enormous 1.5 million dollar project in the serene Pocono countryside. The laying of the cornerstone on May 29, 1960, brought out representatives from the Diocese of Scranton, from the public schools of the area, and many IHM Sisters.

Meanwhile, Monsignor McHugh was making certain that upon completion of the buildings, there would be students in every classroom and IHM Sisters to teach them. He was in frequent communication with the pastors of the six parishes from which he expected students. His letter to Mother Kathleen on April 22, 1961, spoke enthusiastically of the preregistration numbers for the nine grades that would open in September. Already in April, there were 366 registered for the nine grades representing St. Matthew's, Stroudsburg, St. Ann's, Tobyhanna, St. Bernadette's, Canadensis, Our Lady of Victory, Tannersville, St. Rita's, Gouldsboro, and, of course, the home parish of St. Mary of the Mount, Mt. Pocono. (126)

On August 26, 1961, eight IHM Sisters left Marywood to open the new convent adjacent to Pocono Catholic Mission School in Cresco, Pennsylvania. They included Sisters Annette Corcoran, principal and superior, Joseph Gabriel Welsh, Marthine Culhane, Louise Pellow, Immaculate Severino, St. Genevieve (Joanne) Pickard, Michael Marie Hartman, and Ancilla Maloney. The total newness and size of the entire plant brought many exclamations of excitement and joy from the sisters.

August 27, 1961, the day after arrival, dawned quickly and busily for the sisters as they anticipated the influx of visitors for the blessing of the convent, chapel and school oratory that included Mother Kathleen, Sister Beata, Sister Brendan, Sister St. Mary, members of the council; sisters from Stroudsburg and Tobyhanna; Mr. and Mrs. John Martens, donors of the convent chapel in memory of their daughter; and Honorable and Mrs.

Henry L. Ughetta, donor of the school oratory in memory of their son. Monsignor McHugh presided at these blessings. Reverend Harold Durkin, pastor of St. Matthew's, East Stroudsburg, addressed the visitors, and Benediction was offered by Reverend George Jordan, pastor of St. Ann's Tobyhanna. The first Mass offered in the convent chapel was held on August 28, 1961, by Monsignor McHugh. On August 29, he also offered the first Mass in the school oratory. (127)

Five days later, on September 3, 1961, the solemn dedication and blessing of the Pocono Catholic Missions School took place with Bishop Jerome D. Hannan officiating. An elaborate program, preceded by open house from noon to 3:30 p.m., gave two thousand visitors an outstanding opportunity to hear and see the meaningful support given to this new Catholic education endeavor. Participating in the program were Bishops Henry T. Klonowski, Assistant Bishop of Scranton and Patrick O'Boyle of the Archdiocese of Washington, DC; Bishops George L. Leech and Lawrence Schott of Harrisburg; and Monsignor William J. McDonald, PhD, Rector of the Catholic University of America. Letters of praise were read from John F. Kennedy, President of the United States and Governor David Lawrence of Pennsylvania. Mother Kathleen was unable to attend because of illness, but all the members of her council were present. A catered dinner followed the dedication program.

With this full week of whirlwind activity completed, it was probably providential that unfinished construction in the school building delayed the opening until September 18, 1961. But on that date, five parish school buses and many private cars delivered 402 pupils in nine grades to the new school. In addition to the eight IHM Sisters, the following personnel were on hand: Reverend Robert Galligan, school coordinator, Reverend John Walsh, teacher of religion in the elementary school, Reverend William Cusick, cafeteria director, Mr. Philip Walsh, coach and teacher of mathematics and history, Mrs. Jean Burke, fourth grade teacher, and Mrs. Mary Rush, secretary. The first school year was successfully begun.

A month later, on October 21, 1961, open house was held for all religious of the area. Some two hundred religious of various communities were given tours of the convent and school from 2:00 – 5:00 p.m. A buffet luncheon was served during the afternoon. Benediction of the Blessed Sacrament in the school oratory completed the day.

Living in the country had its advantages, such as beautiful scenery and grazing deer in the back yard, but transportation for an eight-person community to catechetical instructions at various sites, to congregation functions whether in Scranton, Stroudsburg, or elsewhere, proved to have its challenges. It was a happy community, therefore, when on November 18, 1961, the pastor, Monsignor Connell McHugh, presented the sisters with a new station wagon.

The sadness experienced by the entire IHM Congregation at Mother Kathleen's death on January 31, 1962, enveloped the Cresco community as well. Additional sorrows came with the death of Sharon Moran, an eighth grade student, in February, and of David Ortoski, a freshman, in June.

The close of the first year found the sisters well established in their new convent home and in their school ministry. Seeing the possibilities in the facilities in Cresco, the Congregation sought Monsignor McHugh's approval for utilization of the spacious convent and school as a summer school setting for the education of sisters. With his approval, sixteen sisters completing their bachelor's degrees spent from June 25 through August 3, 1962, at Cresco, studying English Literature under the instruction of Sister Bonaventure McCloskey, IHM. (128)

Thus began a summer tradition which over the years would see Sister Regina Barrett offering a refresher course for teachers in Language Arts; Sister Samuel McKeown teaching "Methods in Modern Math" for 7th and 8th grade teachers; Sister Mary Peter Doran, "New Math"; and classes in "Typing/Office Practice" with Sister Mary Andrew Earley.

Use of the Cresco facilities was not limited to summers as numerous groups sought the beauty and convenience of conducting events there. The Knights of Columbus, for example, held their picnic for the sisters of the Scranton area at this site in June 1963; the Diocesan Council of Catholic Women, a group of 700 women, spent a full day on April 11, 1964; Sister Clotilde Cullen, IHM, director of IHM Junior Professed Sisters brought forty young IHMs on Ascension Thursday, May 11, 1964; a custom developed of having a group of Marian Convent retired IHMs enjoy the fall foliage in the mountains and visit the Cresco convent for dinner; on October 20, 1978, it was the site of the superiors/principals institute for the IHM Congregation. All of these contacts, in addition to the many individual visitors, gave great visibility to the new Cresco convent and school, and undoubtedly added to the labors of the local community. (129)

By the fourth year of the school's existence, the enrollment had reached 567 pupils in grades 1-12. Accreditation by the Middle States Association of Schools and Colleges had been attained on May 5, 1965, and the first graduating class of twenty-four seniors received their diplomas. On June 12, 1965, the commencement Mass was held at St. Mary of the Mount Church, Mt. Pocono, with the assistant pastor, Reverend

Girard Mulherin celebrant. Monsignor Joseph Quinn, pastor, St. Ann's, Tobyhanna, gave the baccalaureate address. A tradition began as the sophomore class gave a breakfast to the seniors after the Mass.

The following day, June 13, 1965, was graduation day. Bishop Jerome D. Hannan gave out the diplomas, acknowledging each graduate individually. Parents, friends, and all the pastors of the parishes of the graduates were in attendance, as well as representatives from the public school system. The speaker for this occasion was Mr. James Norris, assistant director of Catholic Relief Services in Washington, DC.

A justifiable pride swelled in the hearts of the sisters as they witnessed the fruit of their labors in these graduates, and they were keenly aware of the significant role played by Monsignor Connell A. McHugh. They wrote:

> We looked forward with happy anticipation to this month and year when our first graduating class would receive their diplomas from Pocono Catholic Missions School—a monument to the vision and deep faith of our beloved pastor, Right Reverend C.A. McHugh, PS, VF. (130)

That the school was blessed with vibrancy and growth is evident in the fact that its graduates nearly doubled to forty-five in the very next year, 1965-1966.

Sister Annette Corcoran's term as principal and superior ended in June 1967. The school's size by this time warranted separate principals for the grade and high schools. Sister Laurentia Mayan was appointed coordinator of the elementary faculty of six IHMs and two lay teachers. Sister Mary Joan Kelleher, principal of the secondary school, was fortunate in having four IHMs as homeroom teaches who also were instructors in home economics, music, business subjects, languages and mathematics. (131)

In 1971, the beloved founder and pastor, Monsignor Connell A. McHugh died. Bishop McCormick renamed the elementary school "Monsignor McHugh Elementary School" in his memory. (132)

Sister Virginia Mary Schaefer became principal of the high school in September 1971, with the office of superior being held by Sister Marya Foley. Sister Laurentia Mayan continued as elementary principal.

By 1974-1975, the high point of nineteen IHM Sisters in residence in the Cresco convent was reached with fourteen of that number in the school. Sister Christella Duggan, education consultant for the congregation, Sister Mary Howard Krotzer, CCD coordinator for St. Ann's Parish, Tobyhanna, and Sister Brigida Strome, instructor of private music pupils, were in residence. The high school faculty's labors during this year to attain reaccreditation by the Middle States Association bore fruit in May 1976, when approval was again obtained. (133)

It is difficult to imagine the changes that would occur in the next twelve-year period leading to the closing of the high school and the presence of only four IHM Sisters in the elementary school and convent in 1988-1989. But changing demographics, changes in the economy of the region, and the competitive presence of Notre Dame Junior/Senior High School in nearby Stroudsburg, Pennsylvania, all had their impact.

On May 19, 1987, Reverend John Jordan, Scranton Diocesan Superintendent of Schools, announced to the parents of the Pocono Central Catholic High School students that the high school was no longer viable with its declining enrollment. Students were encouraged to transfer to Notre Dame High School or to other schools in the area. Pastors of feeder parishes were urged to expand the elementary school that remained strong. (134) Father Jordan met again on June 15, 1981, with the parents, but in light of data provided, closure of the school was a foregone conclusion. With a year's notice, the shock experienced by faculty, parents and students was gradually absorbed. The principal, Sister Rose de Fluri and four IHMs on the high school faculty would be assigned elsewhere; the librarian, Sister Angelisse Boyce, was transferred to Notre Dame, East Stroudsburg.

Thus Monsignor McHugh Elementary School became a K-8 school with 259 students in 1988. Four IHM Sisters remained, namely, Sisters Kathleen Kelly, principal; Leon McConnell, junior high; Raymond Mary McIntyre, intermediate; Rita Mary Naughton, fourth grade. Promise of a healthy enrollment future was seen in the double tracks needed for two kindergartens and two first grades. (135)

The following year, 1989, Sister Ann Marie Lynott became principal. There were three kindergartens, with grades one through three on double track. The total enrollment was 315. There were only three IHMs in the school.

The annals reflect the concerns these remaining sisters had over the unutilized space in the convent. So it was not surprising that on September 6, 1989, the sector superior, Sister Janet Jeffers, met with the sisters to discuss a proposal for future use of the convent as a spiritual renewal center for the congregation, in tandem with continuance of the elementary school ministry.

At this time the congregation administration was considering closing the existing retreat center at Verona, New Jersey, to make a more accessible site at Cresco. Throughout 1989-1990, discussions continued with the sisters and with the Pocono pastors regarding the terms of utilization of the convent for this additional purpose.

In February 1990, discussions were held by the sisters of the Verona community with the Cresco sisters. Sisters Patricia Tippen, Eleanor Mary Marconi, and Janet Jeffers from the IHM administration were present. As the annals report, "Much brainstorming occurred as the future of the Center began to take shape. What a magnificent experience of collaboration!" (136)

The convent was in need of much renovation, so at the urging of the IHM Congregation, agreements were reached with the pastors that before the Spiritual Renewal Center would be initiated a total refurbishing should take place, with the congregation and diocese sharing expenses. This being accomplished, a further long-term agreement was made which provided that the diocese be responsible for major problems, such as heating, plumbing, and roofing, and the IHM Congregation for the ongoing upkeep of the convent. There was no term limit for the agreement as ownership continues in the Diocese of Scranton, and utilization at the Bishop's discretion. (137)

By June 12, 1990, the furnishing and household appliances were moved from Verona, New Jersey, to Cresco. As it happened that date was also the busy day of the closing of the school year. Work on the convent continued into September, but the community of eight IHMs managed in spite of obstacles like green water, no laundry facilities, and other inconveniences. Summing up the situation, the annals state, "These prelude days were exciting, exhausting, and also evoking all the faith we could muster." (138)

The core group of sisters for the Spiritual Renewal Center included Sisters Beatrice Caulson, director, Mary Peter Doran, Catherine Ann Gilvary, and St. Mel Wright, local assembly coordinator. Faculty for Monsignor McHugh Elementary School included Sisters Ann Marie Lynott, principal; Ann Grayeski, junior high; Thomas Aquinas Kielceski, junior high; Raymond Mary McIntyre, intermediate.

School opened on schedule on September 7, 1990, and, as a good omen of things to come for the Spiritual Renewal Center, the first retreatant, Sister Aileen, CP, a Passionist Sister from the monastery in Clarks Summit, Pennsylvania, arrived. From that date on a steady flow of priests, religious and laity sought the serenity of this site for retreats, in directed, private, and group settings. Bible study was initiated for the laity on a weekly basis. The center received sister jubilarians, sisters in formation, those in prayer ministry in the congregation, and local assemblies of sisters seeking assistance in goal setting for their communities. (139)

The annals are replete with descriptions of the activities of both the school and spiritual renewal personnel. The members of the community participated together in such activities as the 125th anniversaries of Catholic education in the Scranton Diocese and of the Catholic Church of Monroe County. As always, the sisters were involved in parish activities and IHM Congregation meetings, in addition to their other ministry. There were catechetical instructions followed by First Communions and Confirmations in five different parishes. There were jubilees of pastors, preparations for art festivals, spring concerts, Christmas plays, and sports contests. There were convent activities such as retreats and visitors added to the "regular" spiritual life and schedule of the sisters.

But a well-balanced community will find time for recreation, and so invitations to attend dinners at outstanding Pocono restaurants or to attend shows at the famous Pocono Playhouse were accepted gratefully.

Between 1993-1998, there would be three changes of principals in the school. Due to ill health, Sister Audrey McHale, appointed in 1993, would be unable to continue after one year. She was replaced by Sister Rosemarie Mozzachio who served until 1998 when she was appointed as congregation vocation director. Kathleen Serafin become principal in 1998 and continues as of this writing. In 1998-1999, there were four IHMs in the school, namely, Sisters Thomas Aquinas Kielceski, Michael Marie Hartman, Patricia Stack, and Kathryn Rolley. Sister Michael Marie was also teaching Spanish each week at Marywood College and reaching out to the Hispanic people of St. Ann's, Tobyhanna.

With Sister Patricia Tippen's appointment as formation director, Sister Katherine Sugrue was added to the core group and Sister Jeanne Tubach as a support staff member for the Spiritual Renewal Center. (140)

A significant sadness for the sisters at Cresco and for the entire congregation was the shocking death of Sister Katherine Sugrue on July 10, 1999. An apparent heart attack caused her to lose control of the car she was driving. She was killed when the car lunged into a tree. With this loss and with Sister Michael Marie's appointment as director of Hispanic ministry for the Pocono parishes, both the school IHM faculty and the Spiritual Renewal Center were reduced to three members.

In spite of these reverses, the twentieth anniversary of the IHM Spiritual Renewal Center was celebrated on September 11, 1999. Reverend Hugh Brogan offered the Mass in the convent chapel. Sister Anne Munley, congregation president, and all IHMs once stationed at Verona and Cresco were present for the occasion. (141)

Under the principalship of Kathleen Serafin, the school continued in 2001-2002 to enroll record numbers, necessitating double tracks in the kindergarten and five other grades. Although only one IHM, Sister Patricia Stack, continued in the school, there were seven IHMs in the local community, three of whom were in the Spiritual Renewal Center; two, Sisters Regina Burns and Joel Marie Sheehe in Hispanic ministry in St. Matthew's, East Stroudsburg and St. Ann's, Tobyhanna, respectively; Sister Estelle Gavel in family ministry.

The Spiritual Renewal Center continues its success story with the added attraction of two hermitages on the convent grounds. During 1999-2001, these were used by 84 different people for a total of 393 days. (142)

Monsignor McHugh Elementary School continues to be supported by five parishes: St. Mary of the Mount, Mt. Pocono; St. Ann, Tobyhanna; St. Bernadette, Canadensis; Our Lady of Victory, Tannersville; St. Rita, Gouldsboro. The Board of Pastors has described the school as a Christian community, stating their mission, in part, as follows:

> Since students lives are directed by their values, we strive to lead them to develop their spiritual, scholastic and cultural values in accordance with right reason and the teachings of the Church. Through these efforts to develop sound values, we hope to influence their families, our community and our nation. In a word, we endeavor to create an educational environment that is conducive to the development of Christian living, intellectual growth and emotional maturity. (143)

Closed Residences and Schools: 1956–1960

The following four residences and schools are listed in the archives as having been discontinued from 1956–1960:

1925–1956: St. Agnes Place, Elmhurst, Pennsylvania
1920–1956: St. Joseph's Shelter and Day Nursery, Scranton, PA
1872–1958: St. Cecilia High School, Scranton, Pennsylvania
1903–1960: St. Lawrence Convent, Portland, Oregon

Two of these have been discussed previously, namely, St. Agnes Place and St. Lawrence, since their closing was related to the opening of other facilities. This was true also of the long history of St. Cecilia Academy in Scranton, Pennsylvania. Sister Immaculata Gillespie, IHM and Sister Zita Marie Kane, IHM have both written the early history of St. Cecilia Academy. (144) The present account begins in 1930. (145)

In 1930, Bishop Thomas C. O'Reilly, during the pastorate of Monsignor Paul Kelly at Cathedral Parish, Scranton, decided to close the high school department of St. Cecilia Academy and convert the entire building to a parochial grade school. Bishop O'Reilly had conferred with Mother Mary William, superior general, as her letter of June 5, 1930, indicates:

> . . . The St. Cecilia Academy is very dear to us all because it abounds in sacred memories of our good old sisters who gave the best that was in them in building up this school in the pioneer days of the Diocese, and in the event you decide to make the change you will have our whole hearted cooperation in perpetuating the glory of the old school and in making the new parochial school an honor to the Cathedral Parish. (146)

By the time Mother Kathleen came to office as superior general in 1955, the Scranton Diocese had already embarked upon a very large educational project, the consolidation of parish high schools as central Catholic or area schools. Bishop William J. Hafey had, by 1947, set the diocese in the direction of central Catholic high schools by establishing South Scranton Central Catholic High, and by 1952, Kingston Central Catholic. Bishop Hannan, his successor, continued the consolidations of parochial facilities by establishing Cathedral High in 1953; Pocono Central Catholic in 1961; and Dunmore Central Catholic in 1964. Bishop J. Carroll McCormick would follow the two-decade trend and establish Notre Dame Central Catholic, Stroudsburg; West Scranton Catholic, and additional facilities in Wilkes-Barre, Hazleton, and Williamsport. (147)

The first step toward a new Cathedral High School was to obtain land in the vicinity of the Cathedral in downtown Scranton. As it happened, an old building owned by the Catholic Daughters of America, located on the corner of Wyoming Avenue and Mulberry Street, had became available to the parish. This building and the adjacent Comerford home were demolished in July 1956, making space diagonally across the street from St. Peter Cathedral for the one million dollar high school. (148)

Two years later, on August 31, 1958, Bishop Jerome D. Hannan dedicated the new Cathedral High School. Mother Kathleen, Sisters St. Mary Orr, Beata Wertz, Mary Kevin Nagle and Aquina Whalen attended the ceremonies in the new high school auditorium. They walked in procession from the convent to the school with all the officiating dignitaries. It was a day of thanksgiving as students, parents, the pastor, Monsignor McNulty, and the bishop all expressed their gratitude for the benefactors who had supported the dream that was realized in the new Cathedral High School.

The school chapel was dedicated to Mary Immaculate, so on September 1, 1958, the first Mass offered there reflected the desire of the sisters and of the pastor to honor the presence of the Blessed Sacrament and the Blessed Virgin Mary in their midst. The Holy Sacrifice of the Mass was to be offered in the school chapel every Tuesday, with classes attending on a rotation basis.

The following day, September 2, 1958, the official opening of the new Cathedral High School was observed. Two hundred students were enrolled. The seven IHM Sisters on the high school faculty included Sisters Mary Peter Doran, Nadine Moran, Josine Shannon, Mary Talbot Keliher, Danielle Vacca, Henriette Kramer, and St. Helen Sullivan, principal. (149)

The school would be renamed in 1969 as Bishop Hannan High School.

In 1970 the sisters would move from the former St. Cecilia Convent that was demolished to make room for the Diocesan Chancery Building. The move took them just across the street to what is today Cathedral Convent. The spot on which this convent is located was once LaSalle Hall, a main building for St. Thomas College. It was also once the location of Scranton Preparatory School, a Jesuit high school for boys. (150)

The former St. Cecilia Academy is no more, but a vibrant education ministry continues in Cathedral Parish as the IHM Sisters still serve at Bishop Hannan High School in downtown Scranton.

St. Joseph's Shelter and Day Nursery, Scranton, Pennsylvania

The early history of St. Joseph's Shelter and Day Nursery in Scranton, Pennsylvania has been treated briefly by Sister Immaculata Gillespie in her book *The Sisters of the I.H.M.* and augmented by notes from her files. (151) The charitable services begun by the St. Joseph's Society of laywomen in 1890 had, by 1915, achieved such sufficient recognition in Scranton that Bishop Michael J. Hoban asked them to administer St. Joseph's Shelter at 332 North Washington Avenue. The committee chosen to supervise the management of the shelter included Mrs. P. J. Horan, Mrs. T. P. Hoban, and Mrs. W. B. Duggan.

Additional space at 317 Linden Street was procured, and it was at this site in 1918, during the influenza epidemic, that 163 persons were cared for by the members of the St. Joseph's Society and the Sisters of IHM who came from the various area convents to care for the stricken.

As the opportunities for women to work outside the home expanded, it was clear that a day care center for children was needed. Bishop Hoban sought Mother Casimir's help, asking her to send IHM Sisters to manage the shelter and to open a day nursery. So it was that on April 20, 1920, Sisters Clare Howard, Melanie Rowan, and Consolata Ball initiated the

IHM presence at St. Joseph's Shelter and Day Nursery. Financial support came from the St. Joseph's Society, from small payments by mothers utilizing the facilities and from donors, until the Community Chest came to their assistance in 1921. (152)

For thirty-six years the Sisters of IHM provided transient women and recuperating mothers with a place of safety and care, while at the same time ministering to some fifty children daily, with physical care, nursery school classes, and religious instruction. Vast changes in the availability of day care for children, and the emergence of new facilities in the Scranton Diocese gave support to Mother Kathleen's decision to close St. Joseph's Shelter and Day Care Center in 1956. Sister Dominica Sullivan was superintendent at the time of the closing.

Letters to Pastors of Parishes Where IHM Sisters Served

The period in which Mother Kathleen served as superior general of the Congregation, 1955—1962, was one characterized by the expansion and construction of schools in the Catholic parishes of the United States. Returning veterans of World War II and the Pacific conflicts of the 40s were establishing their families, creating the generation later to be called "baby boomers." The desire of parents to reinforce religious values of the home in the formal education program of the school brought about wholesale parish building response, and a resultant demand for sisters, religious brothers, and priests as instructors.

Mother Kathleen was in a somewhat different situation as the Congregation's "second generation" of sisters was experiencing the onset of illness and aging. Simultaneously, the Church was moving to extend the spiritual formation of the newly professed sisters, giving them a thorough basis in theology and community life. Mother Kathleen rightly judged that it was a time to shore up existing apostolates and to resist the excitement of venturing into expanding horizons. Dozens of letters reveal her determination to persevere in this conviction, responding with graciousness and firmness to the many requests for sisters.

St. Rita School in Dundalk was typical of the times. On February 28, 1956, Father Joseph Weidenhan, pastor, wrote to Mother Kathleen as follows:

> To meet the heavy enrollment in our school we have gone to the expense of building four new classrooms that will be in operation next fall. That will bring our school capacity to sixteen rooms. <u>Naturally these new rooms will have to be staffed by teachers</u>. Could I please request that you send me two additional Sisters for

> two of these rooms, while I try to supply the other two with lay teachers? (153)

In response Mother Kathleen was able to promise one sister, noting with a fine stroke of diplomacy that "this addition may appear small from the point of view of your school needs; but it is large when viewed from the point of view of our limited supply and the pressing needs of the one-hundred schools we serve." (154) And, then, lest the pastor forget, Mother Kathleen reminds him of his part in the matter: "It is our prayerful hope that soon we will have more vocations from your fine parish, and thus be better able to staff our schools. I know that you will help greatly in fostering these vocations." (155)

In another case, Monsignor Thomas O'Shea of Bellefonte wrote movingly of his need for more sisters in Bellefonte, Pennsylvania. It must have been difficult for Mother Kathleen to say "no" to a pastor who was building a new convent for the sisters, who was in the midst of putting an addition on the school, and who was also so deeply concerned about the loss of faith in the parish. Monsignor O'Shea wrote:

> I know what you are up against, Mother, with so many demands from so many quarters, yet in view of the unique situation present which is really and truly missionary territory, in view of the unusual opportunity to salvage souls which would otherwise be lost, I make bold to beg you to send us one more Sister in September. (156)

Mother Kathleen's empathy for the situation is evident in her response:

> I share your deep concern for the children of your parish. Certainly I would be pleased to send you another Sister in September. However, I cannot make such a promise . . . I wish it were possible for me to meet all the needs of our schools . . . (157)

A similar response was made by Mother Kathleen to Reverend Vincent Luther, principal, Bishop Guilfoyle High School, Altoona, Pennsylvania:

> It is with regret that I must tell you that we are not able to send more Sisters to your high school. I realize your needs and would be very happy to send help to meet them. No amount of good will on my part can compensate for the losses we have suffered by death and illness during the past few years. (158)

Testing Mother Kathleen's resolve, Father Luther appealed to Bishop J. Carroll McCormick, then bishop of the Altoona-Johnstown Diocese. But even Bishop McCormick's plea and his reminder that "some sixteen vocations have gone into your Community from Altoona," (159) Mother Kathleen responded, "Our supply of Sisters is not sufficient to enable me to accede to your esteemed request. I am very sorry that we cannot better serve you." (160)

In her communications with pastors, Mother Kathleen showed a dedication to excellence in the apostolates of the Congregation and a concern for future staffing needs, balanced by a desire to protect the religious and professional life of the sisters.

Inadequate housing conditions in convents, double grades and over-enrolled, crowded classes were targets of her expressed concerns with pastors. Her struggle to move the salary of sisters from thirty to fifty dollars per month was won, probably at great cost to her own fragile health. Pastors, already burdened with building projects which included convents and schools, and unaccustomed to having to hire lay teachers, respected Mother Kathleen's reasons for seeking higher stipends for the sisters, but did not greet the new expenditure with enthusiasm.

But Mother Kathleen, a future-looking administrator, was thinking of the Congregation's need to support its elderly sisters at the new Marian Convent and its young members in formation in the new novitiate building.

Annual Retreat Challenges to the Sisters

The Constitutions and Customs of a Congregation, known as the Holy Rule, have always been a centerpiece in the life of the Sisters of IHM. Spiritual writers, saints, and popes down the ages have extolled the strict observance of the Rule as the sure path to holiness, happiness in the religious life, and sainthood. Each sister, in making her profession in the Congregation, knows that she makes her vows to God in accordance with the Constitutions of the Sisters, Servants of the Immaculate Heart of Mary, Scranton, Pennsylvania. Thus, she assumes the responsibility of living her vowed life not only as an individual but also as a member of a Congregation whose Rule, based on the law of love of God and neighbor, is the bond of unity among the members and the source of apostolic effectiveness.

The general superiors of the IHM Congregation have conscientiously urged the sisters to love, respect, and live the Rule. From Mother Mary's exhortations in the 1890s, Mother Cyril's in the early 1900s, Mother Josepha's in the 1930s and 1940s, to Mother Marcella's directives in the 1950s–and to the present day–all reecho the theme expressed from the beginning: "I entreat you all to begin anew, with your first fervor, to practice with love and earnestness our Holy Rule." (161)

Mother Kathleen, too, was most zealous in her promotion of the strict observance of the Rule. Sisters remember well her repeated phrases at the close of the annual retreats, "It has come to my attention that . . . ," "I am grieved that . . . ," "It distresses me to hear . . .," as Mother Kathleen never wavered in pointing out to the sisters the importance of the Rule in the life of the Congregation and of each sister. She often paraphrased St. Alphonsus Liguori, saying, "You will be a saint if you keep your Holy Rule. Follow it, and you will practice the prayer and penance so necessary to make you a saint." (162)

Influenced by Pope Pius XIIs stern admonitions to religious superiors of the day and by her reading of St. Catherine de Ricci, St. Alphonsus, St. John of the Cross, St. John Berchmans, and other spiritual writers, as well as her own lived experience, Mother Kathleen's tendency was to emphasize the penitential aspects of a religious life lived strictly in accord with the Rule. In September 1960, for example, she wrote, "But make no mistake about it, the following of Christ demands this daily taking up of His yoke; and the harder it seems, the more Christ like we become, and the greater generosity we can give to our apostolate." (163)

As the process for the pontifical approval of the Rule moved slowly along in Rome, Mother Kathleen used her annual retreat exhortations to deepen the sisters' understanding of religious life, the central place of the Rule, and its relationship to the apostolate. In September 1959, she said:

> Our first duty and great privilege is, then, to live the full life of the Gospel, walking in the footsteps of Christ. From this fundamental duty, the Church has derived the whole program of perfection. This program she put before us in our Holy Rule as a unique and inexhaustible source of the religious life, a blue print of our pathway to the full imitation of Christ. We have vowed to live as He lived, to set our feet in His footsteps, to attach ourselves to Him, to follow Him . . . We must realize that while our religious vocation is essentially an individual, intimate call to personal sanctification, it is at the same time an apostolic mission . . . In Christ's words, we are His 'witnesses' in this twentieth century, just as truly as were the apostles in their time. (164)

Mother Kathleen was jubilant upon receiving news of the Decree of Praise on December 2, 1960, approving the Rule and entitling the Sisters of IHM to be a papal Congregation. In what would be the last of her September letters to the sisters, she rejoices over this approbation by the Church and once again focuses on the importance of the Rule. She wrote:

> The Congregation is a living organism; the Rules are the nerves keeping the Congregation alive and giving it vigor and strength . . . The religious who lives by faith and whose observance of the spirit of the Rule has caught a spark from the fire of Christ and is a match for the doubts and disbelief of the times.

Let us rededicate ourselves to the apostolate to which we have been assigned and continue the splendid tradition that has characterized our Congregation from the beginning. Let us initiate our work with enthusiasm, for nothing great was ever accomplished without a 'flaring of the spirit'. (165)

One of the sisters who lived on mission at St. John, Susquehanna, and St. Ann, Scranton, when then Sister Kathleen was principal and superior, said of her:

> Mother Kathleen believed 100% that one's joy in religious life was in proportion to one's fidelity to the Rule. She practiced what she preached to the letter . . . she provided treats on appropriate occasions, and enjoyed a good time; within the limits of the Rule and Customs . . . She was generous, loving, and genuinely concerned for the good of the Congregation. (166)

Mother Kathleen's Reelection in 1961

The General Chapter of 1961 opened on June 25, 1961. At a preliminary session, Mother Kathleen delivered her "State of the Congregation Report" to the delegates and expressed her gratitude to God, to Our Lady for guidance, and to the sisters for their faithful cooperation. Her first term was to end on June 27, 1961.

In his remarks to the sisters serving as delegates, Bishop Jerome D. Hannan of Scranton spoke of the importance of the election of the superior general and the council. He enunciated clearly the qualities to be sought in making this selection: "great love for, and loyalty to, the Congregation; a desire for the fulfillment of the purposes of the Congregation; the necessary intellectual competency; training necessary to promote this fulfillment; and the ability to lead and direct others toward it." (167)

The delegates believed that Mother Kathleen fulfilled these qualities. So it was that just six months from her seventieth birthday and her fiftieth year of profession as a sister of IHM, Mother Kathleen was reelected on June 27, 1961 for a second term as superior general of the Congregation. After taking the oath of office, Mother Kathleen then presided over the election of the general councilors and treasurer general. The results of these elections were:

Sister Beata Wertz – First Councilor
Sister St. Mary Orr – Second Councilor
Sister Felicitas Ryan – Third Councilor
Sister Brendan O'Brien – Fourth Councilor
Sister Aquina Whalen – Treasurer General

While some positions had changed among the councilors, the only new member was Sister Felicitas Ryan. (168)

Congratulatory messages poured in from bishops, pastors, and sisters from across the country where IHMs served and from other congregations. Among these was a letter from Mr. William Connolly, president of the Fathers and Friends organization that Mother Kathleen had formed to assist in raising funds for the novitiate building. He wrote, in part:

> This is to express the admiration of the Father's Club for the sisters who have elected you for a second term as their Mother. It is to tell you that we, who have gotten to know you, a little, over the past three years, have come to admire your straight-forward ways, your gentle, gracious humility tempered with steel and courage when they are indicated . . . If we have made your part a little easier, you have shown us an example of splendid womanhood in the tradition of the Mother of God. (169)

Mother Kathleen accepted all this praise graciously, but by 3:00 p.m. on this very date of her reelection she moved on with the Chapter of Affairs for discussion of the many proposals received by the delegates. The 9:15 a.m. to 5:00 p.m. schedule continued over the following four days.

Approximately one hundred twenty proposals were discussed. From these, the chapter delegates issued nine decrees as a result of the intense work by the chapter delegates. Several of these decrees recognized the need for greater mobility, communication, and information for a congregation whose primary apostolate was teaching. Permission to drive cars, to watch cultural and informational programs on television, to listen to the radio, to attend school programs, musicals, and other events on Sundays, and to make an annual home visit of three days – all were approved. Permission to wear wristwatches, however, was not given approval at this time. It was this chapter that approved the congregation's future acceptance of a South American mission.

It was at this chapter also that proposals had been received regarding changes to the habit and to the cloak. Wisely, Mother Kathleen proposed that a referendum be conducted on this matter throughout the Congregation, and that a committee then be appointed to explore the desired changes, if any. (170)

The chapter being over, the promulgation of the Decrees and Recommendations was an immediate task that Mother Kathleen and the council undertook. The records show that from June 27 through December 26, 1961, Mother Kathleen attended and presided at eight meetings of the General Council of the Congregation. Routine matters and extraordinary matters were her daily challenge. The appointment of local superiors for the entire Congregation, the admission of novices to temporary profession; special appointments such as that of Sister Brendan O'Brien as secretary general of the Congregation; Sister Adalbert (Mary) Schelb as mistress of novices; of Sister Liguori Farnon as mistress of postulants; and Sister Clotilde Cullen as mistress of junior professed sisters.

It was at the December 26, 1961 meeting that council approval was given to expand significantly the Marywood College facilities by the addition of a dormitory, student union, and a faculty residence. (171)

It appears that the final general council meeting attended by Mother Kathleen was this December 26, 1961 meeting, about one month before her death.

The Final Days of Mother Kathleen Hart, IHM

The serious condition of Mother Kathleen's health was made know by her physician, R. F. Cooney, M.D. on December 9, 1961 in a letter to Sister Beata Wertz, first councilor. His letter encouraged Sister Beata to inform the Congregation about Mother Kathleen's "total disability" resulting from rheumatic heart disease. His words were frank and direct, stating, "Unless we have a miracle, I don't expect that she (Mother Kathleen) will increase her activities any more than she is now doing." (172)

Having received this word, Sister Beata, on the very same day, wrote to all the sisters conveying Dr. Cooney's message and preparing them for what lay ahead. She wrote:

> Today we learn that the improvement in Mother's condition has been meager, and that the outcome is questionable. The council feels that we should share this information with you. We consider this communication reserved for own Sisters, because Mother is not aware of the fact that we are writing this letter. (173)

Mother Kathleen had been a patient at St. Joseph's Hospital in Carbondale for a number of weeks, requiring prolonged rest and quiet and the curtailing of visits from the sisters. But, as Sister Beata assured the sisters,

> In dealing with necessary community business, Mother has manifested her customary patience and cheerfulness. She has read and dictated her own mail, and has asked us to express her deep gratitude for the good wishes, the prayers and the Masses offered for her by the Sisters. (174)

It was nearing Christmas time, a time when each year Mother Kathleen had written to the sisters of the Congregation. These letters were always about Our Lady and stressed Mary's exemplary qualities. "Bring God to others, like Mary, especially to our own sisters"; (175) "Be a Christ-bearer, just as Mary was God's Tabernacle and Monstrance"; (176) "Imitate Mary's meekness and humility which bring peace to self and the world." (177)

Mother Kathleen's final Christmas letter, written from the hospital in December 1961 was no exception. In it she notes the honor and glory given to God by Mary's life and by every action of the Infant Jesus. "We, too, were created to give glory to God," she writes. "May the homage, the love, and the adoration which God asks of us, be our generous gift to our Infant King." (178)

Christmas passed. Mother Kathleen's family visited her at the hospital and she seemed very much better. By January 26, she felt sure the doctor would approve her return to Marywood. But on Sunday, January 28, a change came in her condition. That evening she was anointed. The council members were present and remained at the hospital until Monday afternoon. During this time, amazingly, she dictated letters and was also involved in discussions and decisions. On Tuesday, January 30, she rested quietly and had no visitors.

One account tells of her final day. "Wednesday morning, January 31, after a good breakfast, she was chatting with Sister Cor Mariae when a sudden change came, and in a few seconds she was with God." (179)

A viewing was held at the Marian Convent on Wednesday afternoon, after which she was moved to the parlor of the motherhouse for viewing until Saturday morning, February 3. A Solemn High Mass of Requiem was celebrated in St. Peter Cathedral, Scranton, with Bishop Jerome Hannan presiding. Reverend Leo W. Gildea, pastor of Our Lady of Sorrows Church, West Wyoming, was celebrant of the Mass. He was originally from Ashley, as was Mother Kathleen, and had become a personal friend. Monsignor John J. Maher, diocesan superintendent of schools, preached the sermon. Eight members of the Fathers and Friends served as pallbearers. These included Joseph Rooney, Edward Rock, Aloysius Wilson, William Connolly, Dr. John Swift, Joseph Bohan, Horace Franco, and Gerald Corcoran. (180)

Even Mother Kathleen, a truly humble religious, would have been impressed in seeing that five bishops and four personal representatives of bishops, numerous clergy, leaders of many religious orders of women and men, civic leaders, and hundreds of her own IHM Sisters were present for the funeral. Wyoming Avenue in front of the Cathedral was blocked off to provide standing room in the street for the numbers of people who could not get inside the crowded Cathedral. With police escorts from Dunmore and Scranton leading the way, Mother Kathleen was buried in St. Catherine Cemetery, Moscow, Pennsylvania.

The esteem in which Mother Kathleen was held is revealed in letters received by the Congregation. Bishop Jerome D. Hannan of Scranton wrote to Sister Beata:

> I offer you and the entire Community my sympathy in your bereavement at the death of your Mother General, Mother M. Kathleen. I shall offer my Mass for the repose of her soul on Thursday and Saturday. I shall cherish with the members of your Congregation the memory of the edifying example of her life and especially of its fidelity to the spirit of her vows. (181)

Mother Maria Alma, former superior general of the Philadelphia IHM Congregation, had been a close friend of Mother Kathleen's for many years. She wrote to Sister Beata:

> Our thoughts and prayers go out to you and your saddened Congregation in the loss of dear Mother Kathleen . . . My personal memories of Mother Kathleen are singularly happy, happy ones; I was privileged to know her. My debt of gratitude to Mother is very deep because of her many kindnesses to me. Her last inspiring letter came several weeks ago; it contained no intimation of her serious illness. (182)

On behalf of the Fathers and Friends of the Novitiate, Mr. William Connolly wrote: "We shall miss Mother very much and we know all the members of our organization will remember her soul in their prayers.

Mother is in a better position to help us to complete the project so dear to her heart. We can still count on her good assistance." (183)

One IHM sister, perhaps a council member, authored a piece entitled "In Memoriam" for the Congregation publication, *The Distaff,* which captured the essence of Mother Kathleen's life. Some excerpts follow:

> Her deep religious spirit and her loyalty to the Church and its laws, motivated her decisions . . . Her prayer life and her official acts were all of one stamp, for they were done with God and for God. God had blessed her with a splendid mind, a strong will, and the ability to see the wholeness of a problem, and to make valid decisions. Hers was a life of complete dedication to God's work, as it presented itself in our beloved Congregation. (184)

Tributes such as these honored the life of Mother Kathleen Hart, the eleventh canonical superior of the Congregation of the Sisters, Servants of the Immaculate Heart of Mary, Scranton, Pennsylvania.

References

1. Mother M. Marcella Gill. Letter to delegates, April 2, 1955. General Chapter, 1955
2. *IHM Constitutions*, 1943, Chapter V, Article 207, p. 6.
3. General Chapter, 1955. Archives, IHM Center.
4. Mother M. Marcella Gill. Report to General Chapter, 1955, p. 8-9.
5. General Chapter, Third Session. June 27, 1955.
6. Mother Kathleen Hart.Letter to Congregation, March 19, 1957 and Opening Remarks to Delegates, June 29, 1957.
7. Bishop Jerome D. Hannan, Bishop of Scranton. Address to Extraordinary Chapter, June 29, 1957.
8. Minutes of Extraordinary Chapter, 1957. IHM Archives.
9. Mother Maria Alma, IHM (Phila.) Letter to Mother Kathleen from Rome, April 22, 1957.
10. Rev. Bernard Ransing, CSC. Letter to Mother Kathleen, January 9, 1958.
11. Rev. Bernard Ransing, CSC. Letter to Mother Kathleen, October 16, 1960.
12. Mother Kathleen Hart. Letter to Rev. Bernard Ransing, CSC. December 16, 1959.
13. Mother Kathleen Hart. Letter to Rev. Bernard Ransing, CSC. June 30, 1960.
14. Mother Kathleen Hart. Cablegram to Rev. Bernard Ransing, CSC. December 3, 1960.
15. Mother Kathleen Hart. Letters to Diocesan Bishops, December 16, 1960.
16. Mother Kathleen Hart. Letter to Rev. Bernard Ransing, CSC. December 20, 1960.
17. Mother Marcella Gill. Report to the General Chapter, 1955.
18. Bishop Jerome Hannan. Address at Marian Convent Dedication, April 9, 1956.
19. Monsignor Thomas Cawley. "The Spotlight," *The Catholic Light,* April 10, 1956.
20. History of the Marian Convent, IHM Archives.
21. Mother Kathleen Hart. Report to the General Chapter, 1961. IHM Archives.
22. History of St. Agnes Place, Elmhurst, PA. IHM Archives.
23. General Council Minutes, July 17, 1957. IHM Archives.
24. Sister Cor Mariae Schroth. IHM, *An Autobiography,* 1981, p. 77.
25. General Council Minutes, January 30, 1956. IHM Archives.
26. History of Old St. Rose Convent, Carbondale, PA. IHM Archives
27. Monsignor Joseph Madden. Letter to Mother Kathleen, August 26, 1957.
28. Mother Kathleen Hart. Letter to Monsignor Joseph Madden, August 27, 1957.
29. Annals of Our Lady of Lourdes Convent, Tobyhanna, PA, 1958-968.
30. Annals of IHM Academy, Coeur d'Alene, ID, 1903-1960.

31. Bishop Edward Kelly. Letter to Sister Mary Kevin Nagle, April 29, 1953.
32. Mother Kathleen Hart. Letter to Sister Rebecca Doyle, IHM, December 8, 1955.
33. Annals of IHM Academy, Coeur d'Alene, Idaho, 1956-1957.
34. Ibid.,1957.
35. General Council Minutes, July 28, 1957 and January 22, 1958.
36. Mother Kathleen Hart. Letter to Sister Rebecca Doyle, IHM, January 28, 1958.
37. Sister Rebecca Doyle, IHM. Letter to Mother Kathleen, September 28, 1960.
38. Annals of IHM Academy, Coeur d'Alene, ID, 1961.
39. Ibid. 1961-1962.
40. General Council Minutes, October 31, 1955.
41. General Council Minutes, December 17, 1957.
42. Monsignor Joseph Madden. Letter to Mother Kathleen, November 14, 1959.
43. General Council Minutes, March 15, 1957.
44. Financial records of IHM Congregation, 1951-1969.
45. "Fathers and Friends," IHM Novitiate dedication booklets, 1962.
46. Mother Kathleen Hart. Letter to Mr. Edward Rock, president of "Fathers and Friends," November 1958.
47. IHM Novitiate dedication booklets, 1962.
48. Bishop Jerome Hannan. Letter to Mother Kathleen, January 13, 1960.
49. Bishop JeromeHannan. Letter to Mother Kathleen, February 11, 1960.
50. Mother Beata Wertz, IHM. Address at dedication of IHM Novitiate and letter dated May 30, 1962.
51. Mr. J. Peter Grace. Letter to Mother Kathleen, January 6, 1959.
52. Mother Kathleen Hart. Letter to Bishop Jerome D. Hannan, January 15, 1959.
53. General Council Minutes, February 1, 1959.
54. General Council Minutes, March 15, 1959.
55. Attorney Oakey McKnight. Letter to Dr. Robert Boggs, New York City, NY, March 13, 1959.
56. *The Sign Magazine,* March 1958.
57. General Council Minutes, May 8, 1959.
58. Annals of Our Lady of Grace Convent, 1959.
59. Ibid., 1959
60. Annals of St. Joseph's Maternity and Children's Hospital, 1888-1920.
61. Annals of St. Joseph's Maternity and Children's Hospital, 1956-1959
62. General Council Minutes, May 17, 1957,
63. Report of Mother Kathleen to Chapter, 1961.
64. General Council Minutes, July 7, 1960.
65. General Council Minutes, December 26, 1961.

66. General Council Minutes, January 1963.
67. Ibid.
68. Reverend M. J. Quinn. Letter to Mother Kathleen, December 17, 1957.
69. Mother Kathleen Hart. Letter to Reverend M. J. Quinn, May 9, 1958.
70. Annals of Christ the King School, Dunmore, PA, 1959-1960.
71. Op. cit., 1961-1962.
72. Op. cit., 1962-1963.
73. Op. cit., 1963-1964.
74. Sister Rosemary Casey, IHM. Conversation on May 1, 2001.
75. Annals of St. John the Baptist Convent, Pittsburgh, PA, 1959.
76. Ibid.
77. Sister Carole Griffin, IHM. Conversation on May 5, 2001.
78. Monsignor McDowell, Superintendent of Schools, Pittsburgh, PA. Letter to Reverend Joseph A. Raynak, pastor. Annals 1960.
79. Reverend Joseph A. Raynak, pastor. Letter to Mother Kathleen, August 6, 1960.
80. Annals of St. John the Baptist Convent, 1960-1962.
81. Op. cit., 1962-1963.
82. Op. cit., 1959-1997.
83. Annals of St. Lawrence Convent, Portland, OR, 1957-1958.
84. Op. cit., 1960.
85. Annals of St. Anthony Convent, Portland, OR, 1960.
86. Ibid. 1960
87. *The Catholic Sentinel,* newspaper of the Archdiocese of Portland, OR, June 8, 1961.
88. Sister Immaculata Norton, IHM. Conversation on May 10, 2001.
89. Annals of St. Anthony's Convent, Portland, OR, 1960-1961.
90. Ibid. 1961
91. Op. cit., 1961-1962.
92. Ibid.
93. Annals of St. Anthony's Convent, Portland, OR, 1965-1968.
94. Louis J. Putz, CSC, editor. *The Catholic Church, USA,* 1956, pp. 39-40.
95. Op. cit. p. 23
96. www/adw/org/about/history.jhtml. "A History of the Archdiocese of Washington." p. 2, February 20, 2004.
97. Mother M. Kathleen Hart, IHM, superior general. Report to the General Chapter, June 25, 1961.
98. Annals of St. John the Evangelist Convent, Clinton, Maryland, 1961-1962.
99. Ibid.
100. Ibid.
101. Annals. 1966-1967.

102. Ibid. 1972-1973.
103. Ibid. 1974-1975.
104. "Twenty-fifth Jubilee Booklet." St. John the Evangelist School, 1966.
105. Annals of St. John the Evangelist Convent, 1994-1995.
106. Cinnamon Burnim. "Clinton Principal Returns to Florida". *The Catholic Standard,* Spring 1995.
107. Annals of St. John the Evangelist Convent, August 3-13, 1995.
108. Annals. 1995-1996.
109. Ibid., 1996-1997.
110. Ibid., 1998-1999.
111. Ibid., 1999-2000.
112. Reverend Thomas Pollard, pastor, St. John the Evangelist Church Bulletin, May 28, 2000.
113. Annals of St. John the Evangelist Convent, 1999-2000
114. Ibid.
115. Ibid., 2000-2001.
116. Ibid., 2001-2002
117. Ibid.
118. Ibid.
119. Ibid., 2002-2003.
120. Reverend Thomas Pollard, pastor, St. John the Evangelist Church Bulletin, May 2003.
121. St. John the Evangelist Elementary School Web Site Data, February 20, 2004.
122. The Archdiocese of Washington—History: www/adw/org/about/history.html. February 20, 2004.
123. Dedication Booklet of Mt. Pocono Catholic Missions, Cresco, PA. Chronological History. 1961, p. 17
124. Mother M. Kathleen Hart, IHM, Superior General. Letter to Monsignor Connell A. McHugh, Pastor, St. Mary of the Mount Parish, Mt. Pocono, PA. September 30, 1958.
125. Dedication Booklet, op. cit. pp. 20-22.
126. Monsignor Connell A. McHugh, Letter to Mother Kathleen. April 22, 1961.
127. Annals of Pocono Catholic Missions Convent. 1961-1962.
128. Ibid.
129. Annals. 1963-1978.
130. Annals. 1964-1965.
131. Annals. 1967-1968.
132. Monsignor McHugh Elementary School Facts. www.monsignorMchughElem.com (internet web site)
133. Annals. 1974-1975, 1975-1976.

134. Annals. 1986-1987.
135. Annals. 1988-1989.
136. Annals. 1989-1990.
137. Sister Barbara Jablonski, IHM, Councilor for Temporal Resources, telephone conversation, March 16, 2004.
138. Annals of Monsignor McHugh Elementary School Convent, Cresco, PA. 1990-1991.
139. Ibid.
140. Annals. 1993-1999.
141. Annals. 2000-2001.
142. Annals. 1999-2001.
143. Board of Pastors. "Pocono Central Catholic High School and Monsignor McHugh Elementary School—A Christian Community, Cresco, PA (undated)
144. Sister Immaculata Gillespie, IHM. *The Sisters of the IHM,* 1921, pp. 145-151. Also unpublished notes, 1930. IHM Archives.
145. Sister Zita Maria Kane, IHM. Unpublished monograph, 1995. IHM Archives.
146. Mother Mary William Craig, IHM. Letter to Bishop Thomas C. O'Reilly, June 5, 1930.
147. Monsignor John P. Gallagher, PhD: *A Century of History: The Diocese of Scranton, 1868-1968,* pp. 378-379.
148. Annals of St. Peter's Convent, Scranton, PA, 1956-1957.
149. Annals of Cathedral Convent, Scranton, PA, 1969-1970.
150. Ibid.
151. Sister Immaculata Gillespie, IHM. Unpublished notes. IHM Archives.
152. Sister Immaculata Gillespie, IHM. op. cit. pp. 477-478.
153. Reverend Joseph Weidenhan. Letter to Mother Kathleen, February 28, 1956.
154. Mother Kathleen Hart. Letter to Reverend Joseph Weidenhan, March 8, 1956.
155. Ibid.
156. Monsignor Thomas J. O'Shea, pastor, Bellefonte, PA. Letter to Mother Kathleen, January 27, 1960.
157. Mother Kathleen Hart. Letter to Monsignor Thomas O'Shea, February 1, 1960.
158. Mother Kathleen Hart. Letter to Reverend Vincent Luther, Altoona, PA, June 7, 1961.
159. Bishop J. Carroll McCormick, Altoona-Johnstown Diocese. Letter to Mother Kathleen, June 26, 1961.
160. Mother Kathleen Hart. Letter to Bishop J. Carroll McCormick, July 22, 1961.

161. Mother Mary Jackson, IHM. Retreat notes to the sisters, August 12, 1892.
162. Mother Kathleen Hart. Retreat exhortations to the sisters, September 12, 1957.
163. Mother Kathleen Hart. Letter to Congregation, September 15, 1960.
164. Mother Kathleen Hart. Retreat exhortations to the sisters, September 24, 1959.
165. Mother Kathleen Hart. Letter to the Congregation, September 24, 1961.
166. Sister Josine Shannon, IHM. Written recollections, May 2001.
167. Bishop Jerome D. Hannan. Address at the Chapter of Elections, June 27, 1961.
168. General Chapter Minutes, June 27, 1961.
169. Mr. William G. Connolly. Letter to Mother Kathleen, July 1, 1961.
170. General Chapter Minutes, June 27, 1961.
171. General Council Minutes, June 27-December 26, 1961.
172. R.F. Cooney, MD, Mayfield, PA. Letter to Sister M. Beata Wertz, IHM, December 9, 1961.
173. Sister Beata Wertz, IHM. Letter to Congregation, December 9, 1961.
174. Ibid.
175. Mother Kathleen Hart. Christmas letter to the sisters, December 1956.
176. Mother Kathleen Hart. Christmas letter to the sisters, December 1957.
177. Mother Kathleen Hart. Christmas letter to the sisters, December 1960.
178. Mother Kathleen Hart. Christmas letter to the sisters, December 1961.
179. "In Memoriam," *Strands from Mary's Distaff,* March 1962.
180. *The Scranton Times,* February 3, 1962.
181. Bishop Jerome D. Hannan. Letter to Sister Beata Wertz, first assistant, January 31, 1962.
182. Mother Maria Alma, IHM, Philadelphia, PA. Letter to Sister Beata Wertz, February 5, 1962.
183. "Fathers and Friends" Organization. Postscript to minutes, January 26, 1962.
184. "In Memoriam," *Strands from Mary's Distaff,* by IHM Sister, March 1962 .

Mother M. Beata Wertz
1962 - 1974

BORN:	Berenice Wertz — July 28, 1898, Bedford, PA
PARENTS:	Charles A. and Margaret C. Schenck Wertz
EDUCATION:	A.B., Marywood College, Scranton, Pennsylvania M.A., Marywood College, Scranton, Pennsylvania LL.D. Honorary, University of Scranton, Pennsylvania
RELIGIOUS LIFE:	Entered IHM Congregation, December 8, 1919 Reception of Habit, August 2, 1920 First Profession of Vows, August 15, 1922 Final Profession of Vows, December 8, 1930
MISSIONS:	1922—1923 St. Patrick, White Haven, PA 1923—1932 St. Ephrem, Brooklyn, NY 1932—1935 St. Rose, Carbondale, PA *1935—1941 St. Charles, Sugar Notch, PA *1941—1944 Our Lady of Good Counsel, Inwood, NY *1944—1947 St. Ephrem, Brooklyn, NY 1947—1948 St. Ann, Nyack, NY *1948—1951 St. Peter of Alcantara, Port Washington, NY *1951—1954 Our Lady of Mt. Carmel, Asbury Park, NJ *1954—1955 Nativity of Our Lord, Scranton, PA 1955—1962 Marywood, Scranton, PA, Council Member 1962—1974 Marywood, Scranton, PA, Superior General **1974—1977 St. Thomas, Bedford, PA **1977—1981 St. Joseph's Hospital, Carbondale, PA **1981—1989 Marian Convent, Scranton, PA *Served as Principal of Elementary School and Convent Superior **In Residence Served as Teacher in all other Missions
MEMBER OF THE GENERAL COUNCIL	Second Assistant to Mother M. Kathleen, 1955 First Assistant to Mother M. Kathleen, 1961
SUPERIOR GENERAL:	1962-1968 (first term) 1968-1974 (second term)
DIED:	September 14, 1989 - 91 years of age

TABLE OF CONTENTS

Mother Kathleen Hart had died on January 31, 1962, just six months after her election to a second term as superior general. In accord with the Constitutions of 1960, Article 204, a special election to fill this vacancy was required within six months. As first assistant on the existing council, Sister Beata Wertz informed the Congregation by letter dated February 13, 1962, that a General Chapter would be convened at Marywood on March 24, 1962. Three days later, a packet of materials for use at the election of delegates to the Chapter was sent to each convent with instructions regarding the election process. The election of delegates was scheduled for February 24 indicating the priority that the council gave to this matter. Sisters elected as delegates were informed by letter on February 27, 1962, were directed to specific reading material and invited to the Preliminary Session of the Chapter on March 23 at 3:00 p.m.

On March 24, 1962, at 9:15 a.m., Jerome D. Hannan, Bishop of the Scranton Diocese, presided at the Chapter of Elections in the motherhouse chapel. Sister Beata Wertz was elected superior general. After a short intermission, Mother M. Beata, newly elected superior general presided at the election of the general councilors and the treasurer general. The following were elected: Sister John Francis Marley, first councilor; Sister St. Mary Orr, second councilor; Sister Brendan O'Brien, third councilor; Sister Felicitas Ryan, fourth councilor; Sister Aquina Whalen, treasurer general.

These were the women chosen to guide the IHM Congregation in the exciting and tumultuous years of 1962-1968. It was a time of amazing developments in the space program of the United States, with Colonel John Glenn, orbiting the earth three times on February 20, 1962. There were medical miracles as Houston, Texas surgeon, Michael E. DeBakey implanted an artificial heart in a human for the first time in April1966; followed in 1967 by the first successful heart transplant performed by Dr. Christian Bernard of South Africa.

Everything seemed possible except peace among peoples. There were international and local tensions. President John F. Kennedy had imposed a missile blockade on the Russians who were invading the waters between the United States and Cuba. At home, there were racial riots in Los Angeles, California and organized hatred in Mississippi and Alabama as federal marshals forced the admission of black students into public schools and universities.

Change was in the air, even in that most stable and predictable of bulwarks, the Catholic Church. The elderly Pope John XXIII, elected in 1958 at age seventy-seven knew that not much was expected of him. He himself wrote, "When the cardinals designated me to the supreme responsibility of the government of the Church, at seventy-seven years of age, the belief was widespread that I would be a provisional pope of transition." (4)

A Vatican journalist writing at the time just prior to the election of John XXIII said, " . . . after the long reign of Pius XII most cardinals . . . will favor not a strong or willful man but a less talented cardinal, of proven reliability, who will ploddingly but surely put through unexciting but badly needed reforms." (5)

An American journalist's observation of Cardinal Roncalli (later Pope John XXIII) was "Roncalli probably is too old at 77 to become pope, surely too old to make his mark if elected." (6)

But, as Pope John XXIII he did "make his mark" in surprising ways. On October 11, 1962, he convened the Second Vatican Council, by-passing the advice of his conservative counselors. It had been ninety-three years since the First Vatican Council of 1869. Who would have thought that Pope John XXIII would be the one to call fifty-one Cardinals to Rome from all over the world for this significant event?

According to an observer, Wilton Wynn, Pope John XXIII had no specific agenda for the Second Vatican Council. He knew intuitively that the Church needed renewal, or "aggiornamento." So his directive to the participants was to excercise "holy liberty" in their deliberations and let events take their course. (7) As is now known, the various commissions of Vatican II produced both refreshing and unsettling papers. After much heated debate these eventually became *The Documents of Vatican II.*

As Wynn says,

> The stifling atmosphere of the old Church of pomp and special privilege was given a good airing by Pope John. He changed almost nothing structurally, but through his style, his spirit, and his deeds he opened windows to winds of change that blew through the Church long after his death. (8)

John XXIII was Pope for only five years, having died in 1963. In that short time he left an indelible mark on the Church and the world. "This interim pope brought such change into the Church that his three successors spent most of their time coping with forces that he set in motion." (9)

Mother Beata Wertz was thrust into this era of change by her election as superior general in 1962. Of her, the biblical injunction "be wise as serpents and humble as doves" could be applied. She was a woman religious whose wisdom came from deep and constant prayer; whose simplicity and humility were natural attributes of true wisdom. In disdain of honors, pomp, or privilege she had the spirit of Pope John XXIII. Like him, she was a politician whose quiet persuasion would reconcile disparate viewpoints as the IHM Congregation sought to fulfill the spirit of Vatican II in its own renewal.

General Chapter of Affairs 1962

The election of Mother Beata Wertz and the four council members having been completed at the 9:15 a.m. session of the Chapter of Elections, the thirty delegates assembled for the first session of the Chapter of Affairs at 2:00 p.m. on March 24, 1962. (10)

Faced with 115 proposals from the members of the Congregation the delegates began their deliberations in earnest. The first matter was a review of the status of the decrees passed at the Chapter of 1961. Of the twenty decrees, fourteen had been promulgated. Among these were such matters as directives regarding the use of television, driving cars, attending school programs, a three-day home visit, changes in the horarium, and a referendum on the habit and cloak. Among the six decrees from 1961 not yet addressed were such larger issues as the development of a Sister Formation Program for the junior professed sisters; exploration of the opening of a South American mission; development of models for school contracts; and, not surprisingly, a proposed "Manual of Etiquette" had not been written! (11)

The referendum on changes in the habit revealed that of 908 replies received, only 381 or 42% favored any change. The highest number, 150, voted for change in the bonnet only. In regard to the cloak, 757 replies were received, with 564 voting against any change and 253 favoring change, 248 of whom preferred a military cloak or Peter Pan collar on the existing cloak. Only two opted for a coat. (12) This ripple of movement for change in the habit would continue to gather momentum, however, and would be faced by Mother Beata at a later time.

At the closing session of the Chapter of Affairs, March 25, 1962, the capitulars affirmed the election of Mother Beata and the Council, saying, in part, "Under your enlightened leadership and through your well-known dedication to the interests of our Congregation, we are assured of continued growth in all fields, but above all in greater love of God and of His Church." (13)

Mother Beata's closing message expressed her gratitude for the dedication of the delegates, who, it must be remembered, disposed of 115 proposals in two days! She said:

> We thank you for all you have done for our beloved Congregation, and we pray that the holiness of our lives and our zeal for the way of life to which God has called us, will shine forth so resplendently that many other chosen souls will be attracted to our Congregation, and that all of us will merit the 'well done' of our divine Master. (14)

Dedication of the IHM Novitiate

Among the earliest official actions of Mother Beata was the dedication of the new IHM novitiate building. Five weeks after her election, on May 30, 1962, this event was held.

An historic path had led from the founding novitiate in 1845 at Monroe, Michigan to a new founding in St. Joseph, Susquehanna County, Pennsylvania in 1858, followed by another thriving novitiate by 1859 in Reading, Pennsylvania. With the division of this large Pennsylvania territory into several dioceses in 1868, Bishop Wood of Philadelphia and Bishop O'Hara of Scranton wanted separate foundations of IHM Sisters in each diocese. The novitiate for the Scranton foundation was temporarily established at Laurel Hill (St. Alphonsus Academy) in Susquehanna, Pennsylvania. By September 8, 1872, a new structure was built in Scranton and the motherhouse and novitiate was opened as St. Cecilia's Academy in downtown Scranton.

As St. Cecilia's Academy grew and seeing the need for a quieter and more remote setting for the novitiate, Bishop O'Hara approved the purchase of the Brennan estate in Carbondale, Pennsylvania for this purpose. On August 30, 1876, the novitiate and motherhouse were once again moved. The convent was named St. Rose in honor of America's first canonized saint.

For twenty-six years, until it became too small to serve as the center of the rapidly growing Congregation, St. Rose remained the novitiate and motherhouse. In 1902 upon completion of Mount St. Mary's (Marywood), the Congregation returned its motherhouse and novitiate to Scranton. For sixty years Mount St. Mary's housed the novitiate where the majority of today's members spent their early religious training years. (15)

It was with a touch of sadness, then, that the sisters gathered with Mother Beata, Bishop Jerome Hannan, clergy, members of the Fathers and Friends organization, and hundreds of friends from the surrounding area to dedicate the new novitiate building. Standing on the hill above the Marywood campus on the site of the new building, the vision that Mother Kathleen and her council had demonstrated in providing for the future growth of the IHM Congregation could be recaptured by all present.

Now, four months after Mother Kathleen's death, it became Mother Beata's role as superior general to preside at the dedication of Mother Kathleen's favorite project.

Mother Beata would not forget, as with mixed emotions she said,

> . . we rejoice in the dedication of this splendid building. It is a monument to our revered Mother M. Kathleen, who devoted herself wholeheartedly to its planning and construction. Every detail was of vital interest to her. Always in our memories, it will express to us the zeal with which she toiled in the care of our novices and postulants. (16)

Mother Kathleen's part in the planning of the new novitiate was recalled also by Monsignor William K. Dolan, Vicar for Religious of the Scranton Diocese, who wrote:

> Some years ago, I was conducted through the old novitiate quarters by your predecessor of happy memory, Mother M. Kathleen. I saw the great need for such a building as has been provided; I listened with keen interest to the plans that were being made for its construction. I shared the hopes that have now been realized. (17)

Bishop Hannan, too, remembered Mother Kathleen while giving credit also to the council and to the entire Congregation for persisting in pursuing its goal of a new novitiate. (18) He was undoubtedly aware that this project had been approved by Bishop William Hafey, his predecessor, and had been the object of Congregation frugality since Mother Marcella's time.

The forty-six page dedication booklet for the occasion was replete with pictures of diocesan and Congregation administrators, members of the Fathers and Friends who had labored through years of fundraising activities, and extensive views of the chapel, the classrooms, dining and recreational areas of the building. Four pages of the dedication booklet listed patrons and other donors solicited by direct letters from Mother Beata. Eight additional pages related an abbreviated history of the IHM Congregation.

An accounting of the dedication booklet project, prepared by Sister Celine Duffy, shows $30,073 in receipts from donors, and expenditures of $2,177, a very successful net of $27,896 for the novitiate building. (19)

The dedication ceremony included the placing of the cornerstone. Mother Beata placed the following items, together with Congregation data, in the cornerstone of the novitiate building: a copy of the IHM Constitutions, the manual of prayers, grace book, statue of Our Blessed Mother, statue of St. Joseph, Sacred Heart badge, brown and green scapulars, medals of St. Benedict, the Little Flower, Mother of Perpetual Help, St. Michael, St. Raphael, St. Anne, Our Lady of Lourdes, and a Miraculous medal. Other items were the dedication booklet, the article from *The Catholic Light* containing the write-up of the dedication ceremony, and a memorial card of Mother Kathleen's death. (20)

Monsignor Joseph G. Quinn, Scranton Diocesan Director of the Propagation of the Faith, was the principal speaker for the occasion. He reviewed briefly the history of the IHM Congregation, paid tribute to the foresight of Mother Kathleen and her council and to the generosity of so many benefactors who helped to realize their vision. His prayerful closing included these words, "May this new novitiate, dedicated to Jesus through Mary, be a power house spreading light and power and divine love . . ." (21)

On June 4, 1962, at 2:00 p.m., seventy-one novices and thirty postulants moved into the new novitiate building. Sister Adalbert (Mary) Schelb was reappointed mistress of novices; Sister Liguori Farnon reappointed as mistress of postulants. (22) Sister Lucetta Butler was appointed superior of the novitiate. Other professed sisters assigned to residence in the novitiate were Sisters Amabilis Conlan, Laetitia Caulson, Yvette Ireland and Florence Langan. (23)

For twenty-eight years this building served as the home and educational center for the novices. On July 27, 1990, Sister Redempta Sweeney, then superior general, and her council, made a decision to move the novitiate to the IHM convent on River Street in Scranton.

Community Board of Education/Tri-Community Education Conference

The delegates of the General Chapter of 1961 had established the Community Board of Education as the result of a unanimously approved proposal. Its first meeting, under the chairmanship of Sister Felicitas Ryan, a council member, was held with the sixteen initial board members present on October 28, 1961, at Our Lady of Grace Convent, Manhasset, New York. (24)

During Mother Beata's terms of office the Board of Education continued its excellent work in the development of the IHM teaching apostolates. Board members conducted numerous studies throughout the schools of the Congregation obtaining vital information for administrative planning and for decision-making by future General Chapter bodies.

Twice annually the Board of Education offered conferences for IHM teachers and principals on important educational issues at primary, elementary, secondary and college levels of instruction. Among these were textbook evaluation, teaching techniques, grading, certification, and the documents of Vatican II. (25)

Always alert to the "bigger picture," Sister Felicitas was more than happy to announce at the March 14, 1964, meeting of the Board of Education that the idea of an Inter-Community (three IHM Congregation branches) Board of Education had been approved by the major superiors at Monroe, Michigan, West Chester and Scranton, Pennsylvania.

Not wishing to claim credit for the idea, she nonetheless acknowledged later that she had written to the three major superiors, Mother Anna Maria, Mother Maria Pacis and Mother Beata on November 9, 1963. Her words were:

> In these days when the spirit of ecumenism breathes so blessedly upon the world and upon us in a special way, do you think we could explore the possibility of forming an inter-community education conference? There would, it seems, be much to gain in uniting the spiritual and the intellectual strengths that each of our three communities has developed over the years since our holy founder, Father Gillet, gave us a common rule, and the Church accepted our common apostolate. (27)

Within five days of her letter, enthusiastic responses were received, all bearing the same date, November 14, strangely enough, the date of Father Louis Florent Gillet's death.

Meetings began in earnest with representatives from the three Congregations, beginning in April 1964 after the NCEA Convention in Atlantic City, New Jersey. The following delegates, two from each Congregation, were appointed by the superiors general: Sisters Marie Isabel and Thomas Aquinas, Monroe, Michigan; Mother Boniface and Sister Lalande, West Chester, Pennsylvania; Sisters St. Mary Orr and Felicitas Ryan, Scranton, Pennsylvania. (28)

At this initial meeting the preparation of by-laws was begun. Two of the basic objectives formulated were: (1) to encourage the spirit of unity and cooperation among the Congregations of the Sisters, Servants of the Immaculate Heart of Mary; (2) to promote the scholarship and professional growth of the members of the Congregations. (29)

The August 26-27, 1964, meeting at Our Lady of Grace Convent, Manhasset, New York was considered "history-making," both because of the rapport among the representatives, and the decision to conduct a significant evaluation of the schools in which the three Congregations served. At this meeting also the theme of the first institute was chosen "The Sister in the School of Tomorrow." (30)

Additional planning meetings were held on October 17, 1964, in Scranton; on December 12-13, 1964, at St. Rosalia's Convent in Pittsburgh; on April 23, 1965, at the Pittsburgh Airport; and on July 25, 1965, at Marywood. (31)

Meanwhile, since the Scranton IHMs were hosts for the first biennial institute, there was much activity on the home front as committees were set into motion. Every aspect of a successful gathering was anticipated from "hospitality," headed by Sister Joanella Ryan, local superior at Marywood; registration, Sister Margrete Kelly; transportation, Sister Aquina Whalen; entertainment, Sisters Marie Cecilia Macmillan and Maryla Farfour; publicity, Sister Celine Duffy; menu, Sister Eva Connors; and many more. While the committee directors were Marywood sisters, committee members were drawn from the entire Congregation. (32)

Mother Beata appointed fifty official delegates, with instructions regarding their duties during the meetings, in a letter to the Congregation dated May 8, 1965. An invitation was also extended to all sisters to attend all or some of the sessions of the institute. (33)

When the historical day, August 19, 1965, arrived it was Mother Beata's task to welcome a Marywood theatre-packed audience of some eleven hundred sisters from the three IHM Congregations. Her message acknowledged the "lively feeling of oneness and of belonging to a unity" which was evident as the three Congregations came together from a common root. Looking to the future, Mother Beata said:

> Now, as our Holy Founder looks out on this changing world, he knows we must prepare to meet this challenge in a new way. But just as Father Gillet met the needs of his day by the formation of a teaching community, so now on this historic occasion marking the first joint conference of his three Congregations, we shall arm ourselves to meet whatever needs will arise in the future. Our objective is clear B to make a more profound, a more deeply spiritual impact on a world that is basically materialistic. (34)

In her usual humble, yet forthright manner, Mother Beata was facing directly a matter of significant disagreement existing between the West Chester IHMs and the other two Congregations, namely, the assuming of varied ministries, along with education, by the Monroe and Scranton groups. "Meeting whatever needs will arise in the future" was not an idea whose time had come for many sisters in the three Congregations in 1965, or indeed, for many years thereafter.

Evidence of the need at that tenuous time to give each Congregation equal participation in the institute program is seen in the fact that the August 20, 1965, program records that on each topic addressed, there were three representative speakers. The verbatim material presented on August 20 is a matter of record and totals 102 pages! (35) It is recalled that it was not until 2:00 p.m. that a break for lunch could be had.

Special evening events, the songfest and the Tri-Community string ensemble under the direction of Sister Consilia (Anita) Brotherton of Scranton were very important in generating admiration and respect for the talents of each sister. Judging by post-institute letters received by Mother Beata, the first objective of the Tri-Community Education Conference, namely, "to encourage the spirit of unity and cooperation among the Congregations of the Sisters of IHM," was already well on its way to realization. Mother Maria Pacis, IHM, of West Chester wrote:

> If an award were to be given for perfect hostesses, you would be the first to receive it! We were thrilled beyond words with the warm hospitality extended to all at the Biennial Institute conducted at Marywood . . . the bound copy of the Proceedings of the Institute is simply inspiring. It is most gratifying to see the spirituality, dedication, and talent manifested in this work. We certainly can be justly proud of our IHMs (36)

Second Biennial Education Institute

Within two years, on August 17-19, 1967, the hospitality of the Monroe, Michigan IHMs was to be experienced by some 175 Scranton IHMs, and a like number of West Chester IHMs who journeyed, most for the first time, to Monroe for the Second Biennial Institute of the Tri-Community Education Conference. Those who traveled by way of Canada recall that the border guards were amazed at all the sisters crossing over into Michigan. One remarked "Is anyone home minding the store?"

Appropriately, at Monroe, the site of the founding of the IHM Congregation, the institute's theme was "The Past is a Prologue to Today's Meaning." The original log cabin, the memorial chapel where Father Gillet was buried, the River Raisin, so often recalled in historical notes, and the hundreds of items of memorabilia displayed in the Pioneer Room of the Monroe Motherhouse—all spoke of past common bonds.

The institute speakers, while paying homage to the IHM past, moved to the present and future of Catholic education and the challenges for IHM sister-teachers in a changing Church and a changing world. Possibly the most inspiring, daring, and insightful of these was the closing address of Mother Benedicta (Margaret) Brennan of Monroe. Entitled "Alphonsian Spirit in Christian Education," her words recalled the teaching and fervor of St. Alphonsus Liguori and Father Gillet on the necessity of personal holiness and the challenge to serve the ever-changing needs of the Church, especially in the poor. "We must serve the poor wherever we find them," she said. "We have not always been as careful as he (St. Alphonsus) was in our preferences." Mother Benedicta asked many hard, thought-provoking questions, among which was, "Will we be willing to rethink even radically if need be the place of the Catholic school in a Post-Conciliar Church?" She emphasized the apostolic nature of our Congregations, balanced with contemplation, in accord with Alphonsian teaching. Then, referring to the challenges of Vatican II, she said:

> The spirit of our Congregations reminds us through the voice of the Church that all renewal is essentially self-renewal and that new directions in Catholic education will have to take their direction from changes in attitude on the part of Catholic educators themselves. (37)

On these notes the Second Biennial Institute came to a close, with bonds of unity strengthened among the sisters.

Third Educational Institute

The 125th anniversary year of the founding of the IHM Congregation and the 50th anniversary of Immaculata College were the occasions for the Third Biennial Institute of the IHM Education Conference at Immaculata, West Chester, Pennsylvania on August 18-21, 1970. Mother Beata invited all Scranton IHMs to attend in a letter dated July 17, 1970. (38)

Detailed planning for the Third Institute had been on the agenda of IHM Education Conference meetings in February, March, and April 1970. The theme chosen was "IHMs in a Decade of Promise," and Dr. Clarence Walton, president of Catholic University, Washington, DC, and Dr. James Hanlon of Marquette University in Wisconsin were selected as keynote speakers. Sisters from the Congregations were to be involved in topics such as "New Dimensions in Education," "Innovations in Schools," and "Issues and Solutions."

Some 1,200 IHMs from the three Congregations found their way to the "city of brotherly love," Philadelphia, and on to Immaculata. Sister Mary of Lourdes, president of Immaculata College, chaired the institute. The welcome address was given by Mother M. Claudia, superior general, West Chester.

Once again, the three Congregations experienced a call from their roots as the words of Father Gillet were recalled: "The fruit is in the seed . . . now is the time for sowing." (39) The fact that Mother Theresa Maxis Duchemin's burial place was on the grounds of the West Chester Motherhouse brought an overwhelming desire to learn more about her part in the founding of the original Monroe community in 1845, to understand better her long, painful years of separation, when, almost as an orphan and beggar she sought refuge with the Grey Nuns in Canada, and finally was able to return to West Chester where she died.

Once again, the IHM Education Conference proved its unifying strength as sisters from the three branches celebrated both their history and their future. Knowledge does bring us together!

Educational Institutes 1972-1974

The Fourth Tri-Community Education Institute was held in Scranton in 1972 under the general chairmanship of Sister Espiritu Dempsey, academic dean, Marywood College. The theme of this institute was "Valuing in Education," chosen, as Sister Espiritu explained, "because the sisters felt that the particular uniqueness of the education offered by the IHM Sisters is in its value orientation for the students." (40)

Once again, over one thousand sisters from the three branches came to Scranton for this bonding and educational experience. This was to be the final Tri-Community Institute during Mother Beata's term of office, which would end in 1974. Mother Beata's closing words were significant and memorable as she expanded on Soren Kierkegaard's theme "To Will One Thing," saying:

> In all this I am only challenging you to capture again for the 1970's the single-mindedness of purpose and persevering spirit which characterized Father Gillet and the first Sisters of the Immaculate Heart of Mary. This does not mean that we should long for the past, nor for the external simplicity of life in those days . . . It is, rather, a challenge to discover what constitutes the central dynamism, which moved the seedling Congregation forward. (41)

And further: "Would our holy founder recognize us today as having that spirit— the desire and the will to become Saints? . . . For such a value there will always be searchers; and for such a_Congregation there will always be a future!" (42)

Subsequently, the by-laws of the IHM Education Conference would change to meet the changing interests of the sisters. Annual meetings of official members, two from each Congregation, continue as of this date in 2002.

Regional Government Established

With all of the time-consuming projects, such as the completion of the novitiate building, the move of 105 novices and postulants from the old motherhouse, exploration and acceptance of the new mission in Peru, and the requirement of visitation to some one hundred houses of the Congregation, Mother Beata's first years as superior general were far from placid.

Prompted by the Awinds of change@ begun by Pope John XXIII and the results of the Vatican II Council, Mother Beata's efforts were also directed at initiating some of these changes in the life of the Congregation. The spirit of collegiality being exemplified by Pope John XXIII in the Church was catching hold at all levels, including religious life. Wilton Wynn, writing of Pope John XXIII said:

> Pope John did not dismantle the imperial papal court, but his democratic style and obvious contempt for protocol showed how out-of-date it was and pointed the way toward its end . . Without issuing any new laws on the subject, John broadened the base of participation in Church decisions . . . (43)

Mother Beata's letter of June 5, 1964, to all the sisters announced the General Council's approval of a new government structure in the Congregation, reflecting this more collegial, participatory style of governance. (44)

Four regions were established across the Congregation's widely dispersed geographic areas. These regions were named Immaculate Heart, Our Lady of Lourdes, Our Lady of Grace, and St. Joseph. Sisters Lucian Reddington, Robertine Fox, and Georgina Wertz were appointed superiors of these regions, respectively, with a term of three years. Mother Beata herself was responsible for Immaculate Heart Region that included the motherhouse, Marian Convent, Marywood Seminary and College, Ponce, Puerto Rico, and the novitiate and juniorate communities. Sister

Lucian's area included all houses in the Scranton Diocese; Sister Robertine, all houses in the Archdioceses of Hartford, Connecticut and New York, and the dioceses of Bridgeport; Brooklyn; Providence, Rhode Island; Raleigh, North Carolina; Rockville Centre and Syracuse, New York. Sister Georgina was responsible for all houses in the Archdioceses of Baltimore, Maryland; Portland, Oregon; and Washington, D.C., and the Dioceses of Altoona, Pennsylvania; Boise, Idaho; Greensburg; Harrisburg; Pittsburgh, Pennsylvania; Trenton, New Jersey, and Wilmington, Delaware.

With a total of 1,139 professed sisters in the Congregation at the time, the new government provided for much greater contact with each individual sister than was previously possible for Mother Beata alone. The regional superiors were required to visit each sister at least once annually.

While Mother Beata's authority as superior general remained intact for major issues, seven areas were delineated in which the regional superior could grant permissions, thus dispersing authority, and relieving the burden on Mother Beata, as well. These areas were: (1) home visits; (2) attending conventions, accompanying school children to cultural activities, applying for a license to drive a car; (3) hospitalization, convalescence, retirement; (4) overnight visit to another convent; (5) dispensation from observance of some particular prescription of the Constitutions for an extended period; (6) recreational or educational trip as a community; (7) attendance at silver or golden jubilees of other IHM Sisters. (45)

It was clear that the newly established regions were not to be considered as independent provinces. All significant appointments, transfers, educational assignments and financial matters remained the prerogative of the central administration, namely, Mother Beata and her council. The regional superiors were not members of the council. They were required to make periodic reports to Mother Beata on their visits to the sisters.

Yet, the regional structure made it possible for the individual sister to become better known by the administration, thus enhancing the apostolate by a better utilization of the talents of the sisters. The new regional government also laid the groundwork for greater shared authority and collegiality in the future.

Habit Experimentation

As seen above in the introduction of regional government, Mother Beata did not wait for a General Chapter to keep the Congregation moving with the Church and the winds of change coming from Vatican II. So it was also with proposing changes in the habit worn by the IHM Sisters.

The question of change in some parts of the habit, namely, the bonnet, cape, or sleeves had been proposed in the General Chapter of 1961 during Mother Kathleen Hart's time. On June 27, 1961, the chapter delegates decided to conduct a referendum across the Congregation to determine the sisters' opinions regarding change in the habit. (46)

In the Chapter of 1962, at the beginning of Mother Beata's term of office as superior general, the results of the referendum were presented. In spite of the fact that 58% of the sisters opposed any change of the habit, it was nevertheless clear that Mother Beata would soon need to address this matter in which nearly one-half of the Congregation desired some change. (47)

Support for some change in the habit was building as sisters became more imbued with Vatican IIs call for adaptation and modernization of dress. Seeing changes among the many other Congregations was also a strong influence for change.

Early in 1966, Mother Beata appointed a committee of ten sisters to conduct further study of the possible modification of the habit. The following sisters were members: Sisters John Francis Marley, Alma Marie Morgan, Lucetta Butler, Timothy Smyth, Liguori Farnon, Rose Angela Ruddy, Amata Jordan, Marie Rooney, Marysia Reilly, and Cor Immaculatum Heffernon. A detailed questionnaire was developed and sent out to the entire Congregation. Of the 1196 questionnaires sent out, a response of 1,120 was received.

At the January 29, 1966, meeting, these responses were tabulated, showing more than a two-thirds majority, 1,055 sisters in favor of change. The majority of these indicated "moderate" change, a desire to retain the scapular, some modification of the bonnet, and change from the cape to a collar.

The next step was to seek models of habits, head dresses and coats which incorporated the sisters' suggestions for "moderate" change. The habit committee set a deadline of March 19, 1966, for these suggestions to be sent to Marywood. (48)

The minutes of the general council for July 21, 1966, record that action for change would not await the next General Chapter in 1968. "The modification of our own habit until final decision is made was discussed at length. All members agreed that some change should be made *this year* (author's emphasis) in order to test appropriate dress." (49)

"This year" turned out to be somewhere between August 15, 1966, and December 8, 1966! The letter sent to the Congregation by the habit committee, with Mother Beata's approval on August 15, 1966, informed the sisters that the "year of experimentation" had begun, that modifications were to be made to the present habit and head dress in accord with the specifications and drawings included in the letter. The statement read: "This habit and headdress may be worn as soon as each local community has completed the necessary alterations. All modifications should be finished by December 8, 1966." (50)

For most local communities the changes were made during the two or three weeks remaining before school opened in September. Seamstresses were in great demand, and ripping, cutting, sewing and pressing were the major activity of the day and night.

The annals of the local communities reveal the experience of the sisters as they returned to school and other assignments in September 1966. For example:

> School opened on September 7, and we made our first public appearance in our "new" habits. The children were surprisingly nonchalant at the strange sight that greeted them. (51). When had so much been accomplished in so short a time! Were we to wear our "new" habits on September first? Yes! . . . But feeling very much like new novices the day after Reception, we wore our renovated habits to the Diocesan Institute on September first. Almost everyone was happy that we, too, were heeding the advice of the Council Fathers. Of course, most glances centered around the hairline. (52)
>
> September 8th, Our Lady's Feast Day, found us donning the new habit for the first time. At first we missed our beautiful old ones but gradually we began to feel very much at home in our "new look." Its practicality came forward when we saw the smaller wash each sister had to do, as well as the few minutes it took to iron. The people here accepted it without question . . . in fact, we had a sneaking suspicion they really liked it . . .Truly we were loved and wanted by all . . . in our old habit or new. (53)

Similar experiences were had everywhere, as blushing boys in classrooms wouldn't raise their eyes to look at sister, who, to their astonishment, had shapely legs showing beneath the shortened dress and a visible hairline.

One sister, returning to graduate school as a student just after the changes in the habit was questioned by her professor as to whether she was "wearing new glasses, or something." (54)

Being women, as well as religious, the sisters were naturally self-conscious and many longed for the more settled past or for the period of experimentation to end. As is now realized, this was not to happen.

By January 1967 the habit committee was again in touch with the sisters, informing them that tailor-made samples of habits would be displayed during the summer retreats. "At this time you will cast a final vote." (55) This was not to happen either. Throughout the year 1967 position papers were sent in to the habit committee from sisters, some calling for retaining religious dress, and others citing the need for further experimentation with various styles and materials.

At the General Chapter 1968 there was no special report from the habit committee, nor was there any great desire on the delegates' part to give much time to this matter in light of the enormous tasks of renewal of the Constitutions, government, formation and apostolate before them. By initiating experimentation in 1966 Mother Beata had effectively diverted major concern from the habit issue. The chapter delegates, on July 19, 1968, heard proposals on the habit as presented by Sister Eva Connors, discussed them, and then voted 45 to 1 to entrust further habit experimentation to the Central Administrative Assembly. (56)

The CAA issued guidelines for habit experimentation on December 5, 1968. These guidelines broadened the options to include various patterns, with or without the scapular, a jacket, if desired, and religious symbols meaningful to the individual sister. (57)

The sisters continued to wear the veil and variations of the basic habit, or blue suits and blouses until the Chapter of 1986 decided on complete option of dress.

Vatican II: Further Renewal and Adaptation

"The Council must produce a new Pentecost of faith . . . like the dawning of a new day, a living dawn of the Catholic Church," wrote Pope John XXIII in early 1962. This was his hope, but he hardly dreamed that a gathering of some 2,500 Bishops from around the world would last more than a few weeks—certainly not for four years as it did, with an impact that would resonate down the decades thereafter. (58)

The same was true for the Sisters of IHM as, under Mother Beata's quiet leadership, they began what would not be a short process into renewal and adaptation, in accord with Vatican II. As soon as the Vatican Council was over and the *Documents of Vatican II* were published in 1966, Mother Beata inaugurated a study process throughout the Congregation.

Citing the "Document on Religious Life," Mother Beata, as early as October 15, 1966, urged the sisters to enter into the spirit of renewal by study and prayer. She wrote, "Each Sister throughout the Congregation is asked to unite in prayer and acts of self-denial, especially on Saturdays.

Successful renewal and adaptation cannot be achieved unless every member of the community co-operates and assumes her share of the responsibilities." (59) She also announced that Bishop J. Carroll McCormick of the Scranton Diocese had given approval for Exposition of the Blessed Sacrament at the motherhouse chapel on all Saturdays from November 5, 1966, to March 23, 1968.

The first step in eliciting the participation of all the sisters was the preparation of a self-study questionnaire, giving each sister the opportunity to suggest ideas for renewal and adaptation. The areas covered in the self-study were (1) administrative structures; (2) formation; (3) apostolate; (4) community life and worship. The questionnaires were sent out to the Congregation on October 24, 1966. Responses were due to Mother Beata on October 29. (60) Many excuses could have been given for not responding at this busy time of year, but none were given, and the sisters entered wholeheartedly into the process.

One week later, Mother Beata and members of the general council met to read, discuss, and tabulate the returns from the questionnaire. At this very meeting the Commission on Revision and five committees were named. (61)

A letter was sent from Mother Beata to the entire Congregation on November 8, 1966, thanking the sisters for their participation in the self-study and announcing the members of the committees. (62) The Commission on Revision of the Constitutions was composed of fourteen sisters: Sisters Benedictus Philpot, Alma Marie Morgan, Jane Kehoe, Stella Devers, Nadine Moran, Helene Coyle, Celine Duffy, Judith Gavigan, Angela Hughes, Francella Shaughnessy, St. Denis (Marian Denise) Walsh, Kevina (Joan) Mooney, Bernardinus (Gloria) Frank, and Marise (Dorothy) Haney.

One or more of the commission members was also a member of each of the five committees formed. Forty-six additional sisters from across the Congregation were members of the committees. The five committees were: (1) Spirit and Purpose; (2) Implementation of Spirit and Purpose; (3) Formation for Apostolate; (4) Works of the Apostolate; (5) Nature and Exercise of Authority in the Congregation.

One month after their appointment, the committee members received a letter from Mother Beata inviting them to Marywood for the first meeting on December 17, 1966. (63) As a result of this meeting the work of the committees swung into high gear. Ideas were needed from the Congregation at large by each of the committees, and so the seemingly endless questionnaires were sent out, the first of which was from the committee on the election of delegates to the General Chapter, dated

December 18, 1966, the very next day after the first meeting was held. Information from the October 1966 self-study had been shared at this first meeting of the committees, and it was evident that there was widespread support for a change in the method of obtaining delegates to the General Chapter. If there were to be any change effected for the General Chapter of 1968, approval would have to be obtained from the Sacred Congregation for Religious in Rome in time for the election of delegates; hence the rush to get the approval of the entire Congregation for a new process.

To their credit, the committee members, Sisters Edgar (Marian) Flannery, Coleman Nee, Jane Kehoe, and Phyllis McCarty developed five possible alternatives for the election of delegates, submitted them to the Congregation, obtained support for two of the plans, resubmitted these to the Congregation, and arrived at 87% approval by the Congregation of what came to be called Plan 2. Briefly, this plan incorporated the desire of the sisters to have representation from five age groups, to minimize the number of ex officio delegates, and to drop the geographic and apostolate representation that had been used previously.

The new plan for the election of delegates to the General Chapter was sent to Rome and was approved nearly nine months later. A letter from Mother Beata to the Congregation, dated September 1, 1967, informed the members that approval had been given for this change in the Constitutions. (64)

Meanwhile, in order to provide updated spirituality for the sisters, Mother Beata continued to encourage the reading of the *Vatican II Documents* and planned a fifteen-lecture renewal program by videotape, copies of which were sent to each convent for viewing and discussion. Lectures were also held at various sites around the Congregation, bringing theologians of the prestige of Bernard Haring, CSsR and canon lawyers, such as Reverend Joseph Gallen, SJ. Every opportunity was provided for the sisters to understand the direction given by Vatican II for renewal of religious customs, dress, government and *Constitutions.*

After nearly a year of study, responding to questionnaires, and holding local and area discussion sessions, Mother Beata again acknowledged the cooperation of the sisters in the work of renewal and its importance as preparation for the General Chapter of 1968 that she knew would bring momentous change. She wrote: "What is evolving is a Congregation confirmed in observance of gospel precepts and faithful to the age-old traditions of our founder." (65)

Mother Beata knew, however, that the "signs of the times" and the spirit of "aggiornamento" prompted by John XXIII would put a new face on the traditions of our founder. In fact, she expected that all the study, reflection and discussion of our roots, nature and purpose were already causing motion (sometimes, motion-sickness) in the sisters. She had no fear of the outcome, in tune as she was with the Church. She refers to this, saying: "If in meditating on the essence of community, you have found your way of thinking radically changed, here is a certain sign of the workings of the Holy Spirit." (66)

The work of the committees continued assiduously for a second year, studying, compiling data, discussing, and finally developing proposals for the General Chapter of 1968. One hundred-seventy pages of minutes of meetings held by the committees are on record. The fruit of this work was finally coordinated under five commissions: Apostolate, Formation, Government, and Religious Life. At the time of the opening of the Chapter in June 1968 the number of proposals received from the total Congregation was 1,877. The commissions had dealt with many of these during the two years prior to the chapter, either incorporating them into their recommendations or rejecting them as not in line with renewal.

The General Chapter of 1968

The General Chapter re-elected Mother Beata Wertz as superior general on June 24, 1968. She was seventy years old at the time, but neither the delegates who elected her, nor she herself, thought the challenge too great. The election of the council members was delayed until the Chapter of Affairs would make a decision on the proposed new form of government. (67)

Mother Beata wasted no time in opening the Chapter of Affairs the following morning, June 25, 1968, at 9:30 a.m. After a few brief introductory business matters, the first agenda item was the presentation of the Resolution for Collegial Government by the chairperson of the Commission on Government, Sister M. Felicitas Ryan.

The *Documents of Vatican II* had introduced the vocabulary for reform of governmental structures in religious life, especially in apostolic institutes. Words such as "collegiality," "participatory," "decentralization," together with "subsidiarity," conveyed a new concept of authority for religious communities. The form of government proposed by the Commission on Government in Chapter 1968 was a response to these new concepts. While there had been a minority of delegates in support of provincial government, this proposal did not gain acceptance.

The plan submitted by the Commission on Government, called "Collegial (Sector) Government" was as follows: The Congregation would be divided into four geographic areas called sectors. A superior would be elected by and from the Congregation at large for each sector. Each sector would have approximately 260 sisters. The four sector superiors, together with the superior general and her assistant would constitute the Central Administrative Assembly, formerly known as the Superior General and Council. The term of office remained six years, with possibility of re-election for another six years.

The sectors were not independently governed entities, as in provincial government, but were linked to the total Congregation by three increasingly wider participatory assemblies, namely, the local assembly, district assembly, and sector assembly.

The local assembly embraced each local community of sisters, and became more independent in matters of permissions previously requiring the regional superior or superior general's decision. For the first time, the local community had the option of electing its own superior from the local members, instead of their being appointed by the superior general and approved by the council.

The district development assembly was composed of one representative from each local assembly within a given geographic area. Their purpose was to plan, coordinate, and evaluate apostolic works and opportunities in the district, and to serve as a liaison from the local assemblies to the sector coordinating assembly.

The sector coordinating assembly included the sector superior, the chairpersons from each district and two additional elected representatives from each district.

The General Chapter of the Congregation remained the highest internal authority in the Congregation, representing every member through its elected representatives, forty in number, plus the ex officio members — the superior general, assistant general, and the four sector superiors.

After a one-day interim in which amendments to the Government Commission proposal were submitted and considered, the Chapter delegates voted for the adoption of the new government by 46 to 1 on June 27, 1968. (68)

With the new government approved, the responsibilities of the assistant superior general and the sector superiors were now clear, and the delegates could begin to identify sisters who could fill these positions. The date set for these elections was July 9, 1968. The new assistant superior general elected was Sister Nadine Moran, whose term would be six years, concurrent with that of Mother Beata. The new sector superiors were: Sister Nora Clarke, Northeastern Pennsylvania Sector; Sister Jane Kehoe, Western Sector; Sister Mary Martin O'Dea, Eastern Sector; and Sister Adalbert (Mary) Schelb, Southern Sector.

The existing regional superiors were to serve until September 8, 1968, at which time the new sector superiors would begin an initial two-year term, after that, if re-elected, would serve a three-year term. (69)

Provisional Constitutions and Chapter Decrees – 1968

While considerable space has been given to the adaptation of religious dress and to renewal of government structures in the Congregation, these were only facilitative measures to support the essence of religious life, namely, life lived in community, committed to the vows of poverty, obedience and chastity.

The Commission on Religious Life presented the Chapter of 1968 with Part I of the Provisional Constitutions, the fruit of nearly two years of work. Both communal and individual means to support the many dimensions of religious life were provided. The focus was on following Christ as seen in the Scriptures and a return to the initial inspirations of our founder. Recommendations encompassed communal and private prayer, Eucharistic celebration, spiritual reading, monthly and annual retreats, silence, and healthy recreation.

The vows were redefined in accord with the *Vatican II Documents*, especially "Lumen Gentium" and "Perfectae Caritatis."

In promulgating the Provisional Constitutions and Chapter Decrees to the Congregation, Mother Beata wrote, in part:

> The General Chapter has accepted Part One of the Constitutions that evolved from the work of the Commission on Renewal. These Constitutions and the Decrees of the General Chapter constitute our interim rule of life. The General Chapter suspends our former Constitutions and abrogates the book of Customs. It is understood that Church law and Canon Law related to religious life have binding force. The Constitutions and Decrees promulgated by the General Chapter have a binding force for each Sister. (70)

And further,

> The Constitutions and Decrees will become effective on the feast of the Nativity of the Blessed Virgin Mary, September 8, 1968. (71)

The General Chapter of 1970

The General Chapter of 1970 would continue the work of the Chapter of 1978, giving more permanent form to the documents referred to above as *Provisional Constitutions* and "interim" way of life.

The sector form of government introduced in 1968 was reaffirmed by the 1970 Chapter delegates. One hundred and eleven proposals for change in the original government description had been received by the Government Commission. Thirty of these related to local government indicating the tension between sisters desiring change to a more collegial authority at the local level, and those wanting no change. Twenty-two proposals addressed the role of the sector superiors. These, too, reflected the "more" or "less" concept of authority and independence of the sector from the Central Administrative Assembly.

An amended resolution was, therefore, presented by the Commission on July 31, 1970. Among these amendments, the description of the office of sector superiors was expanded, and the term extended to four years with possible re-election for a second four-year term.

The Commission on Religious Life presented 102 amendments to the *Provisional Constitutions* based on proposals received from the Congregation membership. Topics included were worship, prayer, spiritual reading, the Sacrament of Penance, retreat, the evangelical counsels (vows), community living, silence, mortification and recreation. It was understandable that the sisters would have shown so much interest in these matters that are at the heart of religious life.

The Finance Committee provided the delegates with a progress report and responses to the 1968 proposals. The Committee members had produced a "Temporal Affairs Manual" which included motivational statements on individual and corporate poverty, and detailed procedures and forms for use by the local assembly in dealing with financial matters.

The work of these three Commissions: Government, Religious Life and Temporal Affairs constituted a major contribution to the direction of the IHM Congregation for years to come.

The General Chapter of 1970 closed on August 4, 1970. By September 8, 1970, the revised *Constitutions,* Enactments and Decrees of the Chapter were promulgated by Mother Beata.

New Missions

It is amazing to note that with all of the activity of the immediate post-Vatican II period described above, Mother Beata and her council were able at the same time to give attention to the expansion of the Congregation's ministry locations. Between 1962 and the Chapter of 1968, thirteen new schools were opened. These included the missions in Ponce, Puerto Rico; Lima, Peru; St. Pius X, Coeur d'Alene, Idaho; St. Aloysius, Cresson, Pennsylvania; Dunmore Catholic High School, Dunmore, Pennsylvania; St. Lawrence, South Williamsport; St. Thomas,

Bedford, Pennsylvania; Maria Regina High School, Uniondale, New York; Our Lady of Mercy, Forest Hills, New York; St. Raphael's, St. Petersburg, Florida; Sts. Philip and James, James, New York; Notre Dame High School, Stroudsburg, Pennsylvania, and Our Lady of Grace Montessori School, Manhasset, New York. In addition, the Child Care Center in Hollidaysburg, Pennsylvania was opened.

Convento Cristo Rey, Ponce, Puerto Rico

A letter dated October 19, 1963, from Reverend Higinio Madrazo, CM., pastor of the new Christ the King Parish in Ponce, Puerto Rico, solicited at least three sisters needed by May 1964 to staff a K-5 school in the parish of Cristo Rey. He described Ponce as the second largest city on the island, having a Catholic University and 150,000 people in the parish. "The new convent is the best in the Island of Puerto Rico," he added. (72)

Mother Beata replied on November 9, 1963, posing many questions. (73) Thus began a monthly correspondence between the pastor of the Parish of Cristo Rey, Reverend Angel Echeverria, CM, and Mother Beata from November 1963 to April 1964. The interest engendered by this correspondence led to the decision-making visit of Mother Beata and Sister John Francis Marley, first assistant, to Ponce on April 13, 1964. The warm welcome they received from the priests, people of the parish of Cristo Rey, and other religious communities of sisters in the area was moving and impressive.

The Sisters of St. Joseph of Brentwood provided hospitality for the travelers. Their superior in Ponce was Sister Ursula Marie, SSJ, who, as it happened, was a niece of IHM Sister Terence McGirr. Sister Ursula Marie was an experienced guide, as Mother Beata and Sister John Francis were introduced to Puerto Rican culture and beauty. The decision to send IHM Sisters to serve in the parish of Cristo Rey was undoubtedly crystallized during this visit. (74)

Two months later, on June 22, 1964, Sisters Mary Gordon (Jeanne) Tubach, Aquinas Shilling and Teresa Mary Gilhool were saying their farewells as they left Marywood in Scranton to travel to New York to join their fourth traveler, Sister Theodore (Maria) Voorneveld, who was then stationed at St. Alphonsus in New York. The little band stayed overnight at St. Alphonsus. Early on the morning of June 23, 1964, they flew from New York to San Juan, then on to Ponce, a bumpy twenty-five minute ride by small plane.

What a welcome awaited the four IHM Sisters, as throngs of children, parents, priests and sisters serving at other parishes on the island greeted their arrival! Speeches, music, flowers and food were part of this sincere and warm welcome. (75)

Eight days later, stern reality set in as the sisters began Spanish classes at the University of Puerto Rico, aware that school would be starting on August 16, just six weeks away.

The patron of languages was surely on their side as they successfully negotiated the challenge of teaching in the Spanish language, and the sisters endeared themselves to the students who politely corrected any small grammatical errors made by their teachers.

The first year of the IHMs in Ponce, Puerto Rico had its share of recreational experiences as the sisters were gradually introduced to cultural events, people, and places to be remembered on the island. There was an excellent rapport developed with other religious communities, especially the IHMs from Monroe and the Brentwood Sisters of St. Joseph. The first visitor from the States was Mrs. Gilhool, mother of Sister Teresa Mary, who arrived on December 29 for a visit. On January 12, Sister Brendan and Sister Aquina came from Marywood for a two-week visit. In February, Betty Braun, sister of Sister Karen Braun, stopped by. All of these visits brought a touch of home to the sisters and provided an opportunity for them to be the new tourist guides. (76)

Throughout the year the sisters were becoming more and more aware of the poverty of some of their near neighbors, and the distinctions being made even by the Church between academy children and barrio children. Separate classes were given, for example, in preparation for First Communion, and separate ceremonies held for such occasions. Mother Beata had been made aware during her visit of the needs of the barrio children, but her advice to the sisters was that they not undertake the extended work for a few years until the school was firmly established. However, some of the priests of the mountain parishes who were dedicated to the work in the barrios pressured the sisters for assistance. By October of the second year in Ponce, the Sisters were deeply involved in catechetical instructions in the barrios. (77)

The second year of IHM presence in Ponce, Puerto Rico saw the addition of Sister LaSallette Connell to the faculty at Cristo Rey, which now numbered five sisters, including the principal, Sister Mary Gordon (Jeanne), and four lay teachers. There were 244 pupils enrolled. The pastor, Father Echeverria, CM, always full of gratitude for the Sisters, wrote to Mother Beata, "Thanks for the new Sister. We have now five angels in the Parish. We are very happy with their work in the past school year." (78)

It was an exciting fall as construction of the new wing on the school proceeded. The first floor included a Salon Iglesia, and three large classrooms made up the second floor. A completely new lavatory section was built for the older children. The highlight of the fall semester was the visit of Mother Beata and Sister St. Mary Orr from December 9 to December 18, 1965. With the sisters already experienced tour guides, the visitors enjoyed seeing Puerto Rico through their eyes. During this visit, plans were made for the building of a chapel in honor of the Immaculate Heart of Mary in Barrio Layuca to be sponsored by the IHM Congregation. Mrs. C. Bruce of Long Island, New York gave $2,000 toward this project.

At this time the Congregation at large was studying possible modifications or changes to the habit and veil worn by the sisters. The sisters in Puerto Rico volunteered to experiment with some of the suggested variations, since there was a need for them to change the blue serge habit to white because of the intense heat in Puerto Rico. Their suggestions for Puerto Rico included lighter weight materials and a change from the bonnet to a light band and veil. Mother Beata and Sister St. Mary approved these. The sisters would wear their new habits for the first time on December 26, 1965.

While Sister St. Mary was in Puerto Rico, the Marywood College Alumnae held a luncheon at the Hilton Hotel to which all the IHMs were invited. As Marywood College president, Sister St. Mary addressed the alumnae, updating them on college news. (79)

Events moved quickly over the holidays, and the sisters were happy to greet Mr. And Mrs. Tubach and their daughter who visited with Sister Jeanne from December 28 to January 7. When the holidays were over, the sisters plunged into preparing the children for the Sacrament of Confirmation. On January 23, 1966 Bishop Torres administered Confirmation to 654 youngsters.

The school year 1966-1967 saw 293 pupils enrolled. Five sisters and six lay teachers comprised the faculty. In addition to the regular classes at Cristo Rey, the sisters provided religious instructions for 590 children at five sites. The largest group, 310 children, were at Maraguez where Sister Aquinas and Sister Theodore (Maria) taught, together with fourteen Catequistas. (80)

November 24, 1966, saw the arrival of the Congregation's school supervisor, Sister Felicitas Ryan. Her six-day visit provided much support for the work of the sisters, as well as much enjoyment as they celebrated Thanksgiving together.

This third year in the history of the IHMs in Puerto Rico saw several crises. On March 18, 1967, Sister LaSalette requested a change to return to the States. On May 20, Sister Teresa Mary requested a dispensation from her vows and left Puerto Rico for the States. These events were devastating to the little community and were complicated further by Mother Beata's decision to transfer the superior and principal, Sister Mary Gordon (Jeanne) from Puerto Rico. On June 4 Sister Mary Gordon said her sad farewells and accompanied by Sisters Theodore (Maria) and Aquinas, who were making home visits, left for the States. The annals attempt to capture the situation, saying only "It is impossible to explain the heaviness of heart that these days have brought and it is better to refrain from comments, as words are inadequate and could not convey the true picture." (81)

By 1967-1968 the school at Cristo Rey included nine grades, a pre-kindergarten and kindergarten. Sister Michael Marie Hartman who had been in Lima, Peru, was appointed superior and principal, as well as first grade teacher of forty pupils. Her facility in Spanish was a great aid to the sisters and faculty. Sister Theodore (Maria) continued as sixth grade teacher. Teachers for all other elementary classes were laywomen. Grades seven, eight and nine, considered secondary school in Puerto Rico, were staffed by Sister Aquinas, Sister Charles Mary (Eileen) Stanley, and Senora Velma Garcia, teacher of Spanish and Science.

Plans for construction of the third section of the Academia were underway. The school's growth to 353 pupils necessitated more space. The urgent need was for three more classrooms, two laboratories, a library, two additional lavatories and two shower rooms. A secondary school office and guidance room were to be located temporarily in a section of the library. (82)

During 1967-1968 the sisters had many opportunities to attend professional and cultural meetings. This beautiful setting continued to attract many visitors, among them Sister Hyacinth Serafini, Sister Charles Mary's mother and aunt, Bishop Carberry from St. Louis, Missouri, Sister Anysia Donohue, superior in Lima, Peru, and Sisters Louisa (Theresa) McElroy, Ann Charles (Mary) Reap, and Amator (Agnes) Shaw who were studying Spanish at the Inter-Cultural Institute in Ponce.

A highlight of the year was the dedication of the Immaculate Heart of Mary chapel in the Layuca barrio. The men of the parish had constructed it, brick by brick. Sister Theodore (Maria) deserves much credit for obtaining gifts from the Congregation and friends in the States for this project. This chapel continues to the present date. (83)

The support of Mother Beata and the Council for the mission at Ponce, Puerto Rico was evident in the 1968-1969 assignment of six IHM Sisters to serve there. New to Cristo Rey were Sisters Gloria Frank, Joan McAndrew, and Bernadette Hamilton. Continuing were Sisters Michael

Marie, Maria, and Eileen. Three hundred-ninety pupils were registered from pre-K to 10 as grade ten was added. Eight lay teachers, plus two part-time physical education teachers rounded out the sixteen-member faculty. In addition to their teaching duties and religious instructions in the barrios, the Sisters were asked to take the parish census. The Trinitarian Sisters instructed them in this process. (84)

October 24, 1968, saw the happy return of Sister Mary Gordon (Jeanne) Tubach to Puerto Rico for a two-week visit. The PTA had invited her as the former principal to the dedication of the new addition to the school. At the ceremonies, Sister Jeanne was presented with red roses from the school children, and an engraved plaque expressing the gratitude of the people for her service there. (85)

The annals of Convento Cristo Rey record a steady flow of visitors to the sisters from mid November 1968 to the end of February 1969. Families and friends of the Sisters, as well as the Congregation sector superior and school supervisors were on the list. During this period the serious business of the evaluation and accreditation of the elementary school proceeded. A team of four from the Department of Education in San Juan visited the school from December 4 through 6. Special commendation was given to Sisters Maria and Bernadette for their teaching of English as a second language. The long-awaited word finally arrived on March 14, 1969: the elementary school had received its accreditation! (86)

It is understandable that the sisters of Cristo Rey wrote no Annals for 1969-1970. This was to be the final year of IHM presence in Ponce, and undoubtedly signs of the eventual closure were felt throughout the year and colored much of the community and school activity. The minutes of the Central Administrative Assembly carry no reference to the impending closure until May 4, 1970, when it is clear that three of the six sisters in Ponce had recently requested changes, one sister seeking exclaustration from the Congregation. The discussion of this serious situation comes to the same conclusion regarding each case, namely, that "at this time we have no Sister sufficiently prepared either in the Spanish language, or in a subject matter area or professional responsibility to replace these three Sisters." (87)

On a motion by Sister Mary Martin O'Dea, seconded by Sister Jane Kehoe, and carried unanimously by the entire Central Administrative Assembly, the decision was made "to withdraw from Academia Cristo Rey, Ponce, Puerto Rico as of June 1970." (88) Sister Nadine Moran, assistant to Mother Beata, was designated to go to Ponce to discuss the matter with the sisters and with the pastor, Reverend Echeverria. Her report to the CAA on May 12, 1970, indicates that several hours had been spent in discussion with the sisters, and in acknowledgement of the late timing of the communication of their decisions, four sisters offered to stay in Ponce to continue the work. No solution was reached regarding possible replacements.

After due consideration the CAA reaffirmed their first decision to withdraw the sisters as of June 1970. This decision was confirmed again after Sister Nadine's second official visit to convey this news to Bishop Juan Torres, to the pastor, and to the sisters. (89)

The annals of Cristo Rey indicate that letters dated May 5 and May 12, 1970, were received by the sisters as a local assembly, by the superior/principal, Sister Michael Marie, and by Sister Joan McAndrew, principal of the secondary school. The pastor and the bishop also received written confirmation of the decision. The reasons cited accurately portrayed the situation:

> The timing of this decision may appear unjust and hasty. However, since three members of your local assembly requested transfers from this mission, two of these requests having been received very recently, there was no alternative left but for us to withdraw all the Sisters. You realize, perhaps not so fully as we do, the difficulty we are experiencing in staffing this mission with Sisters competent in their field of concentration and also trained to be fluent enough to be effective in their apostolic endeavors. (90)

It was clear also in this letter that the members of the CAA understood the sisters' sincere requests for changes and appreciated the work they had done in Puerto Rico. The final word on this mission was a letter from the pastor, Reverend Angel Echeverria recognizing the outstanding work of the sisters over their six years at Cristo Rey. He wrote:

> It is with great sorrow that we, at Academia Cristo Rey, say goodbye to the Sisters of IHM after the six fruitful years that they have stayed with us. Their self-sacrifice, devotion, enthusiasm, faithfulness, and ability made them very dear to all the students, parents and the community of Cristo Rey . . . (91)

In this letter, Father Echeverria notes that he has already obtained the Sisters of St. Francis of Buffalo, New York, to replace the IHM Sisters in the school. Cristo Rey in Ponce, Puerto Rico was obviously an attractive missionary spot that had been enhanced by the work of the IHM Sisters.

Santisimo Nombre de Jesus, Lima, Peru

As early as 1958 there was correspondence between Reverend Joseph Nangle, OFM and Mother Kathleen Hart regarding the possibility of sending IHM Sisters to Lima, Peru. (92) Again in 1960 Reverend John Waldie, pastor of Parroguia de Nuestra Senora Del Pilar in Arequipa, Peru, wrote seeking two or three sisters for March 1962 with a long-term goal of eleven sisters for a school operated by the Maryknoll Fathers. (93)

Mother Kathleen's response indicated the shortage of personnel being experienced at home. (94) The urgent need for nursing sisters and teaching sisters was also set forth in appeals made to Mother Kathleen by Romolo Carboni, Apostolic Nuncio in Lima. (95) In April 1962 three weeks after Mother Beata's election he directed his renewed appeal to her. (96)

Nearly two years passed without further activity regarding a possible IHM mission in Peru. However, in a letter of January 31, 1964, informing Bishop Jerome Hannan of the Congregation's intent to staff Puerto Rico and Lima, Peru, Mother Beata mentions that negotiations are in process with the Franciscan Fathers of New York City regarding the Lima, Peru mission. (97) In a letter to Reverend Donald Hoag, OFM. provincial, dated February 4, 1964, Mother Beata also expressed interest in staffing a school in Peru under the jurisdiction of the Franciscan Fathers of New York. Father Hoag expressed his gratitude to Mother Beata, but it was evident that he was far from ready to begin the project, since the land for the proposed school had not yet been acquired. (98) A flurry of correspondence between Father Hoag, provincial in New York, and Father Joseph Nangle in Lima during February and March 1964 as well as Father Hoag's visit to Mother Beata at Marywood in May, indicate an expediting of plans for the IHMs to go to Lima.

The first communication from the pastor, Reverend Jeremias Nangle, OFM. came to Mother Beata in June 1964. His gratitude for the coming of the sisters is expressed, as well as his disappointment that they would not arrive in April 1965 for the opening of the school year. "We shall begin with lay teachers," he writes. (99) Details are then given of the fact that a new Friary is being built for the Franciscan Fathers so that the sisters will have the Fathers' present residence upon arrival. "Construction of a permanent convent will not begin for at least two years yet," he states. (100)

That this new mission was a priority to Mother Beata is seen in the fact that nearly nine months prior to the sisters' departure for Lima, she had assigned four sisters. Those named were: Sister Ramona Scanlon, superior and principal, Sister Anysia Donohue, Sister Michael Marie Hartman, and Sister Joel Marie Sheehe. (101).

By November 1964 Father Nangle was able to write that " . . . The plans for the school have been completed and construction on the classrooms needed for the coming school year is due to begin in December." (102)

In order to see with her own eyes the mission so far away to which she was sending sisters, Mother Beata planned to visit Lima in advance. So, with a stopover in Miami at the Philadelphia IHM Notre Dame Academy on February 15, 1965, Mother Beata and Sister John Francis Marley, first assistant, were on their way to Lima, Peru. They left Miami on February 18 and were met at the airport in Lima by the Philadelphia IHM Sisters who provided generous hospitality to them during their visit. (103)

It appears that this visit was highly successful and paved the way for the arrival of the sisters who would staff Colegio Parroquial Santisimo Nombre de Jesus. Sisters Ramona, Anysia, Michael Marie and Joel Marie left Marywood at 10 a.m. on Friday, July 16, 1965, for the Newark Airport. They were given a rousing send-off by a large gathering of sisters, friends, and families as they boarded an Eastern Airlines Jet for Miami. Changing planes in Miami to a Panagra Jet, they arrived in Lima at 7:30 a.m. on Saturday, July 17. Again, there was a large delegation, including the pastor, Father Nangle, OFM, a group of school children and adults from the parish, and a large group of Philadelphia IHMs stationed in Lima.

The rented house where they were to reside looked very welcoming, and as the sisters assisted at their first Mass in Spanish in the chapel, they were grateful to be part of the Congregation's first venture into Peru. (104)

The whirl of the next few days must have left the new "missionaries" in a daze. After Mass on their arrival day, Saturday, there was breakfast at the Franciscan friars' house and dinner at Villa Maria with the Philadelphia IHMs. On Sunday, they attended four Masses at the Church in order to meet the parishioners; and later, 7:30 - 9:00 p.m., they were introduced at a parish reception. Monday found the sisters in school for a full schedule of classes from 8:30 a.m. to 11:30 a.m. and 2:00 p.m. to 4:00 p.m. What courage it took to begin teaching in a new school, in a new country, in a new language, going through the processes of becoming legal residents of Peru, obtaining visas for travel, and for Sisters Anysia and Joel Marie to attend language school besides! Such involvement made the months fly by and after their retreat with the Philadelphia IHMs in Callao, the Sisters were ready for their summer work.

Sisters Anysia and Joel Marie taught religion to the poor children of the parish. Sisters Ramona and Michael Marie visited the homes of the poor to "procure the regularization of marriages and the baptism of children." (105)

In 1966 a third class was added, bringing the total school registration to 126 pupils. Sister Joel Marie taught the Kindergarten, Sister Michael Marie, Transicion, and Sister Anysia, Primer Ano.

The third year of Scranton IHM presence in Lima, Peru, saw personnel changes, with Sisters Ramona and Michael Marie returning to the States on July 24, 1967. It will be recalled that Sister Michael Marie was appointed superior and principal in Puerto Rico in August 1967. Sister Anysia was appointed the new superior in Lima, and Sister Louisa (Theresa) McElroy replaced Sister Michael Marie as Transicion teacher. This was another busy year as forty-four children from the second grade were prepared for first Holy Communion; musical programs were presented; service was given to the poor outside the school, and visitors were welcomed. In February, Sister Anysia was able to make a one-month visit home to the States. Thanks to the generosity of the CSMC students at St. Mary's, Manhasset, New York, under the guidance of Sister Johann Barry, a project was begun which provided a trip to the States each year for one of the sisters in Peru.

On May 15, 1968, Mother Beata and Sister John Francis arrived for a one-week stay. Their visit supported the little community and was followed on July 22 by the arrival of Sister Joan of Arc (Jacque) Servick, the fourth member of the community. There were now five classes in the school, so Sister Louisa had a double grade, second and third. (106)

Life was never dull in Lima and October 1968 saw a military coup take place, overthrowing the President Fernando Belaunde Terry and installing General Juan Velasco Alvarado in his place. One interpretation of the reasons for this coup is given by Myron Frankman, stating:

> The 1967 devaluation of the Peruvian sol by over forty percent was one of a number of factors which contributed to the ouster of President Fernando Belaunde Terry by the Peruvian military in October 1968. The military, having been critical of the Belaunde devaluation, appear to have been committed to maintain the value of the sol . . . (107)

According to Frankman, the revolutionary objective was to break Peru's historic dependence on, and domination by the industrialized capitalistic nations. Only time would tell whether the means used would achieve these ends.

In spite of soldiers and tanks in the streets, life went on as Sister Joel Marie visited the States from December 28 to February 26; Sisters Joan of Arc (Jacque) and Anysia were taking Spanish courses; and from April

14, 1969, to April 24, Sisters Mary Schelb, sector superior, and Coleman Nee, coordinator of apostolic works, visited in Lima.

On May 5, 1969, Sister Louisa (Theresa) began the school annex, teaching the very poor during the school day, instead of after school. Thirty-two children, ranging in age from six to fourteen, were included in this program. For a time Sister Louisa also had charge of the Vespertina Program, an evening school for girls aged fifteen or older, many of whom were servants in the homes of the wealthy in the area. (108)

Reaching out to the people further, the Congregation sent Sister Mary Martha Gardiner to work as a nurse in the Posta Medica, in the basement of the church. She arrived on August 26, 1969. Especially the poor sorely needed the services of this clinic. Records show that by 1972 the clinic was open 202 days a year, serving 3,646 persons who received diagnosis or treatment from one of seven volunteer doctors. Another 1,000 received nursing care from Sister Mary Martha, who also conducted classes in health care. (109)

December 1969 brought news of Sister Anysia's change to Williamsport, Pennsylvania, and Sister Joel Marie's appointment as superior in Lima. Sister Coletta Kearney was to replace Sister Anysia in the school and arrived January 2, 1970. (110) This was to be a year of exceptional and memorable weather in Lima. The first rainstorm in forty-five years came on January 15, causing much havoc in this arid area. An earthquake on May 31 from which the sisters and the school escaped harm devastated the surrounding areas. The annals record that 50,000 people died in the Chimbote-Huraz area. Sister Mary Martha and other nurses from Lima went to serve there from June 4 to 9, with Sisters Joel Marie and Joan of Arc (Jacque) taking supplies on June 6 and 7. The Franciscan brothers and the pastor also responded to this situation. (111)

Earthquakes were a recurring phenomenon in Lima as subsequent records relate, and always the after-shocks, instilling fear into the students and teachers alike. (112) But various forms of human violence were even more frightening. One such example was the February 5, 1975, wave of violence between the government and striking workers when government tanks were sent to fire on the strikers. After this uprising, a curfew was imposed on the entire city for three weeks. (113) Again in July 1976 there was a nationwide bus strike and rioting over the devaluation of the Peruvian sol. Schools were closed for eight days and strict curfews imposed at night. (114) There were constant threats of new military coups and the prevailing questions "Do we or don't we have a president? A government? A free country?" (115)

Amidst all this turmoil the work of the sisters continued, with the school enrollment mounting in 1970 to 850 pupils, with three sections of each grade, served by four IHM Sisters, seventeen lay teachers and a part-time psychologist. Vespertina classes had an enrollment of 415 in that year.

There would be many changes in personnel serving the school in Lima as the sisters identified new areas of service in Peru, and gradually prepared the lay faculty to assume full responsibility for the operation of the school. Throughout Mother Beata's tenure, Colegio Parroquial Santisimo Nombre de Jesus flourished and the outreach of the sisters beyond the school would lay the foundation for future ministries in Peru.

Sisters who served in Peru during and after Mother Beata's terms included the following: Sister Ramona Scanlon, 1965-1967; Sister Anysia Donahue, 1965-1969; Sister Michael Marie Hartman, 1965-1967, and returning 1980-1988; Sister Joel Marie Sheehe, 1965-1973, and returning 1976-1998; Sister Louisa (Theresa) McElroy, 1967-1978, and returning 1989-1991; Sister Joan of Arc (Jacquelin) Servick, 1968-1980, returning 1983-1994; Sister Mary Martha Gardiner, 1969-1982; Sister Jeanne Marie (Coletta) Kearney, 1970 to date; Sister Maria Goretti Timperio, 1973-1976.

Additional IHMs serving at Santisimo Nombre de Jesus, and in new ministries in Peru will be discussed in the historic time frame in which they occur.

St. Aloysius, Cresson, Pennsylvania

The story of the founding of St. Aloysius School and Convent in Cresson, Pennsylvania actually begins in another location, the St. Mary-John School of Cresson. This school, opened on November 15, 1928, by Bishop John McCort of the Altoona-Johnstown Diocese, was built to provide elementary school education to the orphans of St. John's Home for Boys and St. Mary's Home for Girls. Until St. Mary-John School opened, there had been separate schools operating in the two orphanages, with the first year of high school offered at St. John's Home open also to the orphan girls.

The new St. Mary-John School solved the problem of double staffing needed in maintaining the separate schools. It also opened a Catholic school for St. Aloysius Parish children. At the time of the opening of the new school there were 274 pupils, 56 of whom were children from St. Aloysius Parish, and 218 from St. Mary's and St. John's Homes. The IHM Sister-teachers were Sisters Uriel Hurst, Robert Gerrity, Dunstan Gallagher, Matilda O'Boyle, Geraldine Tessier, Irenaeus Turner, Macaria

Mooney, and Kevin Maria McMullen. Sister Claudia Whalen taught the pre-school children. Sisters Anna Maria Hayes and Myra Haggerty taught religious instructions on Wednesdays and Saturdays. (116)

Over the years that followed there was a shift in the enrollment to the extent that by 1944
there were 114 children from St. Aloysius Parish and only 71 from the orphanages. Noting this, Bishop Richard T. Guilfoyle, successor of Bishop McCort, designated St.Mary-John School a parochial school for St. Aloysius Parish. The school continued to be supported by the Diocese with annual contributions from all the parishes. (117)

This arrangement continued until 1964 when Bishop J. Carroll McCormick's plans materialized. A new complex, the Catholic Child Care Center in Hollidaysburg, Pennsylvania, was built to house the remaining orphan children, and the 55 year-old buildings at St. Mary's and St. John's Homes, together with the school, were sold to the State of Pennsylvania. At the time of the sale in 1962, there were 215 children from St. Aloysius Parish enrolled in St. Mary-John School.

To replace St. Mary-John School, Bishop McCormick urged the pastor of St. Aloysius Parish, Reverend Bernard J. O'Malley, to seek the support of the people of the parish in building the new St. Aloysius School and convent. Father O'Malley had just arrived as pastor in January 1962. Of Father O'Malley one writer said, "with him began what might be referred to as the most startling of the 125 years the parish has been in existence." (118)

Father O'Malley arrived at a parish, St. Aloysius, whose 125-year history had been one of continuous financial struggles to build a church; had witnessed the church's destruction as a result of a sudden storm; had survived a decision-making process related to closing the parish altogether; and had, with volunteer labor, finally completed a new church in 1957, just five years before Father O'Malley's arrival.

It was to this faith-filled people that Father O'Malley made his urgent appeal for the building of St. Aloysius School and convent. The response of the people was so positive that by November of that year work began on the project. In less than a year, the solemn blessing and dedication took place, bringing deep joy to the pastor and his people. It is understandable that this joy was tempered with the awareness of the burdens that had been assumed. Father O'Malley writes, "No one but God can know the heartache and extent of sacrifice that have put each brick in place in the short space of one year." (119)

While St. Aloysius School opened on schedule, the convent was not completed until October 1963. During this period the sisters resided at

St. Mary's Home and commuted daily to the school. The first group assigned to St. Aloysius included Sisters Marie Imelda Callahan, superior and principal, Leonilla Connors, deRicci Baker, Corona McDonald, Florine Madigan and Anthony Bailey.

The appreciation of the sisters for the new school and the pastor's interest in education is reflected in the following:

> The new St. Aloysius School is something that one must see to appreciate. It is modern, simple, plain, yet, beautiful. Our school is equipped with the latest facilities and textbooks. Our Pastor, Father O'Malley, is a teacher, therefore, nothing is left out where the education of the child is concerned. (120)

This statement refers, of course, to the plan that provided a ground floor for cafeteria/assembly hall, kitchen, lavatories, boiler room, stage and storage rooms; and a main floor containing eight classrooms, library, principal's office, health room, lavatories and storage rooms. Within the spacious classrooms no detail to facilitate teaching was overlooked.

This fortunate group of sisters also enjoyed the beauty of a well-planned and well-furnished convent. The ground floor contained the native cherry-paneled chapel, office, ten bedrooms, kitchen, dining room, two parlors, utility and storage rooms, and lavatory. An indoor staircase from the convent to the second floor of the school provided ready access to the school. (121)

One month after the sisters' arrival, an "open house" was held for the parishioners in November. "Everyone seemed very proud and pleased with everything. It is the first time this parish has had sisters, and they were very happy to see the beautiful furnishings they so willingly contributed to the convent and school." (122)

Many spiritual and professional opportunities were available to the sisters because of the proximity of St. Aloysius to St. Francis College and Seminary in Loretto, Pennsylvania. Monthly retreats were often scheduled with the Franciscan Fathers, and students from both St. Francis and Mount Aloysius Junior College did their practice teaching with IHM Sisters as observers and evaluators in the classrooms.

St. Aloysius School had an excellent educational reputation, and by 1968 its enrollment reached 310 pupils. From the beginning, the sisters were very active in diocesan educational events. Sister Florine Madigan and Sister Immaculate Severino, for example, presented workshops to diocesan teachers in religion and in music, respectively. IHM community supervisors were also called upon to offer lecture-demonstration workshops in music, art, and language arts for the teachers of the Altoona-Johnstown Diocesan Catholic schools. There was no sense of isolation from the Congregation for the IHMs on the Cresson "mountain-top" as the records show a steady stream of visitors— Mother Beata, Sister Felicitas Ryan, Sister Brendan O'Brien of the Congregation's Council; Sister Georgina Wertz, Regional Superior; supervisors, including Sisters Nora Clarke, Sheila Reilly, Maria Regina Loures, Eleanora Whalen, and Maryla Farfour. (123) Visits between the Cresson sisters and the IHMs stationed in Hastings, and later at St. Thomas, Bedford, were marked by celebrations of Congregation feasts and sisters' jubilees.

In 1974, St. Aloysius Convent was designated as a site for a summer-house of prayer. The members included Sisters Conrad Schaefer, Sabina McHale, Perpetua Little, Carol Bender, Maria Eucharia Ward, Elsa Eckenrode, and Vincent dePaul Bonanza. In addition to the meditations and music prepared by the sisters themselves, several Franciscan Fathers from St. Francis Seminary and several sisters of other congregations were available as resource persons to the group. The five-week program was a rich source of spiritual renewal for all participating. (124)

The sisters at St. Aloysius, Cresson, experienced many changes over the years with the deaths of Sisters Georgina Wertz and Jane Kehoe; the replacement of the school's founding pastor, Father O'Malley in 1976 with Father Paul Robine, former vicar for religious of the Altoona-Johnstown Diocese; and the appointment of Bishop James J. Hogan in 1966 to replace their founding Bishop, J. Carroll McCormick, who was made Bishop of Scranton, Pennsylvania.

Seven principals served St. Aloysius School, Cresson, over its twenty-one year history:

Sister Marie Imelda Callahan, 1963-1967; Sister Marie Elise Regan, 1967-1971; Sister Jean Mary Ottman, 1971-1973; Sister Mary Bride O'Malley, 1973-1976; Sister Gabrielis Marley, 1976-1980; Sister Gregory Marie Schwalenberger, 1980-1982; and Sister Laura Booth 1982-1984.

The IHM Sisters were withdrawn from St. Aloysius in 1984.

The Catholic Child Care Center, Hollidaysburg, Pennsylvania

Acknowledging that conditions had changed considerably since St. John's and St. Mary's Orphanage Homes were erected, J. Carroll McCormick, Bishop of the Altoona-Johnstown Diocese outlined his plans in a letter December 12, 1961 to Mother Beata while she was still first assistant to Mother Kathleen. He was aware of the serious illness of Mother Kathleen, superior general, but wished to keep the Congregation informed that he had to move ahead with opportunities at hand. In this letter he notes that the State of Pennsylvania has offered some $550,000 for the orphanage buildings and the school and writes:

> I believe we should accept the offer in order to dispose of these old, oversize structures which will be more and more a burden to us as time goes on. They were built to care for 300 orphans; we now have 38 children there. (125)

After expressing his hope to have a new parochial school in St. Aloysius Parish, Cresson, he mentions that "I should like to build . . . a small orphanage to take care of the few children who will be in our care, i.e. infants awaiting adoption and children who will be assigned later to foster homes." (126)

Eight months later, Bishop McCormick had completed the sale of the buildings to the State of Pennsylvania and informed Mother Beata of the arrangements made for the interim placement of the orphans:

> The State Authority is leasing Saint Mary's Home to us until January 1, 1963. We are to vacate Saint John's Home by September 1, 1962. All the Sisters and orphans at Saint John's will move into Saint Mary's until next January. (127)

Needless to say, there was a flurry of activity, as there remained only about three weeks to vacate Saint John's Home and move to Saint Mary's. St. John's Home was to become a residence for girls aged twelve to sixteen, to be cared for by the State of Pennsylvania. The sisters and the ten remaining boys at St. John's accomplished the move by August 30, 1962, closing fifty-five years at St. John's Home, Cresson. The sisters at St. John's Home at the closing were: Sisters Marie Augustine Maher, deRicci Baker, Clotilda Bubenko and Anthony Bailey.

St Joseph's Foundling Home in Ebensburg, Pennsylvania, operated by the Sisters of St. Joseph of Baden, had also closed three years previously, on July 2, 1959. So, with twenty-five tots under two years of age already transferred to St. Mary's Home, the IHM Sisters became indeed the refuge of the homeless.

It would be a year and seven months before the new Catholic Child Care Center in Lakemont would open. Ground was broken on April 19, 1963. A year later, on March 14, 1964, the new facilities were completed and blessed by Bishop McCormick. Designed as a complex of small, home-like cottages, the new buildings housed the boys, girls, and sisters in separate cottages, with the nursery an extension of the sisters' building. There were live-in quarters for the house-parents of each cottage, giving the children a family-like situation.

In addition, each cottage was complete with living room, dining room, recreation and kitchen areas. Each group had meals in its own residence. The sisters' building included eight bedrooms, a chapel, community room, reception rooms, kitchen, dining room, laundry and administrative offices. The infant nursery accommodating eight infants occupied one section of this building and included a nurse's station, isolation , treatment and formula rooms. (128)

Sister Joyce McQuaide served as administrator and superior of the new facility. Sisters Jamesella McAwhinney, RN, Irene (Eleanor) Flynn, and Maris Law were assigned as staff. Sister Georgina Wertz, as regional superior, was in residence.

The dedicated work of the IHM Sisters at the Child Care Center in Hollidaysburg continued until June 15, 1979.

Dunmore Central Catholic High School (Bishop O'Hara), Dunmore, PA

The decision to consolidate the small parish high schools in the Diocese of Scranton was made as early as 1947 by Bishop William J. Hafey. Looking at the comparatively small enrollments, the financial outlay required in operating these high schools, and the competition being offered by new public school buildings, Bishop Hafey convinced area pastors to pool their finances and support centralized high schools. The first of these was South Scranton Catholic in 1947, later named Bishop Klonowski in 1973, and followed by Kingston Central Catholic in 1952, later named Bishop O'Reilly in 1973.

Bishop Jerome D. Hannan followed this trend to centralized high schools, establishing Cathedral (later Bishop Hannan) in 1958; Pocono Catholic Missions, 1961; Dunmore Catholic (Bishop O'Hara) in 1964; and Notre Dame in East Stroudsburg, Pennsylvania in 1967. (129)

Exercising his best diplomacy, Bishop Hannan was able to obtain the support of five pastors in the Dunmore area to build and support an imposing new high school building, with the assistance of the Scranton Diocese. Based on potential enrollments, Monsignors William A. Crotti, pastor, St. Anthony of Padua Parish and Raymond E. Larkin, pastor, St. Mary of Mt. Carmel Parish would bear 82% of the cost. (130) The sacrifices of the Catholic people of the Scranton Diocese made these efforts possible, together with the generous response of several religious congregations to supply sister-faculty for the school. The five Dunmore parishes raised a major part of the $1,250,000 cost of the new building.

Mother Beata had promised sisters for September 1965 and showed her support for the project by attending the October 7, 1963, ground-breaking ceremony, together with the council members. (131)

In spite of the fact that the building was still under construction, Dunmore Central Catholic High School opened in September 1964 accepting a freshman class of 109 pupils. Reverend Joseph Adonizio was appointed principal by Bishop Hannan. Faculty members included four Filipini Sisters, two Mercy Sisters, one layman and four diocesan priests to teach religion classes. (132)

The first IHMs to be assigned to Dunmore Catholic High in 1965 were Sisters Albertus (Anne) Fulwiler to teach science classes and Samuel McKeown for mathematics. These sisters resided at nearby St. Mary of Mt. Carmel Convent. The local community there included six IHMs teaching in the parish elementary school. Sister Stella Devers was superior and principal at St. Mary's.

In 1966-1967 two additional IHMs were assigned to the Dunmore Central Catholic High. They were Sisters Bernardinus (Gloria) Frank for chemistry classes and Stanley Marie Swaboski for biology. By 1967-1968 six IHMs were on the faculty, the two additions being Sister Macrina Crowe for mathematics and a Monroe, Michigan IHM, Sister Mary Paulus for science. The year 1967-1968 also saw the addition of two Sisters of Sts. Cyril and Methodius to the faculty. This was the year of the first graduating class, with 82% of the original 109 students completing their four years. The June 9, 1968, ceremonies celebrated the graduation of ninety-nine students. (133)

Reverend Joseph Adonizio completed his four-year term as principal in 1968. Reverend Gerald Burns, who also served four years, replaced him. Under Father Burns' leadership, and with the work of a highly dedicated faculty, Dunmore Central Catholic received accreditation from the Middle States Association in 1970. This approval was based on "the school facilities and educational environment; the diligence and competence of its faculty and staff; the professional competency of its administrative unit and the warmth and loyalty of its student body." (134)

Reverend Kenneth Kizis who served for eleven years from 1971-1982 followed Father Burns in the principalship. In this period he saw the school through another Middle States evaluation in which high praise was given for the school's administration, the support of the Board of Pastors, and the support of the Fathers' and Mothers' Clubs. The financial support of the latter assisted in adding two new classrooms, allowing expansion of the library, a key component of the school. (135)

The high point of IHM staffing of Dunmore Central Catholic High was reached in 1972-1973 when eight IHMs were assigned. These included three in mathematics, namely, Sisters Imelda Sharpe, Anita Brown, and Mary Elizabeth Ehling; four in science—Sisters Judy Romans, Joseph Maher, Teresa Moran, and Patricia Tippen; and Sister Marion Irving in religion. It was in 1972-1973 also that Sister Mary Elizabeth Ehling was appointed assistant principal of the school. (136) The school was renamed Bishop O'Hara High School in June 1972.

Reverend Nick Lorenzetti served as principal from 1982-1985, followed by Sister Claudette Naylor, the first IHM principal of Bishop O'Hara High School whose leadership spanned ten years, from 1985-1995. Middle States accreditation was again awarded in 1990, with developments in staffing, physical plant, fiscal stability, and enrollment noted. Sister Claudette resigned in 1995 at which time Mr. Joseph Casciano became principal.

As recently as November 2001, Bishop O'Hara High School has again received the coveted Middle States Association accreditation. (137)

Accreditations like these speak to the overall excellence of the school. From its beginnings, the academic requirements of Bishop O'Hara were rigorous, with credits required in mathematics, science, social studies, languages and religion. A wide array of electives was available in numerous fields from art and music to photography and computer science. In addition, a variety of clubs, honor societies, and athletics provided extracurricular involvement to fit all abilities. A comparatively small high school, Bishop O'Hara nevertheless has had its champions in football, boys' and girls' basketball, softball, cross country, and cheerleading over the years. (138)

Bishop O'Hara High School continues to this date in 2002 with a lay principal, Anita Sirak, and the continuing presence of IHMs, although only two in number. Sister Fidelis Flannery serves in the school office and Sister Ann Marie O'Brien teaches Spanish classes. (139)

IHM Sisters who have served as assistant principals at Bishop O'Hara High School include: Sisters Mary Elizabeth Ehling, Maria del Rey Shevlin, and Claudette Naylor.

St. Pius X, Coeur d'Alene, Idaho

With the growth of the long-established St. Thomas Parish in Coeur d'Alene, Idaho, and the enrollment impact on St. Thomas Elementary School, it was only a matter of time until talk of a second parish and school would begin. Talk quickly turned to action as the new Bishop of the Boise, Idaho Diocese, Sylvester Treinen, became aware of the situation. New parish lines were drawn along the northern half of the city of Coeur d'Alene, land for the new parish was acquired, and a pastor appointed. Writing to Mother Beata on September 13, 1962, Bishop Treinen said:

> The Sisters may have written to you about the new parish that we have just set up in Coeur d'Alene. It will be known as St. Pius X Church. Father Thomas Lafey, a very wonderful priest, is the first pastor. He has nothing at present there, of course, except a piece of ground and a zealous soul. (140

Bishop Treinen then outlined details as to the immediate plans for an elementary school and combination church, as well as long-range plans for a permanent church, rectory and convent. The next expected request, of course, was carefully phrased:

> You will understand, I am sure, how good it would be to have your Sisters staff the new St. Pius X School . . . It would surely be wonderful if you can say that you will be willing to give Sisters to what should be one of the finest grade schools in northern Idaho. (141)

It is noted that the Bishop did not say when the sisters would be needed. But, at about the same time a letter arrived from the new pastor, Father Lafey, with more specific information. "As soon as possible I hope to start building an eight room school with the intention of opening the school in the fall of 1963." (142)

Father Lafey continues with a sincere appeal for IHM Sisters to staff the school:

> I know how short you are of Sisters but will you please consider carefully the needs of this Missionary Diocese and accept the new school. In Idaho we live in an area surrounded by all kinds of protestant churches; the Mormons are moving in on all sides and our greatest strength against these forces lies in the parish schools . . . Mother, please send Sisters to join us in this particular work for Christ. (143)

Mother Beata's prompt response to both Bishop Treinen and Father Lafey indicated the inability of the Congregation to respond positively to these requests at that time. (144)

Just as promptly, Bishop Treinen made his request again, saying . . . "hope springs eternal in the heart of a Bishop." (145) This time he was seeking a promise from Mother Beata to send sisters in 1964 or 1965. "With such a bright future to look forward to, we would proceed with the building program and attempt to make some temporary arrangement for the intervening years." (146)

Mother Beata and the council must have been moved by the Bishop's understanding of their staffing problems, by his praise of the work already being done by the sisters in the IHM High School and St. Thomas Parish in Coeur d'Alene, and his desire to meet the growing religious challenges in the area. Four days after the date of the Bishop's second request, Mother Beata wrote:

> . . . our General Council proposes that we send three (3) Sisters to this School in August, 1965; if a fourth teacher is needed at that time, a lay teacher will be necessary. As grades are added, we shall do our best to give the needed Sisters, if that is at all possible. (147)

Both Bishop Treinen and Father Lafey responded immediately to the good news that three sisters would be assigned to St. Pius X in 1965. (148) No delay occurred in starting the school building. Plans were ready for bids by the spring, 1963 and by early December 1964 the outside structure was completed. Throughout the winter months of 1964, the men of St. Pius Parish continued to work on the completion of the inside of the school.

There was no urgency about building a convent for the sisters, since it had been agreed that since the new IHM Convent in Coeur d'Alene had six extra rooms, the sisters teaching at St. Pius X would reside there. (149) The first three sisters sent to staff St. Pius X School were Sisters Francis Borgia O'Donnell, principal, St. Mel Wright, and Marianna Ginalski. With the opening of six grades, a lay teacher, Mrs. Gunnar Nelson was added to the faculty. (150)

One day after a three-day cross-country train ride, the sisters were thrust into the beehive of last minute activity in preparation for the opening of school. In the midst of scaffolding, they found the pastor, Father Lafey, scrubbing the hallway. They received a thousand welcomes! Two days before classes were to begin Bishop Treinen arrived from Boise to see that all was in readiness for launching his favorite project. His visit on August 30, 1965, was the first of many that he would make, demonstrating his support for the pastor and the sisters.

Other visitors during this first year included Sister Felicitas Ryan on September 22, and Sisters Lucian Reddington and Georgina Wertz on

April 4, 1966. The North Idaho Deanery Meeting brought Bishop Treinan, thirteen priests, and 148 women delegates to St. Pius School on April 19. (151) Mother Beata and Sister St. Mary Orr visited in November of the second year, 1966-1967.

By the second year, each sister's class had an enrollment of forty-two pupils, and thirty-eight in Mrs. Robert Meyer's class. Reaching these limits by the second year demonstrated the effectiveness of the faculty and the desire of the parishioners to support a Catholic education for their children. Bishop Treinen administered confirmation to forty-three pupils on November 8, 1966, and on April 30, 1967, thirty youngsters received First Holy Communion.

This second year was one of basic organization and development in the school. The faculty was given the task of developing the philosophy and objectives of St. Pius X School, as well as a process for evaluating pupil progress in each of the subject areas of the curriculum. Sister St. Mel organized a program for teaching religion to small groups of retarded children from both St. Pius X and St. Thomas Parishes. Sister Marianna's special project was the school library. She was able to augment the library collection through donations from parish families, and by obtaining federal Title II funds for the purchase of books. (152)

This second year, 1966-1967 also saw the fulfillment of Bishop Treinen's desire for the formation of a school board in each parish. Father Lafey sought nominations from the entire parish community, then conducted a total parish election. Father Lafey, as pastor, and Sister Francis Borgia, as principal of the school, were ex officio members. The five elected members were Mr. Louis Spinozza, chairman, Mr. Neil Pyle, Mr. Jim Jaeger, Mrs. Norman Petersen, and Mrs. James Elgee.

In addition to the school board, parents were involved in many supportive activities through the newly organized Home-School Association. This group donated equipment and books to the school as their first project.

St. Pius X School continued with four faculty members teaching four double grades, and Sister Francis Borgia serving as principal in addition to her class of fifth and sixth graders. In spite of these conditions, the pupils were challenged to compete in statewide and regional contests in which they won top honors in science and in various essay contests. At the North Idaho Science Fair "Top Grand Prize" in group awards in elementary grades went to Sister St. Mel and her classes. (153)

The school continued to graduate about twenty students each year from the eighth grade. As was predicted, ninety-nine percent of these graduates went on to the IHM High School in Coeur d'Alene.

The first changes in personnel came to St. Pius X for the 1969-1970 year as Father Lafey, pastor, was transferred to Pocatello, Idaho, and Father John Morgan became the new pastor. Among the IHMs, Sister Francis Borgia was replaced by Sister Bernardus Dwyer as principal and Sister Eleanor Mary Horn was assigned in place of Sister Marianna Ginalski. Sister St. Mel Wright continued as teacher of grades one and two. (154)

Mother Beata and Sister Seraphia Gallagher visited the Coeur d'Alene schools and IHM Convent, arriving on October 2, 1970. Their ten-day visit included appointments with the pastors and with Bishop Treinan. (155) This visit is significant since Mother Beata gave a report of it on October 22, 1970, to the Central Administrative Assembly. It appears that Mother Beata had serious concerns about finances at both St. Pius X and at the IHM High School. The new pastor at St. Pius X, Father Morgan, was willing to increase payments for the living expenses of the three sisters teaching at St. Pius X and residing at the IHM Convent. He was also willing to begin paying hospitalization insurance for the sisters. It seems, however, that Bishop Treinen was not open to a suggestion that the IHM High School become a diocesan responsibility. (156)

After Mother Beata's report on the Coeur d'Alene situation, the minutes state that

> Central Administrative Assembly members suggested that we withdraw the Sisters from the Western missions and try to sell the property belonging to the Congregation through a real estate broker or a lawyer. (157)

This suggestion became a formal motion in the November 27, 1970, meeting of the Central Administrative Assembly when the date for withdrawal of the IHM Sisters from the western missions was set for June 1971. (158)

Three weeks later, on January 18, 1971, Sisters Nora Clarke, sector superior, and Albertus (Anne) Fulwiler, director of apostolic works, met with the Coeur d'Alene sisters. "They had to tell us that the CAA had made the decision to close the western missions. The Coeur d'Alene sisters were given the right to appeal the decision and to offer proposals to help the situation. These proposals would be considered at a CAA meeting on February 25." (159)

Needless to say, work began immediately on the proposals. Supporting statements for the sisters' continuance were given by Reverend J. Donoghue, superintendent of schools for the Diocese of

Boise, by pastors of both schools, by presidents of the parish councils, as well as by Bishop Treinen. A well-prepared document was written, setting forth the special conditions existing, such as the need to combat an active schismatic group in the area, and five alternative plans to continue the schools, to support increased numbers of lay faculty, or to provide for a catechetical instruction program. The main point was to retain at least some of the sisters. (160)

In a separate letter, Reverend John W. Morgan, pastor, St. Pius X made a deeply moving appeal to Mother Beata, saying in part:

> May I say only that St. Pius X Parish would be seriously set back by the loss of its school. This is all we have—no church and no permanent rectory—only a school not yet completely paid for. St. Pius X School, built brick by brick by our own people so few years ago, stands as living proof of our esteem for Catholic Education. Closing our school now would be a drastic blow to the faith of our people. (161)

Sister Mariel Dougher flew to Scranton from Coeur d'Alene, carrying these proposals and letters, which she presented to Mother Beata at a meeting on February 9, 1971. The Central Administrative Assembly's reconsideration of the withdrawal decision was scheduled for February 25. Strikingly, the motherhouse in Scranton was destroyed by fire on February 21, 1971. This historic event will be treated separately in this work. Obviously, the resultant concerns for the welfare of the sisters, the hospitalization of some of the junior professed sisters, the relocation of sisters who had resided in the motherhouse, business matters relating to property and insurance, and a host of immediate problems took priority over all other matters. There was no February 25 CAA meeting about the Coeur d'Alene proposals.

The sisters and people in Coeur d'Alene, aware of the tragedy occurring at the Scranton motherhouse, joined in prayer for the safety of all involved in the fire. Their patient waiting for word about the future of the Coeur d'Alene schools came to a sad conclusion when the bishop, pastors and the sisters received a letter from Mother Beata dated March 2, 1971, stating:

> Our Central Administrative Assembly today reached a final decision to withdraw our Sisters from IHM High School, St. Thomas and St. Pius Elementary Schools, Coeur d'Alene, Idaho. This matter was brought up for reconsideration and will not be reversed. The withdrawal will take place as of June 1971. (162)

It is never easy for any of the parties involved when sisters are withdrawn from the schools. The Coeur d'Alene situation was made more difficult both because of the lengthy history of IHM presence in Coeur d'Alene, and their very short history at St. Pius X Elementary School.

Bishop Treinen was deeply sensitive to the loss being felt by all, especially the sisters. He wrote to the sisters:

> Previously I have told you of my sincere thanks for all you have done for God and the Church in Coeur d'Alene through the years. Now, just before you leave, I want to assure you of this again. Even though you are leaving, I know your heart remains. The Lord, Who has been your strength until now, will continue to strengthen you. Never fear. You are doing His will . . . (163)

St. Pius X School closed in June 1971. The school building continued to be used as a catechetical center serviced by the laity of the parish under the direction of Lidwin Dirne, a member of the Secular Institute of Mary of the Annunciation. Later she was joined by Sister Nancy MacLean and Sister Helen Mason, Sisters of Providence. Twenty-five years later, in September 1996 the three parishes of St. Pius X, St. Thomas of Coeur d'Alene, and St. George, Post Falls, jointly sponsored Holy Family School at the former St. Thomas School location. Holy Family School continues today with an all-lay faculty. (164)

The story of the withdrawal of the IHM Sisters from the other western missions will be considered separately.

Maria Regina Convent, Uniondale, New York

"The realization of Bishop Walter P. Kellenberg's dream" was the heading given to the editorial in the November 3, 1966, issue of *The Long Island Catholic* newspaper (165) describing the remarkable achievement of the construction of four new diocesan high schools in the Rockville Centre Diocese, New York. Maria Regina High School, Uniondale, New York, was one of the four.

Bishop Kellenberg had announced plans for the four schools on March 12, 1963, and with the pledged support of 109,000 families, over twenty million dollars was raised. Maria Regina High School was the first of the four to be started. It was an imposing structure situated on a 22-acre plot between Hempstead Turnpike and Front Street, overlooking the southbound lane of the Meadowbrook Parkway. The groundbreaking took place on May 11, 1964, and the school opened for a freshman class of 700 students on September 8, 1966.

The first principal was Reverend John J. Mullen, aided by two assistant principals, Sister Dermot (Jean) Toolan, IHM and Sister Mary Elise, OP. The initial personnel included sisters from the Amityville Dominicans and twelve IHMs, eleven lay teachers, two priests, and twenty-seven clerical and maintenance employees. (166)

Most of the IHM appointments had been made and communicated to Reverend David Farley, superintendent of schools for the Rockville Centre Diocese, by December 1965. (167) In addition to Sister (Jean) Dermot, assistant principal, the following sisters were assigned: Sisters Lucille (Marion) Irving, Maria Concetta Dell, Clarice Reddon, Beatrix Cawley, Gabriel Kane, Edith Halligan, Mary Thomas Murphy, Josefita (Janice) Heisey, Norbert (Marlyn) DeWitt, and Kevin Mary Norton. (168)

Moving into the third floor convent above the new Maria Regina High School was a major undertaking that engaged the sisters for many months, but received maximum focus from August 19, 1966, until school opened on September 8. As the convent annals report:

> Under the direction of Sister Lucille, Superior, the ceiling-to-floor pile of cartons was opened and contents carefully arranged in the spacious stainless steel cabinets; the first meal was served in our wide-open-spaces refectory due to the kindness of our generous neighbors at St. Raymond's Convent in East Rockaway . . . Five junior professed sisters assisted in cleanup on Tuesday, August 23. (168)

The chapel was as yet incomplete, with pews scheduled for delivery in late September. It would be nearly a year later before the statues and stained-glass windows would be added.

It must be remembered that the Dominican Sisters were also housed on this third-floor penthouse, and all facilities—bedrooms, chapel, kitchen, refectory, community room and laundry were duplicated to provide for both communities. Planned for extensive growth, this huge complex contained ninety-two bedrooms and six suites. (170)

A good relationship was had between the two communities with frequent invitations extended for shared meals, feast-day celebrations, and holiday breakfasts. Faculty gatherings and professional exchanges made for a supportive atmosphere.

With so much space available, Maria Regina Convent became a hospitality center for many visitors. Congregation meetings were held there, bringing ten or more guests at a time.

This first year at Maria Regina Convent brought its sorrows also with the deaths of Sister Gabriel's father, Mr. Thomas Kane on September 19 and Sister Edith's father, Mr. Michael Halligan on May 13. Sister Kevin Mary's father, Mr. C. J. Norton suffered a massive stroke, and Sister Beatrix was called home frequently because of her Aunt Beatrice's serious illness. (171)

Mother Beata's support for Maria Regina High School was evident as the second year, 1967-1968 saw ten additional sisters assigned to this mission, bringing the total number to twenty-one. These were: Sisters David Marie (Mary Ann) Remus, Maria Rose Kelly, Josine Shannon, Josepha Marie Darminio, Dorothy Ann Sheehan, Mercita (Ann Marie) O'Brien, Maureen Therese Harun, Claudette Naylor, deMontfort Babb, and Florent (Margaret) Loftus. This influx of faculty augmented the departments of religion, English, science, and modern languages in the high school.

In addition to their regular teaching schedules, several sisters participated in the CAUSE Program sponsored by St. John's University. This adult education program was held at St. Monica's Parish Hall in Jamaica, New York every Monday evening. Other sisters provided religious instruction at Our Lady of Victory Parish in Floral Park and at St. Mary's, Manhasset.

With many higher educational institutions nearby, the sisters were able to enrich their own backgrounds by taking courses at Nassau Community College, Manhattan College, Fordham and St. John's Universities.

The IHM community at Maria Regina was decreased by one when on June 13, 1968, Sister Maria Concetta Dell received exclaustration for one year. As noted in the annals, this was "of great sadness to us because of the personal loss to our community." (172)

The stresses of change in the Church and in religious life were evident in all congregations, and the IHM Congregation was not exempt. The sadness mentioned above was multiplied six times over in the following year, 1968-1969 at Maria Regina. The annals express the matter in this way:

> Little did we suspect that Sister Theresa Greggo's departure the Sunday before Christmas was a foreshadowing of the departure of five more wonderful people at the close of the school year. Sisters Jacquelyn Norton, Patricia Darminio, Eileen Schiller, Jeanne Walsh, and Catherine Austin all returned to secular life in June, and their leaving naturally affected the lives of all here who know and love them very much. (173)

The emotional effect on a local community of such an exodus is obvious; the disruptive effect on a high school faculty cannot be measured, as students and faculty colleagues try to understand and absorb these events.

In light of the already upsetting situation it would not be expected that the Congregation administration would initiate additional personnel changes at Maria Regina High School. Yet, this was the case. Sisters Gabriel Kane, Janice Heisey, Mary Murphy and Dorothy Ann Sheehan were transferred, effective August 1969.

A full complement of twenty-eight IHM Sisters began the school year 1969-1970 with an almost equal number of Dominican Sisters and lay faculty serving 2,050 students. The academic strengths of the faculty were seen in awards they received for summer study in science, modern languages, and English at universities across the country. Preparation of students for competitions led to student awards in forensics, in band performance, and for the school paper. Adaptability to several educational experiments, such as modular scheduling, initiated by Sister Dermot (Jean) Toolan, assistant principal, was the mark of a secure faculty. (174)

Sister Jean Toolan served as assistant principal for ten years from 1966 throughout Mother Beata's terms until 1976. Her successor in this role was Sister Ann Marie O'Brien who had served on the faculty since 1967-1968. Sister Ann Marie would continue as assistant principal for five years, through the 1981-1982 school year. Sister Mary Elizabeth Ehling succeeded her. (175)

The eighteen-year life of this innovative high school and vibrant local community would come to an abrupt end in 1984 under circumstances to be described in the history of that period.

St. Thomas the Apostle, Bedford, Pennsylvania

The history of the early development of the Catholic Church in the County of Bedford, Pennsylvania is entwined with the life of a young twenty-year old, Prince Demetrius Augustine Gallitzin, who arrived in the United States from Holland in 1790. Bishop John Carroll of Baltimore welcomed the Prince and within five years, on March 18, 1795, ordained him to the priesthood.

The "Prince Priest of the Alleghenies," as he was called, was assigned first to Conewago, Pennsylvania, and later, in 1799 to Loretto, Pennsylvania where he built that town's first Catholic Church. His ministry took him often to Bedford, and he was instrumental in building St. Thomas the Apostle Church, Bedford's first Catholic Church.

A record still extant of the donors and their contributions to the building of St. Thomas the Apostle Church is dated February 2, 1816. Father Gallitzen, known from the book title of his biography as *The Prince Who Gave His Gold Away*, labored zealously, and wore himself out at seventy years of age. He died on May 6, 1840. (176)

The first little church which Father Gallitzin built would be preserved, but replaced by a larger structure, and with renovations in 1895 and 1924, St. Thomas the Apostle Church in Bedford became known as an "artistic jewel." Decorators and architects from Cincinnati and Pittsburgh worked under the supervision of the New York firm of Irving and Casson to beautify the extensive wood carvings in the church. (177)

Several religious congregations had sent sisters over the years to give religious instructions to the parish children on Sundays and in summer vacations. IHM Sisters, Mercy Sisters and Ursulines from Cumberland, Maryland had served the parish in this way. The latter had been regular religious education instructors from 1957 until 1966. As the enrollment reached 258 children under the Ursulines' instruction, and another sixty high school students being taught by the pastor, the situation required a costly solution:

Father O'Connell, the pastor, describes matters in these words:

> The task of teaching so many children with so little physical facilities soon became apparent to all, particularly the pastor and the Ursuline nuns. The children were crowded into five inadequate areas which was (sic) conducive neither to learning nor discipline . . . A suitable building with adequate facilities now has become a necessity . . . (178)

There was a further reason for having increased space, namely, the great influx of summer visitors to the well-known vacation spot of Bedford Springs close by. So, in 1963 Bishop J. Carroll McCormick approved the plans of the parish to construct an all-purpose building that could be used for Mass, religious instructions, and eventually, a parochial school. By the summer of 1965 the building was completed and was used for Sunday Masses. In January 1966 it began its use as a catechetical center. (179)

It is noted that other factors at work in the Altoona-Johnstown Diocese a year prior to the events just described in Bedford, had their impact on the building of "an eventual school" in St. Thomas the Apostle Parish. Mother Beata had asked Sister Georgina Wertz, then regional superior, and Sister Joyce McQuaide, superior at Cresson, to meet with Bishop McCormick as her representatives to discuss the proposed withdrawal of the IHMs from St. Patrick's School in nearby Spangler, Pennsylvania. This meeting occurred on February 4, 1965.

The four major reasons given for withdrawal of the sisters were (1) the enrollment had declined to less than 100 pupils at St. Patrick's School in

Spangler; (2) a new public junior high school had been erected in Spangler, attracting the junior high level pupils from St. Patrick's School; (3) the future, as indicated by the baptismal records of the parish (only one infant in 1964), seemed uncertain; (4) a second elementary school in Spangler, namely, Holy Cross, operated by the Mercy Sisters, was experiencing the same conditions with declining enrollments.

Bishop McCormick concluded that the pupils from the two schools should be combined. In accord with Mother Beata's proposal the IHMs would be withdrawn from St. Patrick's in June 1966. Holy Cross School would continue. (180) The pastor of St. Patrick's, Reverend William McGovern, would be notified by the Bishop.

With four IHM Sisters now being available from Spangler, Bishop McCormick immediately introduced the subject of the availability of four IHMs to staff the proposed parochial school in Bedford, which he hoped would be ready in September 1966. Records from St. Thomas the Apostle Parish indicated that there had been 185 infant baptisms in the six years prior, and that there was a total of 258 children enrolled in catechetical classes in 1965. (181) The prediction was that if the new school in Bedford were to begin with four grades, there would be a possible enrollment of some 160 pupils.

A month later, on March 15, 1965, Mother Beata's letter to Bishop McCormick indicates her acceptance of St. Thomas School in Bedford for September 1966. She wrote:

> Your willingness to combine the two schools at Spangler enables us to promise to send four Sisters to staff St. Thomas School in Bedford, as requested by Reverend Edward McConnell. If the Bedford school and the convent for the Sisters are ready in September 1966, we shall send the four Sisters requested. (182)

Subsequently, at St. Thomas the Apostle Parish in Bedford there must have been mixed reactions to the news that their school would open in September 1966 and that a convent would have to be built in the interim. What a pastor does under such circumstances was seen when a year later, on April 14, 1966, the groundbreaking for the new convent was held, with no prospect or promise that it would be ready for the coming of the IHMs in September.

But the sisters did come, arriving on August 19, 1966, to the welcome of a parish that for the first time in its 150-year history had a school and resident sisters. The first community in Bedford included Sisters Justine (Audrey) McHale, Theresa Bernard Yates, Eleanor Marie Malanaphy and Almarita

(Mary Alice) Wheatley. With the convent at mid-stage of completion, the rectory became the interim sisters' residence. The pastor, Father McConnell, moved next door with a neighbor, Mr. Joseph Armstrong. (183)

A series of welcoming events in late August included a tour and dinner at the Bedford Springs Resort, a picnic at Camp Sunshine, a visit to the mission church in Everett, Pennsylvania, and a sewing bee with the sisters in Hollidaysburg, readying the sisters for the change to modified habits before classes would begin.

The fact that 1966 was the sesquicentennial year of St. Thomas the Apostle Parish (1916-1966) has been noted previously. The whirl of activity its celebration would bring could hardly be anticipated, however, as the sisters opened St. Thomas School to ninety-two students of the first four grades on September 7, 1966. Tours of the school were given for visitors almost daily. (184)

The formal, four-day sesquicentennial celebration of St. Thomas the Apostle Parish began with a bazaar on October 13, 1966. On October 14, tree-planting and flag-raising events were held as local and national civic leaders participated. Trees were donated by the Fungaroli Family in memory of their mother, Mrs. James Fungaroli, Sr., and by Mrs. John R. Blackburn, Jr. in memory of her father, Raymond Larney. Open house and a tea were held for the community. The bazaar continued from six p.m. to midnight with square and round dancing beginning at 9:00 p.m. (185)

Homecoming Day was held on October 15 with commemorative services held in the original church on East Street. Following this, a reception and tea were held at the new St. Thomas School on West Penn Street. Sister Augustus McLaughlin, IHM, a native of Bedford and Sister Leon McConnell, IHM, sister of the pastor, Father McConnell, were present for the festivities.

Finally, the capstone ceremonies were held on October 16. The new Bishop of the Altoona-Johnstown Diocese, Most Reverend James J. Hogan celebrated a Pontifical Mass at 10:30 a.m. The dedication of the school and convent by the Bishop was held at 3:00 p.m., followed by a dinner in the school auditorium. Mother Beata and Sister Georgina, natives of Bedford, as well as Sister John Francis, first assistant to Mother Beata, and many other IHMs, Mercy and Ursuline Sisters who formerly taught religious instructions in Bedford, were present. The speaker at the dinner was another former resident of the area, Reverend Aloysius J. Hankenson, TOR, provincial. (186)

Both the school and the convent were built in colonial style to match the architecture of the existing buildings in the town of Bedford. The first floor multi-purpose room of the school was designed to be used, not only for a school lunchroom and auditorium, but also for Sunday Masses in the summer. This room had a 600-person capacity, with adjacent rooms for the sacristies, kitchen facilities, storage, and mechanical rooms.

The second floor of the school included eight classrooms, large enough to accommodate 316 pupils. The administration area contained an office, faculty room and health room. The library, lavatories and storage areas completed the second floor. (187)

The convent was not completed by the time of the sesquicentennial celebration, but its progress was evident to all at the time of the dedication on October 16. The pastor, Father O'Connell, was aware of the importance of the convent's completion. Linking his December 5 and 12, 1966 requests for an additional sister for the fall 1967 term with a promise of the convent's completion, he wrote to Mother Beata:

> We have builded (sic), with a great mortgage . . . and excellent eight grade school, and a just as excellent ten-room convent. We have high hopes for the future. (188)

And again:

> Excepting the unexpected, the Sisters will be in their convent January16th. Furniture has been arranged. Because of custom-built parts in the chapel, and delays, it may not be completed, although they may use it. (189)

The annals record that the actual move occurred on February 11, 1967. "The long awaited day was finally here. We moved into the new convent. What a delight to have our own home!" (190)

One can imagine that Father O'Connell, too, was delighted to be able to return to the rectory.

The generous parishioners held a shower for the sisters and supplied hundreds of items for the chapel, kitchen, and bedrooms. Everything from paring knives and ironing boards to pillows, blankets and bedspreads, as well as beautiful vessels for the chapel were donated.

When the chapel was completed the sisters finally felt completely "at home." On March 24, Holy Saturday, 1967, the pastor brought the Blessed Sacrament to the convent for the first time. The annals record this event, saying "Easter was truly a day of Thanksgiving for having Our Lord once more in our midst." (191)

In addition to the regular classroom teaching the sisters were involved in catechetical instructions after school and on weekends. The Sacrament of Confirmation was received by 118 youngsters, and there were 54 children who received First Holy Communion. The first year of IHM presence at St. Thomas the Apostle in Bedford was exciting and fruitful.

Father O'Connell's request for an additional sister for 1967-1968 could not be filled. The school year began with the same four IHMs and a lay teacher, Mrs. Georgiana Connell, as the fifth grade instructor, was added. The school year began with an early visit from the IHM supervisors, Sisters Felicitas Ryan, Eleanora Whalen, Sheila Reilly and Nora Clarke. (192) Open house was held on October 28 for all the sisters of the area. Over seventy sisters came and were given tours of the convent and school, and enjoyed refreshments. (193)

Ever hopeful to obtain more sisters, the pastor, Father McConnell, wrote again to Mother Beata: "Next September we will add another grade to our school—the sixth. Most earnestly do I hope you will send us another Sister." (194) The opening of school in September 1968, found, however, that only four IHMs were assigned to St. Thomas, Bedford. Sister Justine had been transferred to Dundalk, Maryland. The new superior and principal was Sister Liguori Farnon. Sisters Almarita (Mary Alice), Theresa Bernard and Eleanor Marie continued for the third year. This would be Sister Almarita's last year in Bedford since she would be transferred to Upper Marlboro, Maryland, and replaced by Sister Adele Mullen in 1969. (195)

In March 1969 Mother Beata communicated to Father McConnell and to Sister Liguori the decision of the Central Administrative Assembly that it was their belief that the sixth grade should be the terminal grade at St. Thomas School. Since the Junior High School of the public school system began with seventh grade, it seemed a wise suggestion that pupils transfer at the close of sixth grade. (196) Father O'Connell was in agreement with this suggestion.

By September 1969 there was a registration of 190 pupils in the six grades. The unevenness of distribution of students across the grades, however, was evident in the lower numbers in the upper grades. On June 1, 1972, the first graduation for sixth graders of St. Thomas the Apostle School was conducted. There were 22 graduates, all of whom were to continue at the public Junior High School. (197)

Although the enrollment declined to 172 pupils in 1972-1973, an additional sister, Sister Marie Patrick Comey, was sent to St. Thomas, bringing the number of sisters to five. Father McConnell was not to enjoy for long the benefit of having five sisters for the six-grade school, since he was transferred to Barnesboro, Pennsylvania, on September 8, 1972. Reverend Raymond G. Crosser was appointed pastor of St. Thomas Parish. (198)

The local community would number six sisters by 1974-1975 as Mother Beata, having completed her time as superior general in 1974, was assigned to "home country" in Bedford.

IHM presence at St. Thomas the Apostle School and convent continued for a total of seventeen years. In 1983 the final three IHMs, Sisters Eileen Miller, Joyce McQuaide, and Theresa Bernard Yates, were transferred to other missions. Sisters of St. Francis from Scotland replaced the IHMs in 1983, sending a member of their group, Sister Martina, a year in advance to serve as principal for the final year, 1982-1983. The IHMs had completed their fruitful years at St. Thomas the Apostle Convent and School in Bedford, Pennsylvania. (199)

Our Lady of Mercy, Forest Hills, New York

In the beauty and elegance brought by gradual historical developments, the humble origins of places and initial struggles of peoples are often lost. So it seems as pertains to Our Lady of Mercy Parish, Forest Hills, New York. It is a long road of dreams, struggles, discouragement and perseverance from the small Chapel of the Little Flower, built in 1927 as a mission of Our Lady Queen of Martyrs Parish, to the dedication of the magnificent church of Our Lady of Mercy on September 26, 1937.

Those ten years saw the first chaplain, Reverend James B. Collins, living in a rented house near the Little Flower Chapel and worrying about how to crowd hundreds of parishioners into the small space. A wing was added to the chapel in 1929.

With the assignment of Reverend Edward P. Costello as first pastor, the Little Flower Chapel was rededicated officially on October 6, 1930, as Our Lady of Mercy Church. It was the height of the depression in the United States; it was not a time to begin a fund-raising campaign to build a parish church. But Father Costello was undeterred. "We will build it," was his message to the people. (200) "No depression could dampen the ardor with which the parishioners addressed themselves to the task at hand . . . additional property was purchased at Continental Avenue and Kessel Street, and a drive for funds brought promises of $72,000." (201)

For six years the dreams and the financial struggles went on. Our Lady of Mercy Parish had grown so large that Sunday Mass had to be held in the Inwood Theater on Metropolitan Avenue in Forest Hills. (202) Meanwhile, the economy of the country was improving and workers were again finding jobs, many of which were federally funded projects under the National Recovery Act initiated by President Franklin D. Roosevelt.

Bishop Thomas E. Molloy, Bishop of Brooklyn, dedicated the new church of Our Lady of Mercy on September 26, 1937. The church stands as a tribute to the fine artistic sense of Father Costello and the elegant designs of the architects of the Italian-Romanesque style structure. Marble altars, carved wooden statues, stained-glass windows depicting the beatitudes, the mysteries of the rosary, the baptism of Jesus and other New Testament events—all added to a most impressive, yet devotional environment.

The construction of a rectory was next on Father Costello's agenda. By the close of 1938 this dream was accomplished. He was not destined to move into his new home, however, because a few days after being stricken with a heart attack he died on January 6, 1939. He was fifty-one years old. (203)

Reverend Christopher T. Molloy was appointed pastor on January 23, 1939. He was to serve Our Lady of Mercy Parish for twenty-four years. His hope was to build a parish school, but the conditions were not right during his time. He worked zealously and paid off the parish debt first, but then came World War II and the focus of the people's energies and finances were on the war effort. By 1941 many were answering the call to service in the armed forces. (204) Father Molloy died on February 12, 1963. Of him, it was written, ". . . he left the parish of Our Lady of Mercy in sound condition, so paving the way for the next great building project, not to be accomplished during his lifetime." (205)

The next building project was, of course, the parish school. The new pastor, Very Reverend Monsignor Matthew E. Hickey, MA, was more than willing to assume this challenge. On his first day in Our Lady of Mercy Parish in June 1963 he announced the new school building project. Observing that the parish census recorded 4,553 Catholics in the area and 847 school-age children, Monsignor Hickey launched his school building campaign saying, "No parish is complete without a school." (206)

Realizing that having a Catholic school meant, in those days, obtaining sisters to staff it and building a convent, Monsignor Hickey obtained a commitment from Mother Beata to send three sisters for the opening of the first four grades in the fall of 1966. By February 1966 groundbreaking was held for both the school and the convent. There was, of course, no hope that these buildings would be ready seven months later for a September 8 opening of school. But, somehow, Monsignor Hickey did manage to persuade Mother Beata to send three sisters anyway. The first group of sisters at Our Lady of Mercy included Sisters Francis de Sales (Michlyn) Grella, principal and superior, Aloysius (Mary Rita) Mayan, and Maron (Mary) Rassley. Arrangements were made with Our Lady Queen of Martyrs Convent to house the sisters there. (207)

Not only was there no convent yet, but neither was there a completed school building when the sisters arrived. Monsignor Hickey's plan was for the two sections of first grade to be schooled in the auditorium of the church; second, third and fourth grade students were to be sent by bus to Resurrection-Ascension School in Rego Park, New York where three rooms had been rented from Father Weber, pastor.

With Sister Francis de Sales serving as half-time first grade teacher, and with two first grade classes, the actual number of teachers required was six. Mrs. Annette Primois also served halftime in first grade; Miss Dona McDermott in second grade; and Mrs. Diane Rowan in third grade. Actually, Miss Marianne Manley replaced Dona McDermott on October 31. Sister Aloysius (Mary Rita) Mayan taught the second section of grade one, and Sister Maron (Mary) Rassley, grade four. (208)

The daily commute of the sisters from their residence at Our Lady Queen of Martyrs, and the seven months of bussing three classes of youngsters and their teachers to Rego Park would have been unmanageable but for the zeal and enthusiasm of Monsignor Hickey, the patient endurance of the sisters, and the supportive understanding of the parents of the school children. Daily they would witness the building progress being made and were able to keep their focus on the future. Monsignor Hickey's gratitude was often expressed, but as early as September 11, 1966, his message in the Church Bulletin read:

> We are thankful to God for the blessings attendant on the opening of Our Lady of Mercy School. We are grateful to our many parishioners for their prayers, their financial assistance and their unselfish cooperation, especially during the difficult time of our beginnings. Most of all we want you to know that our Sisters have been heaping up graces for themselves spending their strength, their talent and their ingenuity as they bring a new spiritual warmth and life to our parish . . . (209)

The year moved along with many educational and social activities. Friday, February 10, 1967, was the last day of classes in the temporary school facilities. Monday, February 13 was moving day as the new Our Lady of Mercy School was completed. The formal dedication of the school by Archbishop Bryan McEntegart of Brooklyn was scheduled for May 14, 1967, but on February 14, 1967, Monsignor Hickey, assisted by the priests of the parish, conducted a blessing of each room of the school, anxious to have the 223 pupils of the school sit for the first time in their own new desks in their own new school.

Many years later, at the twenty-fifth reunion of graduates of Our Lady of Mercy School it would be recalled that "Today we are celebrating a gift of love given to students on Valentine's Day in 1967 . . . We know that the seed planted by Monsignor Hickey blossomed into something wonderful." (210)

The stresses accompanying the many involvements of the sisters this first year at Our Lady of Mercy can hardly be imagined or appreciated. An open house on March 5 brought parents and other parishioners to view the school; attendance at regular educational events, such as the National Catholic Educational Association in Atlantic City, New Jersey; selection of furnishings for the chapel and bedrooms of the convent, and the subsequent arrival and storage of these furnishings; preparation of the children for the Forty Hours procession in April, and of sixty-five youngsters for First Holy Communion on May 6—all of these events were crowded into the spring months of 1967. The week of May 7 was overwhelmingly filled with pre-dedication tasks for the coming of the Archbishop for the May 14 school and convent dedication.

At the height of all this bustle a change of personnel was required because of the illness of Sister Francis de Sales. Sister Maron assumed the duties of principal and superior; Sister St. Imelda (Mary Elizabeth) Costello was assigned to teach first grade. The sisters continued to live at Our Lady Queen of Martyrs Convent until the end of the school year.

May 14, 1967, at 4:00 p.m., the memorable dedication date for Our Lady of Mercy School and Convent saw an honor guard of third and fourth graders in school uniform lining the walk to greet Archbishop McEntegart of Brooklyn. One hundred sisters attended the catered banquet in the multipurpose room of the school after the dedication. One hundred-fifty priests were served in the church auditorium. (211)

Ten weeks later, on July 25, 1967, the zealous, tireless pastor, Monsignor Hickey died, having accomplished his building plans at Our Lady of Mercy. But, as the annals state, "For Monsignor Hickey the treasured dream of seeing the sisters move into the new convent never became a reality." (212) Ironically, within a few days, on July 31, 1967, Sister Maron (Mary), accompanied by Sister St. Virginia (Maureen) Cryan, arrived to open the convent. On August 4 Father John J. Johnston, assistant pastor, offered the first Mass in the new convent chapel in memory of Monsignor Hickey. By August 21, 1967, the local community of four IHMs was complete: Sister Maron (Mary) Rassley, principal and superior, Sister Aloysius Mary (Rita Mary) Mayan, Sister St. Lucy (Jeanetta) Kearney, and Sister Melita (Kathleen) Hassett. (213) Father Johnston was installed as pastor on September 29, 1967.

Classes began on September 11, 1967, with the four sisters and six lay teachers managing five grades in nine classrooms. There were two sections of each grade, except fourth grade. In addition to their regular classes, each sister conducted classes in the parish CCD program. Open school day was held for the parishioners on October 22, giving them the opportunity to observe the beauty and practicality of the facilities that their sacrifices had made possible.

It should be noted that the convent was not yet complete. So while there were small inconveniences, there were also on-going surprises as the stained-glass windows were installed in the chapel, draperies were hung throughout the convent, carpeting was laid, and new furniture arrived. Throughout January, February and March there was a steady stream of Congregation supervisors, and a capacity group of sisters from Clinton, Maryland, and Williamsport, Pennsylvania, who were in New York for a lecture by Reverend Eugene Kennedy.

On April 28, 1968, the convent open house was held. There were 125 sisters in attendance. Father Johnston arranged for a catered luncheon for all. (214)

By the fall 1968, the enrollment in the six grades, with two sections of each, necessitated opening four more classrooms on the second floor of the school, for a total of twelve classrooms in use. The faculty now included five sisters and eight lay teachers. Sister Maria Benedict Russell was the newly assigned IHM for sixth grade. Sister Theodosia (Patricia Ann) Matthews was assigned in residence at Our Lady of Mercy Convent while attending St. John's University. (215)

A high of ten teaching sisters was reached in the school year 1972-1973. These included Sisters Pauline Langan, remedial reading program instructor and Timothy Marie (Jane) Hardison, full-time music instructor. In 1974-1975 Father Johnston, pastor, engaged two Dominican sisters for visitation work with the elderly of the parish. The IHMs were happy to add them to the local community. (216)

In 1975-1976 Sister Nadine Moran, who had been the first assistant to Mother Beata from 1970-1974, was appointed principal of Our Lady of Mercy School. From the time of her surgery on September 26, 1975, however, Sister Nadine spent most of the year in recuperation, returning to the hospital for over a month in the spring of 1976. She resigned as principal in the fall, 1976, leaving Our Lady of Mercy on September 10 to return to St. John Hospital, Elmhurst, New York. Sister Nadine died there on September 26. A vigil was held one night in Our Lady of Mercy Convent and the Mass of Resurrection celebrated at Our Lady of Mercy Church on September 27 at 9:30 a.m. The final Mass from the IHM Generalate Chapel at Marywood in Scranton, Pennsylvania, was held on September 29. Burial was in the IHM Sisters' section at St. Catherine Cemetery in Moscow, Pennsylvania. (217)

Up to the year 1982-1983 there were eight IHMs serving in Our Lady of Mercy School, including Sisters Jacqueline Cunningham and Paulina Langan who instructed small groups of youngsters in math and reading, respectively. By 1985-1986, however, the shortage of sisters that was affecting all IHM schools, found only four IHMs at Our Lady of Mercy School. (218)

Monsignor Johnston retired in May 1984 having served Our Lady of Mercy Parish for a total of thirty-three years, seventeen of which were as pastor. On June 9, 1984, Monsignor Gerald Langalier was installed as the new pastor. It would fall to him to prepare the parish for the celebration of its fiftieth anniversary in 1988. His first step in this direction was to organize the "50th Anniversary Refurbishing Fund Campaign" in the parish. On October 5, 1987, the D'Ambrosio Ecclesiastical Art Studios of Mt. Kisko, New York, were commissioned to design the plans for an expansive liturgically and artistically appropriate renovation of Our Lady of Mercy Church. Preserving many of the original features of the structure's interior, yet updating lighting and furniture, the result was beautiful and impressive. The work in detail is described in the rededication booklet published for the occasion held on January 31, 1988. (219)

Monsignor Langalier would move from the church project to the refurbishing of the convent chapel, utilizing the same artistic experts from the D'Ambrosio Art Studio for the task. The work was begun with the removal of the chapel pews on January 24, 1990, and concluded with the reposition of the Blessed Sacrament on May 14, 1990. During the interim the sisters at Our Lady of Mercy set up a makeshift chapel in one of the convent parlors. Extensive renewal was done, including complete repainting, new altar, tabernacle and stand, carpet, light fixtures, pews and other furnishings. (220) It had been twenty-two years since the 1968 construction of Our Lady of Mercy Convent, so the following year, 1991-1992 would see new drapes and the painting of the dining room, as well as new carpet in the first floor hall.

The year 1991-1992 was the twenty-fifth anniversary year for Our Lady of Mercy School. Special activities were scheduled beginning with a parish liturgy on February 8, tours of the school, and a catered reception in the school gym. The following week was Catholic Schools Week, which provided many opportunities to showcase the philosophy of the school and the work of the students. (221)

The spring of 1993 brought sorrow to the Our Lady of Mercy community once again in the sudden death of Sister Gervase Callahan. She died in the convent of a heart attack on April 3. The vigil was held in the convent chapel and the Mass of Resurrection celebrated at Our Lady of

Mercy Church. The sisters accompanied her body to St. Catherine's Cemetery in Moscow, Pennsylvania, where she was buried. The esteem and love in which Sister Gervase was held was evident in the sincere expressions of sadness from Monsignor Langalier, hundreds of sisters, friends, and former students. (222)

As in all IHM houses, the years at Our Lady of Mercy Convent have been a history of the joys and sorrows of the sisters, the parish family, and their own families. Our Lady of Mercy had its share of all of these, but seems singularly blessed in the generosity of its pastors, in the joyous celebrations of spiritual and temporal events, including Sister Benedict Hore's sixtieth jubilee of religious profession in May 1995.

At this writing in 2002 there are four IHMs teaching in Our Lady of Mercy School: Sister Mary Ellen Malloy, principal, Sister Marylin Grosselfinger, Sister Francis Rose Lapitano, and Sister Franziska Laudacher. In addition, Sisters Ann Barbara DeSiano, IHM serves as a pastoral associate, Sister Noemi Kreppein, OP, as parish visitor, and Sister Mary Edward Loftus, IHM, librarian at Our Lady Queen of Martyrs, Forest Hills, is in residence. Sister Maria Regina Loures, IHM, associate retreat director at Bishop Molloy Retreat House, is also in residence.

Over the years, since 1966, nine IHM Sisters have served as principal of Our Lady of Mercy School. They include: Sisters Francis de Sales (Michlyn) Grella, Maron (Mary) Rassley, Fidelis Flannery, Norita Corrigan, Nadine Moran, Maria Regina Loures, St. William Lynch, Maria Lourdes Vanston and Mary Ellen Malloy, present principal in 2002.

St. Raphael, St. Petersburg, Florida

Unlike most of the new missions accepted by the IHM Congregation, St. Raphael's in St. Petersburg, Florida was a well-established school with a lay faculty before the IHMs arrived in 1966. It was an unusual circumstance that brought about the fortuitous meeting of Mr. and Mrs. Harold Mostyn of St. Raphael's Parish, St. Petersburg, Florida, with the Sisters of IHM for the first time in the summer of 1965.

The Mostyn's were on vacation, visiting the Pocono Mountain area near Scranton. When dining at the Blue Shutters Inn they met several IHM Sisters from the area who were having a farewell dinner for one of the group leaving for Peru. The Mostyn's inquired about the availability of IHMs to staff their parish school in St. Petersburg, and were given the name and address of Mother Beata. Subsequently, Mother Beata was contacted by the pastor of St. Raphael's, Reverend William J. Weinheimer. (223)

As early as October 10, 1965, there is a record of the Central Administrative Assembly's consideration of Father Weinheimer's request for sisters, and a decision to send four sisters to St. Raphael's School in 1966. (224)

The next correspondence of record occurs four months later on February 13, 1966, when Father Weinheimer submitted to Mother Beata the plans for the convent to be built and sought suggestions regarding the adequacy of the plan. His comment that "We are just now beginning a fund drive to provide the money to build the convent and if possible also the rectory," must have signaled the slow pace of the project. (225)

Mother Beata accordingly postponed any action until the CAA (Central Administrative Assembly) meeting of March 6, 1966, at which the plan for the convent was discussed and suggestions made. These suggestions focused on a trunk room, cloak closet, and supply room in the convent. Mother Beata's letter of March 9, 1966, to Father Weinheimer indicated that she would share the suggestions for changes with him when she arrived in St. Petersburg. (226) A week later, letters to Father Weinheimer and to Bishop Joseph P. Hurley in St. Augustine, Florida, indicate the dates of her visit to Florida to be from March 21 to March 24.

The success of Mother Beata's visit to St. Raphael's School in St. Petersburg, Florida, was evidenced in the fact that five months later, on August 19, 1966, the first Scranton IHMs assigned to Florida arrived in Tampa at 6:20 p.m. The new Floridians were Sisters Paracleta (Irene) Gallagher, principal and superior, Mary Paulo McAndrew and St. Bernadette Hamilton. The pastor, Father Weinheimer and his assistant, Reverend Leo Flood, CSC, and the former principal of the school, Miss Elizabeth Sabathe welcomed the sisters.

The drive to St. Petersburg afforded the sisters a view of Tampa Bay and the unfamiliar palm trees along the way. Arriving in St. Petersburg, the sisters were given a quick tour of the church and school. Since the arrangements for even a temporary convent residence were not yet completed, the sisters were lodged in a three-bedroom suite with living room and dinette in the Edgewater Beach Motel. (227)

It would be three years and five residence moves later before the sisters would eventually move to a permanent convent home. The first of these moves came on August 30, one day after school had opened on August 29. This first rented residence was located at 1297 Eden Isle Boulevard next to the school and provided space for three bedrooms, a chapel, community room and large living room. Because of the lack of furnishings it was necessary to shop for basic items. A shower conducted by the Women's Guild supplied bed linens, cooking utensils, glassware and many other necessities. (228)

Although diocesan consent was given to Father Weinheimer in February of 1967 to proceed with the building of a convent, the actuality was still only a remote possibility.

The attractiveness of Florida weather in mid-winter and early spring brought many visitors from the "north" to St. Raphael's. Among these were the parents of Sister Mary Paulo and of Sister St. Bernadette, as well as IHM Congregation school supervisors, Sisters Felicitas Ryan, Sheila Reilly, Dermot (Jean) Toolan, and Eamon O'Neill.

In this initial year of IHM presence in St. Petersburg the sisters were involved in several educational events, attending the teachers' institute in Orlando, speaking at the Women's Guild meetings, attending lectures in spirituality, hosting the principals' meeting for the diocese, preparing a song and dance festival, and observing the operations of ungraded and team teaching schools in the region.

At the close of the school year, its owner was selling the temporary residence of the sisters, so the sisters were on the move again. The annals record the on-going hope of the pastor: "Suitable quarters were found at 3731 Huntington Avenue. No chapel was provided due to the restricted room. But the community was assured by the pastor that a permanent residence will be available within the next few months." (229)

The Huntington Avenue house was not in good condition, but the sisters, together with friends like Mrs. Mary Marchinko and Mrs. Agnes O'Shea, soon put it in good order. The house was closed for the summer as the three sisters left on June 14 for their summer study assignments.

The school year 1967-1968 saw the addition of Sister Maria Regina Loures to the faculty. This brought the total faculty to nine, with four IHMs and five lay teachers. Events of this year were to have their impact on the little community as the month of October brought news of the death of Bishop Joseph P. Hurley one week after his return from a visit to Rome. Until the appointment of a new bishop and the obtaining of new approvals, the building plans for the convent had to be postponed. (230)

In March 1968, another more personal loss occurred as Sister Mary Paulo decided to leave the IHM Congregation. There are never adequate words to explain the pain experienced within the community when a sister leaves. The annals make a brief statement:

> Needless to say, the Sisters and parishioners were very sorry to lose such a wonderful Sister and friend, but wishing her only

> happiness, accepted her decision. Sister Mary Paulo made a wonderful impression on the people and children here. (231)

On March 27, 1968, His Excellency Paul F. Tanner was installed as the new bishop of St. Augustine, Florida. Sisters Paracleta (Irene) and St. Bernadette attended the ceremonies. Bishop Tanner's jurisdiction was soon to change, however, when in May 1968 Pope Paul VI divided the Diocese of St. Augustine, making St. Petersburg a new diocese with His Excellency Charles McLaughlin named as new bishop. Since Bishop McLaughlin had been the former pastor of parishes in Rocky Mount and Greensboro, North Carolina, where the IHMs were located, the sisters at St. Raphael's were happy indeed. (232)

At the close of the school year, the sisters' residence #3 was returned to its owners, and the furniture was put in storage for the summer. Since construction of the convent had not yet begun, the "pilgrim" community left for summer assignments not knowing where they would live in the fall. That a permanent convent would be an eventuality was clear, however, when Mother Beata received a telegram from Father Weinheimer on August 16, 1968, saying: "Happy to report convent contract signed today. Construction immediately." (233)

Of course, the sisters were leaving Marywood for Florida the very next day, August 17, 1968. Sister Paracleta (Irene) Gallagher, continuing principal and superior, was bringing three new sisters to St. Raphael's, namely, Sisters Grace Marie Campbell, Sue Ann Steves, and Laura Booth. Sister St. Bernadette Hamilton had been assigned to Puerto Rico. Aware that their fourth temporary residence would not be ready until August 21, the travelers enjoyed the hospitality of IHMs in Upper Marlboro, Maryland and in Rocky Mount, North Carolina enroute. Residence #4 on Dover Street was a four-bedroom home with a large room overlooking the water reserved as the chapel. The parishioners had cleaned the house, so it was ready for the arrival of the four sisters. (234)

Classes began on September 3, 1968, with over two hundred pupils. On September 6 the sisters rejoiced at having the Blessed Sacrament reserved in the chapel of the Dover Street residence.

As hurricanes were an annual natural phenomenon in Florida, the sisters seemed to accept serenely the fact that hurricane Gladys was a stormy October visitor that brought "the gradual rising of the bayou in our backyard." (235)

February was a good, warm month in Florida for visitors from the wintry north. Again, the first IHM visitors were Congregation supervisors, Sisters Felicitas, Eleanora, Sheila, and Cor Immaculatum. In March,

Sisters Mary Martin O'Dea, sector superior, and Sister Coleman Nee, coordinator of apostolic works, were additional Congregation visitors.

The long-awaited completion of the convent came and the sisters made their final move on May 15, 1969. (236) This Spanish-style structure with red-tiled roof included the entry hallway and office, parlor, kitchen, dining room, laundry, storage and trunk room, chapel, and sacristy on first floor. The second floor had six bedrooms, community room, sewing room and exterior porch. All of the suggestions made to Father Weinheimer by Mother Beata three years before in March of 1966 had been included in the construction plan. (237)

By October 1969 the chapel furnishings arrived. The Mass and dedication of the convent were held on December 9, with Bishop Charles B. McLaughlin officiating. Open house for the sisters of the area was held on February 8, 1970.

All of these exciting events did not deter the sisters from their educational mission as they prepared the students at St. Raphael's for oratorical and poetry contests, a film festival, and science fair, with the resultant capturing of five prizes at the county level. The girls' basketball team also took second place in the Florida West Coast League. Students in the annual art festival won two first place trophies and thirty-two ribbons. Participating in a diocesan contest to design a letterhead for the educational bulletin, Sisters Paracleta (Irene) and Grace Marie Campbell won first and second place, respectively. (238)

In the fall 1970 Sister Paracleta (Irene), the first principal and superior at St. Raphael's was assigned as a school supervisor for the Wilmington, Delaware Diocese. Sister Sue Steves was appointed in her place at St. Raphael's, and Sister Jamesann McCue was welcomed as the fourth IHM for the school faculty. Sister Paul Joseph McArdle and Sister David Marie Scanlon, a Monroe, Michigan IHM, were in residence at St. Raphael's while teaching adult education in several centers throughout the diocese.

Father Weinheimer's silver jubilee was celebrated by the sisters and students in spring of 1970. It was a joyful prelude to the sadness they would experience in June when Father Weinheimer was transferred from St. Raphael's. His initial work in the development of the school and the construction of the convent was deeply appreciated, especially by the IHM Sisters. The new pastor assigned was Reverend Anton Dechering. (239)

The focus of the faculty of St. Raphael's School for the 1971-1972 year was on obtaining accreditation by the South States Association. With an enrollment high of 262 pupils, the support of the parish for its school was evident. Diocesan and Congregation supervisors had affirmed the quality of education being offered, and by the spring of 1972, so had the South States Association by its accreditation of St. Raphael's School. (240) The school would also be accredited by the Florida Catholic Conference in January 1973. (241) Mother Beata's praise and words of encouragement for the sisters was expressed in a letter of January 18, 1973:

> My warm congratulations to each one on the full accreditation of St. Raphael's School by the Florida Catholic Conference. I am sure all—Father Dechering, parents, students, and friends—are pleased with this good word. Such unqualified approval is evidence of the fine work and cooperation of all concerned. God bless you! (242)

St. Raphael's School continued to thrive throughout Mother Beata's tenure as superior general and beyond, to 1984. Four capable principals provided excellent leadership over that time, Sisters Paracleta (Irene) Gallagher, Sue Ann Steves, Grace Marie Campbell, and Florence Ann Marino.

St. Lawrence School, South Williamsport, Pennsylvania

The first parishes established in Williamsport, Pennsylvania, were St. Boniface, founded by Reverend John Bach in 1857 and Annunciation, founded in 1865. The Diocese of Scranton was established on March 3, 1868, but it was not until 1928, in the administration of Bishop Thomas C. O'Reilly, that the need for another parish to serve South Williamsport was addressed.

On July 13, 1931, Bishop O'Reilly established St. Lawrence Parish and announced that Reverend Raymond E. Larkin would be the first pastor of the new parish. His installation was held on August 10, 1931. (243) Father Larkin had been administrator of Annunciation Parish in Williamsport for a time and later served as assistant pastor there until his appointment as pastor of St. Lawrence. He was involved in planning the boundaries of the new parish and had purchased land on which to build a church. This was done on June 26, 1931, prior to his appointment as pastor.

Having the land was one step, but in the height of the economic depression when jobs were scarce, it would take enormous sacrifices to take the second step of actually building a church. "In South Williamsport, as elsewhere across the country, many Americans were barely scratching out subsistence for themselves and their families." (244)

In the year that followed, South Williamsport Community Hall was utilized for Sunday Masses and other services. The first Mass in this hall was celebrated on August 15, 1931. Father Larkin continued to live at Annunciation Parish rectory while a neighborhood house was renovated for his residence. Nine months later, on May 1, 1932, groundbreaking ceremonies for the church were held and on July 10, 1932, the cornerstone was laid. Many of the parishioners fulfilled their pledges to the building fund by actually working on the construction. St. Boniface and Annunciation Parishes each contributed $5,000 to the fund. (245)

> Thus Father Larkin saw his dream of the church of his new parish come true less than eighteen months after the parish was created. The building was completed in September of 1932 and dedicated on October 2 by Bishop O'Reilly. (246)

It was well known that Father Larkin was anxious to establish a parish school, but in light of the economic circumstances mentioned above, and the need to reduce the accumulated parish debt, he addressed the religious education of the children of St. Lawrence in another way. He persuaded the IHM Sisters from St. Joseph's School in Williamsport to conduct classes in catechism on Sundays and during the summer. The IHMs began to offer religious instruction in St. Lawrence Parish in 1933. (247)

Father Larkin was transferred from St. Lawrence Parish in 1938. He was succeeded by Reverend Joseph A. Reilly (1938-1946), Reverend James H. O'Hara, PhD. (1946-1951), Reverend Thomas J. Knight (1951-1966) and Reverend Joseph W. Breslin (1966-1974). It was Father O'Hara who had the church renovated and who purchased the land on Winthrop Street that would later become the site of St. Lawrence Convent. (248) Father Knight, in turn, enlarged the rectory and made additional improvements to the church. It was Father Knight who was to realize the dream of all the former pastors to provide a school for St. Lawrence Parish children.

From its founding in 1931 to 1964 the parish had quadrupled in membership, and having survived the flood of 1936, the economic depression and World War II, and having reduced the debt acquired in building and renovating the church over the years, it was time to build the school and convent. (249)

Father Knight had no concern about obtaining IHM Sisters to staff a school in St. Lawrence Parish since his 1960 request for sisters (250) was responded to in the affirmative by Mother Kathleen, who had promised sisters for the opening of the school in 1966. (251)

Pursuing this promise, Father Knight wrote to Mother Beata on October 15, 1963, enclosing the letter from Mother Kathleen. Knowing that the passage of years and a change of administration in the Congregation may have altered the availability of sisters for St. Lawrence, Father Knight sought a definite commitment for the future. He wrote:

> In a recent letter to His Excellency, Bishop Hannan, I asked permission to begin planning for a school. A reply from Monsignor Madden, acting for His Excellency and the building Commission, instructed me to request a firm commitment from you on the staffing of a school in September 1966. (252)

Mother Beata was in Oregon at the time and having received the letter forwarded to her, she promised Father Knight to present the request to the general council when she returned. (253) This she did. On November 9, 1963, she wrote the good news to Father Knight:

> This morning at a meeting of our General Council, it was decided that our community would assign three of our Sisters to staff your school in September 1966. This assignment will enable you to start the lower grades of your new school. (254)

One month later, on January 8, 1968, Father Knight announced to the parishioners of St. Lawrence Parish by letter the joyful news: "In September of 1966 we hope to open a Parochial School. The school will be staffed with the Sisters, Servants of the Immaculate Heart of Mary." (255)

The following year and seven months found Father Knight, the parish building committee members, and the total parish deeply involved in construction plans and the acquisition of additional land for the school playground. On August 24, 1965, Father Knight turned the first shovel-full of earth for the school (256) and a year later, on August 30, 1966, Bishop J. Carroll McCormick dedicated St. Lawrence School and Convent. It was a festive occasion followed by a dinner in the parish hall. The founding pastor, Monsignor Larkin and the second pastor, Reverend Joseph Reilly were among the distinguished guests. (257) Attending from Marywood were Mother M. Beata, Sister Seraphia Gallagher, Mother Adalbert (Mary) Schelb and Sister Cor Immaculatum Heffernan. Sisters from the neighboring parishes also attended.

The three IHM Sisters who were to staff the new school had arrived on August 26 and had been welcomed at each Sunday Mass on August 28.

So, for Sisters Demetria (Elizabeth) Sciulli, St. Imelda (Mary Elizabeth) Costello and Frances Mary Rundell it was an exciting five-day introduction to the new convent and school. (258)

As more furnishings arrived each day for the convent, the sisters were beginning to feel at home. On September 7, 1966, when school opened with 9:00 a.m. Mass and seventy-five pupils for the first three grades arrived, the sisters knew their mission had begun. There were 28 pupils in first grade under the care of Sister St. Imelda (Mary Elizabeth); 16 in second grade with Sister Frances Mary Rundell; and 31 in third grade with Sister Demetria (Elizabeth) Sciulli, who also served as principal and superior.

The following day, September 8, Father Knight and the parishioners held a welcoming event for the sisters. At this gathering Father Knight announced his transfer to St. John's Parish, Pittston, Pennsylvania. It was difficult for the sisters to balance the emotions of "welcome" and "farewell" on that day, but there were so many things for which to be grateful that by September 13 they were able to enter joyfully into the farewell events honoring Father Knight in the Crown Room of the King's Motel in South Williamsport.

> The new school and convent were the climax of his work at St. Lawrence Parish, but the warmth of the gratitude and friendship felt in the Crown Room on that September evening was an equally important measure of what he had accomplished during his fifteen years of service to the parish. (259)

The very next day, September 14, 1966, Father Joseph W. Breslin, the new pastor, arrived. Since both the school and convent were newly constructed, Father Breslin turned his focus to renovation of the church.

Meanwhile, throughout October, furnishings for the convent chapel continued to arrive: on October 1 the chapel pews were installed; on October 19 the statues arrived. In the school also, each day brought its challenges with "newness." Card tables which had been utilized for pupils' desks were gladly exchanged when the new desks arrived on September 20. The teachers' desks followed a month later, arriving on October 20. (260)

In addition to their regular classroom teaching at St. Lawrence School the sisters also provided catechetical instruction in Resurrection Parish, Muncy. They prepared the children of both parishes for First Communion. Three groups were involved in these ceremonies that were held on October 29 for fifty children of St. Lawrence, on May 28 at Resurrection Parish, and again on June 3 at St. Lawrence Parish.

Open house was held for the sisters of the region on December 28. As the visitors came from far and near, there was no doubt that the efforts of Father Knight in building St. Lawrence School and Convent were appreciated by the IHMs.

The second year of IHM presence at St. Lawrence School saw Sister Mary Claude (Edith) Opferman replacing Sister St. Imelda (Mary Elizabeth) Costello. Sister Maria Gabriel McQuade was added to serve as school secretary. Since there were now four grades, it was necessary to hire a lay teacher, Mrs. Nancy Higgins for the fourth grade. The year was filled with spiritual and professional activities. The Diocesan Teachers Institute in Scranton, music workshops in Williamsport, retreats, visits of Congregation supervisors Sisters Nora Clarke, Sheila Reilly and Eleanora Whalen, and feast day celebrations with the IHMs at St. Joseph's, Williamsport, climaxed by the May 14 confirmation of 120 children and 20 adults—all were part of a busy, normal year at St. Lawrence. (261)

Illness and personnel changes were to invade the little community from 1968-1969 through 1970-1971. Sister Elizabeth Sciulli resigned on September 8, 1968, and was replaced by Sister Lucian Reddington until the close of the year when Sister Dorothy McCaffrey was assigned as principal and superior. Sister Frances Mary Rundell was transferred to Port Washington, New York, in May 1969. The next two years saw the sisters bravely carrying on in spite of the rotation of three lay teachers and seven sisters in the school over this period.

By 1970-1971 the enrollment at St. Lawrence School had increased to 123 pupils. Bishop J. Carroll McCormick held confirmation on May 10 for 156 children and 8 adults. The sisters prepared 53 children to receive First Holy Communion.

Events of larger scope that would impact St. Lawrence School had been gradually evolving. The Diocese of Scranton had decided to sponsor a central junior-senior high school in Williamsport that opened in the fall of 1969-1970. It was to be staffed jointly by the IHMs and the Sisters of Christian Charity (SCC). Four IHMs were requested for the faculty of the new Bishop Neumann High School. The initial impact was felt by St. Joseph's High School, which was closed, and St. Joseph's Elementary School that became a K-6 grade school, with seventh to ninth graders being absorbed by the new junior high at Bishop Neumann.

Letters from the Scranton Diocesan Superintendent of Schools, Monsignor William L. Donovan, Mother Beata, and Sister Eleanor Desaulniers, sector superior, to the pastor of St. Lawrence Parish, Father Joseph Breslin, indicate that a merger of St. Lawrence and St. Joseph's Schools was imminent.

Efforts made by members of St. Lawrence Parish to prevent the loss of their school were discussed at several meetings in the spring of 1972 with Monsignor James Timlin, Monsignor John Dougherty, Sister Willemyn Gambrill, IHM, and Monsignor Donovan. Monsignor Donovan summed up the conclusion of these meetings:

> We realize that no one solution is perfect, nor will it be acceptable to all concerned. We sincerely wish that we could keep both schools in operation. Nevertheless, we must be realistic and accept the decision we feel best serves the greater number of students. (263)

Copies of this letter were sent by Monsignor Donovan to Mother Beata, Sister Dorothy McCaffrey, principal of St. Lawrence, and to Monsignor Joseph Shaughnessy, pastor at St. Joseph's Parish, Williamsport.

It was proposed that St. Lawrence Convent be utilized as a faculty house for the IHM Sisters teaching at Bishop Neumann High School who had been residing at St. Joseph's Convent, Williamsport. These sisters would also be responsible for religious instructions for the children of St. Lawrence Parish on a schedule to be mutually arranged by Father Breslin and the sisters. (264)

These plans materialized when St. Lawrence School was closed on June 14, 1972. The parishioners and the sisters were deeply saddened, but appreciative of all that had been accomplished in the short six-year existence of St. Lawrence School. The final letter of the Central Administrative Assembly to the sisters at St. Lawrence School captured the sentiments felt by all: "We fervently pray that the years of loving service which you have rendered will continue to influence and direct the lives of those with whom you have worked." (265)

The IHM faculty of Bishop Neumann High School became the new residents of St. Lawrence Convent in September 1972. These included Sisters Alphonsine Kelley, elected superior, Rosela McFadden, Gabrielis Marley, Ann Therese (Anne) Munley, and Rosemary Stankis. All of the sisters taught religious instructions at St. Lawrence School and Sisters Rosemary and Ann Therese (Anne) also taught at Ascension Parish on Sunday mornings. (266)

These arrangements continued until 1985 when the number of IHM Sisters at Neumann High School was reduced to two, namely, Sisters Franceline Krug and Kathryn Kurdziel. These two sisters moved to St. Joseph's Convent, Williamsport for the school year, 1985-86. St.

Lawrence Convent was utilized by Sister Natalie de Luca of the Mission Helpers of the Sacred Heart and Sister Loretta Beznar of the Franciscan Sisters of the Atonement. They served St. Lawrence Parish children by providing religious instructions over a three- year period. (267)

In 1993 the pastor, Reverend Tomalis, decided to move the parish rectory to the convent. The former St. Lawrence Convent remains the parish rectory until this day in 2002.

Notre Dame High School, East Stroudsburg, Pennsylvania

Reverend Harold G. Durkin, third pastor of St. Matthew's Parish in East Stroudsburg, Pennsylvania, had succeeded Reverend John T. Butler who died in 1943. It was Father Butler who had led the parish in building St. Matthew's Church, school and convent over the years 1932-1934. (268)

Having inherited this imposing physical plant, Father Durkin's thoughts turned to building a parish high school. This was an eighteen-year dream that never reached fruition before the September 8, 1961, death of this beloved pastor. (269)

About a month later, on October 12, 1961, Right Reverend Monsignor Thomas J. Cawley was appointed pastor of St. Matthew's. There must have been more than a dream left behind by Father Durkin, since important background planning for a high school was underway within seven months of Monsignor Cawley's arrival. On May 2, 1962, Monsignor Cawley met with newly elected Mother Beata about the possibility of procuring IHM Sisters for the proposed high school. She promised sisters for 1967. By September 11, 1962, Monsignor Cawley had also obtained Bishop Jerome D. Hannan's permission for a fund-raising drive for the new school. (270)

Anticipating that additional space would be needed for the sister-faculty for the high school, phase one of the total building project became the renovation and expansion of the existing convent. On March 3, 1963, Monsignor Cawley presented the sisters with the first draft of the new addition to the convent. The plan included a remodeled kitchen, enlarged community room, new chapel, sacristy, sewing room, an all-purpose room, six bedrooms, lavatory facilities, and a garage. (271)

With plans advancing rapidly, it was time for Monsignor Cawley to share more widely with the parishioners of St. Matthew's. The first meeting was held in the parish auditorium on July 21, 1963. One hundred seventy-two men of the parish attended the meeting at which spirited talks were given by Monsignor Cawley and by the parish assistant priests, Fathers Barrett and Essef. After lengthy discussion, the men unanimously agreed that a high school should be built. (272)

At subsequent meetings, the men addressed the issues of size of the school, location, fund-raising and costs. It was projected that the school would serve students from a radius of 200 miles, including St. John's Parish, Bushkill, St. Mark's, Delaware Water Gap, St. Luke's and St. Matthew's, East Stroudsburg. They estimated a twenty-five year goal of one thousand students. The structure envisioned, with large library, cafeteria, and gym facilities, was estimated to cost $1,300,000. (273)

The addition and renovations to the convent were to begin in the summer of 1964. After school closed in June, the sisters dismantled the entire convent, covering furniture, packing dishes, removing pictures and clearing the way for the workers. On June 22, 1964, the doors were locked and the sisters all left for other residences for the summer. No surprise to those who had experience with construction delays, upon the sisters' return in August, nothing was done except a back wall removed and plaster torn from the ceiling in the kitchen.

Yes, things were at a standstill because the Diocesan Building Committee had not approved the plans and new plans had to be submitted. (274) The sisters adjusted, setting up a temporary kitchen and refectory in the basement laundry. Construction continued through the winter months and by May 1964 they were able to say, "Nothing is wanting to make the convent home comfortable and attractive. Everything is in excellent taste and will be a monument to our worthy pastor, Monsignor Cawley." (275) Amazingly, the total cost of the addition and renovation was only $103,750 including furnishings—and it was entirely paid for by October 1964. (276)

A forty-acre plot was purchased in East Stroudsburg, about two miles from St. Matthew's Rectory, as the site for the new high school. The site had easy access from several main streets and a view of the Delaware Water Gap. Ground was broken on April 22, 1966, with priests, sisters, officers of parish organizations and pupils from St. Matthew's grades five through eight in attendance. Monsignor Cawley, pastor, conducted the ceremony. (277)

The IHM faculty for this opening year of Notre Dame High School were Sisters Immaculee Cavanaugh, principal and English teacher, St. Genevieve (Joanne) Pickard, mathematics, Helaine O'Dea, history, and Antonina Williamson, librarian. (278) In 1968-1969, Sister Mary Frances Krystofik was added to teach science classes for grades seven through ten. (279)

The high point in IHM staffing of Notre Dame High School was reached in 1971-1972 when ten sisters were assigned. Sister Mary John (Jean) Conaty was appointed principal with the following IHM faculty:

Sisters St. John Ortner, Elizabeth (Edwarda) Collins, Marinus Krumenacker, Theresa O'Malley, Helene Fee, Jean Leonard, Margot Worfolk, Kathleen Joy Steck and Marylin Grosselfinger. (280)

From the beginning of the school, art and music classes were offered by Sisters Joanne Pickard and Mary Frances Krystofik. A lay teacher, Mr. Allsworthy formed and directed the band classes. Sister Marie Lourdes Vanston, prinicipal of St. Matthew's Elementary School, assisted with the glee club. Dramatic and musical productions were an annual event at the high school.

In addition to these involvements, the sisters from both Notre Dame High School and St. Matthew's were engaged in religious education in St. Matthew's Parish, in music ministry at St. Luke's Parish, in interfaith activities in Stroudsburg, and in campus ministry on the East Stroudsburg State College campus. (281)

IHM principals who served at Notre Dame High School included Sister Immaculee Cavanaugh, 1966-1970; Sister Jean Conaty, 1970-1972; Sister Electa Schmidt, 1972-1976; Sister Margo McCormick, 1976-1980; Sister Mary Persico, 1980-1986; Sister Rosemarie Mozzachio, 1986-1990. Mr. Jeffrey Lyons became principal in September 1990 and continues to serve in this role as of this date in 2002.

Throughout Mother Beata's tenure, and on the present date in 2002, Notre Dame High School continues as an outstanding high school. Only one IHM, Sister Carol Lubas, continues as a junior high teacher at Notre Dame at this time. (282)

Saints Philip and James, Smithtown, New York

Two congregations of sisters had served Saints Philip and James School prior to 1967 when the IHMs accepted this mission—the Sisters of the Holy Names of Jesus and Mary, from 1922 to 1939; and the Sisters of the Holy Union of the Sacred Hearts from 1939 to 1967. The latter began their first school year with seventy-six students enrolled and a faculty of five sisters. Their duties included religious instructions at St. Patrick's, a mission of Smithtown, care of the church—altar boys, sacristy, choir, and playing the organ, as well as the regular classroom teaching.

The parish of Saints Philip and James during the 40s and early 50s was a quiet, rural hamlet, but by 1951 was becoming a larger town. There were 150 students in the school. It was during her visit on May 1, 1951, from Belgium that Reverend Mother Marie Therese of the Holy Union Congregation discussed the possibility of a new school and auditorium with the pastor, Father Murphy. Father Murphy with his own funds had already purchased land, but it was apparent that it would take some time to raise the funds needed for a new school. Father Murphy's death on May 10, nine days after Mother Marie Therese's visit, did not deter the parishioners from forwarding his plans.

Under the leadership of the new pastor, Father Otto Froelich, the first part of the school was built by 1953. By the time of Father Froelich's death in 1957 enrollment in the school was overflowing. Reverend Charles Carow succeeded Father Froelich. It was he who saw to the completion of the new school, the church and auditorium, all of which were dedicated in April 1962, providing a beautiful and complete parish plant. (283)

The school grew to over 300 students by the 60s necessitating the hiring of lay teachers. Unable to continue their commitment to Saints Philip and James School, the Holy Union Sisters were withdrawn on June 24, 1967. The pastor, Father Carow, held a farewell reception for the sisters and paid tribute to their service to the parish saying, "The past twenty-eight years have been filled with their offerings of talent, spirituality, guidance and training of many members of this parish." (284)

Correspondence between Father Charles Carow and Mother Beata began with a letter of request for sisters in September 1965 when Father Carow became aware that the Holy Union Sisters were intending to withdraw because of a shortage of personnel. Father Carow's initial contact was prompted by a suggestion from Sister Phyllis McCarty, IHM, then stationed at St. Leo's in Ashley, Pennsylvania, whose brother Bob McCarty was a member of Sts. Philip and James Parish. (285)

Mr. McCarty and Father Carow had their first appointment with Mother Beata on September 27, 1965. Prudently, Mother Beata cautioned, "But please do not raise your hopes, as I can offer no assurance of help to you . . . " (286)

The meeting must have gone well, for a promise of sisters was forthcoming in a letter from Mother Beata by October 11, 1965. Referring to the council's decision, she wrote: "Our quota is filled not only for this year, but for 1966 as well. If you can find it possible to wait until September 1967, I shall then be able to send you three Sisters, adding to the number later on." (287)

Father Carow's gratitude and delight were evident, even in light of a two-year wait for IHM Sisters. His prayerful acceptance was expressed in these words:

> . . This is only another proof of the great favor that our humble parish has with the Holy Ghost Who has carried us through so

> many impossible situations in the past and still has an open ear for the miracles we dare to request. (288)

By January 1966 a letter to Mother Beata from Reverend David G. Farley, superintendent of schools for the Rockville Centre Diocese, confirmed diocesan approvals for the staffing of Sts. Philip and James School by the IHM Sisters beginning in September 1967. His support was clear:

> May I thank you for your great generosity demonstrated in your willingness to accept this mission. I am certain you will be extremely pleased with Sts. Philip and James School, and with Father Carow who is one of the finest pastors on Long Island. (289)

The generous spirit of the parishioners of Sts. Philip and James was reflected in a steady flow of correspondence and donations to Mother Beata from Mr. Bob McCarty throughout 1966 and 1967. Upon the departure of the Holy Union Sisters, he prevailed upon the pastor for the formation of a parish committee to renovate the convent and provide appropriate furnishings, particularly new kitchen cabinets and a new sink, washer and dryer in the basement laundry. Mr. McCarty personally built a new altar and tabernacle for the chapel and a bookcase along the entire side of the room for the library. (290)

The little IHM community arrived at Sts. Philip and James Convent on August 2, 1967. Sisters Anton (Jeanne) Albrittain, Marthine Culhane, and Anthony (Mary Ruth) Bailey comprised the community. The convent had been vacant since June and the renovation activities mentioned above were in full swing. Cleaning and picking up were the order for many days, with assistance from IHMs from nearby missions.

Many celebrations were held over the ensuing months as the pastor provided many surprises—a new car, chapel carpeting, drapes for each sister's room, new furniture for the community room, stations of the cross, and new chapel statues. The Christmas present from the school children was wall-to-wall carpeting for the community room.

Visitors for the year included Sisters Felicitas Ryan, Robertine Fox, regional superior; Eleanora Whalen, IHM Congregation music supervisor, and the sisters from Oyster Bay and Our Lady of Grace, Manhasset. Sister Phyllis McCarty and several other sisters from Ashley, Pennsylvania, visited over Founders' Day in November. With the McCarty family and the sisters in attendance, the first Mass in the convent chapel was offered on the new altar made by Mr. McCarty.

The first year's work of the sisters in preparing the children of Sts. Philip and James Parish for the sacraments climaxed in the May 14, 1968, with Confirmation of 325 children and the May 25 First Holy Communion of 309 children. (291)

In June of 1968 Sister Marthine was reassigned and Mother Beata appointed Sister Timothy Marie (Jane) Hardison to the faculty as a first grade teacher and music teacher. Sister Alice Marie Kelly was also appointed as the new principal, with Sister Jeanne Albrittain remaining as superior. This brought the total faculty to four IHM Sisters and five lay teachers. Father Carow could not believe his good fortune and wrote: "Knowing the shortage of Sisters and the many problems that face you in various arrangements I am most grateful for this kindness extended to our parish school." (292)

Again, a year later Father Carow was the recipient of good news in Mother Beata's assignment of Sister Maria Magdala as an additional teacher for Sts. Philip and James School. He wrote:

> I do want you to know how grateful I am for your kindness in arranging to send Sister Maria Magdala to us as an additional Sister. I had hoped and prayed for this and can hardly believe our good fortune, knowing the many obligations and demands made upon your services. (293)

Sister Anthony (Mary Ruth) Bailey had been reassigned, but in addition to Sister Maria Magdala, mentioned in the pastor's letter, Sister Jean Marie McAuliffe was also added. This brought the number of IHMs to five. (294)

Responses to a school survey conducted by the IHM Congregation in late 1969 give indication of reasons for what might otherwise appear to be precipitous action in the withdrawal of the IHMs from Sts. Philip and James School in June 1970. With 1800 families in the parish and more than 300 pupils in the school, a long-range plan would have required the parish to address the needs of over 300 additional children attending public school and receiving after school religious education because the capacity limits of the school had been reached. The school survey indicated that only about 20% of the parish children were served by the school, since many were not attending religious instruction classes after school. (295)

Seeing the inability to continue increases in IHM personnel for Sts. Philip and James School, Mother Beata, citing the shortage of sisters, informed the pastor, Father Carow, and all other concerned administrators of the Congregation's decision to withdraw the sisters in June 1970. (296)

Scores of letters and telegrams poured in to Mother Beata seeking a reversal of the decision. Tributes were paid by parents of school children, lauding the excellent work of the sisters in the school. "Your sisters are doing a wonderful job here. Maybe you will see a way to keep them here. We need them," wrote one parent. "We have been so pleased and gratified with not only their efficiency, but also the educational and cultural opportunities the sisters offered to our children. In short, it seemed like a 'Jewel of a School,'" wrote another. (297)

It must have been difficult indeed for Mother Beata to read the pleas of these sincere parents, but the decision was not reversed, and the IHMs left Sts. Philip and James School in June 1970.

The convent in which the sisters had resided became a residence for the Franciscan Brothers when their residence at St. Anthony's High School burned down.

True to his pledge to the parishioners, Father Carow kept the school open. In 1970 he hired the first lay principal in the Catholic school system of the Rockville Centre Diocese, Mary B. Monte. Her twenty-six years of service as principal of Sts. Philip and James brought stability to the school and preserved the Catholic atmosphere, sharing her values with an all-lay faculty. Mary Monte retired in 1996.

To date, in 2002, Sts. Philip and James School continues under the leadership of a lay principal, Mr. Anthony Giordano. (298)

St. Stephen's School, New York, New York

There are many chapters to the story of IHM involvement in St. Stephen's School, New York City. The initial contact was made by Monsignor Raymond P. Rigney, superintendent of schools for the New York Archdiocese on November 5, 1964. Writing to Mother Beata, he said:

> I write now to place before you formally a request that you appoint a sister of your community to help with our efforts in this undertaking. We are hoping to establish an additional center in mid-town Manhattan, possibly at St. Stephen's School on East 29th Street. (299)

He was referring, of course, to the Cardinal Spellman Program for Retarded Children in the Archdiocese that would eventually include nine centers, staffed by sisters from eight religious congregations and two lay teachers.

Mother Beata's response on December 16, 1964, expressed the Congregation's interest in special education and promised to assign a sister for the program at St. Stephen's School. (300) As it happened, Sister Alphonsus Mary (Mary Ellen) Malloy was assigned in September 1965 as special education teacher in the New York Archdiocese, not to St. Stephen's School, but to St. Joseph's School located on East 86th Street. St. Joseph's School was staffed by School Sisters of Notre Dame and had just one special education classroom. Sister Alphonsus Mary (Mary Ellen) resided with the IHM Sisters at Sacred Hearts Convent on 33rd Street and continued to teach at St. Joseph's School until September 1968.

The second chapter of the St. Stephen's story begins again with a letter from Monsignor Rigney to Mother Beata in April 1967 informing her of the consolidation plans for the smaller elementary schools of the New York Archdiocese. Included in these plans were the closings of St. Alphonsus and the Sacred Hearts Elementary Schools, both IHM staffed. (301)

At this time, the Sisters of Charity at St. Stephen's School located at 141 East 28th Street, Manhattan, were no longer able to staff this school. With this in mind, Monsignor Rigney wrote to Mother Beata: " . . . it is my hope that your Sisters, now assigned to these schools (Sacred Hearts and St. Alphonsus) can replace the Sisters of Charity who now staff St. Stephen's School . . ." (302)

It was undoubtedly Monsignor Rigney's hope to obtain the full complement of nine IHM Sisters from the closing elementary schools, but Mother Beata's reply promised seven IHMs due to the retirement of one sister and the departure of another. In the same letter, Mother Beata asked that renovations be made to the St. Stephen's School plant, especially improved lighting and reconditioning of the floors. She also made it clear that the sisters could not take on the responsibility of maintenance of the school building. (303)

These matters being taken care of, St. Stephen's School opened on September 11, 1967, under the direction of the Sisters of IHM. Sister Jeannine Parry was appointed principal, and Sisters Canice Riordan, Suzanne McCarthy, Maurice Hartnett, Marguerita Carbone, Amator (Agnes) Shaw, and Callista Ryan composed the IHM faculty. All resided at Sacred Hearts Convent, 33rd Street, New York, and commuted daily to St. Stephen's. Nine other IHMs teaching in Immaculata High School, adjacent to Sacred Hearts Convent, also resided at Sacred Hearts Convent, making a local community of sixteen sisters. (304)

St. Stephen's was an eight-grade school in a building having four floors. Grades six, seven and eight were located on the fourth floor; grades two through five on the third floor where were also located two bathrooms. First grade, staff offices, and the gymnasium were housed on the first floor. The cafeteria and additional bathrooms were on the basement level. Monsignor James Kenney, pastor, was very anxious to meet the educational expectations of the IHM Sisters and had the entire school cleaned and painted for their arrival.

Since both St. Alphonsus and Sacred Hearts Elementary Schools had closed, there were many parents seeking their children's admission to St. Stephen's. A difficult decision had to be made, since the children who had previously attended St. Stephen's had priority claim on admission. Sister Jeannine had previously served as principal of St. Alphonsus Elementary School and had assisted students from there to be relocated in schools closer to their residences in lower Manhattan. St. Stephen's School was, however, a natural substitute locale for the children formerly of Sacred Hearts Elementary School. Sister Jeannine opened the school to many of these students, increasing the enrollment to nearly three hundred pupils. (305)

A year later St. Stephen's would also open its doors to two special education classes. It was the hope of Monsignor Rigney, superintendent of schools, and Walter A. Kelley, director of special education for the New York Archdiocese to have St. Stephen's become also a center for special education classes. Having asked Monsignor James V. Kenney, pastor of St. Stephen's for classroom space for the special education program, Monsignor Rigney was delighted to inform Mother Beata of the availability of two classrooms at St. Stephen's for special education. In his December 1967 letter he wrote, "With your approval this would make it possible for Sister Alphonus Mary (Mary Ellen) Malloy and the new Sister to teach at St. Stephen's." (306) This meant that the diocesan plans were for the special education center at St. Joseph's School to be discontinued and replaced by St. Stephen's, and that Sister Alphonsus Mary (Mary Ellen) Malloy and an additional special education teacher were to serve there.

Correspondence indicates that Sister Felicitas Ryan, then IHM supervisor of schools, based in New York City, had prepared the way for these decisions by communicating the IHM Congregation's interest in special education to Monsignor Rigney. So, Mother Beata's approval of the plan, although it called for two additional sisters, was given on February 26, 1968. So it was, that Sister Alphonsus Mary (Mary Ellen) Malloy and Sister Marie Redempta (Helen) Kaizer were assigned to the two special education classes at St. Stephen's School in September 1968.

Sister Mary Ellen Malloy describes the program as involving twelve to fifteen students in two classes, divided by chronological ages. Sister Mary Ellen taught the older youngsters; Sister Marie Redempta, the younger. All of the pupils were bused in from East Harlem and represented many ethnic groups, chiefly Spanish speaking. Sister Mary Ellen recalls that "they were really nice children, very docile." Since most of these children lived in apartments with elevators, they were not used to walking up and down stairs. At St. Stephen's, however, their classrooms were located on the second and third floors, and with the cafeteria in the basement, they had to learn how to manage stairs, and lots of them. (306)

The special education program followed the curriculum outlined by the Archdiocese of New York and was supervised by Mr. Walter Kelly, its archdiocesan director. In other matters, the faculty and classes followed the regular schedule of St. Stephen's School.

Sister Mary Ellen Malloy served St. Stephen's special education program until June 1979. Other IHMs who taught in this program were Sister Marie Redempta Kaiser, 1968-1970; Sister Eleace King, 1970-1974; Sister Barbara O'Brien, 1974-1979; and Sister Stephanie Corbett, 1979-1980.

Sister Jeannine Parry served as principal of St. Stephen's from 1967-1971, and, as she remarked "I had four happy years there." (308) That the pastor, Monsignor James Kenney appreciated her work is evident in his words to Mother Beata:

> I feel I must say a special word about our principal, Sister Jeannine. Without her St. Stephen's School would be in dire straits. By her dedication she managed to keep the school functioning. I cannot praise her too highly . . . The school needs someone like Sister Jeannine . . . (309)

Following Sister Jeannine in administration were Sister Bernardus Dwyer, 1971-1974; Sister Timothy Smyth, 1974-1977; Sister Marianne Knight, 1977-1979; Sister Gertrude Hopkins, 1979-1988; and Sister Eleanor Marie Malanaphy, 1988-1990. Correspondence between Monsignor Kenney and Mother Beata indicates that this inner city parish was in dire financial condition, unable to afford lay teachers. Hence there was a continued plea over the years for additional sisters to staff the school.

The sisters, too, were pleading with Mother Beata for additional sister-teachers for St. Stephen's. Describing the conditions under which the majority of their ethnic minority students lived and the sacrifices being made by their parents to send them to St. Stephen's School, the entire sister faculty signed a letter addressed to the Central Administrative Assembly, saying in part:

> . . . We feel that this school is vital to our apostolate. If we are truly committed to this mission and the work of the community here in the only inner-city school we have, it would seem a matter of justice to give these children the best possible education and to staff this school properly . . . (310)

In spite of the staffing problems, Monsignor Kenney had nothing but praise for the sisters, who, indeed, were working far beyond their own strength and acting in dedication and love of these needy children. As he wrote in 1970 to Mother Beata, "It is impossible to estimate the good that has been done by the Sisters of IHM in Saint Stephen's School. These dedicated women of your order have given themselves unstintingly in the service of our children . . ." (311)

And again in 1973:

> If it were not for the Sisters of IHM, Saint Stephen's School would be out of existence. The Sisters have not only provided a school, but also have done a splendid job educating the children. The people and myself appreciate this and are grateful to you and the Sisters. (312)

St. Stephen's School would continue under IHM direction until 1990 in spite of many hardships, not the least of which was the problem of housing the five sisters teaching at St. Stephen's once the IHM Sisters were withdrawn from Immaculata High School in 1971. Immaculata High School was to continue, but with a total lay administration and faculty. The pastor of Sacred Hearts Parish, Monsignor Dunn, was asked by Monsignor Kenney of St. Stephen's to continue housing the sisters teaching at St. Stephen's, even though the convent would now be half empty. Monsignor Dunn generously agreed to this. (313)

Sacred Hearts Convent's third floor was not vacant for long. In the spring, 1971, six Sisters of Charity visited Sacred Hearts Convent with the view to renting the third floor as housing for their sisters serving in the New York area (314) This did in fact occur, and September found the IHMs hosting a buffet supper for the Sisters of Charity, the new residents of the third floor. (315) The Sisters of Charity, reciprocated, observing the IHM feast day on December 8 with a third floor convent party. These exchanges continued over the years.

This arrangement continued for nearly ten years, but not without its concerns, since the new pastor, Monsignor William J. Rinschler, had indicated as early as 1974 that since the sisters living in Sacred Hearts

Convent had no duties in the parish, and since the parish priests were housed in a small "firetrap" building, a move by the sisters to a nearby available convent might be considered. (316) This suggestion was placed before the archdiocesan officials by Sister Anne Fulwiler, then superior general of the IHM Congregation. In spite of the fact that Monsignor Rinschler claimed that the parish could not afford the convent expenses, the archdiocesan officials denied his request.

However, to his credit, when the sisters teaching at St. Alphonsus High School in New York City were forced to an immediate move on February 15, 1980, because of the danger to nearby buildings of the condemned St. Alphonsus Church, Monsignor Rinschler generously offered to accept some of them at Sacred Hearts Convent. (317)

As can be seen, this story of St. Stephen's School and its IHM sister-faculty that began in Mother Beata's time, had its continuance in the terms of three more major superiors. By 1980, the archdiocese offered a housing solution at St. Joseph's Convent, Waverly Place, New York City. The Sisters of the Holy Child, living at Waverly Place were asked to exchange residences with the IHMs at Sacred Hearts Convent. This move provided for the consolidation of housing for some seventeen IHMs in various ministries in the city.

The seven sisters teaching at St. Stephen's who moved to Waverly Place on August 15, 1980, included Sister Gertrude Hopkins, principal; Sisters Ricardus Tuskey and Eleanor Marie Malanaphy, primary; Sisters Beatrix Cawley and Joann Bellomo, intermediate; Sister Jeanetta Hughes, library; and Sister Stephanie Corbett, special education. They joined ten other IHMs who were teaching at Cathedral High School, Loyola High School, All Hallows High School, and doing parish work at Our Lady of Good Counsel Parish. (318) All of the sisters used public transportation to these ministry sites.

At the close of the 1989-1990 school year, faced with declining enrollments, the sisters now only five in number at St. Stephen's were withdrawn. Sister Gertrude Hopkins obtained a teaching position at Cathedral High School, and Sister Maristella Walsh at St. Ann's in the Bronx, hence both were able to remain in residence at St. Joseph's, Waverly Place. A new experience of inter-community living began at St. Joseph's in 1990 as seven sisters from other communities joined the nine IHMs in residence there. June 30, 1997, with the New York Archdiocese desiring to sell the Waverly Place property, the sisters were asked once again to relocate. (319)

St. Stephen's School building was leased by nearby Epiphany Parish to augment space for Epiphany School's upper elementary grades. Special education classes, however, were discontinued at this site. St. Stephen's School continues under the name of Epiphany School to this date.

Our Lady of Grace Montessori School, Manhasset, New York

Mother Kathleen Hart had received word on January 6, 1959, that Mr. Peter Grace, president of the Grace Shipping Line of New York, had gifted the Congregation with a French chateau and eight acres of land adjoining his estate in Manhasset, Long Island, New York. Formerly the estate of Mr. Cornelius Kelly, Chairman of the Anaconda Copper Company, this property was magnificent in size and architecture. (320)

After obtaining the permissions of both Bishop Jerome Hannan of the Scranton Diocese and Bishop Walter Kellenberg of the Rockville Centre Diocese, approval of civil authorities for tax-exempt status and zoning approval, Mother Kathleen accepted this very generous gift from Mr. Grace. It was not long before she declared that the house would be ready for use by June 1959. (321)

The original intended usage was to provide a secluded locale for summer spiritual renewal programs for the IHM Sisters, and to serve as a house of studies for the Sister Formation Program. Given the proximity of several major universities, the location would also serve as a residence for sisters pursuing higher degrees. The main building has continued to serve in these and many more ways.

By 1966, the Congregation, with a two-fold purpose of bringing a quality pre-school program to the local community, and providing a stable source of income to maintain the convent building and land, began the renovation of the garage and stable buildings on the property. The renovated buildings would become Our Lady of Grace Montessori School. Sisters Joanne Madden and Sarah Ann Holmes were put in charge of the planning.

It was expected that the school would open in September 1967, but because of legal problems there was a delay of several months. As indicated in a letter sent by Sister Felicitas Ryan, IHM, the assistance of Mr. Peter Grace was sought. As she explained, the North Hills ordinance relating to school zoning provided "only for elementary and secondary schools, public and private, which lead directly to a New York Regents diploma." (322) Of course, the planned Montessori School did not fit the ordinance requirements. Mr. Grace was able, with the approval of the Board of Trustees of North Hill to have the words "Montessori School" inserted into the ordinance.

With two classrooms, a cloakroom and a bathroom carved out of the two garages, Our Lady of Grace Montessori School opened on January 22, 1968. Forty students were enrolled. Sister Sarah Ann Holmes became acting administrator with Sister Marilyn Muro as faculty member. Sister Joanne Madden continued at Xavier University, Cincinnati, Ohio, during 1968. In September 1969 the three sisters conducted classes in the original renovated rooms with an enrollment of sixty children. (323)

So great was the instant reputation of the new school that in 1970 work was begun to enlarge the setting to four classrooms, observation rooms and an office. Sister Mary Ellen Downing was added to the faculty in 1970 and Sister Sharon Kelly in 1971 when the enrollment rose to one hundred pupils. By the tenth anniversary of the school in 1978 a capacity enrollment of 120 children was reached, served by Sisters Marilyn Muro, Sarah Ann Holmes, Sharon Kelly, Constance Wilt, Laura Booth and Ann Michael Zaytoun. (324)

Plans to expand the school program to a full day kindergarten were realized when one of the two second-floor apartments, once used as employees' residences in the glory days of Cornelius Kelly's ownership, was renovated for classroom space in 1982. Again in 1986 further improvements and expansions were made. In 1989-1990 a new building was constructed, providing sufficient classrooms for an enrollment up to 240 pupils. (325)

The dedication of the new school building was held on September 23, 1990. Bishop John McGann of the Rockville Centre Diocese celebrated the liturgy for the occasion. Sister Redempta Sweeney, superior general and the council members, former principals of the school, and the mayor of North Hills were among the special guests. (326)

In 1996 an elementary program for grades one through three was added. The excellence of Our Lady of Grace Montessori School is attested to by the parents of the pupils, by its certification by the New York State Education Department, the Middle States Association, and the American Montessori Society. All teachers in the school hold New York State/American Montessori Society credentials.

Throughout Mother Beata's tenure and beyond to this date in 2002, Our Lady of Grace Montessori School has fulfilled the vision seen by its promoters. Under the leadership of dedicated, competent principals and faculty, children receive outstanding instruction.

The following principals served at Our Lady of Grace Montessori School: Sister Sarah Ann Holmes, January, 1968-September, 1969; Sister Joanne Madden 1968-1976; Sister Marilyn Muro, 1976-1980; Sister Margaret Mary Kane, 1980-1989; Sister Dorothy Kibler, 1989-1994; Sister Mary Ellen Downing, 1994-1995 (died August 2, 1995); Sister Eleanor Marie Malanaphy 1995-1996; Sister Kelly Quinn, 1996-present date.

Bishop Neumann High School, Williamsport, Pennsylvania

On January 25, 1968, Bishop J. Carroll McCormick announced a Scranton Diocesan fund-raising effort entitled Project Expansion. Among the projects included was a central diocesan high school for the Williamsport area. (327) News reporting for *The Catholic Light* was evidently ahead of the actual plans for the high school as a February 8, 1968, article reported that the school would be located in St. Boniface Parish, would be called St. Mary's School, and would utilize an existing structure. (328) The facts, of course, turned out later to have been premature, as the actual Bishop Neumann High School was to be a newly constructed facility located on Penn Street in Williamsport.

It was about a year after the original announcement that Mother Beata Wertz and Sister Nadine Moran visited Williamsport on January 31, 1969, to see the new high school plant that would open for classes in September 1969. Neumann High School was to be a co-instructional school conducted jointly by the Sisters of IHM and the Sisters of Christian Charity, and supported by eight Williamsport area parishes.

St. Joseph's High School in Williamsport, open since September 14, 1878, and staffed by the IHM Sisters would close after an outstanding ninety-one year history. Over the years there had been changes in St. Joseph's, even an entirely new school building in 1900, renovations, and renovations to the renovations. (329) With the building of Bishop Neumann Diocesan High School, St. Joseph's School would continue with kindergarten through sixth grades. Grades seven and eight would become the junior high level at Neumann High School.

Bishop Neumann High School opened officially on September 8, 1969; the open house and dedication was held on September 21. Months would pass before the equipment and furniture arrived. Students and faculty adapted, using borrowed desks and folding chairs, and happy to be in the new, spacious quarters regardless of inconveniences.

The IHM Sisters assigned to the faculty of Bishop Neumann High School in its first year were: Sisters Albrette Rouleau, business; Rosemary Stankis, science; Antonina Williamson, library; Mary Ann Adams, social studies. Before the opening of school, however, Sister Mary Ann Adams was reappointed to Ponce, Puerto Rico, and replaced at Bishop Neumann High School by Sister Anne Therese Munley. These four sisters resided at St. Joseph's Convent, joining the seven IHMs serving at St. Joseph's Elementary School. (330)

By the second year of IHM presence at Bishop Neumann High School (1970-1971) there were already two personnel changes as Sister Electa Schmidt replaced Sister Albrette Rouleau and Sister Alphonsine Kelly replaced Sister Antonina Williamson.

News of the closing of St. Lawrence School in South Williamsport also had its impact on the IHM community at St. Joseph's Convent, Williamsport. The Congregation and Diocesan administrators had arranged with the pastor of St. Lawrence, Reverend Joseph Breslin, that religious instruction for the children of St. Lawrence Parish would continue under the direction of the IHM Sisters on the faculty at Bishop Neumann High School. St. Lawrence Convent would remain open and become the residence for these sisters. So it was that the opening of classes at Bishop Neumann in September 1972 saw Sisters Alphonsine Kelly, Rosela McFadden, Gabrielis Marley, Ann Therese Munley and Rosemary Stankis—all Neumann High faculty—in residence at St. Lawrence Convent, South Williamsport. (331)

Since eight parishes in the Williamsport area supported Bishop Neumann High, bonds developed among the sisters and these parishes. Religious instructions were provided, not only at St. Lawrence Parish, but also at Annunciation Parish. When, on December 5, 1972, St. Boniface Church, the oldest Catholic Church in Williamsport, burned to the ground, the IHMs were responsive to the needs of the people and to the Sisters of Christian Charity whose convent was located very near the burned out church.

The joys of these parishes were also shared. In May 1973 the IHMs celebrated the silver jubilee of ordination of the pastor of Annunciation Church, Reverend William Fleming. The sisters prepared a special dinner at St. Lawrence Convent for the occasion.

On June 2 and 3 the sisters, as Neumann High faculty, also attended the graduation exercises at which Sister Dorothy Haney, IHM, from Marywood College was the speaker. Other IHM guests at the graduation were Sisters Willemyn Gambrill, Katherine Sugrue, Mary Schelb and Margaret Gannon. (332)

In 1973-1974 there were again five IHMs assigned to Bishop Neuman High School. Although Sisters Alphonsine Kelly and Gabrielis Marley had been reassigned, Sisters Helene Fee and Jane Francis Dunnigan replaced them, and together with Sisters Rosela McFadden, Rosemary Stankis, and Ann Therese Munley constituted the total group residing at St. Lawrence Convent and teaching at Bishop Neumann High. (333)

With a forty percent increase in the junior high enrollment, Reverend John W. Jordan, Neumann High administrator, wrote to Mother Beata requesting an additional sister for social studies. His request cited the excessive teaching load of the existing faculty, as well as the financial burden of the parishes subsidizing Neumann High. (334) It was with regret that Mother Beata could not respond affirmatively to Father Jordan's request.

Throughout Mother Beata's administration there continued to be five IHMs assigned to Bishop Neumann High School. Their visibility at liturgies in the various supporting parishes, their assistance in fund-raising events such as the annual October fest, and their expertise in the classroom endeared them to students, pastors, and people of the Williamsport area.

The IHM Sisters would serve at Bishop Neumann High School until 1986 and return on an individual basis in later years.

St. Mark's High School, Wilmington, Delaware

Bishop Michael J. Hyle of the Wilmington, Delaware Diocese had decided that the need for a Central Catholic High School in Wilmington was a priority. While his public announcement of the construction of a $6.8 million school structure did not come until 1966, (335) the preparatory work had begun as early as 1961. In that year, Reverend Edmund F. Julian, superintendent of schools for the Wilmington Diocese, began to contact religious orders to staff the future school.

It is almost impossible to imagine the disheartening work of Father Julian as throughout 1961-1962 he contacted seven religious teaching orders of brothers seeking faculty. Religious orders from Pennsylvania to Rhode Island, from New York to California were contacted with the same result—a letter of "regret." (336)

It was a time of change in the Catholic Church after Vatican II, a time of change in religious orders of men and women, with resultant decline in the number of candidates entering religious life, increased departures, and the simultaneous lengthening of formation programs, postponing the availability of religious for ministry service.

From 1963-1967 Reverend Howard T. Clark, the new superintendent of schools for the Wilmington Diocese, continued the quest begun in 1961. Eleven more communities were contacted, including sisters from Maryland, New York, Pennsylvania, Connecticut, New Jersey and priests from Toronto, Canada, and Brooklyn, New York.

First to respond affirmatively to Father Clark's July 14, 1963, request for sisters was Mother Beata Wertz of the Sisters of IHM of Scranton, Pennsylvania. In a letter of July 20, 1963, she expressed a willingness to provide staff for the new high school that would open in 1969. (337) The general council minutes of December 31, 1966, confirmed this position as Mother Beata reported, "A new 2,000-pupil coeducational Catholic High School in Woodcrest, Wilmington, Delaware, will be opened in 1969. Four communities of Sisters will be on staff. We are committed to give four Sisters the first year, September 1969." (338)

This commitment triggered a flow of correspondence that would continue from January 3, 1966, when preferred curriculum areas of the faculty were discussed, through February 29, 1968, when specific four-year commitments were spelled out. Fifteen IHM Sisters were promised over the first four years—four in 1969 (two in mathematics, one in religion, and one in business), four IHMs in 1970 and 1971, and three in 1972. (339)

Father Clark made similar contacts in this same time period with the Sisters of Notre Dame de Namur, Sisters of St. Joseph, and the Bernardine Sisters of North Stamford, Connecticut. (340) Each group was asked to provide fifteen sisters over the four-year period, 1969-1972.

Meanwhile, plans for the construction of the new school were progressing. In October 1967 the groundbreaking ceremony was held. Bishop Michael Hyle, however, was not to see the completion of his dream. His death on November 27 of that year was a striking example that "man proposes, but God disposes." (341) Bishop Thomas Mardaga succeeded Bishop Hyle and at the school's dedication on May 24, 1970, acknowledged the significant contribution of his predecessor, saying:

> The need for a Catholic secondary school under Diocesan auspices had been talked about for many years. Before I came to Wilmington, the plans had been laid and the work was begun. Today we can see the results of the hopes and dreams of Bishop Hyle, my beloved predecessor. (342)

The realization of this dream began with Bishop Hyle's acquisition of fifty-five acres of land in Pike Creek Valley, Wilmington, Delaware. His vision was to build a facility for 2000 students, with a library housing 30,000 volumes. This vision took form in the architect's plans and in the work of many area craftsmen and builders. The campus of St. Mark's High School includes playing fields for football, baseball, softball, girls' hockey, and a running track. Basketball and tennis courts are also available.

St. Mark's High School is completely air-conditioned and carpeted. It includes laboratories for art, science, mechanical drawing, language listening, photography, home economics, and business. In addition, there are three lecture halls with tiered seating for seventy-seven persons for large group instruction. An audio-visual center, 1000-seat auditorium, a 600 capacity cafeteria, and a 2,500-seat gymnasium, the largest high school gym in Delaware, are all part of this amazing structure.

St. Mark's educational philosophy embraces many innovative techniques, such as team teaching, modular flexible scheduling of classes, independent study options, and a multi-phased curriculum to address individual student needs. Religious activities, such as retreats and spiritual counseling, as well as formal religious instruction are central in the curriculum.(343)

When St. Mark's Central Catholic High School opened in September 1969 seven religious communities of sisters were represented on the faculty. They included Scranton IHM Sisters, Franciscans of Glen Riddle, Pennsylvania, Sisters of St. Joseph from Chestnut Hill, Pennsylvania, Sisters of Notre Dame de Namur of Ilchester, Maryland, School Sisters of Notre Dame from Baltimore, Maryland, Daughters of Charity of Emmitsburg, Maryland and Benedictine Sisters of Ridgeley, Maryland. (344). The four IHM Sisters appointed to St. Mark's for that first year, 1969, were Sisters Mary John (Jean) Conaty, Ignatius (Ann) Seguljic, Dolores Filicko and Isabel Schratwieser. For the year 1969-1970 these Sisters resided at St. Matthew Convent in Wilmington with a community of twelve other IHMs, eleven of whom were teachers at St. Matthew's Elementary School, and one, Sister Eamon O'Neill, served as assistant superintendent of schools and reading consultant for the Diocese of Wilmington. (345)

By the fall of 1970, the new faculty house at St. Mark's was completed. As an inter-community residence this house was unique to living arrangements for religious at the time, but surely forecast things to come. The large, rectangular-shaped structure contained seven, five-bedroom apartments to house each of the communities as a group. All, however, shared the chapel, dining room, kitchen, laundry, storage room and parlors. (346) In 1970, this arrangement was undoubtedly experimental for all communities involved, as indicated by the minutes of the organizational meeting conducted by Father Howard T. Clark on January 12, 1970. Sisters representing each of the seven communities were present at the meeting.

It was obvious from the discussions that the sisters wished to preserve the spirit and customs of their own communities, and while open to shared liturgies and prayer, were anxious about other aspects of the situation. Father Clark suggested that a handbook of procedures be developed by the sisters to address any potential problems and emphasized that "we are all one community in a sense; yet we have individual differences which we want to preserve without excluding others." (347)

In actuality, whatever concerns may have been anticipated this "experiment" in shared inter-community living proved over the years to work out exceptionally well, even with the comings and goings with which religious personnel are familiar. It is a tribute to all of the sisters who lived at St. Mark's Faculty House that the overriding religious spirit and shared mission to the students of St. Mark's High School drew them all together.

By the second year, 1970-1971, there was a total of twenty-seven sisters in residence at St. Mark's Faculty House, six of whom were Scranton IHMs. Sister Mary John (Jean) Conaty had been transferred to be principal at St. Matthew's in East Stroudsburg, Pennsylvania. Three additional IHMs were assigned, namely, Sisters Andre Davoren, Joanne Pickard, and Catherine Anne Mullaly. (348)

On September 20, 1970, Bishop Thomas Mardaga blessed the faculty house. Guests from all seven communities were present. IHM visitors included sisters from St. Matthew's, Wilmington; St. Ephrem's, Brooklyn; Sacred Hearts, New York; St. Agnes, Baltimore, Maryland; Silver Springs, Maryland, and council members from Scranton, Pennsylvania.

On October 1, open house was held for the lay faculty and on October 4, for the people of the Wilmington Diocese. (349)

Already in this first year of inter-community living at St. Mark's Faculty House it was evident that there was a great rapport developing among the sisters. Sharing of special occasions, patronal feasts of each community, and jubilees provided means of getting to know one another better. Sharing of concern in times of stress was also obvious when the tragic fire destroyed the IHM Motherhouse in Scranton, Pennsylvania, on February 22, 1971. As the IHMs noted:

> The kindness, sisterliness and concern of all our Sisters here at St. Mark's was shown in the clothing and useful items that all the Sisters brought to our apartment to be taken up to Marywood, as well as the prayers for the safety and recovery of the victims. (350)

Mother Beata's visit to the Wilmington Convents on March 16, 1971, gave her an opportunity to express her gratitude to all and to relate the details of the tragic fire as known at that time.

In the third year, 1971-1972, there were eight Scranton IHMs and one Monroe, Michigan IHM serving on the faculty at St. Mark's. Included were Sisters Andre Davoren, Verena O'Callahan, Chrysostom Roberts, Isabel Schratwieser, Michaeline Macedonio, Joanne Pickard, Ignatius (Ann) Seguljic, Marguerite Green, and Sister Sienna from Monroe, Michigan. In May 1972 Father Delaney resigned as principal of St.

Mark's to become director of the diocesan radio and television ministry. Reverend Thomas Cini became principal in the fall of 1972. Under his guidance, and with the cooperative efforts of the religious and lay faculty, St.Mark's was awarded full accreditation by the Middle States Association in May 1975.

The commitment of seven or eight IHM Sisters to St. Mark's was to continue during Mother Beata's tenure and until 1977-1978 when it decreased to six; then to five IHMs from 1979-1983; to four, from 1985-1988; then to three, from 1988-1991. This was the case for all the religious communities serving at St. Mark's as the number of vocations to religious life was declining. (351)

Throughout all the years the IHM Sisters at St. Mark's were very active participants in the district and sector assemblies of the IHM Congregation's government, as well as in many diocesan groups. For example, Sister Norita Corrigan was president of the Sisters' Council of the Diocese of Wilmington and Sister Mary Hugh Placilla was a member of the Diocesan Due Process Board, the Resurrection Parish Board of Religious Education, and the Curriculum Committee for Religious Education on the secondary level. (352) Sister Marguerite Green represented the Diocese on the Council on Mathematics and the State Council on Computers in Education. (353)

In addition to the IHMs already named through 1971-1972, the following sisters have served at St. Mark's: Sisters Lillian Marie Farrell, Lucy McGrath, Mary Newett, Catherine Ann Gilvary, Norita Corrigan, Mary Hugh Placilla, Louise Connolly, Marguerita Carbone , Mary Howard Krotzer, Margaret Loftus, Janet Milan, Ann Newell, Mary Elizabeth Almy , and Redempta Sweeney. (354)

The IHM Sisters teaching at St. Mark's High School as of 2002 are Sisters Marguerita Carbone and Redempta Sweeney. The total number of sisters from all communities at St. Mark's has declined from a high of thirty-four in 1973-1974 to the present four sisters teaching in the school, two of whom still reside at St. Mark's Faculty Residence. The faculty residence is scheduled to be closed at the end of the 2002-2003 school year as a residential facility, but will be utilized for activities related to the high school curriculum. (355)

St. Rocco's, Pittston, Pennsylvania

St. Rocco's Parish, Pittston, Pennsylvania, was founded in 1919 to serve the families of Italian immigrants who had settled in the area and whose numbers were dramatically increasing. There were eighteen Italian parishes in Luzerne and Lackawanna Counties, and one in

Lycoming County by 1928. (356) Monsignor Gallagher describes the Scranton Diocese as a rarity with its multiplicity of national (ethnic) parishes. He comments:

> Lay sensitivities were such that none of the priests could be assigned to a specific pastoral appointment unless he first satisfied the ethnic test. Everyone took it for granted that somehow or other, the Ordinary would be able to turn up 89 Irish priests, 44 Poles, 23 Slovaks, 18 Italians, 14 Lithuanians, 21 Germans, 3 Maronites, 2 Magyars, 1 Syro-Melchite, 1 Slovenian, and 1 Tyrolean. . . . it was expected that where assistant pastors were needed they too would have the proper birthright. (357)

For many years the bishop met these demands as immigrant priests provided the number of clergy needed for each ethnic group. At times of shortage, however, both Bishop Michael Hoban and Bishop Thomas O'Reilly invited religious communities of priests, such as the Passionists, Stigmatine fathers, Franciscans, and the Oblates of St. Joseph to the Scranton Diocese. This latter group, the Oblates, took over the pastorates of the Italian parishes of St. Anthony of Padua, Exeter, Pennsylvania, Our Lady of Mt. Carmel and St. Rocco's, Pittston, Pennsylvania, in March 1929. (358)

It would be twenty years before the first St. Rocco's parochial school would be initiated. On September 7, 1949, four classrooms were opened in the basement of St. Rocco's Church at 51 Tompkins Street in Pittston. Three hundred pupils were enrolled from kindergarten through fourth grade. An easy calculation would convince the reader of the immediate need for an expanded facility. So it was that construction of the new St. Rocco's School was begun in that very year, 1949, at 63 Tompkins Street, Pittston. (359)

The new school, completed by September 1950 was constructed of steel and brick and housed eight classrooms, a kindergarten, and a large assembly hall. Bishop William J. Hafey presided at the school's dedication on September 10, 1950. The Maestre Pie Filippini Sisters served as faculty of the school. (360)

All of this history would not have related to the IHM Sisters were it not for the fact that by the 1960s the survival of St. Rocco's was a concern. Discussion of consolidation with other parochial elementary schools led to the formation in 1969 of Pittston Catholic Elementary School, a joint endeavor of the Filippini and IHM Congregations. Since the IHM Sisters were already located at St. Mary, Help of Christians

School in North Pittston, grades five through eight were assigned to them; grades one through four were located at St. Rocco's with the Filippini Sisters. The possible complications of such an arrangement are obvious. Class scheduling, separation of children from the same family, with the inherent transportation problems for parents, not to mention the differing administrative styles involved with two principals—all of these, and many more made this a short-lived experiment, lasting only until 1970. Mother Beata's decision to withdraw the IHM Sisters from this consolidation with St. Rocco's in effect caused the closing of the school. Subsequently the school building was razed. (361)

According to one source, it was Mother Beata's concern for the religious education of the children of St. Rocco's Parish, together with changes brought about by Vatican II, which would lead to her decision a year later to return IHM Sisters to St. Rocco's Parish in a new role. (362)

With Vatican II documents bringing an emphasis on collegiality and personal responsibility to the structures and former monastic-like regimen of apostolic religious life, various new ministries, as well as "experimental" living arrangements, were approved by the IHM central administration. In the 1970s these latter were not drastic, but minor facilitative changes which sought to bring the sisters together in smaller communities.

Such was the case when on October 12, 1971, five sisters from St. John the Evangelist Convent in Pittston, Pennsylvania received approval to move to St. Rocco's Convent, Pittston. (363) They were leaving a large community of twenty-one sisters at St. John's to assume the responsibilities of a small five-member community at St. Rocco's. This move was termed "experimental" in that these five sisters, with the approval of the Central Administrative Assembly, initiated their own coming together by volunteering for membership in the new community. (364) It would also have been customary to reside in the parish where the sisters served full time. In this case, the five sisters taught at St. John the Evangelist School and were assuming also the teaching and coordination of the late afternoon and evening religious instruction classes for the children of St. Rocco's Parish who did not attend Catholic school. Those involved in the St. Rocco "experiment" were Sisters Jane Driscoll, Pauline Kelly, Mary Pio Ferrario, Martha McAndrew and Diane Saracini.

On October 21, 1971, at the first local assembly meeting at their new residence the sisters elected Sister Jane Driscoll, superior; Sister Pauline Kelly, treasurer; and Sister Mary Pio Ferrario, secretary. Within a week both the pastor, Reverend Serra and the assistant pastor, Reverend Paul Mazzochi had held several meetings with the IHMs and the lay religious education instructors of the parish, organizing the classes. Each sister was placed in charge of a grade level, with Sister Diane Saraceni responsible for the music for all grades. Sister Pauline Kelly was named coordinator of the program, under the pastor. (365)

The sisters soon saw what a challenge small community living would be as they quickly became immersed in the activities of St. Rocco's Parish, continued their primary teaching ministry at St. John's School, participated actively in diocesan and Congregation committee work, provided a welcoming home for their many visitors and continued their own religious and professional development. Their first year at St. Rocco's passed rapidly indeed.

The annals of 1972-1973 reflect the effort of the sisters to balance their commitments to St. Rocco's Parish and to St. John's. Many activities were planned for the students, including a trip to New York to see the play "Godspell" in December and another April trip to broadway for a performance of "Jesus Christ, Superstar." Several special liturgies and prayer group activities were planned for the students, with novices, postulants and junior professed sisters from Marywood assisting. The pastor, Father Serra, was most appreciative of the work of the sisters. (366)

It was with mixed emotions, then, that the sisters received the news that Father Serra had been appointed provincial of the Oblates of St. Joseph and would move from St. Rocco's to St. Joseph's Oblate Seminary on June 11, 1973. His successor, Reverend Paul Pavese, former rector of the Oblate Seminary and a religion teacher at St. John's High School, Pittston, was no stranger to the sisters.

As the 1973-1974 school year began, the new pastor wasted no time in organizing the catechetical classes. He scheduled a meeting with all CCD teachers of the parish on September 5, 1973, at which all classes, textbooks and future activities for the students were organized. As a special welcome to Father Pavese, the sisters planned a liturgy in the convent chapel for September 12 and invited him to dinner after the liturgy. The generosity of the sisters was evident in their willingness to go beyond a minimal ministry at St. Rocco's. Father Pavese, as a new pastor, having no priest assistant in the parish, eagerly accepted the sisters' offer to assist in the work of the parish in any way possible. (367) So, it was not surprising that in addition to the CCD instruction, they were found boarding a bus with St. Rocco's students and parents bound for Scranton to see a Billy Graham film "A Time to Run," a spiritually inspiring experience, or helping with fund-raising projects, or visiting the sick.

Meanwhile, the sisters were involved in district assembly meetings, study preparations for the Chapter of 1974, their commitments at St.

John's School, and their continuing professional and social ties to the sisters at St. John's Convent. Many meaningful liturgies, discussions, retreats and socials were initiated by the St. Rocco's community for the members of both convents. (368)

This was the year of preparation for the Middle States Evaluation of St. John's High School and by March 25-28, 1974 the faculty was more than ready. Comments in the annals indicate the tremendous amount of work done by all and the spirit engendered by this cooperative endeavor:

> . . . No other single event has brought to light so vividly the strength that lies in community loyalty, the rewards of group sacrifice, and the appreciation of fellow-workers for their ability to work unstintingly for the good of an institution beyond individual needs. It was a three-day evaluation—but its implications have altered lives! (369)

Sister Jane Driscoll was transferred to Syracuse, New York, at the close of the 1973-1974 school year. As part of the "experimental" community living arrangement, letters were sent to all houses of the Congregation inviting sisters to apply for the opening at St. Rocco's. At the completion of this process, Sister Patricia Huhn was added to the St. Rocco community. (370)

Mother Beata's tenure in office concluded in 1974. Sister Anne Fulwiler as superior general of the Congregation succeeded her. Support for experimentation in community living, such as that at St. Rocco's continued. However, changes in 1976-1977 brought a reduction in the community to three sisters for several months as Sister Eileen Mary Coleman, newly assigned to St. Rocco's, moved to St. John's Convent, Pittston, in October. Another October departure was that of the pastor, Reverend Paul Pavese, OSJ who was changed to Our Lady of Mount Carmel Parish, Pittston. The new pastor was the former superior general of the Oblates of St. Joseph, Reverend Mario Buttini, OSJ. The IHM community increased to four again after Easter when Sister Joanne Campanini changed residence from St. John's to St. Rocco's.

Several announcements made by the central administration during 1975-1976 would impact significantly the St. Rocco's community. St. Rocco's had been designated as a formation residence for the candidates and their director, Sister Jane O'Neill. This move of the candidates to a residence outside of the novitiate building in Scranton was in accord with the 1974 General Chapter recommendations which encouraged the superior general to locate the candidacy and novitiate groups in local assemblies which would include a number of professed sisters. "These professed sisters, whose number would be about comparable to that of the candidates or novices, will pray, dine and recreate with the latter, supplying a supportive community for them and creating an opportunity for realistic, less institutional interchange." (371)

The St. Rocco's community welcomed the possibility of serving as a formation community. They also welcomed the appointment of a full-time coordinator of the parish CCD program in the person of Sister Joan Bastress, while each Sister continued to assist with classes, choir and folk group activities. Not so welcome was the news that St. John's Elementary School, grades one to six, would be discontinued in June 1976. St. John's High School was made a central diocesan high school and renamed Seton Catholic High School that same year. The closing of the elementary school affected two of the four sisters at St. Rocco's, namely, Sister Joanne Campanini who was transferred to Monsignor McHugh Elementary School, Cresco, Pennsylvania, and Sister Diane Saraceni who had been responsible for music instruction at both the elementary and high school levels at St. John's. (372)

In the fall of 1976 anticipation was high as Sisters Mary Pio, Diane Saraceni, Jane O'Neill and Maura Delaney, a candidate of eight months, prepared for the formal entrance day of the three new candidates, Anne Tupper, Kim Casher and Nancy Kilmer.

These candidates were all enrolled as students at Marywood College in Scranton, so their mornings were spent attending campus classes, and afternoons were spent at the novitiate pursuing formation program studies and activities. In spite of their heavy study schedule it was soon evident that the candidates would find their niche in St. Rocco's Parish activities and as full members of the local community, preparing liturgies, praying, cooking, cleaning, and recreating with the sisters.

St. Rocco's Convent became a hub of activity as the usual visiting Congregation administrators and supervisors were augmented by frequent "live-in" groups of young women interested in religious life. All of these visitors were given generous IHM hospitality and shared in the life of the local community.

Highlights of this first year of the candidates' residence at St. Rocco's were the January 22, 1977, ceremony of entrance to the novitiate for Maura Delaney and that of Kim Casher on June 4. Each of the St. Rocco's sisters participated in the liturgies on these occasions. (373)

St. Rocco's continued to be a residence for IHM candidates in formation until June 12, 1982. Sister St. Mel, director of candidates, had been elected as a sector superior and would begin her new ministry on August

1. The last two candidates at St. Rocco's, Judith Ann Hessert and Kathleen Clancy, were received into the novitiate at Marywood on June 12, 1982. The new candidates, scheduled to come in September 1982 were to live at Immaculate Heart Convent, River Street, Scranton, with Sister Francis Xavier Grieb as director. (374)

This move provided a solution to the growing concerns about the living conditions of the sisters teaching at Seton Catholic High School and residing in St. John's Convent. An early September cold spell and faulty furnace at St. John's necessitated many of the sisters moving temporarily to other area convents. They were gradually able to return to St. John's as repairs were made. (375) Assessment of the long-range implications of the deteriorating condition of St. John's Convent led to the decision to move the sisters to St. Rocco's Convent on June 15, 1982. Thus the new community at St. Rocco's in September 1982 included the IHMs teaching at Seton Catholic High School and Sister Celesta Sinisi, new CCD director for St. Rocco's Parish. Sisters Marita Gill, Mary Peter Doran, Geraldine Marie Dranginis, Lillian Marie Farrell, Margo McCormick, Eileen Mary Coleman, and Sandra Grieco were members of the Seton Catholic faculty. (376)

Sister Celesta Sinisi was to continue as CCD director at St. Rocco's until July 31, 1997, completing fifteen years in this ministry. (377)

St. Rocco's Convent continues to this date in 2002 as a residence for two IHM faculty for Seton Catholic High School, namely, Sisters Mary Pio Ferrario and Claire Marie Kulp. It serves also as residence for IHM Sisters in other ministries in Luzerne County, including Sisters Ellen Maroney and Mary Howard Krotzer. (378)

St. John the Baptist Convent, 418 South Main Avenue, Scranton, Pennsylvania

St. John the Baptist Convent located at 418 South Main Avenue in Scranton, Pennsylvania became the residence of five IHM Sisters on August 10, 1973. (379) Formerly occupied by the Sisters of Christian Charity, the convent had been empty for seven years until Sisters Margaret Potthast, Maria Rose Kelly, Margot Worfolk, Joan Zang and Marion Irving identified it as the answer to their search. Mother Beata and the council members, in accord with the 1972 Chapter guidelines, had given approval on November 22, 1972 (380) for this group of Sisters to come together as an "experimental" community living arrangement.

As was explained in another section, "experimental" was the term used to describe chiefly the fact that the sisters had not been assigned, but had come together voluntarily, had set their common goals, and, as in this case, were serving in various ministries. Such "experiments" required, of course, the collaboration of the pastor in whose parish the convent was located. Having been without the services of sisters for seven years, Reverend Francis J. Merkel, pastor of St. John the Baptist Parish, saw that even the part-time services of five IHM Sisters would revive the religious instruction program in his parish, as well as provide for the upkeep of the convent that was in dire need of repairs and refurbishing.

So it was that August of 1973 saw five IHMs, friends, family members, and professional workmen from Marywood engaged in the transformation of St. John Baptist Convent to a "house with somebody in it," which the sisters named "friedenshutte," a German word for house of peace. (381)

The first local assembly was held on August 24 after a day of private and communal prayer. It was obvious from the goals reached that it was important to this group to affirm the gifts and uniqueness of each member, while achieving unity in community through prayer, Eucharist and shared activities. Sister Margaret Potthast was chosen by consensus as superior, Sister Margot Worfolk, treasurer, and Sister Marion Irving, secretary. (382)

True to IHM heritage the sisters welcomed the coming of the Blessed Sacrament to their convent chapel.

> Father Merkel brought the Blessed Sacrament to the house on August 31,1973. The Eucharistic presence of the Lord brought us comfort and joy. It wasn't until September 20 that we had our first Mass in the convent, but a few weeks later Father Merkel began to come every Tuesday evening at five o'clock for the liturgy. (383)

The special challenges that accompany living in a long-vacated house soon came to light. There were crying cats in the cellar, skunks to be trapped, a broken furnace, lack of hot water, and at one point, a broken sewer main. In addition, there was the anxiety of an often broken-down car, and the expenses that go with repairs.

In spite of all, the sisters managed with a sense of humor and deep commitment to be engaged in Congregation committee work and to carry out their obligations as full-time teachers—Sisters Margot and Margaret at Bishop Klonowski High School, Sisters Maria Rose and Joan at West Catholic, and Sister Marion at Bishop O'Hara. In addition, their weekly involvement in the religious instruction of the children of St. John the Baptist Parish was significant. Sister Maria Rose coordinated the total program with lay teachers and sisters each responsible for teaching a particular grade level.

The sisters were called upon to assist with the Scranton Diocesan input into the National Catechetical Directory. Several were also active in the local work of the National Assembly of Women Religious; others were engaged in the Youth Encounter Program to assist the elderly in the Valley View Housing Development.

There would be changes at the close of this first year as Sister Margot obtained a new position as director of campus ministry at Mansfield State College. Sisters Jeanne Drummond and Mary Persico would be added to St. John the Baptist community. Sister Margaret Potthast would continue to reside there, but had been appointed as vocation director for the Congregation.

The spirit of the community is evident as the year was summed up in these words:

> Because it is in the ordinary events of our lives that God speaks to us, our greatest joy and fulfillment this year was in the ordinary everyday-ness of our lives . . . We tried to live simply. We wanted to reach out to others less fortunate. We led a life of presence to one another. We tried to create an at-home-ness that enabled each one to be herself. We challenged one another to greater goodness by our very being. (384)

By mid-year of 1975-1976 Sister Margaret Potthast as vocation director for the Congregation was asked to move to the Generalate. However, the little community at St. John the Baptist retained its membership of six as Sister Joan Coyne joined the group. The sisters were drawn closer together as they participated in many activities for the Congregation and St. John the Baptist Parish over the year. Their joys and sorrows, especially the February 19 sudden death of Mr. Persico, Sister Mary's father, called forth deep support for one another. (385) Their hospitality extended to all, but in a special way to the young women in the affiliate program who were discerning religious vocations.

The same community of six, including Sisters Marion Irving, Joan Zang, Jeanne Drummond, Joan Coyne, Mary Persico and Maria Rose Kelly continued in 1976-1977. Ministry roles changed for some, as Sister Jeanne Drummond was named academic principal at Bishop Hannan High School, with Sister Marion Irving as a new faculty member there; Sister Joan Coyne was assigned to teach at St. Mary's Elementary School in Dunmore; Sisters Maria Rose Kelly and Sister Joan Zang were assigned to Bishop Klonowski and Bishop O'Hara High Schools, respectively.

Signs of the coming termination of IHMs in residence at St. John the Baptist Convent came early in October 1976 when Father Merkel, pastor, declared that he could no longer bear the financial burden which the convent placed on the parish. His dissatisfaction with the CCD program was expressed by removing the program from the sisters entirely, his own need for updating in post-Vatican II content and methodology causing much of the tension. These and other concerns relating to the upkeep of the convent increased over the year, reaching a climax on New Year's Eve when the dining room ceiling fell down and the water pipes burst.

This difficult year was made more difficult by the sickness of several of the sisters, and by the February announcement by Sister Joan Zang that she had reached a decision to leave the Congregation. All of these events affected the life of the little community to the extent that they sought and obtained permission to find a new residence. With the help of Sister Anne Fulwiler, superior general and Bishop John Dougherty, a new home was found in Immaculate Conception Parish, where Reverend Alan Conlan was pastor.

On August 12, 1977, the five IHMs moved from St. John the Baptist Convent at 418 South Main Avenue to the hill section of Scranton and began life together at 1000 Webster Avenue. Their final word sums up their situation:

> We stand at the end of a year that has been long and hard—we leave our beloved 418, but we are still together more than ever filled with love and trust for each other and looking forward to a new year and a new beginning. (387)

Withdrawal from Missions 1961-1974

The IHM Congregation has always been alert to the signs of the times and indicators of the emerging needs for the services of the sisters. In opening the thirty new missions previously described, Mother Beata, faced with declining numbers of sisters, obviously had to weigh the reasons for withdrawing sisters from some long-established missions in order to respond to new calls. Between 1962 and 1973 forty-three missions were affected by these decisions.

Often withdrawals came as a result of decisions reached by diocesan bishops and school administrators, bringing about school mergers, and actually improving local situations where enrollments were small. This was true of the nine missions from which IHMs withdrew between 1962 and 1967. Included were St. John Boys' and St. Mary's Girls' Orphanage Schools in Cresson, Pennsylvania, in 1962 and 1964, respectively; Resurrection in Muncy, Pennsylvania, and St. Patrick's, Spangler, Pennsylvania, in 1966. Withdrawal from five missions occurred in 1967: St. Patrick's, White Haven; St. Joseph High School, Renovo; St. Agnes, Lock Haven—all Pennsylvania schools; St. Alphonsus Elementary and Sacred Hearts Elementary and High School in New York City, New York. Several of these missions had been in existence since the first decade of the twentieth century, making the decision to withdraw the sisters all the more difficult both for the parishes and for the congregation. (388)

After one hundred eight years of pioneer service at Laurel Hill Academy, the IHM Sisters were withdrawn from the high school in 1968. Letters of protest from students, parents, and even the sisters reflected the genuine sadness and shock that closure would come to so much history entwined with the IHM Congregation. The original Laurel Hill Academy, an old hotel, had served also as the motherhouse and novitiate of the IHM Sisters, with Mother Theresa, co-foundress, as first superior there.

The "new" Laurel Hill Academy was built in 1923 in the pastorate of Reverend Dennis J. Bustin. This $150,000 structure housed St. John's Elementary School on the first floor and Laurel Hill high school classes on the second floor. Obviously, the number of students was never very large. But, in 1968, with only sixty-five students in the entire high school and a faculty of four IHMs, five lay teachers, and one part-time priest, the decision made by Mother Beata to withdraw was a reasonable one.

The IHM Sisters on the high school faculty at its closing were Sister Christella Duggan, principal, Sister Alphonsine Kelly, Sister John Joseph Moore, and Sister Aurelia Mary (Eleanor Mary) Marconi.

The high school was continued for two additional years with an all-lay faculty. These included Mrs. Michael Varcaro, Mr. and Mrs. John Chianese, Richard Pescatore, and Frederick C. Hough. Reverend Thomas O'Malley, assistant pastor, was also a part-time instructor of religion.

Laurel Hill Academy saw its final day when the graduation ceremony for seventeen students was held on June 7, 1970. The seventh and eighth grades were also discontinued. St. John's Elementary School continued with grades one through six until 1975. (389)

The fifty-two year old structure was then demolished and became the site of the present Simon H. Barnes Memorial Hospital.

Regarding the withdrawals from the western missions, one pastor, using a military analogy, remarked, "When the troops are in decline, the outposts are robbed to beef up the homefront." (390) This seems to have been the case as thirty-three IHMs were reassigned from the western missions. The first withdrawals were from Central Catholic High School and St. Anthony's Elementary School in Portland, Oregon, in 1968. Three years later, in 1971, withdrawal was made from the four remaining western missions, namely, St. Edwards in Twin Falls, Idaho; St. Henry's, Gresham, Oregon; St. Pius X, Coeur d'Alene, Idaho, and the IHM Academy, Coeur d'Alene, Idaho. This latter was possibly the most painful departure of all since the IHM Academy and convent were Congregation-owned properties to which hundreds of IHMs had committed their services and energies over the years since 1903. (391)

However, after the tragedy of the motherhouse fire in Scranton in that same year, 1971, Mother Beata had many other difficult decisions to make. Because of the fire a landmark institution, Marywood Seminary, begun in 1902, and housed in the motherhouse building, was destroyed. The decision not to rebuild must have been a tortured one as this renowned institution had its strong and vocal public supporters in Scranton, ready to build a new Marywood Seminary at once. (392)

Seven other high schools staffed by IHMs were closed in 1969 and 1970. These included St. Paul High School, Scranton and St. Joseph's, Williamsport in 1969, both of which were replaced by Scranton Diocesan High Schools. William Gaston High School in New Bern, North Carolina, and Mother of Mercy, Washington, North Carolina, were victims of severe enrollment decline due to desegregation adjustments. In 1970, St. Bernardine's in Baltimore, Maryland, similarly, declined as private education was unaffordable for the emerging black population surrounding St. Bernardine's changing parish. By contrast, St. Basil's High School in Dushore, Pennsylvania, a small country area, also closed in 1970, having had IHMs for ninety-three years, since 1877.

Altogether, ten missions were withdrawn from in 1970, among them St. John the Evangelist in Scranton which had opened in 1887, and Immaculate Conception, West Pittston, with a fifty-nine year history. Holy Name of Mary, Montrose, Pennsylvania, and Our Lady of Good Counsel, Inwood, New York, were additional 1970 withdrawals by the IHM Congregation.

Three additional high schools were subject to IHM withdrawal in 1971, namely, Immaculata in New York City where the IHMs had served since 1925, St. Rosalia High School, Pittsburgh, Pennsylvania, dating back to 1913 and Holy Rosary High School, Scranton, where IHMs had served since 1882. St. Patrick's High School in Olyphant, Pennsylvania, opened in 1893, was closed in 1972. These latter two were subject to the centralization of high schools by the Scranton Diocese. (393)

It must be remembered that many of these old, old school buildings were in need of tremendous infusions of funds from the parishes if they were to meet continually rising criteria for approval by educational accreditors, as well as to compete with new, modern facilities being built by the public educational system. Many parishes, lacking such funds, had mixed emotions about the loss of their school, since it brought relief from the financial burdens associated with the upkeep of the school buildings. Sadness at the loss of the sisters and the value that their example, religious instruction, and high academic standards brought was, however, widely felt.

In many cases the Congregation was able to help parishes bridge the loss of the sisters by sending teachers for religious instructions in the summer months. At Mother of Mercy in Washington, North Carolina, for example, Sisters Eileen Egan, Moira McMonagle, Edith Marie Smith and Babette Opferman taught the children in the summers without remuneration, so great was the Congregation's commitment to this parish.

For several years Sisters Bernita McDonough and Mary Zita (Caroline) Cossack traveled to St. Edward's, Twin Falls, Idaho, at the request of the parishioners so that the children, surrounded by strong Mormon believers, would study the Catholic religion and be prepared to receive the sacraments. Father Dodd, the pastor, summed up his gratitude in these words:

> We need the Sisters in Twin Falls; we want them...and are convinced that things will never be the same without them. So we continue to pray for the return of the Sisters, and to be enormously grateful that they could be here . . . if only for six short weeks. (394)

There were many positive results of these changes along with the pain of withdrawals and the departure of the sisters. Several schools were able to continue with an all-lay faculty and lay principals. The laity also assumed leadership of CCD programs. Educational opportunities for students were enhanced in most cases by mergers and centralization of small schools.

Perhaps without knowing it, Mother Beata and her council were preparing for a future in which fewer IHM missions, staffed by smaller numbers of IHM Sisters, would be the norm.

St. Joseph's Hospital Convent, Carbondale, Pennsylvania

Sister Cor Mariae Schroth had been administrator of St. Joseph's Hospital (now Marian Community Hospital) in Carbondale,

Pennsylvania, since 1950, following the very successful administration of Sister Lucina Mullen, who had cleared the hospital of debt.

It was not surprising, then, that the first word of the possibility of a new convent for the sisters serving at St. Joseph's Hospital would come from Sister Cor Mariae. In a letter to Mother Beata dated March 17, 1963, she indicated that the financial report did not include the amount of the sisters' salaries, $102,913 that was placed "in a savings account for a convent." (395) Each year thereafter until the convent was a reality she reported on the increased amount in the "convent building fund."

There was no doubt that a new convent was needed. With IHM sister personnel at the hospital averaging twenty sisters each year, the fact was that the sisters were scattered in various living accommodations. Some resided on the first floor of the hospital in an area later occupied by the pharmacy; some lived in the nursing school; others in St. Mary's Convent, actually a home located on the block in front of the hospital.

Responding to a clear call for the expansion of St. Joseph's Hospital, including several service areas, enlargement of the chapel, and the need for a new convent, the Central Administrative Assembly gave approval on November 21, 1965, for plans to go forward. (396) By December 5, 1965, Sister Cor Mariae Schroth, as administrator and Sister Christine Clarkin, as superior, cosigned a letter to Bishop Jerome D. Hannan seeking permission to proceed with plans, not only for the convent, but also for building a nursing home for the aged. (397) It is noted that at this time the "convent fund" had a total of $200,000. Nevertheless, Bishop Hannan gave an affirmative response within eleven days, on December 17, to the building of a new convent. (398) By March 19, 1966, groundbreaking ceremonies took place.

As expected, numerous meetings were held with the architect, Mr. Russoniello, throughout 1966-1967, and as always in mining locales, drilling was done to determine the underground conditions of the total property to be utilized for the new convent. (399)

The next step was to move the six sisters residing in St. Mary's Convent so that this structure, located on the site of the new convent, could be razed. On August 1, 1967, the sisters moved to a small rented house on High Street in Carbondale, which they called St. Mary's Hall. The razing process for the old convent did not begin until January 3, 1968, and was finally completed on April 9, 1968. (400)

After eighteen years as administrator of St. Joseph's Hospital, Sister Cor Mariae Schroth was assigned as administrator of the Marian Convent on the Marywood campus in Scranton, Pennsylvania. The doctors, nurses and friends established a memorial scholarship in Sister Cor Mariae's honor. Sister Cephas (Mary C.) Ryan assumed the responsibility of administrator of St. Joseph's Hospital on September 8, 1968. (401)

Taking on a new administrative role at the start of a $1,050,000 building project is no easy task. Sister Cephas, desiring to have all the sisters involved in the plans for the future convent, reviewed the plans with them. Not surprisingly, some very practical suggestions were made, for example, the inclusion of a laundry room and kitchenette on each floor, and other changes. Sister Cephas, together with Sisters Christine Clarkin, Wendelin Casey, Michaela Mollica and Carleen Boehlert then met with Mother Beata and the council members on October 30, 1968. After discussion and deliberation, unanimous approval for the suggested changes was given. (402)

To the joy of the sisters it was only about a month later, on November 25, 1968, when the steel began to be delivered for the new convent. It seemed that all aspects of the project were in high gear, pushing toward completion that would come one year later, in December 1969.

As the sisters wrote:

> First Friday of December brought good news to us. The day so long anticipated had arrived and we were informed that the convent was now ready for occupancy . . . Saturday night six Sisters slept in the convent and before the end of the week all were enjoying their new convent home. (403)

As often happens, Sister Christine Clarkin, who had been superior for six years, completed her term of office in August 1969 and was assigned to Holy Rosary Convent, Scranton, Pennsylvania. Her successor was Sister deNeri McLane, who with twenty-three other IHM Sisters assigned to St. Joseph's Hospital, would occupy the newly built Immaculate Heart of Mary Convent.

On December 21, 1969, the chaplain, Reverend Kenneth Kizis, blessed the altars and the chapel. The Blessed Sacrament was then transferred from the hospital chapel to the beautiful new tabernacle in the new chapel. As Father entered, carrying the Blessed Sacrament, the sisters sang, "O Come, O Come, Emmanuel." The joy of all was beyond description. (404)

In order to meet the challenging fiscal responsibilities of renovating large sections of the hospital, reducing the original mortgage, and meeting construction payments on the new convent, Sister Cephas revamped the hospital accounting system so that the IHM Congregation was reimbursed for the twenty-four IHM Sisters at professional-level salaries for the first time. This income helped finance the new convent as well as the many additional hospital projects underway, so that only $147,841 had to be borrowed from Northeastern National Bank and Trust Company of Scranton on March 30, 1970. (405)

As of 2003, the dedication of the IHM Sisters to the hospital continues. Eight IHM Sisters now reside in St. Joseph Convent, five of whom serve on the hospital staff. These include Sisters Margaret Loftus, Laurentia Mayan, Anne McDonald, Josine Shannon, Ann Lucille Bohn, Maria Rose Kelly, Jacinta Guinther and Lila Sciabica. (406)

In their annals, the sisters express their connection to the hospital, now named Marian Community Hospital, this way:

> Our convent is a welcoming place to our Sisters who are coming for treatment, to needy co- workers, to families and loved ones of our Sisters and others in the Hospital, to those companioning our Sisters for tests or doctors' visits. Hospital activities, especially those of the auxiliary, receive the strong support of the Sisters here. Way beyond the physical connection, St. Joseph Convent is an extension of Marian Community Hospital. Its mission is ours. (407)

In line with the desire of many sisters to live in smaller community settings, four IHMs also serving at Marian Community Hospital are living in nearby locations in Carbondale. These include Sister Jean Coughlin, administrator, Sister Mary Joy O'Neill, Sister Mary Alice Jacquinot and Sister Theresa Frere. (408)

Marian Convent Addition

The original Marian Convent building had been dedicated on April 9, 1956, in Mother Kathleen's time as superior general. It was built at a cost of approximately $1,700,000 to house some seventy infirm and aged IHM Sisters. Previously these sisters resided either at St. Agnes, Elmhurst, Pennsylvania, or at St. Joseph's Hospital, Carbondale, Pennsylvania.

Maximum occupancy was reached within ten years, and discussion of construction of an additional wing had taken place in council meetings as early as May 1966. (409) Plans were announced to the General Chapter of 1968 by Mother Beata. In her report to the Chapter on June 23, 1968, she cited the fact that seventy elderly sisters, plus the IHM staff were in residence at the Marian Convent. She described plans to build a new wing to provide fifty additional sleeping rooms, offices, and a pharmacy. "Work on this building will begin in the fall of 1968," she stated. (410)

Six months later, bids on the building project were submitted by various construction companies and opened in the presence of the members of the Central Administrative Assembly, Sister Romuald Doyle, superior of the Marian Convent, Sister Cor Mariae Schroth, administrator of the Marian Convent, Mr. Louis Russoniello, architect, Mr. John Domanish and William Brosch, consulting engineers, and Attorney Robert O'Brien. "After some study and discussion, it was agreed that the lowest bidder in each case should be awarded the contract." (411) Even with that decision the cost of the addition, including furnishings, would amount to about $1,700,000. (412)

As construction began, so did negotiations to secure funds for the ongoing costs being incurred. A temporary loan of $300,000 without interest was made by Marywood College in September 1969. By September 10, 1969, a loan agreement for $1,500,000 at 6 1/4 percent interest was signed between Mother Beata and Monsignor Joseph Madden, representing the Diocese of Scranton. (413) Bishop J. Carroll McCormick had approved the monthly disbursement of funds over the year 1969-1970 in amounts ranging from $55,000 to $225,000. (413) In a later letter Monsignor Madden expressed a veiled concern when he said, "I hope that somebody leaves the Marian Convent a substantial legacy to help you with your financial problems." (415)

The completed new wing provided additional sleeping rooms, a medical laboratory, physical and occupational therapy space, space for doctors to see patients, improved pharmacy facilities, and last, but not least, space for a fully-equipped beauty salon. (416)

Bishop J. Carroll McCormick conducted the blessing ceremony on January 20, 1971. Open house took place on Sunday, March 7, 1971. (417)

Sister Cor Mariae Schroth was administrator, Sister Joyce McQuaide, superior, and Monsignor William K. Dolan, STD was resident chaplain of the Marian Convent. In 1971, IHM Sisters on the nursing staff included Sisters dePaul Dougherty, RN, Marie Helen Dougherty, RN, Reparata Callen, RN, deLourdes Makstutis, RN, Lenore Thomas, LPN, and Eleanor Flynn, Nurses Aide. (418)

The now thirty-year old east wing of the Marian Convent, together with the forty-four year old west wing has provided an outstanding facility in which dedicated professionals, both lay and religious, have given the care of elderly and ill sisters. Many renovations have been made, as well as updating of equipment over the years. IHM Sisters serve in a variety of roles at the Marian Convent in 2003. Sister Rosemary Goulet, administrator; Sister St. Mel Wright, coordinator; Sister St. Henry Haiss, assistant administrator; Sister Ann Michael Zaytoun, director of food services; Sister Cecilia Marie Tippen, computer operator; Sister Harriet Jackson, administrative secretary; and Sister St. Kenneth, administrative assistant. Additional IHM staff include Sisters Anita Maleski, nurse practitioner; Mary Ellen James, medical technician; Damian Marie Dlugos, coordinator of nursing systems; Patricia Hauser, LPN; Barbara DuMont, pharmacy assistant; Mary Rassley, director of transportation; and three nurses aides Sisters Eileen Miller, Jeanne Albrittain, and Raymond Mary McIntyre. Sisters of IHM also serve as part-time aides as companions, drivers, ancillary services, receptionists, dietary assistants, occupational therapy, and medical records.

Marywood Motherhouse Fire

Dramatic photographs of wind-whipped flames swallowing up the huge sixty-eight year old motherhouse buildings tell the story better than any words can portray. Headlines of national and local newspapers shouted various aspects of the tragedy: "Marywood's Motherhouse Destroyed by flames"; "Nine Nuns Injured in Marywood Fire"; "About 140 Removed By Police, Firemen in General Alarmer"; "Pope Paul's Sorrow Passed to Marywood." These, and many, many more columns announced the news of the devastating fire at the Marywood Motherhouse in the early morning hours of February 22, 1971.

In addition to housing sisters on the faculty at Marywood College located on the same campus, the huge motherhouse building was the site of Marywood Seminary, an outstanding high school for girls. This building also housed the junior professed Sisters of IHM who were pursuing their higher education and spiritual formation program.

While no one died in the fire, it was this latter group, housed on the fourth floor of the seminary wing, who suffered the greatest trauma and injury. Forced to jump from the fourth floor to a roof below, after being trapped by flames, two junior professed sisters were listed in critical condition. Sister Lisa Barnes suffered a broken leg and Sister Sharon Kelly first-degree burns of the legs and back. Multiple burns and smoke inhalation caused the hospitalization of Sisters Rosemary Ludwick and Mary Violet Sloat. Five others were also taken to the hospital for treatment: Sisters Jean Coughlin, Sheila Cashera, Bernadette Thomas, Immaculate Severino, Maureen Schrimpe and Camille Lacosto. At least five firemen also suffered in fighting the blaze, receiving a range of injuries from facial and body burns to broken and sprained backs from falls out the windows and smoke inhalation. (419)

With the destruction of the west wing of the motherhouse, some 120 sisters, chiefly faculty of Marywood College and Seminary, were in need of immediate housing. Mother Beata arranged for many of them to stay in the newly completed wing of the Marian Convent, and others to live at the novitiate building. Eventually, dormitories in the novitiate would be converted into private rooms for the permanent housing of these sisters.

Housing was, of course, a major item, but myriads of minor losses were immediately obvious as sisters had lost clothing, eyeglasses and other personal effects, in addition to books, research materials, and other academic work. Addressing some of these personal needs, donations from every diocese where our sisters were located poured in, ranging from five dollars to nine thousand dollar gifts. The Marywood College faculty donated nine thousand dollars to the sisters; the Globe Store in Scranton donated five thousand dollars in gift certificates to be used by the sisters for new clothing. Mother Claudia, superior general of the Philadelphia IHMs sent five thousand dollars, as did the Daughters of Charity of Emittsburg, Maryland. Among the donors were organizations and people of every faith. Alumnae of the college and seminary, Knights of Columbus, members of Temple Israel in Scranton, the faculty and administration of the University of Scranton, and many more. Sisters from nearby and far distant missions, IHMs and other religious congregations, provided funds, clothing, and prayerful moral support.

A day after the fire, on February 23, 1971, Mother Beata somehow found strength to write to the total congregation. She asks and answers an important question in the midst of so much suffering:

> What is the spirit of our Congregation? The question is often asked. No definition could possibly interpret the spirit that characterized your response to the tragedy that struck Marywood early Monday morning, February 22.
>
> How shall I say thank you for all the ways in which you responded to the needs of the sisters? . . . your selfless coming and giving and sharing have truly shown the beautiful spirit of unity and love for which our Congregation is known.
>
> Please join us in thanksgiving to Almighty God for preserving the lives of our sisters. Though eight of the Junior Sisters are hospitalized and still being examined to determine the extent of injuries and burns, their wonderful, brave spirit rises above their suffering. Pray for them.
>
> As one sister was heard to say, "Our buildings may burn, but our spirit cannot be destroyed." (420)

This spirit was acknowledged also in the visit to Marywood of Most Reverend Archbishop Luigi Raimondi, Apostolic Delegate to the United States on May 7, 1971. In his homily at the Mass offered in the novitiate building, Archbishop Raimondi conveyed the solicitude and concern felt by Pope Paul VI in learning of the tragic fire. He also expressed his own desire to pay tribute to the Sisters of IHM for their "extraordinary and meritorious work over a long period of time." (421) His genuine feeling for the shock being experienced by the sisters was evident in his visit with Mother Beata, groups of sisters, and with the victims of the fire in several different hospitals in Scranton.

Bishop J. Carroll McCormick, acknowledging the long and fruitful service of IHM Sisters in the Scranton Diocese, announced "IHM Day" on March 21, 1971, a day of coordinated diocesan effort to respond to the needs of the IHM Sisters. (422) The response to this appeal was $120,126. "the largest special diocesan collection ever received in the history of the Diocese of Scranton."(423)

Mother Beata's gratitude was expressed as follows:

> . . . We are deeply grateful to our Bishop for his efforts, as we are to the Pastors and Assistant Pastors, and the generous people of the parishes for their overwhelming response. (424)

The extent of the damage would not be determined for several months. Magnificent paintings and furnishings in the reception hall, adjoining first floor rooms, and the central chapel were destroyed. Immediate estimates put the building loss alone at nearly two million dollars. Nearly a year later *The Scranton Times* of November 29, 1971, carried pictures of the slow progress of the tremendous job of razing the remains of the structure. (425)

Fortunately, Mother Beata and the council members had moved to the novitiate building, together with some of the congregation records, in the fall of 1969. (426)

It would be difficult to assess the long-range impact of the loss of the motherhouse building

to the Sisters of IHM, most of whom had known only this site since 1903 as their motherhouse. It would be difficult also to assess the long-range impact of the loss of the high school, Marywood Seminary, housed on the lower two floors of this building. Two hundred eight young women students were displaced as a result of the fire. Sister Marianne Addy, principal of the school, accepted the offer of Phil Brady, president of the Scranton Central Labor Union, to use the seven meeting rooms in the basement of the International Brotherhood of Electrical Workers' (IBEW) Building at 431 Wyoming Avenue in downtown Scranton.

The location of the IBEW Building, just a block away from Bishop Hannan High School, also served by the IHM Sisters, made this site a good temporary solution for Marywood Seminary students to complete the 1971-1972 academic year. The cafeteria, library, gymnasium, and business department equipment at Bishop Hannan High School were shared with the Marywood Seminary girls. (427)

Over the months that followed numerous pleas were sent to Mother Beata about the continuation of Marywood Seminary. Judge Richard P. Conaboy, Jr., president of the Fathers' Club of the Seminary, expressed the concern of the area community, saying:

> . . . not only the parents and the students at the Seminary feel deeply about its continuation, but rather, it has achieved a position in this community of such stature that its loss would be something no one would want to contemplate. (428)

Sister Marianne Addy's appeal, as principal of the Seminary, set forth important reasons for rebuilding: (1) the number of graduates who entered the IHM Congregation; (2) the fact that fifty percent of the graduates enrolled in Marywood College; (3) the financial assistance provided to the Congregation by the Seminary; (4) the need to staff a school for the educational needs of our benefactors. "The parents are waiting only for the word that you will rebuild and they will arrange donations." (429)

It must have been very difficult for Mother Beata and the council barely two weeks after a two million dollar property loss to even think of rebuilding Marywood Seminary. But, even Sister Marianne's later modified request that some existing building be leased or purchased for the high school, found no support in the Central Administrative Assembly. While expressing understanding that the sisters and students wished to continue the school, the CAA members agreed unanimously that Marywood Seminary be discontinued as of June 1971, and "that no project or plan for rebuilding or relocating be considered." (430)

Mother Beata in a letter dated March 15, 1971 communicated this decision to Sister Marianne Addy, principal. (431) Heartbroken as she was at the news, Sister Marianne accepted the decision, responding to Mother Beata's letter, "I am at peace with your decision and thoroughly understand the reasoning and wisdom that necessitated your making it." (432)

In the months that followed Mother Beata, trying to hide her own suffering over the loss of the motherhouse, led the sisters by her example in spiritualizing the tragic events. Her letter of May 10,1971, told the story of the Easter retreat master, Reverend Timothy McGough, OCD finding on campus a partially burned leaf of paper that had blown out of the ruins. The leaf of paper bore these words from St. Paul: "One thing I do; forgetting the things that are behind, and stretching forth myself to those that are before, I press towards the mark, to the prize of the supernal vocation of God in Christ Jesus." The little piece of burned paper was copied and enclosed in Mother Beata's letter. (433)

Events would indeed be put into perspective and life would go on, but it would not be the case that the Sisters of IHM could "forget the things that are behind." Knowing this, Mother Beata planned for a memorial, marking the site of the former motherhouse and Marywood Seminary, with a picture etched into the marble facade and a brief history of the Sisters of IHM. The total plan provided for a huge circular design with elevated steps, and concrete walks in web-like fashion leading from the circle to many points on the Marywood College campus. (434) This project later became known as the Marywood Commons and provided a location for many outdoor activities. The memorial was completed in the spring 1973.

Scranton Diocesan Centenary Celebration (1871-1971)

Mother Beata, a quiet, humble person was, however, one who loved joyous celebrations. And, of course, most IHM Sisters could always find a reason to celebrate some occasion! But no occasion seemed so compelling a time to celebrate as the one-hundredth anniversary of the IHMs association with the Diocese of Scranton. September 8, 1971, was the official date set by Mother Beata for the observance of this historic occasion.

Pope Pius IX, who also appointed Very Reverend William O'Hara, first bishop of the new diocese, formally established the Diocese of Scranton on March 3, 1868. (435) The Sisters of IHM, of course, had come from Monroe, Michigan, in 1857 and were located in Susquehanna County at St. Joseph, Pennsylvania, which was then in the Diocese of Philadelphia. Mother Theresa Maxis Duchemin had responded to the call of Bishop John Neumann to send sisters from Monroe to the Diocese of Philadelphia, which then included what later became the Diocese of Scranton.

IHMs had staffed Laurel Hill Academy in Susquehanna in 1860, Haycock in 1862, Manayuak in 1863, St. John's in Pittston in 1864, and other missions throughout eastern Pennsylvania prior to the establishment of the Scranton Diocese.

Seeing the young congregation's potential, the zealous Bishop O'Hara of the new Scranton Diocese proposed that the sisters, who were already canonically separated from the original foundation in Monroe, Michigan, would now separate from their companions in the Philadelphia Diocese and establish their own foundation in the Scranton Diocese.

On August 15, 1871, after serious reflection, twelve of the sisters voted to become an independent congregation, leaving twelve in the Philadelphia Diocese. Bishop O'Hara appointed Mother Joseph Shaughnessey as their first canonical superior and established St. John's Convent, Susquehanna, as their first motherhouse and novitiate. Providentially, six novices were accepted into the fledgling community one month later on September 8, 1871. By 1872 Bishop O'Hara had provided St. Cecilia's Convent in the heart of Scranton as the new motherhouse of the Sisters of IHM. (436)

With one hundred years of history from 1871-1971 as their legacy to the Scranton Diocese, it was fitting that a centenary celebration be held. September 8, 1971,was set as the date for special prayer throughout the congregation, for a celebratory liturgy at the IHM Generalate, and an evening banquet at Nazareth Hall, Marywood College. Bishop J. Carroll McCormick presided at the liturgy with concelebrants Reverend Kenneth G. Kizis, Generalate chaplain, Reverend William M. Mellody, Marywood College chaplain, Reverends Gerard M. Gannon and Joseph A. Fadden, faculty members at Marywood College. Monsignor Vincent P. Burke, pastor of St. Patrick's Parish in Scranton delivered the homily, and Sister Judith Gavigan directed the all-IHM choir. (437)

Bishop McCormick gave the invocation and the closing benediction at the dinner in Nazareth Hall where some two hundred guests were gathered. Monsignor John M. Dougherty, vicar for religious, delivered the centenary address. He spoke to the appropriateness of celebrating the occasion, saying:

> Indeed, then, you are compelled to celebrate. Surely, to thank God, to rejoice in God, to be strengthened by God; but before, above and after all, you celebrate to see, to see yourselves in the reality of being part of one hundred years of history . . . who are you, then? You are God's gift, in every sense of the word. God's gift in the sense that only God's giving explains you; God's gift in the sense that only God's giving to others fulfills you. (438)

Bishop McCormick had sent his congratulatory message by letter to Mother Beata. He wrote, in part:

> Mere words are certainly incapable of conveying adequately the sentiments of admiration and appreciation that the people of our Diocese share with me on this joyous anniversary. We are all aware of the countless apostolic endeavors, outstanding achievements and noble service whereby your congregation has enriched the Diocese of Scranton for the past one hundred years. (439)

He then mentioned the various ministries in which IHMs were engaged in the diocese, noting especially the sisters' work in education, health care, and social works for orphans, exceptional children, the homeless, and unwed mothers. He expressed genuine gratitude for the presence of the IHMs in the Scranton Diocese over the century. Looking ahead, he said, "We not only acclaim the accomplishments of the past, but we also anticipate a yet unwritten record of a glorious future." (440)

Mother Beata's closing remarks responded to all these expressions of gratitude to the IHM Congregation with her own litany of thanks to God, to Pope Paul VI, Bishop McCormick, the pastors and priests of the diocese, other religious congregations, the laity, and all those served by the IHMs. She gave tribute to the pioneer IHMs, as well as to "our Sisters of this decade, who have so faithfully followed the Church through trying days of Renewal and Adaptation . . ." (441)

As always, Mother Beata's message was also one of hope and trust in God's support. It will be recalled that this September 1971 centennial celebration came only six months after the devastating motherhouse fire. It would seem almost impossible, but for the deep faith of Mother Beata, that she could at this time call the sisters to be women of hope. Her closing remarks were:

> We close a century of loving service with grateful hearts for all our past blessings as we look forward with simplicity, humility, faith and hope toward our future. Amid a diversity of complex questions that present themselves in the present day, we trust in God for His light and wisdom to lead us to our final goal. (442)

The Wyoming Valley Flood

On Thursday, June 22, 1972, deluge-type rains from hurricane "Agnes" caused the west branch of the Susquehanna River to overflow its banks. Ravaging floods raged throughout the Wyoming Valley, moving south and west before subsiding. Sixty-eight thousand persons were evacuated from their homes in the Wyoming Valley alone. Communication lines were cut and transportation through the streets by boat was the only choice. Cars were overturned, bridges washed out, homes broken apart, gravestones upended, and even caskets were floating in the streets.

Evacuees had to be provided for immediately in the Wilkes-Barre and Scranton areas, so centers were set up at the Red Cross offices, Pocono Downs Racetrack, public schools, the National Guard Center at the Wilkes-Barre/Scranton Airport, Misericordia College, Dallas, Pennsylvania, St. Joseph Seminary in Pittston, and at the Catholic Youth Center and Marywood College Residence Halls and Athletic Field House in Scranton.

At these centers evacuees were provided with medicines, food, clothing, bedding, furniture, cleaning utensils, and financial aid. Immediate assistance came through hundreds of volunteers.
Only months later was the impact of federal and state aid felt.

The full-hearted response of the IHM Sisters to this crisis is noteworthy. IHMs were found wherever there was a need. They cooked meals at the centers, organized the incoming overwhelming donations of food, clothing and furniture. They were out soliciting supplies from stores and factories, shopping for cleaning utensils, manning telephones and performing clerical tasks for the Red Cross. IHMs were shoveling mud from homes and churches, and scrubbing floors for victims unable to handle these tasks.

IHM sister-nurses were on the front line, giving nursing care and medical supplies where needed. On June 23 at 7:00 p.m., a request came to Marywood for nurses to report to evacuation areas in Wilkes-Barre. Sisters Wendelin Casey, Reparata Cullen, St. Gerard Meyers, Damian Marie Dlugos and Jamesella Mawhinney, all of whom were on retreat at Marywood at the time, left retreat to take up duties at the G.A.R. School and the Jewish Synagogue in Wilkes-Barre. Throughout the night they settled evacuees on cots, providing blankets, pillows, baby bottles and many caring words to people in shock and sorrow. Insulin and other medicines, lost in the flood, were provided by St. Joseph's Hospital, Carbondale, and other area hospitals. (443)

Several IHM missions in the flood area sustained considerable damage. Sisters from the IHM novitiate in Scranton were sent to help clean in convents and churches in Forty Fort, Kingston and Exeter.

In Forty Fort, for example, the first floor and basement of Holy Name of Jesus Convent were a disaster, except for the kitchen that was the only useable room on the first floor. "We were happy to enjoy that," they wrote, "especially when we realized that our loss was nothing compared with the losses suffered by parishioners and the other people in the valley." (444) The first floor and basement of the school were badly damaged. Books in the library, first and second grades had to be disposed of. The pastor, Reverend Aloysius Boylan and his assistant Reverend Edward Lyman worked daily to restore the school. Monsignor Thomas Horan and many parishioners from St. Rose, Carbondale, Pennsylvania, came to assist. Mennonites from Allentown, Pennsylvania, and IHMs from several convents also helped clean and shovel the mud. A Philadelphia parish sent donations totaling $15,000.

While restoration work was to continue for several years, Holy Name of Jesus School opened for classes on September 26, 1972. (445)

The events at St. Ignatius Convent in Kingston were similar. Since most of the eleven members of the local community were away on summer assignments, only Sisters Mary Roche, Xavier Gibbons and Martin Marie Stanwich were at home when the floodwaters came to Kingston. The convent was evacuated at 7:30 a.m. and the sisters moved to St. Leo's Convent in nearby Ashley. A week later, Sisters Xavier, Josefa Connolly, Aquin Theobald and Mary Roche began clean- up of the mud deposited on the first floor of the convent. Without water or electricity, however, their work was slow and discouraging.

By July 5, however, it became possible to work in the school where significant losses were experienced. With great assistance from other IHMs, students from Central Catholic High School in Kingston, and the Grosek Brothers Construction Company hired by the pastor, Monsignor Matthew F. Boylan, classes began at the high school on September 13, 1972. Religious instruction classes for public school students were postponed until February 3, 1973, due to repair and renovation of areas ordinarily used for these classes.

While the sisters were already residing in the convent by September 3, it was not until October 6 that heat and hot water were restored. Since most of the first floor was still too damp to be carpeted or to set new furniture in place, the kitchen became the gathering spot of the sisters. By November 30 the Blessed Sacrament was placed in the chapel, but it was not until February 1, 1973, that the pews were installed and the renovations completed in that area. Mass was celebrated on February 15 for the first time since the flood. (446)

The resiliency of the sisters was notable in the face of so many inconveniences and so much destruction. As the annals report, "Despite any inconveniences still prevalent we are deeply grateful for the progress that has been made and we hope will continue to be made in the days to come, not only for ourselves but for all the flood victims of the Wyoming Valley area." (447)

In her letter to the congregation on July 1, 1972, just two weeks after the flood, Mother Beata praised the response of the sisters to the tragedy.

She wrote:

> The generous response to this intense suffering was immediate. Each day we witnessed our Sisters manifesting their concern for these stricken people by their prayers, contributions, hospitality and generous service. (448)

Mother Beata also expressed her desire to assist families of IHM Sisters who were in need, saying:

> Our special concern extends to the families of our Sisters whose homes are ravaged by the recent flood. If those Sisters whose families are suffering and in need would contact us, we would have a beautiful opportunity to gladly share our abundance with them. (449)

Both the Congregation and Marywood College united to provide $10,000 to the flood relief fund, as well as housing and meals for flood victims for a month after the flood occurred. Sister Coleman Nee, president of Marywood College, also made a personal call on the presidents of Wilkes, King's and Misericordia Colleges in the flood area, presenting each with a check for $1,000. From the Marywood Field House eight tractor-trailer loads of clothing, boxed and sorted by IHM Sisters, went out to the evacuee centers.

In her letter of July 13, 1972, Mother Beata detailed many of the activities of the sisters during the aftermath of the flood. Using the maxim "The need of the hour is the Will of God," she expressed her personal gratitude for the sacrifices made by the sisters:

> Clearly our Sisters are not working for an expression of gratitude, but we feel obliged to communicate to you the tremendous impact that the Sisters are making in the various agencies and institutions where they serve. Doing those things which Sisters do best— organizing, encouraging the young and old, comforting the distressed, working and praying—the challenge of Vatican II to be a witness to Christ is being lovingly and capably met. (450)

In addition to all that the congregation did during the immediate aftermath of the flood, Mother Beata and the council also notified the bishop and the pastors in the flood areas that salaries and fringe benefits of all sisters in the flood-stricken areas (Kingston, Forty Fort, Lock Haven, and

Wilkes-Barre) would be waived from September 1, 1972, to August 31, 1973, and that these sisters would be supported from the Generalate in Scranton. (451) This gesture brought hope to discouraged pastors and parishioners in the Wyoming Valley. God's Will was found in the need of the hour.

Education of Sisters from Foreign Countries

"If you want to love Christ, extend your charity over all the earth, for the members of Christ are throughout the world." (St. Augustine: Letters)

Realizing this truth and the call of Pope Paul VI to serve the peoples of the world in foreign lands, both Mother Kathleen and Mother Beata caught the missionary spirit of the Church. They responded, with Marywood College administration and faculty as supportive allies, by initiating a higher education scholarship program for sisters of foreign congregations.

In 1961 Mother Kathleen arranged for two Sisters of the Immaculate Heart of Mary of Nagaski, Japan, to begin study for their Master's degrees at Marywood College. (452) Over the years, other Japanese sisters would follow.

Again in 1963 two sisters, Daughters of the Cross from Chanthaburi, Thailand, were sponsored by the IHM Congregation for study at Marywood College. The sentiments of gratitude of these congregations are reflected also in correspondence from the Bishop of Thailand:

> I want you to know how grateful we feel for the great help you are giving not only to the sisters and their Congregation, but to the whole ApostolicVicariate of Chanthaburi and the mission of Thailand, as it is here that the Sisters will come to work for the Faith after their training in the States. (453)

It will be recalled that Mother Beata had opened two IHM missions outside of the United States, Puerto Rico in 1964 and Lima, Peru in 1965. In addition, she promoted the missionary work of the Church by responding to the requests of three congregations from India to send sisters to Marywood College to study. During the years 1966-1974 five Sisters of the Franciscan Clarist Congregation of Polai, Kerala, South India, came to the United States to study. Some of these attended Duquesne University in Pittsburgh, Pennsylvania, and lived at St. Mary of the Mount Convent in Pittsburgh with the IHM Sisters. Others attended Marywood College in Scranton. From Changanacherry, Kerala, India, were also two Sisters of the Adoring Blessed Sacrament.

From 1969-1973 two Sisters of Mary Immaculate of West Bengal, India, were students at Marywood College. Letters from these former students after their return to India express their love for the Scranton IHMs and their gratitude for the education they received.

In August 1972 Sisters Lourdes and Rosita wrote to Mother Beata from Krishnagar, India:

> . . . once again we thank you for your kindness and generosity toward us. Please pray that we may use all that we have received from you and your sisters in service of God and our fellow men. May we find happiness in our selfless giving to our church in India. Although far away, we are united with you in spirit. (454)

In addition to their education at Marywood College, many of these young sisters participated in the religious formation program for IHM Sisters not yet finally professed. In this program they received instruction in theology, in prayer, religious life, and the vows. Mother Beata, acting in place of major superiors of these congregations in foreign lands, received the first vows of many of these sisters while they were students here.

From Micronesia four Sisters of the Congregation of Mercedarian Missionaries of Berriz, Spain, came in 1971. Two of these sisters had finished their junior college years at Donnelly College, Kansas City, Kansas; others were missionaries from Lima, Peru.

One cannot but admire the perseverance with which native Spanish-speaking, Chinese and Japanese sisters mastered the English language, and succeeded in adapting to the food and other cultural dimensions of life in the United States. Even sisters from India found American English strange and difficult because of a difference in rhythm and accent.

Some of the problems experienced by the sisters would be true of all foreign-born students studying in the United States. One Indian student, writing home to India from New York made these comments:

> . . . time is an extremely important element in American life. No words of excuse can remedy the fact that if you miss an appointment, or if you are slightly late, they will consider you extremely rude . . . Americans live a fast and strenuous life. Because you come from a culture where life is much slower and more relaxed, you are not well prepared for the speed, the competitiveness, the 'rugged individualism' which are the major elements of American life . . .Here you will have no servant to clean your dishes, kitchen

> or bathroom. Americans usually set aside a day for cleaning . . . American education is indeed excellent, but it requires much harder work than education in our country . . . To maintain the required standard is a full-time occupation in itself. (455)

The student-sisters may have been sheltered from some of these cultural differences because of the kindness shown them by the IHM Sisters. Sister Mary Paul, OLC, American director of the sisters of Our Lady of China, studying in the United States, wrote to Mother Beata:

> Would also like to take this opportunity to mention the wonderful spirit of charity and friendship expressed to our Sisters by all the IHM Sisters we met. Have traveled widely throughout the world, have never before witnessed such a friendly spirit among a group of Sisters as have known while visiting Scranton! (456)

Several of the Sisters of Our Lady of China from Taiwan attended Marywood College between 1971 and 1990. Degrees were earned in nursing and in education. This community of sisters had escaped communist China and were trying to establish a nursing school, clinic and hospital in rural Taiwan. As Sister Mary Paul wrote: "We will be better prepared for our mission apostolate, and can also give better medical care to the sick poor." (457)

From 1973 to the present the IHM Congregation has also sponsored the education of sister-students from Africa. The list of sisters from many congregations native to Africa is impressive. Represented are sisters from Ghana, Nigeria, Tanzania, Uganda and Kenya, many of whom obtained both undergraduate and graduate degrees from Marywood College.

Mother Beata chose a highly practical and blessed way to support the missionary activity of the Church and to make the IHM presence felt in so many corners of the world.

Mother Beata Wertz, IHM: A Summary

Having guided the Scranton IHM Congregation for twelve historic years, from 1962 to 1974, through the dramatic period of Vatican II and its immediate aftermath, Mother Beata Wertz, IHM, completed her terms as superior general. She was seventy-six years of age and had celebrated her golden jubilee of profession in 1972.

From 1922 to 1955 for thirty-three years, she had served in the teaching apostolate of the Congregation in ten different missions. For nineteen years, from 1955 to 1974 she was engaged in the administration of the

Congregation, making a gentle, yet firm imprint on the spirit of the membership. After her time in office, she had fifteen additional fruitful years, serving at St. Thomas the Apostle Parish in Bedford, Pennsylvania, from 1974-1977, then as a visitor of the sick at St. Joseph's Hospital, Carbondale, Pennsylvania, from 1977-1981. Her last eight years, from 1981-1989 were spent in prayer ministry at the Marian Convent .

Mother Beata had participated fully in the preparations for the General Chapter of 1974, meeting with pre-chapter committees as early as November 1972. In her address to the opening meeting she recalled all the adaptations and changes that had taken place and the very real suffering experienced by most religious during the post-conciliar years. As was her custom, she called the sisters to deepen their spiritual roots, as well as to address external changes. She repeated this plea in several different ways:

> Be especially concerned about those things which will make the Congregation a better instrument for the sanctification of the Sisters . . . We want to shape the Congregation to serve the future needs of the Church and the people of God in the best possible manner, but not to the detriment of the holiness of the sisters . . .
>
> Change that brings about destruction of the interior life for the sake of efficiency should not be accepted. The point is not the disappearance of personal sanctification, but the shift of perspective to the apostolic viewpoint. The interior life remains indispensable; one cannot bring to one's neighbor what one does not possess oneself. (458)

At the General Chapter of 1974, prior to giving the required report of the spiritual and temporal aspects of the congregation, Mother Beata gratefully acknowledged the contribution of each sister to the accomplishments of her twelve years in office. She stated:

> I should like first to express my deep gratitude to all the members of the Congregation for their fidelity and perseverance during these turbulent times of renewal in religious life. It is the constant and consistent prayers of the individual Sister and our community prayers that have kept our Congregation vital and alive while generously embracing the faith in our Consecration to Christ as members of His Church. (459)

In her humility, she made herself one with all who suffered during this time of change, saying,

> When there was doubt and discouragement—and, Sisters, there were times—my hope was reaffirmed and reassured at the thought and by the example of our many dedicated Sisters who serve and have served Christ constantly . . . to each and every one my humble and heartfelt 'thank you, Sister.' (460)

In thanking Mother Beata for her generous participation in the work of the General Chapter, Sister Anne Fulwiler, newly elected Superior General, wrote:

> You rendered a noble service to our beloved Congregation in your prayerful, patient self- giving to the arduous deliberations of this summer. May God reward you by His blessing and the assurance that you have contributed tremendously to a precious heritage. (461)

The characteristics, which were the essence of Mother Beata's leadership, were captured in the citation written by Sister Paulinus Sullivan, IHM, and presented at the joint meeting of the Sector Coordinating Assembly on March 30, 1974. The full text of the citation follows:

> Greetings! All Discerningly and Low, Blow, O Love and Gladness, Blow. Holy Spirit, help those who would honor Mother Beata on this occasion to understand ever more fully her whom they honor. Help them to know the depths of discernment with which Mother Beata fulfilled her role as Superior General of the Sisters, Servants of the Immaculate Heart of Mary from 1962 to the present time. Truly forgetful of herself, Mother Beata shared the joys and sorrows of those fortunate enough to live within the range of her influence—and that influence was wide, including not only the members of her own congregation, but sisters who came from other communities as far away as Thailand and Japan to share in the formation program at Marywood.
>
> Moreover, Mother Beata's sense of discernment is not merely humanitarian; hers is a spirit that searches out God and the ways of God. The sixties were not easy for anyone; for a superior general they were traumatic. To understand and to implement the decrees of Vatican II with regard to religious life; to understand and cope with change in the modern world; to reconcile the urgencies of the young and the nostalgias of the old; to curb the

> radical and move the conservative—all this required insight into both the human heart and the incandescent heart of God.
>
> And what is the secret of this abundance of the gifts of the Holy Spirit shared in by Mother Beata? Perhaps the word "unassuming" would be the key. Perhaps the last pew in the chapel is a symbol of this secret of what any superior should be and of what Mother Beata is. Day after day she might be found there—in the place of the lowly publican—pleading before God and for man to understand and to be understood, to accept and to be accepted.
>
> And she is glad in the Spirit. We marvel at the youthful resilience characteristic of Mother Beata, which keeps her upright under weighty responsibility, even tragedy. We marvel at her common sense, her rich wisdom and her sense of humor.
>
> As we admire this great soul that is Mother Beata's today, and praise not only what she has done but what she is, we pray that the Holy Spirit will remain with her always
>
> We pray: All Discerningly and low, Blow, O Love and Gladness, Blow. (462)

The praise that came from her own sister-IHMs was significant, and only added to the recognition Mother Beata had received over the years from bishops, pastors, civil authorities, and administrators of other religious congregations, as they observed her election, re-election, her golden jubilee of religious profession, and her courageous leadership in difficult times.

On June 4, 1967, at the annual commencement held by the University of Scranton, Reverend Aloysius C. Galvin, SJ, president of the University, bestowed the degree of Doctor of Laws, Honoris Causa, on Mother Beata. The insightful words of the citation include, in part, the following:

> Her (Mother Beata's) maternal, gentle, firm, efficient competence fused with her vision of the new as also true, as she guided her community through progressive new programs in Sister formation, through expansion from Marywood College to Latin America, through post-conciliar religious experimentation and the challenge of vital renewal. (463)

Mother Beata was also honored on the occasion of the 60th Anniversary of Marywood College, October 4, 1975. In awarding the Presidential Medal to Mother Beata, Sister Coleman Nee, president, said

> As a woman of faith, Mother Beata was that 'new light on everything' as she guided the Congregation in its response to the call of the changing Church and changing religious life. As a woman of faith, she demonstrated a constant readiness to begin anew and adapt . . . Combining the attributes of deep personal interiority with concerned service for others, Mother M. Beata is at home and at peace with all—herself, her associates and her God. Her genuine humility puts at ease all who come into contact with her. (464)

It was no wonder that at Mother Beata's death on September 14, 1989, the world seemed a bit darker and less secure. She had spent sixty-eight years as a Sister, Servant of the Immaculate Heart of Mary and had reached ninety-one years of age. Yet, even in death, so brightly did the example of her life shine that those attending her funeral on September 16, 1989, were able to sing Beethoven's "Ode to Joy" as her final hymn. (465)

References

1. Sister M. Beata Wertz, IHM. Letter to Congregation, February 13, 1962
2. Sister M. Beata Wertz, IHM. Letter to Congregation, February 16, 1962
3. Sister M. Beata Wertz, IHM. Letter to Chapter Delegates. February 27, 1962
4. Wilton Wynn. *Keeper of the Keys.* 1988. P. 23
5. Ibid.
6. Op.cit. p. 21
7. Op.cit. p.52
8. Op.cit. p.236
9. Op.cit. p.44
10. General Chapter Minutes. March 24, 1962
11. Ibid.
12. General Chapter Notes on Habit and Cloak Referendum. 1962
13. General Chapter Notes. "Note of Appreciation of Capitulars." March 25,1962
14. Mother Beata Wertz, IHM. Closing Message to Chapter. March 25, 1962
15. Sister Immaculata Gillespie, IHM. *Sisters of IHM.* 1921. p. 48-88
16. Mother Beata Wertz, IHM. Letter to Sisters and Dedication Address. May 30, 1962
17. Monsignor William K. Dolan, STD. Letter to Mother Beata Wertz, IHM. March 27, 1962
18. Bishop Jerome D. Hannan. Letter to Mother Beata Wertz, IHM. April 2, 1962
19. Archives. Land and Buildings—Novitiate
20. Ibid.
21. Monsignor Joseph G. Quinn. Dedication Sermon. *The Catholic Light*, June 7, 1962
22. General Council Minutes. March 26, 1962 and May 20, 1962
23. Archives. Land and Buildings—Novitiate
24. Board of Education of IHM Congregation. Minutes. October 28, 1961
25. loc. cit., 1961-1968
26. loc. cit., March 14, 1964
27. Sister Felicitas Ryan, IHM. Address to the First Biennial Institute of the IHM Education Conference, August 19, 1965
28. "Horizons Newsletter" Vol.II, April 1964, No.3, p.1
29. Ibid.
30. Ibid.
31. Community Board of Education Minutes, 1964-1965
32. Community Education Conference. First Biennial Institute Materials. August 1965
33. Mother Beata Wertz, IHM. Letter to Congregation. May 8, 1965

34. Mother Beata Wertz, IHM. Welcome Address to First Biennial Institute of The Tri-Community Education Conference. August 19, 1965
35. Proceedings of the First Biennial Institute of the IHM Education Conference, Scranton, PA. October 6, 1965
36. Mother Maria Pacis, IHM, Superior General, West Chester, PA, October 6, 1965
37. Mother Benedicta (Margaret) Brennan, IHM. Closing Address to the Second Biennial Institute of the IHM Education Conference. Monroe, MI, August 19, 1967
38. Mother Beata Wertz, IHM. Letter to Scranton IHMs. July 17, 1970
39. Reverend Louis Florent Gillet. Cited in the 125th Anniversary Liturgy Booklet
40. Sister Espiritu Dempsey, IHM. Fourth Biennial Tri-Community Institute. Marywood. July 1972
41. Mother Beata Wertz, IHM. Closing Address at Fourth Biennial Tri-Community Institute. Marywood. July 1972
42. Ibid.
43. Wilton Wynn. *Keepers of the Keys.* Random House, New York, 1988, p.236
44. Mother Beata Wertz, IHM. Letter to IHM Sisters, June 5, 1964
45. Ibid. Materials enclosed with June 5, 1964 from Mother Beata Wertz, IHM
46. Minutes of the General Chapter, 1961
47. Minutes of the General Chapter, March 23-25, 1962
48. Sisters John Francis Marley and Amata Jordan. Letter to Congregation, January 29, 1966
49. Minutes of the General Council, July 21, 1966
50. Sisters John Francis Marley and Amata Jordan. Letter to Congregation, August 15, 1966
51. Annals of Epiphany Convent, Sayre, Pennsylvania. 1966-1967
52. Annals of Little Flower Convent, Washington D.C. 1966-1967
53. Annals of St. Paul Convent, New Bern. North Carolina. 1966-1967
54. Conversation with Sister Espiritu Dempsey, IHM. September 1966
55. Sister Amata Jordan, IHM. Letter to the Congregation. January 21, 1967
56. Minutes of the General Chapter of Affairs. July 19, 1968, p.2
57. Central Administrative Assembly. Letter to Congregation. December 5, 1968
58. Wilton Wynn. Op.cit. 1988. p.104
59. Mother Beata Wertz, IHM. Letter to the Congregation. October 15, 1966
60. General Council Minutes. October 25, 1966
61. General Council Minutes. November 5, 1966
62. Mother Beata Wertz, IHM. Letter to Congregation. November 8, 1966
63. Mother Beata Wertz, IHM. Letter to Committees on Renewal. December 17, 1966

64. Mother Beata Wertz, IHM. Letter to Congregation. September 1, 1967
65. Mother Beata Wertz, IHM. Letter to Congregation. September 18, 1967
66. Ibid.
67. General Chapter Minutes. June 24, 1968
68. General Chapter Minutes. June 27, 1968
69. Ibid.
70. Mother Beata Wertz, IHM. Promulgation of Constitutions and Decrees of the General Chapter, August 2, 1968
71. Ibid.
72. Reverend Higinio Madrazo, CM. Letter to Mother Beata Wertz. October 19, 1963. Annals of Convento Cristo Rey, Ponce, Puerto Rico
73. Mother Beata Wertz, IHM. Letter to Rev. Higinio Madrazo, CM. November 9, 1963. Annals of Convento Cristo Rey, Ponce, PR
74. Annals of Convento Cristo Rey, Puerto Rico, 1963-1964
75. Ibid.
76. Ibid.
77. Sister Jeanne Tubach, IHM. Notes of June 11, 1995. Archives
78. Reverend Angel Echeverria. Letter to Mother Beata Wertz, IHM. July 7, 1965
79. Annals of Convento Cristo Rey, Puerto Rico, 1965-1966
80. Ibid.
81. Ibid.
82. Annals of Convento Cristo Rey, Puerto Rico, 1967-1968
83. Ibid.
84. Annals of Convento Cristo Rey, Puerto Rico, 1968-1969
85. Ibid.
86. Ibid.
87. Central Administrative Assembly Minutes. May 4, 1970
88. Ibid.
89. Central Administrative Assembly Minutes, May 26, 1970
90. Central Administrative Assembly. Letter to Local Assembly, Cristo Rey, May 12, 1970
91. Reverend Angel Echeverria. Letter to Mother Beata Wertz, May 26, 1970
92. Mother Kathleen Hart. Letter to Reverend Joseph Nangle, OFM, October 15, 1958
93. Reverend John Waldie, Pastor. Letter to Mother Kathleen Hart, August 9, 1960
94. Mother Kathleen Hart. Letter to Reverend John Waldie. August 25, 1960
95. Romolo Carboni, Apostolic Nuncio, Lima, Peru. Letters to Mother Kathleen Hart. March 17 and April 27, 1961
96. Romolo Carboni. Letter to Mother Beata Wertz, April 15, 1962

97. Mother Beata Wertz, IHM. Letter to Bishop Jerome Hannan, Scranton, PA. January 31, 1964
98. Reverend Donald Hoag. Letter to Mother Beata Wertz, IHM. February 6, 1964
99. Reverend Jeremias Nangle, OFM. Letter to Mother Beata Wertz, IHM, June 22, 1964
100. Ibid.
101. Mother Beata Wertz, IHM. Letter to Reverend Jeremias Nangle, OFM September 29, 1964
102. Reverend Jeremias Nangle, OFM. Letter to Mother Beata Wertz, IHM November 25, 1964
103. Mother Beata Wertz, IHM. Letters to Mother Marie Stanislaus, Miami, Florida, and to Archbishop Romolo Carboni, Lima, Peru. February 12, 1965
104. Annals of Convento Nombre de Jesus, Lima, Peru, 1965
105. Ibid.
106. Ibid. 1968-1969
107. Myron Frankman, "Foreign Exchange and Revolution: Peru, 1968-1973." McGill University, May 1975
108. Annals of Convento Nombre de Jesus, Lima, Peru, 1968-1969
109. *Close Up*, October 5, 1973, p.5
110. Annals, 1969-1970
111. Ibid.
112. Annals, 1974-1975
113. Ibid.
114. Annals, 1976-1977
115. Ibid.
116. Sister Anna Maria Hayes. Letter to Sister Immaculata Gillespie, IHM. March 5, 1944, citing the diary of Sister Sebastian Murphy
117. Ibid.
118. Unknown editor. "History of the Parish" brochure. Dedication of St. Aloysius School, Cresson, PA. September 1, 1963, p.11
119. Reverend Bernard O=Malley, Pastor. Foreword to Dedication Brochure. September 1, 1963, p.2
120. Annals of St. Aloysius Convent, 1963-1964
121. Dedication Brochure. Architect's description., September 1, 1963
122. Annals of St. Aloysius Convent, 1963-1964
123. Ibid.
124. 1963-1970
125. Bishop J. Carroll McCormick. Letter to Mother Beata Wertz, IHM. December 12, 1961
126. Ibid.

127. Ibid. August 10, 1962
128. "Altoona Catholic Register," April 26, 1963
129. Monsignor Joseph P. Gallagher. *A Century of History*, 1868-1968, p.378-379
130. Op.cit. p. 435
131. Right Reverend Monsignor R. E. Larkin. Letter to Mother Beata Wertz, IHM October 14, 1963
132. Annals of St. Mary of Mt. Carmel Convent, Dunmore, PA, 1963-1964
133. Ibid. 1966-1967 and 1967-1968
134. Bishop O'Hara High School Handbook for Students and Parents, AThe History of Bishop O'Hara High School, 2002-2003, @ p.2
135. Ibid.
136. Annals of St. Mary of Mt. Carmel Convent, 1972-1973
137. Middle States Association. Evaluation of Bishop O'Hara High School, November 7-9, 2001
138. 30th Anniversary Booklet of Bishop O'Hara High School, 1994, p.ix,x
139. Annals of St. Mary of Mt. Carmel Convent, 2000-2001
140. Bishop Sylvester Treinen. Letter to Mother Beata Wertz, IHM, September 13, 1962
141. Ibid.
142. Reverend Thomas J. Lafey, Pastor, St. Pius X, Coeur d'Alene, Idaho. Letter to Mother Beata Wertz, IHM. Undated.
143. Ibid.
144. Mother Beata Wertz, IHM. Letters to Bishop Sylvester Treinen and Reverend Thomas J. Lafey, September 18, 1962
145. Bishop Sylvester Treinen. Letter to Mother Beata Wertz, IHM. September 21, 1962
146. Ibid.
147. Mother Beata Wertz, IHM. Letter to Bishop Sylvester Treinen. September 25, 1962
148. Bishop Sylvester Treinen. Letter to Mother Beata Wertz, IHM, September 27, 1962 and from Father Lafey, undated
149. Bishop Sylvester Treinen. Letter to Mother Beata Wertz, IHM. December 15, 1964
150. Annals of St. Pius X Convent, 1965-1966
151. Ibid.
152. Ibid.
153. Annals, 1967-1968
154. Annals of IHM Convent, Coeur d=Alene, Idaho, 1969-1970
155. Ibid. 1970-1971
156. Central Administrative Assembly Minutes. October 22, 1970
157. Ibid.

158. Central Administrative Assembly Minutes. November 27, 1970
159. Annals of IHM Convent, 1970-1971
160. Reverend John Morgan, Pastor, St. Pius X, Reverend Bernard Mulligan, CSsR Pastor, St. Thomas Church and Presidents of Parish Councils. Letter to Mother Beata Wertz, IHM, February 7, 1971
161. Reverend John Morgan, Pastor, St. Pius X. Letter to Mother Beata Wertz, IHM. February 8, 1971
162. Mother Beata Wertz, IHM and Central Administrative Assembly members. Letter to IHM Sisters, Father Morgan and Father Mulligan, CSsR, March 2, 1971
163. Bishop Sylvester Treinen, Diocese of Boise, Idaho. Letter to the Sisters of IHM. Coeur d'Alene, Idaho, May 24, 1971
164. "History of St. Pius X Parish." Insert in St. Pius X Parish Bulletin, September 15, 2002
165. Editorial. "The Long Island Catholic," vol.5, No. 27, November 3, 1966
166. Dedication Booklet. Maria Regina High School. October 16, 1966
167. Mother Beata Wertz, IHM. Letter to Reverend David Farley. November 22, 1965
168. Annals of Maria Regina Convent, Uniondale, New York. 1966-1967, p.1
169. Ibid.
170. Mother Beata Wertz, IHM. Letter to IHM Sisters assigned to Maria Regina High School, November 22, 1965
171. Annals of Maria Regina Convent, 1966-1967, p.2, 3
172. Annals, 1967-1968, p.1-5
173. Annals, 1969-1970
174. Annals, 1970-1971
175. Annals, 1981-1982
176. Sesquicentennial Booklet of St. Thomas Church, Bedford, PA, p.21-33
177. Ibid. p.35
178. Reverend Edward F. McConnell, Pastor, St. Thomas Church, Bedford, PA Sesquicentennial Booklet, p.37
179. Ibid., p.39
180. Sister Georgina Wertz, IHM. Letter to Mother Beata Wertz, IHM. February 11, 1965
181. Ibid.
182. Mother Beata Wertz, IHM. Letter to Most Reverend J. Carroll McCormick, Bishop of Altoona-Johnstown Diocese, Altoona, PA.March 15, 1965
183. Annals of St. Thomas the Apostle Convent, Bedford, PA. 1966-1967, p.1
184. Ibid. p.2
185. Sesquicentennial Dedication Booklet. p.28

186. Ibid. p.3
187. Ibid. pp. 40-43
188. Reverend Edward McConnell, Pastor, Letter to Mother Beata Wertz, IHM. December 5, 1966
189. Ibid. Letter to Mother Beata Wertz, IHM. December 12, 1966
190. Annals of St. Thomas Convent, Bedford, PA. 1966-1967, p.4
191. Ibid. p.5
192. Annals, 1967-1968, p.1
193. Ibid. p.2
194. Reverend Edward McConnell, Pastor. Letter to Mother Beata Wertz, IHM. March 25, 1968
195. Annals of St. Thomas Convent, 1968-1969, p.1, 5
196. Mother Beata Wertz, IHM. Letter to Reverend Edward McConnell, Pastor. March 21, 1969
197. Annals of St. Thomas Convent, 1971-1972, p.3
198. Annals, 1972-1973, p.1
199. Annals, 1981-1982, p.3
200. Dedication Booklet of Our Lady of Mercy School, Forest Hills, New York.1967, p.17
201. Ibid.
202. Dedication Booklet, p.18
203. Ibid. p.19
204. Ibid. p.20
205. Ibid.
206. Ibid. p.21
207. Annals of Our Lady of Mercy Convent, Forest Hills, New York, 1966-1967
208. Ibid. p.2
209. Ibid.
210. Reverend Krische quoted in undated newspaper article by Vera A. Peracchio. IHM Archives
211. Annals of Our Lady of Mercy Convent, 1966-1967
212. Ibid. 1967-1968
213. Ibid.
214. Ibid.
215. Ibid. 1968-1969
216. Ibid. 1972-1973; 1974-1975
217. Ibid. 1976-1977
218. Ibid. 1982-1983; 1985-1986
219. Anthony D'Ambrosia. Rededication Booklet. January 31, 1988
220. Annals of Our Lady of Mercy Convent, 1989-1990
221. Ibid. 1991-1992

222. Ibid. 1992-1993
223. Anonymous account of IHMs meeting Mr. and Mrs. Harold Mostyn, Summer, 1965. IHM Archives
224. Central Administrative Assembly Minutes. October 10, 1965
225. Reverend William J. Weinheimer. Letter to Mother Beata Wertz, IHM. February 13, 1966
226. Mother Beata Wertz, IHM. Letter to Reverend W.J. Weinheimer. March 9, 1966
227. Annals of St. Raphael Convent, St. Petersburg, Florida, 1966-1967, p.1
228. Ibid. p.2
229. Ibid. p.5
230. Annals, 1967-1968, p.1, 2
231. Ibid. p.3
232. Ibid. p.4
233. Reverend W. J. Weinheimer. Telegram to Mother Beata Wertz, IHM. August 16, 1968
234. Annals of St. Raphael Convent, 1968-1969, p.1
235. Ibid.
236. Annals, p.2
237. Plans of Anderson, Bruce, Henry, Johnson, Parish and Bodo, Architects, St. Petersburg, Florida. IHM Archives
238. Annals of St. Raphael Convent, 1969-1970, p.1
239. Ibid.
240. Ibid. 1971-1972 p. 2,3
241. Charles John O'Malley, Coordinator of Education, Florida Catholic Conference. Letter to Sister Sue Ann Steves. January 8, 1973
242. Mother Beata Wertz, IHM. Letter to Sister Sue Ann Steves and Faculty. January 18, 1973
243. St. Lawrence Parish Publication, p.4-5. Based on thesis by Sister Mary Edith Opferman, IHM. "The Origin, Growth and Development of St. Lawrence Parish, South Williamsport, PA, 1931-1968"
244. Ibid. p. 8
245. Ibid. p. 7
246. Ibid.
247. Ibid.
248. Ibid. p. 9
249. Ibid. p. 12
250. Reverend Thomas J. Knight. Letter to Mother Kathleen Hart, IHM. April 26, 1960
251. Mother Kathleen Hart, IHM. Letter to Reverend Thomas J. Knight. May 3, 1960

252. Reverend Thomas J. Knight, Pastor. Letter to Mother Beata Wertz, IHM. October 15, 1963
253. Mother Beata Wertz, IHM. Letter to Father Knight. October 22, 1963
254. Ibid. November 9, 1963
255. Reverend Thomas J. Knight. Letter to St. Lawrence Parish parishioners. January 8, 1964
256. St. Lawrence Parish Publication, op.cit. p. 12,13
257. Ibid. p. 13
258. Annals of St. Lawrence Convent, South Williamsport, PA. 1966-1967
259. St. Lawrence Parish Publication, op.cit. p. 13
260. Annals of St. Lawrence Convent, 1966-1967
261. Ibid. 1967-1968
262. Ibid. 1968-1971
263. Monsignor William L. Donovan, Superintendent of Scranton Diocesan Schools. Letter to Reverend Joseph W. Breslin, Pastor, St. Lawrence Parish, March 30, 1972
264. Sister Eleanor Desaulniers, IHM, Sector Superior. Letter to Reverend Joseph Breslin, Pastor, St. Lawrence Parish, April 5, 1972
265. Central Administrative Assembly. Letter to Sisters of IHM, St. Lawrence Convent, South Williamsport, PA. April 20, 1972
266. Annals of St. Lawrence Convent, 1972-1973
267. Telephone conversation with Sister Gabriel Kane, IHM, Vicar for Religious, Scranton Diocese, September 2002.
268. Sister Immaculata Gillespie's file on St. Matthew's School, East Stroudsburg, PA. p. 2, 4. Archives
269. Annals of St. Matthew Convent, East Stroudsburg, PA, 1961-1962
270. "The Story of a High School." January, 1964, p.2
271. Annals of St. Matthew Convent, 1962-1963
272. "The Story of a High School." op.cit. p. 4
273. Ibid. p.8-9
274. Annals of St. Matthew Convent, 1963-1964
275. Ibid.
276. "The Story of a High School." op.cit. p. 2
277. Annals of St. Matthew Convent, 1965-1966
278. Ibid. 1966-1967
279. Ibid. 1968-1969
280. Ibid. 1971-1972
281. Ibid. 1977-1978
282. Ibid. 2001-2002
283. Reverend Brian McQuade. Sts. Philip and James Convent: "A History of Faithful Witness." 1997

284. Ibid.
285. Reverend Charles Carow. Letter to Mother Beata Wertz, IHM. September 12, 1965
286. Mother Beata Wertz, IHM. Letter to Reverend Charles Carow. September 23, 1965
287. Ibid. October 11, 1965
288. Reverend Charles Carow. Letter to Mother Beata Wertz, IHM. October 17, 1965
289. Reverend David G. Farley, Superintendent of Schools, Rockville Centre Diocese. Letter to Mother Beata Wertz, IHM. January 19, 1966
290. Annals of Sts. Philip and James Convent, 1967-1968
291. Ibid.
292. Reverend Charles Carow. Letter to Mother Beata Wertz, IHM. June 19, 1968
293. Ibid. July 13, 1969
294. Sister Jeanne Albrittain. Telephone conversation. May 8, 2002
295. IHM School Survey. 1969. IHM Archives.
296. Mother Beata Wertz, IHM. Letter to Reverend Charles Carow. February 18, 1970
297. Parents of Sts. Philip and James School children. March 1970. Archives
298. Reverend Brian McQuade. Commemorative Historical Journal.1922-1997. IHM Archives.
299. Very Reverend Monsignor Raymond P. Rigney, Superintendent of Schools, New York Archdiocese. Letter to Mother Beata Wertz, IHM. November 6, 1964
300. Mother Beata Wertz, IHM. Letter to Monsignor Rigney. December 16, 1964
301. Monsignor Raymond P. Rigney. Letter to Mother Beata Wertz, IHM. April 27, 1967
302. Ibid.
303. Mother Beata Wertz, IHM. Letter to Monsignor Rigney. May 11, 1967
304. Annals of Sacred Hearts Convent, New York, NY. 1967-1968
305. Sister Jeannine Parry, IHM. Telephone conversation. December 20, 2002
306. Monsignor Rigney. Letter to Mother Beata Wertz, IHM. December 15, 1967
307. Sister Mary Ellen Malloy, IHM. Telephone conversation. December 21, 2002
308. Sister Jeannine Parry, IHM. Telephone conversation. December 20, 2002
309. Monsignor James V. Kenney, Pastor, St. Stephen Parish. Letter to Mother Beata Wertz, IHM. January 5, 1971
310. IHM Sisters at St. Stephen School. Letter to Central Administrative Assembly, May 1, 1972
311. Monsignor James V. Kenney. Letter to Mother Beata Wertz, IHM. June 10, 1970

312. Ibid. March 6, 1973
313. Ibid. January 5, 1971
314. Annals of Sacred Hearts Convent, New York, N.Y. 1970-1971
315. Ibid. 1971-1972
316. Monsignor William J. Rinscheler, Pastor, Sacred Hearts Parish, New York, NY. Letter to Sister Anne Fulwiler, Superior General. September 25, 1974
317. Sister Michel Keenan, IHM, Superior General. Letter to Monsignor Rinscheler. December 31, 1979
318. Annals of St. Joseph Convent, New York, NY. 1980-1981
319. Ibid. 1990
320. Mother Kathleen Hart, IHM. Letter to Bishop Jerome Hannan, Scranton, PA. January 15, 1959
321. Mother Kathleen Hart, IHM. Letter to Bishop Walter P. Kellenberg, Rockville Centre Diocese, NY. May 23, 1959
322. Sister Felicitas Ryan, IHM. Letter to Mr. Peter Grace, Manhasset, NY. July 9, 1967
323. Tenth Anniversary Pamphlet of Our Lady of Grace Montessori School. "History of Our Lady of Grace Montessori School," p.6-7
324. Ibid.
325. Information Brochure on Our Lady of Grace Montessori School. Undated, circa 1998, 3rd anniversary publication
326. Annals of Our Lady of Grace Community. 1990-1991
327. Annals of St. Joseph Convent, Williamsport, PA. 1967-1968
328. *The Catholic Light*, February 8, 1968
329. Sister Immaculata Gillespie's Notes. IHM Archives. St. Joseph's Convent, Williamsport, PA
330. Annals of St. Joseph Convent, Williamsport, PA, 1969-1970
331. Annals of St. Joseph Convent, 1972-1973
332. Ibid.
333. Ibid. 1973-1974
334. Reverend John W. Jordan. Letter to Mother Beata Wertz, IHM. March 22, 1974
335. Reverend James T. Delaney, Principal, St. Mark's High School, Wilmington, DE Dedication Program. May 24, 1970
336. Reverend James T. Delaney. Report on the Staffing of the Diocesan High School. 1961-1968. Archival material provided by Donn Devine, Archivist, Diocese of Wilmington, Delaware. May 2002
337. Ibid.
338. IHM Congregation General Council Minutes. December 31, 1966
339. Ibid.
340. Ibid.

341. Annals of St. Matthew Convent, Wilmington, DE 1967-1968
342. Most Reverend Thomas J. Mardaga, D.D., Bishop of Wilmington. Dedication Booklet, May 24, 1970
343. Reverend James T. Delaney. Descriptive materials of St. Mark's High School prepared for Religious Communities, 1972-1973.
344. Annals of St. Mark Faculty Residence, Wilmington, DE. 1969-1970
345. Annals of St. Matthew Convent, Wilmington, DE, 1969-1970
346. Annals of St. Mark Faculty Residence, 1969-1970
347. Sister Dolores Filicko, IHM. Minutes of Organizational Meeting for St. Mark's Faculty Residence, January 12, 1970
348. Annals of St. Mark Faculty Residence, 1970-1971
349. Ibid.
350. Ibid.
351. Ibid. 1971-1993
352. Ibid. 1979-1980
353. Ibid. 1983-1984
354. Ibid. 1972-2000
355. Sister Redempta Sweeney, IHM. Information received by e-mail, June 2002
356. Reverend John P. Gallagher. *A Century of History - The Diocese of Scranton 1868-1968,* p. 298
357. Op. cit. p. 301
358. Op.cit. p. 302-303
359. Charles McCarthy. "History of Parochial School Education in Pittston City," Chapter IX, *Sunday Dispatch*, 1959
360. Ibid.
361. 150th Anniversary Booklet, St. Mary, Help of Christians Church, Pittston, PA. (1851-2001)
362. Conversation with Sister Pauline Kelly, IHM Center, Scranton, PA. August 2002
363. Annals of St. Rocco Convent, Pittston, PA. 1971-1972
364. Central Administrative Assembly. Minutes of October 12, 1971
365. Ibid. October 6, 1971
366. Annals of St. Rocco Convent, 1972-1973
367. Ibid. 1973-1974
368. Ibid.
369. Ibid.
370. Ibid. 1974-1975
371. Ibid. 1975-1976
372. Ibid.
373. Ibid. 1976-1977

374. Annals, 1981-1982
375. Annals of St. John Convent, Pittston, PA. 1981-1982
376. Annals of St. Rocco Convent, 1982-1983
377. "The Spotlight," *The Sunday Dispatch*, Pittston, PA. May 18, 1997
378. Annals of St. Rocco Convent, Pittston, PA. 2000-2001
379. Annals of St. John the Baptist Convent, Scranton, PA. 1973-1974
380. Central Administrative Assembly Minutes. November 22, 1972
381. Annals of St. John the Baptist Convent, 1973-1974
382. Ibid.
383. Ibid.
384. Ibid.
385. Ibid. 1975-1976
386. Ibid. 1976-1977
387. Ibid.
388. IHM Archival Records. 1962-1967
389. St. John the Evangelist Church 100th Anniversary Bulletin, 1976
390. Reverend Perry W. Dodds, Pastor, St. Edward Parish, Twin Falls, ID Personal conversation with Sister Michel Keenan, IHM
391. IHM Archival Records. 1968-1971
392. Parents of Marywood Seminary students. Letters to Mother Beata Wertz, IHM March, April, 1971
393. IHM Archival Records. 1969-1971
394. Reverend Perry Dodds, Pastor, St. Edward's Parish, Twin Falls, ID Letter to Sister Anne Fulwiler, September 9, 1977
395. Sister Cor Mariae Schroth, IHM. Letter to Mother Beata Wertz, IHM March 17, 1963
396. Central Administrative Assembly Minutes. November 21, 1965
397. Sister Cor Mariae and Sister Christine Clarkin, IHM. Letter to Bishop Jerome D. Hannan, Scranton, PA. December 5, 1965
398. Annals of St. Joseph's Hospital Local Community. 1965-1966
399. Ibid. 1966-1967
400. Ibid. 1967-1968
401. Ibid. 1968-1969
402. Central Administrative Assembly Minutes. October 30, 1968
403. Annals of St. Joseph's Hospital Local Community, 1969-1970
404. Ibid.
405. Attorney Robert E. O'Brien. Letter to Mother Beata Wertz, IHM. April 3, 1970
406. IHM Congregation Directory, 2002-2003
407. Annals of St. Joseph's Convent, 2001-2002
408. IHM Congregation Directory, 2002-2003

409. Central Administrative Assembly Minutes. May 5, 1966
410. Mother Beata Wertz, IHM. "Report to the General Chapter, 1968". June 23, 1968
411. Central Administrative Assembly Minutes. December 6, 1968
412. Marian Convent Construction Notes, May 31, 1970. Land and Buildings Book 1. Archives.
413. Mother Beata Wertz, IHM and Monsignor Joseph Madden, Chancellor, Scranton Diocese. September 10, 1969. Land and Buildings, Marian Convent, Book 1. Archives.
414. Sister Martin dePorres McHale, IHM, Treasurer General. Letters to Monsignor Madden, Chancellor. November 22, 1969
415. Monsignor Joseph A. Madden, Chancellor. Letter to Sister Martin dePorres McHale, IHM, Treasurer General, March 13, 1970
416. *The Catholic Light,* May 16, 1991. 30th Anniversary Review.
417. Sister Zita Marie Kane, IHM. *History of the Marian Convent*, 1956-1996. p.3
418. Sister Cor Mariae Schroth, IHM, Administrator, Marian Convent. Letter to all IHM Sisters. October 11, 1969
419. *The Scranton Times,* February 23, 1971
420. Mother Beata Wertz, IHM. Letter to Congregation. February 23, 1971
421. *The Catholic Light,* March 11, 1971
422. Bishop J. Carroll McCormick. Letter to the priests and people of the Diocese of Scranton. March 2, 1971
423. Bishop J. Carroll McCormick. Comment on presentation of check to Mother Beata Wertz, IHM. March 29, 1971
424. Mother Beata Wertz, IHM. Comment on receiving check from Bishop McCormick. March 29, 1971
425. *The Scranton Times.* November 29, 1971
426. Central Administrative Assembly Minutes. October 6, 1969
427. *Scranton Tribune.* February 28, 1972
428. Judge Richard P. Conaboy, Jr. Letter to Mother Beata Wertz, IHM. March 2, 1971
429. Sister Marianne Addy, IHM, Principal, Marywood Seminary. Letter to Mother Beata Wertz, IHM, March 4, 1971
430. Central Administrative Assembly Minutes. March 8, 1971
431. Mother Beata Wertz, IHM. Letter to Sister Marianne Addy. March 15, 1971
432. Sister Marianne Addy, IHM. Letter to Mother Beata Wertz, IHM. March 24, 1971
433. Mother Beata Wertz, IHM. Letter to the Congregation. May 10, 1971
434. Ibid. November 6, 1972
435. Monsignor John P. Gallagher. *A Century of History: 1868-1968*, p.117
436. Sister Immaculata Gillespie, IHM. *Sisters of IHM.* 1921, p.139

437. *The Scranton Times*, September 9, 1971
438. Monsignor John M. Dougherty. Centenary Address. September 8, 1971
439. Bishop J. Carroll McCormick. Letter to Mother Beata Wertz, IHM. September 8, 1971
440. Ibid.
441. Mother Beata Wertz, IHM, Centenary Remarks, September 8, 1971
442. Ibid.
443. Archival Reports of IHM response to the flood. June 1972
444. Annals of Holy Name of Jesus Convent, Forty Fort, PA. 1972-1973
445. Ibid.
446. Annals of St. Ignatius Convent, Kingston, PA. 1972-1973
447. Ibid.
448. Mother Beata Wertz, IHM. Letter to the Congregation. July 1, 1972
449. Ibid.
450. Ibid. July 13, 1972
451. Mother Beata Wertz, IHM. Letter to Sister Daniel Turner, President, CMSW, Washington, DC. September 29, 1972
452. Sister Agatha, ICM, President, Junshir Junior College, Kagoshima City, Japan. Letter to Sister St. Mary Orr, President, Marywood College, Scranton, PA. April 14, 1962
453. Bishop Francis Xavier Songuon. Chanthabury, Thailand. August 26, 1963
454. Sisters Lourdes and Rosita, CMI., West Bengal, India. Letter to Mother Beata Wertz, IHM.August 16, 1972
455. Indian Student. Letter to Indian friends. May 1962
456. Sister Mary Paul, OLC, Taiwan, Free China. Letter to Mother Beata Wertz, IHM. September 21, 1971
457. Ibid.
458. Mother Beata Wertz, IHM. Address to Pre-Chapter Meeting. November 12, 1972
459. Mother Beata Wertz, IHM. Report to the General Chapter of 1974. June 25, 1974
460. Ibid.
461. Sister Anne Fulwiler, IHM, Superior General. Letter to Mother Beata Wertz, IHM. August 15, 1974
462. Sister Paulinus Sullivan, IHM. Citation written for Mother Beata Wertz, IHM Presented at the Joint Sector Coordinating Assembly. March 30, 1974
463. Reverend Aloysius C. Galvin, SJ. Citation for Mother Beata Wertz, IHM University of Scranton, Scranton, PA. June 4, 1967
464. Sister Coleman Nee, IHM, President, Marywood College, Scranton, PA. Citation for Mother Beata Wertz, IHM. October 4, 1975
465. Mass of Resurrection Booklet for Mother Beata Wertz's funeral, IHM Center. September 16, 1989